A COMMENTARY ON
HOMER'S ODYSSEY

A COMMENTARY ON
HOMER'S ODYSSEY

VOLUME III
BOOKS XVII–XXIV

JOSEPH RUSSO
MANUEL FERNÁNDEZ-GALIANO
ALFRED HEUBECK

CLARENDON PRESS · OXFORD

OXFORD

UNIVERSITY PRESS

Great Clarendon Street, Oxford OX2 6DP

Oxford University Press is a department of the University of Oxford.
It furthers the University's objective of excellence in research, scholarship,
and education by publishing worldwide in

Oxford New York

Athens Auckland Bangkok Bogotá Buenos Aires Calcutta
Cape Town Chennai Dar es Salaam Delhi Florence Hong Kong Istanbul
Karachi Kuala Lumpur Madrid Melbourne Mexico City Mumbai
Nairobi Paris São Paulo Shanghai Singapore Taipei Tokyo Toronto Warsaw

and associated companies in Berlin Ibadan

Published in the United States
by Oxford University Press Inc., New York

Originally published in Italian under the title Omero: Odissea
© Fondazione Lorenzo Valla
English edition © Oxford University Press 1992

ISBN 0-19-814953-0

Printed in Great Britain
on acid-free paper by
Bookcraft (Bath) Short Run Books
Midsomer Norton

CONTENTS

BIBLIOGRAPHICAL ABBREVIATIONS

The abbreviations used for ancient authors correspond to those employed in the ninth edition of Liddell and Scott, *Greek–English Lexicon* (LSJ) and in the *Oxford Latin Dictionary*, for periodicals to those of *L'Année philologique*.

Editions of the *Odyssey* referred to in the Commentary:

Allen	T. W. Allen, *Homeri Opera*, iii², iv² (Oxford Classical Text), Oxford, 1917, 1919.
Ameis–Hentze–Cauer	*Homers Odyssee* f. den Schulgebrauch erklärt von K. F. Ameis u. C. Hentze, bearbeitet von P. Cauer, i 1¹⁴, 2¹³, ii 1⁹, 2¹⁰, Leipzig, 1920, 1940, 1928, 1925.
Bérard	V. Bérard, *L'Odyssée*, Paris, 1924–5.
Hainsworth*	*Omero, Odissea, libri v–viii: Introduzione, testo e commento* a cura di J. B. Hainsworth, Fondazione Lorenzo Valla, Rome, 1982.
Heubeck*	*Omero, Odissea, libri ix–xii; xxiii–xxiv: Introduzione, testo e commento* a cura di Alfred Heubeck, Fondazione Lorenzo Valla, Rome, 1983, 1987.
Hoekstra*	*Omero, Odissea, libri xiii–xvi: Introduzione, testo e commento* a cura di Arie Hoekstra, Fondazione Lorenzo Valla, Rome, 1984.
Merry–Riddell	W. W. Merry and J. Riddell, *Homer's Odyssey: Books i–xii*, Oxford, 1886.
Monro	D. B. Monro, *Homer's Odyssey: Books xiii–xxiv*, Oxford, 1901.
Russo*	*Omero, Odissea, libri xvii–xx: Introduzione, testo e commento* a cura di Joseph Russo, Fondazione Lorenzo Valla, Rome, 1985.
Stanford	W. B. Stanford, *The Odyssey of Homer*², Macmillan, London, 1959.
van Leeuwen	J. van Leeuwen, *Homeri Carmina, cum prolegomenis, notis criticis, commentariis exegeticis, Odyssea*, Leiden, 1917.
von der Mühll	P. von der Mühll, *Homeri Odyssea*³, Basel, 1961 (Stuttgart, 1984).
S. West*	*Omero, Odissea, libri i–iv: Introduzione generale di*

* The present volume is the third in the English edition (introductions and commentary only); the first volume (Books i–viii) was published in 1988, and the second (Books ix–xvi) in 1989 (both from OUP).

S. West (*cont.*) | *Alfred Heubeck e Stephanie West, introduzione, testo e commento* a cura di Stephanie West, Fondazione Lorenzo Valla, Rome, 1981.

Works mentioned by abbreviated title:

Allione, *Telemaco*　　　　　L. Allione, *Telemaco e Penelope nell'Odissea*, Turin, 1963.

Ameis–Hentze, *Anhang*　　　K. F. Ameis and C. Hentze, *Anhang zu Homers Odyssee*[3], Leipzig, 1889, 1895[3].

Archaeologia　　　　　　　*Archaeologia Homerica: Die Denkmäler u. das frühgriechische Epos*, ed. F. Matz and H. G. Buchholz, Göttingen, 1967.

Arend, *Scenen*　　　　　　W. Arend, *Die typischen Scenen bei Homer*, Berlin, 1933.

Austin, *Archery*　　　　　N. Austin, *Archery at the Dark of the Moon: Poetic Problems in Homer's* Odyssey, Berkeley–Los Angeles, 1975.

Bechtel, *Lexiologus*　　　F. Bechtel, *Lexilogus zu Homer*, Halle, 1914.

Beekes, *Laryngeals*　　　R. S. P. Beekes, *The Development of the Proto-Indo-European Laryngeals in Greek*, The Hague–Paris, 1969.

Besslich, *Schweigen*　　　S. Besslich, *Schweigen–Verschweigen—Übergehen: Die Darstellung des Unausgesprochenen in der Odyssee*, Heidelberg, 1966.

Bethe, *Homer*　　　　　　E. Bethe, *Homer: Dichtung und Sage*, i–iii, Leipzig–Berlin, 1914, 1922, 1929[2].

—— *Odyssee*　　　　　　—— ibid. ii: *Odyssee, Kyklos, Zeitbestimmung*[2], Leipzig, 1929.

Blass, *Interpolationen*　　F. Blass, *Die Interpolationen in der Odyssee*, Halle, 1904.

Bolling, *Evidence*　　　　G. M. Bolling, *The External Evidence for Interpolation in Homer*, Oxford, 1925.

Bona, *Studi*　　　　　　　G. Bona, *Studi sull'Odissea*, Turin, 1966.

Bowra, *HP*　　　　　　　C. M. Bowra, *Heroic Poetry*, London, 1952.

Büchner, 'Penelopeszenen'　W. Büchner, 'Die Penelopeszenen in der Odyssee', *Hermes*, lxxv (1940).

Burkert, *Religion*　　　　W. Burkert, *Greek Religion: Archaic and Classical*, trans. John Raffan, Blackwell, 1985.

Cauer, *Homerkritik*　　　P. Cauer, *Grundfragen der Homerkritik*[3], Leipzig, 1921–3.

CEG　　　　·　　　　　　*Carmina Epigraphia Graeca*, ed. P. A. Hansen (Berlin–New York, 1983).

Chantraine, *Dictionnaire*　P. Chantraine, *Dictionnaire étymologique de la langue grecque*, Paris, 1968–80.

—— *Formation* —— *La Formation des noms en grec ancien*, Paris, 1933.

—— *Grammaire* —— *Grammaire homérique* i³, ii², Paris, 1958, 1963.

—— *Morphologie* —— *Morphologie historique du grec*, Paris, 1967.

Clay, *Wrath* J. S. Clay, *The Wrath of Athena: Gods and Men in the* Odyssey, Princeton, 1983.

Companion *A Companion to Homer*, ed. A. J. B. Wace and F. H. Stubbings, London, 1962.

Delebecque, *Télémaque* E. Delebecque, *Télémaque et la structure de l'Odyssée*, *Annales de la faculté des lettres d'Aix-en-Provence*, NS xxi, 1958.

Denniston, *Particles* J. D. Denniston, *The Greek Particles*², Oxford, 1954.

Ebeling, *Lexicon* H. Ebeling, *Lexicon Homericum*, Leipzig, 1880–5.

Eisenberger, *Studien* H. Eisenberger, *Studien zur Odyssee*, Wiesbaden, 1973.

Erbse, *Beiträge* H. Erbse, *Beiträge zum Verständnis der Odyssee*, Berlin–New York, 1972.

Fenik, *Studies* B. Fenik, *Studies in the* Odyssey, *Hermes* Einzelschriften, xxx, Wiesbaden, 1974.

Finley, *World* M. I. Finley, *The World of Odysseus* (second revised edn.), Harmondsworth, 1979.

Finley Jun., *Odyssey* J. H. Finley Jun., *Homer's Odyssey*, Cambridge, Mass., 1978.

Finsler, *Homer* G. Finsler, *Homer*, i 1–2, ii, Leipzig, ²1918, ³1924.

Focke, *Odyssee* F. Focke, *Die Odyssee*, Stuttgart–Berlin, 1943.

Fränkel, *Gleichnisse* H. Fränkel, *Die homerischen Gleichnisse*, Göttingen, 1921.

Friedrich, *Stilwandel* R. Friedrich, *Stilwandel im homerischen Epos* (Heidelberg, 1975).

Frisk, *GEW* H. Frisk, *Griechisches etymologisches Wörterbuch*, Heidelberg, 1954–73.

Germain, *Genèse* G. Germain, *Genèse de l'Odyssée*, Paris, 1954.

Goodwin, *Syntax* W. W. Goodwin, *Syntax of the Moods and Tenses of the Greek Verb*, London, ²1889, repr. London, 1965, 1966.

Hainsworth, *Flexibility* J. B. Hainsworth, *The Flexibility of the Homeric Formula*, Oxford, 1968.

Heubeck, *Dichter* A. Heubeck, *Der Odyssee-Dichter und die Ilias*, Erlangen, 1954.

Hoekstra, *Modifications* A. Hoekstra, *Homeric Modifications of Formulaic Prototypes*, Amsterdam, 1965.

—— *Epic Verse* —— *Epic Verse before Homer: Three Studies*, Amsterdam, 1981.

ix

Hölscher, *Untersuchungen*   U. Hölscher, *Untersuchungen zur Form der Odyssee*, Leipzig, 1939.

Kirchhoff, *Odyssee*   A. Kirchhoff, *Die Homerische Odyssee und ihre Entstehung*, Berlin, 1879.

Kirk, *Commentary*   G. S. Kirk, *The* Iliad: *A Commentary*, i. *Books 1–4*, Cambridge, 1985.

—— *Songs*   —— *The Songs of Homer*, Cambridge, 1962.

Kl. Pauly   *Der Kleine Pauly: Lexicon der Antike in 5 Bänden*, ed. K. Ziegler and W. Sontheimer, Munich, 1964–75, DTV Munich, 1979.

Kühner–Gerth   R. Kühner, *Ausführliche Grammatik der griechischen Sprache*, i–ii. *Satzlehre*³, besorgt v. B. Gerth, Hanover, 1898–1904, repr. Leverkusen, 1955.

Leaf, *Iliad*   W. Leaf, *The* Iliad², London, 1900–2.

Lesky, *Homeros*   A. Lesky, *Homeros*, *RE*, Supplementband xi, Stuttgart, 1967.

Leumann, *Wörter*   M. Leumann, *Homerische Wörter*, Basel, 1950.

LfgrE   *Lexicon des frühgriechischen Epos*, ed. B. Snell and H. Erbse, Göttingen, 1955– .

Lord, *Singer*   A. B. Lord, *The Singer of Tales*, Cambridge, Mass.–London, 1960.

Lorimer, *Monuments*   H. L. Lorimer, *Homer and the Monuments*, London, 1950.

Ludwich, *AHT*   A. Ludwich, *Aristarchs Homerische Textkritik*, i, ii, Leipzig, 1884–5.

Marzullo, *Problema*   B. Marzullo, *Il problema omerico*², Milan–Naples, 1970.

Mattes, *Odysseus*   W. Mattes, *Odysseus bei den Phäaken*, Würzburg, 1958.

Meister, *Kunstsprache*   K. Meister, *Die homerische Kunstsprache*, Leipzig, 1921, repr. Darmstadt, 1966.

Merkelbach, *Untersuchungen*   R. Merkelbach, *Untersuchungen zur Odyssee*², Zetemata, ii, Munich, 1969.

Monro, *Homeric Dialect*   D. B. Monro, *A Grammar of the Homeric Dialect*², Oxford, 1891.

Nilsson, *Geschichte*   M. P. Nilsson, *Geschichte der griechischen Religion*³, i, Munich, 1967.

Onians, *Origins*   R. B. Onians, *The Origins of European Thought*, Cambridge, 1951.

Page, *Folktales*   D. L. Page, *Folktales in Homer's* Odyssey, Cambridge, Mass., 1972.

—— *Odyssey*   —— *The Homeric* Odyssey, Oxford, 1955.

—— *PMG*   —— *Poetae Melici Graeci*, Oxford, 1962.

Parry, *Blameless Aegisthus*   Anne Amory Parry, *Blameless Aegisthus*, Leiden, 1973.

Pocock, *Odyssean Essays* — L. G. Pocock, *Odyssean Essays*, Oxford, 1965.

Ramming, *Dienerschaft* — G. Ramming, *Die Dienerschaft in der Odyssee*, Erlangen, 1973.

RE — *Paulys Realencyclopädie der classischen Altertumswissenschaft*, ed. G. Wissowa, W. Kroll, K. Mittelhaus, and K. Ziegler, Stuttgart, 1893– .

Reinhardt, 'Abenteuer' — K. Reinhardt, 'Die Abenteuer des Odysseus', in id., *Von Wegen und Formen*, Godesberg, 1948, 52–162 = *Tradition und Geist*, Göttingen, 1960, 47–124.

Risch, *Wortbildung* — E. Risch, *Wortbildung der homerischen Sprache*[2], Berlin, 1973.

Rüter, *Odysseeinterpretationen* — K. Rüter, *Odysseeinterpretationen. Untersuchungen zum ersten Buch u. zur Phaiakis*, Hypomnemata, xix, Göttingen, 1969.

Ruijgh, *Élément* — C. J. Ruijgh, *L'Élément achéen dans la langue épique*, Assen, 1957.

—— *Études* — —— *Études sur la grammaire et le vocabulaire du grec mycénien*, Amsterdam, 1967.

—— τε *épique* — —— *Autour de 'τε épique': Études sur la syntaxe grecque*, Amsterdam, 1971.

Schadewaldt, *Welt* — W. Schadewaldt, *Von Homers Welt und Werk*[4], Stuttgart, 1965.

Schulze, *Quaestiones* — W. Schulze, *Quaestiones epicae*, Gütersloh, 1892.

Schwartz, *Odyssee* — E. Schwartz, *Die Odyssee*, Munich, 1924.

Schwyzer, *Grammatik* — E. Schwyzer, *Griechische Grammatik*, i–iii, Munich, 1939–53.

Shipp, *Studies* — G. P. Shipp, *Studies in the Language of Homer*[2], Cambridge, 1972.

Simpson–Lazenby, *Catalogue* — R. Hope Simpson and J. F. Lazenby, *The Catalogue of the Ships in Homer's* Iliad, Oxford, 1970.

Stella, *Ulisse* — L. A. Stella, *Il poema di Ulisse*, Florence, 1955.

Thompson, *Motif Index* — Stith Thompson, *Motif Index of Folk Literature*, Copenhagen, 1955–8.

Thornton, *People* — A. Thornton, *People and Themes in Homer's* Odyssey, London, 1970.

Trümpy, *Fachausdrücke* — H. Trümpy, *Kriegerische Fachausdrücke im griechischen Epos*, Basle, 1950.

van der Valk, *Textual Criticism* — M. van der Valk, *Textual Criticism of the* Odyssey, Leiden, 1949.

van Leeuwen, *Enchiridium* — J. van Leeuwen, *Enchiridium dictionis epicae*, Leiden, 1918.

Ventris–Chadwick, *Documents* — M. Ventris and J. Chadwick, *Documents in Mycenaean Greek*[2], Cambridge, 1973.

von der Mühll, 'Odyssee'   P. von der Mühll, 'Odyssee', *RE*, Supplementband, vii, 696–768, Stuttgart, 1940.

von Kamptz,   H. von Kamptz, *Homerische Personennamen*, Göt-
Personennamen   tingen, 1982.

Wackernagel,   J. Wackernagel, *Sprachliche Untersuchungen zu*
Untersuchungen   *Homer*, Göttingen, 1916.

Werner, *H u. ει vor*   R. Werner, *H u. ει vor Vokal bei Homer*, Fri-
Vokal   bourg, 1948.

Wilamowitz, *Heimkehr*   U. von Wilamowitz-Moellendorff, *Die Heimkehr*
des Odysseus, Berlin, 1927.

—— *Glaube*   —— *Der Glaube der Hellenen*, i–ii, Berlin, 1931–
2, reiss. Darmstadt, 1959³.

—— *Untersuchungen*   —— *Homerische Untersuchungen*, Berlin, 1884.

Woodhouse, *Composition*   W. J. Woodhouse, *The Composition of Homer's*
Odyssey, Oxford, 1930, repr. Oxford, 1969.

Wyatt, *Lengthening*   W. F. Wyatt, jun., *Metrical Lengthening in*
Homer, Rome, 1969.

BOOKS XVII–XX

Joseph Russo

INTRODUCTION

I

Books xvii to xx of the *Odyssey* provide the vital turning-point for the second half of the epic, the story of return, revenge, and reunion. Immediately after these four pivotal books, the unusual stranger manages in xxi to string Odysseus' bow and make the near-impossible shot; stands revealed as Odysseus at the opening of xxii and goes on in that book to kill all the suitors; is finally recognized by and united with Penelope in xxiii; and in xxiv is reunited with his father, with whose help he successfully meets the challenge of the suitors' families' attempt at retaliation. These successes of the final four books are all made possible because the lowly vagabond who entered the royal halls in xvii has been gaining power by degrees, acquiring increasing influence and intimacy with Penelope and the few faithful servants while simultaneously compelling increasing respect from the suitors, who begin by mocking him but gradually learn to respect his abilities and eventually realize (xxi 285–6, 323 ff.) that he is quite likely to string the bow. It is the actions and reactions of all persons involved in this escalation of the beggar's importance in the royal household that give us the major events of xvii to xx.

Book xvii begins at Eumaeus' hut and brings Telemachus, and then Odysseus and Eumaeus, to the palace. Only Telemachus knows the beggar's identity at this point; but a curious recognition takes place when Odysseus' old dog Argus recognizes his returning master and dies overwhelmed by emotion. Odysseus himself is assailed by strong emotion at this encounter, but Homer uses the dramatic occasion to highlight the hero's famous self-control: Odysseus suppresses his tears, channels his feelings into speech in the form of laudatory comments on the dog's career, and is thus able safely to cross the threshold he has sought for ten years. The encounter with Argus has allowed the poet to mark this important moment with a brief but unforgettable little drama of hidden meanings, a fitting prelude to the many such dramas that will be enacted once Odysseus is inside the palace.

Having entered, Odysseus makes the threshold his regular seat, a symbolic statement of the 'liminal' position of a king who has returned home but not assumed his royal authority, and of a vagabond who has no fixed place in any community and no social role except that of 'outsider'. (The word commonly used to refer to the beggar is ξεῖνος, which here denotes a 'stranger' or 'outsider' rather than its more favourable meaning of aristocratic 'guest' whose rank would entitle him to guest-gifts, ξενία.) For the remainder of xvii, Odysseus' lack of rank and status exposes him to the hostility of Melanthius, who had abused him earlier in this book on the road to the palace, and to the jibes of Antinous, who in exasperation at the beggar's verbal audacity hits him with a footstool. The book concludes with Penelope's attempt to invite the stranger to tell her his story. The invitation, relayed through Eumaeus, is declined for the moment, to be accepted only when the suitors have gone home for the night (xix).

The eighteenth book begins with the arrival of Irus, the old 'established' beggar, who serves as a stepping-stone for Odysseus in his incipient rise in status: the new beggar displaces the old, revealing in the process that both his physique and his sense of self-importance are stronger than anyone would have expected. He trades insults with Eurymachus as with an equal, gives Amphinomus sage advice, from the vantage point of a more experienced peer, about the vicissitudes of life, and makes it clear again, as he did in xvii 419 ff., that except for the bad luck dealt by Fortune he would still be a member of the nobility and the equal of Penelope's suitors (xviii 138 ff.). In a bitter exchange with Eurymachus near the end of the book he again implies that he is the peer of the leading suitors, this time specifically in military prowess (376 ff.). This image of an Odysseus armed with spears, shield, and helmet is prophetic of the reality to come in the twenty-second and twenty-fourth books.

Still awaiting the disguised Odysseus, however, is a chance to talk to the queen and 'test' her fidelity (cf. xiii 336, xix 45).[1] He finally sees his wife when in the middle of xviii she comes down into the main hall to charm the suitors into giving her expensive courtship gifts. Odysseus admires her cunning, since he is the only one in the hall who recognizes exactly what she is doing.[2] His recognition of her true

[1] At xiii 336 Athena anticipates Odysseus' future testing of Penelope with the Greek verb πειρήσεαι ('test, make trial of'), while at xix 45 Odysseus, describing this forthcoming encounter to Telemachus, uses the verb ἐρεθίζω ('provoke, irritate'). See the commentary at each passage for the significance of these two verbs, and H. Vester, 'Das 19. Buch der Odyssee', *Gymnasium* 75 (1968), 419 n. 13.

[2] Critics have been bothered by Homer's failure to tell us explicitly that Odysseus 'rejoices' *because* he grasps Penelope's hidden purpose, and they object that he should instead have been troubled by her apparent interest in a new husband. But it is natural for Homer (and us) to assume that Odysseus knows his wife well enough to understand

character is a fitting beginning for the process of rapprochement in which their knowledge of one another will grow by degrees, to culminate in the full recognition of Odysseus by Penelope in book xxiii. The scene of Penelope's beautification by Athena and her appearance before the suitors (158–303) has had a mixed reception from scholars. Once suspected as an interpolation, it is now usually esteemed as a superb example of Homer's story-telling art, although there remain obscurities of character motivation that require special explanation (see nn. at 160–2, 160, 163, 164–5). The underlying problem may be termed 'narratological': Homer attempts to construct a plot sequence that both allows Odysseus' identity to remain concealed from Penelope and yet shows her reacting to his presence with a renewal of emotional energy that points to a kind of psychological or spiritual revival. Such a sequence is nicely served by her decision at this point to show herself in the main hall and beguile the suitors into giving her courtship gifts; and because it has no natural motivation, Homer makes Athena the source of the irrational impulse. Penelope herself wonders aloud at the strangeness of her impulse (163–5), and feels the need to rationalize it to her servant Eurynome (166–8); but the unexpected decision does make good narrative and psychological sense. In the words of a recent interpreter, 'It is the first response to a cluster of events that have brought Odysseus to her notice: Telemachus' report of what he learned on his journey, Theoclymenus' "prophecy" that Odysseus has already returned, Odysseus' actual entrance into the house in disguise, and Eumaeus' praise of his guest of the night before.'[3]

The nineteenth book brings us finally to the long-awaited interview, previously deferred. The queen and the beggar have two lengthy dialogues, divided in the middle by the footbath administered by Eurycleia, the occasion for one of Homer's most famous

when she is feigning or posturing; and it is a common enough narrative device for a major character to share the author's omniscient point of view with no explanation provided (Fenik, *Studies*, 119–20; U. Hölscher, 'Penelope vor den Freiern', in *Lebende Antike: Symposion f. R. Sühnel* (Berlin, 1967), 27–31). C. S. Byre, 'Penelope and the Suitors before Odysseus: Odyssey 18. 158–303', *AJPh* 109 (1988), 169–73, reaffirms this explanation but then adds the less convincing one that Odysseus' joy is the sign of a pent-up rage against the suitors.

[3] S. Murnaghan, *Disguise and Recognition in the Odyssey* (Princeton, 1987), 48–9. See also the good discussion at 46–7 of the series of episodes in which Penelope experiences something less than recognition but analogous to it, an ambiguity arising from 'the narrative accommodation of a certain necessary paradox' (47): Penelope must somehow acknowledge that Odysseus is back without recognizing him.

episodes, the digression on the scar of Odysseus. In the first dialogue Penelope describes her predicament: courted by the leading nobles of Ithaca and the nearby islands, she is being urged to marry by both her parents and her son. She describes the deception of the web and its discovery, making it clear that her strategies for delaying the marriage are used up and her condition is desperate. The beggar then identifies himself as a Cretan noble, Idomeneus' younger brother, former guest-friend ($\xi\epsilon\hat{\imath}\nu\sigma$) of Odysseus, whom he entertained when Odysseus was on his way to Troy. Penelope, believing that she is finally speaking to a friend of her husband's, weeps profusely and asks for a more detailed description of Odysseus as proof of this man's former intimacy with him. The beggar gives a description so detailed that it drives the queen to further weeping as she recognizes the 'sure signs' he gives (xix 249–50), and she elevates the newcomer from merely $\epsilon\lambda\epsilon\epsilon\iota\nu\delta s$, an object of her pity, to $\phi\iota\lambda os$ and $\alpha\iota\delta o\hat{\imath}os$, a man close to her family and worthy of her respect (253–4). Now that he enjoys her respect and confidence, Odysseus goes on to assure her that her husband is alive and recently with the Thesprotians, who will soon convey him to Ithaca. He will in fact be home during the forthcoming period called the $\lambda\nu\kappa\dot{\alpha}\beta\alpha s$, between the waning of the old moon and the waxing of the new (see the note to 306–7 for this obscure word and the problems of interpreting the passage). Penelope finds this news too exciting to accept, too good to be true (309–16), and so deflects the conversation to the beggar's need for a bath and a bed. When he insists that only an old servant equal in suffering to himself be allowed to wash his feet, Eurycleia is called forth, and in washing him discovers the scar that points to his true identity.

  'She recognized the scar which the boar inflicted' (393): this phrase introduces the famous digression, concluded at 467–8 when similar words are used ($\check{\epsilon}\gamma\nu\omega$ $o\dot{\nu}\lambda\dot{\eta}\nu$, $\tau\dot{\eta}\nu$, 393; $\tau\dot{\eta}\nu$ ... $\gamma\nu\hat{\omega}$, 467–8). Within this digression, to explain how the adolescent Odysseus was wounded, Homer needs to retreat further into the past and tell us of Odysseus' birth and naming. His maternal grandfather Autolycus gave him a name, 'Odysseus', that would commemorate Autolycus' own career as a trouble-maker ($\dot{o}\delta\nu\sigma\sigma\dot{\alpha}\mu\epsilon\nu os$, 407); he then added that upon reaching puberty ($\dot{\eta}\beta\dot{\eta}\sigma\alpha s$) Odysseus should seek out his maternal grandfather again to receive gifts (406–12). It was in fulfilment of this baptismal injunction that the adolescent Odysseus went to Parnassos in what became a rite of passage from boyhood to manhood: he made his first kill in the men's hunt and received his first wound. This narrative structure with elaborate flashback suggests that Homer feels the need at this point to re-establish Odysseus in his full biographical identity before continuing the forward movement of rapprochement between the hero and his wife. We have been told of Odysseus' birth, naming, and entry into manhood. All that is lacking now to complete the heroic identity is the reacquisition of his wife and his royal power over the Ithacans. The remainder of the interview makes significant moves toward these goals.

What follows is a sequence of complex and puzzling statements and responses, which have drawn a wide range of diverse and contradictory interpretations from critics. With an intimacy that develops with amazing speed, the queen tells the stranger about her dream, which he confirms as prophetic of Odysseus' return and slaughter of the suitors. This prophecy Penelope claims she does not accept, taking refuge behind a theory of true and false dreams that allows her flatly to assert (with no explanation) that this dream is among the false ones. She moves immediately to the announcement that she has decided to set an archery contest for the very next day: she will marry whichever suitor most easily strings Odysseus' old bow and shoots through the twelve axes. The stranger endorses this decision, asserting that Odysseus will be with her before any suitor can manage to perform these acts. Penelope's decision to accept a likely remarriage in one day,[4] after successfully stalling the suitors for so long, and while still having no clear evidence that her husband has returned or is about to, is without evident motivation in our text and has never been successfully explained (see Commentary at 572–81 for a survey of current opinion).

Since Penelope's decision represents the key turning-point in the plot, the obscurity of its motivation deserves our full attention. Some readers have sought an explanation in the dubious theory that she recognizes her husband during the interview; but it is thoroughly alien to Homeric narrative habit to allow an event of this magnitude to pass without comment. Others have sought a neo-Analytic solution, positing an earlier version of the epic in which the interview of xix did in fact lead to Penelope's recognition that the beggar was Odysseus and to their collusion in setting the bow-contest (the

[4] That she assumes some suitor is likely to succeed with the bow and marry her is most clearly inferred from xix 571–2, 'this dawn ... will take me from Odysseus' house', and from the whole tenor of her desperate prayer for death at xx 61–90, including the specific hope of meeting Odysseus in the underworld rather than being alive to 'gladden the mind of some inferior man [husband: ἀνδρί]', 80–2. Some readers would also cite her tears of xxi 55–6 as indicating grief over prospective remarriage; but the very act of removing Odysseus' bow from its storeroom and handling it for the first time since he left for Troy could easily be sufficient cause for these tears.

7

erroneous interpretation offered by the suitor Amphimedon at xxiv 167 ff.). This other version would have been largely but not entirely superseded by our 'revised' version, with Penelope's unmotivated decision upon the bow-test and Amphimedon's reconstruction of events persisting as vestiges of this original plot. Such an explanation is perhaps plausible, and might find support in the tendency for oral traditions to retain earlier, sometimes incongruous, material, and for oral performances to contain occasional lapses or inconsistencies (note the argument that our *Odyssey* may represent an oral dictated text, a possibility discussed below). Yet it remains hard to believe that Homer, whose control of details and human psychology is so subtle throughout xix, would maintain such an incongruous remnant of an earlier version.

More recent attempts to explain Penelope's decision may be classed under four different schools of interpretation: 'narratological', folkloric, psychological, and literalist. Exponents of narratological criticism allow the inconsistency or ambiguity to stand as the inevitable consequence of alternative potential plots that are never fully harmonized by the narrator, who is moreover less able or willing to give us as full and consistent a portrayal of Penelope's mind as he is of Odysseus'.[5] The folkloric approach is essentially a form of German neo-analysis, most recently applied by U. Hölscher, who posits an earlier folk-tale pattern based on the clever and duplicitous wife-heroine, reworked by the epic poet to fit the more aristocratic portrait of a noble Penelope who is steadfast in her rejection of any possible marriage to one of the suitors.[6] The literalist approach is distinguished by lack of any theoretical base, and in its 'minimalist'

[5] N. Felson-Rubin, 'Penelope's Perspective: Character from Plot', in J. M. Bremer, I. J. F. De Jong, and J. Kalff, eds., *Homer: Beyond Oral Poetry* (Amsterdam, 1967), 62-3: 'In plot language, [Homer] assigns [Penelope] more than one plot'; and 'by keeping her ignorant as to her marital status, Homer represents Penelope as uncertain as to which of her several plots she is in at any moment'. Cf. Murnaghan (op. cit., n. 3 above), in a similar vein: 'In its account of Penelope's encounters with her disguised husband the poem gives us the complex depiction of someone involved in a plot of which she is unaware' (127). Regarding the timeliness of Penelope's decision to set the bow-contest when she does, Murnaghan interprets the successful outcome as emerging 'from a fortuitous combination of her despair and his improvisation', so that this crucial turning-point in the plot is 'brought about neither by Odysseus' or Penelope's cleverness in devising a strategy against the suitors, but rather by the lucky chance that at the point when Penelope feels she can no longer hold out against the suitors, Odysseus is there to take advantage of the means she devises to replace him' (134). I agree, but would add that Penelope acts from despair *combined with* the intuition that something may happen to save her from remarriage.

[6] Hölscher, op. cit. (n. 2 above), and 'The Transformation from Folk-Tale to Epic', in B. Fenik, ed., *Homer: Tradition and Invention* (Leiden, 1978), 51-67.

8

stance towards the use of interpretative methods represents a safe and
conservative methodology, least likely to lead to exaggerated readings
but also least likely to penetrate a complicated text. Literalist interpreters strive for intelligent common-sense reading and accumulation of observations taken from the surface of a text which is viewed as
having no sub-text, just as the poet is viewed as having little or no
interest in multiple levels of representation, whether of plot patterns
or of human motivation. Such an approach arises naturally from a
straightforward philological tradition of exegesis, but is in my view
the least rewarding critical method to use when facing the most
difficult problems of interpreting a storyteller as subtle as Homer in a
tradition as complex as the one from which his poems derive. It is not
surprising, then, that two recent essays of this type, although useful
on other points, fail to shed new light on the mystery of Penelope's
motivation.[7]

For unravelling the complexities of Penelope's relationship to
Odysseus, and in particular her 'submerged' recognition of his
identity and their discussion of her dream and the setting of the bow-
contest, more imaginative critical methods are needed. Neo-
Analytical interpretations carry a certain plausibility, and the
narratological analyses of Murnaghan and Felson-Rubin offer
perhaps the best explanation available for the apparent incomplete-
ness of the *Odyssey*'s textual surface. Yet all these interpreters share
the view—arrived at from different theoretical perspectives—that
Homer has imperfectly orchestrated and articulated some of his
major plot structures. In this they resemble the Analysts before them,
taking a critical position that faults Homer, or the *Odyssey* text, for
awkward or incomplete integration and mastery of materials and
form. Although it is not rare for Homer to 'nod' on small points of
consistency, in his characterization of Penelope and Odysseus it may
be best to assume that he knows what he is doing, and to apply whatever critical methods we find most rewarding in bringing his full
meaning to light.

I believe that a psychological interpretation permits us to account
for the many signs of unexpected rapport between Penelope and
the stranger without assuming that recognition has taken place,
and might also make her decision to stake her future on the bow-
contest easier to understand. This is the theory that Penelope has,
during her interview with the stranger, become progressively aware,
on an intuitive or unconscious level, not that this man *is* her

[7] C. Emlyn-Jones, 'The Reunion of Penelope and Odysseus', *G&R* 31 (1984), 1–18;
P. Marquardt, 'Penelope Πολύτροπος', *AJPh* 106 (1985), 32–48.

husband,[8] but that he has an uncanny familiarity about him, that he stirs up the same feelings that her husband does, and is in some sense his like or his near-equivalent (cf. ἔοικας and ἐοικότα used by Eurycleia to describe the stranger at 380–1, and εἴκελος used by Penelope at xx 88 to describe the Odysseus-like figure who sleeps next to her in the dream inspired by her dialogue with the stranger). Homer clearly makes us aware of the beggar's close physical resemblance to Odysseus, strongly remarked on by Eurycleia just before the footbath (378–81), intensifying her comments about the parallel circumstances in which the two ageing men are likely to find themselves (370 ff.).[9] Because this stranger has such power to evoke the image and presence of Odysseus, his emphatic interpretation of Penelope's already self-revealing dream must impress her more strongly than her guarded reaction would suggest at first reading. Her invocation of the fabled Gates of Horn and Ivory should not be taken as a firm disclaimer of belief in her dream's clear prediction, but as a defensive verbal stance. It is characteristic of Penelope to use the language of scepticism to shield herself from a belief she would love to accept (cf. 569, 'that would be welcome to me and my son') but which would render her vulnerable to the kind of false hopes that have deceived her before.[10] Her decision to tell the stranger she has

---

[8] Such is the interpretation of Anne Amory, 'The Reunion of Odysseus and Penelope', in C. Taylor, ed., *Essays on the Odyssey* (Bloomington, 1963), 100–36, followed by Austin, *Archery*, 232. My view (first set forth in J. Russo, 'Interview and Aftermath: Dream, Fantasy, and Intuition in *Odyssey* 19 and 20', *AJP* 103 (1982), 4–18) differs in assuming not outright recognition, albeit unconscious, of the beggar as Odysseus, but of the beggar's qualities and presence as evocative of Odysseus in various subtle ways (as they are for Eurycleia at xix 378–81). Of course my interpretation would not be possible without Amory's groundbreaking study, which opened the way for psychologically sophisticated readings of the interview in xix as a welcome alternative to Harsh's clever but misguided argument for full recognition (P. W. Harsh, 'Penelope and Odysseus in *Odyssey* xix', *AJPh* 71 (1950), 1–21).

[9] Throughout xix we find an intensification of a central concern of the *Odyssey* which distinguishes it in one important respect from the *Iliad*: a concern with truth and appearance as seen in the crucial distinction between reality/identity and its (mere) approximation in likelihood/similarity. Note the ψεύδεα that are ἐτύμοισιν ὁμοῖα at 203, following the significant verb ἴσκε (related to ἔοικα and εἴκελος) at 202; the beggar's description by Penelope as ὁμήλικα to Odysseus at 358 and by Eurycleia as ἐοικότα to him at 380–1; the idea that there exist separate Gates for True and False Dreams, which are none the less hard to tell apart; and Odysseus' careful distinction between two kinds of vision in defining Penelope's dream as οὐκ ὄναρ ἀλλ' ὕπαρ at 547.

[10] At xiv 124 ff. Eumaeus describes how Penelope in the past was often deceived by vagabonds with lying tales about Odysseus; and in xxiii 215–17 we hear in her own words that she has 'constantly been afraid that some mortal would come and deceive me with words'. The self-protective stance she has learned to adopt has been evident throughout the epic: at xix 309–16 she responds to the stranger's emphatic oath and

decided on a marriage contest, coming as it does immediately after
her assertion that her dream of rescue was a false one, seems on the
surface an act of total surrender to a hopeless situation: she will
finally accept marriage to the best of the suitors. But it is in keeping
with the complexity of Penelope's character that she hopes for more
than her words reveal. She cannot remain totally unaffected by the
dream's optimistic vision and the stranger's emphatic endorsement
of it, coming as they do after the prophecy of Theoclymenus (xvii
151–62) and the stranger's earlier affirmation of Odysseus's return
(xix 262–307). Her decision to set the bow-test allows her action that
resolves an impasse that had reached the breaking point (the suitors
are now prepared to murder her son) while keeping open the possibility that the dream and the mysterious stranger are telling the
truth. Her decision thus reveals her willingness to take a risk, to
commit herself to life and to life's chances after years of defensive,
calculated manœuvring. And it is her attraction to the stranger and
her intuitive sense of his latent power that move her now to act in a
way that accords perfectly with his prediction, even as her words say
the opposite.

As a former ξεῖνος of her husband who has now become φίλος and
αἰδοῖος to her, this stranger has come to mean much more to
Penelope than would normally be possible in a relationship between
a famous queen and a wandering stranger.[11] Penelope seems to
acknowledge this unusual and almost improper intimacy in her
closing speech to the beggar at the end of Book xix:

> Stranger, if you were willing to sit by me in the hall
> and give me pleasure, no sleep would fall on my eyelids.
> But there is no way for people to be constantly without sleep:
> the immortals have given it to each human
> as allotted portion upon the nourishing earth.
> So then I, for my part, am going upstairs
> to go to bed in my chamber, my bed full of weeping . . .

assurance that Odysseus will soon arrive by wishing this were true but immediately
coming up with the opposite hypothesis that it will never happen; and in xxiii she
responds to Eurycleia's news that Odysseus has returned and killed the suitors by *three
times* offering alternative explanations (10 ff., 58 ff., 80 ff.) for this supposedly most
welcome news.

[11] See W. Büchner, 'Penelopeszenen', 133–4, for an excellent analysis of the
unusually rapid growth of this attachment. As he notes: 'It is after all her husband
sitting before her; and even if a divine influence has altered his appearance to keep her
from recognizing him, the core of his being, the spirit [das Geistige], has remained the
same' (134).

There I will lie down; but you make your bed here in the house,
either spreading your own bedding, or let them set up a bed for you.

(589–95; 598–9)

Her imagination would have them, for a moment, spending a sleep-less night in intimate talk, which she says would give her great pleasure; but then she grows more realistic and specifies not only that each must retire, but that each has his and her own resting place, clearly defined and far apart. It is time to break the spell of increasing intimacy and fascination with this extraordinary stranger. Penelope has now had her husband called to mind several times with great vividness. Her imagination and her unconscious mental processes have been vigorously stirred up in xix, and the following book will continue to show the effects of this intense stimulation after so many years of impasse.[12]

Book xx begins with a depiction of Odysseus and Penelope in parallel states of mental agitation. At first each is too excited and upset to sleep, and when they finally are at rest, the sleep of each is filled with the presence of the other. Odysseus dreams that Penelope is standing by his bed, while Penelope dreams that 'someone just like him (εἴκελος αὐτῷ) as he was when he went off with the army' (88–9) is now sleeping beside her. Homer is showing us that Penelope has some kind of intuitive awareness of her husband's presence but, as suggested above, it is active on a less than conscious level. Some modern readers may be surprised at the suggestion that an eighth-century BC poet has the psychological insight to recognize the forces of the human unconscious, and the narrative subtlety to show those forces at work through the agencies of intuition, dream, and fantasy. But it should not surprise us that great storytellers have long under-stood the deeper sources of human motivation, and the obvious importance of dreams as wish-fulfilment and as commentary, in a transposed mode, upon significant daytime events.[13]

[12] The above description of xix assumes without question that it is a carefully conceived artistic whole, free from the structural blemishes imagined by earlier scholars who believed that the interview was originally designed as a recognition-scene. See Vester (op. cit., n. 1 above) for a summary and repudiation of the German Analyst tradition and a perceptive discussion of xix and its place in the overall plot design; and the similar approach of Büchner, 'Penelopeszenen', who defends the integrity of the Penelope-scenes in xviii and xix, and the references to her Web in ii, xix, and xxiv, against the strictures of the Analysts.

[13] Argued at length by Russo (op. cit., n. 8 above). Some present-day critics may still find it difficult to accept that a distinction between conscious and unconscious motives has any place in the narrative vision of an archaic poet, even a great one like Homer. Hence the emphatic criticism by Emlyn-Jones (op. cit., n. 7 above) of 'the intuitive

Now the action moves toward resolution. Telemachus and Odysseus both become bolder in their dealings with the suitors. Telemachus amazes them with his threat of violence against anyone who harms the beggar (262–74). Odysseus again has an object thrown at him, this time a cow's hoof; but this throw is distinctly more ineffective than the two previous ones (he easily dodges it), and Telemachus uses the occasion to threaten to kill the man who threw it and to berate the group with his most forceful language so far.

There now follows a series of portents and other reminders that the suitors are very near destruction. Athena creates a scene of supernatural eeriness, which the suitors cannot understand. The prophet Theoclymenus leaves the palace immediately as he sees their doom rushing upon them; but the suitors remain oblivious to the rhythm of their fate and show only incomprehension at the seer's abrupt departure. All they can do is complain to Telemachus that he chooses his guests badly, and then resume their feasting, which Theoclymenus' vision has shown us is closely tied to their forthcoming slaughter ('The meat they ate was a meal of blood . . . their laughter sounded like lamentation', 348–9). To conclude the twentieth book and intensify his portrayal of the contrast between the suitors' declining fortunes and the growing success of Odysseus, Homer leaves us a final image of father and son closely bound in silent communication based on a shared understanding (385–6), while Penelope has moved her chair to a position right outside the door so that she can hear all that has been said (387–9). Thus the three family members have a position of privileged understanding while the suitors, now more hapless than menacing, are about to 'eat

Penelope' and the 'extreme psychological interpretation' of her dream. His view (16, n. 19) is that because Penelope publicly *says* she loathes the suitors, the poet means this to represent her entire and uncomplicated psychological reality. Such an interpretation fails to deal with the fact that Homer has also made her 'say' something important through her dream of the geese: her bitter weeping over their slaughter can only point to some ambivalence in her true feelings toward them and their courting presence in her halls (Russo, op. cit., 8–10). Emlyn-Jones (op. cit., 2, nn. 7 and 8) notes with scepticism the recent tendency among American Homerists to accept some form of unconscious or intuitive recognition of Odysseus by Penelope before the full recognition of xxiii. This tendency no doubt reflects the high degree of integration of basic Freudian theory into American intellectual life in general and our interpretation of literature in particular. Whether it is 'extreme', at least as applied to the study of early epic, is a matter of individual judgement. All interpretations are constructs that must convince by their capacity to account for all the phenomena. I believe that many significant features of the queen's relation to the beggar, and especially her instant acceptance of his proposal of the bow-contest, are best accounted for by what is in fact a very moderate application of the theory of the unconscious.

their most unpleasant meal' (392). Homer has brought us, in these four books, from a situation where the suitors ruled in the house of Odysseus to a situation where the hero has returned, used his god-given disguise skilfully to win a place in the household and in Penelope's affections, and now stands ready, with the help of his son and the co-operation of a few loyal servants, to pass the test of the bow and turn that weapon to the task of eliminating the hated usurpers. Books xvii to xx have masterfully set the stage for the great denouement.

II

The reader deserves a brief statement of the principles that have determined the form of my commentary and the approach to Homer emphasized therein. Given the abundance of possible information and existing scholarship that one could cite in connection with Homer's text, I have tried to concentrate on what the attentive reader, with or without a scholarly background in Greek, needs to know for a good appreciation of Homer's narrative artistry. I have, naturally, imagined this ideal reader according to my own inclina-tion. While the *Odyssey* is an important source of linguistic, historical, and archaeological information, it is above all else a work of literary art, a narrative about human character and situation rendered in a traditional yet distinctive poetic style. Since I consider myself primarily a literary critic, my commentary gives special emphasis to literary interpretation, although not, I hope, at the expense of other, sometimes more technical, information when it is pertinent.

I have assumed that the text commented upon is almost entirely Homer's, and that its overall cohesiveness has been created by a master storyteller who was usually in full control of his technique. There is a long tradition in Homeric scholarship of suspecting and suggesting deletion of many passages in our received text, a tradition from which I wish to distance myself. These modern-day *atheteses* take their origin in the practice of Aristarchus and his fellow learned Alexandrians, who were quick to condemn what failed to appeal to their stylistic taste. Most of the verses bracketed, condemned, or suspected by earlier editors and commentators gave offence only because they are common repetitions or are not smoothly integrated into a seamless rhetorical flow. Today we know that such repetitions and occasional stylistic and narrative awkwardness are typical of oral compositional technique and natural in poetry that was recomposed or slightly modified in one performance after another. Rather than run the risk, therefore, of casting doubt on words and passages that are quite possibly Homer's, I have preferred to trust, for the most part, in the inherited manuscript tradition. I do not doubt that there are interpolated verses in our text; but I do not share the facile confidence of earlier editors that these can be easily identified. Therefore I have chosen not to use my commentary to rehearse what I consider to be vain speculations of other scholars about authenticity, nor to make any additions of my own to this unhappy scholarly genre.

Whether the Homeric poems were composed in a purely oral manner has been a much debated, and not yet satisfactorily answered, question.[14] But whatever we think about the genesis of the texts before us, there can be no doubt that their style has some resemblance to an oral style and some indebtedness to a long oral tradition. Naturally such a style, particularly if the text before us bears some marks of live performance,[15] will lack the consistent smoothness and felicity of a text of Theocritus, Callimachus, or Vergil. My personal view is that the Homeric epics were composed without the aid of writing, but with a high degree of deliberate artistry.[16] The *Iliad* and *Odyssey* must have been viewed by Homer

[14] A good summation of this issue, with detailed bibliography, is given by Hainsworth, pp. xvi–xxx, restated with minor changes in his essay 'The Epic Dialect' in vol. i of this commentary, 24–32. He inclines cautiously to the belief in an oral Homer who dictated his poems to a scribe. See also the wide-ranging and judicious review by J. Latacz in his introductory essay and his review of the history of the oral theory ('Einfuhrung' and 'Tradition und Neuerung in der Homerforschung' in J. Latacz, ed., *Homer: Tradition und Neuerung*, Wege der Forschung cdlxiii (Darmstadt, 1979), 1–44). An earlier overview of the controversy is given by Lesky, *Homeros*, who prefers a literate Homer.

[15] The first argument for this possibility was made by A. B. Lord, 'Homer's Originality: Oral Dictated Texts', *TAPhA* lxxxiv (1953), 124–34. Among the most fruitful applications of his theory are D. M. Gunn ('Narrative Inconsistency and the Oral Dictated Text in the Homeric Epic', *AJP* xci (1970), 191–203; 'Thematic Composition and Homeric Authorship', *HSPh* lxxv (1971), 1–31), who shows some minor narrative inconsistencies to be a kind of characteristic of oral performance, and argues on this basis that our text derives from the transcription of a real performance. The theory receives further support from the fieldwork observations of M. Skafte Jensen, *The Homeric Question and the Oral-Formulaic Theory* (Copenhagen, 1980), 81–95. For a recent application of the thesis see J. Russo, 'Oral Style as Performance Style in Homer's *Odyssey*', in J. M. Foley, ed., *Comparative Research on Oral Traditions: A Memorial for Milman Parry* (Columbus, Ohio, 1987).

[16] This position is argued very well by Anne Amory, 'The Gates of Horn and Ivory', *YCS* xx (1966), 35–40, and can be successfully combined with J. B. Hainsworth's observation ('Criticism of an Oral Homer', *JHS* xc (1970), 90–8) that oral stylistic traits dominate the small-scale construction of the epics, while qualities we associate with literary composition dominate the large-scale structures.

and his audiences as his masterpieces, and in a successful career as singer of tales he must have been called upon to perform them many times. Such repeated performance amounts to a form of rehearsal whose final product, while retaining small imperfections, would achieve impressive dimensions and large-scale design. It is such a text that I believe we have before us.

J.R.

Haverford, Pennsylvania
July 1989

POSTSCRIPT

I should like at this time to give thanks to all the friends and colleagues, too numerous to name, who have encouraged my work and furthered my understanding of Homer's *Odyssey* over the years. I owe a particular debt to two scholars who gave me helpful advice at different stages: Jenny Strauss Clay, who read through most of the epic with me at a preliminary stage and helped me focus on those issues in the text that deserved comment; and Henry Hoenigswald, who was most forthcoming recently with linguistic information and references. I also am grateful to the students to whom I have taught the *Odyssey* at Haverford College over the last twenty years, and in graduate seminars at the University of Michigan, the Johns Hopkins University, and the University of California at Berkeley, for deepening my knowledge of the poem through their comments and questions. The constant support of my wife, Sally Wise Russo, was not only essential but decisive in helping me complete the commentary at a time when I seemed in danger of extending the task indefinitely. As a final act of homage I wish to dedicate this book to the memory of my father, Joseph H. Russo, native of Sicily and lover of language.

August, 1990

BOOK XVII: COMMENTARY

Book xvii can be summarized in twelve narrative units, varying in length from simple twenty-line scenes to more complex scenes of 100 or more verses. Some alternative divisions could be imagined, but most of the units would be substantially the same in any scheme.

1. 1–27 Eumaeus, Telemachus, and Odysseus confer at Eumaeus' hut.
2. 27–62 Telemachus goes to the house, is curt in refusing Penelope the news she expected, and departs to fetch Theoclymenus.
3. 63–84 Telemachus talks to the loyal Ithacans at the agora; Peiraeus brings Theoclymenus.
4. 85–166 Telemachus returns home with the seer, bathes, tells Penelope the news she has been eager to have.
5. 167–82 The suitors begin gathering at the house.
6. 182–203 The scene shifts to Eumaeus' hut. Odysseus and Eumaeus prepare to leave.
7. 204–54 On their way, Melanthius insults and kicks Odysseus.
8. 255–327 Their approach to the house. First Melanthius, then Eumaeus and Odysseus arrive. The dog Argus knows Odysseus.
9. 328–68 The disguised Odysseus enters the megaron and begins begging food at Athena's prompting, to test the suitors' character.
10. 369–491 Hostility from Melanthius, and incidents of increasing abuse from Antinous, who hits Odysseus with a stool instead of giving him food. This maltreatment is criticized by the other suitors.
11. 492–588 Penelope from her chamber has followed the action in the megaron. She hears Eumaeus' account of the stranger and is eager to meet him. Odysseus replies, through Eumaeus, that a private interview would be best, after dark, with the suitors gone. Penelope agrees.
12. 589–606 Eumaeus returns to the countryside, Telemachus assuring him all will be well. The suitors take their pleasure in dance and the bard's songs.

1. This line occurs twenty times in the *Odyssey*, but only twice in the *Iliad*, and the phrase ῥοδοδάκτυλος Ἠώς occurs in five additional Homeric verses. It is probably the best-remembered and most cited Homeric line among the 'general public', and for good reason: the image is captivating and the assonance in the Greek is striking (A. Shewan, 'Alliteration and Assonance in Homer', *CPh* xx (1925), 199–200, notes Homer's partiality to the sound of η). It illustrates perfectly the conservatism of Homeric diction: once the perfect way is found to say something, the phrase is kept and repeated; there is no fear of the cliché.

2–5. Telemachus now begins to carry out the plans made in private with his father in the preceding book (270ff.). Odysseus wanted Telemachus to go first, and he would follow later with the swineherd, so as not to seem connected with Telemachus.

3. This whole verse is used six times in the *Odyssey* (including one instance in the accusative (iii 398); the hemistich Ὀδυσσῆος θείοιο is used another eighteen times, always to complete a verse after the trochaic caesura of the third foot; and one of these verses precedes the phrase with φίλος υἱός: ἔνθ' ἦλθεν φίλος υἱὸς Ὀδυσσῆος θείοιο, xxiv 151. Thus we see illustrated the same conservatism noted above for verse 1, the tendency toward verbatim repetition of the same words for the same thought, usually (but not always) keeping the same position and rhythm in the line. Against this normative background, however, the poet can innovate: the verse spoken by Zeus at i 65, πῶς ἂν ἔπειτ' Ὀδυσῆος [note -σ- for -σσ-] ἐγὼ θείοιο λαθοίμην, reveals a skilful variation on this formula. The fact that it is the only such example shows it to be a relatively new verse, created after the end-line formula had become familiar.

The purpose of Homer's frequent verbatim repetition, according to Milman Parry, was the practical one of facilitating composition; dramatic effect in the choice of epithets was not supposed to concern the poet. But critics have often demurred from Parry's absolutism (see, for example, William Whallon, 'The Homeric Epithets', *YCS* xvii (1961), 97–142; Parry, *Blameless Aegisthus*, esp. introduction and chapter I; and for the most total theoretical rejection of Parry, P. Vivante, *The Epithets in Homer* (New Haven–London, 1983), *passim*). Here in verse 3, calling Telemachus 'Odysseus' own dear son' must have special emotional force, in addition to metrical convenience, after the moving reunion in the preceding book. There is an ironic tension between formula and narrative here, in that Odysseus' 'own dear son' cannot acknowledge the bond (nor can the disguised beggar), but must energetically dissemble (12–15) to keep Eumaeus from suspecting anything.

3a. One codex includes this stock verse, which is identical to ii 3, just as xvii 1 = ii 1, and xvii 2 and ii 4 end with identical half-lines. The opening descriptions in each book of Telemachus' actions at dawn belong to the same general scene type, and we should remember that while we exclude verse 3a from our 'normative' text, there may well have been genuine Homeric *performances* in which this verse about Telemachus' sword did precede verse 4 describing his spear. Note that Book ii is again recalled briefly here when Telemachus goes to the ἀγορά (marketplace) and meets his father's loyal friends, Mentor, Antiphon, and Halitherses (68–70), the three Ithacans who spoke in his support at the assembly in ii.

6. ἄττα: 'father' is the basic meaning, but the nuance is more difficult to capture in modern translation: 'papa' comes closest. Linguists are agreed that this is a word from child's language with the meaning 'nurturing father' and the expressive gemination typical of similar words (Eng. *mamma, pappa*; Old High German *amma*, '(nurturing) mother'; Old Icelandic *amma*, 'grandmother'; Ital. *babbo*; and so on). The word is widely represented throughout Indo-European, cf. Latin *atta*, 'grandfather', Gothic *atta*, Hittite *attaš*, Old Slavic *otici*. Eustathius 777. 54 calls the word Thessalian, and at 1793. 12 says it is the term a young brother uses addressing an older (brother). Chantraine, *Dictionnaire* s.v., says that Eustathius calls it 'le terme employé par un jeune homme, comme s'il s'addressait à son père nourricier', which is incorrect rendering of Eustathius, although an accurate description of Greek usage. In Homer, it is used by Telemachus to Eumaeus six times, and by Achilles to Phoenix twice.

10. **τὸν ξεῖνον:** the article in Homeric Greek usually retains some of its original demonstrative force, and in fact should not be viewed as an article but as a demonstrative pronoun in a specialized 'deictic' usage that is in the process of developing into the definite article as we know it in later Greek (Monro, *Homeric Dialect*, 224–34; Chantraine, *Grammaire*, ii 158–66). The meaning here is probably somewhere between 'him, the stranger' and 'that stranger', but we cannot be sure, since there are also instances where Homer seems to approximate the Attic usage (Chantraine, *Grammaire*, i 276; ii 164–5). An interesting fact noted by both Monro (230) and Chantraine (164–6) is that this 'weakened' or Attic usage tends to be more frequent with certain nouns, in certain books of the *Iliad* (x, xxiii, xxiv), and in the *Odyssey* generally as compared with the *Iliad*. The nouns favoured for the *Odyssey* are ὁ ξεῖνος, ἡ νῆσος, τὰ μῆλα, ὁ μόχλος, and τὸ τόξον. Yet if we count the actual uses with the article contrasted with those without it, we find much less distinct a predilection than the wording of Monro and Chantraine would lead us to believe, with the sole exception of ὁ ξεῖνος. Singular forms of νῆσος show the article 6 of 56 times, of τόξον 2 of 50, of μόχλος 3 of 7. (Plural forms reveal only τὰ τόξα in one of 10 occurrences, and no articles used for other cases or for any forms of νῆσοι.) μῆλα is preceded by τὰ in 4 of its 34 occurrences, while μήλων has no article in 10 appearances. But when we look at ξεῖνος we find for the two commonest forms, the nominative and accusative singular, 32 of 76 instances with the article! Adding the relatively infrequent genitive and dative singular, we get 33 of 95; and we note again that plural forms show very little use of the article (one of 37, including the dual). We must conclude that the process of evolution toward an Attic usage of the definite article is markedly pronounced in one area only, that being the use of the word ξεῖνος; and it must be the special importance that the story of the *Odyssey* gives to (disguised) strangers that has generated this linguistic habit, in which Homer has left behind the norms of traditional epic diction and taken advantage of a current development in the language spoken around him.

20-1. **τηλίκος:** governs both μένειν and ὥς τε . . . πιθέσθαι as 'consecutive' infinitives (Chantraine, *Grammaire*, ii 314). This construction, which occurs only here and at *Il.* ix 42, has not yet become common like the familiar Attic ὥστε + inf., but it reveals the origin of that construction. This syntax is analysed by Ruijgh, *τε épique*, 616. **πάντα:** adverbial, 'obey him in all respects'.

23. **πυρὸς:** best taken as a partitive genitive, as in *Il.* vi 331: ἄστυ πυρὸς

COMMENTARY

δηίοιο θέρηται; xi 666–7: νῆες θοαὶ ἄγχι θαλάσσης | Ἀργείων ἀέκητι πυρὸς δηίοιο θέρωνται. We translate 'be warmed *by* the fire', but the Greek way of conceiving the relationship is to be warmed '*of* the fire', as if the fire is a substance from which one takes a share of the warmth. **θερέω**: this verb is naturally associated with πυρός, as the examples given above show, but the form is puzzling, since a passive is expected. Chantraine, *Grammaire*, i 71, 401, 459, identifies this as an aorist passive with -ηω shortened to -εω by a metathesis well attested for subjunctives (θέωμεν, κτέωμεν, στέωμεν, etc.; and see Meister, *Kunstsprache*, 161–3, for further details). This would then be the only evidence for such an aorist passive of θέρεσθαι. Monro, ad loc., suggests it may be a present tense intransitive form, equivalent in meaning to θέρεσθαι. **ἀλέη**: this noun is a *hapax*, although several verbal and adjectival forms exist (Chantraine, *Dictionnaire* s.v. ἀλέα). The Scholia, the *Etymologicum Magnum*, Ameis–Hentze–Cauer, and Monro ad loc., understand it as 'the sun's warmth', as do Frisk, *GEW* and *LfgrE*. The more general meaning 'warmth' has been advocated by LSJ, Stanford, and Chantraine (loc. cit.), all of whom take it to mean the warmth of the fire in this passage. That gives an awkward sentence, whereas 'sun's warmth' gives a much more natural sequence, where Odysseus goes on to cite the poor condition of his clothes and the threat of morning frost in the next two verses. We should recall that seasonal references to cold weather have been made throughout the poem (v 467–9, vii 7, xi 373, xiv 457, 529, xv 392, xvii 191, 572–3, xviii 328–9, xix 64), and the warmth of the rising sun would be a significant factor in taking the chill off the land in the early morning. Some scholars have inferred from these details that the *Odyssey* takes place between September and November. See J. A. Scott in *CPh* xi (1916), 148–55, and Hainsworth's comments at v 272–7 and vii 7.

29. Some scholars have been needlessly bothered by an apparent inconsistency with Book i. At i 127–9 Telemachus first enters the house and then puts Athena–Mentes' spear into a spear-holder (δουροδόκη) located inside the megaron. Here, he rests it against a column outside the hall before entering. I see no reason why Telemachus cannot do two different things on two different occasions. Stanford prints a variant reading, ἔγχος μὲν στῆσε πρὸς κίονα μακρὸν ἐρείσας, following Ludwich and Ameis–Hentze–Cauer, which has seemed to some editors (I know not why) to mitigate the supposed difficulty over the location of the spear-holder. Monro, ad. loc., strangely takes this line as showing that the spear-holder was outside the megaron, even though the receptacle is not mentioned and we are specifically told that he simply placed the spear against a column. As so often with Homer, scholarly ink has been wasted combating shadows.

32. **καστορνῦσα**: a Scholiast glosses with the more familiar καταστρωννῦσα. Homer knows only forms of this verb with the stem στορ-, never the form στρώννυμι common in later Greek. The final -α of κατά is lost by *apocope*, loss of a final vowel before a consonant (whereas elision is loss of final vowel before a vowel), very common in Homeric Greek for the

20

prepositions ἀνά, παρά, κατά (cf. the familiar forms ἄμ πεδίον, παρθέμενοι, κακκείοντες). Normally after loss of -α the final -τ of κατά assimilates to the following consonant and doubles it, but where the consonant is already double, the τ is simply dropped, as in κάσχεθε. Further details in Chantraine, *Grammaire*, i 87–8.

35. **κύνεον**: the scansion ∪ ∪ – is unexpected, since metrical position before final ν is not among the special conditions that allow lengthening (Meister, *Kunstsprache*, 34–42; Chantraine, *Grammaire*, i 97–105; initial ν, on the other hand, like the other liquids λ, μ, ρ, and the spirant σ, often has the power to lengthen preceding short vowels: Monro, *Homeric Dialect*, 344). It is the interesting observation of Monro, ad loc., and *Homeric Dialect*, 349, that a distinct tendency exists for 3rd-plural forms of secondary tenses (-ον and -αν) to count as long, but it is confined to the *Odyssey* (eleven times) and the Iliadic Catalogue of Ships (seven times), with another example at *Il.* vii 206.

37. **Ἀρτέμιδι**: with long -ῐ, which may be the original quantity (Chantraine, *Grammaire*, i 217; *Dictionnaire* s.v., notes a possible Mycenaean *Atimite* = Ἀρτεμίτει); but it is also common for dat. sing. -ι to be long by metrical convenience. In this case the digamma of (ϝ)ἰκέλη would prevent correption. Monro, *Homeric Dialect*, 346–7, is no doubt correct in envisaging an original long -ῐ which epic poets came to treat as a poetic licence available when they needed it.

The choice of Artemis and Aphrodite together as a comparison for Penelope is especially felicitous. Earlier in vi 102, Homer had used a simile of Artemis to describe the young and virginal Nausicaa, and later Odysseus uses the same comparison directly addressed to Nausicaa (vi 149–52). In our passage, Penelope has been a chaste Artemis-figure during Odysseus' twenty-year absence, but she is at the same time a desired sexual object or Aphrodite-figure every time she appears before the suitors. Hence the dual comparison (repeated at xix 54) is most apt.

39–42. These four verses are identical with xvi 15, 22–4. In xvi a simile (16–21) separates the first verse from the next three, a simile in which Eumaeus tearfully greets Telemachus as a father receives a beloved only son who returns from dangers in a distant land, after a ten years' absence. Here in xvii the simile has become reality: Penelope tearfully greets her only son who has, indeed, narrowly escaped death returning from a distant land. (47: φυγόντι περ αἰπὺν ὄλεθρον; xvi 21: ὣς ἐκ θανάτοιο φυγόντα). Penelope knew about the danger of the suitors' ambuscade, while Eumaeus did not; hence in xvi the danger is expressed in the world of the simile, since it could not find expression in the conscious mind of one of the characters.

46. **μοι ... μοι**: the first μοι can be understood as a dative of interest, designating 'the person who is particularly interested in the statement' and 'especially common with the unaccented pronouns μοι, τοι, οἱ' (Chantraine, *Grammaire*, ii 71; or possibly as the closely related ethical dative, as in vii 303, ix 42 (cf. Chantraine, op. cit. 72). Its meaning approaches that of 'please'. The second μοι is a simple possessive dative, 'my heart in my chest'. The closely related verbs ὄρνυμι and ὀρίνω show a

COMMENTARY

subtle distinction here, the first meaning 'to set in motion', the second 'to put in commotion, to trouble'.

47. περ: here intensive rather than concessive (contra Ameis–Hentze–Cauer, ad loc.): 'since I have (barely) escaped'. The same intensive meaning of περ holds for 13 above. These two instances are good examples of what Denniston, Particles, 482, distinguishes as 'determinative' περ, closely related to the intensive function, signifying that 'the speaker concentrates on [something] to the exclusion of other things'.

48–53. Telemachus' full ascendancy to power within his household is now seen, completing the process begun by his new independence (inspired by Athena) as revealed in his trip to Pylos and Sparta. His independent strong-mindedness looks to us like rudeness: he not only refuses to answer his mother's question, he refuses to acknowledge it. His only concern is to complete what he considers more urgent business of his own, the reclaiming of Theoclymenus from Peiraeus.

57. Ὣς ἄρ ἐφώνησεν, τῇ δ' ἄπτερος ἔπλετο μῦθος: this much-discussed line is one of the great cruces of the Odyssey. It reappears at xix 29, xxi 386, and xxii 398, where Eurycleia is addressed by Telemachus, Eumaeus, and Telemachus again. Scholarly opinion has been divided on two distinct problems: (1) does the μῦθος belong to the speaker or to the person addressed? (2) what does ἄπτερος mean? A likely answer to either question would help answer the other.

Many have thought that since Penelope and Eurycleia, when addressed in these passages, make no answer and proceed to carry out Telemachus' or Eumaeus' orders, the phrase must prepare for this action and mean 'she made no response (but did as she was told)'. On this reading the μῦθος belongs to the woman addressed and ἄπτερος means it goes unspoken. This view is favoured by Monro ad loc., Ameis–Hentze–Cauer (and defended at length in the Anhang), and is argued with skill and subtlety by J. Latacz in Glotta xlvi (1968), 27–38, interpreting the silence of Penelope and Eurycleia as pregnant with an unexpressed emotion which unexpected coldness or surprising content in the utterance of an intimate person has forced the women to repress. (The hemistich thus becomes another of the 'silence-formulas' studied by S. Besslich, Schweigen.) Other scholars, however, emphasizing the regularity of Homer's dictional habits, have made a convincing argument for referring the μῦθος to the speech just made (P. Mazon, RÉG lxiii (1950), 14–19; J. B. Hainsworth, Glotta xxxviii (1960), 263–8). In similar situations we find a verse whose first half says 'so he (she) spoke' and whose second half describes the effect of this utterance using the word μῦθος. Cf. ὣς ἔφατ' Ἀλκίνοος (Ἀντίνοος, Ἀμφίνοος), τοῖσιν δ' ἐπιήνδανε μῦθος (7 ×); ὣς φάτο Σαρπηδών, δάκε δὲ φρένας Ἕκτορι μῦθος (Il. v 493); ὣς φάτο Πουλυδάμας, ἅδε δ' Ἕκτορι μῦθος ἀπήμων (2 ×). It is most likely that our verse should be interpreted analogously.

But if the μῦθος is the speech of Telemachus, what does it mean to call it ἄπτερος? The α- can be privative or intensive, and ancient lexicographical tradition is aware of both possibilities. (Modern scholarship is similarly

22

divided over whether ἄπτερος at A. Ag. 276 means 'swift' or 'unfledged', although at Eu. 51 and 250 it clearly means 'without wings'.) Schol. on this line agree with the Etymologicum Magnum in glossing ἄπτερος as (1) 'swift (as flight)'—ταχύς, ἰσόπτερος—and (2) 'abiding, not flying away'; the EM adds (3) 'pleasing' and Schol. (4) 'ready' (ἕτοιμος, a meaning attributed to Herodian); and finally the Lexicon of Apollonius the Sophist has 'swift' followed by 'pleasing' or 'gentle' (προσηνής). It is noteworthy that nowhere does the meaning 'wingless' = 'unexpressed' or 'ineffective' appear. Meanings (3) and (4) are generally found useless. Meaning (2) makes the assumption that the function of wings or feathers, πτερά, is to help the word fly away so as to be lost. Such an interpretation would make the familiar formula ἔπεα πτερόεντα rather peculiar (pace F. M. Combellack, 'Words that Die', CJ xlvi (1950-1), 21-6, who argues for precisely this interpretation).

Let us clarify πτερόεις as part of the problem of interpreting ἄπτερος. J. A. K. Thompson, CQ xxx (1936), 1-3, and J. Latacz, loc. cit., have made a strong case for ἔπεα πτερόεντα as 'feathered words', ascribing the metaphor to arrows not birds (cf. Il. iv 117, v 171, xvi 773, xx 68). They are followed by S. West on Od. i 122, q.v. Leaf, Iliad, on v 453 (= xii 426), glossing the obscure λαισήϊα πτερόεντα used of shields, suggests 'fluttering' as the meaning that suits all the applications of πτερόεις, and it is attractive to avoid a forced choice between 'winged' and 'feathered' as the sole alternatives. Chantraine, Dictionnaire s.v. πέτομαι, defines πτερόν as 'that which is used to fly', i.e. neither wing nor feather but a broader meaning that encompasses both and is not easily translated. I would render πτερόεις, then, as 'flying easily' or 'equipped to fly', applicable to both words and arrows and suggesting swift motion. (The λαισήϊα πτερόεντα remain a special case whose meaning is unclear.)

How then should we understand ἄπτερος? Any idea that the μῦθος just spoken does not fly easily to its goal is refuted by the context: Penelope and Eurycleia clearly receive the message, and proceed to obey it. We must choose, finally, to accept the first meaning, 'swift', with intensive alpha. The persuasive evidence is in the phrase τοὶ δ' ἀπτερέως ἐπίθοντο in Hesiod, fr. 204 MW, line 84, which describes the speedy compliance of Helen's suitors with the oath that Tyndareos makes them swear. The phrase comes from the same formulaic nexus as Homer's τοὶ δ' ὀτραλέως ἐπίθοντο, Il. iii 260, τοὶ δ' ἐσσυμένως ἐπίθοντο, Od. xv 288. The adverb ἀπτερέως is also found in archaic Greek in Parmenides fr. 1. 17 DK, where the meaning 'swift' seems certain, and it reappears in several Hellenistic authors. We should therefore probably accept in Homeric diction the coexistence of two words, ἄπτερος and πτερόεις, of approximately the same meaning ('swift as/in flight'), which can seem to be opposites and have for centuries confused interpreters. The 'winged words' and 'wingless speech' familiar from some English versions would then be the products of inaccurate etymologizing.

Among modern authorities only Mazon offers the interpretation

COMMENTARY

favoured above. Hainsworth agrees that the μῦθος belongs to the speaker and that ἄπτερος is 'swift', but on the basis of an original lost *ἀπτερόεις, from which ἔπεα πτερόεντα would derive via false division of ἔπε' ἀπτερόεντα. For other discussions see M. Durante, *Rendiconti dell'Accademia dei Lincei* xiii (1958), 3–14 (repr. in German in R. Schmitt, *Indogermanische Dichtersprache* (Darmstadt, 1966), 242–60); M. van der Valk, *AC* xxxv (1966), 59–64; E. C. Yorke, *CQ* xxx (1936), 151–2; M. R. Jacks, *CR* xxxvi (1922), 70–1; S. West, i 122 n.; Hainsworth, viii 346 n.; Hoekstra, xiii 165 n.

62. **κύνες ἀργοί:** this phrase and κύνες πόδας ἀργοί are descriptive formulas commonly used to name dogs in Homeric narrative. In this epic style familiar things all have their standing epithets, which relate them to the world of heroic action. So just as spears are long, or sharp, or fitted with bronze, so dogs are always 'swift' or 'swift in their feet'. Here the MS variant 'swift-footed dogs' is in terms of Homeric style as 'authentic' as the reading we have printed (following the greater MS authority), and we must remember that in the Homeric 'original', which means a *performance*, the replacement of a standard phrase by its equivalent would not be unusual. See further 292 n. for ἀργός.

63–4. It is one of Athena's characteristic services to enhance her favourites by pouring 'divine grace' upon them. The recipients are Telemachus (here and ii 12) and Odysseus (vi 235, viii 19; and cf. vii 42 for a variant with a disguising mist), which underscores their closeness and the fact that the son, in the course of the story, is growing increasingly like his father. A different enhancement formula is used for Penelope at xviii 192.

66. **βυσσοδόμευον:** a most interesting word, used seven times in the *Odyssey* (cf. below 465, 491; also iv 676, viii 273, ix 316, xx 184), never in the *Iliad*, and in Hesiod only at *Scut.* 30. The meaning, 'to meditate secretly', is derived by combining the etymological sense, 'to build in the deep', with the idea of mental space, here specified by φρεσί but normally not verbally expressed. It is always meant *in malam partem* and joined with κακά (*Scut.* 30 has instead δόλον). This word is at home in the *Odyssey*, which contains so much disguise, dissembling, and intense secret planning, and employs a correspondingly more elaborate vocabulary in this area than does the *Iliad*. This whole verse is unusual in contrasting good specious things spoken with evil thoughts hidden in the speaker's mind. The heroic epic norm is quite the contrary, with its expected unity of word and deed, summed up in Phoenix's statement of Peleus' charge to him concerning the education of Achilles: μύθων τε ῥητῆρ' ἔμεναι πρηκτῆρά τε ἔργων, *Il.* ix 443. Words are also expected to be commensurate with the quality of one's thoughts, so that Alcinous can say to Odysseus: σοὶ δ' ἐπὶ μὲν μορφὴ ἐπέων, ἔνι δε φρένες ἐσθλαί, *Od.* xi 367. We see then that in epic terms Homer is making a serious criticism of the suitors.

72. **ἔτι δήν:** the scansion of this common phrase is always ∪ – –, with the digamma (δήν < *δϝην) keeping its force to make position.

85–95. Descriptions of guests' arrival, their reception, their hand-washing, and their being served food by servants, are among the common repeated

24

passages in Homer. They are analysed and discussed, together with other such 'typical scenes', by Arend, *Scenen*. For a full discussion of composition by theme as a device of oral poetics, see Lord, *Singer*, ch. 4.

87. ἀσαμίνθους: on this pre-Greek word for 'bath-tub' and its importance in Mycenaean culture, see S. West, iii 468n. and Hainsworth, viii 450n.

101-6. Another example of how the tension between mother and son leads Penelope to communicate by indirection. Her statement, 'I am returning to my bed and my weeping now; and you didn't tell me the news about your father', is her way of suggesting that although he refused to answer her question earlier (44 ff.), she is now giving him a second chance. In being indirect, she avoids the risk of encountering, a second time, the direct rebuff that a direct request might bring.

119. θεῶν ἰότητι: is this a reference to the Judgement of Paris, where it was the clash of the goddesses' wills that led to the abduction of Helen and the Trojan War? Or is it merely the stock phrase for the theological suggestion that divine will is behind all significant human travail? I incline to the former, partly because it gives more meaningfully coherent syntax for the whole relative clause from ἧς εἵνεκα, and partly because the one clear reference in Homeric epic to the Trojan War (*Il.* xxiv 31-2) is also oblique, which suggests that the legend was so well known it needed almost no mention in the epics and could be evoked by the slightest allusion.

124-41 = iv 333-50. Telemachus repeats Menelaus' speech verbatim.

130. ἀμφοτέροισι: presumably two young fawns are meant, the νέβρους of 127. Ameis–Hentze–Cauer and Monro both understand ἀμφοτέροισι to refer to the combination of 'both' doe and fawns, which is unidiomatic as well as improbable because we were told at 128-9 that the doe was βοσκομένη elsewhere. The scholia on iv 339 show that Aristophanes was the first critic to interpret ἀμφοτέροισι this way, but referring to the doe and only one fawn, influenced by Aristotle's belief (cited in the same scholia) that does normally bore single offspring (presumably then Aristophanes read νέβρον at 127). Stanford's note (which seems to misread the opinions of both Aristophanes and Aristotle) makes the convincing point that since the simile equates the fawns with the suitors, their mother, like the suitors' parents, would be removed from danger.

133. ἐϋκτιμένη: seems to have remained a favourite epithet of Lesbos, if we can take Anacreon's Λέσβου ἐϋκτίτου (fr. 358 P) as continuing the tradition.

134. Philomeleides is explained by Eustathius as a king of Lesbos who challenged every newcomer to a wrestling match. We know nothing else about this exploit of Odysseus.

140. τά: Homeric use of the definite article as relative pronoun is normally restricted to cases where the noun or pronoun immediately precedes, as seen in ἔτος . . . τῷ and Αἰθίοπας, τοί at i 16-17 and 23. For the rule, see Monro, *Homeric Dialect*, 231, who cites this verse (= iv 349) and *Il.* i 125 as the sole exceptions. He suggests the possibility of reading ἀλλά θ' ἅ, which is developed further by G. M. Bolling ('Wackernagel's Psilotic Homer',

CPh xli (1946), 233), who points out that this could have been written *ΑΛΛΑΤΑ*, facilitating the corruption to ἀλλὰ τά.

153. ὅ γ᾽: does this refer to Menelaus or Telemachus? Commentators have been divided over this point, but the reference must be to Menelaus for several reasons: (1) It would be awkward and rude for Theoclymenus to refer thus to the deficiencies of his host Telemachus. (2) ὅδε not ὅ γε would be more likely if Telemachus were the one meant. (3) Since the contrast is between one whose knowledge is partial and limited, and one who is clairvoyant (the speaker), the most fitting reference would be to the contrast between Menelaus, whose report of what Proteus said is both second-hand and already dated, and the direct testimony of Theoclymenus, which comes through no intermediary and is completely new. This contrast is pointed by the repetition of οὐδ᾽ ἐπικεύσω, 141 and 154, which shows that Theoclymenus' revelation of the truth concerning Odysseus is to be taken as a replacement for the earlier version received from Menelaus.

160-1. The scholiast notes that in the 'common' (κοινοτέροις) editions lines 150–65 are athetized, while in the 'better' ones (χαριεστέροις) it is only 160–1 (Theoclymenus' statement that he was *on the ship* when he saw the bird). These two verses are inconsistent with xv 499 ff., where Telemachus and Theoclymenus have already disembarked and are on shore when the omen appears (cf. esp. 527–8); but I see no good reason to doubt the lines if we keep in mind two important points: (1) The word *athetized* (ἀθετοῦνται) represents, as Monro in his commentary ad loc. reminds us, 'the judgement of a critic, not the reading of a manuscript'. That is, the received text known to Aristarchus contained all these lines and critical doubt was focused on them, especially 160–1, because of the factual inconsistency with Book xv. (2) A few small inconsistencies of detail occur throughout the *Iliad* and *Odyssey*, as they do in all epic poetry that is composed not for a readership but for an audience that is to follow with their ears in recitation by instalments. A slip like the inconsistency at 160–1 is by no means a sign of spuriousness, but on the contrary it can be taken as evidence for the 'oral' conditions of creation or performance of this episode. As van der Valk puts it, this kind of 'inaccuracy' shows merely 'the poet's neglect of former data in order to stress the present situation' ('The Formulaic Character of Homeric Poetry', *AC* xxxv (1966), 228), which is one of the cardinal features of oral narrative.

163-5. These same three lines are spoken earlier by Telemachus to Theoclymenus at xv 536–8, and will be spoken later by Penelope to the disguised Odysseus, xix 309–11. In such recurrences we are sometimes justified in seeing more than formulaic repetition for the kind of merely functional convenience that was noted above in the comment on 85–95. These three lines have a different context each time they are spoken, and acquire a more powerful dramatic irony in each successive context, as the crisis of Odysseus' return builds to its climax.

182. A change of scene at mid-verse is unusual, but seems to appeal to the poet in this section of the narrative, since he does it again at 260 and did it earlier at xv 495.

191. **ποτὶ ἔσπερα**: 'towards evening'. The sole use of πρὸς/ποτὶ with temporal sense in Homer, see Chantraine, *Grammaire*, ii 133. **ῥίγιον:** 'colder'. The comparative ῥίγιον is normally metaphorical in Homer and means 'worse', 'rather unpleasant' (xx 220; *Il.* i 325, 563, xi 405; and cf. ῥίγησε(ν), which always means 'shuddered with distaste'). The fact that this passage offers the one exception is another sign of the poet's determination to emphasize the chilly weather, noted in the comment on 23 *ad fin.*

196. **οὐδόν:** οὐδός is for ὁδός, a scholion tells us, but commentators have been unhappy with this explanation, since the word normally means 'threshold' in Homer. Monro suggests if it were an Ionicism for ὁδός it should have become the main form, like κοῦρος and ξεῖνος. We must conclude either (1) with Monro, that it is the word 'threshold' in a special restricted sense applied to a road, and means 'road-way' (Monro compares Latin *agger viae*); or, with more likelihood, (2) that it is indeed an Ionic form of ὁδός, but was inhibited from spreading in the Epic language because of the possibility of confusion with οὐδός = threshold. A third alternative, to prefer the reading οὖδας of a few MSS, has nothing to recommend it. Below at 204 we have ὁδόν παιπαλόεσσαν referring to this same road (it is this rockiness that makes it 'very treacherous', ἀρισφαλής), which strengthens the likelihood that οὐδός and ὁδός are exactly the same thing. This is the view of Chantraine, *Grammaire*, i 104, who explains the lengthening as analogical influence of οὐδός, 'threshold', an interpretation supported with detailed analysis by Wyatt, *Lengthening*, 226-7.

207. Ithakos, Neritos, and Polyktor are identified by scholion V as the founders first of Cephallenia and then of Ithaca, who gave their names first to the islands and then to Mt Neritus. The story is attributed to Acusilaus. Scholia BQ add that Polyktor gave his name to Polyktorion, a place in Ithaca of which nothing else is known. The name Polyktor appears as father of the suitor Pisander, xviii 299, xxii 243; but since the name also appears at *Il.* xxiv 397, this Odyssean appearance may carry no special significance and may simply be a typical heroic 'significant' name, 'Muchpossessing'.

208. **ἦν:** although all the MSS read ἦν, it is quite possible that Homer originally said ἔεν, a common form elsewhere, which here would have the virtue of avoiding a spondee in the fifth foot.

212. Enter Melanthius the palace goatherd, the one male servant who has allied himself with the suitors. Conspicuous for his disloyalty, he is the exact negative counterpart of loyal Eumaeus, just as his sister Melantho (xviii 321 ff., xix 60 ff.) is the bad counterpart of the faithful Eurycleia. Here as elsewhere, the *Odyssey* shows a certain curious taste for doublets and opposing pairs. To the doublet Melanthius/Melantho add Circe/Calypso, Demodocus/Phemius, Cyclopes/Laestrygonians, Antinous/Eurymachus, Eurycleia/Eurynome, Mentes/Mentor; and perhaps the pairing of

27

Phemius and Medon as two professionals (δημιοεργοί, see note on 383) who served the suitors but were not disloyal, are accordingly spared at xxii 330–80, and are still treated as a duo at xxiv 439.

As opposed pairs, consider Clytemnestra/Penelope and Agamemnon/Odysseus, Circe (Calypso)/Nausicaa, Polyphemus/Alcinous (who share descent from Poseidon but are antithetical hosts), Melanthius/Eumaeus, Melanthius/Philoetius, Melantho/Eurycleia, Antinous/Amphinomus, Sirens/Leucothoe.

218. This verse seems to be a proverb, and is quoted as such by later authors. All recent editors accept the MSS' ὡς τὸν ὁμοῖον, while acknowledging that there is no evidence for ὡς = εἰς before Attic Greek. Stanford notes that Plato (*Lysis* 214a) and Hippocrates (Kühn 1, 390 and 392) quote the line with ὡς, and he suggests that their influence, together with 'Aristotle's citation of the line with ὡς τὸν' (*Rh.* i 11. 25. 1371b), has eliminated an original Homeric ἐς τόν. I believe this is so (with one correction: Aristotle quotes not the line but just the proverbial phrase ὡς αἰεὶ τὸν ὁμοῖον, the first hemistich). That a blatant Atticism has crept into our text is further suggested by Callimachus fr. 178 Pfeiffer, 9–10 (cited by von der Mühll and Stanford as fr. 8): ἀλλ' αἶνος Ὁμηρικός, αἰὲν ὁμοῖον | ὡς θεός, οὐ ψευδής, ἐς τὸν ὁμοῖον ἄγει. This final piece of evidence is sufficient, in my judgement, to warrant the unusual step of restoring ἐς to the text against all the MS testimony.

219. μολοβρὸν: an abusive term of uncertain meaning, used again by Irus of Odysseus at xviii 28. The scholia give what seem to be silly etymologizing explanations, deriving the word from μολοῦντα πρὸς τὴν βρῶσιν or μολίσκοντα ἐπὶ βοράν, one who goes after food, someone with a raging belly (γαστρίμαργον). The same meaning, 'glutton', is suggested by Chantraine, *Minos*, xii (1952), pp. 203–5. Modern commentators have related it to μολόβριον, a young wild pig (Ael. *NA* vii 47). Aelian goes on to say that Hipponax (68D = 114bw) refers to the pig (boar) itself as μολοβρίτης. Either meaning would be appropriate here: calling Odysseus a seeker after food would accord with the abusive words that follow at 220 and 228, and would also anticipate Odysseus' own characterization of himself as driven by a hungry belly (473, 559; xviii 364, 380); while, as Stanford points out, calling him a kind of pig would be a joke on Eumaeus' position as swineherd. An alternative meaning for μολοβρός, 'hairless', 'pest-ridden', or 'diseased', is suggested by E. Coughanowr, 'The Meaning of ΜΟΛΟΒΡΟΣ in Homer', *CQ* xxix (1979), 229f., based on interesting linguistic evidence from modern Greek and the suitability of this meaning for uses of μολοβρός in post-Homeric Greek.

220. δαιτῶν ἀπολυμαντῆρα: ἀπολυμαντήρ is found only here and at 377, and this expression has been interpreted two ways: either 'spoiler (destroyer) of feasts' or 'lick-plate', i.e. one who eats the left-over food. Both glosses are in the scholia and both meanings are cited by LSJ, who seem, like most translators, to favour the less convincing first interpretation, while Ebeling, *Lexicon*, and Ameis–Hentze–Cauer favour the second. The issue seems settled by T. A. Sinclair, 'On Two Words in Homer', in *Festschrift F. Dornsieff zum 65 Geburtstag* (Leipzig, 1953), 330–3, who shows that the meaning 'spoiler' or 'destroyer' must have come from confusion with Attic λυμαίνομαι (from λύμος), 'to damage', and that the ἀπολυμαντήρ is one who cleans up the discarded scraps (cf. ἔκβολα λύματα δαιτός, Call., *Cer.* 115) after a meal, a likely function for beggars in Homeric society.

221. πολλῆς φλιῆσι … θλίψεται ὤμους: 'will rub his shoulders on many doorposts', i.e. will many times be rubbing his shoulders on doorposts, a metonymic transfer of temporal πολλά to πολλῆς modifying φλιῆσι. The MSS divide between φλίψεται, an old Aeolic form, and the better-known θλίψεται. I suspect, following van der Valk, *Textual Criticism*, 101, and Shipp, *Studies*, 344, that the more common form has driven out the rare and authentic one, probably a change made by Zenodotus (so von der Mühll, apparatus, and Ludwich, *AHT* i 619). In support of φλίψεται I note that it is the form recorded in Apollonius the Sophist's *Lexicon Homericum*, and that it adds more alliterative force to Melanthius' abusive outburst. Echo and alliteration are characteristic of his abuse (κακὸς—κακὸν 217, ὁμοῖον—ὁμοῖον 218, τόνδε μολοβρὸν ἄγεις, ἀμέγαρτε 219, αἰτίζων—ἀκόλους—ἄορας 222, ἐρίφοισι φορῆναι 224, βούλεται αἰτίζων βόσκειν 228), and seems part of Homer's careful, consistent delineation of this minor character. See further comment on Melanthius' rhetoric in the note to 231–2. For more detail on the linguistic peculiarities of Melanthius' speech, see Shipp loc. cit.

225. ἐπιγουνίδα: γουνός is a knoll or swelling of the ground, and so ἐπιγουνίς is the swelling of the upper thigh caused by the large muscle there. Again, as so often in xvii and xviii, echo of phrase or of narrative motif links the two books: at xviii 74 the suitors will marvel that the old man has such a powerful thigh (οἵην … ἐπιγουνίδα) when he pulls back his ragged clothing, girding for the fight with Irus.

231–2. Although accurately characterized by Monro as 'a piece of exaggeration or inversion of the natural statement, suited to the rough humour of the speech', these verses have seemed to critics (beginning with the scholia) as awkward or strained, for two reasons: (1) it seems inconsistent for stools to be simultaneously *around the head* and *hitting the ribs*; (2) the ribs are said to wear out the stools, whereas the naturalistic truth would have the stools wearing out the ribs. Solutions have been sought in the MS variants πλευράς and πλευρά (neut. pl. as at *Il.* iv 468, xi 437), both of them unnecessary and unattractive. πλευράς, which would give the more credible picture of the stools wearing out the ribs, must scan with short final syllable -ᾰς, giving us an a-stem with short acc. pl., a phenomenon found at least eight times in Hesiod (G. P. Edwards, *The Language of Hesiod* (Oxford, 1971), 140ff.) but never in Homer (W. F. Wyatt, 'Short Accusative Plurals in Greek', *TAPhA* xcvii (1966), 617ff., esp. 618f.). The form πλευρά has very weak MS authority and would introduce an 'illegitimate' hiatus before ἀποτρίψουσι (although such hiatus does occur occasionally in Homeric diction: Chantraine, *Grammaire* i 90–2). Alternatively, one could read πλευρά τ' with Bothe. But I find the majority reading πλευραί quite attractive. Melanthius' language is characterized by strong and even excessive metaphors (see 218, 221–2, 225, 228). He is an impressive rustic rhetorician, and in this case he has made effective use of the syntactic ambiguity inherent in the Greek neuter plural, by beginning his statement as if πολλά οἱ ἀμφὶ κάρη σφέλα were to be his subject and he were about to describe what the stools flying about the beggar's head would do; and then he surprises his audience by revealing that the stools are the object and are acted upon by the ribs. The result is a crudely conceived exaggeration, to be sure, but it suits the speaker and is more effective for its roughness. As for the inconsistency in the stools being both around the head and at the ribs, we might be justified in taking ἀμφὶ κάρη as not literal and local but as a phrase expressing the looser sense of 'around you', as if κάρη were metonymic for the whole person, as is idiomatic in Greek.

235–8. ὁ δὲ μερμήριξεν ... φρεσὶ δ' ἔσχετο: an interesting deviation from the Homeric norm for describing the act of 'pondering' (μερμηρίζειν) alternatives. The person always weighs *two* alternatives, and regularly chooses to act upon the second named, as for example at xviii 90–4, in a confrontation between Odysseus and Irus similar to this one with Melanthius. Here, however, both alternatives are disregarded in favour of a third possibility, which is a unique feature for such μερμηρίζω-scenes. Another unusual feature is that the new alternative chosen is not action but the suppression of action, literally the repression, by an act of will, of the normal impulse to act. Hence the novel phrase combination, ἀλλ' ἐπετόλμησε, φρεσὶ δ' ἔσχετο. μερμηρίζω-scenes are discussed as one of the 'typical scenes' in Arend (see note to 85–95), and in fullest detail by Christian Voigt, *Überlegung und Entscheidung* (Berlin, 1933), esp. 47 n. 2 and 80–1, where deviations from the basic pattern are discussed.

237. ἀμφουδὶς: a hapax of disputed meaning. Bechtel, *Lexilogus* s.v., accepts Fick's proposal of an original spelling ἀμφωδίς from *ἀμφωϝαδίς and the meaning 'by both ears'. Such a comic image would have been appropriate to the tone of Melanthius' mocking speech, but I find it hardly consonant with the serious and angry mood provoked in Odysseus, who, we must note, is seriously considering killing the man. Perhaps more likely is the interpretation (LSJ, followed by Stanford) that takes ἀμφουδίς as an adverbial derivative of ἀμφί, like ἀμυδίς from ἅμα and ἄλλυδις from ἄλλος, with the meaning 'around the middle'. With ἀείρας this would describe a wrestling hold on the body and then ἐλάσειε κάρη would be the fatal dashing of the head against the ground. Ameis–Hentze–Cauer cite a parallel from Terence, *Ad.* iii 2 18: sublimem medium arriperem et capite in terram statuerem, ut cerebro dispergat viam. One obstacle to this adverbial interpretation is the -ου- in place of the -υ- found in the normal adverbial formation. The fullest discussion of this problematic passage is by A. G. Tsopanakis, Ἀμφουδίς, *Hellenika*, xii (1951), 79–93, who prefers the v.l. ἀμφ' οὔδας ἐρείσας.

248. ὀλοφώϊα εἰδώς: it is a typically Homeric habit of language to describe someone's state of mind or character as 'knowing' plus a neuter plural object of the participle. Thus men who are friends are described as φίλα εἰδότες ἀλλήλοισιν; a 'good' woman is κεδνὰ ἰδυῖα; and a variety of temperaments are described in phrases like πεπνυμένα (ἀποφώλια, ἀθεμίστια, ἤπια) εἰδώς, regularly constituting the fourth colon of the verse.

This habit of language is discussed by Hermann Fränkel, *Early Greek Poetry and Philosophy* (New York–London, 1975), 79–83, who skilfully relates it to the characteristic Homeric (and primarily Iliadic) world-view, in which 'there is no cleavage between feeling and the corporal situation . . . If what man wills and is, is straightway and without hindrance transformed into action, then every human trait and every character passes unchecked into outward expression and achievement' (79; and see esp. 82. For the different Odyssean conception of man, see pp. 85-93, and my note above on line 66). ὀλοφώϊος is a word of some ambiguity. It is either related to ὄλλυμι (cf. ὀλώϊος) and means 'destructive' (but then where does the -φ- come from?), or, perhaps more likely, to ἐλεφαίρομαι (xix 565; *Il.* xxiii 388) and means 'deceitful, tricky'. LSJ s.v. ὀλοόφρων says the Iliadic meaning is 'destructive-minded' while the Odyssean meaning is 'devious, deceitful'.

257. τὸν: at first sight one would think τὸν = Eurymachus, the person mentioned immediately preceding. But the pronoun must refer to Melanthius, since we can see from passages like vii 171 and *Il.* iii 388 that this kind of abrupt change of subject is typical of Homeric diction, and furthermore that φιλέεσκε more likely refers to the more powerful party favouring the dependent and weaker one.

262. γλαφυρῆς: this adjective, regularly translated 'smooth' or 'hollow', is most frequently applied to ships, but also used of caves, once of rock (πέτρη), and twice (here and viii 257) of the bard's lyre (as also at *h.Ap.* 183 and *h.Merc.* 64). The quality that suits all three must be that of being *hollowed out*, rather than smooth or polished. ἀνὰ . . . βάλλετ' ἀείδειν: Phemius is 'striking up' the preliminary musical phrases (ἰωή φόρμιγγος 261-2) to his actual recitation (ἀείδειν). The same meaning suits ἀνεβάλλετο καλὸν ἀείδειν at i 155, but seems somewhat less appropriate to viii 266 ff., where the sequence ἀνεβάλλετο καλὸν ἀείδειν | ἀμφ' Ἄρεος φιλότητος ἐϋστεφάνου τ' Ἀφροδίτης, | ὡς τὰ πρῶτ' ἐμίγησαν moves so quickly from ἀνεβάλλετο into the *content* of the song, that we may be justified in taking the phrase in a different, more general, sense, 'started up singing about Ares and Aphrodite . . .'

263. Φήμιος: Stanford translates 'Fame-giver, son of Delight' (see xxii 330-1, where his patronymic Τερπιάδης is given with his name), stressing Homer's constant attention to significant names, which we have noted often.

266. ἐξ ἑτέρων ἕτερα: the antecedent is δώματα in 264. The interconnection of halls suggests an elaborate architecture and elevated life-style sufficient to impress even a former Cretan nobleman such as the beggar claims to be. οἱ: like μιν in 268, refers back to δώματα viewed now as a collective singular.

267. εὐερκέες: the majority of MSS read εὐερκέες, although the fairly well-attested variant εὐεργέες ('well-built') is attractive for several reasons. εὐερκής normally means 'well-fenced' as at xxi 389, xxii 449, *Il.* ix 472, describing a courtyard (αὐλή). Its use to describe doors, with a shift in meaning to 'well-protecting', is certainly possible; but in a context here that stresses the craftsmanship and style of construction of the palace, εὐεργέες seems the more perfectly chosen word. See also the following note.

268. ὑπεροπλίσσαιτο: commentators divide over whether this word, a *hapax legomenon*, means 'would scorn it' (from ὑπέροπλος, 'arrogant') or 'would overpower it' (from ὅπλον, 'weapon'), a division that goes back to the scholia and admits no easy solution. Apollonius the Sophist's *Lexicon*, s.v., records that Aristarchus gave the second interpretation. I would call attention to the reappearance of ὁπλίζονται twenty lines later at 288, joined with ἐΰζυγοι just as ὑπεροπλίσσαιτο is associated with εὐερκέες (εὐεργέες?). In both instances good construction is emphasized, which leads me to suggest a different meaning for 268: 'no man could equip it better', i.e. no man could surpass it in accoutrements. This interpretation is supported by ὁπλίσθεν δὲ γυναῖκες, xxiii 143, describing the serving-women of the household adorning themselves, in order to give the illusion of a wedding feast as ordered by Odysseus. Since ὁπλίζω is to adorn or equip finely, then ὑπεροπλίζομαι is 'to surpass in adornment or equipment'. This interpretation has been largely overlooked in the past, the only exception I could find being van der Valk, *Textual Criticism*, 127, who simply translates 'to surpass', with no discussion of its being a *hapax* and no explanation of how it comes to have this meaning.

270. ἐνήνοθεν: 'has risen into the air'. I should prefer the vulgate ἀνήνοθεν to Aristarchus' ἐνήνοθεν. Both variants (sometimes compounded with ἐπ-) occur several times in Homer. Most scholars have favoured ἀνήνοθεν (Leaf, *Iliad*, on ii 219, xi 266; Chantraine, *Dictionnaire* s.v.) as a reduplicated o-grade pf. or ppf. from the same stem as ἄνθος (ἀνεθ-, ἀνθ-; see Risch, *Wortbildung*, para. 121b), the meaning being 'rose up', 'appeared on the surface', just as ἄνθος is that which appears on the top of a growing plant. This interpretation (V. Pisani, *Rendiconti dell'Istituto Lombardo* lxxvii (1944), 548) finds further support in the metaphoric verb ἐπανθεῖν, 'to be on the surface', common in later (Classical) Greek. This whole line of interpretation is doubted by Frisk, *GEW* s.v., who would connect ἀνήνοθε/ ἐνήνοθε with ἐνθεῖν, 'come, go', attested in Doric, Delphian, and Arcadian, possibly a by-form of ἐλθεῖν.

269-71. A tradition common to the heroic epic of many nations shows the song and harp as natural concomitants of the aristocratic feast. The *locus classicus* for Greek epic is Odysseus' speech to Alcinous, ix 2–11, where this scene is presented not merely from the poet's external and objective point of view, but is commented upon appreciatively from the inside by one of the characters. Odysseus calls such a scene the most satisfying (χαριέστερον) and most beautiful (κάλλιστον) thing he knows of. A good example outside of classical epic is the brilliant scene of the feast in Heorot in *Beowulf*, 116 ff.

272. **προσέφης, Εὔμαιε συβῶτα:** the poet's direct address to Eumaeus is striking. This same verse occurs 13 times in the *Odyssey*, and two others end with *προσέφης, Εὔμαιε συβῶτα* after a different introductory hemistich characterizing the tone of Eumaeus' address (xiv 325, xxii 194). The poet began apostrophosizing the swineherd at xiv 55. This apostrophe is intriguing because (1) the conventions of epic normally prevent the poet from speaking *in propria persona*; (2) a swineherd, or any servant, would seem unworthy of being so singled out, since we must take apostrophe as a form of praise. Homer's purpose in employing apostrophe has been admirably treated by Adam Parry, 'Language and Characterization in Homer', *HSCPh* lxxvi (1972), 9-22. Parry rejects the idea that this use of the second person and vocative is merely a function of metrical convenience; instead, he finds a definite pattern in the way Homer comes to settle on this formula of direct address. Homer first addresses Eumaeus at xiv 55, but when Eumaeus answers at 121, it is *τὸν δ' ἠμείβετ' ἔπειτα*, plus the half-line *συβώτης ὄρχαμος ἀνδρῶν* which was first used at xiv 22. Homer returns to the second-person apostrophe at 165 and 360, but at 401 adopts a different third-person alternative, *τὸν δ' ἀπαμειβόμενος προσεφώνεε δῖος ὑφορβός*, where the final half-line is an exact replacement for *προσέφης, Εὔμαιε συβῶτα*. From this point on, however, every speech of Eumaeus is introduced by the second-person formula (twelve instances). 'Clearly', Parry says, 'the poet simplified his choice, and in this direction [i.e. toward the second person] because the apostrophe, however mildly it is felt, was appropriate to the sense of Eumaeus' character . . . which he wished to impose on the audience' (p. 21). Like Eumaeus, the two people singled out for repeated apostrophe in the *Iliad*, Patroclus and Menelaus, are, as Parry shows, personages that Homer is especially interested in, whose characterization is therefore complex, consistent, and built up with a variety of subtle touches. All three are, in Parry's words, 'altruistic, loyal, sensitive, vulnerable'. Apostrophe is one of the special poetic devices Homer selected (was it in the tradition already, or his own contribution?) for heightening his audience's interest and sympathy for some of his favourite characters. The only restrictions imposed by metre are that such characters come from among those whose names, in the vocative, scan $\overset{w}{\smile} - \cup (\cup)$, so that Menelaus and Eumaeus can be named ending in the feminine third-foot caesura or the first short of the fifth foot, while the longer vocative of Patroclus allows for a greater variety of positions.

287. **οὐλομένην, ἢ πολλὰ:** one cannot help being reminded of *Il.* i 2, *οὐλομένην, ἢ μυρί' Ἀχαιοῖς ἄλγε' ἔθηκεν*. Is it simply a question of recourse to a familiar syntactic pattern, or is some kind of gentle parody intended, through comparison with a greater heroic world which makes the present concern with the belly seem paltry? Cf. the Muses' rebuke to shepherds, including Hesiod, at *Th.* 26, *γάστερες οἶον*, 'mere bellies'. This Odyssean verse recurs at 474. For a more ambitious interpretation that makes *γάστηρ* 'the secret force behind Odysseus' adventures' and an emblem of the

restlessness and wanderings in the *Odyssey*, much as μῆνις epitomizes the
action of the *Iliad*, see P. Pucci, *Odysseus Polytropos* (Ithaca and London,
1987), 173–87.

289. ἀτρύγετον: a common epithet of the sea, of obscure meaning and
etymology. The ancient commentators glossed it variously as 'infertile',
'untiring', 'deep'; modern linguists have proposed 'limpid', 'sparkling',
'fluid', 'dry', with no agreement reached. The epithet is once in Homer (*Il.*
xvii 425) and twice in *h. Cer.* applied to αἰθήρ, so that we must imagine a
meaning applicable to both the sea and the upper air. Further details are
well summarized in *LfgrE*.

290–1. Note the remarkable abruptness of this transition. The background
information that Homer normally gives when introducing a new figure is
here placed *within* the scene, and exploited for dramatic irony as Argus is
described to the master who knows him so well.

290–327. Odysseus' old dog Argus recognizes his master after a twenty-year
absence: one of the most famous episodes in the poem, brief yet highly
effective in its structure, and crucial in its placement here at the moment
that the long-absent king is about to enter his own halls again. This significant moment of returning would otherwise go unmarked by any special
emphasis. Homer's normal emphasizing device is to depict the strong
emotional reaction of one or more characters. But recognition by a person
would risk giving the disguise away, or require special explanations as to
why the person did *not* reveal the truth. The use of the dog is perfect, giving
the suspense and pathos of a recognition without the risk of discovery. This
is the second in the series of recognition scenes that began with recognition
by Telemachus at xvi 187 ff., and continues in the recognition by Eurycleia
at xix 392 ff., by Eumaeus and Philoetius at xxi 205 ff., by Penelope at xxiii
205 ff., and by Laertes at xxiv 320 ff. We might add the recognition by the
suitors at xxii 35 ff., which differs in that it is the one recognition by hostile
rather than by loyal figures, it causes great dismay, and leads to a scene of
extended violence. The recognition by Argus is unique in that it is the only
time that Odysseus' disguise is penetrated without his or Athena's co-
operation or without an obvious clue like the scar. The fact that only the
dog's special sense can penetrate the disguise actually confirms what is
implicit throughout the narrative, that the disguise given by Athena makes
Odysseus magically safe from human recognition for as long as he keeps it,
which is typical of such disguises in folk-tale traditions. (The penetration of
the disguise by Eurycleia is not an exception, since Odysseus in effect
reveals himself by failing to conceal his familiar scar.)

292. Ἄργος: very likely another significant name. The adjective ἀργός is
commonly applied to dogs in Homer, in phrases like κύνες ἀργοί and κύνες
πόδας ἀργοί, but it is also used twice of a goose and once of oxen. ἀργός
has two meanings, 'swift' and 'bright', recognized by lexicographers as
early as Apollonius the Sophist. It is commonly assumed by scholars that
the idea of swift motion naturally passes over into the idea of flashing
brightness. Similarly Chantraine, *Dictionnaire* s.v., who suggests 'originally

a notion that expresses the white burst of lightning and at the same time its speed', as seen in a word like ἀργικέραυνος. Bechtel, *Lexilogus*, on the other hand, believes that there were originally two different words ἀργός, one meaning 'swift' and the other 'white', and that we should continue to distinguish these meanings in Greek. The use of the word to describe oxen (*Il.* xxiii 30) makes it clear that the two meanings, if not independent historically, have certainly become independent in Homeric Greek. That the meaning 'bright' or 'white' has become very prominent in Greek is seen from the early proliferation of words like ἀργής, ἀργεννός, ἐναργής, and compounds like ἀργικέραυνος and ἀργιόδων. For the development of ἀργός from *αργρός and the variation between the -ro and -i suffix, see Bechtel, *Lexilogus* s.v., and Risch, *Wortbildung*, 195. For a detailed survey of the problem of the double meaning and the difficulty of assigning priority in Greek to either meaning, see *LfgrE* s.v.

296. ἀπόθεστος: a *hapax legomenon*, although related compounds ἄθεστος and πολύθεστος are each attested once in later Greek. The etymology usually given is ἀπο- plus -θεστός from θέσσασθαι, 'to pray', and hence the meaning 'prayed away', interpreted as 'wished away' or 'rejected'. This seems a rather roundabout way, however, to reach the meaning clearly needed by the context, 'neglected' or 'uncared-for'. Leumann, *Wörter*, 64–5, proposes the simple solution of α- privative and *πόθεστος, derived from ποθέω, through the intermediary of an infinitive *ποθεσ-σαι that may be assumed to underlie the attested forms ποθέσαι and πόθεσαν. To ἀ-πόθεστος Leumann would give the meaning 'nicht sehnsüchtig vermisst', which does fit the context admirably.

300. κυνοραιστέων: 'dog-destroyers', a *hapax*, which one might imagine Homer coined specially for this passage. Stanford goes further and suggests that Homer is deliberately avoiding a common word for tick or louse and 'coining instead a lordly synonym—perhaps with a touch of humour—on the analogy of θυμοραϊστής, 'soul-destroying', a lofty heroic term used in the *Iliad*. The suggestion of parody here was first made by V. Bérard in his note ad loc., *L'Odyssée*, iii (Paris, 1924–5). Two scholia add that some take the word to mean fleas but Aristarchus said it meant ticks.

304-5. This act of Odysseus' recalls his hiding (ἐλάνθανε) his tears from the Phaeacians (although noticed by Alcinous) at viii 83–95, 521–34, and foreshadows his successful concealment of tears before Penelope, xix 209–12. Similarly Telemachus at iv 112–16 tries to conceal his tears with his cloak, just like Odysseus in viii, but is observed by Menelaus, just as his father was observed by Alcinous. Here we have an important particular detail within the major theme of concealment and disguise that dominates the poem. Tears caused by the painful memory of dear persons lost (cf. iv 183–226), and the constant need for concealment or repression of one's strongest emotions and urges (cf. xx 9 ff.), are two leading motifs that run through the poem and contribute to its more sombre aspect, an aspect which Vergil felt very keenly and which he made central to the tone of his *Aeneid*. Here and elsewhere in the *Odyssey*, concealment of tears is a powerful conjunction of the disguise-motif and the pain-motif, and so heightens considerably the emotional tenor of a scene.

306–10. Homer's psychological portrait is skilful: Odysseus, overflowing with emotion at seeing his dog, channels his feeling into a series of questions about the animal. This allows him to 'manage' his strong emotions by a kind of role-playing in which he deals with the painful subject in the *persona* of an outsider, so that he can keep some distance from it.

308. ἦ: I prefer the εἰ of the MSS, and would resist the normalizing tendency that has led most editors to replace it with ἦ in similar constructions, even where there is no MS authority. The nearest thing to authority for this change is the scholia's statement on iv 712 that Aristarchus read ἦ (found in one MS) for εἰ; and Aristarchus' authority may well underlie schol. Q's discussion on iv 487 of the choice between εἰ (σαναπτικός) and ἦ (σύνδεσμος). Further parallel passages are iii 216, iv 28, 833, xviii 265, xix 237, xxii 158, 202–3.

311. The poet's direct address to Eumaeus (see note to 272) is a subtle touch that contributes to the heightened emotional tone of this scene. It strengthens the dramatic irony by which we (i.e. the poet's audience) are in collusion with the poet and with one character, Odysseus, over the trusting innocence of a second character.

319–23. Eumaeus has answered Odysseus' question pointedly, revealing Argus' sad decline, but now he digresses. Lines 319–21 relate well to the theme of the overall decline of Odysseus' household and hint at the disloyalty of some of the maidservants (cf. xx 6 ff.); but 322–3 have the appearance of a proverbial couplet awkwardly added on. We may blame the associative verbal habits of oral composition or suspect an interpolator, according to our prejudices. The lines were known to Plato as Homer's and are quoted at *Lg.* 777a, which is in turn quoted by Athenaeus vi 18. 264e, and in part by Eustathius 1766. 37 (although we have no certainty that they knew the verses in this same Odyssean context). They have ἀπαμείρεται in place of ἀποαίνυται, τε νόου in place of τ' ἀρετῆς, and ἀνδρῶν, οὓς ἂν δὴ for ἀνέρος, εὖτ' ἄν μιν, changes that suggest Plato was quoting from memory.

324–7. It is a revealing feature of Homer's stylistic artistry that this unusual and rather unformulaic scene should be crowned with four highly formulaic concluding verses. ἐεικόστῳ ἐνιαυτῷ, one of the familiar keynote phrases of the epic, here evokes great pathos by its placement as the last statement in the scene, describing the death of Argus. For analysis of the formulaic content of 303–27 and discussion of its relation to oral technique, see Joseph Russo, 'Is Oral or Aural Composition the Cause of Homer's Formulaic Style?', in B. Stolz and R. S. Shannon, eds., *Oral Literature and the Formula* (Ann Arbor, Mich., 1976).

331. ἔνθα τε: Bekker's emendation (τε for δέ of MSS and papyrus) has been universally accepted because the connective force of δέ is out of place here, while the so-called 'generalizing' τε suits the sense perfectly. See Chantraine, *Grammaire*, ii 239 ff., Denniston, *Particles*, 520–3. The contrary is argued by Ruijgh, τε épique, 392, who finds τε inappropriate in the description of 'temporary facts'. This τε, however, seems not temporary but an expression of the habitual.

339. μελίνου οὐδοῦ: the ashwood threshold is puzzling, since Telemachus entered over a stone threshold at line 30. The oral dimension of Homeric composition may provide the answer: μελίνου οὐδοῦ is a metrical variant of λάϊνον οὐδόν (∪ ∪ − − − for − ∪ ∪ − ∪), just as, e.g., Hera is usually white-armed or cow-eyed (λευκώλενος or βοῶπις) by reason of metrical exigency rather than descriptive accuracy. Traditional scholarship has tried to solve this problem of the stone and wooden thresholds by recourse to a variety of architectural schemes. Monro, 498–500, envisions a wooden threshold as part of the door-frame and resting *upon* the stone threshold (following J. L. Myres, 'On the Plan of the Homeric House', *JHS* xx (1900), 128–50, esp. 136–9). This view is reaffirmed by S. E. Bassett, 'The Palace of Odysseus', *AJA* xxiii (1919), 288–311, who provides a good review of the various reconstructions of the palace offered by different scholars to fit Homer's description of the actions of his characters. Lorimer, *Monuments*, 417–22, notes that this single mention of the ashwood threshold offers the only discordant element in an otherwise consistent picture, and speculates that the lines have intruded from a different traditional context, or that this unique form μέλινος (for μείλινος) 'suggests a later hand' (421). Attributing the novel phrase to oral-formulaic compositional technique would free us from these perhaps needless difficulties. We should remember that Homer's audience, in their enjoyment of the story, would not have had the time or interest to notice such minor discrepancies.

341. Is it merely fortuitous that the language describing the carpenter's making the column perfectly straight with his levelling tool falls into a totally spondaic rhythm?

347. Stanford notes the similarity to Hesiod, *Op.* 317–19. A. Hoekstra, 'Hésiode et la poésie orale', *Mnemosyne* x (1957), 199–200, suggests that the likelihood that this is a proverb is strengthened by the fact that it concludes a speech.

354. μοι: As Ameis–Hentze–Cauer point out, the μοι may be a *double entendre*, ostensibly meant with an implied δός but also meaning 'my' Telemachus.

354-5. The infinitive with subject accusative can be used to express a wish, like the optative γένοιτο with which it is parallel, when the context is a prayer (we may assume an implicit εὔχομαι or δός). For parallels cf. xxiv 376–81, vii 311–13; and *Il.* ii 412–13, iii 285–6, vii 179–80, where the infinitives parallel imperatives earlier in the sentence. As Monro says, *Homeric Dialect*, 207, these infinitives have the force of an indirect imperative. Cf. also Chantraine, *Grammaire*, ii 317–18.

359. We know from the scholium on *Il.* xxii 329 that Aristarchus athetized that verse and this one for the same odd reason: that it was 'ridiculous'—γελοῖος—to ascribe a purpose to acts that are accidental. *Il.* xxii 328–9 says that Achilles' spear did not cut Hector's windpipe, in order that he could still speak to Achilles, ὄφρα τί μιν προτιείποι. The scholiast complains that it is 'ridiculous' if the spear did it purposefully, ἐπετήδευσε. The Aristarchian objection to our Odyssean verse, then, is apparently that the bard is made to stop singing *because* the beggar has finished eating. This objection may have arisen from Aristarchus' text reading δὲ παύσατο, an attested variant, which would suggest that Phemius stopped at the very point when the beggar finished his meal. No problem at all exists if we see ἐπαύετο as logically subordinate and take the true apodosis as coming in 360, μνηστῆρες δ' ὁμάδησαν. So Monro, which is surely right.

364. τιν': any one of the suitors whom Odysseus would recognize (γνοίη) as ἐναίσιμος. The ἔμελλε refers back to Athena. Since she is not going to spare even the right-thinking ones (probably a forecast of the scene with Amphinomus in xviii), we may wonder why she encourages Odysseus to search for the distinction in the first place. A partial answer may lie in the fact that Homer is invoking an old folk-tale motif, in which a king (or deity) goes about in disguise to find out who is loyal (or reverent) among his subjects. The suitors themselves have this idea at 483–7. Homer would be using this motif for its immediate narrative impact, without feeling bound to its logical entailment (i.e. the finding of a right-minded suitor), a characteristic trait of oral poetry.   **κακότητος:** the variant κακότητα is possible if we take τιν' as τινι. The normal construction of ἀλέξειν is in fact with a dative of the person or thing protected and accusative of the thing warded off; but here the prefix ἀπο- justifies the genitive and accusative, as at *Il.* xxiv 371.

366. This whole verse adds a marvellous touch, showing off Odysseus' brilliance at acting the role and imitating the beggar's routines. Remember he has played this role before, at Troy: iv 244 ff. The suitors' natural reaction to this convincing performance is pity, wonder, curiosity (367–8).

375–9. Antinous' speech is characterized by a variety of rhetorical devices which merge with metrical and acoustic devices: synizesis in 375 and 376 (ὦ ἀρίγνωτε, ἦ οὐχ); assonantal echo in τίη δὲ σὺ τόνδε πόλινδε; frequent η and liquid sounds in 376; hyperbole (and solecism?) in δαιτῶν ἀπολυμαντῆρες, 377; sarcasm in 379 in ὄνοσαι and in the mock-critical tone of the reference to the devourers of the master's goods. For the synizesis in 376 cf. ix 311, δὴ αὖτε, in the same metrical position. This all amounts to a very effective characterization of the man through his diction. His arrogance, sarcasm, hostility (note the significant name Antinous, 'counter-minded') are all vividly portrayed. The fact that all this verbal artillery is directed at a lowly swineherd stresses still more the meanness of spirit of this 'lordly' suitor.

380. προσέφης, Εὔμαιε συβῶτα: again the apostrophe adroitly draws us into emotional alliance with Eumaeus at the dramatically opportune moment, when he is under attack.

385. Note how in the succinct list of valuable professionals, Homer reserves an entire verse for describing his own trade in glowing terms. At xix 135 heralds are also named as δημιοεργοί. These verses are our earliest evidence for poets and other craftsmen as wandering professionals for hire in Greek society. See Finley, *World*, 36–7, 56, and Hainsworth's note on viii 62–103.

388. εἰς: this less common form (sometimes εἰς) of the second person sing. of εἶναι is found nine times in Homer. Monro, *Homeric Dialect*, 4, would like to restore an assumed original ἐσσ', which is metrically possible everywhere, he notes, except in this line.

388–9. περὶ πάντων ... περὶ δ' αὐτ' ἐμοί: note the different syntax and meaning of περί in these successive lines. With ἐμοί it means 'and especially to me', while the more familiar περὶ πάντων μνηστήρων means 'beyond the suitors'.

397–404. Telemachus' speech is rhetorically well-structured in an ABAB pattern. He begins with a heavily sarcastic and obviously untrue statement for two and a half verses, then in the second half of the third verse abandons irony for a blunt statement of his true wish, contradicting his preceding words. Lines 401–2 return to the ironic ascription to Antinous of decent motives that he obviously does not have, and 403–4 return again to the blunt truth, denying the kindly motives just ascribed to him. The characterization through rhetoric is again impressive, as Telemachus continues to show the typically adolescent qualities of peevishness, moodiness, and sarcasm that were so evident in the first two books of the poem.

406. ὑψαγόρη: 'lofty (arrogant) speaker'—a perfect and effective compound coined especially for Telemachus by Antinous in i 385 and now repeated, as their hostile relationship is resumed with Telemachus' return to his halls and renewed assertion of his rights.

407–9. τόσσον: this adjective of quantity *seems* to refer back to the issue of how much is being given to the beggar. Only when Antinous holds up his stool from under the table two verses later (ὑπέφηνε τραπέζης, 409) is his true meaning and full irony revealed. This is another example of his meanness of character expressed through his clever handling of language.

410. κείμενον: it is somewhat awkward to describe the stool as 'lying' at the same moment that it is being held up and shown to everyone. We can take this either as hysteron-proteron, in which 410 describes the stool as it is *before* Antinous lifts it; or we can ascribe to κείμενον the function typical of Homeric epithets and sometimes seen in other adjectives, that of describing the normative, enduring quality of an object rather than its momentary state. The relative clause that goes on to describe the stool, ᾧ ῥ' ἔπεχεν, could support either interpretation.

413. γεύσεσθαι: this word, meaning 'to taste of (a thing)', is in Homer always figurative, 'to make a trial or test of', and as such belongs here to what I have called the *testing-motif* associated with the character of Odysseus, usually expressed in the frequent use of the verbs πείρομαι, πειράομαι, πειρητίζω, noted elsewhere in the commentary.

415–44. This fictitious tale is essentially the same story told to Eumaeus at xiv 199–359, and some verses are exact repetitions (427–41 = xiv 258–72).

An overall consistency is necessary, since Eumaeus is still present and the beggar must maintain his plausible role for the faithful swineherd, whose ignorance of the secret, combined with his fidelity, is one source of the complex irony of disguise and revelation that characterizes the whole poem and these latter books especially. The one inconsistency between this account and that told to Eumaeus is 442–4, which cannot be made to square with the earlier story. The other false tales, told to Athena in xiii, Penelope in xix, and Laertes in xxiv, are far less closely related, since there is no need for consistency in those cases.

416. Here all MSS read ὤριστος, whereas at 375 the readings divide between ὢ ἀρίγνωτε (synizesis) and ὠρίγνωτε (crasis). For a succinct account of crasis and synizesis see Monro, *Homeric Dialect*, 350–1.

427. Αἰγύπτῳ ποταμῷ: the 'Aigyptos river' must certainly be the Nile, which is first mentioned by the Greeks, as far as we know, by Hesiod, *Th.* 338 (Νεῖλος).

440. ἡμέων: scanned with synizesis as a spondee.   πολλοὺς μὲν: answered by τοὺς δὲ of the following verse, not a perfectly symmetrical balance but none the less idiomatic: 'many they killed, some they took alive'.

443. Δμήτορι Ἰασίδη: about this Dmetor, ruler of Cyprus, nothing else is known. He has a significant name, meaning 'Subduer' or 'Tamer', from the verb δάμνημι; just as servants, δμῶες, represent the passive side of the action, 'people subdued'.

446–8. Antinous continues his figurative and expressive language. In a series of strong metaphors the beggar is called 'this pain', 'spoiler of the feast', and Antinous threatens to show him a 'bitter Egypt and Cyprus'. This last phrase, as Stanford points out, condenses a physical threat and mockery of Odysseus' story into one sharp statement.

450–2. Antinous would like to separate himself from the other suitors by criticizing their freehanded giving away of Odysseus' goods. This pretended sympathy with the household interests recalls his oblique criticism of his fellow suitors at 378–9, and continues Homer's characterization of this duplicitous figure as one whose ambition leads him to display virtues that he does not possess. As Ameis–Hentze–Cauer interpret his motives (*Anhang*, ad loc.), 'Antinous' disposition makes his summons to moderation merely a mask for his own egoism'. These lines are called spurious by the H Scholiast, echoing Aristarchus; but such a view fails to understand the psychology and rhetoric of Antinous.

454. ἐπὶ εἴδεϊ: ἐπὶ with the dative here means 'in addition to', as earlier at 308 where the identical phrase was used in describing Argus. There it was asked whether the dog, 'in addition to such good looks' (ἐπὶ εἴδεϊ τῷδε), also had speed, the chief virtue of a dog. Here, the corresponding chief virtue of a man is implied as *phrenes*, 'good sense', 'intelligence', which Odysseus accused Antinous of lacking. Each passage calls attention to the relationship between attractive surface appearance and the underlying reality, which is of major importance throughout the *Odyssey*, a corollary of what we have earlier labelled the disguise-motif.

462–3. δεξιὸν ὦμον, πρυμνότατον κατὰ νῶτον: the phrase at first sight looks ambiguous, but πρυμνὸν βάλε δεξιὸν ὦμον at 504 makes it clear that πρυμνὸν or πρυμνότατον to modify ὦμον designates the lower shoulder and κατὰ νῶτον simply means 'on the back', so that the phrase refers to the place where the shoulders become the back. Perhaps we are meant to imagine that Odysseus made a half-turn to protect himself.

463–4. This description recalls Odysseus' similar unflinching stance when kicked by Melanthius at 234–5; a clear thematic echo—the disguised king is abused first by the lower, then by the higher in rank among his disloyal subjects—although there is no verbal echo, as there was between 308 and 454.

465. κακὰ βυσσοδομεύων: see the note at 66. The recurrence of this phrase here and at 491 emphasizes the new intensity of scarcely controlled hostilities in this book. Recall that the suitors have recently tried to murder Telemachus on his return journey; that their ambush was noticed; and that Odysseus has been seeking, at Athena's prompting, to provoke the suitors to reveal their nastiest qualities.

476. τέλος θανάτοιο: a common Homeric phrase, similar to κῆρ (κῆρες . . .) θανάτοιο and μοῖρα . . . θανάτοιο (it is necessary for metre that κῆρες but not μοῖρα be separated from θανάτοιο by one or more words). The genitive is not possessive but explanatory; the meaning is 'the end (or fulfilment) consisting of death'.

475–80. These six lines, the scholia tell us, were athetized: 'For how could Antinous endure such curses, when he was so angered by smaller matters?' The naturalness of the lines was defended by Wilamowitz, *Heimkehr*, 156. Because the Erinyes were born from the first act of violence ever committed by child against parent—Cronos' castration of Ouranos at *Th.* 185—they are normally avengers of crimes against either a father, as at *Th.* 472, or a mother, as at *Il.* xxi 412, *Od.* xi 279–80. The idea that any wronged person has his *erinyes* is common enough in Greek tragedy, but is probably rather original at this earlier period, hence the cautious phrasing with εἴ που and γε.

476. This is the first in a series of wishes uttered as if they were merely vain hopes or fanciful exaggerations, but which are in fact going to come to pass, as the audience knows. These foreshadowings of Odysseus' eventual retribution punctuate the action from the latter part of xvii to the slaying of the suitors, and build an increasing excitement as we (the audience) see further ahead than the characters in the story can. Such dramatic irony is particular to art forms like Greek epic or drama that use stories ('myths') familiar to the audience. It grows naturally from the conditions of performance of epic, reinforced by the repeated recitation of essentially the same tale to what is in part the same audience.

480. πάντα: either agreeing with σε of 479, or neuter pl. accusative of respect, 'in every way', 'completely', adverbial as at 20–1.

484–5. οὐλόμεν' . . . καί τε: οὐλόμεν' may be a vocative addressed to Antinous, or more likely the neuter pl., giving the opposite of the κάλ' in

41

the preceding line, but without formally expressed antithesis. In 485 καί τε would then continue this thought by introducing the general truth from which this particular warning was drawn.

485-7. A clear allusion to the motif of the *theoxeny*, common in myth and literature, in which gods visit certain mortals to test their hospitality. The story of Baucis and Philemon in Ovid, *Met.* viii, is a fully developed example; the wanderings of Demeter and Dionysus among mortals, and the rewards or punishments they give according to the treatment received, are less explicit versions (see E. Kearns, 'The Return of Odysseus: A Homeric Theoxeny', *CQ* xxxii (1982), 2–8, who traces this story pattern in the latter half of the *Odyssey*). The wording and sentiment of 487 are closely echoed in Archil. fr. 177 w, apparently spoken by the fox invoking Zeus' punishment upon the eagle in a fable about abuse of power.

490-1. Two motifs that have occurred earlier in this book are here joined: the suppression of tears and the silent preoccupation with murderous thoughts. Allione, *Telemaco*, 55, observing that verse 491 is identical to 465 describing Odysseus, notes that 'here [Telemachus] appears truly able to suffer and endure in order to attain the opportune moment, just like his great father'.

492-506. The exact location of Penelope's chamber (θάλαμος) has long been disputed, since the testimony of different passages can be used to support different reconstructions of the palace. (See the discussions of Myres, Bassett, and Lorimer (ch. 5) cited in the note to 339; of Monro, app. 5, 493–7; and, more recently, of L. R. Palmer, *TPhS* (Oxford, 1948), 92–120, A. J. B. Wace, *JHS* lxxi (1951), 203–11, and D. H. Gray, *CQ* (1955), 1–12.) We should note that the θάλαμος named in 506 is not necessarily Penelope's own private room. The only certain fact is that it is near to or adjoining the μέγαρον or main hall, since she has been able to follow what has happened to the beggar, which she summarizes in 501–4. How did she acquire this knowledge? At 492–3 I take τοῦ δ'... ἤκουσε... βλημένου to mean that she actually heard the sound, and accompanying shouting, of Antinous hitting the beggar with the stool (rather than give ἤκουσε the different meaning it has at 525–6, 'heard about'). Most of her perceptions are of sounds (cf. her hearing Telemachus' sneeze later at 542), but ἔοικε at 511 implies that she has been able to *see* the beggar, and presumably some of the action. Stanford, on the other hand, would equate this θάλαμος with the ὑπερῷα mentioned at 49 and often in the poem, the private upper bedchamber to which Penelope retires periodically to weep and rest, and from which she was able to hear Phemius' song at i 328. But if she were that distant, it is unlikely that she could say that the beggar looks like (ἔοικε, 511) a wanderer and that Antinous hit him on the *right* shoulder (524). It is more reasonable to suppose that the distinct word ὑπερῷον denotes a distinct room, an upper bedroom connected by a short stairway to one of the ground-floor θάλαμοι, a location from which Penelope could hear the bard singing and be herself heard by Odysseus when she is weeping aloud at xx 92. Although the most plausible picture remains, then, that she is here sitting in a ground-floor θάλαμος close enough to the μέγαρον to hear and see what is happening, we should not press the narrative too closely for verisimilitude and a strict consistency of architectural detail. The recent emphasis of scholarship on the conditions of oral performance adds new force to Monro's remarks of some eighty-five years ago, in which he concludes—and to a large extent undermines—his discussion of hypothetical detailed reconstructions by admitting that Homer's listeners could not have been accustomed to the same consistency of detail that modern readers expect of a book (Appendix, 496–7). In this light, Aristarchus' literal-minded objection to this passage—that Penelope is depicted with knowledge that she could not have—is seen, as so often, to be worthless. Stanford's note to 500–4 refutes Aristarchus effectively by citing Bassett's argument (*The Poetry of Homer* (Berkeley, Calif., 1938), 130ff.) that it is characteristic of Homeric (and, we might add, oral) narrative sometimes to let the characters have the same knowledge that the audience has.

514. θέλγοιτό κέ τοι φίλον ἦτορ: the word θέλγειν, 'to charm', reveals the Greek view of verbal performance as a kind of magical spell, holding its listeners by a power that in part derives from the sheer pleasurableness of the sound itself (ἔπε' ἱμερόεντα, 519). The most pointed description of this poetic power is Hesiod's tribute to the Muses at *Th.* 98–103, where poetic recitation has not only the power to charm but the power to *cure*, to drive out sorrows and restore the mind. The fascinating topic of the *thelxis* of oral performance is first discussed at length by E. A. Havelock, *Preface to Plato* (Cambridge, Mass., 1963), ch. 4, 'The Psychology of the Oral Performance'; and most recently by Charles Segal, 'Eros and Incantation: Sappho and Oral Poetry', *Arethusa* vii (1974), 139–60, who stresses the incantatory and magical background of poetry in archaic Greece. Segal's emphasis is on Sappho and the erotic *thelxis* of lyric; but in comparing lyric to epic *thelxis* he notes that Homer uses θέλγω not only of the power of words to enthral the listener but also in an erotic sense that comes close to that of Sappho (*Od.* i 56–7, iii 264; and the 'charm' of the Sirens' song, xii 44, carries a latent erotic suggestiveness). This erotic aspect of the word θέλγω allows us to see in the present statement of Eumaeus a *double entendre* unintended by the speaker but felt perhaps by both poet and audience: this beggar *will* in fact 'charm the heart' of the queen, in several senses: we shall observe a progression from *thelxis* as persuasion, to *thelxis* as emotional bond, to *thelxis* that wins an erotic goal.

518. ὡς δ' ὅτ' ἀοιδὸν ἀνὴρ ποτιδέρκεται: the comparison of the beggar's recitation to a bardic one contains a hidden subtlety in that it was, literally, a bardic recitation, if we step outside the internal fictional frame of the story and acknowledge the external reality of Homer's recitation to his audience. The similarity of Odysseus to a bard was first suggested by King Alcinous at xi 367–8, was reaffirmed by Eumaeus at xiv 387, and is implied at xix 203, where the verisimilitude of Odysseus' fictions is described in terms that recall the Muses' statement at Hes. *Th.* 27. This simile (518–21) is also noteworthy in that it is spoken by a character in the poem. Normally

similes represent the poet speaking, with the anonymity required by the conventions of epic narrative. But here the simile is able to refer back to its speaker as one of the points of comparison (ὥς ἐμὲ κεῖνος ἔθελγε).

519. ἀείδῃ: the variant ἀείδει, though less well attested, is more normal in relative clause extensions of comparisons. Ruijgh, τε épique, 399–401, documents 17 instances of the subjunctive versus 68 of the indicative.

525. προπροκυλινδόμενος· στεῦται: two strong words in sequence. προπροκυλινδόμενος onomatopoeically recreates the forward rolling it signifies, as it takes us all the way to the penthemimeral caesura in completely dactylic movement. It occurs only here and at *Il.* xxii 221, and nowhere else in Greek literature. στεῦται can have a physical meaning, 'presses forward', like Tantalus eager to drink at xi 584, or can metaphorically suggest aggressive assertion in language or behaviour (cf. the English adjective 'forward'). Eumaeus continues to paint the beggar in bright colours (cf. 513–21), stimulating Penelope's already expressed interest (509–11) in the newcomer.

534–40. The first five of these lines are identical to those spoken by Telemachus complaining to the Ithacan assembly at ii 55–9. ἀρή, 'harm', is not connected with ἀρή, 'curse' or 'prayer'. Penelope's wish that follows (538–40) is essentially the same wish we saw in Telemachus' fancy when Homer first presented him in i 115–17. Now Telemachus is in a position to confirm that wish, expressed by his mother, with his own prophetic or 'kledonic' sneeze.

541. Sneezes were viewed as omens in antiquity (Xen. *An.* iii 2. 9; Catull. xlv 8–9, 17–18; Prop. iii 3. 24; Ov. *Pont.* xviii 152), as in many cultures today. This sneeze is one of a series of omens running through xvii to xx and heightening our anticipation of the climax to come when Odysseus finally reveals himself to the suitors and kills them. Most often the omen is a verbal utterance whose full implications are unknown to the speaker but secretly understood and rejoiced in by his interlocutor—hence by Homer's audience and by us. The first example we saw was Melanthius' statement at 251–4, where the narrative makes no explicit comment on the irony but allows it to stand as self-evident. More commonly, the character who grasps the full significance of the utterance is said to recognize it as a κλεηδών (xviii 117, with note; xx 120; iv 317) or a φήμη (xx 98–119; ii 35).

565. σιδήρεον οὐρανὸν: the whole verse was used in describing the suitors at xv 329, and seems to be an ironical variant on the common epic conceit that the κλέος of great personages reaches to the sky (viii 74, ix 20, xix 108; *Il.* viii 192). One wonders exactly what Homer meant by calling the sky iron. He also refers to it as bronze (iii 2; *Il.* xvii 425), and the underlying idea, as Stanford notes, may be that the sky is a metal dome over the earth. Stanford adds the interesting point that while bronze is the everyday metal for concrete objects mentioned by Homer—as would suit the Bronze Age period he is describing—it is quite different in his imagery, where iron is mentioned fifteen times and bronze only four. The imagery reflects the poet's contemporary world, where iron is the more important metal.

572-3. The idea returns (cf. 23n.) that the season is cold and the beggar must take care to warm himself.

593. σύας καὶ κεῖνα: κεῖνα represents an unusual usage and is awkward coupled with the concrete σύας. The unmetrical variant κύνας reveals a prosaic impulse toward more normal diction and parallel construction. κεῖνα has been understood as a contrast to the ἐνθάδε πάντα of 594 by Ameis–Hentze–Cauer, Stanford, and Ebeling, *Lexicon*, 744b, who translates it τὰ ἐκεῖ and calls attention to τάδε πάντα of Telemachus' answer at 601 as supporting the contrast. The meaning of κεῖνα would then be as general as that of πάντα, embracing all that exists at the farm besides the σύας: τὰ πράγματα, as Eustathius glosses the word.

An ingenious alternative to all this has been offered by M. D. Petruševski (*ŽA* xvi (1966), 349; xvii (1967), 103–4, 108; and *Platon* xx (1968), 289–96), who would replace κεῖνα with the *hapax* *κεῖμα. Although unattested in extant Greek, *κεῖμα was posited by Frisk, *GEW* s.v. κεῖμαι, as the intermediary form on which the noun κειμήλιον is built. (For Frisk's full argument see *Eranos* xxxviii (1940), 42; and for the extension through the suffix ηλ-, see *Eranos* xli (1943), 52.) The hypothetical existence of *κεῖμα is also accepted by Chantraine, *Dictionnaire*. Petruševski's conjecture has been criticized by B. Glavičic, *ŽA* xvii (1967), 81–5 and xviii (1968), 95–111, and by M. Marcovich, *Platon* xli–xlii (1969), 297–301; but it remains linguistically plausible and stylistically attractive, since it would give us a subtle distinction between 'movable' possessions (σύας) and 'immovable' ones (cf. the phrase ὑμέας ἐσθέμεναι κειμήλιά τε πρόβασίν τε, ii 75).

599. δειελιήσας: the verb comes from δείλη, δείελος and refers to late afternoon and early evening, the time near the setting of the sun (δείελον ἦμαρ, 606). Stanford takes it to mean simply 'having spent the afternoon (here)', and doubts a meal is involved. But the common interpretation, that the verb means to have a light meal between δεῖπνον and δόρπον, certainly fits better with the action of 602ff.: Eumaeus takes a seat and eats before leaving. He is told σὺ δ' ἔρχεο δειελιήσας (599), and his *immediate response* is to sit down: ὡς φάθ', ὁ δ' αὖτις ἄρ' ἕζετ'.

605-6. The sequence here gives us an important datum on archaic Greek social habits: the ἤδη γὰρ καί shows that dancing and listening to poetic recitations are typical activities for the close of day, filling in pleasantly the time between the early supper that δειελιάω suggests and the later full evening meal, the δόρπον.

45

BOOK XVIII: COMMENTARY

Book xviii is composed of six episodes. The first and third are long (over 100 verses), the others short. The third (Penelope's scene) is the longest episode and the centrepiece of the narrative structure, after which the action moves more quickly through two short scenes to a still shorter coda in 405–28. The suspicion, once widespread, that the Penelope-scene is an interpolation rests on subjective criteria and reveals a failure to appreciate the overall design of the book.

1. 1–116 The beggar Arnaeus, called Irus, arrives and quarrels with Odysseus. Antinous proposes they fight; Odysseus fells Irus with one blow and drags him out into the courtyard.
2. 117–57 Amphinomus, the best of the suitors, gives Odysseus food, toasts him, and wishes him well. Odysseus reminds him of life's vicissitudes and encourages him to leave. But Amphinomus cannot leave; Athena has fated him to die by Telemachus' spear.
3. 158–303 Athena inspires Penelope to face the suitors and charm them into giving her gifts. The goddess puts her to sleep and beautifies her. The suitors are powerfully charmed by her appearance. She complains to Telemachus over the maltreatment of the newcomer; he wishes the suitors a fate like that of Irus. Eurymachus flatters Penelope. She replies that Odysseus' last advice to her was to remarry when her son was getting his first beard, and that time has come; but the suitors should be following the custom of giving courtship gifts, rather than deplete the household. Odysseus is pleased to observe his wife's clever manipulation of the suitors. Rich gifts are brought to Penelope.
4. 304–45 The suitors feast and dance until nightfall. Odysseus tells the maids that he can tend the braziers himself and they should go to Penelope. Melantho and Odysseus trade bitter words.
5. 346–404 Athena provokes Eurymachus to taunt Odysseus with the accusation that he avoids honest labour. Odysseus answers by saying he would like to compete with Eurymachus in such labour, by vaunting his own valour, and impugning that of Eurymachus, predicting that Odysseus' return would send him rushing out the door in fright. Eurymachus hurls a stool at Odysseus.
6. 405–28 Telemachus accuses the suitors of disorderly behaviour and boldly proposes that they go home. Amphinomus encourages them to comply, and to leave the beggar to Telemachus' care. They agree, make a libation to the gods, and depart.

1. πανδήμιος, ὅς . . .: the relative pronoun is epexegetic of the preceding adjective, a common syntactic pattern of epic style. See S. West's comment

46

on i 300–2 for further examples. The well-known instance of this pattern in i 1–2 (πολύτροπον, ὅς μάλα πολλὰ πλάγχθη) is often discounted by those who wish to limit πολύτροπος to the sense of 'ingenious', since Odysseus' major epithets emphasize such mental qualities (so S. West on i 1). But the physical sense 'much-wandering' is better suited to the context which describes (with πολλῶν and πολλὰ) the many cities and minds of men and the many hardships encountered.

3. **ἀζηχὲς**: a word of uncertain etymology but fairly clear meaning, its context suggesting 'incessant' or 'persevering'. The favoured etymology is ἀ-δια-(σ)εχης, with the a- as privative and the normal Aeolic change of δy- to ζ (so LfgrE s.v., Bechtel, Lexilogus, 14–15) if διέχω is understood as 'keep apart' (cf. later Greek διεχής, 'discontinuous'); or as intensive if διέχω has the common Homeric meaning 'to continue through' (so Stanford, Bechtel, loc. cit., Frisk, GEW s.v., Chantraine, Dictionnaire s.v.). This meaning suits the most common ancient glosses διηνεκές, ἀδιάλειπτον, although Apollonius the Sophist's ἀδιηχές suggests a connection with ἠχέω, and Chantraine notes that the use of this word to describe sounds may have led to ἠχέω and compounds in -ηχής having an influence on its form. This would explain the unparalleled (in epic language) contraction of αε to η, and also the appearance of μεγαλόφωνον among the glosses of Hesychius and Eustathius. Monro accounts for the unparalleled -ηχ- by proposing a different etymology, from the IE root *gʷyē-, Skt. jyā, 'to be strong', 'to live' (Greek ζῆν), with 'formative' -χ- as in νήχω and τρύχω, thus arriving at the meaning 'with unbroken vigour', which could find support in Hesychius' ἰσχυρόν. Still another interpretation (Ameis–Hentze, Anhang) is the simple reliance on ἠχέω, assuming intensive a- and translating 'with penetrating sound'; but this sense would be unsuitable for one of the four Iliadic occurrences of the word (xv 25) and for the present passage.

5. **Ἀρναῖος**: probably a significant name, 'Getter', from ἄρνυμαι, 'to acquire', an apt name for a beggar (so Ameis–Hentze–Cauer, following schol. B). Such a name would fit with the punning sobriquet 'Iros' and with the tendency throughout the Odyssey to use etymologically significant names. The scholia also suggest a derivation from the word for sheep, taking 'Arnaios' as 'sheep-like', 'foolish'. A still more literal interpretation is that of von Kamptz, Personennamen, 285–6, who would derive this name from the city Arne in Boeotia or the spring of that name in Arcadia.

6–7. **Ἶρον ... οὕνεκ' ἀπαγγέλλεσκε**: the connection (οὕνεκ') assumes a playful derivation from Iris, the messenger of the gods, of whom Irus would be a male counterpart. But it is also possible to connect this name to the form *ἶρος that underlies Homeric ἱερός, 'strong' or 'quick' (so von Kamptz, Personennamen, 128–9, 281; see also the note at xviii 60: the ἱερὸς ἰχθύς of Il. xvi 407 shows how these two meanings may fall together). Either derivation, from Ἶρις or *ἶρος, would connect Irus with ἵεμαι, and perhaps 'Striver' or 'Hustler' is the closest English equivalent.

8. **διώκετο**: the verb would normally be διώκε. The scholia give the

47

impressionistic interpretation that the middle voice is more 'pathetic' than the active; but Meister, *Kunstsprache*, 19–20, has a more scientific explanation: alternative verb forms in the middle-passive voice are especially common at this position in the verse, where they meet the need for the rhythm − ∪ ∪. He notes that it is a common trait of Homeric language to have both active and middle forms of the same verb with the same meaning.

11. **ἐπιλλίζουσιν**: this word occurs only here and *h.Merc.* 387 and means to signal by winking or squinting the eyes. It may be connected with εἴλω, 'to press together', like the noun ἰλλάς (*Il.* xiii 572), 'a twisted rope'.

26. **ὁ μολοβρὸς**: the same word used by Melanthius insulting Odysseus at xvii 219 (see note). Here the definite article seems emphatic and mocking in its deictic force (see note to xvii 10). **ἐπιτροχάδην ἀγορεύει**: here the phrase is pejorative as used to describe an 'old woman at the oven': presumably we should translate ἐπιτροχάδην 'glibly', 'talkatively'. But at *Il.* iii 213–15 the same phrase is used to describe Menelaus in positive terms as a 'fluent' speaker, this fluency consisting of brevity, clarity, and the absence of awkwardness. It is often the case that the meaning of a word evolves in a pejorative direction, and in the semantic shift of ἐπιτροχάδην we may have an example of the relative lateness of Odyssean diction compared to Iliadic.

27. **καμινοῖ**: the scholia say Aristarchus and Herodian understood this as a hypocoristic form of καμινο-καύστρια, 'one who heats an oven'. Meillet, *REG* xxxii (1919), 387, is inclined to accept this explanation, adding 'en tout cas καμίνω est une formation familière, servant à la raillerie'. The word occurs only here in Greek literature.

29. **συὸς ὣς ληϊβοτείρης**: an odd comment, explained by the scholia and Eustathius as reflecting a Cyprian law that permitted any landowner who caught a pig eating his crops to pull its teeth out. Why a Cyprian law should be so well-known as to be a commonly understood reference is unclear. Perhaps the reference to such a law is only a guess, based on what may have been a widespread ancient practice among farmers to protect their crops from foraging pigs.

33. **οὐδοῦ ἐπὶ ξεστοῦ**: the repeated mention of the threshold (xvii 339, 413, 466, 575; xviii 17, 33, 110), together with other references to the entry (πρόθυρον 10, 101; προπάροιθε θυράων 32, xvii 297), builds a cumulative emphasis on the 'liminal' position of the beggar: he is held at the outer limit of *social* membership in the community of which he is, ironically, not just a legitimate member but the true leader; and simultaneously held at the *physical* edge of occupancy of the house of which he is, ironically, the master. The importance of the palace threshold as a symbol marking Odysseus' transitional state is emphasized by Charles Segal, 'Transition and Ritual in Odysseus' Return', *Parola del Passato* xl (1967), 337–40. The theoretical scheme for such an interpretation is derived from the well-known *Rites de Passage* of A. van Gennep, where the three states of ritual passage are identified as *separation*, *threshold* or *margin*, and *reaggregation*.

An important elaboration of the threshold or liminal state is given by Victor Turner, *The Ritual Process* (Chicago, 1969), 95-130, where liminal personages are assigned many attributes similar to those of Odysseus in his socially excluded role as beggar (note especially 102-11). Turner's observation (110), 'Folk literature abounds in symbolic figures, such as "holy beggars" . . . who strip off the pretentions of holders of high rank and office and reduce them to the level of common humanity and mortality', applies to Odysseus' speech to Amphinomus at 125 ff., to Eurymachus at 366 ff., and to Melantho at xix 71 ff. Odysseus exercises what Turner calls 'the ritual powers of the weak', the power to insult, curse, bless or in some way pass judgement on those of high social status. Note the suitors' fear, at xvii 483-7, that the beggar may be a disguised deity who wanders among men to judge their virtues and vices.

The threshold is associated with Odysseus again at xx 258; with his bow and the unsuccessful attempts made to string it, at xxi 43, 124, 149; and with his own successful use of the bow against the suitors as he regains his full identity and power, at xxii 2, 72, 76, 203. Cf. also xxii 127 and 182 where a threshold is involved less directly in the combat.

34. **ἱερὸν μένος Ἀντινόοιο**: seven of the eight occurrences of this formula in the *Odyssey* have Ἀλκινόοιο; the similar formula ἱερὴ ἴς Τηλεμάχοιο occurs seven times and is restricted to Telemachus (see 60 below, with note); and both formulas are absent from the *Iliad*. While the exact meaning of this archaic expression may be obscure by Homer's time, the general intention seems clear, to represent a heroic character metonymically by reference to his strength, a metonym appropriate for worthy villains as well as for heroes. μένος combines 'force' and 'impulse' into one word, the force being felt as an urge directed toward a specific action. A full discussion is in R. Schmitt, *Dichtung und Dichtersprache in Indogermanischer Zeit* (Wiesbaden, 1967), 103-12, where μένος is explained in relation to its Indo-European origins and cognates, the latter including the Vedic cognate formula *isirám mánaḥ*. (J. T. Hooker, *Ἱερός in Early Greek* (Innsbruck, 1980), maintains that this is a merely formal identity without semantic equivalence.) The root *men-, whose original meaning is 'to be stirred in one's mind or spirit', is most clearly seen in Greek *μάω; hence Latin *mens* and *memini* are also related, as well as μιμνήσκω, and, with further semantic narrowing, μαίνομαι. For ἱερόν see the note at 60.

44. **γαστέρες**: literally 'stomachs', here referring to intestinal membranes of the kind still used as sausage-casings in many countries. The 'fat and blood', κνίσης τε καὶ αἵματος, of line 45 recall the blood-sausages of modern Europe (French *boudin*, German *Blutwurst*). Passing to the symbolic level, we find that this *gaster*, which represents simply food, recalls Odysseus' earlier complaints about the urgings of the belly (vii 216-21, xv 344-5, xvii 286-9, 470-4), so that when it is used here the word has acquired the symbolic potential of evoking a larger frame of reference: the human need for sustenance and the difficulty of survival in the physically demanding heroic world, especially if one is politically and socially

powerless. (P. W. Rose, in *Historia* xxiv (1975), 129–49, sees in the repeated mention of *gaster* a sensitivity of the poet to the feelings of a hard-working peasantry and a political bias against the idle rich oligarchs who are contemporary with the poem. See further at the note to 366–80.) This *gaster*-motif, in which Odysseus is metonymically represented by his belly (xvii 228, 559; xviii 53, 364, 380), reaches its culmination at xx 25 ff., where a striking and unexpected simile directly equates Odysseus with a *gaster*. See further xvii 287 n.

53. **ἀρημένον:** this perfect passive participle is the only surviving form of a verb related to ἀρή, 'harm' (Apollonius the Sophist and the scholia on vi 2 gloss with βεβλαμμένος); but initial η- rather than ἀ- would be expected. Bechtel, *Lexilogus* s.v., posits an Aeolic ἄρημι, which he thinks accounts for the retention of ἀ.

56. **ἐπ᾽ Ἴρῳ ἦρα φέρων:** ἦρα is a strange noun found only in the accusative; and in Homer only with forms of φέρω and usually preceded by ἐπί, to give the meaning 'show favour to'. Herodian (398) explained it as the accusative of ἦρ (otherwise unattested), 'referring to aid' (ἐπὶ τῆς ἐπικουρίας). Hesychius glossed it with ἤτοι ὄντως· ἢ χάριν βοήθειαν ἐπικουρίαν, 'either truly; or favour, aid, assistance'. The first words could support an etymological connection with Latin *vērus*, Old High German *wār*, Old Irish *fír*, Old Slavic *věra* ('belief'). The gloss with χάριν, however, suggests a different root **wer-*, seen in Old Icelandic *voerr*, 'friendly', Old High German *wāri* as in *ala-wāri*, 'kind', and Latin *se-vērus*, i.e. 'without friendliness'. The Homeric usage makes the second interpretation far preferable (and cf. ἐπιήρανα, xix 343). The root in either case is **wer-*, and Homeric metre suggests initial digamma, as does the persistence of the adjective ἐπίηρος in classical Greek: there is never elision of ι before η. The use of ἦρα as equivalent to χάριν in the construction with the genitive to mean 'for the sake of' (Bacchylides x 20–1, but not again until Callimachus) is further evidence for favouring the second **wer-* meaning 'pleasing' (so Bechtel, *Lexilogus* s.v. ἐρίηρ, ἐρίηρος, following Jacob Grimm); cf. also the Hesychian gloss βρίηρος· μεγάλως κεχαρισμένον ('briēros: greatly pleasing').

60. **ἱερὴ ἴς Τηλεμάχοιο:** 'the prodigious strength of Telemachus', an archaic-seeming periphrasis used uniquely for this hero (but cf. ἱερὸν μένος, 34 above with note). The formula may allude to a special vigour believed to inhere in royalty (Wilamowitz, *Glaube* i 21–2, considers it fitting for Telemachus as heir to the throne). But the precise meaning of ἱερός remains elusive because of the wide range of nouns attached to it in Homeric language. Many of these nouns allow the standard post-Homeric meaning 'sacred', but others make this sense unlikely, such as 'dusk' (κνέφας), 'gate-guardians' (πυλαωροί), 'army' (στρατός), 'band of guards' (φυλάκων τέλος), and 'fish' (ἰχθύς). It is generally agreed that the semantic range of ἱερός extends from 'sacred' to 'vigorous', with the latter extending from 'strong' to 'active', the second of these being especially apt for the ἱερὸς ἰχθύς of *Il.* xvi 407 which is being pulled from ocean onto land.

Scholars have debated whether one original word can account for such breadth of meaning or whether two words should be posited. The Sanskrit cognate *iṣirá-* does not clarify the question since its meaning seems also to be broad. (See J. Duchesne-Guillemin, 'Gr. ἱερός ~ skr. *iṣiráḥ*' in *Mélanges Boisacq* (Brussels, 1937), i 333–8; P. Ramat in *Die Sprache* viii (1962), 4–28. It is noteworthy that the Greek formula ἱερὸν μένος has the Sanskrit cognate (in form if not necessarily in meaning) *iṣirám mánaḥ*; also that the Sanskrit meaning tends toward 'strong', 'fresh' rather than 'sacred'.) A lengthy case for multiple origins was made by Schulze, *Quaestiones*, 207–16, who thinks four or five different words may be involved to account for the semantic variation, the metrical variation between *i-* and *ī-*, and the shorter form ἱρός. But recent opinion has preferred to see a single original word: thus A. Pagliaro, *Saggi di critica semantica* (Messina–Firenze, 1962), 93–124 and esp. 104–7, following Wilamowitz, *Untersuchungen*, 106 n. 17, argues that ἱερός originally refers to the wonder which archaic man felt to reside in the phenomena of nature and their inexplicability. The meaning 'sacred' then would be the end-point rather than the beginning of the semantic evolution of this word, an argument echoed by Ramat, op. cit. The opposite is argued by P. Wülfing-von Maritz in *Glotta* xxxviii (1960), 272–307 and xxxix (1961), 24–43, and is further supported by the opinions reached independently by Gallavotti in *AC* xxxii (1963), 422–3, and J. P. Locher, *Untersuchungen zu ἱερός hauptsachlich bei Homer*, diss. (Bern, 1963), that the Mycenaean *i-je-ro* occurs in cultic contexts and suggests 'sacred' as the earliest documented meaning. Gallavotti adds, however (427), that this evidence does not suffice to invalidate the theory of a development from a general meaning 'vitally vigorous' to the more specific 'ritually efficacious' and finally 'sacred'. J. T. Hooker (op. cit., n. to 34) argues well for just such a primary meaning ('strong', especially 'as expressed in vitality, activity, or motion', pp. 26–7), which allows him to account for all Homeric instances except *Il.* xviii 504, the 'sacred circle' (ἱερὸς κύκλος) of judgement seats in the legal session depicted on Achilles' shield.

Historical–etymological explanations, it would seem, must remain inconclusive, and we may agree with Gallavotti (423, 427) that ἱερός in Homer tends toward a general 'elative' meaning that allows its application to an extraordinarily wide range of objects. Telemachus' 'prodigious' strength, therefore, most likely makes no allusion to sacral kingship but is simply a verbal gesture conferring honour on this uniquely important character through a unique formular combination.

69–70. Athena here reverses the changes in Odysseus' physique that she had created at xiii 430ff. There she 'shrivelled the skin on his limbs' to give them the strengthless, thin look of an old man's; here, she restores the fullness of their flesh and muscle. The 'large and beautiful thighs', 'broad shoulders', and 'sturdy arms' that Odysseus reveals here in 67–9 must all be the result of Athena filling out his limbs at 69–70, which gives us an example of Homeric hysteron-proteron. Her actions in 69–70 are meant to *account* for, rather than literally to *follow*, the changes of 67–9.

COMMENTARY

73. Ἶρος Ἄϊρος: 'Irus non-Irus'. The poet and his audience enjoyed such verbal wit, especially that which played with personal names. Homer's penchant for significant and punning names is illustrated—to choose only a few examples—by Echetus at 85 below, Odysseus' false name and father's and grandfather's names at xxiv 305–6, 'Phemius Terpiades' at xxii 330–1 (see note at xvii 263), the many significant names borne by members of Alcinous' court, and the fact that Irus' name is already a punning variant on the divine messenger Iris. A more specialized kind of name-play is illustrated by 'Irus-non-Irus', the deliberate distortion of familiar names as a sarcastic expression of hostility: cf. δύσπαρι spoken by Hector to Paris at *Il.* iii 39 = xiii 769; Κακοΐλιον, *Od.* xix 260 = 597 = xxiii 19.

79. βουγάϊε: this word is used only here and *Il.* xiii 824, Hector rebuking Ajax, and its meaning is problematic. The *Odyssey* scholia and Eustathius take the Iliadic usage to mean 'rejoicing in your (oxhide) shield', as if βουγάϊε = ἐπὶ τῇ βοΐ (ἀσπίδι) γαίων, an expression parallel to κύδεϊ γαίων. Eustathius believes that the *Odyssey* passage needs a totally different interpretation, and suggests that here the word means either 'a weight upon the earth (because Irus is fleshy)' or 'one who does an ox's labour'. Hesychius and Apollonius say that a plough-ox (ἐργάτης βοῦς) was called γάϊος or βουγάϊος because it worked the ground, γαῖα; hence the word may have become a pejorative term for an ox-like person (so Monro). Ameis–Hentze–Cauer take it differently, as 'one who swaggers like a bull', and LSJ, *LfgrE*, and Frisk, *GEW*, define the word as 'braggart', all understanding the second element of the word (from γαίω) to mean 'exulting'. J. Latacz, however (*Zum Wortfeld 'Freude' in der Sprache Homers* (Heidelberg, 1966), 128–30), argues well for the meaning 'proud of' rather than 'rejoicing' or 'exulting' for the second element, and argues that the βου-element is augmentative as it is in later Greek. This view accords with Apollonius' gloss τὸν ἐφ' ἑαυτὸν μεγάλως γαυριῶντα, 'one who bears himself very proudly'. Whatever meaning we give to βουγάϊε, it is likely that βου- is intensive and pejorative, marking the beginning of a trend that becomes quite pronounced in late fifth- to fourth-century Greek. For Aristophanes it is an augmentative abusive prefix, seen in the words βούπαι, *V.* 1206, and βουλαμάχου, *Pax* 1292 (a punning reference to Lamachus as βου-Λάμαχος). Note also the verb βουλιμιάω in Xenophon *An.* iv 5. 7–8. L. J. D. Richardson in *Hermathena* xcv (1961), 53–65, discusses βου- compounds from Homer to comedy and concludes that this prefix has not yet acquired intensive or pejorative meaning in Homer but had the concrete meaning 'ox', so that βουγάϊε here means 'clumsy' or 'stupid ox'. But see Latacz's counter-arguments, 129 n. 2.

85. Ἔχετον: traditionally taken to be an imaginary person, whose significant name means 'Holder' (cf. 'Hector', also formed from ἔχω, 'to hold'). Such a traditional figure may be like the familiar wicked king in folktales who puts all newcomers to death. The scholia, however, believe Echetus to be an historical figure, a king either of Sicily or of Epirus and son of Echenor and Phlogea, and having a daughter called Metope or

Amphissa. The scholia emphasize his cruelty, but this may be made up to support Homer's allusion. The reference to Sicily recalls Homer's mention of that place at xx 383, where the suitors in anger suggest sending Telemachus' guests (the beggar and Theoclymenus) 'to the Sicilians' to be sold. Echetus is mentioned again at 116 and xxi 308.

90-4. A typical pattern of pondering and decision. See xvii 235-8 n.

95. ἀνασχομένω: 'having their hands up', i.e. having assumed the standard boxer's stance (at 89). Cf. xiv 425; *Il.* iii 362, xxii 34, xxiii 660, 686.

98. κὰδ δ' ἔπεσ' ἐν κονίῃσι μακών: a formula used elsewhere only of a mortally wounded animal (x 163, xix 454, *Il.* xvi 469), as noted by D. B. Levine, *CJ* lxxvii (1982), 201. Irus' threat (27-9) ironically rebounds upon him, and the description of him knocking his teeth together, σὺν δ' ἤλασ' ὀδόντας, Levine notes, echoes his own words ἐκ πάντας ὀδόντας . . . ἐξελάσαιμι in 28-9.

100. γέλῳ ἔκθανον: 'they died with laughter', a surprisingly exact correspondence with our modern idiom. Eustathius observed (twelfth century) that it 'has continued in use up to the present day as a proverbial way of speaking about great and concentrated laughter' (1839. 30-1). In an oddly parodic way, this metaphor anticipates the literal death of the suitors, also to be caused by Odysseus, in reality rather than in a figure of speech.

108-9. These two verses describe the wretched beggar's wallet in detail, recalling the scene where Athena first transformed Odysseus into the beggar and equipped him with this ragged wallet and strap (109 = xiii 438). In passing on to Irus the most obvious and degrading token of his beggar's status, Odysseus takes a symbolic step toward leaving that condition and moving upward to a higher one, on the way to full recovery of his true identity. Now he has moved from itinerant beggar to 'established' household beggar (cf. 110: he is now the sole and legitimate occupier of the threshold), and in the latter part of this book and throughout xix he becomes a trusted confidant of Penelope.

111. δεικανόωντο: see the note to 121.

111a. This line, absent from most MSS, is also missing from the earliest evidence for our text, the fourth-century Papyrus Ross. Georg. 7 and the sixth/seventh-century Papyrus Oxyrhyncus 1820. It is very likely an intrusion (the identical verse occurs at ii 324) placed here by a copyist or a reciting rhapsode.

117. χαῖρεν δὲ κλεηδόνι: cf. xvii 541 with note. 'He rejoiced at the verbal omen' is the nearest translation, but κλεηδών/κλήηδών has no exact equivalent. It is formed from the group κλέος, κλέω/κλείω (stem κλεϝ-), whose meaning runs the semantic gamut 'to name/make known/make famous'. The specialized meaning 'verbal omen, presage' follows the habit of nouns in -δων, -ηδών (Chantraine, *Formation*, 360-2). Earlier in the poem this word meant 'news', the sharing of what has been heard (iv 317; cf. iv 322-4 which serves as a perfect gloss on what Telemachus means by κληηδών). But here, in the books nearing the climax of the poem, the word is drawn into that part of its semantic range that best serves the narrative

COMMENTARY

needs for suspense and irony, referring to something uttered that can be fully understood only by a *privileged* audience, here Odysseus. The phrase recurs at xx 120, again referring to Odysseus. It has long been noted (Ebeling, *Lexicon*, 812 col. 1) that κλεηδών and φήμη largely overlap in meaning: cf. ii 35, χαῖρε δὲ φήμῃ; and Eust. 1884. 50 ff. (ad xx 120), where the similarity of κλεηδών and φήμη is maintained in the light of their distinction from τέρας. Homer brings these three terms together, and adds a fourth, σῆμα, in a sustained description of an omen at xx 100–20.

119. Ἀμφίνομος δὲ: the introduction of Amphinomus seems sudden, since he has not been mentioned since xvi; but Homer does often use the bucolic caesura as a point of syntactic and narrative juncture. When the suitors in xvi were disgruntled over the failure of their ambush, it was Amphinomus who dissuaded them from adopting Antinous' proposal that Telemachus be murdered outright (xvi 361–406). Here he is again introduced for a scene of major importance, to provide a strong contrast to the suitors' wickedness. His toasting the old beggar stands out as a gesture quite the opposite of Antinous' and Eurymachus' throwing stools at him at xvii 462 ff. and xviii 394 ff. And while we are saddened at the inevitability of the death which Amphinomus does not fully merit, his situation offers a good opportunity for Homer to add some theological and existential commentary (130–42) that deepens and enriches the action.

121. δειδίσκετο: a word of confused etymology and elusive meaning, probably related to δεικανόωντο at 111 above: there the suitors make a 'toast' in words, ἔπεσσι, and here Amphinomus does so with a golden cup, δέπαϊ χρυσέῳ, to accompany his verbal declaration. Authorities divide over whether both verbs derive from δείκνυμι (so Monro, *Homeric Dialect*, 23. 6, 24. 3), or from δέχομαι (LSJ takes δειδίσκομαι from δέχομαι and δεικανάομαι from δείκνυμι), or from still another verb stem, δηκ- and related to Sanskrit *dāsnóti*, 'to give homage' (so Schwyzer, *Grammatik*, i 648, 697; Bechtel, *Lexilogus*, 96). Chantraine, *Dictionnaire*, 270–1, believes that no clear etymological explanation is possible because of extensive conflation (for morphological details see his *Grammaire*, i 317–18, 359–60, 303 n. 3), and that all these verbal forms (including δεικνύμενος, *Il.* ix 196, which belongs semantically to this group and not to δείκνυμι 'to show') share an idea that extends from offering formal greeting with words to doing so with a cup of wine in hand (xv 150), like our own ritual toasts, or simply with a hand gesture, as at xx 197. Modern translations unfortunately fragment this idea into particular aspects, such as 'greet', 'pledge', 'with a gesture', because our modern social interactions lack what the social anthropologist, speaking of tribal societies, notes as 'the relatively great development of special customs and stylized etiquette to mark the different roles which a man or woman is playing at any one moment' (Max Gluckman, 'Les rites de passage', in *Essays on the Ritual of Social Relations* (Manchester, 1962), 27; and cf. 24–5 for further definition of 'the ritualization of social relationships').

125–50. Odysseus' speech to Amphinomus has often been singled out for

54

comment upon its 'philosophy of life' and theological vision. See R. B. Rutherford, 'The Philosophy of the Odyssey', *JHS* cvi (1986), 156, who uses this speech to argue for Odysseus' evolution in the course of the poem from a reckless adventurer to a man who has learnt the wisdom of restraint. A striking and original theoretical discussion, J. M. Redfield's 'The Economic Man', in C. A. Rubino and C. W. Shelmerdine, edd., *Approaches to Homer* (Austin, Tex., 1983), finds in this speech a perfect illustration of the central Odyssean concern with 'economics' conceived as an ethic of struggle between labour and saving, scarcity and plenty, aimed at 'developing a *noos* to some degree independent of the day Zeus brings us, able to confront scarcity and plenty without despair or insolence'.

126. τοίου ... πατρός: supply ἐσσί, 'you are', which is understood, and rendered less necessary by the εἶναι which concludes the preceding verse.

128. ἐπητῆ: a word of disputed etymology and meaning. The most likely derivation is from the root (ϝ)επ-, which connects this word to εἶπον and ἔπος and suggests the meaning 'very proficient in speech', a *nomen agentis* parallel to ἀγορητής. This ancient interpretation, found in the scholia, the *Etymologicum Magnum*, and Eustathius, is renewed and ably defended by A. T. Dale, *Glotta* lx (1982), 205–14, who argues against those who would translate 'polite, affable' (based on derivation from the root *sep- of ἕπω) and suggests further that the πεπνυμένος of 125, indicating a virtue normally manifested through proficiency in speech, is nearly synonymous with and anticipates the ἐπητῆ of 128. Examining the only other Homeric use of ἐπητής, xiii 332 where Athena uses three adjectives to characterize Odysseus (ἐπητής, ἀγχίνοος, ἐχέφρων), Dale makes a plausible connection between ἐπητής and Athena's commending Odysseus' skill at μῦθοι at iii 298; she then interprets the closely related but problematic ἐπητύς of xxi 306 as the *conversation* that is the normal component of a banquet, as described at xxi 290–1.

130. ἀκιδνότερον: this unusual word occurs only at v 217, viii 169 (each referring to εἶδος), and here, always a comparative in form, with the apparent meaning 'feeble' or 'slight'. Apollonius' *Lexicon* glosses it ἀσθενέστερον, 'weaker', for this passage, εὐτελεστέρα, 'less noteworthy', for v 217; both Hesychius and *EM* gloss ἀσθενής, and Hesychius adds εὐτελές; while the scholia gloss it as 'more patient' or 'more enduring', ὑπομονητικώτερον. It does not reappear in Greek until the Hippocratic corpus (*Praec.* 8, *Nat. Puer.* 30), where ἀκιδνός seems to mean 'weak' (and one MS at *Praec.* 8 reads ἀσθενής).

133. ἀρετή: this word has a wide range of meanings, from the more physical 'prowess', 'manliness', to the more general idea of 'prosperity' or 'success'. Either meaning would fit here; but the habits of Homeric style make the following words, καὶ γούνατ' ὀρώρῃ, 'and his knees have spring in them', most likely a gloss or expansion of the statement 'so long as the gods give ἀρετή', so that ἀρετή most likely means physical prowess.

136-7. The νόος of humans here means their disposition or cast of mind. Cf. i 3, πολλῶν δ' ἀνθρώπων ... νόον ἔγνω, with S. West's note, and Solon fr.

4. 7 w, where an ἄδικος νόος describes the unjust mentality of the leadership of the demos. A full discussion of this word is given by K. von Fritz, *CP* xxxviii (1943), 79–93 (for Homer), xl (1945), 223–42 and xli (1946), 12–34 (for later authors), improved by T. Krischer, *Glotta* lxii (1984), 141–9. For the same sentiment in similar wording, perhaps a deliberate echo, cf. Archilochus fr. 131 w, where θυμός replaces νόος.

137. ἐπ' ἦμαρ ἄγῃσι: tmesis for ἐπάγω. The word ἦμαρ, as Stanford notes, often approaches the meaning 'daily condition', the quality of life in one's day. Homer usually achieves this meaning by using a modifier + ἦμαρ to describe significant events by giving that day a sharply defined character, e.g. δούλιον ἦμαρ, 'the day of enslavement', νόστιμον ἦμαρ, 'the day of homecoming', νηλεὲς ἦμαρ, 'the day without pity'. For these formulaic usages, see R. A. Santiago in *Emerita* xxx (1962), 139–50. The conception of the human condition thus implied (man's 'ephemeros' nature) is discussed by H. Fränkel, *TAPhA* lxxvii (1946), 131–45, esp. 135–6 (slightly revised in *Wege und Formen frühgriechischen Denkens* (Munich, 1968), 23–39. Fränkel points out that a Zeus who sends upon us, and in effect is, the day, is implicit in the very name Zeus *patēr*, Latin *Diespiter* > Iuppiter, equivalent to the Sanskrit *dyauti pitā*, a sky-god or sky-Father who represents the physical weather. The connection of this weather to our 'inner weather' or state of mind, here νόος, is a natural one. Man's mind, his thoughts and feelings, are subject to as much change as the succession of days brings: life is unpredictable, a wheel of fortune. Thus did Odysseus (as the lowly beggar) move abruptly from good fortune to bad. (Note, however, the argument of M. W. Dickie, 'On the Meaning of ἐφήμερος', *Illinois Class. St.* i (1976), 7–14, who points out that the adj. ἐφήμερος does not yet exist for Homer, and that when used by Pindar and other archaic and classical period poets to describe the human condition, it most likely means 'lasting for a day', 'short-lived'.) This passage is one of Homer's most profound and lyrical expressions of the generally pessimistic epic view of life; consequently it was imitated by Archilochus (68 D = 131 w; cf. also 58 D = 130 w) and later echoed but transformed by Parmenides (B 16) and Heraclitus (fr. 17). Verses 130–7 are quoted by Plutarch, *Consol. ad Apoll.*, 104 d.

138. ἔμελλον: as earlier at 19, μέλλω + pres. inf. conveys likelihood deriving from what should be or, in a past tense, should have been. Here the idiom combines the sense of our two statements 'I was supposed to be prosperous' and 'I was on my way to being prosperous'. If the future infinitive is used, it accentuates the forthcoming development as representing what is inevitable or destined in a situation, as at x 477, xiii 293 and 383–5. A full discussion of the nuances of μέλλω is in Chantraine, *Grammaire*, i 307–9.

141–50. Here the reasoning changes from the more archaic 'wheel of fortune' conception of the universe seen in 132–40 and summarized epigrammatically in 136–7 where man's fortune changes almost with the weather, to a more morally conceived system where people receive their 'just desserts'. In the first model a man's fortune swings from good to bad

simply because 'the gods bring to pass evils for him'—ὅτε δὴ καὶ λυγρὰ θεοὶ
μάκαρες τελέσωσι, 134. No attention is given to what misdeeds the man
might have committed to bring these evils on himself. But when Odysseus
now turns to specifics and uses his own case to illustrate his point (καὶ γὰρ
ἐγώ, 138), he introduces a moral causality by admitting he acted badly
(ἀτάσθαλ' ἔρεξα, 139), having acted as if, in our modern idiom, 'might
makes right' (βίῃ καὶ κάρτεϊ εἴκων, 139). Such a moralized scheme is
necessary as foundation for his judgement on the suitors, introduced by τῷ
μή τις . . . ἀθεμίστιος εἴη, 141, and then given specific focus by οἷα beginning 143. The repetition of ἀτάσθαλα in 143 equates their violations with
those ἀτάσθαλα of 139 which we were told led to the beggar's downfall. It is
interesting that this moral cosmic model of justice can coexist with the
relatively amoral one of 132–40; archaic thought was less troubled by
logical contradiction than is our own thinking. We are justified in seeing in
this important speech of Odysseus one of the first examples of early Greek
speculative thought striving to articulate a morally justifiable theodicy. For
an excellent example of this 'double theodicy' see Clay, Wrath, 227–9, who
suggests that Odysseus' shift to the more ethical conception is motivated by
his wish to encourage Amphinomus to leave.

144-7. Note how as the argument moves from the general principle to the
problem at hand—the impending danger of a confrontation between the
suitors and an angry, returned Odysseus—the relation of sentence-
structure and phrase-pattern to verse boundaries is altered. The normative
tendency for the verse-end to correspond with the end of a sentence or
clause (visible in the fact that most lines are printed with some punctuation
at the end) here yields to a series of varied enjambments (144–5 ἄκοιτιν/
ἀνδρός, possessive genitive; 145–6 φημὶ . . . ἀπέσσεσθαι, complementary
infinitive; 146–7, σε δαίμων/οἴκαδ' ὑπεξαγάγοι, completion with verb
phrase after both subject and object have been expressed). The final two
verses of Odysseus' warning also show grammatical enjambment.

151-2. Odysseus completes the conventional, even ritual, sequence of acts
begun with Amphinomus' toast at 121. There Amphinomus' address to
the beggar, containing a wish for his future success (ὄλβος), is framed
within the pattern of a formal toast (δέπαϊ χρυσέῳ δειδίσκετο); here, the
beggar's response continues an important ritual pattern designed to
involve the gods' power in fulfilling human wishes: σπείσας ἔπιεν, he pours
the gods a libation, then drinks from the cup over which the wish was first
pronounced, then returns the cup to the donor. The modern reader needs
to appreciate this ritual sequence in its full formal structure in order to
realize how it succeeds in giving special strength to the theological vision of
forthcoming retribution revealed in the speech (130–50; note esp. 149–50)
that it serves to frame. Benveniste, Le Vocabulaire des institutions indo-
européennes (Paris, 1969), ii 211–12, discussing libations, stresses that their
purpose is always that of protecting someone engaged in a dangerous
enterprise (cf. Xerxes' libation at Hdt. vii 54). Odysseus is then reinforcing
his verbal warning with a warning conveyed through ritual gesture.

158–303. This memorable episode used to be suspected as an interpolation, by critics as renowned as Wilamowitz (*Heimkehr*, 19–26) and Page (*Odyssey*, 124–6), although Wilamowitz admired it as a well-wrought scene. A sensible review and appraisal of these arguments is given by A. Heubeck, *Die Homerische Frage* (Darmstadt, 1974), 126–7, who judges it one of Homer's 'masterpieces'. Besslich, *Schweigen*, 138–43, also defends the narrative coherence of this scene against earlier German scholarship. Suspicion has been aroused by the appearance of several linguistically late or rare forms in a short space (see 172, 173, 179, 190, 191, 192); but in the absence of any sure criteria for determining the source of such rare forms, their weight as evidence for post-Homeric composition remains uncertain.

160–2. An ambiguous sequence, which, if we mistakenly take the ὅπως-clause to depend on φανῆναι instead of ἔθηκε, would seem to attribute to Penelope the highly implausible intention of wishing to excite the suitors and impress her husband (of whose pretence she is unaware) and son. Another source of confusion is that the construction of ὅπως with following optative can describe either the intention behind an action or the result of the action. (That the scholiasts were bothered by this ambiguity is seen in their comments on similar constructions—with ἵνα and ὄφρα instead of ὅπως—at ix 154–5, xii 426–8, and *Il.* xxii 328–9, where they puzzle over whether the poet is representing deliberate intent or simply the causal sequence.) It is also possible to imagine these verses to be the vestige of an earlier version of the poem in which Penelope has already recognized Odysseus and they are now acting in concert against the suitors (other traces of this earlier version would be the suitors' ghosts' remark at xxiv 167–9 that Penelope plotted with Odysseus to slaughter them).

But here it is best to follow most perceptive commentators since van Leeuwen and understand ὅπως and its following two optatives to depend grammatically on ἔθηκε and to indicate intention rather than result, the intention being Athena's and not Penelope's. It is the goddess who is engineering this scene: we see her strong control in her decision (ἀλλ' ἐνόησε, 187) to overcome Penelope with sleep and the continuation of her purpose in the optative clause ἵνα μιν θησαίατ' at 191.

Allione, *Telemaco*, 76–7, offers the unconvincing argument that it is both Athena and Penelope who share in the intention of the ὅπως-clause, and that the queen's intention to be 'more honoured by her husband' refers not to the scene at hand but to the future time of Odysseus' return, when he will find her in possession of these impressive gifts. Such a reading misses Homer's strong dramatic focus on the enhanced status attained by Penelope in the present scene, and also fails to explain why her son is mentioned together with her husband in 162.

It should be noted that Athena's threefold purpose regarding Penelope in 160–2 is in fact fulfilled at three points in the ensuing narrative: at 212–13 the queen enflames the suitors; at 215–42 she earns Telemachus' acknowledgement that it is she who runs the house and that he has been managing it badly; and at 281–3 she earns Odysseus' respect for her clever manipulation.

160. πετάσειε: there is a tradition of translating 'might flutter' (so Monro, LSJ s.v. πετάννυμι) which has, however, no basis in the Greek, and may derive from an early confusion of πετάννυμι (Latin *pateo*) 'expand' with πέτομαι (Latin *peto*) 'to fly'. Thus the scholia gloss ἐκπλήξειεν. ἀναστήσει πρὸς ἐπιθυμίαν. θέλξει, all of which assume that πετάσειε θυμόν has a meaning similar to Sappho's καρδίαν ἐν στήθεσιν ἐπτόαισεν, 31. 6 L–P. But πετάσειε here means she would 'enlarge' or 'open up' the suitors' spirit, the metaphor being to expand it with a new influx of strong emotion. Wilamowitz, *Heimkehr*, 19 n. 1, explains the metaphor as that of opening up a door.

163. ἄχρειον: literally, 'useless', but here usually understood as 'inappropriate', 'pointless', perhaps describing what we call an embarrassed laugh. The common-sense reading is that Homer uses this unusual word to show that Penelope is uncomfortable with the bold impulse planted in her by the goddess (so Hölscher, *Untersuchungen*, 62). A full discussion of the difficulty in ascertaining the exact sense of ἄχρειον is given by Büchner, 'Penelopeszenen', 141–3.
More recently, D. B. Levine, 'Penelope's Laugh: *Odyssey* 18. 163', *AJPh* civ (1983), 172–80, citing many places in Greek literature where laughter accompanies deception, argues that this laugh expresses the queen's confidence in and appreciation of her own trickery regarding the suitors. J. S. Clay, 'Homeric ἄχρειον', *AJPh* cv (1984), 73–6, accepts this interpretation and attempts to supply the linguistic argument that Levine lacks, deriving ἄχρειον from the Homeric expression οὐδὲ τί σε (με) χρή, which she translates as 'it does not befit you (me)'. She then translates ἄχρειον as 'inappropriate to one's character', 'uncharacteristic', a meaning she argues would also suit the ἄχρειον that describes Thersites' look at *Il.* ii 269 (the only other Homeric occurrence of this word). While the sense may be attractive for the characterization of a more assertive Penelope than critics customarily allow, Clay's proposed derivation is less so. Since the nouns χρείη/χρέος mean 'need' and not 'appropriateness' or 'characteristic', it seems strained to find this second meaning in an idiomatic extension of οὐδὲ τί σε χρή, lit. 'you ought not' or 'you need not', to mean 'it is uncharacteristic of you', and then to apply the meaning 'characteristic' back to the root χρει-.
The exact meaning of ἄχρειον, then, must remain elusive. The word is best analysed as 'not needed' (*LfgrE*) and understood as indicating either the embarrassment or discomfort described above, or perhaps a laugh that is unnecessary or forced because it is feigned, Penelope's purpose being either to offer a lighthearted façade to Eurynome or to get herself 'into character' for the superior tone she is preparing to adopt toward the suitors and her son.

164–5. Since Athena has put this unusual urge in Penelope, the queen has to explain her surprising decision to Eurynome with οὔ τι πάρος γε to stress

COMMENTARY

its novelty and ἀπεχθομένοισι περ ἔμπης to stress that she is *not* departing from her position of contempt for the suitors and loyalty to her husband.

These verbal touches, prepared for by the ἄχρειον of 163, are needed to explain the contradiction between Penelope's normal stand and her sudden and abnormal willingness to entice the suitors and declare herself ready for remarriage—a contradiction well described by U. Hölscher, 'Penelope vor den Freiern', in *Lebende Antike: Symposion für R. Sühnel* (Berlin, 1967), 27–33. Hölscher explains it as deriving from the poet's revival of a Märchen-like aspect of Penelope (the 'clever wife' familiar from the ruse of the web) at a point in the narrative where he has been emphasizing her nobility and lofty aloofness, qualities more suited to the high tone of epic than to the familiar tone of folktale.

166-8. The fact that Penelope never voices this advice (not to associate, ὁμιλεῖν, with the suitors) when she eventually addresses Telemachus at 215–25, has led some critics to question the coherence and even the authenticity of this entire episode. But the topic of that eventual speech—chiding Telemachus for allowing the suitors to maltreat the beggar—amounts to a criticism for going along with the suitors' manner of behaviour. As Besslich, *Schweigen*, 141, notes, Telemachus in 64–6 expressly joined the suitors in allowing the fight with Irus, and such collaboration is seen as the ὁμιλεῖν that Penelope will object to more explicitly in 215–25.

172. χρῶτ': χρῶτα (also at 179) is usually labelled post-Homeric and Attic (Shipp, *Studies*, 345; Wackernagel, *Untersuchungen*, 146–7 [306–7]), despite the occurrence of this form at *Il.* x 575 and Hesiod, *Op.* 556. While the more common epic inflection of χρώς is χροός, χροΐ, χρόα, there is no way to prove that the stem χρωτ-, which is well-established in the language of Empedocles and Pindar, did not attain sufficiently wide diffusion in poetic diction at a period early enough to coincide with the last stages of Homeric composition (*c.*700). Wackernagel, on the other hand, would assign these verses (172, 179, *Il.* x 575) to an Attic interpolator, noting that the stem χρωτ- is found early only in West Greek poets, and does not enter Attic until Aeschylus.

173. δακρύοισι: this form is a *hapax*, the dat. pl. being regularly δάκρυσι. All forms of δάκρυ elsewhere have a long first syllable, but here we have a rare -άκρ-; although the same irregularity is paralleled in δάκρωπλώειν at xix 122. Mute + liquid normally make a long syllable in Homer (aside from names like Ἀφροδίτη that could not be used metrically unless shortened; for the norm, see Chantraine, *Grammaire*, i 108–9); but shortening is occasionally allowed before τρ, πρ, κρ, πλ, κλ. The metrical and morphological irregularity here has often been adduced, together with other rare forms like χρῶτα (and cf. notes to 179, 190, 191, 192) and supposed thematic awkwardnesses (in the eye of the beholder rather than in the text), to argue that this scene is an interpolation. But the Homeric language is a mixed and artificial language, abounding in varied and inconsistent forms, and arguments from supposed linguistic anomalies

60

have less force today than they used to. And the scene is one of Homer's finest.

175-6. It is not immediately apparent to us—although it must be to Penelope—that Eurynome is alluding to Odysseus' instructions when he left for Troy, which Penelope will quote verbatim at 257–70.

178-84. Penelope is retreating now from the momentary and unnatural boldness inspired by Athena. Her normal diffidence and sense of vulnerability in the face of the suitors reassert themselves: she needs the supporting presence of her familiar attendants.

179. ἀπονίπτεσθαι: most of this verse is quoted by Apollonius, *Lex.*, 23 (s.v. ἀλοιφῇ), but with ἀπονίψασθαι and ἐπιχρείσασθαι. Wackernagel, *Untersuchungen*, 74 [234], calls ἀπονίπτεσθαι 'a quite recent addition', but this is relative chronology and does not necessarily deny Homeric authorship.

190. κλιντῆρι: a *hapax* for the usual κλισμῷ. τέως: most often scanned – ◡, as if we had a scribal transformation of the original τῆος (the same is true of ἕως); but here it is ◡ –. Some have seen in this rarity the sort of irregularity that would help condemn the entire lengthy scene (158–303), but this datum is scarcely compelling. The facts are that τέως and ἕως appear as – ◡, –, and ◡ –. The iambic form is the least frequent and clearly 'late' (such quantitative metathesis is one of the latest linguistic innovations in Homeric Greek; see Hoekstra, *Modifications*, 31–41); but 'late' is only a relative term and need not mean post-Homeric. Hoekstra follows Meister, *Kunstsprache*, 163–4, in assuming that quantitative metathesis was already present in the dialect of the epic singers; thus the passage under consideration is most likely to belong to the latest stages of the *Odyssey*'s composition. Insofar as the enhancement of Penelope and her appearance before the suitors is a tightly constructed scene of fine descriptive detail and dramatic power added to the basic story line, we may with good reason think of it as Homer's own embellishment upon the traditional tale.

191. θησαίατ': an irregular form for θηησαίατο, the epic third-plural aorist optative. Page, eager to emphasize its oddness and the linguistic unorthodoxy of this episode, calls it 'a monster' (*Odyssey*, 133 n. 27), and Shipp quotes this judgement (*Studies*, 345). But the contraction of disyllabic -ηη- to single -η- is not so monstrously odd: see Chantraine, *Grammaire*, i 30, who notes that two vowels of the same timbre present a favourable case for contraction. Thus, while the forms ἄαται and ἀασάμην are normal, we do find also the rare ἄσατο, *Il.* xix 95, and ἄσε, *Od.* xi 61; and the form ἄτη is always found contracted (from an original *ἀϝάτη). Since θηέομαι also has an original digamma (stem θαϝε-) the contraction from θηϝησαίατο to θησαίατο is not really surprising.

192. προσώπατα: an irregular pl. generated as if from a sing. πρόσωπα. Cf. the similar dat. pl. προσώπασι at *Il.* vii 212. Such a formation suggests the spontaneously created neologism of the oral poet, relying on his ear rather than on conscious grammatical rules.

194. χρίεται: by this word we see that the κάλλεϊ of 192, continued in the relative οἵῳ of 193, is envisaged by the poet as a concrete object, a sort of divine beauty cream. This is the only instance of κάλλος having this meaning, a semantic *hapax*. An alternative, metaphorical interpretation is conceivable, but unlikely in view of κάθηρεν (192) which suggests literal cleansing, as in the famous 'Adornment of Hera' at *Il.* xiv 170 ff., where we find a more explicit statement with 'dirt', λύματα, as the object of κάθηρεν.

195. πάσσονα: Wilamowitz speaks for many who have erroneously condemned this word as an awkward transfer of *male* standards of beauty to a *female* context (*Untersuchungen*, 31 n. 2). But size was a component of female beauty for the Greeks, as noted by Pasquali, *Terze pagine stravaganti* (Florence, 1942), 141–2, n. 2; K. Jax, *Die Weibliche Schönheit in der Griechischen Dichtung* (Innsbruck, 1933), 9 with the references in notes 53–7; W. J. Verdenius, in *Mnemosyne* iv (1949), 294–5; and M. Treu, *Von Homer zu Lyrik* (Munich, 1955), 35–52, especially p. 51 where Wilamowitz is refuted concerning this very verse.

196. λευκοτέρην: whiteness is the conventional attribute of women's skin, both in the Homeric world and later in the archaic and classical periods. Homer repeatedly uses the epithet λευκώλενος of Hera, Andromache, Helen, Arete, Nausicaa, and various female attendants; and the arms of Aphrodite and of Penelope are white in the conventional formula πήχεε λευκώ (*Il.* v 314, *Od.* xxiii 240). Greek vase painting of the eighth and seventh centuries represents women's skin as white and men's as reddish-brown: see J. D. Beazley and B. Ashmole, *Greek Sculpture and Painting to the End of the Hellenistic Period* (Cambridge, 1932), 6–7, 23; J. D. Beazley, *The Development of Attic Black Figure* (Berkeley, 1951), 1; E. Buschor, *Griechischen Vasen* (Munich, 1940), 67; E. Irwin, *Colour Terms in Greek Poetry* (Toronto, 1974), 112–14. It should be noted that this stereotyping begins as early as Minoan palace painting. M. Treu, op. cit. 52, 75–6, stresses that white skin for women and dark skin for men (cf. *Od.* xvi 175) are aesthetic ideals in Homeric epic; but he notes that white skin is often attributed to heroes also, citing Jax, op. cit. 31–2, n. 131, who suggests, no doubt rightly, that in such cases the poet is emphasizing the vulnerability of the hero's skin. πριστοῦ ἐλέφαντος: ivory is mentioned six times in the *Odyssey* as a material used by craftsmen in decoration, and again twice as the material of which the gates of deceptive dreams are made, at xix 563–4. Cf. the note there for the possible symbolism of the substance ivory. In the *Iliad*, ivory is mentioned only at iv 141 and v 583. See Lorimer, *Monuments*, 507, who finds the higher frequency in the *Odyssey* a sign of its later composition; and further in M. Treu, *Philologus* ic (1955), 149–58.

202. Penelope will repeat this wish for death by Artemis' arrow at xx 61 ff., 80. Artemis is regularly a bringer of 'gentle death' with her painless arrows, usually for women as at xi 172–3, 198–9, 324, xv 478; and once for a man, the death of Orion described at v 121–4. Normally men receive the same 'gentle death' from Apollo, as at iii 279–80, *Il.* xxiv 758–9. At *Od.* xv 410–11 Artemis and Apollo jointly bring such a death to the elderly. Penelope's immediate association of sleep with death is not surprising, since they are established in Homeric thought as close kin: at *Il.* xiv 231 they are called 'brothers' and at xvi 682, 'twin brothers'. Cf. Hes. *Op.* 116, *Th.* 212; and *Th.* 756–66 for a description of their kinship and contrasting attributes. Their similarity is a commonplace throughout all literature and all metaphoric thinking, appearing as early as the Gilgamesh epic, where the hero fails Utnapishtim's 'sleep test' and thereby fails to evade mortality.

209-10. A physical attitude that is characteristic of Penelope throughout the epic (i 333–4, xvi 415–16, xxi 64–5), and may be seen as the outer manifestation of an inner attitude of mind. As A. Amory notes (*YCS* xx (1966), 55–6), Penelope tends to look at things only intermittently, to look away from that which is important for her to perceive (cf. xix 478, xxiii 106–7). From these observations Amory builds a suggestive contrast of the difference between Odysseus and Penelope in the way they look at, and deal with, the world around them. A different interpretation is given by H. Haakh, *Gymnasium* lxvi (1959), 374–80, who argues that her gesture is one of holding the veil *away* from her face.

212. λύτο γούνατ': the knee joints are a critically vulnerable point of the body in the Homeric conception of man as a psychosomatic totality. Just as one's peak of vigour and self-confidence was expressed in the phrase γούνατ' ὀρώρῃ, 'the knees have spring' (above, 133), so one's being overwhelmed by strong emotion is also depicted in the effect upon the knees, which in this case go slack. In the *Iliad* the knees are made slack or loose in numerous passages as the result of a deadly wound or intense fear. In the *Odyssey* this is a common reaction to fear (iv 703, v 297, 406, xxii 68, *et al.*), but the present passage is unique—and achieves a powerful effect—in attributing the cause to the power of *eros*. For detailed documentation of the knees as a special seat of strength and spiritual force, see Onians, *Origins*, 174–97.

213. παραὶ λεχέεσσι: 'to lie beside ⟨her⟩, in bed'. The παραί is adverbial, not a preposition, while λεχέεσσι is locative. This line = i 366, describing the suitors' reaction to Penelope the first time in the epic that they see her.

224. ῥυστακτύος: ῥυστακτύς, found only here in Greek, means 'a dragging about' and derives from ῥυστάζω, 'to pull about, maltreat', a frequentative form of ἐρύω, 'to drag, pull'. Odysseus uses ῥυστάζω joined with the equally expressive στυφαλίζω at xvi 108–9, and Telemachus at xx 318–19 (a verbatim repetition), to criticize the suitors' maltreatment of guests and servant women, an important emphasis of this section of the story.

234. μνηστήρων ἰότητι: the fight did not turn out 'according to the will (or wish) of the suitors', that is, Telemachus imputes to them an initial preference for Irus, which has made critics uncomfortable because they cannot find it in the text of the earlier scene. The suitors seem impartial, as Stanford and earlier commentators note; but we must remember that Telemachus sees things from the viewpoint of his father's interests. Despite the suitors' words, they clearly expected the younger, stronger-seeming Irus to defeat the old man (until the relevation of Odysseus' physique at 67–74); and we must recall that Odysseus feels it necessary to extract an oath that they will not intervene on Irus' side (55–8). We must also note that Telemachus makes this statement, with its emphatic explanatory οὐ μέν τοι, in the context of a complaint about the suitors' hostile intentions (οἵδε κακὰ φρονέοντες), and he goes on to identify them with Irus in his prophetic wish (235–42) that they be physically undone just like him. It is natural, then, for Telemachus, who knows the beggar's identity and views the suitors as his father's antagonists, to impute to them a stronger wish for his father's defeat than they actually had. This interpretation keeps to the usual translation of ἰότης as 'will', with an etymology that connects it either with ϝίεμαι or with Sanskrit iṣ-, 'to wish'. In view of the scholia's gloss κατὰ τὴν βούλησιν and Hesychius' ἰότητι: βουλήσει θελήσει αἰτίᾳ ὀργῇ χάριτι, it is difficult to accept Leumann's argument, Wörter, 127–33, that the basic meaning of ἰότης is 'hostility' or 'anger', for which he finds support in Hesychius' ὀργῇ and in the possibility that 'hostility' might better suit a few of the other Homeric contexts (notably Il. v 874). But his proposed etymology, a false division of δηϊότητι into δὴ ἰότητι, does not convince.

238. λελῦτο δὲ γυῖα ἑκάστου: earlier at 212 the suitors' knees were made slack by the force of ἔρως, a unique combination in Homeric epic. Here we are back to the more conventional agency of a mortal wound slackening the limbs. The former passage and the present one—a mere wish—both foreshadow the inevitable slaughter of the suitors, whose knees and heart will 'go slack' (λύτο γούνατα) for the last time at xxii 68 as they face their death.

246. Ἴασον Ἄργος: ancient commentators are agreed in understanding this phrase as denoting the Peloponnese, since the phrase μέσον Ἄργος refers to a very large region, apparently all or most of the Peloponnese, at i 344, iv 726, 816, xv 80. Argos is called 'Iason' after the name of its legendary King Iasos, identified as the son of Io by the scholia and as her father by Apollodorus (ii 1. 30) and Pausanias (ii 16. 1). Since Io is the mythical founder of the Ionian race, we have in the unusual phrase Ἴασον Ἄργος, which occurs only here, the trace of an old tradition that would describe the early inhabitants and rulers of Argos as 'Ionian'. Stanford points out that attempts to connect 'Iason' with 'Ias', the term for 'Ionic', 'are linguistically and historically unsatisfactory'. But there is evidence for believing in an early Ionian settlement in Argos or the Peloponnese in the statements of Herodotus (vii 94) and Pausanias (ii 37. 3) that the people of Argos (Achaia) and of Athens used to speak the same language before the Dorian invasion. Furthermore, the decipherment of Mycenaean has given us a picture of an 'Achaean' linguistic unity at an earlier period than was formerly believed. J. Chadwick, 'The Greek Dialects and Greek Pre-history', in The Language and Background of Homer, ed. G. S. Kirk (Cambridge, 1964), 117–18, shows that we can explain the ancient tradition that puts Ionians in the Peloponnese by accepting 'Ionian' as the name for a branch of the Mycenaean ruling class, i.e. what they called themselves and were called by others. He supports this theory with W. Brandenstein's observations (Festschrift Debrunner (Bern, 1954), 66–70) that the Hebrew Yavan designated the Greek settlements on the south coast of Asia Minor—Rhodes, Pamphylia, and Cyprus—which were Mycenaean colonies. The

Mycenaeans' real name, then, would have been Ἰάϝονες (cf. Ἰάονες at *Il.* xiii 685) and they inhabited 'Ionian' Argos, which is what *Iason Argos* must mean.

247. πλέονές: scanned − −, taking -εο- as long by synizesis. Such monosyllabic pronunciation of the vowel combinations εο, εα, εω is not unusual: see the discussion of Monro, *Homeric Dialect*, 351 (cf. also 55, 87). It is a common Ionic feature to contract εο to ευ, as in ἐμεῦ, σεῦ, τεῦ, and so perhaps πλέονες here was in effect πλεῦνες.

251-3. Cf. 180-1, xix 124-6.

260. ἀπονέεσθαι: scanned ἀπονέεσθαι wherever it occurs in Homer, an irregularity that has been 'regularized' because it is localized as a lineending formulaic word and therefore *must* be pronounced with long ā *metri gratia* (five occurrences in the *Odyssey*, plus ἀπονέωνται v 27; ten occurrences in the *Iliad*, plus ἀπονέοντο three times, ἀπονεοίμην xxi 561).

263. ἵππων τ' ὠκυπόδων ἐπιβήτορες: 'riders on chariots with swift-footed horses'. The use of 'horses' metonymically to mean 'horse-drawn chariot' is a common Homeric idiom, so that ἵππων ἐπιβαίνειν is to mount a *chariot*. Cf. *Il.* viii 128-9: ὅν ῥα τόθ' ἵππων | ὠκυπόδων ἐπέβησε, δίδου δέ οἱ ἡνία χερσίν. **οἵ κε:** although this is the reading of all MSS, Monro's οἵ τε has found widespread acceptance (Ruijgh, τε *épique*, 432). Such a use of τε with noun or pronoun to express an essential or permanent characteristic of a person or thing is common to epic diction, and well described by Chantraine, *Grammaire*, ii 239ff., and Denniston, *Particles*, 520-3.

264. ὁμοιΐου πολέμοιο: this phrase (with -ἴ- in ὁμοιΐου) is found eight times in Homer, while ὁμοίϊος (short -ἴ-) occurs three more times modifying νεῖκος, γῆρας, and θάνατος, plus once in the hymns (*h. Ven.* 244). Meaning and etymology of ὁμοίϊος have been contested since Apollonius' *Lexicon*, where it is reported that some grammarians equate the word with κακός, but Apollonius glosses it as τὸ ὁμοίως συμβαῖνον. Leaf's *Iliad*, Commentary ad iv 315, takes it as a separate word from ὁμοῖος, with irregular metrical lengthening; and Monro's suggestion that ὁμοιΐου πολέμοιο replaces an original ὁμοίοο πτολέμοιο (the variant πτολέμοιο is attested in all eight occurrences of this formula) is repeated by LSJ at the end of an entry that begins by calling ὁμοίϊος an 'Epic adjective of uncertain meaning'. An etymology relating ὁμοίϊος to ὁμός/ὁμοῖος would allow the meaning 'the same for all, impartial', which suits the sense of all Homeric instances; but it would fail to explain both how ὁμοῖος gained the extra syllable to become ὁμοίϊος, and why the iota is most often long. An ingenious solution is proposed by A. Athanassakis (*RMus* cxix (1976), 4-7), who suggests we have a compound of ὁμός and the root ϝῐ/ϝῖ of ϝίς, ϝίεμαι, Latin *vis*, etc. The steps would be *ὁμοι+ ϝι + yo + ς > ὁμοίϊος as the intervocalic digamma and the y disappeared. The etymological meaning, 'forcing to the same place', suits all Homeric instances admirably (but not Hesiod *Op.* 182, where, as Athanassakis notes, ὁμοίϊος is used as if a synonym of ὁμοῖος), and Athanassakis' proposed translation, 'levelling', matches the intuition of both Stanford (who understood πόλεμος as 'the equalizer') and Leaf, *Iliad*, ad ix 440, who lacks Athanassakis' etymology but has anticipated his translation 'levelling'.

265. ἀνέσει: the verb form is uncertain. Ancient commentators and some moderns assume a short-vowel form of the future ἀνήσει from ἀνίημι, 'will send back (home)'; but Monro raised serious objections both to the use of a future with εἴ κεν instead of a subjunctive to parallel ἀλώω, and to the meaning 'send home' for ἀνίημι. A subjunctive ἀνέῃ was proposed by Thiersch and adopted in the texts of Cauer, Nauck, and van Leeuwen–Mendes da Costa. Ameis–Hentze (*Anhang*) cite the doubtful argument of J. Savelsberg that ἀνέσει can stand as it is and be understood as an uncommon first aorist subjunctive (< ἀνέσεσι, with substitution of short vowel for long as a common epic subjunctive trait). Monro argued for a different verb, ἀνίζω from the root *sed-*, the active form of the middle ἔζομαι (*hesd-* < *se-s(e)d-*), as seen in the aorist εἶσα and in a single attested future at *Il.* xi 455, ἐφέσσεσθαι. Monro would restore the subjunctive of this verb, ἀνέσῃ, and translate 'seat me again', 'restore to my place'.

269. Cf. the note to 176. In view of the instructions, we see that Penelope has been delaying the suitors by keeping this information back from them, for surely Telemachus must have begun his beard before the age of 20! Her policy has consistently been to forestall remarriage indefinitely, preferring, as she says later, 'to keep safe all my possessions, my property, servants, and high-roofed house, respecting my husband's bed and the voice of the town' (xix 525–7). An alternative interpretation is that Penelope is deceiving the suitors by inventing a false story of Odysseus' last words to her, and making her remarriage seem likely in order to fan their hopes and extract gifts from them. Such an interpretation is harmonized with Penelope's series of stalling tactics by W. Büchner, 'Penelopeszenen', 137–41. But it is not necessary to interpret this as a *lying* speech in order to see it as a speech intended to deceive and *mislead* the suitors (cf. 282–3).

275. μνηστήρων … δίκη: the 'way' or 'custom' of the suitors. In the *Odyssey* this meaning of δίκη is the regular one (cf. xix 43) and approximates that of θέμις (see Hoekstra, xiv 59 n.). The meaning 'justice' and its expansion into an abstract or cosmic principle or personification is developed first in Hesiod, later in Pindar, Aeschylus, and the pre-Socratics (e.g. Heraclitus ' fr. 94, where he says that the Erinyes, 'helpers of Justice', Δίκης ἐπίκουροι, would punish the sun if it deviated from its course). See further in H. Lloyd-Jones, *The Justice of Zeus*[2] (Berkeley–Los Angeles, 1983), 35–6, 86–7, 99–101, and *passim*; E. A. Havelock, *The Greek Concept of Justice* (Cambridge, Mass., 1978), 206–7, 217 on Hesiod, 264–8 on Heraclitus, and *passim*.

281-3. A brilliant narrative sequence: Penelope appears for the first time in the main hall since the beggar's arrival, and her disguised husband's first view of her shows her engaged in clever manipulation of the suitors, which has characterized her handling of them all along, from the ruse of the web to her recent speech at 259–70. This cleverness confirms for us that she is the perfect wife for Odysseus. And because they are so alike she is transparent to him. He immediately grasps what she is doing—and rejoices in it—because this masking of inner motives is exactly the kind of stratagem Odysseus himself likes to use, and in fact will soon use, at 344–5, where he too will be intending things quite 'other'—ἄλλα—from the appearance he gives outwardly. The suitors, by a pointed and obvious contrast, have no idea they are being played with.

It is unfortunate that several scholars of note have complained that Odysseus' rejoicing at his wife's cleverness (281–3) is out of place because he would have no way of knowing that she is not acting in earnest. Such a view fails to appreciate the instinctive ὁμοφροσύνη between husband and wife (see vi 180–5, which shows that such mental harmony is an important part of Odysseus' conception of the ideal marriage; and such a couple is a 'grief to their enemies', which the present passage illustrates perfectly!). An excellent elucidation of these lines and their relation to the whole scene is given by Bona, *Studi* 151–2. See also Büchner, 'Penelopeszenen', 138–46; Allione, *Telemaco*, 65–70, and xix 137 n.

283. νόος δέ οἱ ἄλλα μενοινᾷ: 'her mind was after other things'. It has been disputed whether this means that Penelope has a specific plan in mind like her earlier stratagem of weaving the shroud, or whether the phrase has simply the general sense that her words were insincere. Allione, *Telemaco*, 67–9, emphasizing Theoclymenus' recent assurances at xvii 151–61 and the queen's positive interpretation of Telemachus' sneeze at xvii 541–50, points out that Penelope by now has good reason for believing in Odysseus' imminent return; thus she takes ἄλλα μενοινᾷ to represent *both* Penelope's general intention to deceive the suitors as to her true feelings *and* her more specific plan to put off any immediate choice of a new husband in the clear expectation that Odysseus will soon return. Bona, *Studi*, 151–2, and Erbse, *Beiträge*, 82–7, take these words not to refer to any specific plan but to mean simply that the queen was masking her true feelings. The identical phrase occurs also at ii 92 and xiii 381, where Penelope is described as using the clever strategy of giving hope and encouragement to all the suitors but intending something else. Since no other more specific plan is envisaged in these earlier parallel passages, it is best to understand the phrase in the general sense, 'but her intention was otherwise'.

291-2. It is un-naturalistic that no time elapses between the order given to each suitor's herald and the herald's return with a gift. Homer has chosen to telescope his narrative sequence so as to give prominence to the description of the gifts.

291-301. The gifts are of the kind meant specifically for winning a woman's favour. Gold is prominent, together with elaborate and skilled craftsmanship (ποίκιλον, 293; πολυδαίδαλον, 295; ἐϋγνάμπτοις, 294); appeal to the eye is paramount, as noted in the words ἠέλιον ὥς, χάρις δ' ἀπελάμπετο πολλή. These gifts (δῶρα) are *not* those gifts (ἕδνα) whose exchange is a formal and integral part of the marriage agreement. For a full discussion of the distinction, see W. K. Lacey in *JHS* lxxxvi (1966), 55–68, esp. 58.

296. ἠλέκτροισιν ἐερμένον: 'studded with amber (beads)'. The word ἤλεκτρον means amber (cf. xv 460 with Hoekstra's note), but can also denote a gold–silver alloy (possible at iv 73, but see S. West's note) which is still called *electrum* today. The sun is called ἠλέκτωρ at *Il.* vi 513, xix 398, *h.Ap.* 369, and Empedocles 22. 2, so it clearly describes a substance that appears brilliant or flaming; hence the poet's addition, ἠέλιον ὥς. The etymology is a mystery, to which an imaginative solution is proposed by M. S. Ruipérez, 'Sur ἠλέκτωρ et ἤλεκτρον, "ambre"', in *Mélanges de linguistique et de philologie grecques offerts à Pierre Chantraine* (Paris, 1972), 231–41, who relates the words to the group ἀλέξω, ἀλαλκεῖν, ἀλκή, because of the apotropaic powers he assumes amber had for the ancients. The change ἄ > η, however, is hard to explain.

298. μορόεντα: an obscure word, the likeliest meaning being that derived from μόρον, 'mulberry', and denoting berry-like clusters. With τρίγληνα it suggests three beads (γλήνη literally = 'pupil of the eye'), each fashioned like a berry cluster. E. Bielefeld, in *Archaeologica* C, 4, suggests that the appearance of mulberries was achieved either by dark-coloured glass or stone or by granulated gold beads.

308. κάγκανα: 'dry' is the universally accepted meaning for this word (LSJ, Eustathius), and Hesychius offers a related verb καγκαίνω; but this meaning has hitherto been essentially a good guess based on context. The explanations of Frisk, *GEW* s.v., and Chantraine, *Dictionnaire* s.v., relate κάγκανος to Indo-European cognates meaning 'hunger' or 'pain'. Derivation from καίω/κάω makes much better semantic sense, and is well argued by A. Athanassakis, *TAPhA* cvi (1976), 1–9, who postulates reduplication from an intermediate *κάνος.

310. δαῖδας: normally 'torches', but here the context strongly suggests a meaning like 'kindling', denoting small strips of wood, coated with resin (so Ameis–Hentze–Cauer), mixed in with the larger ξύλα κάγκανα to help them ignite. Some have understood the δαῖδας to be small torches mixed in among the braziers (λαμπτῆρες), but μετέμισγον is too concrete a term, suggesting *physical* mixture. Moreover, ἀμοιβηδὶς δ' ἀνέφαινον gives clearest sense as a description of the maids standing by to take turns in adding the fuel mixture to the braziers.

317–19. Odysseus' statement here is aggressive in both tone and content, so as to incite the mean-spirited Melantho to react harshly. (We see Homer deliberately working to motivate this hostile encounter.) Odysseus has ordered the servants (313ff.) with authority, almost revealing the master beneath the disguise (he seems to become aware of this excess at the end of the speech and to pull back his assertiveness with the last half of verse 319). The speech itself is ironic and ominous: φάος, 'light' is a common metaphor for victory in combat (cf. *Il.* vi 6, viii 282, xv 41, xvi 95, xviii 102, xx 95), and the metaphor, as C. H. Whitman notes (*Homer and the Heroic Tradition* (Cambridge, Mass., 1958), 121–2), eventually turns into a miracle at xix 34–40 where Athena creates an unnaturally bright light for Odysseus, symbolizing his impending victory.

319. πολυτλήμων: that Odysseus is in effect punning on his common epithet πολύτλας is suggested by J. Griffin, 'Homer and Excess', in Bremer, de Jong, and Kalff, eds., *Homer: Beyond Oral Poetry* (Amsterdam, 1987), 100–1, where he relates the passage to an interesting general tendency for the *Odyssey* to play with its own formulas.

321-6. A miniature ring-composition frames the portrait of Melantho as an ingrate. She scolds Odysseus (ἐνένιπε) at 321, but instead of this phrase introducing her speech, Homer gives us a short but incisive digression containing the background information necessary to appreciate the extent of her disloyalty. Then 326 repeats the idea of 321 (again, ἐνένιπε) and introduces the speech we have been waiting for.

327. ἐκπεπαταγμένος: ἐκπατάσσω is a Homeric *hapax*. With the specifying accusative φρένας it is equivalent to ἐκπλήσσω, 'to knock someone out of his wits'. Hesychius and Apollonius gloss ἐκπεπληγμένος, and Hesychius adds ἔκφρων. This perfect passive participle affords Melantho a most effective and lengthy word of abuse, rich in alliteration (note that the φ of φρένας is echoed in the two π's).

328-9. χαλκήιον ... δόμον ... λέσχην: a λέσχη is any public lounge or gathering place (from λέχομαι, 'to repose'), and the close association with the blacksmith's house, χαλκήιον δόμον, seems natural, since in cold weather people would find the foyer near the smithy an appealing location because of its warmth. This very association is in fact made by Hesiod, *Op.* 493-5, where cold is specifically cited as driving men indoors to such gathering-places. Thus we have a further confirmation that Odysseus' return takes place in winter or early spring (see note to xvii 23, ἀλέη). This passage is quoted by Pausanias, x 25. 1, describing a 'club-room' or λέσχη at Delphi.

333. τὸν ἀλήτην: 'that beggar': emphatic and contemptuous. For this use of the definite article, see note to xvii 10.

334-6. Melantho concludes her speech with a hail of alliterative abuse: 334 has three consecutive words beginning with τ- and three with α-; 335 is conspicuous for κ-χ and σ; 334 is filled with labials, π, μ, φ, ψ.

343-5. Odysseus' taking up a position by the flaring lamps, himself illuminating the room (φαείνων) as if he were a light, offers a forceful image, suggestive of his growing power and forthcoming triumph. This description achieves the bright clarity of an epiphany. Cf. 317-19 n.

346-8. These same lines recur at xx 284-6, where again the provocation culminates in an object hurled at Odysseus. A modern reader may puzzle over the desire of a deity to incite the suitors so that Odysseus be caused more pain. One obvious reason for this pain is that it helps justify the total, unsparing revenge Odysseus will later take against the suitors (cf. the concluding line of xx: πρότεροι γὰρ ἀεικέα μηχανόωντο, one of the few times the poet offers his own comment on the plot). A second, more submerged reason is that pain fulfils a premise implicit in Odysseus' name: he is a figure who gives and receives *abuse* (the likely meaning of ὀδύσασθαι, cf. note to xix 406-9). Odysseus carries some traces of an early

COMMENTARY

Greek incarnation of the 'Trickster' figure found in all the folklore and mythology of the world, a figure whose nature is, mysteriously, both to give and to receive pain and humiliating treatment. (The classic study is P. Radin, *The Trickster* (London–New York, 1956).)

350. **γέλω**: note how often laughter has been directed against Odysseus in this book: 35, 40, 100, 111, 320, and here. The other major concentration of laughter is in xx (346, 347, 358, 374, 390), describing the abnormal laughter Athena inspires in the suitors, a reversal and horrible parody of their earlier laughter at Odysseus. It is worth noting that laughter in the Homeric world is usually hostile, at the expense of one of the characters; and it is twice as frequent in the *Odyssey* as in the *Iliad*. Again we may suspect a latent connection to the archetypal Trickster figure, among whose chief characteristics are the stimulation of laughter and an ironic mode.

353–5. The connection in thought is not at first sight obvious. Eurymachus, seeking to be ironic at Odysseus' expense, pretends to voice the traditional sentiment expressed by the suitors earlier at xvii 483–5, that gods go among men in disguise. But then abruptly (with ἔμπης, 'just so', stressing the connection) he turns to mocking the idea of a divine presence, asserting that the light apparently radiating from Odysseus (cf. 317, 343–4) must come from his bald head. Since Homer has been giving increasing emphasis to the symbolic equation of light = victory (see note to 317–19), the attempted irony he puts in the mouth of Eurymachus turns around and becomes an irony at the suitor's expense.

357. **θητευέμεν**: 'to be a θής', a hired day-labourer, the lowest position in the social order (Finley, *World*, 53–4, 71). When the ghost of Achilles in Hades is searching for a point of comparison to explain to Odysseus that even the lowest social role on earth is preferable to ruling over all the dead, he uses the life of a θής as his comparison (xi 488–91).

359. **αἱμασιάς τε λέγων**: λέγω here means 'to collect, gather', but αἱμασιάς remains obscure and its etymology unknown. The scholia think it means a fence made of small stones or fragments; Monro, 287, compares the later Greek λιθολόγος, 'builder'. The phrase probably describes a technique for building a 'dry wall', i.e. without mortar, by collecting small stones (so P. K. Buttmann, *Lexilogus* (London, 1846), para. 78. 8; Stanford, ad loc., who notes similar construction in the Irish and English countryside). A divergent tradition is that αἱμασιά originally meant 'thorn-hedge' and later, via the more general meaning 'hedge, barrier', came to be transferred to walls made of stone (so Eust. 1851. 30 ff.). But there is no evidence in extant Greek for this theory (Eustathius gives a folk-etymology from αἱμάσσειν, since thorns cause bleeding), and the occurrences of αἱμασιά in Herodotus (i 191, ii 69, 138; and cf. Eustathius 1851. 25–30) clearly denote walls of stone.

362–4. These identical verses were used by Antinous attacking Odysseus at xvii 226–8.

366–80. An amazingly bold speech for a beggar to make to a nobleman! Implicit in the statement is the social ideal that one should be both a good

70

warrior and good at peasant tasks, perhaps a folk motif from the tradition of the 'little people' as opposed to the ruling class, according to W. Donlan, 'The Tradition of Anti-Aristocratic Thought in Early Greek Poetry', *Historia* xxii (1973), 153. Cf. H. Strasburger, *Gymnasium* xl (1953), 97–114, who sees the peasant viewpoint permeating both Homeric epics, but also notes that manual labour and agricultural work are often attributed to members of royal families (104). Both Donlan and P. W. Rose, 'Class Ambivalence in the *Odyssey*', *Historia* xxiv (1975), 129–49, argue well for a peasant-oriented, anti-aristocratic tradition, essentially Hesiodic, that determines the favourable emphasis on the 'lower-class' figures of the *Odyssey* and the very negative portrait of the suitors. H. Münding, *Hesiods Erga in Verhältnis zur Ilias* (Frankfurt, 1959), 12–96, sees this Hesiodic tradition as self-consciously anti-aristocratic, and our *Odyssey* passage suggests that such a tradition was already well-established in two different literary genres by the late eighth century. The ἔρις ἔργοιο of 366 recalls Hesiod's concern, at *Op.* 11–26, to add to the single ἔρις of *Th.* 225 the second, beneficial ἔρις of competitive striving that stimulates people to work, ἥτε ... ἐπὶ ἔργον ἔγειρεν (*Op.* 20).

384-6. A vivid picture, similar in its hyperbolic imagery to the language of Melanthius' attack on Odysseus at xvii 230–2, but much more offensive since directed at a social superior. Eurymachus' violent reaction is not surprising or excessive, given such provocation. The cowardice imputed to this suitor in the hypothetical situation of Odysseus' return is in fact contradicted when the hypothesis becomes reality at xxii 44–78: Eurymachus exhibits commendable bravery. (See especially xxii 73, ἀλλὰ μνησώμεθα χάρμης, with Fernández-Galiano's note on this Iliadic phrase.)

394-8. This hurling a stool at Odysseus repeats the similar incident at xvii 462 ff. where it is Antinous who hits him with a stool. A third use of this same motif is at xx 299ff., where Ctesippus throws an ox's hoof, which misses Odysseus and harmlessly hits against a wall. The repeated insults and stool-throwing are discussed by H. Reynen, in *Hermes* lxxxv (1957), 129–46, who argues, against the earlier German analytic tradition, that this incident in xviii is developed from the earlier incident in xvii. A significant structure and progression in the throwing-scenes is noticed by Fenik, *Studies*, 180–4: the first cast hits Odysseus, the second misses and hits a retainer, and the third is most ineffective of all and harmlessly hits a wall. Thus the suitors are depicted as growing increasingly powerless, while the criticism which their hostility evokes grows stronger and stronger (compare Telemachus' criticism at xviii 405–9 to his even more powerful statement at xx 304–19).

402. μετέθηκε: the MSS' μεθέηκε has been displaced in all modern editions by this variant, which schol. H asserts was the reading of 'all', πᾶσαι. This πᾶσαι is generally accepted as Aristarchus' observation based on the MSS available to him (so Monro, 432–3; but Ludwich, *AHT* 119, thinks it refers only to a *majority* of the earlier editions known to Aristarchus, and included his own editions) and so μεθέηκε has regularly been taken to be an easy corruption that spread to all the now extant codices. But those who follow Aristarchus overlook the fact that μετατίθημι elsewhere in Greek always means to *change* the position of something, and so this alleged Homeric usage would constitute a semantic *hapax*. On the other hand μεθέηκε commonly means to let loose as if from a restraining leash, as μεθεῖται στρατός, A. *Th.* 79, and also can refer to letting *sound* fly forth, as in E. *Hipp.* 499, μεθήσεις ... λόγους, *id.* 1202 βρόμον μεθῆκε; S. *OT* 784, μεθέντι τὸν λόγον, and the description of shouting (in Persian) at Hdt. vi 29, Περσίδα γλῶσσαν μετιείς. The object κελαδόν would therefore fit quite well with μεθέηκε (so van der Valk, *Textual Criticism*, 159), despite Stanford's claim that 'it hardly makes adequate sense'; and I believe that we must distrust the scholiast's allegation of universal testimony for μετέθηκε, and should return to the reading of the vulgate.

403-4. Monro suggested that these two lines contained an imitation, perhaps a parody, of *Il.* 574-6, where Hephaestus intervenes to calm the argument between Zeus and Hera, pointing out that they should not spoil the divine feast by quarrelling over mortals: νῦν δὲ περὶ πτωχῶν ἐριδαίνομεν would echo εἰ δὴ σφὼ ἕνεκα θνητῶν ἐριδαίνετον, and the clausula of 403 plus all of 404 is identical to the clausula of 575 plus all of 576. Certainly the language is very close, but the assumption of deliberate imitation or parody belongs to the world of written epic, self-consciously literary and evocative of its predecessors, as Vergil or Apollonius Rhodius consciously allude to Homer. Such a specific and subtle Iliadic allusion here would be foreign to the style of oral epic, even the polished and carefully composed oral epic of Homer. Instead, we should assume that similar thoughts tend to find similar, and often identical, expression. These two lines are, however, significant for another reason: they underline an important development in the narrative, showing emphatically how the lowly beggar who entered the palace early in xvii has become a major presence in the household, an important force for the suitors to contend with.

406-7. μαίνεσθε ... θεῶν νύ τις ὕμμ' ὀροθύνει: this is one of the earliest clear instances of madness, μανία, explained as divine interference, a view that was to become common in the classical period and is discussed at length in Plato's *Phaedrus*, 244a-245c (where μανική and μαντική are joined etymologically, 244 c 1-5). E. R. Dodds, *The Greeks and the Irrational* (Berkeley–Los Angeles, 1951), 67, noting that the idea of 'possession' is largely absent in Homer although slight traces of it are found in the *Odyssey*, cites the word ἐκπεπαταγμένος (327 above) as such an oblique reference; the present verses, however, would have served him as better evidence. Further discussion of madness (primarily its absence) in Homer in B. Simon, *Mind and Madness in Ancient Greece* (Ithaca, NY, and London, 1978), 65–71.

408. κατακείετε: either an imperative or the future indicative used to express a milder, more polite command. Monro argues for the future both here and in 419 below (see note there), and the more polite form certainly accords better with 409.

408-21. Telemachus makes his strongest assertion yet of his right to command in his own house, and the suitors are amazed at his new boldness (410–11). The intervention here of Amphinomus, the best of the suitors, recalls his intervention at xvi 394–406 to dissuade the others from the murder of Telemachus, and suggests that a hostile clash between Telemachus and the suitors is a possible outcome of the high temper displayed in this scene. We recall that Athena incited this development (346–8 above), and only now do we see the full consequences of her instigation: the latent tension in the household of Odysseus continues to grow, with the presence of the beggar a major catalyst.

410. ὀδὰξ ἐν χείλεσι φύντες: literally 'fastening into their lips with their teeth', a most vivid expression to show the degree of the suitors' anger, which they must 'bite their lip' (to use our modern idiom) to keep from expressing openly. This striking phrase occurs again only at xx 268, when Telemachus' assertion of his prerogatives grows still bolder and the suitors react similarly. For a full discussion of 'lip-biting' and the broader issue of facial and non-verbal communication as depicted in Homer, see D. Lateiner, 'Teeth in Homer', *LCM* xiv (1989), 18–23.

414. ἐπὶ ῥηθέντι: the original digamma is preserved in the scansion ἐπίϝρηθέντι. δικαίῳ: as Stanford notes ad xiv 90, δίκαιος refers to the 'customary' or 'proper' thing rather than to what is 'just'. Cf. the meaning of δίκη at xix 43, 168.

419. κατακείομεν: as noted at 408, Monro argued for future indicative as the likely form here (see his *Homeric Dialect*, 297, for examples of ὄφρα introducing the future tense); but in his note to xiv 532 he concedes that Homeric usage would give us to expect a subjunctive after ὄφρα (cf. xix 17), and so we may have here a short-vowel subjunctive of the aorist ἔκεια (Hesychius preserves the infinitive in his gloss κακκεῖαι· κοιμηθῆναι). For the possible subjunctive form, see Chantraine, *Grammaire*, i 453.

423. κρητῆρα κεράσσατο: the *schema etymologicum* as at 361 (εἵματα δ' ἀμφιέσαιμι), xix 72 (εἵματα εἵμαι) and 92 (ἔρδουσα ἔργον).

428. κείοντες: here, as earlier at xiii 17, the context allows the possibility that we have a *desiderative* form of the verb, with loss of the characteristic sigma (Chantraine, *Grammaire*, i 453). On the thematic level, it is noteworthy that thirteen of the twenty-four books of the *Odyssey* conclude with the actors going to bed, passing the night, or meeting the dawn. Such a closing 'cadence' suggests that many of our book-divisions represent units of narrative performance, and—to speculate further—that this performance took place in the evening, serving the audience (unconsciously) as a preparation for going to bed.

BOOK XIX: COMMENTARY

Book xix displays a carefully arranged structure, which includes two scenes showing the closing of the distance between Odysseus and Penelope and two scenes of a similar movement involving Odysseus and Eurycleia. The first two are balanced on either side of the second two, giving an ABBA pattern. At the very centre of this structure is the digression on Odysseus' scar, which extends the symmetrical pattern to ABCBA. These are the final five scenes of the book. They are preceded by two short scenes: Odysseus and Telemachus plan the removal of the weapons, then Melantho enters and rebukes Odysseus, for which she is herself rebuked by Penelope. The seven scenes may be summarized as follows.

1. 1–52. Odysseus and Telemachus plan the removal of the weapons from the main hall (anticipated at xvi 281–98).
2. 53–95. Penelope enters the hall (for the interview proposed by the beggar at sunset, xvii 582–4); her serving maids as they leave her encounter the beggar, whom Melantho reviles. Odysseus answers in kind, drawing the attention of the queen who intervenes to chide Melantho.
3. 96–316. Lengthy interview between the beggar and the queen. He gives three descriptions of Odysseus. Penelope weeps at the first and second, and upon hearing the third firmly declares that she knows Odysseus will not return.
4. 317–93. Penelope turns to the maids and orders them to bathe the beggar and prepare his bed. He refuses to be bathed by the servants, unless there is an old woman who has suffered as he has. Eurycleia is summoned, comments on his similarity to Odysseus, begins to bathe him, and notices the scar.
5. 393–466. A flashback to the boar hunt, then further back to the birth and naming of Odysseus, then back to the boar hunt and his wounding.
6. 467–507. Odysseus is recognized by Eurycleia; he threatens her and swears her to silence.
7. 508–604. Another lengthy exchange between Odysseus and Penelope, based on a developing intimacy and trust. In three speeches, she compares herself to the nightingale and then tells him of her dream of the eagle slaying her geese; she disparages her dream's obvious interpretation by applying the typology of horn and ivory, and then turns to the idea of setting an archery contest to decide which suitor will win her; she comments on the unavoidability of sleep, wishes they could continue conversing all night, and decides it is time to retire.

1–50. The plan to remove the arms to prevent the suitors from using them in the forthcoming fight was conceived earlier at xvi 281–98 (xix 5–13 = xvi

286-94). When such repetitions were suspect, before the Homeric style was appreciated as an oral style, critics used to debate over which passage was original and which interpolated. Recent critics tend to defend the authenticity of both: Erbse, *Beiträge*, 3-41; Bona, *Studi*, 131-41 (who thinks, however, that xvi 295-8 may be interpolated); Stanford, 315 (defending linguistic and thematic details against Monro's objections). There are two inconsistencies: the anticipation in xvi that the suitors will notice the absent arms and ask about them never in fact comes to pass; and Odysseus' directions there to reserve two swords, spears, and shields are never again referred to. I understand both anticipations in xvi to be precautions against what Odysseus thinks is *likely* to happen. While such anticipations are usually fulfilled in Homeric narrative, their non-fulfilment is not a serious blemish. The narrative reveals the characteristically oral tendency to achieve detailed vividness for the immediate moment, at the expense of total consistency with what preceded or will follow, so long as enough time intervenes so that these inconsistencies do not force themselves on the listeners' attention by their proximity (cf. the inconsistency noted at xvii 160-1). Kirk, *Songs*, 242-4, explains this passage by assuming that the poet made small changes in his narrative plan as he went along, and a similar explanation is given by Eisenberger, *Studien* 228-9. Such minor inconsistencies distinguish Homer or the poet of *Beowulf* from poets like Vergil or Milton who can review their composition *verbatim* and arrive at a completely consistent, fixed text (see Bowra, *HP*, 299-306; *Homer* (London, 1972), 32-8, emphasizing Homer's concentration on the dramatic present).

9. That this is a very plausible excuse is evident from the description of the similar old-fashioned Yugoslav house, as given by I. M. Garrido-Bozic, *G&R* xv (1946), 108-13. Such houses have no chimney, only a smoke-hole in the roof, so that 'the ceiling, beams, and pillars, all of oak, are blackened with smoke' (109).

13. αὐτὸς γὰρ ἐφέλκεται ἄνδρα σίδηρος: 'iron of itself draws a man to it', apparently a proverb, used here to add persuasiveness by an appeal to traditional wisdom (cf. note to xvii 347, where an apparent proverb also closes a speech). Although meant as a warning against the temptation to resort to weapons in a drunken quarrel—a common danger in heroic societies—this proverb may have older origins in an awareness of the magnetic, and hence magical, properties of iron. So M. Cary and A. D. Nock, *CQ* xxi (1927), 125-6. And perhaps the early availability of meteoric iron contributed to this belief: G. A. Wainwright, *Antiquity* x (1936), 6: 'Iron was the thunderbolt, one of the most appalling powers in Nature'. The use of 'iron' as the word for an unspecified weapon, instead of the more normal 'bronze' (cf. xi 120, xix 522, xx 315, and throughout the fight in xxii), is criticized by Lorimer, *Monuments*, 510, as 'an unexampled breach of epic convention' (but see 119-20 for what she admits are 'partial exceptions'), but this is hardly an adequate reason for doubting the line's authenticity.

25-9. There will be no maids to carry the light because Telemachus has just asked Eurycleia to detain them (ἔρυξον, 16) in the palace. Her question at 24–5 may imply that she expected Telemachus to answer that she, of course, as a trusted and motherly figure, will carry the light for him; and if this is so, his answer at 26–8 is still another example of his newly acquired independence and cool aloofness. Thus interprets Latacz, *Glotta* xlvi (1968), 36–7, who believes the *apteros mythos* of 29 represents speechlessness on the part of one stunned into silence by such a rebuff (for my divergent interpretation of *apteros mythos*, see the note to xvii 57).

28. χοίνικος: χοῖνιξ occurs in Homer only here, obviously denoting grain or food. In later Greek it referred to a specific measure of wheat (Hdt. i 192), the quantity considered sufficient for one man's daily maintenance (ibid. vii 187, Th. iv 16, D.L. viii 18). We have no way of knowing if the word denoted a measure in Homeric Greek.

34. χρύσεον: with synizesis of εο, χρύσεον is scanned – –. See at xviii 247. λύχνον: this 'golden lamp' of Athena has led both ancient and modern critics to question this passage. Athenaeus, xv 700E, declared that the λύχνος was οὐ παλαιὸν εὕρημα, adding that 'the ancients for lighting used [instead] the flame of a torch and other woods' (as at xviii 307–11). His words are echoed by Eustathius (1571. 22, ad vii 101), and both the scholia and Eustathius (1854. 51) note that Homeric heroes do not use lamps. Modern archaeological opinion agrees: M. Nilsson, *Opuscula Archaeologica* vi (1950), 98–101, and Lorimer, *Monuments*, 509–11, suspect this passage as a late interpolation on the grounds that while lamps are frequent in Minoan and Mycenaean sites, they disappear from use until the latter half of the seventh century. But H. J. Rose, *Classical Bulletin* xxviii (1951), 1–2, suggests that the use of lamps *as cult objects* would survive in old religious shrines long after their secular use was discontinued; and R. Pfeiffer, *Studi Italiani di Filologia Classica* xxvii–xxviii (1956), 426–33 (= *Ausgewählte Schriften* (Munich, 1960), 1–7), makes the same distinction still more forcefully, arguing that a lamp seems to be associated with Athena continuously from Mycenaean times down to Hellenistic and later literature. The *Odyssey* here would be drawing upon that tradition for a piece of striking imagery turned to good dramatic use.

36-40. It is the goddess' *own presence*, and not the lamp, that fills the hall with a supernaturally intense light. Such a flooding of light is characteristic of a divine presence in *h.Cer.* 189 (see the commentary ad loc. of N. J. Richardson, ed., *The Homeric Hymn to Demeter*, Oxford, 1974, 208) and 280, *h. Ven.* 86–90, *h.Merc.* 440 ff., S. *OC* 1650–2, and other ancient authors (further citations in Richardson). Here the light acquires the symbolic suggestion of forthcoming victory for Odysseus, a common metaphor in heroic epic (see n. to xviii 317–19), an interpretation developed by Focke, *Odyssee*, 315, and M. Müller, *Athene als göttliche Helferin in der Odyssee* (Heidelberg, 1966), 125–6. Cf. the uncommonly bright radiance of Achilles' helmet at *Il.* xxii 133–6, which overwhelms Hector with fear and is clearly meant as a portent of Achilles' impending victory.

45. ἐρεθίζω: this word normally means 'irritate, provoke'; but what exactly does Odysseus mean by it here? LSJ cite this line and the object μητέρα σήν for the meaning 'provoke to curiosity', but this interpretation has two weaknesses: (1) it fails to account for the other object, δμωάς, the servants, who are in no such way provoked; (2) it assumes that in the ensuing two interviews with Penelope, Odysseus is trying to arouse her curiosity about his identity, which is not evident in the text (although argued ingeniously by P. W. Harsh, *AJPh* lxxi (1950), 9–17). It is better to take ἐρεθίζω as close to πειράομαι in meaning, understanding Odysseus' statement here as a fulfilment of Athena's prediction at xiii 336, πρίν γ' ἔτι σῆς ἀλόχου πειρήσεαι, and of his intentions as stated to Telemachus at xvi 299–307 (so Schwartz, *Odyssee*, 106, followed by H. Vester, *Gymnasium* lxxv (1968), 419–20 n. 13): he will keep everyone in the household from knowing that he has returned, while using his hidden presence to discern the 'direction' or 'course' of the women (γυναικῶν γνώομεν ἰθύν, xvi 304; cf. xix 501) and to 'test' (πειρηθείμεν, xvi 305) the male servants. The meaning of ἐρεθίζω, then, is something like 'prod', a combination of the idea of testing the loyalty and feelings of Penelope and the servants with that of stimulating his wife to think of the likely return of her husband. For a different interpretation see Thornton, *People*, 84–7, who takes ἐρεθίζω in the more normal sense of 'provoke to anger' and argues that this meaning (δμωὰς ἐρεθίζω) anticipates Odysseus' provocation of Melantho. For the less apparent 'provocation' of Penelope (μητέρα σήν), Thornton finds justification in Odysseus' statement to Melantho at xix 83: 'I fear your mistress may be angry with you and rage against you', which does in fact happen at 91–5. It remains unlikely, however, that Odysseus would use the phrase 'I shall provoke your mother' to Telemachus to mean that he will bring about Penelope's chastisement of Melantho.

51-2. Note how verses 1–2 are repeated, rounding off this scene as a complete unit. Such a stylistic marker is not common, but recurs later at 393–4 partially echoed in 465–6.

53-4. Identical to xvii 36–7. See the note at xvii 37.

56. δινωτὴν: as Stanford notes, this word suggests inlay of gold and ivory spirals or circles. Cf. 67.

57. Ἰκμάλιος: the artisan Ikmalios is known only from this passage, and his name is probably the poet's ad hoc creation to help explain the marvellous chair. Stanford sees Ikmalios as one of Homer's many significant names, etymologically connected with Cypriot ἰκμάω and Latin *ico*, 'to beat, strike' (a similar etymology is given by Ruijgh, *Élément*, 136), a good name for a master of metal and ivory inlaying. A full discussion by L. Lacroix in *Hommages à Waldemar Deonna*, Collection Latomus xxviii (Brussels, 1957), 309–21, bases the etymology instead on ἰκμάς, 'moisture', a term used to denote human sweat and the juice of a plant. Since the ἰκμάς of the oak is called εὔκολλος by Antipater of Sidon (*AP* vi 109) and glue is once called the 'sweat of the oak' in a fragment of Ion of Chios, Lacroix suggests that the name conceals a reference to the technique of using glue to apply ivory and metal inlays. He notes that such a technique existed in Greece and is especially well-documented for Egypt, where glue was extracted from animal hides as a kind of 'sweat'. Pliny (*HN* vii 198) credits Daedalus with the invention of glue, but Lacroix suggests that Homer may here preserve a dim memory of an almost forgotten Ikmalios as the earliest Greek furniture craftsman.

62. δέπα: this form represents a contracted neuter pl. with correption of ά. Alternatively, we could read δέπα', representing δέπαα, the uncontracted pl. The same word occurs at xv 466, and the same choice between -α and -α' in κέρα at 211 below.

63–5. Here the serving-maids refill the braziers that they set up at xviii 307–11 when evening first came on. Now it is quite late. The suitors had gone home for the night with the last verse of xviii. Telemachus has just gone to bed (47–50). Only Odysseus and Penelope are still awake, and now the interview proposed and postponed at xvii 508–11, 529, 561–73, and held in abeyance throughout the activities of xviii, can finally take place. But Homer has one more narrative embellishment: he will bring back the sharp-tongued Melantho and use her attack as a device for bringing Penelope and Odysseus together in a state of heightened sympathetic rapport.

66. ἀνιήσεις: from ἀνίη, 'pain': 'will you be a pain?' Antinous similarly called the beggar a 'pain' at xvii 446.

67. δινεύων: 'circling' (through the house). **ὀπιπεύσεις δὲ γυναῖκας:** 'and you will give the women the eye'. Melantho's language is sharply spiced with strong descriptive words, which convey admirably her antagonism. It is unusual that δινεύσεις should occur so soon after δινωτήν at 56, since these words are used only rarely. A subliminal association was at work in the poet's mind, a not uncommon phenomenon.

71. δαιμονίη: Homer's characters often use the vocative of δαιμόνιος in a state of heightened emotion to address someone familiar who is behaving unexpectedly. Presumably the locution originates in the notion that the addressee has been momentarily possessed by some supernatural power (δαίμων), causing her or him to act or speak out of keeping with the customary manner or cultural norm. In such cases the word amounts to a rebuke (see iv 774 with S. West's note) and a good colloquial translation might be 'What's gotten into you?' Other instances exist, however, where no rebuke is conceivable (e.g. *Il.* xxiv 194, Priam's speech to Hecuba, where it is *his* behaviour that seems inexplicable and is divinely prompted, and *she* might well be expected to use this term of address). The study of E. Brunius-Nilsson, *ΔΑΙΜΟΝΙΕ* (Uppsala, 1955), suggests that no universally valid translation is possible, and that the constant element of meaning is an intensity on the speaker's part meant to create an atmosphere of intimacy that might oblige the addressee to co-operate.

75–9. Interestingly enough, these lines are the literal truth, although employed as part of a larger falsehood. This conflation of truth and false-hood on a small scale anticipates the more elaborate tales that Odysseus will tell to Penelope later in the book, and recalls the tales told to Eumaius and Antinous earlier (verses 75–80 were used at xvii 419–24). The mixture of truth with falsehood is an important feature of the process Odysseus called ἐρεθίζω (45, above): the verisimilitude of his self-portrait prods both maids and Penelope to reveal their degree of loyalty to Odysseus and to the beggar who claims his ξενία.

79. εὖ ζώουσι ... καλέονται: these verbs lack an expressed subject, 'people', which we must supply from the context.

84. Odysseus in disguise enjoys dropping hints about his likely return (cf. xvii 525–6, xviii 145–6, and the series of hints, turning into assurances, here in xix). The irony thus engendered functions both as an excellent device by which the poet titillates his audience, and an effective personal trait of the beggar that gives vividness to his characterization.

86. τοῖος: a 'proleptic' use of the word: exactly what quality τοῖος describes is forthcoming in verses 87–8.

92. ἔρδουσα ... ἔργον: the schema etymologicum, a favourite Greek rhetorical device even at this early date. Cf. xviii 423n. and vi 61n.

ὃ σῇ κεφαλῇ ἀναμάξεις: this metaphor seems to allude to a ritual custom by which wiping blood from a sacrificial knife on to the victim was a means of transferring the guilt to the victim (so Stanford, citing Hdt. i 155 and S. El. 445–6). Such a custom would form part of the Unschuldskomödie, the 'comedy of innocence', performed in ritual slaughter as a device for warding off the guilt-feelings that must inevitably attach to the 'murderer' (cf. K. Meuli, 'Griechische Opferbrauche', in Phyllobolia: Festschrift von der Mühll (Basle, 1946), 275–6; W. Burkert, Homo Necans (Berkeley, Los Angeles, and London, 1983), 4ff., 46 n. 46). As used here by Penelope, it means that the blame will not be transferred but placed on the head of the doer of the deed, Melantho. The metaphor gets its strength from a reversal of the ritual habit.

98. καθεζόμενος εἴπῃ: the scansion shows that the digamma was felt in Ϝείπῃ.

99. ξεῖνος ἐμέθεν: scanned − − ∪ ∪ −. The lengthening before -ν is irregular but not unexampled. The lengthening before final -ς is extremely rare. Both irregularities can occur only in the first syllable of the metron.

107-14. All this preamble avoids answering the direct question as to his identity and origin, substituting flattery of Penelope and a short excursus on the virtues of a good king and the way nature responds bountifully to a just regime. The portrait drawn of harmony between the natural order and the politically just civic order reminds us of Hesiod's insistence on connecting the two throughout his poem and especially at Op. 225–37. That they were a commonplace of Greek and early European thought is stressed by M. Nilsson, Homer and Mycenae (London, 1933), 220. (Plato refers to both the Homeric and Hesiodic passages together at R. 363b.) This ideal also, ironically enough, gives us from Odysseus' mouth a portrait of his own regime as it was in the past (cf. ii 230–4 = v 8–12; iv 687–93) and as he will re-establish it. Further, as an example of Odysseus' rhetorical habits, it repeats the patterns of his reply to Arete at vii 241 ff. and to Alcinous at ix 2 ff. In each situation Odysseus is asked his identity, and to Arete as to Penelope here he gives an answer that evades the direct question τίς ποθεν εἰς ἀνδρῶν; (vii 237–8a = xix 104–5a). With Alcinous he responds first with flattery, then with a description of the ideal harmonious banquet as exemplified in the one present before them, and finally he gives Alcinous his name. Here he describes his unhappiness but still holds back his identity, which he will reveal in his next speech.

109. ὥς τέ τευ ἢ βασιλῆος: the MSS give ἢ but, as Stanford notes, this phrase is awkward because there is no alternative given to βασιλῆος. Monro emended to ἢ (following Bekker, *Homerische Blätter*, ii 200), which (even with another ἢ in the preceding line) seems preferable.

113. παρέχῃ: scanned – ◡ ◡, as if a trace remained of the original -σ- of (σ)έχω (so Monro, *Homeric Dialect*, 359). Stanford compares the similar lengthening in σύνεχές at ix 74.

122. δακρυπλώειν: the shortening of α in δάκρυ is unusual, but was seen in δακρύοισι at xviii 173. The verb, unique to this passage, is a strongly metaphorical compound of δάκρυ with πλώω (Ionic for πλέω), which can have the meaning 'swim' or 'float', as at v 240 and *Il.* xxi 302. The compound would mean 'to be afloat with tears' or 'to be swimming in tears'. This verse is quoted by Aristotle, *Pr.* 953 b 12, in a partial paraphrase, καί με φησὶ δάκρυ πλώειν βεβαρημένον οἴνῳ.

124–9. These same verses were spoken, nearly verbatim, by Penelope to Eurymachus at xviii 251–6. Spoken here they are of course much more dramatic and powerful, since the husband whose return she wishes for is in fact the very person she is addressing! As often happens, a Homeric repetition acquires new force from its new context.

130–3. Again, Homer reuses earlier statements, this time taken from the speech of Telemachus to Odysseus before the beggar's identity has been revealed to him, xvi 122–5, and also spoken earlier by Telemachus to Athena disguised as Mentes at i 245–8. Here the echo does not carry the dramatic significance of the echo noted above in 124–9, and it was suspected in antiquity as an interpolation: schol. H (as emended by Porson to indicate 4 not 30 verses athetized) records that these lines were not in 'the majority' of MSS, and Aristarchus athetized them. But they have the appearance of the kind of non-essential 'filler' that is easily added or dropped in the process of a living performance, be it of a ballad, folk-song, or oral epic.

135. δημιοεργοί: at xvii 383–5 we had a listing of four categories of these 'public-working' professionals: the prophet, physician, carpenter, and the 'divine bard'. Here the herald is given the same social status designation.

137. δόλους τολυπεύω: 'I spin out deceptions'. This metaphor is well-established in Homeric diction, in the widely-used phrases δόλον ὑφαίνειν and μῆτιν ὑφαίνειν. Here it gains added significance from the fact that Penelope's most renowned δόλος was in fact the web which she spun out by day and unravelled by night, her literal actions paralleling her metaphorical description. Penelope may be an especially appropriate 'spinner', of both webs and deceptions, if we follow the etymology that would connect her name with πήνη, 'thread' or 'woof', discussed by E. Wüst in *RE* 19 col. 461 ff. Recently von Kamptz, *Personennamen*, 29 f., 70, has revived an earlier speculation (Kretschmer, *Anz. Wien. Ak.* 82 (1945), 80 ff.) that the second element -ελοπεια may be derived from ὀλόπτω, 'to pluck out', giving the possibility that 'Penelope' means 'Weaving-Unraveller'. But von Kamptz seems to incline elsewhere (pp. 139, 275) to the more conventional etymology that 'Penelope' is one of the many names of individuals and populations derived from animals, in this case the wild duck or goose called πηνέλοψ (so tentatively Chantraine, *Dictionnaire*, s.v. πηνέλοψ).

Penelope's use of the plural δόλους suggests that, beyond the trick of the web, deception has characterized her lengthy dealings with the suitors. She has stalled their designs with various evasions (cf. Antinous' complaint at ii 91–2, echoed by Athena's description at xiii 380–1; also Amphimedon's retrospective assessment at xxiv 126–8, which echoes Telemachus' earlier comments at i 249–50 and xvi 126–7), and most recently has raised their hopes with her seductive appearance that inflamed their desire and extracted valuable gifts, xviii 158–303. Thus her use of the phrase 'I spin out deceptions' further strengthens the view that her exchange with Eurymachus at xviii 245–80 represents calculated deception on her part, and that Odysseus' observation and reaction at 281–3 reveal a wily husband's appreciation of a kindred wiliness in his wife.

139–56. These verses are almost *verbatim* repetition of ii 94–110 in which the ruse of the web is first described, in the complaint made by Antinous to the Ithacan assembly convened by Telemachus. Here only verse 153 has no counterpart in the earlier speech. Since it is omitted in many manuscripts, it may be a later interpolation, or a verse that was added in some performances but omitted in others.

141. ἐπεὶ θάνε δῖος Ὀδυσσεύς: the flat factual tone of this statement is far removed from Penelope's real feelings, in which some hope for Odysseus' return is always present (cf. 127–8, above; xviii 254–5). She is deliberately deceiving the suitors, and Homer skilfully conveys this in her diction.

143. μεταμώνια: 'in vain, ineffectual', always neut. pl. in Homer. The original meaning is probably 'gone with the wind', the original form *μετα-νεμώνιος (from μετ' ἀνέμων), which lost the -νε- by dissimilation. This etymology is already in Apollonius' *Lexicon* and is supported by Bechtel, *Lexilogus*, 226, and Chantraine, *Dictionnaire* s.v., among modern authorities. It receives ancient support in Simonides fr. 16D = 516 PMG, κονία μεταμώνιος ἀέρθη, 'the dust was raised high by the wind', where a connection with ἄνεμος is clearly assumed. Compare the synonymous ἀνεμώλιος, and the phrases ἀνεμώλια βάζειν (*Il.* iv 355, *Od.* xi 464) and μεταμώνια βάζειν (*Od.* iv 392).

145. τανηλεγέος θανάτοιο: 'death with extended grief', a noun-epithet formula found eight times in the *Odyssey* and twice in the *Iliad*. τανηλεγής is most likely from ταναός (τείνω) and ἄλγος (the adjectival ἀλεγεινός), as Hesychius saw when he glossed this word with παρατεταμένην ἔχοντος τὴν ἀλγηδόνα. Similar lengthening of α to η in a compound is seen in the Homeric δυσηχής, from δυσ- plus ἄχος; and in δυσηλεγής, which, although apparently similar, may not be built on ἄλγος but on ἀλέγω, with the meaning 'uncaring, pitiless', which would suit its frequent application to πόλεμος (see Leumann, Wörter, 45; Chantraine, Dictionnaire, s.v. ἄλγος, ἀλέγω).

147. κῆται: found in only one MS, the others giving κεῖται. The form is a subjunctive, contracted from κέεται or κείεται (see Chantraine, Morphologie, 259). Monro believes the true Homeric form was κέεται, which van Leeuwen prints in his text, and which can be substituted metrically for κῆται/κεῖται in all Homeric occurrences but one (Il. xxiv 554).

149–50. Van Leeuwen, Odyssea (Leiden, 1917), 521, offers a fanciful symbolic interpretation in which a 'celestial' myth is deeply buried under this narrative element: Penelope represents the moon, whose waxing and waning is represented as the weaving and undoing of the web (μηνῶν φθινόντων of 153 could be added in support of this interpretation). Presumably the recurrent waning of the moon was a symbolic representation of the fact that Penelope's web would never be finished. Thus we would have a lunar counterpart of the solar myth upon which the return of Odysseus (and all heroes) was once thought to be based (cf. van Leeuwen ad v 467 ff.; and for a survey and critique of this 'solar mythology' made famous by Max Müller, see R. Dorson, 'The Eclipse of Solar Mythology', in Myth: A Symposium, ed. T. Sebeok (Indiana, 1958), 25–63). A more sensible investigation into the weaving–unweaving motif is E. S. McCartney, 'Undoing by Night Work Done by Day: A Folklore Motif', in Studies Presented to D. M. Robinson, ii (St Louis, 1953), 1249–53, who finds this motif in many European and Arabian folktales. Penelope's web is a motif perfectly adapted to function on both the literal and symbolic levels: it is the activity of a good housewife and here is performed in filial piety, yet at the same time spinning commonly has a metaphoric dimension in many languages, and in Greek is part of a standard metaphoric expression for deception (cf. note to 137).

157–61. Penelope here gives a realistic, and pessimistic, assessment of her situation vis-à-vis the suitors: both her parents and her son are pressing her to remarry, and she has run out of stalling devices. It is a rather candid account to give to a stranger; but she accepts him as someone to whom Telemachus has chosen to extend guest-hospitality (ξενία), and in the course of this long interview she will grow increasingly to trust and confide in him. We may assume a strong intuitive feeling is at work, which draws the queen to this interesting newcomer.

160–1. οἷος τε ... κήδεσθαι: an early example of this construction (found also at xxi 117, 173 but not in the Iliad), and similar to ὥς τε + inf. commented on at xvii 20. See further in Ruijgh, τε épique, 48–9, 541–3.

161. τῷ: the antecedent is probably ἀνήρ, although Monro takes it to be οἴκου.

163. ἀπὸ δρυὸς ... οὐδ' ἀπὸ πέτρης: apparently a proverbial expression referring to the old belief that the human race originated from these natural sources. Penelope is using gentle irony to imply that the stranger has real family origins, which etiquette now suggests he reveal. The phrase occurs also at *Il.* xxii 126, and in the related περὶ δρῦν ἢ περὶ πέτρην at Hesiod, *Th.* 35, both of which seem less appropriate to their context than does the present passage, and have given rise to debated interpretations (for which see W. J. Verdenius in *Mnemosyne* xi (1958), 20–4; Hesiod, *Theogony*, ed. M. L. West (Oxford, 1966), 167–9). For the myths of human origins from trees or stones, see Roscher, *Lexicon* vi 500–2; F. Specht, *Zeitschrift für Vergleichende Sprachforschung* lxviii (1944), 191–200; G. Bonfante, in *Die Sprache* v (1959), 1–8; and on the name 'Dorian' and its relation to δόρυ and δρῦς through the root *derw-, P. Ramat, *La Parola del Passato* xvi (1961), 62–5.

170. This verse recalls the phrases πολλῶν δ' ἀνθρώπων ... ἄστεα and πάθεν ἄλγεα in the famous prooimion of the *Odyssey* (i 3–4). Odysseus' ability to spin lies that resemble the truth (203 below) comes in part from his incorporation of many real experiences into his narrative.

172. Κρήτη: at xiv 199ff. Odysseus also idenfies himself as a Cretan, when giving his history to Eumaeus. There he names Crete as if it is a well-known place; but here he describes it as if to someone who might have heard the name before (Κρήτη τις γαῖ' ἔστι) but would need to be informed about the island's geography, inhabitants, resources, and political leadership. Presumably a woman, even a queen, paid little attention to international politics and geography, whereas a man, even a swineherd, spent a good part of his time exchanging such information and gossip with his friends—as remains true of Mediterranean cultures today.

172–9. This passage, together with *Il.* ii 645–52, is the earliest description we have of Crete and one of the most important pieces of historical information in Homer. He describes a society of mixed, international composition, the only such settlement known in early Greece, whether we assume the description to be valid for the Bronze Age, for Homer's time, or for some period in between. The Achaeans are the Mycenaeans, who seem to dominate central Crete under the leadership of Idomeneus according to the tradition presented at *Il.* ii 645 ff. 'Eteocretans', meaning 'true Cretans', obviously refers to the aboriginal inhabitants. Their non-Greek language is preserved in inscriptions at Praisos that continue to the third century BC, and Herodotus (vii 170) identifies the Praisians as descendants of the original Minoans. The Cydonians are mentioned also at iii 292 where they are placed at the river Iardanos, at the western end of the north coast. According to Pausanias viii 53. 4 they originated in Arcadian Tegea. Most striking is the inclusion of Dorians among Cretan populations, since Homer mentions them nowhere else and shows no knowledge of the supposed 'Dorian invasion'. *Il.* ii 653–6, however, seems to refer to the Dorian settlement of Rhodes, identifying the Rhodian leader

COMMENTARY

Tlepolemus as a 'son of Heracles' and describing the Rhodians dwelling 'arranged in threefold division', τρίχα κοσμηθέντες, ii 655. This phrase, taken with the τρίχα of ii 668, might be related to the τριχάικες of *Od.* xix 177, suggesting that both epics are consistent in their awareness of the three Dorian tribes—unless we derive τριχάικες from θρίξ and ἀίσσω (see n. on 177) and translate 'with waving (horsehair) plumes'. For further discussion see Kirk, *Commentary*, 225–7, and R. F. Willetts, *Cretan Cults and Festivals* (London, 1962), 131–7.

Strabo (x 4. 6–7) commenting on this important passage identifies both Eteocretans and Cydonians as autochthonous and cites the authority of the lost historian Staphylos for assigning the Cydonians to the western part of Crete (modern Khania), the Dorians to the east, and the Eteocretans to the south where they occupied Praisos. In the classical period, and perhaps as early as Homer's time, Dorians occupied much or most of Crete, so that this tradition preserved by Strabo and Homer may accurately reflect the time when the Dorians gained their first foothold on the island. See further in R. W. Hutchinson, *Prehistoric Crete* (London, 1962), 317–20. As for the ubiquitous Pelasgians, Herodotus (i 56–8) identifies them as the original non-Greek people from whom the Ionians are descended; elsewhere (ii 52–6) he inclines to the idea that all Hellas was originally called 'Pelasgia'; and he mentions them often throughout his History. They remain a mysterious people, possibly connected with the Lydians and Etruscans (cf. Th. iv 109), whom modern research has not successfully identified. The full-length study of historical evidence is F. Lochner-Hüttenbach, *Die Pelasger* (Vienna, 1960), where this passage is discussed on 99–100. The earlier authoritative discussion is by J. L. Myres in *JHS* 27 (1907), 170–225. See also W. How and J. Wells, *A Commentary on Herodotus* (Oxford, 1912), 442–6 (based on Myres), and R. F. Willetts, *Ancient Crete* (London, 1965), 25–35. For a linguistic argument for 'Pelasgian' as a pre-Hellenic Indo-European language that left many traces in Greek, see A. J. van Windekens, *Le Pélasgique* (Louvain, 1952) and *Études pélasgiques* (Louvain, 1960).

177. **τριχάικες:** an unsolved etymological puzzle. Several recent authorities cite the analogously formed κορυθάιξ, 'with shaking helmet', and derive this word from θρίξ, 'hair', and ἀίσσω, 'to move quickly, leap', and translate 'with flying hair' or 'with waving (horsehair) plumes' (so Chantraine, *Dictionnaire* s.v., Leumann, *Wörter*, 65, Risch, *Wortbildung*, 194, Frisk, *GEW*). But Hesiod fr. 233 M–W, our earliest testimony for epic usage, uses the word to mean 'dwelling in threefold location'. This older etymology, favoured by Bechtel, *Lexilogus*, 317–18, Schwyzer, *Grammatik*, i 93, and Benveniste, *Institutions indo-européennes*, i 311 (= Eng. edn. 253), assumes an original *τριχάϝικες, the second element cognate with οἶκος, Latin *vicus*, Skt. *viś-*. This etymology offers the advantage of a consistent portrait of Dorian tribal division in both Homeric epics (see on 172–9), but faces the obstacle of unexplained long -ᾱ-·and -ι- (metrical lengthening is argued by Bechtel, rejected by Chantraine). I suspect we should follow

84

Hesiod's sense of his own poetic language, and assume metrical lengthening for long -ι- and compound lengthening for long -α- (cf. ἐκάβολος, post-Homeric κρεάνομος).

178. Κνωσός ... Μίνως: Cnossos was the great central city of Crete, and Minos, son of Zeus, its legendary ruler. For his excellence as a just king, he was singled out, according to legend, together with his brother Rhadamanthus, to preside as judge over all the souls of the departed in Hades.

179. Both the meaning of ἐννέωρος and the syntax of the line present ambiguities. This word is most likely derived from ἔννεα, 'nine', and ὥρη, 'season' or 'year', and should mean 'nine years old' or 'in the ninth year'. (Ruijgh, τε épique, 479 n. 17, suggests it may have replaced an original *εἴνωρος, which would account for the synizesis in scansion, − − −.) At xi 311 the context requires 'nine years old', which would hardly suit our passage; but at x 19 and 390, referring to an ox and to pigs, the meaning 'of mature age' is commonly assumed (Cunliffe, LSJ), although 'in the ninth year' also gives good sense if we understand it as the traditionally 'perfect' age for symbolic or ritual reasons. At *Il.* xviii 351 the word is applied to the oil that is used to stop the ears of Patroclus' corpse, and while the exact meaning remains obscure some ritually appropriate attribute seems to be designated. For the present passage, we must either follow Plato's interpretation, in *Min.* 319 and *Lg.* 624 (echoed in Strabo x 4. 8 and xvi 2. 38), that 'every ninth year' Minos went up to the cave of Zeus to talk with the god and bring back laws to his people; or say that Minos ruled 'in nineyear cycles', taking ἐννέωρος with βασίλευε, which is more natural, rather than with ὀαριστής, as Plato does; or say simply that Minos ruled for nine years. The existence of nine-year cycles has been often attested for Greek festivals, based on an early octennial calendric rhythm (M. P. Nilsson, *Die Entstehung und religiöse Bedeutung des griech. Kalendars* (Lund, 1962), 46–7, 150–1; G. Thomson, *JHS* lxiii (1943), 63; an eight-year period could be called either ὀκταετηρίς or ἐνναετηρίς, since the ninth year marked the beginning of the new cycle but could be counted inclusively with the concluded cycle; thus an eight-year cycle could be said to proceed δι' ἐνάτου ἔτους). Nine is generally a favoured number throughout antiquity in Greece, the Near East, and Rome (F. B. Anderson, *CJ* l (1954–5), 131–8) and may have been a 'sacred' number in Minoan–Mycenaean religion (Thomson, op. cit. 64, denied by Nilsson, op. cit. 30 n. 4). The safest interpretation, then, is that ἐννέωρος refers generally to a nine-year period, and means 'nine years old' when referring to animals but 'in nine-year units' when describing how King Minos ruled. S. Marinatos, *Studies Presented to D. M. Robinson* i (St Louis, 1951), 131–2, speculates that the so-called eleven-year rainfall cycle lies behind this; that in Greece it approximated nine years and led to the belief that King Minos (and elsewhere Aeacus: Paus. ii 29. 7) had interceded with his father Zeus to bring a good rainfall.

181. Here Odysseus claims not just a noble background—which he has already implied by his courtly manner and concern for proper behaviour at 107–22—but that he is younger brother to the King of Crete. At xiv

199–242, telling his story to Eumaeus, he depicted himself as the illegitimate son of a Cretan nobleman and a concubine, a man who attained high esteem despite his mixed background and eventually was given joint command, with Idomeneus, of the Cretan expedition to Troy. That story was a fiction well-chosen to ingratiate himself with Eumaeus, who similarly has had a mixed career, but of reverse pattern, beginning as a true-born prince but spending most of his life as a servant, albeit a highly respected one. Here with Penelope, however, Odysseus claims a flawless royal lineage, which will help win the queen's full confidence and begin the progression of sympathy and trust that leads to her accepting him as a friend and equal by the end of this book.

183. **Αἴθων:** no doubt Homer intends a 'significant name', but the exact meaning here may elude us. R. J. Edgeworth, 'Terms for "Brown" in Ancient Greek', *Glotta* 61 (1983), 31–40, argues well that αἴθων (together with αἴθοψ) is primarily a colour term and not the equivalent of 'shining' or 'blazing' (for which αἰθόμενος would be the normal participle); hence its meaning as a personal name would be 'dark-complexioned' (a typical male physical trait: see xvi 75, μελαγχροιής and xix 246, μελανόχροος with note), or, with metaphorical extension, perhaps 'vigorous' (the meaning that the related αἴθοψ must carry at Hes. *Op.* 363, αἴθοπα [MSS, αἴθονα Bergk] λιμόν, 'intense hunger'). The exact meaning of Homeric αἴθων remains problematic because the adjective is attached to so many different objects: lion, horse, oxen, eagle, tripods, cauldrons, iron. Its common use to modify metallic objects has been used to support the translation 'shining'; but Edgeworth seems correct in claiming that it is the red-brown colour of bronze that is denoted, and that in the case of iron we have an instance of the frequent formulaic conflation of bronze and iron (noted by Lorimer, *Monuments*, 119).

185. **Ὀδυσῆα ἐγών:** a rare instance of 'illicit' hiatus. According to Leaf, *Iliad*, vol. i 123 (ad iii 46), it is found only at *Il.* ii 8, iii 46, v 118, xix 288, xxiii 263, and *Od.* iii 480, vi 151, and here.

188. **σπέος Εἰλειθυίης:** Eileithyia is the goddess with the power to facilitate childbirth, a function which Artemis gradually assimilates in later tradition. This cave of Eileithyia at Amnisos was excavated by S. Marinatos in 1929–30 and evidence was found for continuous cult use from the third millennium BC to the fifth or sixth century AD. The goddess's name, believed to be pre-Indo-European, is found on several Linear B tablets from Amnisos and Knossos, and Eileithyia probably descends from a neolithic prototype of the Great Goddess or Magna Mater of nature and fertility, whose figurines were widely distributed in prehistoric times. Her cave at Amnisos must have been well-known for Odysseus to use it to lend credence to his account. For further information see M. P. Nilsson, *Minoan–Mycenaean Religion* (Lund, 1950), 73, 521–2; R. F. Willetts, *CQ* viii (1958), 221–3, and *Cretan Cults and Festivals* (London, 1962), 168–72. Both Nilsson and Willetts see an etymological connection between Eileithyia and Eleusis, while L. R. Palmer, *The Interpretation of Mycenaean Greek Texts*

(Oxford, 1963), 238, connects the name to ἐλεύθερος and Latin *Liber*, the god of generation and growth, and *liberi*, 'children'. Either etymology allows us to see a relationship between Eileithyia and the widespread cult of the earth-mother, and perhaps to assume that the reference to this goddess' cave is a subtle omen of Odysseus' eventual success.

203. Ἴσκε: a much-disputed word. Ancient commentators already noted that some authorities said it meant εἴκαζε, ὁμοίου, while others equated it with ἔλεγε. The latter interpretation almost certainly arose from a misunderstanding of ἴσκεν ἕκαστος ἀνήρ at xxii 31, where ἴσκεν means 'conjectured', but was taken as equivalent to ὣς φάτο because it follows and describes a speech. We should understand ἴσκω as a variant of εἴσκω, meaning primarily 'to liken one thing to another', secondarily 'to conjecture'. All other Homeric uses of ἴσκω bear this out (*Il.* xi 799, xvi 41; *Od.* iv 279, xxii 31), and the use of ἐΐσκεις at iv 148, referring back to ἔοικε at 143, shows the secondary meaning emerging from the primary one. The verb is formed as an iterative of (ϝ)εἴκω: ϝίκ-σκω > ϝίσκω, with ϝει/ϝι variation as in εἴκελος/ἴκελος. The misunderstanding of ἴσκε was encouraged by the ambiguous syntax of 203: do we construe ἴσκε ψευδέα ἐτύμοισιν, adding ὁμοῖα as epexegetical of ἴσκε; or ἴσκε (intransitive), ψευδέα λέγων ἐτύμοισιν ὁμοῖα? Hes. *Th.* 27, ἴδμεν ψευδέα πολλὰ λέγειν ἐτύμοισιν ὁμοῖα, shows that the phrasing is traditional and that by adding ἴσκε Homer has rendered the syntax ambiguous. It is interesting for the history of neologisms that the false meaning was accepted and imitated by the Hellenistic poets Theocritus, Apollonius of Rhodes, and Lycophron.

204-8. One of the *Odyssey*'s unforgettable similes. Penelope's 'melting' was anticipated by her statement at 136, κατατήκομαι ἦτορ, and is echoed in Odysseus' μηδέ τι θυμὸν τῆκε at 263-4. A form of τήκω is used in each of these five successive verses, an unparalleled verbal concentration that creates an overwhelming image of melting and overflowing. The verb includes both meanings, which our translation cannot imitate: overflowing is the surface phenomenon; melting is what happens internally. τήκετο δὲ χρώς means her skin ran with liquid from her tears, not that it 'melted'. What does melt is Penelope's long-standing resistance to yielding herself to the belief that Odysseus is alive and will return (cf. n. on 309-16); and as melting snow produces a liquid overflow, so the dissolving of her energies spent in repression of emotion produces an overflow of feeling whose concrete manifestation is tears. Her denial of her true emotions was indeed 'the winter of her soul'. Hence the perfect aptness of this simile representing the release of Penelope's strong innermost feelings through the image of snow dissolving under a warm wind.

209. The irony and pathos of this line are striking. Its power derives from a neat verbal and rhythmical subtlety: παρήμενον states the ironic truth—that the husband for whom Penelope is weeping is in fact sitting at her side, unknown to her—and expresses it in one word. The placement of this word is crucial: it immediately follows the phrase it qualifies so ironically, and is placed just after the mid-line caesura, which normatively coincides with

some semantic division (see H. N. Porter, *YCS* xii (1951), 22–3). The effect is to 'bridge over' this caesura semantically while formally in respecting it formally in the division between words. The effect is sharpened by the full stop after παρήμενον, which makes the overrunning of the caesura especially conspicuous.

211–12. A paradigmatic example of the power of self-control that has made Odysseus one of literature's most famous figures. Homer uses horn and iron to represent the hardness of the hero's will, just as in the simile of the melting snow (204–8) the physical world was used to represent, through externalization, the inner, psychic reality that is normally not accessible to observation. Corresponding to the δόλος of Odysseus at 212, we have the δόλοι of which Penelope boasts at 137 (cf. the μῆτις of Penelope and of Odysseus discussed at 325–6).

215. πειρήσασθαι: the 'testing' of another person (or of an object, like the bow in xxi, or in athletic competition as in viii) is characteristic of Odysseus throughout the epic: the verb πειράω/πειράομαι/πειρητίζω is used by him, or to describe him, more than twenty times. Normally, he is the tester. Occasionally, he submits himself to the test, as at viii 205, 213. Rarely, the test is applied to him against his will or without his awareness of it: by Penelope here and at xxiii 181, and by Athena at xxii 237. (At ix 281 the Cyclops tries to test him but is clumsy and transparent and receives 'deceptive words' for an answer.) This rare reversal of the norm is significant, and the fact that it is given to Penelope to 'test' the wily tester is another sign of her own special gift for guile, which qualifies her perfectly to be Odysseus' wife (cf. 137 n., 325–6).

221–2. Construe ἐόντα as referring to με, the unexpressed subject of εἰπέμεν, while the other accusative τόσσον χρόνον expresses the duration of ἀμφὶς ἐόντα. Less likely, but possible, would be an unspecified subject, τινα.

225. χλαῖναν πορφυρέην οὔλην: οὔλην must mean 'wool', and χλαῖνα designates equally a cloak or a blanket, since the same piece of cloth was used for both. χλαίνας οὔλας are mentioned at iv 299, vii 338, *Il.* x 133–4, *Il.* xxiv 646. A χλαῖνα is described as the ideal protective covering against a severe winter at xiv 520–2. A less likely interpretation would take οὔλην here as 'entire', referring to πορφυρέην and meaning 'entirely of purple'.

226–31. A wonderfully detailed description. The double sheaths, αὔλοι, are the tubes into which the pins fit. The lively naturalism of the dog catching the fawn has some resemblance to animal motifs of Minoan gems and gold work, but brooches of this complex style belong to a much later period, and are most often dated no earlier than the seventh century BC (M. P. Nilsson, *Homer and Mycenae* (London, 1933), 123–5, Lorimer, *Monuments*, 511–15). An earlier date, late eighth to seventh century, is urged by Anne Roes, *Mnemosyne* iv (1951), 216–22, from the comparison of North Italian and Etruscan brooches and the detailed study of a similar type of brooch in the Dijon museum. J. L. Myres, *Annual of the British School at Athens* xlv (1950), 242–3, finds a close parallel in a Greek fibula from Sparta dated about 700 BC, and goes on to suggest that Homer knew *both* Minoan *and* later

Orientalizing styles and techniques and in his descriptions creates imaginary combinations that never really existed.

229–30. It is not certain what the hound is doing to the fawn, since the meaning of λάω is disputed.

Context strongly suggests 'grip', and so the verb λάω, 'to grip', has found its way into LSJ, but there is no evidence (except the present passage) to support this entry. The other early use of the word is h.Merc. 360, where it is said that not even the eagle ὀξὺ λάων could see Hermes hidden in a cave (cf. Il. xvii 675, where the eagle is called ὀξύτατον δέρκεσθαι ὑπουρανίων πετεηνῶν, a characteristic repeated by Aelian, i 42). Clearly the meaning 'see' is intended by the author of the hymn, and is supported by Hesychius' gloss λάετε· σκοπεῖτε, βλέπετε. For the form λάων, however, Hesychius gives three meanings: (1) βλέπων, (2) λάπτων τῇ γλώσσῃ, (3) ἀπολαυστικῶς ἔχων, ἐσθίων. And under λάε he glosses ἐψόφησε, which can be combined with the scholia's equation of λάω with ὑλάω to suggest the possibility that ὀξὺ λάων describes the eagle's shrill cry (cf. S. Aj. 112, αἰετὸς ὀξέα κλάζων). Leumann, Wörter, 233–6, reviews the evidence and, stressing the similarity of ὀξὺ λάων to ὀξὺ λεληκώς used of a hawk at Il. xxii 141, suggests that λάω is a present created erroneously from the pf. λεληκώς (by false division λελη-κώς instead of λεληκ-ώς). But we should note that on Odysseus' brooch it is more difficult to imagine the visual depiction of a dog's bark than of his fierce look. Therefore the balance of evidence inclines toward the meaning 'to see', which receives some small additional support from the papyrus variant γηθήσειε λάων for γηθήσειεν ἰδών at Il. xiii 344. The dog has fixed its eyes intently on the struggling fawn while throttling it. The representation of the dog would have prominent eyes and would gaze directly at its victim, in the manner of the black-figure painting of Achilles killing Penthesileia on the famous neck-amphora by Exekias (British Museum, London) or comparable to the even more dramatic gaze of Achilles and Penthesileia on the red-figure cup by the Penthesileia Painter (Museum Antiker Kleinkunst, Munich).

233. The syntax is ambiguous. The simplest construction, probably to be preferred, is to take κατά with its normal accent as governing the genitive phrase: 'like the skin over a dry onion'. It is possible, but more strained, to accent κάτα and take this preposition as governing λόπον: 'as [sc. the shining] along the skin of a dry onion'. See further Ruijgh, τε épique, 533 n. 17 for the accentuation of κατά (no anastrophe when a word comes between the noun and the governing preposition that follows it), following the authority of J. Vendryes, Traité d'accentuation grecque (Paris, 1904), 246–7.

236–50. The beggar cleverly heightens the verisimilitude of his description by feigning uncertainty as to whether the clothes and brooch might have been acquired by Odysseus after having left Ithaca. He then proceeds to cap the unerringly accurate description with a vivid portrait of the herald Eurybates, a man so singular-looking that his depiction leaves no shred of doubt that this beggar really knew Odysseus. The result of such a cleverly arranged climax of proof is that Penelope collapses in another fit of weeping.

COMMENTARY

246–9. As Pasquali shrewdly observed, *Terze pagine stravaganti* (Firenze, 1942), 139–66, the Greeks tended to describe beauty in conventionalized, general terms that did not give individuals' idiosyncracies, whereas ugliness was always more particularized and vivid, from Homer to classical times. It is nevertheless possible that a conventional typology existed also for the short, stoop-shouldered, unattractive man such as we meet in Eurybates and in Thersites at *Il.* ii 212ff., and in Archilochus' fr. 60D = 114W (where Archilochus emphatically stresses the inner excellence that contrasts with the un-heroic façade, in a manner reminiscent of the portrait of Eurybates here: see J. Russo, 'The Inner Man in Archilochus and the *Odyssey*', *Greek, Roman, and Byzantine Studies* xv (1974), 139–52).

246. **γυρὸς:** 'bent' or 'rounded', which must refer to his back and shoulders, describing a characteristic physique of which we have a more exaggerated version in Thersites, τὼ δέ οἱ ὤμω | κυρτώ, ἐπὶ στῆθος συνοχωκότε, *Il.* ii 217–18. **μελανόχροος, οὐλοκάρηνος:** 'dark-skinned' must mean the same as μελαγχροιής applied to Odysseus at xvi 175 (when Athena restores his handsome appearance), denoting the ruddy tan natural to men who spend much time out of doors (cf. Ar. *Ec.* 385–7, 428, for the unmanly pallor of the women disguised as men). The combination with οὐλοκάρηνος, however, may point to a specific combination of physical traits, 'dark-skinned' and 'woolly-headed', that are meant to suggest an African type, generally thought of as 'Ethiopian' in antiquity. See F. Snowden, *Blacks in Antiquity* (Cambridge, Mass., 1970), 101–2, 122, 181.

248. **ὅτι οἱ φρεσὶν ἄρτια ᾔδη:** another indication that 'harmony of mind', ὁμοφροσύνη (cf. vi 180–5), is of prime importance to Odysseus in personal relationships (see note to xviii 281–3). It was also the similarity of mind between Odysseus and Athena that delighted the goddess and was the reason for her strong support of him (xiii 291 ff., esp. 296–301).

253–4. **ἐλεεινός . . . φίλος . . . αἰδοῖος:** because he has proved his close tie of hospitality (ξενία) to Odysseus (ἐξείνισσα, 194, for twelve days, 199), the stranger is now formally elevated by the queen from the status of pitied (ἐλεεινός) suppliant to that of a dear (φίλος) and respected (αἰδοῖος) friend of the household. This improved status is crucial to a correct understanding of the last scene in this book, where Penelope entrusts to this former stranger her most important thoughts: her prophetic dream and her intuition that the time is right for proposing the contest of the bow. For both the interpretation of her dream and the decision to fix the contest for the following day, confirmation from this increasingly appealing and influential new person is vital.

260. (= 597, xxiii 19.) *Κακοΐλιον:* for verbal play of this sort, which is serious and not humorous in Greek, cf. 'Iros–Airos' at xviii 73, with note.

271–87. Odysseus repeats the same fiction he has told to Eumaeus at xiv 316ff., that he had news of Odysseus from the Thesprotians, and repeats the detail of the accumulation of much wealth for his return to Ithaca. Odysseus' acquisitiveness is conspicuous throughout the *Odyssey*, is a cardinal trait of a folktale hero, and here serves as a detail that adds verisimilitude. The incident of the cattle of Helius is summarized, as is the arrival at Scheria and the Phaeacians' willingness to transport Odysseus home. But, as Stanford observes, Odysseus has conflated into one story the shipwreck off Thrinakia and the wreck of the raft with which he left Calypso. This tactful abbreviation has him going directly from the cattle to the Phaeacians without the intervening sojourn with the beautiful temptress.

275. ὀδύσαντο: the verb *ὀδύ(σ)ομαι involves a pun on Odysseus' name. Homer employs this word-play at several places in the poem, the most significant being xix 407 (see note). Greek puns are not humorous like our own, but point to a coincidence that is supposed to reveal some underlying truth.

288-99. These verses are substantially the same as those spoken by Odysseus to Eumaeus at xiv 323-35, but the order has been changed.

296-7. The oracle of Zeus at Dodona and that of Apollo at Delphi were the two internationally famous oracular shrines of antiquity. Greek literature refers several times to the fact that Zeus' voice was audible from the sacred oak at Dodona. See H. W. Parke, *The Oracles of Zeus: Dodona, Olympia, Ammon* (Oxford, 1967), 11-13, 20-33.

297. ἐπακούσαι: the aorist opt. third-sing. Most MSS read the subjunctive ἐπακούσῃ, but the optative accords better with νοστήσειε in the following line. At xiv 328 the same verse occurs, with a scholium telling us that ἐπακούσαι is read by Aristophanes, ἐπακούσῃ by Aristarchus.

299. ἀμφαδὸν ἦε κρυφηδόν: this phrase recalls that part of Teiresias' prophecy where he predicts that Odysseus will succeed in killing the suitors δόλῳ ἢ ἀμφηδόν, xi 120.

306. λυκάβαντος: many etymological arguments have been fashioned to explain the word λυκάβας as 'day', 'year', 'lunar month', or 'going of the light' (which could denote several possible time periods). None of the Greek etymologies is fully convincing. Ruijgh, *Élément*, 147, argues for a pre-Hellenic root, and O. Szemerenyi, *JHS* 94 (1974), 144-57, for a Semitic origin. Etymology may derive some support from context, which suggests a connection with the festival of Apollo (see on 306-7). The best explanation along these lines is that of J. van Windekens, *BN* v (1954), 31-4, who makes *lykabas* a festival of Apollo Lykeios or Lykios. The wide range of derivations from the root *leuq- (λύχνος, λεύσσω, Lat. lux, luna < *luk-na) shows that Apollo 'Lyk(e)ios' can be both a god of light and of the returning light of the moon.

306-7. This prediction (= xiv 161 ff.), while of crucial importance, remains obscure to us because the time period denoted by λυκάβας is unknowable. In later Greek it was understood as 'year', and many have followed Wilamowitz (*Heimkehr*, 43-4, *Untersuchungen*, 54) in believing that τοῦδ' αὐτοῦ λυκάβαντος means 'within this very year' (Chantraine, *Dictionnaire* s.v., still finds this 'acceptable'). But such a meaning is contradicted by the context, where the stranger is trying to convince Penelope that Odysseus' return is *imminent*. The period denoted in 306 is further defined in 307 as falling within, or being essentially the same as, the space between the waning of the old moon and the rising of the new. Such a period terminates in, or may be equated with, the festival of Apollo referred to at xx 156, 276–8, and xxi 258–9 (Roscher, *Lexicon*, i 424–5, gives evidence for a monthly celebration of Apollo Neomenios, 'of the new moon'; but 425–30 discusses 'Apollo als Gott des Frühlings', and *RE* s.v. *Lykeios* cites evidence—although epigraphical and relatively late—for a spring month Lykeios, connected with Apollo. Since the poem's action has probably taken place during winter (see n. on xvii 23 and van Leeuwen's commentary on v 467), it is tempting to follow Austin, *Archery*, ch. 5, in believing that Homer has given his poem a seasonal rhythm in which the return of Odysseus coincides with the return of spring. A springtime celebration of Apollo would underscore that seasonal rhythm). Since the stranger's prediction is spoken in order to confirm Penelope's decision to set the bow contest for the following day, and is reinforced with assurances that Odysseus will arrive in time for that contest, Penelope certainly understands λυκάβας to specify, or conclude with, that day. And since Odysseus used the same words to Eumaeus at xiv 161–2, we must infer (unless we call the earlier passage an interpolation) that τοῦδ' αὐτοῦ λυκάβαντος cannot mean 'this (next) day' but could mean 'this very day of the Apollo-festival'.

It may be best simply to take λυκάβας as an obsolete word meaning 'interlunar period', the dark moonless night of the new moon (so H. Koller, *Glotta* li (1973), etymologizing *λύκα βάντα, 'the daylight having gone'; similarly Leumann, *Wörter*, 212 n. 4), and to understand it as denoting not the Apollo-festival itself but the interlunar period about to end with the new moon festival of the god.

309–11. Penelope spoke these same lines to Theoclymenus at xvii 163–5. Here the statement acquires heightened significance in the unintended forecast of φιλότητα, and becomes a kind of κληδών to the audience of the poem.

309–16. In these verses we see a psychological pattern that Homer has consistently used in his portrait of Penelope: she lets hope buoy her up briefly, then sinks into pessimism. Such pessimism serves as her protection against being deceived by false hopes, as has happened repeatedly (described at xiv 126–30, xxiii 213–18). Note the same abrupt shift to pessimism at mid-verse in 257, and her sudden assertion that her dream must be a false one at 568.

312. μοι ὧδ' ἀνὰ θυμὸν ὀΐεται: 'so it seems to me in my heart', the only impersonal use of ὀΐομαι in Homer. The normal idiom is seen in μοι ὀΐσατο θυμὸς ἀγήνωρ ix 213, and κατὰ θυμὸν ὀΐσατο at 390 below: the subject of ὀΐομαι is normally either a person or his θυμός. Emendation of ἀνὰ θυμόν to ἄρα θυμός has been proposed, to restore the more common idiom.

315. εἴ ποτ' ἔην γε: a formula, expressive in its simplicity, for referring to a past happiness or a lost beloved person as if the speaker really doubted that it ever existed. The formula is used with typical poignancy by Helen at *Il.*

iii 180 and by Priam at xxiv 426, both characters whose happiness now lies in a lost past.

317. Penelope here, after her self-protective statement of pessimism, protects herself further by abruptly (ἀλλά) turning from the dialogue that was engaging her deepest emotions in a dangerously uncomfortable manner. She breaks off the dialogue by ordering a bath for her visitor.

325-6. It is significant that Penelope wishes to be judged for her outstanding νόος and μῆτις, qualities that are associated with Odysseus. We recall that he is praised as ἀγχίνοος by Athena at xiii 332, and he was presented, through Homer's verbal play on οὔ τις and μή τις, as the embodiment of μῆτις at ix 405-6, 408, 410, 414.

331. τεθνεῶτί: scanned with synizesis as − − ∪.

332. ἀμύμων: this word is the subject of a recent detailed study by Anne Parry (*Blameless Aegisthus*) who argues that ἀμύμων refers not to moral quality, as believed by those who derive it from μῶμος and translate 'blameless', but rather evolves from an original meaning 'physically beautiful' toward a more generalized sense of 'fine, good, excellent'. She examines carefully all Homeric passages containing this word and finds the present passage anomalous in its metrical and syntactic use of ἀμύμων, and in its unique use of the neuter plural. She judges ἀμύμων here to have 'more definite moral connotations than in any other uses in Homer' (ibid. 110–16).

336-48. Why does Odysseus persist in declining all the comforts offered him? At 344–5 the stated motive is to avoid Melantho and her like, but the entire speech is dominated by a determination to keep himself at a low level of physical comfort, which serves both realistic and symbolic purposes. Eustathius suggests the practical motive that Odysseus wishes to avoid anything that makes him more conspicuous and therefore suspect to the suitors. I would add that he acts deliberately to keep himself in total opposition to the suitors regarding physical circumstances as if savouring the irony: the usurpers enjoy all the comforts of the palace while the rightful king has no more than a beggar. It is good story-telling art to exploit this inversion of the norm, so that the final retribution is all the more satisfying.

338. ὄρεα νιφόεντα: the final -α of ὄρεα is lengthened by the following ν-. Liquids and ς often have the power to act like double consonants; but in some cases the lengthening can be attributed to a lost consonant, and here we may have the residual force of an original *σνιφ- (Monro, *Homeric Dialect*, 344–6).

342. ἄεσα: the first aor. of ἰαύω (ἰάϝω): ἄϝεσα > ἄεσα. Cf. ἄσαμεν at xvi 367.

344-5. The allusion is to the verbal indignities inflicted upon him by Melantho at 95 ff. and by her and her cohorts at xviii 320 ff.

346-8. The scholia tell us three verses were athetized, and give as reasons that (1) Odysseus should not be depicted choosing the very woman who can penetrate his disguise; (2) the phrase 'who has suffered as much as I' is ludicrous; and (3) that φθονέω is incorrectly used in 348 since one can 'begrudge' only what is valuable to someone else, and there is nothing valuable in the task of washing the beggar's feet. Such objections are effectively refuted by W. Büchner, *RMus* lxxx (1931), 129–36, who points out that (1) Odysseus has no reason to fear exposure through Eurycleia, until he recalls the tell-tale scar, which comes to mind *suddenly* (αὐτίκα) as a problem he had overlooked (390–1); (2) the assumption that the nurse has had grief comparable to his may seem inappropriate to the role of Cretan wanderer, but is an appropriate assumption for Odysseus as king to make about the utterly loyal and loving servant who would have grieved for her missing king (such small lapses from the assumed disguise are present elsewhere and heighten the dramatic tension); and (3) saying he will not begrudge the touching of his feet is another example of the king in Odysseus overcoming the constraints of the disguise: it is an honour to touch a king's feet.

346. τις γρῆυς ... παλαιή: is Odysseus here specifically thinking of Eurycleia, or is he merely seeking someone totally different from the faithless maids and has he not yet noticed (or remembered) Eurycleia? Büchner, op. cit., argues convincingly that Odysseus has seen Eurycleia and inferred correctly that she will be summoned in answer to his request; that he is confident she cannot recognize him; and that his motive in contriving to have *her* wash his feet is to get the much-needed emotional satisfaction of contact with a dear old figure from his childhood. Homer's narrative art turns this attempted manœuvre of Odysseus into a 'reversal' (peripety) that leads to 'recognition' (anagnorisis). Aristotle cited this very passage as an example of the best kind of recognition, *Po.* 1454 b 25.

358. An exciting moment in the poem as a *heard* narrative, and a good example of the poet playing with his audience's expectations. For a fraction of a second, before ὁμήλικα joins the other members of its clause, we hear a construction that leads us to think Penelope has somehow penetrated Odysseus' disguise and is revealing his secret. Since foot-washing is the topic, and we have heard ἥ σε πόδας νίψει at 356, we (and Homer's audience) expect νίψον to take its most natural object, πόδας, 'wash your master's feet'. Homer teases us and then moves the sentence into a construction that reveals no secrets. Using the word 'age-mate' does, however, require Penelope to explain why she has made this sudden and unexpected comparison between the stranger and her husband; the words καί που introduce such an explanation.

359. Hands and feet are noticed by Homer as commonly as facial features are noticed by us today. Recall that when Telemachus was recognized as Odysseus' son at Sparta, Helen noted their resemblance in hands and feet as well as in eyes, head, and hair (iv 149–50).

363–70. Eurycleia begins her speech by addressing the lost Odysseus, a powerful dramatic device that startles us by its unexpectedness, and derives power from the fact that Odysseus is directly in front of her. Homer teases his audience, as at 358, by manipulating his language to give the illusion— impossible though it be—that Odysseus' disguise has been penetrated and the nurse is addressing the beggar. The verbal surprises continue when at 370 Eurycleia abruptly switches to third person reference to the absent king—cf. κείνῳ to the τοι οἴῳ in the line immediately preceding—and now begins using second person address to the beggar before her (σέθεν in 372).

370-85. The rhetorical devices noted in 358 and 363-70 have begun a process of associating the newly arrived stranger with Odysseus through their *physical* resemblance (earlier their association was based on the guest-friendship alleged by Odysseus) and the interchangeability of their unhappy destinies, subtly reinforced by the interchangeability of the second and third persons in Eurycleia's speech. Now the faithful nurse's statement that the beggar and the absent king have shared similar ill treatment yields the irony that, like Penelope's observation at 358-9, it is truer than the speaker thinks, since their condition and treatment are not *similar* but *identical*. From this she moves to the simplest and strongest point of comparison: the stranger looks remarkably like Odysseus in build, voice, and feet. Odysseus has no choice but to agree, and tries to protect himself by saying that the similarity has often been observed. At this point anyone hearing the narrative must feel that a revelation is about to burst forth. But Homer has other plans. He has led us carefully toward a climax, only to avert it.

389-90. αἶψα· | αὐτίκα: these two words allow us to reject any idea that Odysseus is seeking to bring about a recognition of his identity. Homer emphasizes the *suddenness* with which Odysseus realizes that his disguise can be penetrated. The verb tenses also contribute to this emphasis: his sitting is a continuing condition (impf. ἷζεν), suddenly interrupted by his turning away (aor. ἐτράπετ').

392. Dramatic effect is again served by aspectual contrast in the verbs: the process of Eurycleia's impf. νίζε is interrupted by the aorist in αὐτίκα δ' ἔγνω.

393. οὐλήν, τήν: with this relative clause begins the most famous digression in all literature. The poet has so far been exploiting a variety of small verbal and rhetorical devices to titillate his audience. Now he undertakes a large digression (393-466) on the circumstances behind the scar, a device of retardation of the narrative at just the point where Odysseus' disguise seems to have finally been penetrated. The mixture of emotions in the listener—frustration at the retardation, excitement at the threat of discovery, enjoyment of the digression as a story in its own right—reminds us that the audience and not just the poet contributes to the experience and form of a poetic genre.

393-466. The story, in 'flashback' technique, of the boar hunt on Parnassus. A clear formal analysis is given by J. Gaisser in *HSCPh* lxxiii (1969), 20-1, who follows the lead of W. van Otterlo, *Mededeelingen der Nederlandsche Akademie van Wetenschappen* (1944), nos. 1-6, pp. 131-76; *Mnemosyne* xii (1945), 194-207; and *De Ringcompositie als Opbouwprincipie in de Epische Gedichte van Homerus* (Amsterdam, 1948). Van Otterlo showed that digressions tend to be enclosed or framed by similar language used at the beginning and end of the passage. In this story of the scar, the relative pronoun τήν that opens the digression at 393 returns to close it at 467, and the entire wording of 393–4 is closely echoed at 465–6. The structure of this digression conforms to what Gaisser calls 'the complex cyclic style': two concentric rings frame the story (392–3 ~ 467–8, 393–4 ~ 465–6), which is itself organized into a ring form, in which Odysseus' visit to Parnassus is framed by the four related verses 413–14 and 459–60, which themselves offer an ABBA pattern (414 = 459, 413 ~ 460). Gaisser notes that this complex cyclic composition is rare in the *Odyssey* but characteristic of the *Iliad* (pp. 37–43).

394. Αὐτόλυκον: Odysseus' maternal grandfather is significantly named: αὐτό-λυκος suggests 'the wolf himself' or 'the very wolf'. The brief portrait given in this passage shows a man impressive for his ability to come out on top in his dealings with others, who approaches such dealings always in an adversary manner, whose intelligence is used entirely for self-serving purposes. Autolycus is thus the prototype of Odysseus' personality seen in its most negative aspect. An excellent discussion of Odysseus' 'Autolycan' nature is that of W. B. Stanford, *The Ulysses Theme* (Oxford, 1963), ch. 2. An interesting if speculative interpretation of Autolycus as a folklore figure with magical powers ('ein Hexenmeister') is offered by K. Marót, 'Autolykos', in *Minoica und Homer*, ed. Georghiev and Irmscher (Berlin, 1961). The inauspicious quality of anyone whose name is 'Wolf' is too evident to need elaboration: cf. the well-known myth of King Lykaon who is transformed into a wolf (Apollod. iii 8. 1; Paus. viii 2–3; Clem. Al., *Protr.* ii 36; Ov., *Met.* i 163 ff., and others), sometimes because of the impiety of his sons (so Apollodorus) but in most accounts because he himself tried to deceive a divine guest by serving him a slaughtered human in the guise of food. The offences of Autolycus recorded in Greek tradition are consonant with Homer's description here. In *Il.* x 266 we learn he stole a helmet decorated with boar's tusks from Amyntor; Hesiod, fr. 67b M–W, tells us that he 'made anything invisible that he handled', and comments at *EM* s.v. ἀείδελον and Tzetzes in Lycophron 344 describe Autolycus as a thief of horses, cattle, and sheep, who was successful through his trick of changing the animals' brands so as to deceive their owners. These qualities were commonly connected to the fact that Hermes was not just the patron of Autolycus (as 396–7 suggests) but his *father* (Hes., fr. 64 M–W; Eust. ad xix 416; and the Athenian historian Pherecydes, quoted in the Scholia to xix 432).

403. θῆαι: the second aorist subjunctive, middle voice. Many MSS offer variants with optative forms, but a subjunctive is most natural after the imperative εὕρεο.

404. πολυάρητος: the same adjective, 'much prayed for', is used for the newborn Demophoon at *h. Cer.* 220. It comes near being a proper name (Stanford compares the Biblical 'Samuel' and the modern 'Desirée'; and note that Queen Arete, xiii 57, has a name of similar meaning). Eurycleia may be hinting that Polyaretos would be an appropriate name for the newborn child. If so, the name Odysseus with its negative associations (note to 407), given instead· of Polyaretos, comes as a surprising but meaningful contrast, and strengthens the value of Odysseus' name as an omen of a life that will be filled with trouble.

407. ὀδυσσάμενος: this verb has been used throughout the poem in a punning relationship to the hero's name (i 67, v 340, 423, xix 275). Because all occurrences are in the aorist or perfect tense, we can only conjecture a present *ὀδύ(σ)ομαι, whose meaning is 'to become angry at' or 'to take a dislike to', with some uncertainty as to whether *anger* or *hatred* (a possible cognate with Latin *odium*) or *pain* (a possible cognate with ὀδύνη or ὀδύρομαι) is the fundamental meaning of this word. Autolycus' statement here is the sole use of the verb in a context that makes the pun on Odysseus' name explicit and offers an etymology. Since Autolycus in his career as trickster has dealt harshly with many men and women, the child, as Autolycus' heir, will be 'Odysseus', 'the man who deals out harsh treatment'. The suffix -ευς points to such an active sense. This interpretation is close to that of L. Ph. Rank, *Etymologiseering en verwante verschijnselen bij Homerus* (Assen, 1951), 51–65, who believes that Odysseus' name contains two meanings, 'The Hater' and 'The Hated', with the first meaning clearly predominant. An older view, seen in the scholia and Eustathius and revived by Stanford in his Commentary and in *CPh* xlvii (1952), 209–13, prefers the 'ethical' interpretation of Odysseus as the 'man of suffering', and hence prefers a passive, or reciprocal and generalized, sense for the participle ὀδυσσάμενος, 'having quarrelled', or 'having incurred and expressed wrath'. In this view, Odysseus means 'Child of Woe'. See further Clay, *Wrath*, 54–64. Acknowledging the simultaneous presence of an active and passive meaning in Odysseus' name allows us to see him as a distant relative of the Trickster figure of folklore and mythology, who is both deceiver and victim of deception, both the cause of pain to others and the recipient of pain. See P. Radin, *The Trickster* (New York, 1956), xxiii.

409. ὄνομ'... ἐπώνυμον: the concept of an 'eponymous name' contains a word-play in Greek. It is attractive, but not necessary, to construe ὄνομ' ἐπώνυμον as an accusative of specification, with Ὀδυσεύς as subject: 'Therefore, let him be "Odysseus", as his signifying name.' So Rank, op. cit. 57 n. 83, citing Hes., *Th.* 144, Κύκλωπες δ' ὄνομ' ἦσαν ἐπώνυμον where the pl. ἦσαν shows ὄνομ' to be such an accusative.

413. Here we resume the narrative thread interrupted by the subordinate clause at 395. Homeric digressions like this one serve the important function of providing background information that is vital for a full appreciation of the situation illuminated as foreground. On the narrative level, Odysseus owes Autolycus a visit to claim the promised gifts. On the symbolic level (see G. Dimock, 'The Name of Odysseus', in *Essays on the Odyssey*, ed. C. Taylor (Bloomington, 1963, he is 'earning' the name Odysseus, which promises pain and trouble. The boar hunt and wounding thus have some of the qualities of an initiation.

439-43. The boar's lair described here closely resembles the shelter seen at the end of v, formed by the growing together of two bushes, olive and the obscure φυλίη, in which the exhausted Odysseus finds protection from the cold by burying himself in the leaves, like a seed of fire to be reborn the next day. Verses 440–2 are nearly identical to v 478–80, while 443 reproduces most of v 483. It is surprising that there should be an underlying connection between the lair of Odysseus and the lair of the boar that gave him his identifying wound. The poet has perhaps made an unconscious association based on the concept of birth/rebirth. Just as the 'seed of fire' ensures that a new fire will be born, so Odysseus, in his encounter with the boar, will be (re)born as the man with the scar, which becomes the sign of his identity for those people closest to him.

450. The verb διαφύσσειν is regularly used of 'drawing off' wine from a larger jar into a smaller vessel. In this verse we would seem to have a forceful image, depicting the flesh as scooped out or drawn away as if it were mere liquid in contrast to the hard tusk. Since the same metaphor is used at *Il.* xiii 507, xiv 517, it may have been a conventional part of epic diction and may therefore have been less vivid than it seems to us.

454. The normal Homeric belief was that the θυμός leaves the body or is breathed out when a warrior (e.g. *Il.* xx 403, 406) or an animal (e.g. *Il.* xvi 469) dies. (Further discussion and examples in the note to xx 304.) Of the several Homeric meanings of θυμός, this is probably the most archaic, preserving some of the semantic connection with its Latin cognate *fumus*, which suggests a vaporous animating principle whose loss is the physiological cause of fainting and of death. See Onians, *Origins*, 44 ff.

457-8. ἐπαοιδῇ δ' αἷμα ... ἔσχεθον: a rare reference to the archaic belief in the magical power of sung charms. The use of the ἐπαοιδή to staunch the flow of blood is not, however, an archaic *survival* from a lost past but one of the rare intrusions from the stratum of popular belief and practice into the normally more refined and aristocratic world of the epics. The *Odyssey* is closer than the *Iliad* to this popular world. Faced with a similar medical crisis in the *Iliad*, Patroclus resorts not to magic but to a medicinal root (xi 846–8), knowledge of which goes back to the centaur Cheiron (xi 832). While this root may have power that is supernatural, its use is described in realistic medical terms.

467. τὴν: this substantive pronoun refers to the scar, οὐλὴν, mentioned three lines earlier, and resumes the reference to the scar made at 393, where τήν as a relative pronoun served to introduce the lengthy digression. λαβοῦσα: this word resumes the idea μή ἑ λαβοῦσα | οὐλὴν of 390–1, and fulfils the condition imagined there.

469-72. Homer's description of Eurycleia's reaction attains a high degree of vividness through combination of unusual rhythm, sound, and conceptualization. 469 has the relatively unusual word-end in the first short syllable of the second foot, the sound η four times, and heavy alliteration of κ–κ–χ–χ–κ. 470 has two χ–θ combinations near the verse end. 471 offers the oxymoron of ἄμα χάρμα καὶ ἄλγος. 472 describes Eurycleia's emotions as having the powerful effect of blocking both her speech and her vision.

473. The conventions of supplication were to touch the chin, and often to clasp the knees, of the person supplicated. It is a common attitude depicted on vase paintings, and an important Iliadic motif: see *Il.* i 500ff., viii 371–2, x 454–5, xxi 67ff., xxiv 477–9. See further Hainsworth on vi 110–250.

474–5. The first words Odysseus' old nurse speaks to him are subtly chosen by Homer so as to be quite moving: she calls him both 'dear child' and 'my lord' in the same sentence, beginning with her earliest and most private relationship to him, and then shifting to the external reality of the newly discovered situation (ἄνακτ' ἐμόν).

478–9. These two verses are the biggest obstacle to the theory that Homer has tried to describe in this book a subtle and veiled awareness on Penelope's part of the identity of the stranger.

482. τίη μ' ἐθέλεις ὀλέσαι: it is nicely in character for Odysseus to use mocking irony at the very moment when his safety has been jeopardized and he is most upset. Irony requires deliberate control, a quality that Odysseus never loses.

487–90. Odysseus' statement of intentions may seem excessively cruel if we fail to take into account what is implied by the γάρ: 'for (if you do *not* keep quiet) I declare as follows.'

489. οὔσης: this seems an Attic form, whereas epic should have the uncontracted ἐούσης. Perhaps we should assume ἐούσης with synizesis underlying the οὔσης transmitted by the MSS.

501. φράσομαι καὶ εἴσομ' ἑκάστην: Odysseus' claim to be able to deduce for himself who the offenders are is borne out at the beginning of xx, where he finds the faithless maids conspicuous in their behaviour.

505. λίπ' ἐλαίῳ: a fixed formula: λίπ' is always used in this position in the line, with ἐλαίῳ in 9 of its 10 Homeric occurrences (the exception is λίπ' ἄλειψεν vi 227), always elided. The form is most likely an adv. like κάρτα, λίγα, πύκα, τάχα, possibly the survival of an old instrumental case. Some scholars have proposed the elided -ᾳ (-αι) or -ι of a dative λίπαι or λίπι (Leumann, *Wörter*, 309–10). At a later period Thucydides and Hippocrates use the unelided phrase λίπα ἀλείφεσθαι, which shows they understood λίπα as an adverb or adverbial neuter. Homer's meaning then is 'rubbed him with oil richly'.

513. τέρπομ' ὀδυρομένη: the apparent paradox in construing this phrase—how can one 'take pleasure in grieving'?—has led some commentators to reserve τέρπομαι for the following verse, to be construed with ὁρόωσα, 'I enjoyed looking after my work'. But τέρπομαι often has the special meaning to indulge in something (even grief) to the point of satisfaction, as seen in the common phrase τέρπεσθαι γόοιο, xi 212, xix 213, 257, xxi 57; *Il.* xxiii 10, 98, xxiv 513. τέρπομαι is also used with the datives γόῳ and ἄλγεσι. Onians, *Origins*, 20–1, has an excellent analysis of this word and how it differs from other terms of emotional involvement.

516–17. πυκιναὶ ... ἀδινὸν κῆρ ... μελεδῶναι: an ABA word pattern intensifies the force of an already powerful combination. The adjectives πυκιναὶ and ἀδινὸν are close in meaning and can be translated as 'crowding' and 'crowded'. Penelope uses the similar phrase πυκινῶς ἀκαχήμενος ἦτορ at xx 84, after referring to a different sad episode in the story of Pandareos' daughters to describe her unhappiness.

518–24. The story of Pandareos' daughter, the nightingale, as told here, is not known from any other ancient source. The story familiar to us from Attic authors is of Pandion's two daughters, Procne and Philomela. Procne married Tereus and they had a son Itys. Tereus seduced Philomela and cut out her tongue to prevent her from telling what he had done, but she managed to communicate the truth to Procne by weaving the words in a robe, whereupon Procne took revenge on Tereus by killing their son and serving him as food to his father. Tereus learned the facts, pursued the sisters to kill them, and the gods turned all three into birds. Procne became the nightingale, Philomela the swallow, Tereus the hoopoe. This full account is in Apollod. iii 14. 8. Allusions to the nightingale's lament for her son are a common topos in Greek poetry (A. *Ag.* 1144; S. *El.* 148; Ar. *Av.* 228, E. fr. 773N, 22–5). The scholia on this Homeric passage tell a different story: the nightingale is personified as Aedon, wife of Zethos, who was jealous of her sister-in-law Niobe's large family and attempted to kill Niobe's son, but in error killed her own son. This story may be an earlier variant of the Attic tale, or perhaps a fiction largely invented by the scholia, which misunderstood ἀηδών of 518 as a proper name. The variation in the names Pandareos and Pandion, Itylos and Itys, recalls other examples where Homer's version of a tale or myth seems a variant on the better known version: e.g. Epicaste instead of Iocaste as Oedipus' mother, and the fact that Oedipus continued to rule in Thebes even after his secret was revealed (xi 271–80).

Penelope is probably alluding to a story quite similar to the tale of Tereus, Procne, and Itys, which offers a significant parallel to her own situation in some particulars. She resembles the nightingale in the frequency and intensity of her lamentation (cf. πυκιναί and ἀδινόν, 516, with θαμά, 521). From her admission that her heart is divided, 524, we may read into her account of Pandareos' daughter the implication that the nightingale killed her own son not by mistake, as in the scholia's explanation, but 'in her senseless folly', like Procne, which is a better meaning for δι' ἀφραδίης of 523. Penelope's choice of this comparison to express her mental state is, moreover, appropriate because she harbours a fear that she too may cause the death of her own son, if she continues, by refusing marriage, to exasperate the suitors and drive them to desperate plots against Telemachus. See further 525–34 n.

518. χλωρηΐς: a *hapax*, which some have taken to mean the same as χλωρός. The nightingale, however, is not green. Hesiod, *Op.* 203, calls it ἀηδόνα ποικιλόδειρον, and Simonides also refers to its neck, ἀηδόνες πολυκώτιλοι χλωραύχενες, fr. 45 D (= *PMG* 586), which may refer to a green-necked variety known to him, but more probably is a literary imitation of this Homeric passage. I incline to Monro's view that the longer form χλωρηΐς suggests more than simply 'green', the suffix denoting one who does something related to greenery. This is the view of the scholia, which explain that the nightingale is seen among green foliage, and alternatively that she appears with the first green of spring. Analogous forms like βορηίς, βασιληίς, ποταμηίς, ἀλσηίς (see Buck and Petersen, *A Reverse Index of Greek Nouns and Adjectives* (Chicago, 1945), 418 ff.) are always simple adjectives, but they are all built on nouns and so offer no real parallel to χλωρηίς. Perhaps the closest parallels are Homeric proper names like Chryseis, 'she of Chryses', which suggests that the nightingale is 'she of the green'.

525-34. A clear description of the dilemma that forms the 'political' basis of the plot. The pressure of community opinion, δήμοιο φῆμιν, and her loyalty to Odysseus' memory, εὐνήν τ' αἰδομένη, were sufficient reasons for Penelope to keep the estate intact and refuse to remarry. The needs of the *immature* Telemachus coincided with this choice (530-1). But now Telemachus is a man, and his mother sees his growing anger over the suitors' wanton consumption of his inheritance, and his need to take charge of his property. She also knows clearly that the increasingly open hostility between Telemachus and the suitors can lead to his death: cf. xvi 411-12, 418-23.

530. ἧος: for this single word the MSS have ἕως μεν, scanned – ∪. For ἧος (and τῆος) the MSS regularly give ἕως or εἵως (τέως or τείως), usually disyllabic as trochee or spondee, rarely iambic, and occasionally monosyllabic, as here, with synizesis (see Chantraine, *Grammaire*, i. 111-12). Attempts to correlate these metathesized forms with supposed 'late' passages (Shipp, *Studies*, 8-9) are subjective and inconclusive: ἕως μεν here has apparently replaced the ἧος of an earlier pre-Homeric stage. For further discussion of this vexed question, see nn. at iii 126, iv 90, v 123, 365, xiii 315, and M. L. West, *Glotta*, xliv (1967), 135-9.

535-53. Some readers have thought it inappropriate for the queen to divulge the content of her dream to an unknown beggar; and others have taken it as a sign that she suspects or knows that he is Odysseus and is cleverly asking for his advice and collusion. But Homer has provided fully adequate motivation for this intimacy: see 253-4 (with n.), 350-2, and the content of her speeches, where she has revealed more and more details to him of her situation *vis-à-vis* the suitors and of her innermost feelings.

535. τὸν ὄνειρον: τόν = 'this', as often in Homer, most frequently seen in the references to Odysseus as ὁ ξεῖνος (xvii 10n.). ὑπόκριναι καὶ ἄκουσον: an instance of hysteron-proteron, where the second of two ideas is named first, often because it is felt to be the more important or essential fact. Other good examples are iii 457, iv 50, 208, 723 v 264, *Il.* xxi 537, xxiv 206. The classic study is by S. E. Bassett, Ὕστερον πρότερον Ὁμηρικῶς, *HSPh* 31 (1928), 39-62, who shows that the principle affects not only single words but also larger statements, e.g. questions in a dialogue, which are commonly answered in reverse order. For the semantic range of ὑποκρίνομαι see Hoekstra, xv 170n.

537. ἐξ ὕδατος: construe either with πυρόν, as if the grain was in the trough (the πύελον of 553), or in a general sense with χῆνες describing their

COMMENTARY

location, 'away from (out of) the water', as seen in ἐκ καπνοῦ κατέθηκα, xix
7 = xvi 288, or ἐχώμεθα . . . ἐκ βελέων, Il. xiv 129–30.

539. κατ' αὐχέν' ἔαξε: tmesis for κατῆξε, which normally appears as
κατέαξε. The MSS read αὐχένας ἧξε. **ἐκέχυντο:** the verb χέω
combines the ideas of strewing about and piling up something on the
ground. The dead geese were 'strewn (piled) close together in the hall'.
Homer has sustained a (perhaps unconscious) connection with the suitors
in his choice of verb. After they are slain Homer uses the same verb,
κέχυντο, xxii 389, to describe their bodies, and also of the fish to which they
are likened in a vivid simile: κέχυνται, 387.

541. The fact that Penelope lamented so intensely (κλαῖον, ἐκώκυον, 541;
ὀλοφυρομένην, 543), combined with her statement that her spirit was
cheered (ἰαίνομαι, 537) seeing the geese, reveals—as dreams often do—
feelings kept beneath the threshold of consciousness because they are
unacceptable to the moral censor of the waking mind. The lonely queen
obviously derived some cheer from the attentions of the suitors, and
would, on an unconscious level, regret their sudden slaughter (see G. Devereux, in *Psychoanalytic Quarterly* xxvi (1957), 381–2; but the remainder of
this article, suggesting an earlier tradition of a faithless Penelope, is
totally unconvincing). The symbolism of this dream is reinforced by the
fact that the single activity that characterizes the geese is *eating* (553),
which is the most conspicuous activity of the suitors. Of several dreams in
Homer, only this one resembles a true dream: its message is hidden in a
symbolic code. The other dreams in Homer avoid psychological realism
and follow a literary convention that includes long speeches to the person
sleeping (G. Devereux, *Dreams in Greek Tragedy* (Oxford, 1976), xxv).

543. Penelope's words contain suggestive ambiguities. The μοι can be
understood as simple possessive with χῆνας, as in 536 when they are introduced as 'my geese'. But another association of μοι is with ἔκτανε, 'he
killed them for me', a dative of 'disadvantage'. A third and more
submerged association is found by reading μοι αἰετὸς as 'my eagle', an
irony in that Penelope does not yet know that the eagle is more truly hers
than the geese are. The eagle himself brings forth this latent association in
his choice of words at 548–9, where the suggestive τοι of ἐγὼ δέ τοι αἰετὸς
ὄρνις ἦα πάρος passes into the emphatic τέος of νῦν αὖτε τέος πόσις
εἰλήλουθα.

547. ὄναρ . . . ὕπαρ: ὄναρ is a dream, ὕπαρ, as the scholia say, 'a dream that
appears in the daytime'. Dreams are often deceptive in Homer (see 562–7
below, and recall the dream Zeus sends to deceive Agamemnon at Il. ii
5 ff.), but a daytime vision is more likely to be true. See the note to xx 90.

552. παπτήνασα: the perfect word to describe Penelope's cautious look to
see whether the geese are still alive. It is the same verb used for Odysseus'
cautious peeking out to see whether any of the suitors are still alive at
xxii 381.

555. ὑποκρίνασθαι: this word commonly refers to giving an answer in the form of a response that interprets an oracle or omen. Cf. *Il.* v 150, τοῖς οὐκ ἐρχομένοις ὁ γέρων ἐκρίνατ' ὀνείρους.

562. ἀμενηνῶν: a word of obscure meaning. The dominant view, e.g. Bechtel, *Lexilogus*, 37, sees a privative compound based on μένος, 'energy', 'spirit'. Stanford suggests a compound of α-privative plus μένω, 'remain', meaning 'fleeting'. But 'strengthless' is not only far more appropriate to the contexts where ἀμενηνός is used, it is virtually demanded by the use of the verb ἀμενηνόω at *Il.* xiii 562.

562-3. A doubꞇᴇ set of gates, of which one set is made of ivory and one of horn or horns (the pl. noun κεράεσσι seems to be substitutable for the sing. adj. in Homeric diction, as at xix 211). Generations of scholars have puzzled over the symbolism of this passage and the reasons for associating horn with truth and ivory with deception. An etymologizing connection of ἐλέφας with ἐλεφαίρομαι (565) and κέρας with κραίνω (567) is probably intended by the poet; but whether this causes, or derives from, the horn-ivory symbolism is unclear. The fullest discussion is by E. L. Highbarger, *The Gates of Dreams* (Baltimore, 1940), who takes κεράεσσι as 'horns' not 'horn', referring to a pair of horns which he connects with the Gates of Heaven in Egyptian and Mesopotamian mythology. The prominence given in Crete to sacred horns could well derive from this eastern source. While Highbarger's connections are not fully convincing, I suggest that the importance of horns in early Greek religion raises the possibility that Homer has preserved the memory of the gateway of horns (or horn) as symbol of the passageway to a higher, more permanent reality. A different approach by Anne Amory, *YCS* xx (1966), 1–57, rejects speculation about archaic inherited symbols and argues instead for Homer's use of horn and ivory as antithetical symbols representing Odysseus' and Penelope's contrasting approaches to reality at several places in the poem.

565-7. ἐλεφαίρονται is of disputed meaning and etymology. Most critics see in the present passage a contrast between false or deceptive dreams and true ones, but this distinction may be due to the influence of Vergil's famous imitation, *Aeneid* vi 893–6, with its opposition between *veris umbris* and *falsa insomnia*. Homer's meaning is unclear because each verbal phrase describing what each group of dreams does is open to two interpretations. ἐλεφαίρομαι is defined as 'to cheat' or (its unmistakeable meaning at Hes. *Th.* 330) 'to damage'. But 'to cheat' has no real basis in Greek usage and seems to be the creation of lexicographers based on a misreading of this passage. ἔτυμα κραίνουσι can mean 'fulfil things that are real' or 'really have power' (ἔτυμα as adverbial, κραίνω in its less common meaning shown at viii 390–1, where δώδεκα βασιλῆες κραίνουσι means 'twelve kings have power': see Amory, op. cit., 22–8). Penelope's meaning, then, is that dreams from the ivory gate are harmful because they bring messages that are believed and acted upon but not ultimately *fulfilled* (ἀκράαντα), whereas those from the gate of horn *do* really come true (ἔτυμα κραίνουσι, however interpreted, is antithetical to ἀκράαντα). The assumption is that all dreams are messages to be acted upon, and if

Penelope interprets the dream wrongly and acts upon it, its message will be
'unfulfilled' and the dream, through Penelope's actions, can cause harm
(ἐλεφαίρονται). This interpretation is close to that of Amory, op. cit.

568. αἰνὸν ὄνειρον: commentators have been bothered by the supposed
inappropriateness of αἰνὸν characterizing a dream of Odysseus' much-
awaited return. But if we recall Penelope's deep upset in the dream, we see
that she is here accurately recording her distress at the scene of violence
which led her to weep.

572–81. Why does the queen decide *at this point* to set the contest of the bow
for the very next day and stake her entire future on its outcome? This
question remains one of the fundamental problems for any interpretation
of xix and the consistency of Homer's portrait of Penelope. Since she has
the best reasons now for believing in her husband's imminent return (the
emphatic assurances of Theoclymenus at xvii 152–61, of the beggar at xix
262–307, and the manifest message of the dream itself), why not delay the
marriage for a few more days and expect that Odysseus will arrive in time?
The problem has recently been restated in its full difficulty by F. M.
Combellack, 'Three Odyssean Problems', *California Studies in Classical
Antiquity* vi (1973), 32–40, who provides no answer. Two easy solutions
remain unattractive: (1) that Penelope has seen through Odysseus' disguise
and can assume he will string the bow tomorrow (Harsh, op. cit.); (2) that
we have before us the imperfectly adjusted conflation of an earlier and a
revised *Odyssey*, so that Penelope's decision is the awkward residue of a
version in which husband and wife plot together to kill the suitors (Amphimedon's plausible but erroneous reconstruction of events at xxiv 125 ff.,
and the similar reconstructions of Page, *Odyssey*, 123–4, Kirk, *Songs*, 246–7,
and the German Analytic tradition that preceded them). The second
explanation, while more plausible, assumes a poet or later redactor who
could be content with major narrative inconsistency, an impression belied
by the subtle and effective storytelling technique found throughout xix.
The first assumes that an event of the utmost significance has transpired in
xix but has been kept out of sight by the poet, which is hardly Homer's
manner.

It is tempting to view the bow-contest as another stalling tactic similar to
Penelope's trick of the web, if we can assume that she has genuine hope,
despite her self-protective protestation to the contrary at 568, that her
dream did in fact issue through the gates of horn (her emphatic wish at 569;
we must remember that Penelope often uses speech as a protective shield
rather than as a naïve mirror of her thoughts, as discussed at length in my
Introduction). This interpretation seems weakened, however, by her
apparent belief that the contest will result in her marriage to one of the
suitors (xix 571–2; xx 61–90, esp. 80–2; and possibly her weeping at xxi
55–6). We must concede that Homer keeps us from fathoming Penelope's
mind completely: we cannot estimate the mixture of expectations that
prompts her decision, and so it remains mysterious. See N. Felson-Rubin,
'Penelope's Perspective: Character from Plot', in J. M. Bremer *et al.*, edd.,

Homer: Beyond Oral Poetry (Amsterdam, 1986), for an intriguing 'narratological' explanation in which the unfathomability of Penelope's motives results from her participation in simultaneous multiple marriage-plots, and from a complicity between author and character to keep her from clarifying her motivation by accepting any single plot.

Other explanations include the theory that her unconscious attraction to the beggar and faith in his predictions lead Penelope to a bold intuitive gamble at this point (Russo, *AJPh* ciii (1982), 4–18; that Penelope uses the contest as a test of her own correct reading of the stranger's identity (Austin, *Archery*, 230–2, following Amory, 'Reunion'); that she is carrying out Odysseus' parting request that she remarry when Telemachus gets his first beard, as well as acting to protect her son (Thornton, *People*, 103–5); that we have here the elevation of coincidence to a major structuring device of plot (O. Seel, 'Variante und Konvergenz in der Odyssee', in *Studi in onore di U. E. Paoli* (Firenze, 1956)), or, in more existentialist tonality, that we have a 'self-conscious and disturbing use of chance for the resolution of a plot', a device that 'contradicts the poem's dominant and more comforting assumptions' that strong characters can control the events that shape their happiness (S. Murnaghan, *Disguise and Recognition in the Odyssey* (Princeton, 1987), 134, and see further 133–7).

574. δρυόχους: literally 'wood-holders' or 'ship-holders': the wooden props that support the frame of a ship under construction. To resemble such props, the axes must be aligned in a straight line, the heads down and the handles up. The details given at xxi 120–2, 420–2 (see n.) are not sufficient to allow us to draw this picture with certainty, but it is the likeliest reconstruction.

574-5. ἵστασχ'... διαρρίπτασκεν: the iterative suffixes show that this was a regular performance trick of Odysseus. Exactly what 'shoot an arrow through them' means has been much disputed. The interpreters' crux is the contradiction between Odysseus' statement at 587 that the shot will pass through *iron*, and the actual description of the shot at xxi 421–2 which specifies that he shoots through the *handle* of the axes. The problem vanishes if we assume that the axes are not everyday tools, but *votive* axes whose handle terminated in a metal ring that allowed the axes to hang from a peg. This interpretation, which goes back to C. Blinkenberg, *Archaeologische Studien* (1904), 31 ff., is recently defended in detail by Page, *Folktales*, 94–113 (originally in *Epistemonike Ephemeris* (Athens, 1964)), and A. Sacconi, *Un problema di Interpretazione Omerica* (Rome, 1971). Interesting criticisms of this solution, however, are raised by C. Gallavotti, *Studi micenei ed egeo-anatolici* xv (1972), 17–24, who notes that votive axes found from the Minoan and Mycenaean periods are too small to be used as we have imagined here. We are dealing then with poetic fancy distorting a distant memory of earlier times.

587. διοϊστεῦσαί τε σιδήρου: the argument of the preceding note would allow us to interpret σιδήρου as the series of holes in the iron rings on the handles. An alternative interpretation is given by W. Burkert in *Grazer*

Beiträge i (1971), 69–78, who collects Egyptian evidence to show that Amenophis II (1447–1420) demonstrated his royal strength by shooting through thick sheets of copper. Artistic representations made the targets look like axes, and may therefore have been the source, through Syrian, Hittite, and Hurrian intermediaries, of the Homeric tradition that kings showed their legitimacy by shooting through axes. Such an interpretation requires one, however, to argue that στειλειῆς at xxi 422 means something other than 'handle'.

589–90. A final expression of the degree to which this stranger has entered into the queen's affections. Her instincts draw her to this man who has the power to give her pleasure, τέρπειν, simply by his presence, παρήμενος, and his constant supportive statements (300–7, 557–9, 585–7) that affirm the imminent arrival of Odysseus. We may see here an anticipation of the extra-long night in which Odysseus and Penelope have their full reunion and Odysseus fulfils the wish that his wife voices here: ἡ δ' ἄρα τέρπετ' ἀκούουσ', οὐδέ οἱ ὕπνος | πῖπτεν ἐπὶ βλεφάροισι πάρος καταλέξαι ἅπαντα, xxiii 308–9.

597. Κακοΐλιον οὐκ ὀνομαστήν: (= xxiii 19) Ilion is 'not nameable' because of the intense resentment Penelope has toward that place, and so she substitutes a punning pejorative version of its name. The same verbal device was commented on at xviii 73. Cf. also *Il.* iii 39, xiii 769 for Hector's pun on Paris' name, Δύσπαρι.

598–9. λεξαίμην· σὺ δὲ λέξεο: Penelope's specifying the difference in her and her new friend's sleeping quarters seems to answer to an unexpressed sexual undercurrent that runs throughout their lengthy scene. The poet has brought their hearts close together, and will bring them still closer in the early part of xx. The language of 589–90 shows that Homer is anticipating their long night together in xxiii. Now he is making clear the distance that still separates the two, so that the scene can close, appropriately, with Penelope in her familiar private grief (595–6, 603). This narrative rhythm of approach and withdrawal informs the books from xvii to xxiii with a finely controlled tension and crescendo.

BOOK XX: COMMENTARY

This is one of the shorter books, and has been judged by some scholars as inferior in quality to the excellent books that precede and follow. It contains, however, some of Homer's most incisive description of his characters' deepest feelings. It also recapitulates and draws towards a climax several themes that have characterized the events in Ithaca since Telemachus and Odysseus arrived there. Finally, in the prophetic vision spoken by Theoclymenus, Book xx gives us one of Homer's most intense and unforgettable portrayals of the supernatural.

1. 1–55. Odysseus' seething emotions and active mind keep him from sleep. Athena descends and calms him, reassuring him of her aid for a final victory over the suitors.
2. 56–121. Penelope awakens and laments aloud, praying to Artemis for a painless death. Odysseus hears her, awakens, prays to Zeus for two signs, a verbal φήμη and a visible τέρας, and obtains both.
3. 122–240. The new day begins for the household: Telemachus arises and goes into town, Eurycleia orders the maids to prepare for the feast of Apollo. Eumaeus, Melanthius, and Philoetius arrive and address Odysseus each in his characteristic way.
4. 241–344. The suitors receive an unfavourable omen, abandon the plan to kill Telemachos, and return to feast at the palace. Telemachus asserts his right to protect the stranger; Ctesippus throws a cow's foot at the beggar but misses; Telemachus makes a bold speech, which Agelaus answers in a moderate way.
5. 345–94. Athena sends an unnatural seizure upon the suitors; Theoclymenus sees them as surrounded by portents of death, and leaves the house. The suitors return to mocking Telemachus for the kind of guests he has. The book closes by noting the rapport between father and son, Penelope listening from a distance, and the suitors in their ignorance enjoying their last meal on earth.

1. αὐτὰρ: xx is closely connected to xix, just as xix is to xviii, by this mildly adversative particle. The *Odyssey* six times begins a book with this word, the *Iliad* twice. Such an opening may suggest that the books so connected had come to be recited together as part of a longer recitation, with little or no pause between books. ὁ ἐν: such hiatus is rare, as Stanford notes, but what he cites as parallels (xiv 1, xix 1) are in fact the same formula, αὐτὰρ ὁ ἐν (ἐκ).
4. κοιμηθέντι: an ambiguous word, which would give the impression that Odysseus is asleep (especially following εὐνάζετο), until Homer tells us in the next verses that the hero's active mind is at work, plotting against the suitors.

6. ἐγρηγορόων: this irregular participial form of ἐγείρω, as if from the perf. ἐγρήγορα, occurs only here. The short vowel in -όων is created by *diektasis*, since we expect -άων from ἐγρήγορα (Chantraine, *Grammaire*, i 80, 359).

6-7. ἐκ μεγάροιο ... ἤϊσαν: they have to pass through the entrance-way (the πρόδομος of line 1) in order to leave the palace to keep the rendezvous with their lovers.

7. ἐμισγέσκοντο: normally augment is not used on iterative forms, and in the other exceptions we can usually restore the unaugmented form, as in παρακέσκετ' for παρεκέσκετ' at xiv 521, preserved by one MS.

9-10. θυμὸς ... θυμόν: it is noteworthy that θυμός is used in consecutive lines with different meanings. In 9 it is the *angry impulse* that rises up in Odysseus at the outrageous spectacle; but in 10 its use in a stock formula is equivalent to 'heart' or 'spirit'.

10-35. Such pondering of alternatives is one of Homer's 'typical scenes'. This one, however, is unique in the entire Homeric corpus, because it ends not in resolution or any decision but in the odd metaphor of Odysseus' heart barking. This metaphor then generates a simile, which leads Odysseus to address his heart in an admonishing speech. But even now the anxiety indicated by the introductory verb μεμήριζε does not subside, and the poet gives us another, even more homely, simile, and finally a divine intervention, in which Athena successfully calms Odysseus and puts him to sleep. A sequence of such length, deliberately extended by the juxtaposition of so many distinct units, is totally different from Homer's usual practice and is employed here to achieve an unusually strong intensification of the description of the hero's inner turmoil. The formal idiosyncracy of this scene is analysed by Chr. Voigt, *Überlegung und Entscheidung* (Berlin, 1933), 69–74, its untraditional intensity by J. Russo, *Arion* vii (1968), 275–95 (German version in J. Latacz, ed., *Homer: Tradition und Neuerung* (Darmstadt, 1979), 403–27).

14-16. ὡς δὲ ... ὥς ῥα ... ὑλάκτει: this wording shows how the simile is called forth as in effect a gloss on the striking metaphor κραδίη δέ οἱ ἔνδον ὑλάκτει of 13. For an examination of dogs in the *Odyssey*, as closely identified with Odysseus as protector and avenger, see G. P. Rose, 'Odysseus' Barking Heart', *TAPhA* cix (1979), 215–30. Rose suggests that the dog on the brooch at xix 228 ff. represents Odysseus and its victim, the helpless fawn, represents the suitors.

14. περὶ ... βεβῶσα: περιβαίνω is regular Iliadic usage for the act of standing over ('bestriding') a fallen comrade to protect him. It is easily used metaphorically, as at *Il.* i 37, where Apollo 'stands over' (i.e. protects) the land of Chryse. The transference of this idiom, from the battlefield to the household scene of the bitch with her puppies, is in keeping with the domestic setting and lowly circumstances in which the hero of the Trojan War, lord of this house, is forced to play his new role of beggar. Odysseus' rage at the maidservants reveals the possessiveness of the master beneath the beggar's disguise, and may also hint at sexual jealousy, since it was not uncommon for powerful nobles to have sexual relations with their female servants (i 429–33). In this sense (even though Odysseus did not intend sexual relations with the maids) they 'belonged' to him, which makes his extreme anger here more understandable. βεβῶσα: this form of the fem. participle is unique in Homer, who elsewhere uses βεβαυῖα.

18. τέτλαθι δή, κραδίη: direct address to one's heart or spirit will become a familiar device in lyric and dramatic poetry (e.g. Archilochus 67a D = 128 w, θυμέ, θυμ' ἀμηχάνοισι κήδεσιν κεκωμένε, ἄνσχεο; E. Med. 1056, μὴ δῆτα, θυμέ, μὴ σύ γ' ἐργάσῃ τάδε), but is rare in the epic genre which is more concerned with action than with reflection. Here it helps create a scene of unusual emotional intensity, reinforced by other atypical narrative devices (see 10–35, 24, 30 nn.). **κύντερον:** this comparative adj., 'more offensive', 'more shameless', is formed from the word 'dog'. The process of association by which the Greeks transformed the meaning 'dog-like' to that of 'without shame' is seen in Agamemnon's condemnation of Clytaemestra at xi 424–7, where he calls her κυνῶπις ('dog-faced') and adds that no other woman's deed was κύντερον ('more dog-like = more shameless') than hers. Just as κυνῶπις seems to call forth the word κύντερον in xi, so here the canine simile immediately preceding has apparently directed the poet's choice of language. The word 'dog' has also been much used recently as a term of reproach for Melantho and the other faithless maidservants (xviii 338, xix 91, 154, 372). For an extensive discussion of the range of metaphoric possibilities Homer exploits through the use of the dog (in relation to other animals) as representative of an aspect of human nature, see J. Redfield, *Nature and Culture in the Iliad* (Chicago, 1975), 193–203. Redfield emphasizes the dog's essentially negative image, whereas Rose (op. cit., 14–16n.) argues for a positive value attached to dogs in the *Odyssey* when they are associated with Odysseus.

18–24, κραδίη ... ἦτορ ... αὐτός: it is generally held that the Homeric conception of man is poor in vocabulary denoting the 'self' or whole person, tending instead to conceive of the person as an aggregate of separate parts (B. Snell, *Die Entdeckung des Geistes*⁴ (Göttingen, 1975), 17–23; H. Fränkel, *Dichtung und Philosophie des frühen Griechentums* (Munich, 1962), 83–94; J. Russo and B. Simon, 'Homeric Psychology and the Oral Epic Tradition', *Jour. Hist. Ideas* xxix (1968), 483–98, repr. in J. Wright, ed., *Essays on the Iliad* (Bloomington, Ind., 1978)). In these lines, while Odysseus' rebellious organs, representing emotive aspects of the self, have been subdued, the man 'himself' (αὐτός) is more than the sum of his parts and remains too upset to hold still. This passage seems to represent an advance from the standard Homeric conception toward a more modern one, as the poet presses the word αὐτός into service to denote the 'whole' psychological entity in opposition to its constituent impulses (contrast *Il.* i 3–4 where αὐτούς has the normal, simpler meaning 'them', i.e. the men's bodies as distinct from their ψυχαί which have gone to Hades).

20. μῆτις: in recalling the escape from the Cyclops, Odysseus has recalled the word upon which the elaborate punning sequence was built (οὔ τις/μή τις: Οὖτις/μῆτις); cf. ix 366, 370, 408, 410, 414, and Heubeck, 408–12 n.

23. πείσῃ: this word, a *hapax*, means either 'persuasion' (from πείθω) or 'bondage' (cf. πεῖρα, 'ship's cable'). The scholia support both possibilities, Chantraine, *Dictionnaire*, 869, supports only the first.

25–8. This simile, like the preceding one, arises from the poet's wish to explicate or illustrate a striking detail in his description of Odysseus' emotional turmoil, this time the words ἐλίσσετο ἔνθα καὶ ἔνθα (24). This tossing of Odysseus is likened to a man rolling a sausage back and forth, ἔνθα καὶ ἔνθα αἰόλλῃ. While the primary identification is between the tossing Odysseus and the rolled sausage, the eagerness of the man to have it cooked quickly (27) corresponds to Odysseus' eagerness to find a way to attack the suitors (28–9).

30. ἦλθεν Ἀθήνη: in the formal pattern established by Voigt (op. cit.) for typical scenes of deliberation and choice, the intervention of a deity to settle the choice follows upon deliberation *whether* to do one thing *or* another (as at 10–12, μερμήριζε . . . ἠὲ . . . ἦ), whereas deliberation over *how* to achieve an end (μερμηρίζων | ὅπως, 28–9) regularly leads to autonomous decision, described in the verse ἥδε δέ οἱ κατὰ θυμὸν ἀρίστη φαίνετο βουλή. This lengthy and anomalous scene of Odysseus' inner turmoil has a unique conclusion, in that it is a deity that brings the decision *how* to act. Besides this anomaly in sequence, it is the only Odyssean example of divine intervention to help a character make a decision after the formulaic pondering described as μερμηρίζειν. Such decisions are regularly made autonomously in the *Odyssey*, whereas the Iliadic norm (one exception, xiii 455–9) is for gods to decide autonomously and for mortals to receive divine direction.

32. στῆ δ' ἄρ' ὑπὲρ κεφαλῆς: this is the normal position assumed by figures who appear in dreams (iv 803, vi 21, *Il.* ii 20, xxiii 68).

33. πάντων πέρι κάμμορε φωτῶν: a similar address is used by Odysseus' mother Anticleia at xi 216. On each occasion the hero's upset state calls forth the protective feelings of his mother or patron goddess. The phrase is not mere hyperbole but underlines Odysseus' reputation as a man singled out by destiny for a hard life, as suggested by his very name and its association with a serious wound (see nn. to xix 407, 409). The word κάμμορος (*κατάμορος), 'subject to destiny, ill-fated', is absent from the *Iliad* and used only of Odysseus (ii 351, v 160, 339).

34–5. It seems that Athena is stating what is self-evident. But in this context, where Odysseus is intensely feeling his isolation and helplessness, it is significant that what strengthens his morale is to be reminded of the integrity of his nuclear family.

43. ὑπεκπροφύγοιμι: the compounded prepositions that create this unusually long verb suggest that Odysseus will need to 'get out from under' and then move 'ahead of' the threat of vengeance from the families of the murdered suitors. His analysis is correct, since this vengeance will become a major threat in xxiv and it will need Athena's intervention to finally reconcile the warring parties.

47. διαμπερές: Athena's claim to guard her favourite 'without interruption' in 'all his labours' is shown by allusions elsewhere in the epic to be false (vi 324–31, xiii 316–23). See Clay, *Wrath*, 44–53 and *passim* on Athena's anger at Odysseus and the poet's wish to minimize that traditional story.

49. **μερόπων**: a traditional epithet so old that its meaning has been lost. The etymology of the scholia to *Il.* i 250, combining μείρομαι 'to have a share of' and ὄπα 'voice', is unacceptable, since μείρομαι cannot be forced to mean 'articulate' and the -οψ element is more likely to refer to 'face' or appearance, as in the Homeric compounds οἶνοψ, αἶθοψ, νῶροψ, ἦνοψ. Since these words all describe bright appearance, it is possible that μέροψ means 'bright-faced', the μερ- cognate with μαρμαίρω and Latin *merus*. Other interpretations include 'with thoughtful face' (μερ- as in μέριμνα, μερμηρίζω: Bechtel, *Lexilogus*, 225, repeating the explanation of Fick); 'who look upon death', i.e. 'mortal' (M. Runes, *Indogermanische Forschungen* lii (1934), 216–17; a similar meaning 'vergänglich, sterblich' in H. Koller, *Glotta* xlvi (1968), 18, not from etymology, which he finds unprofitable, but from context, especially the Hesiodic usage that always prefaces γένος or γενεαί to μερόπων ἀνθρώπων); and 'earth-born', equivalent to γηγενεῖς, argued by P. Chantraine in *Mélanges Cumont* (Brussels, 1936), 121–8, based on the same name belonging to the autochthonous hero Merops and the comment of the Venetus A scholium to *Il.* i 250, μέροπες ἀπὸ Μέροπος. Chantraine's general thesis is that names of this type (including δρύοψ and ἀέροψ), which also designate specific types of bird, go back to the most archaic sources of the Greek vocabulary, are probably Thracian or Phrygian in origin, and are distant echoes of an earlier association of humans with images drawn from the animal world (cf. the note on xix 163 for a similar association of humans with trees and to xix 137 for the name 'Penelope'). As to form and frequency, μερόπων ἀνθρώπων is the standard end-line formula (10 ×), while the metrically irregular μέροπες ἄνθρωποι is found once (the irregularity tolerated, no doubt, because the genitive pl. form was so well-established), and once we find the variant μερόπεσσι βροτοῖσι. Of these twelve occurrences, ten are in the *Iliad*, which preserves archaic phrases more than the *Odyssey*. The two Odyssean usages are, curiously, both in xx.

50. **Ἀρηϊ**: Ares is often not conceived as a god but as a metaphor for war or martial spirit. This latter sense is most vividly illustrated by *Il.* xvii 210–12.

52. **ἀνίη καὶ τὸ φυλάσσειν**: either we have here the earliest example of the articular infinitive (so Chantraine *Grammaire*, ii 305); or τό is demonstrative, giving the meaning 'that watching' (like ὁ ξεῖνος, 'that stranger', see note to xvii 10); or we should translate 'a pain is that also, to keep watch', taking φυλάσσειν as appositional to τό.

57. **λυσιμελής**: here, as at xxiii 343, the juxtaposition of this word to the phrase λύων μελεδήματα θυμοῦ raises the possibility that the poet is using the phrase to gloss λυσιμελής, as if he understands the element -μελής to refer to *cares* (from μέλω) rather than to *limbs* (μέλεα). I prefer, however, to keep the traditional meaning 'looser of limbs' for λυσιμελής, and to assign

the homophony to unconscious aural association or perhaps to conscious sound-play on the part of the poet.

57–8. In a perfect complementary narrative and psychological rhythm, once Odysseus is relieved of distress and lulled to sleep, his wife abandons sleep in a state of distress. Homer presents an extended picture of the mental state of the two main characters, which serves two purposes: it develops as a natural consequence of the intense feelings they aroused in each other in the preceding scene (end of xix), thereby illuminating these feelings further, and it also looks forward to the action of xx and xxi, since such growing internal agitation is natural as morning dawns on the day that will bring the decisive and fatal contest of the bow. See further J. Russo, *AJPh* ciii (1982), 4–18.

61. πότνα θεά: πότνα and πότνια, honorific titles given to many goddesses and important mortal women and translated 'lady', 'mistress', or 'queen', may originally be the name of an old Mycenaean goddess, who is perhaps to be equated with the Minoan and middle eastern Mother Goddess. See J. Chadwick in *Minos* v (1957), 117–20. The practice of joining Potnia to the name of an Olympian may already be visible in Knossos tablet v 52. 1, a-ta-na-po-ti-ni-ja, presumably 'Athena potnia' (Ventris–Chadwick, *Documents*, 126–7 and KN 208). But the reading of a-ta-na as Athena is open to doubt: see M. Gérard-Rousseau, *Les Mentions religieuses dans les tablettes mycéniennes* (Rome, 1968), 45–6.

62. ἰὸν ἐνὶ στήθεσσι βαλοῦσι: viz., in her capacity denoted by her familiar epithet ἰοχέαιρα, 'she who showers arrows'. For Artemis as bringer of death to women, see xviii 202n. For Heubeck's alternative etymology, 'having arrows in her hand', see Hainsworth on vi 102, Hoekstra on xv 478.

63. ἤ ἔπειτα: not literally to follow 'after', but rather with the meaning 'or then', as an alternative if the first imagined death is not granted.

64. ἠερόεντα κέλευθα: these 'murky paths' seem to be associated with the river Ocean that encircles the world, because at xi 13–15 Odysseus' ship arrives at the 'boundaries of deep-flowing Ocean' where the city of the Cimmerians is covered with mist.

66–78. This story is not known from any other source, like the story at xix 518 ff. which it resembles. Pandareos' daughter, the nightingale, is not mentioned here nor are any other daughters besides the nightingale mentioned in xix. The two tales do not contradict each other, but neither do they sound like the same story. Penelope seems to be selecting different accounts of disasters that befell Pandareos' various daughters to illustrate her feelings on two different occasions.

66. ἀνέλοντο θύελλαι: this phrase, like the similar ἀναρπάξασα θύελλα, ἀνηρείψαντο θύελλαι, and ἅρπυιαι ἀνηρείψαντο, are common metaphors for saying that someone has permanently vanished from the human world (Odysseus is referred to in such language earlier in the poem, i 241, xiv 371). The daughters of Pandareos still exist, as servants of the Erinyes, but from the viewpoint of human society they have disappeared forever, as stated by the verb ἀϊστώσειαν at 79.

69. These are three of the four ingredients (the fourth being ἄλφιτα, barley) of the commonly drunk mixture called κυκεών (from κυκέω, to mix). It was served by Circe (x 290, 316 ff.) to Odysseus' men with drugs added to enchant them.

70-2. These gifts accord with the nature of each goddess. Hera as Zeus' counterpart is both 'handsome' and 'wise'; Artemis is tall, as emphasized at vi 107; and Athena is skilful at handiwork. The exception is Aphrodite, whose feeding the girls honey, cheese, and wine (68–9) is not a simple extension of her personal attributes but a more complex enactment of her function as surrogate mother and patron goddess of weddings, as shown further by her role in arranging their marriage (73–4).

74. τέλος...γάμοιο: as in the more common phrase τέλος θανάτοιο (see n. on xvii 476), the genitive is not possessive but epexegetical: the 'fulfilment of (consisting in) marriage'.

76. μοῖράν τ' ἀμμορίην: the context, naming Zeus, suggests the meaning 'good and ill fortune' (cf. *Il.* xxiv 527 ff.: Zeus distributes a mixture of good and bad fortune from two urns), and so the scholia interpret. But the Greek more likely means 'what is fated and what is not fated'.

77. The trochaic word-end in the fourth foot is rare (statistics in E. O'Neill, Jun., *YCS* viii (1942), 158), and is here caused by the use of a word of unusual length and shape, ∪ − − − ∪ (O'Neill, 148 and 151, comparing Table 26 with 29), to close the verse.

81. ὀσσομένη: normally this word would mean 'seeing', but the meaning here must be equivalent to the more explicit ὀσσόμενος ... ἐνὶ φρεσί, used of Telemachus at i 115, and refer to an internal image in one's imagination. Penelope wishes to die with an image of Odysseus in her mind's eye.

82. This line clearly shows that in setting the shooting contest for the next day, Penelope is willing, finally, to face the possibility of marrying one of the suitors. Her complaint confirms the fact that she has no suspicion that her husband has already returned in the disguise of the beggar.

83. The syntax is ambiguous. Of several possibilities, the best is to take τό μὲν as subject, ἔχει in the sense (unusual for Homer) of 'brings' or 'involves', and the ὁππότε clause as appositional to τό μέν.

87-90. A most significant dream, which must be interpreted together with the one reported by Penelope at xix 535 ff. There she envisions her husband's return. Here, he is already in his place sleeping beside her. Penelope's premonition of Odysseus' return grows stronger and stronger. The intensity of her desire for his presence is strengthened by παρέδραθεν (88), which connotes sleeping together sexually in its one other Homeric use (*Il.* xiv 163, παραδραθέειν φιλότητι, Hera speaking of her forthcoming seduction of her husband Zeus).

89. This image of Odysseus as he looked when he left for Troy has already been conjured up by Odysseus' description at xix 224 ff., answering Penelope's request for an exact portrait (for τοῖος ἐὼν οἷος ἦεν, cf. αὐτός θ' οἷος ἔην, xix 219). This image now becomes the fantasy that she invests

with the realism of a 'true vision' (ὕπαρ).　　**οἷος**: here with internal corruption, scanned as two shorts, ∪ ∪.

90. οὐκ ... ὄναρ ... ἀλλ' ὕπαρ: the language recalls xix 547. Each of these dreams has an especial vividness not ascribed to the other dreams in Homer.　**ὕπαρ**: a word of curious origin, probably created by word-play on the Aeolic preposition ὄν = ἀνά. Since ὄναρ seemed to contain the word for 'up', a word of opposed meaning was artificially—or playfully—created, based on the preposition 'under', ὑπό, and given the corresponding form ὕπαρ and the sense of a 'real' vision (so Leumann, *Wörter*, 126, following Ed. Hermann, *Nachrichten von der Königlichen Gesellschaft der Wissenschaften zu Göttingen* (1918), 285). When used earlier at xix 547, it is glossed by the phrase ὅ τοι τετελεσμένον ἔσται, which in effect defines ὕπαρ as a vision of what will come true.

92. ὅπα σύνθετο: συντίθεμαι is to 'put together' in one's mind, hence to notice or attend to. Odysseus from the πρόδρομος can hear the queen's weeping in the ὑπερῷον, her upstairs bedroom, just as at i 328 Penelope upstairs could hear the bard singing in the main hall below.

93–4. This is a surprising and unique description of Odysseus' vivid imaginings. We realize as we read the text that Odysseus is not fully awake, but is still in the sleep induced by Athena at 54. The vivid image he sees is best explained as the kind of imagery called *hypnopompic* by psychologists, which is characteristic of the transitional state between sleep and waking (G. Reed, *The Psychology of Anomalous Experience* (Boston, 1974), 37–40). Such images 'often have reference to the subject's anticipations about his forthcoming day' (ibid. 39), so that Homer's description is quite true to observed psychological reality. The poet is obliged to describe this subtle phenomenon in the simple vocabulary available in epic diction for ordinary perception, hence the unelaborated δόκησε δέ οἱ κατὰ θυμόν. He has, however, stretched μερμήριζε to cover a broader category of thinking ('reflect', as at xvi 256–61) than does its more formulaic use ('ponder anxiously') in the traditional type-scenes described in the note to 10–35 above. In these two verses, Homer describes succinctly a phenomenon that a modern writer might depict at length. Into Odysseus' consciousness suddenly enters a vivid image, or fantasy, of an eagerly desired goal that now is growing close: his wife knows him already, so that the anxieties of contriving a revelation of his identity and the task of eliminating the suitors are all by-passed. A more perfect wish-fulfilling fantasy could not be imagined.　**παρεστάμεναι κεφαλῆφι**: this is similar but not identical to the formula with which dreams and visions always appear at the *head* of the sleeper, στῆ δ' ἄρ' ὑπὲρ κεφαλῆς.

100–1. φήμην ... τέρας: The motive for Odysseus' fervent prayer at this moment must be seen in the striking vision he has just had of reunion with his wife. He takes this vision as a kind of omen, and asks Zeus for an unusual double confirmation by two other kinds of omen, the significant verbal utterance (φήμη) and the natural sign or portent (τέρας). See further

114

in the note to xviii 117. **τέρας ἄλλο**, as Monro notes, is 'a sign besides', not 'another *τέρας*'.

104. **ὑψόθεν ἐκ νεφέων**: the phrase *ἐκ νεφέων* contradicts the old woman's statement at 114, *οὐδέ ποθι νέφος ἐστί*, which makes of the thunder a *τέρας*. The poet has been careless here, using *ἐκ νεφέων*, 'from the clouds', metonymically to mean 'from the heavens'.

106. **οἱ μύλαι... ποιμένι λαῶν**: the *οἱ* refers somewhat awkwardly back to Odysseus, with the formular *ποιμένι λαῶν* an appositional gloss on *οἱ*.

108. **ἄλφιτα... ἀλείατα**: the first is the familiar barley-meal sprinkled on meat in sacrifices. *ἀλείατα*, a rare word found only here in Homer, would from its etymology (*ἀλέω*, to grind) mean any ground flour. But the context suggests a different grain, and we should accept the scholia's gloss 'wheat flour', for which the classical Greek word was *ἄλευρον*.

111. **ἔπος... σῆμα**: an 'utterance' that is in effect a 'sign' is a definition of the *φήμη* Odysseus asked for.

112–19. This is an unusual prayer for an old, anonymous servant, as commentators have noted. K. Hirvonen, 'Cledonomancy and the Grinding Slave', *Arctos* vi (1969), 5–21, has a lengthy analysis of the sometimes unusual diction and the practice of 'cledonomancy' referred to by the poet. Hirvonen finds it strange for a slave woman to pray to Zeus rather than to a goddess like Demeter; but the prayer is for *vengeance* and this is Zeus' function, especially when the violation is of hospitality. For revulsion against the suitors to be expressed finally by this humble and anonymous person is a powerful dramatic addition to the negative portrait Homer has painted of the 'lordly' suitors, and is typical of the *Odyssey*'s tendency (as opposed to the *Iliad*) to view things from the position of the powerless classes. See xviii 366–80n.

119. **νῦν ὕστατα δειπνήσειαν**: this phrase and the *πυματόν τε καὶ ὕστατον* of 116 recall Odysseus' language at 13 (referring to the maids) and Penelope's wish earlier at iv 685 that the suitors might be eating their last meal. As the final revenge approaches, the poet alludes to the suitors' end more frequently and multiplies the number of ominous warnings.

120–1. Thornton, *People*, 57, makes the important observation that many omens are prayed for and received from the gods in Homer's epics, but only Odysseus asks for and receives one from Zeus (here and at xxi 413; and Thornton also includes the thunderbolt sent at xxiv 539). A partial exception to her rule is the suitors' wish for a sign from the gods and Zeus at xvi 402–4, which comes in the form of an eagle (from Zeus) at 243 below.

132. **ἐμπλήγδην**: a hapax, probably from *ἐμπλήσσω*, and meaning 'in a striking manner', or perhaps 'in an odd way'. Telemachus' constant critical tone in speaking to or about his mother is spiced by this vivid adverb.

138. **μιμνήσκοιτο**: this reading of the major MSS may be less apt than the v.l. *μιμνήσκοντο*, because of the awkwardness of the optative after *ὅτε*, which should refer to a general or recurring condition. The *ἄνωγεν* of the apodosis clearly requires a single action in the protasis: 'But when their

thoughts turned to bedding and sleep', rather than 'But whenever his thoughts turned to . . .'. The pl. form, which would refer the action to Penelope and Odysseus, also receives some support from the reading τ' ἐμνήσαντο in Apollonius' *Lexicon*.

140–3. It has been characteristic of Odysseus' portrayal of the lowly beggar to refuse comforts that would lessen the contrast between himself and the self-indulgent suitors who have been enjoying all the resources of his house. See xix 336 n.

149. ἄγρειθ': this pl. of the common exclamation ἄγρει ('come', always linked to a command) appears only here in Homer. It is easy to see how Eurycleia's speech, filled with commands to the maids, fostered the creation of a plural, since ἄγρει was still felt as a verbal form meaning 'take' (cf. Archilochus' ἄγρει δ' οἶνον ἐρυθρὸν, 5a.8 D = 4.8 w). Details are in Bechtel, *Lexilogus*, 8–9, who cites Wackernagel's comparison of δεῦρο giving rise to δεῦτε. The recessive accent, ἄγρειτε for the normal ἀγρεῖτε, is preferred by ancient and modern grammarians as proper for Aeolic verbs.

149–56. A speech filled with imperatives, that realistically conveys the bustling activity of a household preparing for a special holiday (πᾶσιν ἐορτή). It contributes to the building of an atmosphere of impending climax for the poem's audience: this will be, as they know, the suitors' last day in the palace of Odysseus.

153. δέπα: see xix 62 n.

156. ἑορτή: the scholia, citing Philochorus as a source, identify this as the festival of Apollo Neomēnios, the first day of the month. The same identification of the νεομηνία as an Apollo-festival is noted for the island of Samos by the author of the 'Herodotean' *Life of Homer*, cited in Monro's commentary (see further xix 306 n.). Preparations for this feast are described below at 276–8 and later at xxi 258. Van Leeuwen, ad loc., connects this new lunar month with the information at xiv 457 that the first night Odysseus spends at Eumaeus' hut is a νὺξ σκοτομήνιος, a night of the interlunar period, the period which (we argued in the n. on xix 306–7) was either called the λυκάβας or concluded with the λυκάβας. The interlunar dark of the moon, which began when Odysseus was with Eumaeus, is therefore about to end with the new moon festival dedicated to Apollo. See further Austin, *Archery*, 245–52, for an elaborately spun theory that we have here the conjunction of the festivals, those of Apollo Neomēnios and the springtime Apollo, fitting into a larger cosmic rhythm involving 'conjunction and opposition in a ceaseless cycle'.

158. μελάνυδρον: water from a spring is always judged 'black' because of the visual effect caused by its depth. The same phrase is found at *Il.* ix 14 and xvi 3.

162–3. At xvii 600 Telemachus told Eumaeus to bring these ἱερήϊα καλὰ at the dawn of the next day.

163. τρεῖς σιάλους: schol. A defines σίαλοι as 'well-fattened and tame', εὐτραφεῖς καὶ ἥμερους, in contrast to 'wild pigs', χλούνας. Eumaeus gives a more relevant distinction at xiv 81, offering his new guest χοίρεα, young pork, and adding as explanation ἀτὰρ σιάλους γε σύας μνηστῆρες ἔδουσιν, the suitors eat all the well-fattened pigs. From xiv 19 and 27 we see that a single well-fattened pig was normally sufficient for the suitors' daily feasting, so that the number three emphasizes the special holiday feast, at which everyone will be fed (πᾶσιν ἑορτή, 156), not just the suitors.

166. μᾶλλον ... εἰσορόωσιν: 'Do they show you greater respect?' This use of εἰσοράω in the sense 'show respect' is unique, since it elsewhere requires a qualifying phrase like θεοὺς (-ον) ὣς or ἴσα θεῷ to achieve this meaning (vii 71, viii 173, xv 520; *Il.* xii 312).

176. κατέδησεν: most MSS read the pl. κατέδησαν, which gives better sense: the two other shepherds mentioned in 175 perform this action, while Melanthius (αὐτὸς δὲ) begins to revile Odysseus again.

178. Melanthius' sister Melantho used the same words in her attack on Odysseus at xix 66. These twin characters with similar names are in effect doublets, and part of a widespread pattern of doubling and tripling of events and personages throughout the epic (see Fenik, *Studies*, 133-230).

181. χειρῶν γεύσασθαι: as noted at xvii 413, this verb is always used metaphorically in Homer, and in the *Odyssey* always for a sardonic or mocking purpose. Cf. xxi 98.

184. κακὰ βυσσοδομεύων: see xvii 465n.

185. Here is introduced the last of the allies that will join Odysseus in his cause against the suitors. The epithet ὄρχαμος ἀνδρῶν is excessive for a herdsman, but similar epic exaggeration was bestowed upon Eumaeus, and we may assume the poet does this for characters he especially favours (see xvii 272n.). The very name Philoetius suggests that this is a 'positive' figure who will help Odysseus to an ultimate victory: φίλος plus οἶτος mean 'a desirable fate', the opposite of the κακὸν οἶτον mentioned three of the five times the word οἶτος is used in the poem.

194. βασιλῆϊ ἄνακτι: these words, both loosely translatable as 'king', have distinct meanings in early Greek. Both are well attested in Linear B, which reveals that a single ϝάναξ was king while several βασιλεῖς were local chieftains. In Homeric Greek this distinction has largely, but not entirely, vanished. βασιλεύς usually means 'king' but is occasionally used in the older sense of 'lord' (cf. Telemachus at i 394-6, who says that in Ithaca there are 'many other βασιλεῖς', one of whom might take Odysseus' place). In view of this semantic background we should understand Philoetius' phrase to mean approximately 'lordly king'.

195. δυόωσι: the only example in Greek of the verb δυάω (formed from δύη, 'misery'). It appears again only in Hesychius' gloss δεδυημένη· κεκακωμένη.

197. δειδίσκετο: see xviii 121n.

199-200. These identical lines were spoken to Odysseus by Amphinomus, xviii 122-3. Their compassionate tone contrasts totally with the mocking greetings Odysseus has received from Melantho and Melanthius, and with the sarcastic comments addressed to him by the worst of the suitors. The poet clearly reserved these lines for his 'good' characters.

201–3. Zeus 'begets' (γείνεαι) men metaphorically, as in the stock formula that calls him πατὴρ ἀνδρῶν τε θεῶν τε, 'father of men and gods'. But more may be implied by the combination of ὀλοώτερος and γείνεαι both said of the chief deity. W. Burkert (personal corresp., 1 Nov. 1989) suggests that this may be the first Greek testimony for the antithesis γίγνεσθαι– ὄλλυσθαι, and finds in the Greek wording an echo of a proverbial expression 'do not destroy what you have created', addressed to a chief divinity in a number of Mesopotamian and Old Testament texts: *Enuma Elish* 1, 45 (Tiamat to her husband Apsu), 'Why should we, what we have created, destroy?'; 'Enlil, my master, do not destroy what you have created' in a Babylonian fable (W. G. Lambert, *Babylonian Wisdom Literature* (Oxford, 1960), 190–1); Job 10: 8 (Job to Yahweh), 'Your hands have formed and made me; and yet you do destroy me'; Psalms 138: 8, 'What your hands have made, do not forsake'.

203. μισγέμεναι: the infinitive is governed by οὐκ ἐλεαίρεις, with the sense 'you don't pity men their mixing with ill fortune and dreadful suffering'. ἄνδρας is first object of ἐλεαίρεις and then subject of μισγέμεναι.

204. ἴδιον: from ϝιδίω, cognate with Eng. *sweat*, Latin *sudare*. Sweating as a symptom of overwhelming emotions is also seen in Sappho's famous ode beginning φαίνεται μοι, where she says μ' ἴδρως ψυχρὸς κακχέεται (31. 13 LP).

205–7. It is noteworthy that characters who are strongly attached to Odysseus are reminded of him when they see the beggar, and draw parallels between the beggar's poor condition and that of Odysseus. We must remember that Odysseus retains some of his natural looks: Athena has *aged* him magically, but not *transformed* him into a completely different person (see the perceptive discussion by Hölscher, *Untersuchungen*, 77–9). Compare Penelope's speculation at xix 358–60 and Eurycleia's speech at xix 363 ff., where their comparisons are like those of Philoetius here. Homer exploits these situations for maximum dramatic irony, since these comparisons are made in the presence of the disguised king.

210. Κεφαλλήνων: it is not clear whether the word here has the same meaning it does in the Catalogue of *Il.* ii 631–4, where it denotes all the people subject to Odysseus' kingship, including the nearby islands and part of the mainland (the same areas as named in the list of Penelope's suitors, i 245–7 = xvi 122–4 = xix 130–2), but not the island later called Cephallenia. It is doubtful that the Cephallenians' district (δήμῳ) would be mentioned if the reference is so broad. The author of the *Odyssey* is probably using the term, as Monro observes, for the mainland where Odysseus' cattle were kept (xiv 100).

211. οὐδέ κεν ἄλλως: 'in no other (better) way'. ἄλλως, 'otherwise', sometimes carries the sense of 'better', as at viii 176. We see this secondary sense clearly emerging from the primary one at *Il.* xix 401, and a semantic midpoint at *Il.* xi 391.

212. ὑποσταχύοιτο: στάχυς is an ear of grain, and the *hapax* verb form means 'to spring up like grain', so that the transfer of reference to cattle constitutes a bold metaphor. Agricultural comparisons come naturally to Homer's people (see xviii 366–80n.). Note the argument over agricultural skills between Eurymachus and Odysseus at xviii 357 ff., and Odysseus' fine metaphor at xiv 214 describing himself as the straw left standing after harvest.

217-25. Philoetius concludes his speech with a wish whose language recalls Telemachus' daydream at i 115–16. The cowherd is, like Eumaeus, a man of strong emotions, deeply loyal to his absent king as a son to his father. Such loyalty is a fitting return for the benevolent rule of a king who was several times described as being 'as kindly as a father' (ii 47, 230, 234; v 8, 12).

230-1. These two lines were spoken by Theoclymenus to Penelope at xvii 155–6 and by Odysseus to her at xix 303–4. They acquire more dramatic force each time, as the revelation of Odysseus' presence draws closer.

232-4. Responding to the intensity of Philoetius' feelings, Odysseus makes a prophecy much more explicit and threatening than any spoken previously. Such a firm promise of death to the suitors can be spoken only to the present company, and even then is slightly out of character for a beggar (cf. xix 348 with note, where the beggar's lordly tone is also out of character).

232. ἐνθάδ' ἐόντος: Philoetius has just been ferried over (187) from the 'Cephallenians' deme' (210) where he normally works.

235-9. Van der Valk, *Textual Criticism*, 213, notes that when Odysseus swore the same oath to Eumaeus (xiv 158–9) and Penelope (xix 312–13), both of them were incredulous and said 'Odysseus will not return'—whereas here both Eumaeus and Philoetius believe the beggar's words. Again, dramatic tension is heightened as the dénouement approaches.

236. τελέσειε Κρονίων: here we are close to the Ζεὺς τέλειος of the classical period, 'Zeus the Accomplisher'. The accomplishment prayed for was often, as here, vengeance, as in Clytaemnestra's prayer in A. *Ag.* 973. Cf. also *Eu.* 28, τέλειον ὕψιστον Δία, and *Th.* 116–17; Pi. *O.* xiii 115, *P.* i 67, Ζεὺς τέλειος. The cult of Zeus Accomplisher was to become widespread throughout classical Greece (Roscher, *Lexikon*, v 255).

240-2. The suitors' plot against the life of Telemachus was first conceived at iv 669 ff. Telemachus was warned by Athena and told how to escape the ambush at xv 28 ff.; the suitors realized their failure at xvi 342 ff., and made plans for a new attempt on his life at 371 ff. These plans were left contingent upon Zeus' approval, presumably to be shown through some omen. Now the poet resumes this thematic thread, with good dramatic purpose, a few lines after Odysseus and his supporters have been envisioning with pleasure the destruction of the suitors. The poet feels the need to revive here the picture of the suitors' murderous intent, so as to show that the murderous wishes of Odysseus and his friends are fully justified. As the great slaughter draws near, Homer is conspicuous in his efforts to introduce enough negative elements into the suitors' behaviour to allow us to view their wholesale murder as an act of *justice*. Note 284–6 below (= xviii 346–8), and the moralizing tone of the last line of this book.

242. ἀριστερός: a bird on the left is an unlucky omen, warning against whatever undertaking is contemplated.

243. αἰετός: the eagle is the bird of Zeus, and this is the response from Zeus stipulated at xvi 402–5. The powerful eagle and helpless dove recall the bird symbolism of Penelope's dream, and point to the destruction of the suitors by the powerful Odysseus. The irony here is that the suitors cannot of course see this implication, while the more perceptive members of Homer's audience and readership can.

244–6. It is natural for the 'good' suitor, Amphinomus, to annul definitely the murder plot. It was he who dissuaded the others from a new plan to kill Telemachus before they had consulted the gods (xvi 394–405).

257–9. κέρδεα νωμῶν: this phrase does not mean 'exercising shrewdness' (Stanford, and similarly Ameis–Hentze–Cauer, van Leeuwen) but 'exercising his advantage'. It refers to the advantage Telemachus has over the suitors in his knowledge of the beggar's identity, which allows him to establish Odysseus in a permanent place in the hall, under his personal protection, in preparation for the final attack. The stone threshold has been the beggar's customary place for some time (xviii 33 n.). The small table and mean chair contribute to the illusion that this is merely a harmless tramp.

262–74. Telemachus' speech is his strongest assertion thus far of his personal authority in the face of the suitors, whose amazement at his boldness (268–9) is described in the same words as xviii 410–11. In both scenes a suitor acknowledges that Telemachus has spoken 'a just word' (xviii 414–17 = xx 322–5), but in the present passage this admission is preceded by Antinous' comment in which he labels Telemachus' utterance 'a strong threat' (μάλα ... ἀπειλήσας, 272) and wishes aloud that Zeus had not restrained them. His allusion to how they would have 'stopped' Telemachus comes close to a public admission of the plot on his life, and is meant as a thinly veiled threat.

271–4. The sequence of clauses proceeds by abrupt transitions that leave certain thoughts unexpressed. The μάλα δ' ἡμῖν of 272 suggests discomfort with the decision to 'accept Telemachus' statement', δεχώμεθα μῦθον, and the following οὐ γὰρ gives the reason for their inability to eliminate him, while this inability is itself never described explicitly. The sense is: 'We must take what he says; he is, however, making big threats. [We have to endure them] because Zeus did not favour [our plan]; in that [hypothetical] case, we would have stopped him.'

275. Telemachus can afford to pay no heed to Antinous' threats because he knows the suitors' death is near. In οὐκ ἐμπάζετο μύθων, Homer has invested a familiar line-ending formula with heightened meaning by using it in a new context.

276. ἱερὴν ἑκατόμβην: a hecatomb was originally the ritual sacrifice of one hundred oxen (ἑκατὸν + βοῦς), although a smaller number could be used to 'represent' one hundred. It was to Apollo that hecatombs were most often offered, and there was an ancient festival called Hecatomboia that may be what Homer means to describe here. The possibility of a symbolic connection between the slaughter of one hundred cattle and the forthcoming slaughter of the approximately one hundred suitors is raised by G. Thomson, *JHS* lxiii (1943), 57 n. 40.

279. κρέ' ὑπέρτερα: the same phrase is used in the descriptions of the eating after ritual sacrifice at iii 65 and 470. It refers to the 'outer meat', which forms the main part of the meal after the preliminary tasting of the entrails (σπλάγχνα, iii 9, 461: this first step is not mentioned in the present passage).

284–6. Athena did the same at xviii 346–8. See the note there.

287. ἀθεμίστια εἰδώς: this phrase is used elsewhere only of the Cyclops, ix 189 (with ᾔδη) and 428. It refers to Ctesippus' nasty mockery of the custom (θέμις) of hospitality, and recalls the Cyclops' offer of a ξείνιον (ix 356, 365, 369–70) that is similarly a horrible parody of the proper procedure for giving guests their due.

292–8. Ctesippus mocks the norms of hospitality first by paying them sarcastic lip-service (292–5). His tactic changes to sarcasm at 296, with the offer of a 'gift' which the beggar may use as an 'honorific gift' (γέρας) for one of his compeers, viz. a household servant. He thus pretends to hold Odysseus at the rank of 'guest of Telemachus' (295) but concludes by equating him with servile rank.

299–300. This disagreeable suitor, as van Leeuwen shrewdly observes, is more contemptible than Antinous and Eurymachus who threw stools at Odysseus (xvii 462 ff., xviii 394 ff.), since they were provoked by an argument with the beggar while Ctesippus is merely looking for amusement. The three throwing incidents show a finely calculated gradation, well described by Fenik, *Studies*, 182–7, who points to the *decrease* in the effectiveness of each throw contrasting with the *increase* in the forcefulness of Telemachus' response. He also notes (181) that each attack is thematically prepared for by verbal abuse from Melanthius or Melantho. It has been debated whether this cow's foot is raw or cooked, and what purpose it served at the feast. It is likely that cooked pieces of such less desirable parts of the animal were brought to the feast in a basket, to be eaten by those of lowest rank. This assumption gives point to Ctesippus' attack, since he resents the beggar's receiving a portion equal to the aristocrats and is now 'giving' him the piece he would have had without Telemachus' special intervention (281–3). In so treating the beggar Ctesippus is attempting to undermine Telemachus' authority.

301. μείδησε δὲ θυμῷ: since θυμός has so many meanings it is difficult to know whether Homer means 'smiled inwardly' or 'smiled with angry (or resolute) spirit'. The first meaning is supported by parallel situations and phrasing where an emotion is clearly intended to be inwardly registered: xix 210, θυμῷ ἐλέαιρε γύναικα, 'he pitied the woman (his wife) inwardly', and Odysseus' command to Eurycleia to 'rejoice inwardly', ἐν θυμῷ . . . χαῖρε, at xxii 411; cf. also the instance of a person praying 'privately' (ὃν κατὰ θυμόν) at v 444 and *Il.* xxiii 769. The second meaning finds support in passages where the unmodified noun θυμός denotes an angry or fighting spirit, such as ii 315, xiii 148, xx 9, xxiv 318, 511, *Il.* i 192, iv 289, v 470, vi 439, ix 637, xiv 459, etc., or (sometimes hard to distinguish) a resolute spirit, such as i 353, iv 713, xvi 99, *Il.* i 228, iii 9, xiii 485, 487, etc. In the present passage the following σαρδάνιον suggests a bitter grimace, so that a likely translation of μείδησε δὲ θυμῷ σαρδάνιον might be 'smiled bitterly in anger' or 'smiled with bitter resolve'. The passage is discussed by Fenik, *Studies*, 180ff., esp. 185 where he emphasizes Odysseus' -'menacing silence'; and D. B. Levine, *TAPhA* cxiv (1984), 1–9, who treats Odysseus' three smiles in xx–xxiii as a closely connected thematic structure that emphasizes the hero's confident superiority over the suitors; but neither raises the question of what 'smiled in his θυμός' really means.

302. **σαρδάνιον**: the first 'sardonic smile' in literature, with σαρδάνιον a Homeric *hapax*. This is the spelling favoured by ancient authors, a few MSS, and a third- or fourth-century AD papyrus of sections of the *Odyssey*, while the vast majority of MSS offer the later spelling σαρδόνιον. The many testimonia preserved in the schol., Hesychius, the *Suda* and several entries in the *Corpus Paroemiographorum Graecorum* for the proverbial phrase σαρδό[ω]νιον γέλως ('sardonic laughter') show that ancient etymology derived this word either from the pf. σέσηρα (σέσαρα) of σαίρω, 'to grin or grimace' (which fails to account for the -δ-), or from the Sardinians, either because they grew a poison parsley which drove those who ate it to bite their own flesh (σαρκάζειν), or because they practised variously described customs of human sacrifice in which it was shameful for the victims to protest, so that they went to their death with a 'sardonic' laugh. Hence a forced smile or laugh in the face of evils is 'sardonic', a meaning which suits our passage well, whether or not we believe any of the etymologies. A different solution is offered by P. Kretschmer, *Glotta* xxxiv (1955), 1–9, who reviews and refutes the ancient etymologies and would derive the word from a Near Eastern people called the Shardana, neighbours of the Egyptians who migrated westward and gave their name to Sardinia and to laughter-provoking performers of south Italian farce. This last connection, however, based on Hesychius' gloss σαρδανάφαλλος· γελωτοποιός, seems tenuous, and so the origin of 'sardonic laughter' must remain obscure.

304–9. This is the strongest speech Homer puts in Telemachus' mouth. The open threat of death to Ctesippus (306) corresponds with Telemachus' acknowledgement that the suitors have planned *his* death (315; cf. 273–4); the blunt truth is now made public, as the adversaries abandon the fictions of politeness and respect for each other's prerogatives that characterized their earlier exchanges. Telemachus is ready to fight and die for his honour, and we feel the climax of the story approaching.

304. To make the best sense of κέρδιον ἔπλετο θυμῷ we should translate 'better for your life', taking θυμός in a specialized sense as the animating or life-principle in one's body, as at iii 455, x 163, xii 414, xix 454, *Il.* xiii 671, xvi 606, etc. Those passages, however, use familiar context and formulas to define this special sense of θυμός, while the present passage, as Monro

notes, conflates two formulas (κέρδιον είσατο θυμῷ and φίλον ἔπλετο
. θυμῷ) that use θυμός in its more ordinary meaning, 'heart', to create an
exceptional instance of the narrower meaning.

311-12. As Stanford and others note, the transition from τάδε to
appositional genitive absolutes is unexpected, and σίτου is deprived of a
proper verb so as to create a zeugma with πινομένοιο. Such ragged syntax
supports the impression that Telemachus is angry and upset.

318-19. (= xvi 108-9). The conclusion of this angry speech gains emphasis
from uncommon colometry: in 318 the mid-line caesura is bridged over by
the long word στυφελιζομένους; in 319 we find the vivid word ῥυστάζοντας
(frequentative of ἐρύω) extending the first colon abnormally to a trochaic
cut in the second foot, a bridged-over mid-line caesura, and the unusual
rhythm of ἀεικελίως (words of this shape normally end in the third or the
fifth foot: of 104 instances in his Homeric sampling, only two were found in
this position by E. G. O'Neill, Jun., *YCS* viii (1942), 146).

321. Ἀγέλαος: the first mention of this person in the *Odyssey*. He will play a
prominent part in xxii, where he emerges as a leader of the suitors in the
fight, after Antinous and Eurymachus have been killed; and his is the first
name in a brief list of the 'best' of the suitors (xxii 241-5). Homer introduces him now, rather than give this speech to one of the already
prominent figures, because he is already looking ahead to the action of xxii.

322-5. These same lines were spoken by Amphinomus at xviii 414 ff., in a
conciliatory statement after Eurymachus has thrown the stool at Odysseus
and provoked an angry outburst from Telemachus. In each case the poet
has made one of the 'better' suitors acknowledge the validity of
Telemachus' angry complaint.

326-33. Agelaus presents himself as a man of moderation who would make a
reasonable assessment (μῦθον ... ἤπιον) of the situation. There is great
irony in the fact that the supposition he takes as 'obvious' (νῦν δ' ἤδη τόδε
δῆλον) is contradicted (for us and Homer's audience) by the presence of
the beggar.

330. μενέμεν τ' ... ἰσχέμεναί τε: the likeliest construction is to assume
Odysseus, named in the previous line, as the unexpressed object of μενέμεν
and the suitors, named in the following line, as object of ἰσχέμεναι: 'to wait
for him while holding off the suitors'. An alternative is to construe μένω in
the sense used for enemies and wild animals as objects, 'stand firm
against', with 'suitors' as the object, which would add an attractive subtlety
to the thought, but is less appropriate as spoken by one of the suitors.

335. The bow-contest has not been announced publicly yet, so the suitors
can still imagine that gifts will determine the queen's choice, as if the
situation had not advanced since xviii 285-303. With nice dramatic irony,
the poet and audience share the knowledge that a totally different device
for deciding the marriage will be announced soon (xxi 68 ff.), a device
which will also, through economical use of plot-elements, become the
instrument of the suitors' destruction.

336-7. Now that the murder plot has been abandoned, the suitors must concede to Telemachus the retention of his inherited wealth and land, as they did at i 402–4, before the independence shown in his journey to Pylos and Sparta made them think he was too dangerous and should be eliminated. Their goal has been the kingship, and either Penelope's hand or Odysseus' estate would strengthen any claim to it, while possession of both would have guaranteed it. They now give up their designs on the estate and concentrate on winning Penelope.

343–4. Telemachus said the same thing at xvii 398–9. There is a quality of *déja vu* in these negotiations for marriage and in the recent quarrelling over Telemachus' rights and the suitors' improper conduct (284 ff., 309–10, 318–19, 322 ff., all repeat lines spoken in recent books; Ctesippus' throw repeats an already familiar incident; and there are many small verbal echoes from Books xvi through xix). This accumulation of verbal and thematic recurrence suggests that the situation *vis-à-vis* the suitors has reached an impasse. It is time for new and different action to break forth.

345–9. Athena's forceful intervention to control the suitors' behaviour is a more intense version of the motif used at 284–5 and xviii 346–7. That was manipulation; this is outright possession.

348. It is not clear to whom the meat appears in its bloody transformation. The scholia say only Theoclymenus sees it. More likely everyone *except* the suitors sees it. Possibly they too see it, but have no memory of it once their seizure has passed.

349. γόον δ' ὠΐετο θυμός: an odd phrase, used also of Eurylochus' agitated state after witnessing Circe's transformation of his comrades, x 248. Since we are told that Eurylochus' anguish made him incapable of speech, we should interpret this phrase as 'their heart imagined crying out', meaning that they wanted to wail but could not make any sound.

350. Theoclymenus has not been heard of since he was brought to the palace by Telemachus in xvii. He has apparently been present since then, and is now 'activated' by Homer to add intensity to the growing mood of crisis. This character seems to have been introduced (invented by Homer?) in xv specifically for this exciting scene, after which he hastily exits. The supposed awkwardness of his integration into the story was once a favourite target of Analyst criticism; but see now Fenik, *Studies*, 233–44, for a well-balanced defence of his place in the story.

351–7. The most eerie passage in Homer. Stanford aptly emphasizes the unusual quality of this prophecy by spontaneous visionary outburst, noting that Homeric prophecy normally operates through omens and reasoned interpretation. See further E. R. Dodds, *The Greeks and the Irrational* (Berkeley, 1951), 64–101, concerning possession and ecstatic prophecy where this passage is contrasted with the Homeric norm (70). Each detail of Theoclymenus' vision is the kind of supernatural manifestation that is found in the folk-beliefs and epic literature of other peoples, and the symbolism is well-nigh universal. The cloud of darkness is found in Celtic tradition (Monro, ad loc.); the walls and beams dripping with blood are similar to Njal's vision, in *Njal's Saga*. ch. 127, that portends the slaughter of his family ('it seems as though the table and the food were gone and everything were covered with blood'), and blood dripping from the hairbrush of the hero Lemminkäinen, in *Kalevala* xv 24–48, is a sign to his mother that he has died. Blood is also seen in Cassandra's vision in Aeschylus' *Ag.* 1090 ff., where the vision includes both past and future murder; and blood is seen dripping from the roofs of temples in an oracle narrated in Herodotus vii 140 (cf. the vision of the prophetess described by Plutarch, *Pyrrh.* 31). For detailed documentation of the universality of this motif see Thompson, *Motif Index*, ii D474: 'Transformation: object becomes bloody', and also under E761. 1, 'Blood as life token'. As for the ghosts, their presence portends the suitors' approaching death and the procession to the Underworld that will take place at the beginning of xxiv. The vanishing of the sun and the dark mist (ἀχλύς) that conclude the vision return to the same ominous dark imagery with which it began. Monro notes that a common Iliadic description of death is κατα δ' ὀφθαλμῶν κέχυτ' ἄχλυς, 'mist poured down over his eyes', and that *Il.* xiii 425 offers the metaphor ἐρεβεννῇ νυκτὶ καλύψαι 'to cover with black night', meaning 'to slay'. Cf. also A. *Eu.* 378 ff. Darkness is appropriate to represent impending death just as the supernatural light was a natural symbol for Odysseus' divine protection and forthcoming victory at xix 33–40.

353. οἰμωγὴ δὲ δέδηε: 'a groan blazes forth', a strong metaphor, probably to be understood as referring to the sudden outburst or the rapid extension of the sound. Cf. the rapid spread of Rumour, described as μετὰ δέ σφισιν ὅσσα δεδήει, *Il.* ii 93. Stanford notes that it is one of the rare synaesthetic metaphors in Homer.

354. ἐρράδαται: third pl. perf. passive of ῥαίνω, 'to sprinkle', of which we had the aorist imperative ῥάσσατε at 150. Chantraine, *Grammaire*, i 435, explains the -δ- as perhaps from the false impression of a dental stem-termination given by the form ῥάσσατε.

358–60. The suitors regard the seer as a madman and laugh at him because they have no awareness of the spell Athena cast on them and of the supernatural phenomena.

367. τοῖς ἔξειμι θύραζε: since ἔξειμι suggests walking, and θύραζε the direction, the τοῖς seems to refer awkwardly back to πόδες of 365. Possibly the intervening line was added as an afterthought, by Homer or a later performer. But Stanford, Monro, and Ameis–Hentze–Cauer are probably right to take τοῖς as referring to *all* the faculties of the preceding two lines, and van der Valk, *Textual Criticism*, 57, gives a good defence of the sequence as typical of the less logical expression found in colloquial speech and often reproduced in Homer.

373–83. The suitors now turn to teasing Telemachus about *both* his odd guests, and they propose packing them both off to Sicily. Lines 373 and 375 are formulas that have been used throughout the poem to introduce their mocking statements. In their final round of flippancy before their sobering inadequacy with Odysseus' bow, Homer portrays them with their familiar sarcasm in an especially self-indulgent form.

376. κακοξεινώτερος: in their mockery the suitors create a wonderful new compound. κακόξεινος, built on the model of κακοδαίμων, means 'unfortunate in one's guests'. The length of the comparative form contributes emphasis to their mockery. The long -ω- has been called 'incorrect' (Shipp, *The Language of Homer* (Cambridge, 1972), 351), but Chantraine, *Grammaire*, i 258, gives parallels that suggest we have a not uncommon adjustment *metri gratia*.

377. ἐπίμαστον: probably from ἐπιμαίομαι, whose two meanings are 'to strive after', and 'to handle'. Ebeling, *Lexicon*, applies a passive sense of the second meaning and renders 'sordid'; but ancient authorities (scholia, Hesychius, Apollonius) agree in translating 'needy', 'seeking food', assuming a probably incorrect derivation from μαστεύω, 'to search after'. Ameis–Hentze–Cauer derive the same meaning from the active sense of ἐπιμαίομαι, which is probably right (cf. the abusive epithets μολοβρός and ἀπολυμαντήρ, which seem to identify a beggar as a good scavenger, at xvii 219, 220 and 377). A less likely interpretation is that which sees a passive sense of 'search after', to give the meaning 'sought out', i.e. brought to the palace by Eumaeus.

379. ἔμπαιον: a rare word, apparently from πάομαι, 'to get possession of', a Doric verb not found in Homer. The compound ἔμπαιον suggests the meaning 'possessed of' or 'experienced in'. It is here scanned irregularly as a dactyl, through internal correption (cf. οἷος at 89 above). In its one other occurrence, xxi 400, the scansion is normal.

380. ἄλλος ... τις οὗτος: the tone in Greek is contemptuous: οὗτος easily assumes a pejorative shading, especially when used of someone present (cf. Italian *costui*). Theoclymenus, recently departed, is vividly evoked as if present: 'And then again some other person, this "type" here ...'

383. Σικελούς: the Greeks called 'Sikeloi' or Sikels all the indigenous people they found in Sicily when they were colonizing its eastern coast in the latter part of the eighth century. Who these people were, ethnically, is not altogether clear, but current opinion is that they did not, as the Greeks thought, inhabit Sicily from Bronze Age times, but were migrants from the mainland who began settling in Sicily about 1200 BC and spoke a language related to Latin (L. Bernabò Brea, *Sicily Before the Greeks* (New York, 1966), 141–3, 165; M. I. Finley, *Ancient Sicily to the Arab Conquest* (London, 1968), 9–14). This is the first time they are mentioned in ancient sources (E. T. Vermeule, *Greece in the Bronze Age* (Chicago, 1964), 271 with n. 11, speculates that among the 'Sea People' named in the Amarna letters of fourteenth-century Egypt, the *Shekelesh* may be *Sikeloi*). In xxiv we find that the servant who takes care of old Laertes is a Sicilian woman (211, 366, 389). To the Greeks of Homer's time, 'to send someone to the Sicilians' apparently meant to get rid of them, and the end of the verse suggests that people were sent there to be sold into slavery. Cf. the threat to send Irus to King Echetus, xviii 85, where the scholia identify Echetus as 'tyrant of the Sicilians'.

383. ἄλφοι: the lack of obvious subject for this verb is awkward, but it is not difficult to supply as subject the general idea of the preceding words, and to translate, with Stanford, 'it would fetch you a worthy price'.

384-6. Again we are told (as at 275) that Telemachus 'paid no heed' to the suitors' words. Here, however, we are given an explanation in the following two verses, which make explicit what was merely implicit in the situation at 275.

387. κατ' ἄντηστιν: the noun is a *hapax* found nowhere else in Greek literature, but context and the root ἀντ- make it clear that the phrase refers to a position in her private room, or θάλαμος, just opposite the doorway to the main hall, from which position Penelope could hear the discussion, as she heard the sound of the suitors maltreating the beggar at xvii 492 (see note there for the relation of the μέγαρον, θάλαμος, and ὑπερῷον).

390-2. δεῖπνον μὲν ... δόρπου δ': the poet points a sharp contrast between their 'dinner', which is described with words denoting delight (γελοίωντες, ἡδύ, μενοεικές), and their 'supper', which they never literally will have, and which is instead made into a metaphor for the death that Athena and Odysseus will 'set' (θησέμεναι) for them. Odysseus revives this grim metaphor at xxi 428.

394. The poet deliberately concludes the scene with an emphasis on the suitors' role in causing their own death. See 240–2 n.

BOOKS XXI–XXII

Manuel Fernández-Galiano

The late Manuel Fernández-Galiano's
Introductions *and* Commentary *on Books xxi and xxii*
were translated for this volume by
Jeremy Lawrance.

BOOK XXI: INTRODUCTION

There is general agreement that Book xxi is one of the finest in the *Odyssey*, full of dramatic suspense in its final unfolding of the plot. The only difficulties of interpretation are the practical details of the contest of the bow, discussed in an excursus below. I shall confine myself in this Introduction to a few general remarks about authorship, placed here to avoid encumbering the notes.

It is now widely accepted that the poem had two main authors: the original poet whom critics call *A*, and one or more later poets known collectively as *B*, who reworked *A*'s nucleus to lengthen the poem and give the adventures a more modern slant. This is not the place to discuss all the arguments on the 'Homeric Problem'; some will be touched upon in the commentary. I shall limit my discussion to the well-known theories of P. von der Mühll and W. Schadewaldt, who agree that there are two hands at work but disagree on which parts of xxi to attribute to each.

Schadewaldt is inclined to accept a broad unity of authorship in xxi, attributing the whole book to *A* with the exception of eight lines: namely, Telemachus' boast in 372–5 (already rejected by Bérard), whose removal requires the further deletion of the suitor's smile in 376–7 and the first foot and a half of 378 (which will therefore have to be rewritten); and Zeus' thunderbolt in 412–15.[1] The latter is a melodramatic interpolation, as von der Mühll observed.[2]

Von der Mühll's *Odyssee* takes a far less unitarian line. Though not all his objections against the unity of the book can be accepted, his arguments are worth summarizing:

The first oddity occurs in 1–4, which read as though the contest had not been previously mentioned in xix 570–81. Line 5, with a choice between two different compounds of the verb (see app. and n. ad loc.), poses a problem about the location of the action. The digression on the history of the bow gives the impression of being an afterthought: 11–41 are marked as suspect by von der Mühll, and other editors reject various lines, especially between the caesurae of 16 and 35. The whole interpolation, and particularly 24–33, would have

---

[1] W. Schadewaldt, 'La Odisea como poesia', *Estudios de literatura griega* (Madrid, 1971), 9–52, fig. on pp. 50–2.
[2] P. von der Mühll, 'Einige Interpretationen in behrümten Stellen der *Odyssee*', *Philologus* lxxxix (1934), 391–6.

been inserted to relate the passage to the epic *Sack of Oechalia*; the story of Eurytus has already been mentioned in viii 224–8, probably by *B*.

On the difficulty of γωρυτῷ in 54 see p. 137 f. In the original poem Penelope's entry into the hall at 58 was perhaps her first appearance there, if xviii 158–305 are removed (on which, however, see xxi 311–53 n.). Bérard also regards 68–72 as suspect, and 73 is repeated in 106.

According to von der Mühll, 80–95 betray the hand of *B*: the original poet imagined Odysseus and Telemachus fighting the suitors alone, without Eumaeus, who is portrayed weeping in 82, or Philoetius, a character invented by *B*, who is also seen weeping in 83. The later poet misunderstood the adjective ἄατος in 91; Antinous' words on his earlier relationship with Odysseus in 94–5, like Eurymachus' in xvi 442–4, are due to *B*'s desire to connect the characters chronologically; the fact that Penelope orders Eumaeus to organize the contest in 81 is contradicted by the fact that it is Telemachus who sets out the axe-heads (no doubt this role seemed unworthy of a prince to *B*); and finally, if 80–95 are removed, 96 must read τοῖς δ' ἄρα.

Furthermore, 98–100 seem to anticipate future events in an unnecessary way; and 101 is wholly corrupt (see apparatus). There are many touches from the hand of *B* in 102–17: Telemachus' words in 106–10, which smack of the auctioneer, have always seemed odd, and include 109, an objectionable line omitted by some papyri and MSS; 111 with the *hapax* μύνῃσι and the following lines, evidently by the same author as 91 ff.; the sense of ἀέθλια in 117, of which I have already spoken (see p. 144), is striking.

In 113 Telemachus announces that he is going to try the bow; but it is probable that in *A* he did not do so. The pedantic remark in 123 may be *B*'s; in 125 the word πελέμιξεν which we have mentioned (see p. 138), found also in *Il.* xxi 176, perhaps fits Asteropaeus' movement as he 'shakes' a spear to loosen it before pulling it out of a wall better than Telemachus', who is pulling a bowstring. Lines 132–3, similar in meaning to ii 60–2 and almost exactly the same as xvi 71–2, are less appropriate to a boy whom circumstances are rapidly bringing to maturity. On Leodes, who appears in 144 as a replica of Amphinomus, see 152–62 nn.; the last two lines of this passage are a calque of xvi 391–2.

Melanthius will not have been one of *A*'s characters either, and so 175 ff. on the picturesque heating and greasing of the bowstring must be an addition, which will mean that the passage in which 246 occurs is also suspect. The two servants' recognition of Odysseus also seems to be the work of *B*: the exit in 188 is not properly explained, the affection expressed in 216 is exaggerated, 219–20 are omitted in one papyrus, the showing of the wound in 221 is unnecessary, and the lamentation in 226 excessive.

Antinous' suggestion of a postponement in 256 ff. lacks point: in his speech he mentions Melanthius and a festival of Apollo which are only found elsewhere in *B*. In 277 it is perhaps better to read Ἀντίνοον first and Εὐρύμαχον second (see apparatus), since the latter has the epithet θεοειδής in iv 628 and xxi 186, whereas the former is never thus described (nevertheless, cf. βασιλῆα in xxiv 179; the two heroes appear together in xviii 65). The hand of *A* is seen again in 281, but 286, removed by Nauck, presents signs of interpolation, as does 289, where the reading of the papyrus may point to serious corruption (see apparatus). The allusion to king Echetus in 306–9 is strikingly reminiscent of xviii 83–7; lines 291–310 have been the subject of several deletions.

There are also several problems in 311–53, as will be seen in the notes to the passage, especially on 336–42. In 350–3 there is an added complication. The lines derive from *Il.* vi 490–3, with changes in the last two lines, and are the origin of 356–9, with a change in the last line; they are followed by 353a, which may be genuine (see apparatus). On the other hand, the excellent passage on Penelope's divinely-induced sleep in 356–8 is necessary to the story; its parallels with i 362–4, xvi 449 (almost identical), and xix 602–4 surely confirm the antiquity of these lines.

However, *B* shows his hand again directly in 359 ff., where Eumaeus is given the task of handing the arms to Odysseus. In the original version it will have been Telemachus who did this, as he himself has already said in 345. If we were to remove 359–91 (see apparatus), the subject of 392, perhaps expressed in a line now lost, would be Telemachus, which would give fine sense to εἰσορόων in 393. Along with these lines would go 372–8, already condemned by Schadewaldt, as we have seen. With a reminder about 412–15, also suppressed by Schadewaldt, and a mention of 427, an obvious echo of xx 376–83 (see apparatus), the main outlines of the book are clear.

The chief problems in this book have to do with the details of the extraordinary test of the bow. Many of them are connected with the layout of Odysseus' palace.

First of all, there is a lively debate about where the contest took place. Modern opinion opts for the μέγαρον or feast-hall, whereas in the past most scholars placed it in the courtyard, αὐλή, xxi 191, or entrance porch, πρόδομος, xx 1, or πρόθυρον, xxi 474. Fries, Stubbings, Page, Sacconi, and Burkert do not come down firmly on either side, though I suspect they mostly incline towards the feast-hall.[3] The main arguments in favour of the courtyard or entrance porch are as follows:[4]

1. The relatively small μέγαρον would be too narrow and short for the dangerous bow-contest in the presence of 108 suitors, ten servants, Odysseus, and his three companions. Bowshots require plenty of space, even if Penelope's πολλὸν ἄνευθε in xix 575 is a nostalgic exaggeration.

2. The plan of the hall would not be suitable, with its columns and hearth, on which in xxi 181 we are told there is a fire burning.

3. The floor of the feast-hall is paved (κραταίπεδον οὖδας, xxiii 46). But Telemachus, as we shall see, is supposed to dig a trench in it (xxi 120–2) and then rake up earth around the axes.

4. In xxii 10 we find Antinous calmly drinking in his seat; this could hardly have been a safe place to sit while arrows were being shot off.

5. The suitors would doubtless have picked up the axes to fight their enemies if these had been to hand.

6. When the hall is cleared up in xxii 448 ff. there is no mention at all of the axes.

7. In xx 258 Telemachus has placed Odysseus παρὰ λάϊνον οὐδόν, next to the door leading from the feast-hall to the porch; and in xxi 422 the hero's arrow flies through the axes and goes out θύραζε, that is out through the doors of the palace into the open.

8. Immediately after this, Odysseus leaps towards the threshold (xxii 2), then turns and confronts the suitors, thus trapping them inside the feast-hall, as emerges from the strategies described in xxii 76 and 172.

9. The hero shoots the first arrow from his stool (xxi 420); this

[3] C. Fries, 'Zur τόξου θέσις', PhW lvii (1937), 1198–9; F. H. Stubbings, Companion, 534–8; D. L. Page, 'A Problem in Homer's Odyssey: The Arrow and the Axes', Ἐπ.Ἐπ.Φιλ.Σχ.Πανεπ.Ἀθ. xiv (1963–4), 541–62, and Folktales, 93–135. A. Sacconi, 'Un problema di interpretazione omerica: la freccia e le asce del libro XXI dell' Odissea' (Rome, 1971); W. Burkert, 'Von Amenophis II. zur Bogenprobe des Odysseus', Grazer Beitr. i (1973), 69–78.

[4] J. van Leeuwen (1897 edn.); V. Bérard (1924 and following edns.), with a daring cj. at xxi 120, for which see app.; H. W. Stubbs, 'The Axes Again', CR lxi (1947), 12–13; J. L. Myres, 'The Axes Yet Again', CR lxii (1948), 113; J. Bérard, H. Goube, and R. Langumier (1952 edn.), 336; E. Delebecque, 'Le Jeu de l'arc de l'Odyssée', in Le Monde grec: Hommages à Claire Préaux (Brussels, 1975), 56–67, J. Bérard, 'Le concours de l'arc dans l'Odyssée', REG lxviii (1955), 1–11.

odd position, with the body and the weapon held low, would be explained by the drop from the hall across the porch down into the courtyard where the axes are fixed.

10. In order to use the bow, both Telemachus, in xxi 124, and Leodes, in xxi 149, have to take up position in the doorway between the hall, where they are standing, and the courtyard, where the axes are placed.

However, a considerable body of opinion supports the theory that the contest took place inside the feast-hall. Some of the arguments are of a general and unconvincing kind. It is said, for example, that Homer, who like Telemachus (xxi 123) had never witnessed a contest of this type, was deliberately vague about the details because the main ingredients of the story were traditional and well known to his listeners or readers as a fantastic or magic folk-tale, even down to the symbolic twelve axes which perhaps represented the twelve months of the year, or the phallic arrow associated with the triumphant husband, and so forth (Germain, *Genèse*, 11–54, adduces numerous mythological parallels from other cultures). Alternatively, emphasis is laid on the disturbing evidence of multiple layers of authorship in the text of the poem.

It is possible, however, to counter the objections against the feast-hall with more specific arguments.[5] My own commentary, with a few reservations, follows the same line. Taking the arguments in order:

1. The archery contests in the parallels adduced by the scholars cited above presuppose quite short distances, no more than eleven to eighteen feet. As for the large number of suitors, it is clear that this is an exaggeration of the original poem by a later hand.

2. The problem of the layout of the feast-hall will be dealt with below.

3. (*a*) The phrase in xxiii 46 does not necessarily refer to a paved floor; it may indicate a flattened and beaten earth floor. Raking is described in xxii 456 (ξύον); Agelaus' head is spattered with dust (κονίησιν ἐμίχθη, xxii 329); the fallen suitors lie in the dust (ἐν αἵματι καὶ κονίῃσι, xxii 383). (*b*) Some of the possible ways of arranging the axes do not require any serious digging, though our interpretation of xxi 120 will'be decisive here. It might have been sufficient simply to pile a little earth brought in from the courtyard on top of the paving

[5] J. van Leeuwen (1890 edn.); Monro; Woodhouse, *Composition*, 102–7; W. B. Stanford (1948 edn.) and his 'A Reconsideration of the Problem of the Axes in *Odyssey* xxi', *CR* lxii (1949), 3–6; L. G. Pocock, 'The Arrow and the Axe Heads in the *Odyssey*', *AJP* lxxxii (1961), 346–57, and his *Odyssean Essays* (Oxford, 1965), 12–22; P. Brain and D. D. Skinner, 'Odysseus and the Axes: Homeric Ballistics Reconstructed', *G & R* xxv (1978), 55–8.

or beaten earth, enough to hold the targets upright. Indeed, it might even have been an advantage not to stand the axes too firm; the toppling of any one of them would then clearly indicate a foul shot.

4. (a) The seating could have been moved to the sides of the hall for the contest. (b) Besides, Antinous' calm is partly explained by the fact that up to that moment only one arrow has been shot.

5. (a) The suitors have no need of the axes, since they carry swords (xxii 74, 79, 90, 98); besides, both are ineffective against arrows. (b) Furthermore, if the axes had no handles, as seems probable, they would have been useless as weapons.

6. (a) It would have been mere pedantry for the poet to have mentioned something which can in any case be inferred; or he may simply have forgotten about the axes. (b) In xxi 260–2, when Antinous suggests postponing the end of the contest to the next day, he proposes leaving the axes standing on the ground, since nobody will remove them ἐλθόντ' ἐς μέγαρον. This argument is weak, however, since it could refer to someone stealing the weapons while walking 'towards the hall' through the courtyard or porch.

7. The word θύραζε may be a technical term for the successful flight of an arrow through all the obstacles, when it could be said to fly 'out'. A parallel expression where the word has lost its semantic connection with 'doors' is v 410, though there are no such parallels in these last books. In xxi 89, 299 the adverb refers to the outer exit from the courtyard (the latter case, διὲκ προθύρου . . . θύραζε, does not refer to Odysseus' palace); in xxi 238, 384 it refers to the exit from the women's quarters to the men's; in xxi 388, xxii 375, 456, to the exit from the feast-hall to the courtyard. In the first of these passages Philoetius goes out to close the gate of the courtyard; it would therefore have been impossible for an arrow to have flown out of the palace altogether. On the other hand, it would be possible for an arrow shot from inside the hall towards the exit to fly into the courtyard (though it is unlikely that the shooting took place in this way, since it would be all the more difficult to shoot against bright daylight from within a dark room).

8, 10. But this last theory would make Odysseus' strategic manœuvre of leaping on to the threshold of the exit impossible. The latter has many arguments in its favour and is compatible with the theory that the contest took place in the hall without any adjustments save that of suppressing the supposed half-turn.

9. (a) Whether or not we assume a sloping row of axes, the shot would have to be aimed from very low unless we imagine very large axes (a point to which I shall return). It appears, however, that

only two maidservants carry them, in a single and not very heavy ὄγκιον (xxi 61, 66). Certain iconographic evidence shows archers crouching down to shoot, and both Achilles, with his famous wound in the heel, and also Diomedes (*Il.* xi 377) are shot in the foot by Paris. The fact that Odysseus throws his arrows on the ground in xxii 3–4 may reflect the fact that this was the most comfortable position for a bowman. (*b*) The slope might after all be explained by the layout of the feast-hall itself, which may have had two levels (see below). That would make the trench necessary, for safety, to prevent arrows flying off course or travelling too far in a straight line. There is no difficulty in accepting the poet's licence in making Telemachus occupy himself with such a job.

11. Perhaps the clinching lines are xix 573 (Odysseus' custom was to set up the axes ἐνὶ μεγάροισιν ἐοῖσιν), xxi 4 (Penelope arranges the contest ἐν μεγάροισ' Ὀδυσῆος), and xxi 229 (Odysseus fears they may be seen by someone ἐξελθὼν μεγάροιο). But the word μέγαρον, in singular and plural, can also have the meaning 'palace' or 'palace buildings as a whole, with all its out-houses'.

The question of how the trial actually took place is also a thorny one. The first part of the test, the stringing of the bow, is the easier: of the abundant work on this I mention only Lorimer, *Monuments*, 298 ff., and, specifically on the last books of the *Odyssey*, Delebecque's article.

In xxi 5 ff., Penelope goes to the treasure-house where the τόξον and the φαρέτρη/ἰοδόκος are kept (11–12), the latter full of ὀϊστοί. In xxi 13–41 we are told the tale of the famous bow, given as a gift to Odysseus by Iphitus, who in turn had received it from the great Eurytus (32–3). It is a magnificent weapon, though impractically large (xxi 74, 405, 409 μέγα), and tough enough to survive the suitors' clumsy treatment unscathed. Odysseus sometimes carries it in Ithaca, presumably for hunting (xxi 41), but does not use it on campaign (xxi 38–40), which is why it has been a little neglected: its owner has to examine it closely (xxi 393–5) in case the horn has been worm-eaten.

Penelope takes the bow down from its peg (xxi 53), which must have been very sturdy, αὐτῷ γωρυτῷ, ὅς οἱ περίκειτο φαεινός (xxi 54). This is difficult: γωρυτός, only here in Homer, referred to the case of metal (hence φαεινός) carried by the Scythians and other nomad tribes to protect their bows in cold northern climates. It had two compartments, one for the bow itself and the other for the arrows; by hanging the case from his saddle, a mounted man could reach the arrows easily. But Homer does not mention the case again; he talks elsewhere of a quiver (xxi 59, 233, 417, xxii 2, 71), which was carried on the shoulder with a strap. It looks as if the anomaly in xxi 54 may be an interpolation (which must extend as far as ἐκ ... ἦρεε in 56). Note that in xi 607, another late passage, Heracles carries his bow in Hades γυμνόν, 'without a case'.

Already in xxi 75 we are told what a feat it is to string the bow. The poet, however, is vague as to the nature of the problem and probably did not understand it. Telemachus tried to string the bow standing (στῆ 124) and his action is obscurely described by the words πελέμιξεν ἐρύσσασθαι μενεαίνων: πελεμίζω is 'to cause to quiver', ἐρύομαι 'to pull'. The suitors suspect that the bow has lost its flexibility, Odysseus strings it (how?) as easily as stringing a lyre. His posture is not directly described but he made his first shot καθήμενος 420. It seems that the poet thought there was some kind of trick involved known only to an expert archer like Odysseus.

Stringing a 'self' bow, such as the medieval long bow, is done by placing one end of the stave against the ground and leaning on the other; it calls for strength rather than any skill or knack. When Pandarus is said to string his bow ἀγκλίνας (Il. iv 113), the poet may refer to this operation, but κλίνας here at 137 certainly does not. The more powerful composite bow is made of a wooden stave supporting an outer layer of sinew and an inner layer of horn (κέρα 395). Early representations of this bow show a weapon of 'normal' shape, but from the late eighth century the Greeks were familiar with the improved 'Scythian' model, characterized when not fully drawn by the double curve, as shown, perhaps rather fancifully, in Figure 1. When unstrung such a bow assumes a reflexed curve which is well described by the regular epithets of the bow, παλίντονα, καμπύλα, and ἀγκύλα. καμπύλα is applied to Odysseus' bow in xxi 359, 362, and to a similar bow used by his companions in ix 156. (In the Iliad it is applied particularly to the bows of warriors with oriental connections, Paris, Pandarus, Dolon, Teucer, and Artemis in xxi 502.) ἀγκύλα alternates with καμπύλα chiefly for metrical reasons, and is found applied to the bows of Pandarus, Paris, and the Paeones ἀγκυλότοξοι.

Because of the reflexed shape of the unstrung composite bow stringing it required a special skill. The archer, sitting, as many classical monuments show, put one end of the bow over one knee, the middle under the opposite thigh, and pulled up (ἀνέλκων 150, ἐρύσσεσθαι 125) the other end. Beside the knack involved, great strength was clearly also required. See further Lorimer, *Monuments* 276–300.

INTRODUCTION

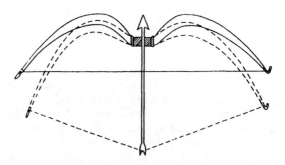

FIGURE 1. The 'Scythian' bow (Delebecque, 'Le Jeu de l'arc de l'Odyssée',
58, fig. 2)

The arrows (on the Greek words used, see xxi 423 n.) consisted of
the δόναξ, 'shaft' (*Il.* xi 584), the ἀκωκή, 'tip, head' (*Il.* xiii 251; *Od.*
xxii 16; of a spear, *Il.* v 67, xi 253, xvii 49, xxii 327, *Od.* xix 453), the
ὄγκοι, either 'barbs' or 'fletchings (flight feathers)' which helped the
arrow to fly true (in *Il.* iv 151 Menelaus is relieved to see the ὄγκοι
have not penetrated the wound, and in *Il.* iv 214 they are broken
when an arrow is pulled out); the νεῦρον, 'cord' used to tie the
components of the arrow together, also mentioned in the first of the
two passages just quoted; and the γλυφίδες, 'notches' (on these last
two parts of the arrow, mentioned in *Il.* iv 122, see below).

Penelope returns, then, with the bow and quiver (xxi 59).
Telemachus tries to brace the bow (πελέμιξεν, xxi 125). When he
fails, he leans the bow against the wall, with an arrow from the quiver
laid out and somehow resting at hand-height on the κορώνη (xxi 138)
as a mark of courtesy to the next contestant.

Leodes' attempt (xxi 149–66) is similar. Then Antinous thinks of
heating and greasing the bow, or rather the string (xxi 179, 184), to
soften and stretch it, but without success, for the other suitors try in
vain to bend the bow (xxi 184–5). At last only Antinous and
Eurymachus remain; the former suggests an adjournment (xxi 257–
68), while the latter, despite heating the string (246), is also unsuccessful (xxi 246–7), and, with temper frayed, no longer rests the arrow
politely on the κορώνη, but leaves it on the table γυμνός, 'out of the
quiver' (xxi 416–17; cf. xi 607 and n.).

Odysseus, on the contrary, does string the bow (xxi 409), as easily
as a lyre-player stringing his φόρμιγξ (xxi 406–8), though this simile
is only partly appropriate since the strings on a lyre are tightened by
turning either one or two pegs (ἀμφοτέρωθεν, 408). Odysseus hooks

BOOK XXI

the string over with his left hand, and then plucks it with his right for tautness (xxi 410), making it sing like a swallow (xxi 411; cf. λίγξε βιός, νευρὴ δὲ μέγ' ἴαχεν in *Il.* iv 125). He picks up the arrow from the table (xxi 416–17), rests it against the hand-grip (ἐπὶ πήχει ἑλών, xxi 419; cf. ἐπὶ νευρῇ κατεκόσμει... ὀϊστόν in *Il.* iv 118, and note that in *Il.* xi 375, when Alexander τόξον πῆχυν ἄνελκε, it must mean he drew the string away from the hand-grip), and shoots.

There are fewer details in this passage than in the ̇one on Pandarus, who draws the string back to his chest and pulls it so far that the head of the arrow is level with the bow (νευρὴν μὲν μαζῷ πέλασεν, τόξῳ δὲ σίδηρον, *Il.* iv 123), though in 124 the bow is described as bent double 'in a circle', which is a physical impossibility given the bow's large dimensions and the necessarily short arrow, which would have to equal the diameter of the circle in this position. The phrase ἕλκεν νευρὴν γλυφίδας τε (xxi 419) is unclear unless we translate 'he pulled the string and [the end of the arrow slotted on to the string with] the notches'. The latter[6] were probably two crossed notches (cf. γλύφω, 'carve, incise') cut into the end of the arrow to rest on the string; in *Il.* iv 122 the phrase γλυφίδας τε λαβὼν καὶ νεῦρα βόεια is a little more logical, since what the bowman pulls back is the whole arrow, the shaft and its fittings as well as the νεῦρον. This raises the question of whether νεῦρα βόεια, if it means a tough tendon (νεῦρον is applied to the human body in *Il.* xvi 316) and not simply gut, is here and here only a synonym for νευρή, 'bowstring' (frequent in the *Il.*, and used in *Od.* xi 607, xix 587, xxi 97, 127, 410, xxiv 171 as well as the passage under discussion). If that is so, then the two passages closely parallel one another.

The important passages on the bowshot itself are these: in xix 572 Penelope declares that she is going to set up a contest (ἄεθλον) involving 'those [well-known] axes' (τοὺς πελέκεας, xix 573; the demonstrative pronoun is important) which Odysseus (xix 574) used to set up ἑξείης, twelve in a row, δρυόχους ὥς, before taking up position 'some way away' (this phrase has been commented upon already) to shoot an arrow at them (xix 575). Now she proposes the same contest (xix 576) for any man ὅς... κε... | διοϊστεύσῃ πελέκεων δυοκαίδεκα πάντων (xix 577–8). In xix 587, xxi 97, 114, 127 we find σιδήρου with various forms of διοϊστεύω; xxi 75–6 are an exact repetition of xix 577–8. In xxi 3–4, the first of which is repeated in xxi 81, we read τόξον... θέμεν πολιόν τε σίδηρον | ... ἀέθλια καὶ φόνου ἀρχήν; in xxi 9–10, ἔνθα... κειμήλια κεῖτο... | χαλκός τε χρυσός τε πολύκμητός

[6] W. McLeod, "Γλυφίδες", *CR* xiv (1964), 140–1.

140

τε σίδηρος; in xxi 61–2, ἀμφίπολοι φέρον ὄγκιον, ἔνθα σίδηρος | κεῖτο; in xxi 120–2 Telemachus πελέκεας στῆσεν, διὰ τάφρον ὀρύξας | πᾶσι μίαν μακρήν, καὶ ἐπὶ στάθμην ἴθυνεν, | ἀμφὶ δὲ γαῖαν ἔναξε; in xxi 135 he says ἐκτελέωμεν ἄεθλον; in xxi 328 Eurymachus fears it may be said a beggar διὰ ... ἧκε σιδήρου; and finally xxi 420–3 describe the great feat, ἧκε δ᾿ ὀϊστόν | ἄντα τιτυσκόμενος, πελέκεων δ᾿ οὐκ ἤμβροτε πάντων | πρώτης στειλειῆς· διὰ δ᾿ ἀμπερὲς ἦλθε θύραζε | ἰὸς χαλκοβαρής. This description of the contest, which is far from pellucid, has been interpreted in many ways. But we can dismiss those explanations which take the impossible feat at face value on the grounds that the whole story is a magic fairy-tale; strictly speaking, the repeated phrases about 'piercing the iron' would have to mean in this case that the arrow went through not just one but twelve solid metal plates in a row. Odysseus' incredible feat of shooting through twelve axe blades would then be comparable to the more or less legendary feats recounted in texts and inscriptions from Egypt and India (Fries, Page, Burkert).

We do not have enough archaeological information to entertain Myres's theories about various different types of perforated axe-blade, which might allow the arrow to pass through a hole of some sort in each blade.

Into the same fanciful category falls van Leeuwen's timid suggestion that the arrow was supposed to pierce not the axe-heads, but the wooden handles. Apart from the fact that this too is an impossible feat, van Leeuwen does not explain why a cylindrical target was chosen, which would make the contest even more difficult, instead of using, say, twelve flat boards.

On the other hand, the description of Telemachus' setting up the axes and the comparison with δρύοχοι imply a single row of targets; they exclude other arrangements, such as a double row where the arrow would have to pass between pairs of blades, or in rows staggered skittle-fashion, and so on.

We are left, therefore, with the more plausible hypotheses:

1. The least acceptable is perhaps Stubbs's passing suggestion that the arrow had to pass between the axe-head, set up with its face side-on to the bowman, and the ground. This would make the low angle of aim referred to above an even more acute problem.

2. A theory which once enjoyed a certain popularity was J. K. A. Goebel's (see Figure 2);[7] though Goebel did not know this at the

---

[7] Last put forward in his *Lexilogus zu Homer u. den Homeriden* (Berlin, 1878), i 488 ff.

time, the double-headed axe was common in Minoan Crete. It was a clever guess to suppose that Odysseus' axes were double-headed, in contrast to the ἡμιπέλεκκον which in *Il.* xxiii 851, 858, 883 denotes a single-headed axe (Finley Jun., *Odyssey*, 191–2 adduces the double-headed axe in v 235, where Odysseus is building his raft, and thinks the δρύοχοι, discussed below, were similar in appearance to this weapon). But Goebel's theory leaves many questions unanswered, such as the meaning of στειλειή in xxi 422, the difficult syntax of this and the following line, the excessive and unlikely curvature of the blade shown in the Figure, the comparative ease of the feat given the necessary diameter of the aperture, the difficulty of reconciling this theory with the phrase 'piercing the iron', and the absence of any need to dig a trench with this kind of target.

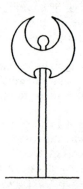

FIGURE 2. The double-headed axe (Page, *Folktales*, 101, fig. 3)

3. Page has drawn attention to the old theory of the Comte de Caylus, which was accepted by Monro and others: namely, that the axes had a kind of metal ring or handle on the blade, such as the one held by an Amazon on the Archaic metope at Selinus. The test would be to shoot the arrow through this handle, the wooden shaft of the axe being stuck in the ground. Against this, the first two and last two objections just mentioned still stand.

4. But Page himself proposes an ingenious theory, partly taken from Blinkenberg and Schuchhardt, which has earned the approbation of Dorothea Grey, *Archaeologia* G, 114–15. This is illustrated in Figure 3. The double-headed axes in question, like those of the Archaic Period known from miniatures and paintings, differed from the wooden-handled domestic axe in having a haft of iron or bronze,

at the end of which there was a ring for hanging them from a nail as votive offerings, like the *pa-sa-ro* which are mentioned, according to A. Sacconi, in Pylos Tablet Ta 716. In this case the axes would be stood on their heads with the haft upwards; only a small amount of earth piled against the head would be needed to hold them upright, and the test would be to shoot the arrow through the rings on the end of the haft. The narrowness of the rings might be an obstacle to this theory; Page suggests a diameter of four inches without advancing any evidence, Stanford speaks of an axe found by Evans which was four feet long with a ring of five inches, and Brain and Skinner consider the shot possible. One might object that the poet does not mention any rings, and that an ὄγκιον with twelve such axes would

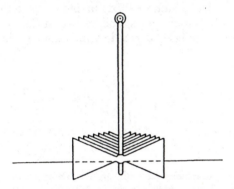

FIGURE 3. The hanging-rings on the handles of double-headed axes (Page, *Folktales*, 112, fig. 6)

weigh a great deal (a point I have mentioned above). Sacconi counters with the suggestion that the ὄγκιον, as the etymology of ὄγκοι indicates, in fact contained only the feathering or barbs of the arrows. In favour of Page's theory are the following points: the possibility that στειλειή is simply a synonym for στειλειόν, 'axe-handle, haft, helve', in which case the difficult phrase in 422 would mean 'and he did not miss [the ring] at the end of the helve of a single axe'; the acceptability of describing this sort of shot in a broad sense as 'piercing [the hole in the haft of] iron'; and the religious function of this kind of axe, which would explain the presence of such a large set of them in the palace.

5. The last theory, however, is the one adopted in my commentary. This theory was widely accepted in antiquity, fell out of favour, and is

now popular once again, being accepted in its general lines by Stanford, J. Bérard, Pocock, Stubbings, and Delebecque. What the arrow has to pass through is the hole or socket in the axe-head where the helve would normally be fitted. The axes used for the contest had no helves, either because these were removed for the purpose, or more likely because the axe-heads were stored without the wooden helves, which would in any case be exposed to rotting by worm and damp in the coffers. These axe-heads were therefore in the technical sense ἀέθλια, 'sports equipment' as we would say today (xxi 4, though not in xxi 117, where the word means 'prizes'), also called more generally σίδηρος (which does not necessarily mean they were not made of bronze). Twelve axe-heads are an easier burden for two serving-girls than twelve enormous axes complete with helves.

The trench, which could be made by piling up earth rather than digging, might be similar to the ones shown in Figures 4, 5, and 6. Figure 4 shows single-headed axes, less likely than the double-headed

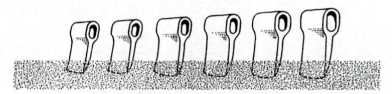

FIGURE 4. Single axe-heads fixed in the ground (Delebecque, 'Le Jeu de l'arc de l'Odyssée', 59, fig. 3)

ones, as I have said; Figure 6 is safer for the spectators, not only if an arrow is deflected sideways but also if it overshoots. In every case, the holes are placed with gaps between them, not hard up against one another.

The comparison with δρύοχοι, 'keel-blocks', refers only to one feature, their careful alignment in a straight line (on which Telemachus is praised, εὐκόσμως xxi 123; cf. v 245, where Odysseus ξέσσε . . . ἐπισταμένως καὶ ἐπὶ στάθμην ἴθυνεν like Telemachus in xxi 121; and *Il.* xv 410, where an evenly-matched battle is compared to the plumb-line accuracy with which a shipbuilder aligns a timber). Accurate alignment was vital when laying the keel of a boat (made, of course, from a tree-trunk, δρυ-), which was therefore fastened (-οχος) into the keel-blocks during building. Even today, the alignment of the blocks is apparently checked by eye, sighting along the line of

FIGURE 5. Double axe-heads fixed in the ground (Stubbings, *Companion*, 535, fig. 62)

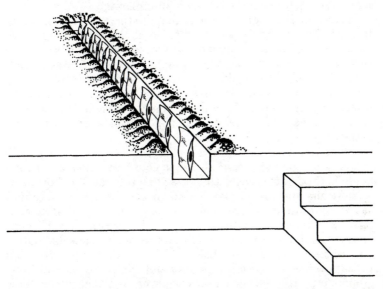

FIGURE 6. Double axe-heads fixed in a trench (Pocock, 'The Arrow and the Axe-Heads in the *Odyssey*', *AJP* lxxxii (1961), 349, fig. 1)

metal shoes (see Figure 7) whose curved shape is rather reminiscent, as noted above, of a double axe-head.

It is not clear, however, that the comparison should be pushed as far as to imagine the axes set up on a slope like the ramp of a dry-dock

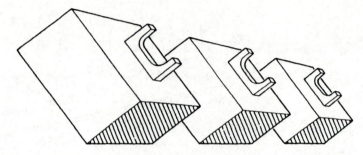

FIGURE 7. The alignment of keel-blocks (Delebecque, 'Le Jeu de l'arc de l'Odyssée', 60, fig. 4)

on the seashore. In this respect, our interpretation of $\sigma\tau\epsilon[\iota]\lambda\epsilon[\iota]\acute{\eta}$ and $\sigma\tau\epsilon[\iota]\lambda\epsilon[\iota]\acute{o}s$ or $\sigma\tau\epsilon[\iota]\lambda\epsilon[\iota]\acute{o}\nu$ is all-important.

Page is certainly correct to note that the three attestations of the feminine form mean simply 'handle, helve', the same as the neuter form in v 236; but these attestations occur not in archaic texts but in classical and Hellenistic authors (Antiphanes, fr. 121 K; Apol. iv 957; Nic. *Ther.* 386). But gender pairs where the feminine denotes the orifice and the masculine the haft or shank that fits it are a common linguistic phenomenon. Indeed, as Stanford wryly notes, sooner or later someone was bound to use this fact for a Freudian interpretation of the kind I have mentioned above.

A more complicated problem is the syntax of xxi 421–2. Goebel's theory (see Figure 2) requires the ingenious translation 'and he did not miss the end of a single axe-helve'; that is to say, the shot was so accurate that the arrow brushed each knob at the end of the handle, as shown in the Figure, without knocking over the axe. Page asks, reasonably enough, whether anyone could have eyesight sufficiently keen to umpire such a contest. His own theory requires the translation we have already given above, which is syntactically correct but which involves a bold assumption about the archaeological background, especially as regards the narrow or variable diameter of the hypothetical apertures, and above all depends on the questionable synonym of $\sigma\tau\epsilon\iota\lambda\epsilon\iota\acute{\eta}/\sigma\tau\epsilon\iota\lambda\epsilon\iota\acute{o}\nu$.

In either case, the two translations given above take $\pi\rho\acute{\omega}\tau\eta s$ in the predicative sense; in Attic prose this would require $\pi\rho\acute{\omega}\tau\eta s$ $\tau\hat{\eta}s$ $\sigma\tau\epsilon\lambda\epsilon\hat{a}s$, not $\tau\hat{\eta}s$ $\pi\rho\acute{\omega}\tau\eta s$ $\sigma\tau\epsilon\lambda\epsilon\hat{a}s$. In all the theories which involve the arrow passing through holes a further translation is possible: 'and he did not miss the edge [top or bottom] of the hole in a single axe'. This would imply that the bowman had to aim the flight of the arrow to compensate for the ballistic curve due to gravity. Such a consideration was surely irrelevant over such a short distance. Besides, any translation which takes πρώτης in the attributive sense is open to objections; thus, for example, 'and he did not miss one of the axes, from the first hole [or helve] onwards' involves a syntax which is anomalous, and even impossible. In my opinion we have to do with a syntactic cross between 'he did not miss the first hole (that is, the hole in the first axe)' and 'he did not miss a single hole (that is, the hole of a single axe)'.

The expression 'piercing the iron' is no obstacle, either to Page's theory or mine, if we take it to mean 'pierce the [aperture surrounded by] iron'. One problem which remains, especially for my theory (Page proposes very large axes), is the low level of the holes in the axes, even with a high trench. Perhaps the axe-heads were mounted on some sort of stick (the *Etymologicum Magnum*, misled by the *Odyssey* itself, mistranslates δρυόχους as τοὺς πελέκεις, but then has a similar idea: οἱ μὲν κρίκους ἀκούουσί τινας μεγάλους ἐπ᾽ ὀβελίσκων κειμένους, οὓς καταπήγνυσθαι εἰς τὴν γῆν ὥστε δι᾽ αὐτῶν τοξεύειν), or even tied to the axe-helves themselves. An alternative explanation, for those who are not convinced by the evidence given above of Archaic bowmen shooting from a crouching position (Brain and Skinner remark that to succeed in shooting through a tunnel at such a low level one would in fact be forced to shoot lying down), is the stepped floor-level shown in Figure 6.

The chief difficulty of the test, apart from the bending of the bow, was to shoot through the first hole without touching the sides, since the arrow which successfully did this would be on course for the succeeding targets. Be that as it may, the feat was an extraordinary one, and the text shows Odysseus taking very careful aim indeed (xxi 421 ἄντα τιτυσκόμενος).

BOOK XXI: COMMENTARY

1–2. = xviii 158–9, where Athena suggests that Penelope should make her first entry into the feast-hall. Here, however, the phrase seems out of context, since it overlooks the fact that Penelope has already mentioned the contest in xix 572 ff. Penelope's motive for proposing the trial may be to gain time in the desperate situation she speaks of in xix 157–61 (at any rate the φόνου ἀρχήν of 4 must refer only to Athena's intentions: see Büchner, 'Penelopeszenen', 153). Or has she in her heart given in to the suitors' adulterous importunities, an echo of the ancient legend which made her a whore (lover of Hermes, mother of Pan, etc.: Merkelbach, *Untersuchungen*, 5, and Heubeck's comments, *Frage*, 126)? The latter suggestion is opposed by P. Kretschmer's 'Penelope', *Anz. Akad. Wiss. Wien* lxxx (1943), 80–93 (see Lesky, 'Homeros', 116), which connects the heroine's name etymologically with the bird πηνέλοψ, model of conjugal fidelity.   **περίφρονι:** see 321 n.

3. **σίδηρος:** the word refers to the axes, most likely without their helves (see Introduction). They are described as 'hoary, grey-haired', that is steel-grey (cf. xxi 10).

4. **ἐν μεγάροις Ὀδυσῆος:** the phrase supports the theory that the contest takes place in the feast-hall (see Introduction, and cf. the first hemistich of xx 117).   **ἀέθλια καὶ φόνου ἀρχήν:** cf. xxiv 169, and n. on 1–2 above. The words are in apposition to τόξον and σίδηρον; I have translated ἀέθλια, somewhat anachronistically, as 'sports equipment' in my Introduction (and cf. xxi 62, 117).

5. **προσεβήσετο:** there is a problem about the direction implied by the prefix. Since Odysseus' departure Penelope has moved her bedroom from the ground floor to an apartment upstairs; in xix 600 she goes up (ἀνέβαινε) to her ὑπερώϊα, and it is there that she sits to listen to the noise of the feasting (xx 387). Now, therefore, she must descend from her chamber (οἷο δόμοιο must be ablative) with the key in her hand (εἵλετο in xxi 6 is pluperfect in sense) to one of the store-rooms which led off the λαύρη, 'corridor, passage'; to be precise, to the furthest and least-used of them (ἔσχατον, 9, perhaps situated outside the palace itself). These store-rooms or θάλαμοι will have been at the same level as the feast-hall: how else could the weapons have been carried back and forth without having to climb the steep stairs (κλίμακα ... ὑψηλήν)? In i 330, where Penelope likewise descends from her chamber, the reading is κατεβήσετο, a possible variant here (see apparatus); otherwise προσεβήσετο must be translated 'proceeded (to descend)' (cf. xiv 1 προσέβη).

6. **παχείη:** the epithet, used of Odysseus' hand in xx 299 and xxii 326, has been held to be inappropriate for Penelope's. *Et. Flor.* emends the word ἵνα

148

μὴ δοκῇ ἀκύρως ἐπὶ γυναικὶ εἰρῆσθαι; but in *Il.* xxi 403 and 424 the same adjective is applied to Athena. A. C. Schlesinger, 'Penelope's Hand', *CPh* lxiv (1969) 236-7 suggests that Penelope had her hand clenched to hide the key from the maidservants; but there is nothing improbable in a tall, well-built, and noble-looking queen having a sturdy hand (W. F. Wyatt Jun., 'Penelope's Fat Hand (*Od.* xxi 6-7)', *CPh* lxxiii (1978) 343-4; cf. xviii 195 μακροτέρην καὶ πάσσονα θῆκεν ἰδέσθαι, of the same heroine). Alternatively, the epithet may be formulaic, or emotional ('mighty', reflecting the decisive moment in Penelope's life, as Austin suggests, *Archery*, 73-4; see Finley Jun., *Odyssey*, 190). T. Eide, 'A Note on the Homeric χειρὶ παχείη', *Symb. Osl.* lv (1980), 23-6, notes that Penelope's hand would naturally be clenched and full, since she is holding a bulky key shaped like an S or Σ (taking the better reading εὐκαμπέα, an adjective applied to a sickle in xviii 368); this key has to be inserted with some difficulty (ἄντα τιτυσκομένη, xxi 48) into a gap or hole in order to shoot back the bolts (ἀνέκοπτεν ὀχῆας, xxi 47) which hold the door on the inside. The key is a work of craftsmanship (καλήν, xxi 7) with a handle of ivory (possibly a sign that this line is late: M. Treu, 'Homer u. das Elfenbein', *Philologus* xcix (1955), 149-58), made not of gold but of bronze (see apparatus). Before opening, Penelope must untie the leather thong (ἱμάντα . . . ἀπέλυσε κορώνης, xxi 46) which passes through a second hole (the one through which the wraith of Iphthime enters in iv 802 παρὰ κληῖδος ἱμάντα), and is fastened on the outside to the κορώνη (on the two meanings of this word see my Introduction) to close the bolt and lock the door from the outside. In i 441-2 Eurycleia pulls the door of Telemachus' chamber shut with the κορώνη, which doubled as a door-handle and was made of silver; and then ἐπὶ δὲ κληῖδ' ἐτάνυσσεν ἱμάντι, 'shot the bolt (note this second meaning of κληῖς) with the thong' from outside, leaving it untied so as not to lock the prince in.

8-9. We must imagine more than one store-room (cf. xxi 5n.), since Penelope would otherwise come upon the hiding-place where Odysseus and Telemachus have stored the arms taken from the feast-hall in xix 31-3, and from which the latter will fetch them in xxii 109. But in ii 337 the poet talks only of Odysseus' ὑψόροφον θάλαμον.

9. κειμήλια: cf. xiv 326 (with a list of metals two lines before) and xix 295.

10. πολύκμητος: the epithet is appropriate, since the metal had to be laboriously extracted from lumps of crude ore, sometimes even from meteorites (cf. the σόλον αὐτοχόωνον offered as a prize in the games in *Il.* xxiii 826), by repeated firings (Hesych. ἐλατρεύς· ὁ τρίτην πύρωσιν τοῦ σιδήρου), coolings, and other processes; see further R. J. Forbes, *Archaeologia* K, 31-2, n. 171.

11. παλίντονον: on the epithet, and on the contradiction between this line and xxi 54, see the Introduction.

12. ἰοδόκος: elsewhere only in xxi 60 and *Il.* xv 444.   **στονόεντες:** 'mournful, laden with grief'; found also in xxi 60 and in nine other places in Homer, of which xxiv 180 and three of the *Iliad* attestations concern arrows.

13. This appears to be the beginning of the interpolation on Iphitus mentioned in the Introduction, of which there are further traces in 15, 18, 20–1, 26, 35, 41 (see nn., and Blass, *Interpolationen*, 239–40, Shipp, *Studies*, 351); on its 'convoluted style suggesting a more extensive poetical model' see Kirk, *Songs*, 370. Iphitus, son of Eurytus, king of Oechalia, a city of unknown location here sited somewhere in the Peloponnese, was killed by Heracles. The chronology is fantastical; in *Il.* xi 690 we find Heracles associated with the deeds of the young Nestor, which looks suspiciously like the work of an interpolator, as does the present unattested episode from the youthful exploits of Odysseus, his diplomatic mission on behalf of Laertes (D. Gray, *Archaeologia* G, 116, 128). Against all these objections, however, it may be argued that the story provides a decent explanation for the apparent improbability of Odysseus having left his best weapon behind in Ithaca when he set out for Troy. There is an inversion of sequence in the syntax of the aorists: the proper chronological order is ἄειραν (18), ἦλθε (17), ξυμβλήτην (15), and δῶκε (13). **δῶρα:** predicative.

15. Μεσσήνη: a nice problem of geography is posed by this name, here only in Homer, in relation to Λακεδαίμονι in 13 (cf. iv 1). Either the poet thought there was a city in Lacedaemon so called (Hoekstra, *Epic Verse*, 61, n. 57, notes the name Hippocoon given to a Thracian in *Il.* x 518 as another allusion to Spartan myths), or this passage was written after 700 BC by an author who was aware of the outcome of the first Messenian War. The problem disappears if we assume that xxi 15 is an interpolation, but keep ξυμβλήτην: this dual does not appear elsewhere. In addition, the line is ὁλοσπόνδειος. Unlike the eight other such lines, including xxii 175, 192, where *αὐτόο is possible instead of αὐτοῦ (D. W. Pye, 'Wholly Spondaic Lines in Homer', *G&R* xi (1964), 2–6), this one cannot be corrected by resolution, unless we accept Nauck's doubtful ξυμβλήατο.

16. The spelling of the names of the two characters called Ὀρτίλοχος or Ὀρσίλοχος causes considerable confusion. The first was the father of Diocles, at whose house in Pherae Telemachus stays in iii 489, xv 187; the second, whose death is described in *Il.* v 542 and 549, was Diocles' son (his grandfather is named there too, 546–7). The testimony of the MSS of both poems is naturally chaotic; the schol., Aristophanes of Byzantium, and Aristarchus were of the opinion that the grandfather should be spelt with -τ- and the grandson with -σ- (followed by Allen, though both his and von der Mühll's editions spell the Trojan hero of the same name in *Il.* viii 274 and the Cretan in *Od.* iii 260 with -σ-); but Zenodotus and Pausanias (iv 30. 2) wrote -τ- in all cases. Wackernagel, *Untersuchungen*, 236, n. 1, is probably right in considering the forms with -σ- to be late.

17. μετὰ χρεῖος: 'after (i.e. to recover) a debt' owed to the Ithacans by the Messenians.

18. ἐξ ... ἄειραν: 'robbed by taking away', a strange phrase without parallels elsewhere. E.-M. Hamm's translation 'hatten ... über die Wasserfläche schweben gemacht' (*LfgrE*, i 165–70, s.v. ἀείρω) is very forced, and iii 312, misspelt and adduced by her as a parallel, has a different meaning.

19. **πολυκλήϊσι:** 'with many benches of oarsmen'; cf. viii 161 and xx 382. The second hemistich = *Il.* xi 697, but there *τρίηκόσι'* follows *κρινάμενος*; Hoekstra, *Epic Verse*, 36-7, suggests that in both places the original formula was *μῆλα τριηκόσι' ἠδὲ νομῆας*.

20. 'went a long way [on] an embassy'; the first accusative expresses content, the second distance. **ἐξεσίην:** a possible reminiscence of *Il.* xxiv 235, where it precedes *ἐλθόντι*.

21. **παιδνὸς:** elsewhere found only in the late xxiv 338, and in tragedy. **ἄλλοι τε:** usually 'and furthermore'.

22. Supply *ἦλθε*. **οἱ:** ethic dative. **ὄλοντο:** pluperfect in sense.

23. = iv 636. **ὑπό:** adv. in the sense 'under [the teat], still suckling'. W. Richter, *Archaeologia* H, 78, n. 562, remarks that Homeric mules are always the offspring of mare and he-ass; that the epithet *ταλαεργοί* refers to their proverbial hardiness at work; and that the small number of animals stolen emphasizes their scarcity, and hence their great value, in the Homeric period: thus in *Il.* xxiii 266, 654 mules are offered as prizes in the games.

24. **γένοντο:** the verb points to a future event, the *φόνος* brought about by *μοίρα*.

25. The line is metrically acephalous; cf. iv 13 n., xxiv 482. **καρτερό-θυμον:** note the formal epithet of praise, even though the passage concerns an evil deed committed by the hero.

26. **φῶθ':** in apposition, the only example in the *Odyssey* of this construction in conjunction with a proper name. **ἐπιίστορα:** not otherwise attested until the Hellenistic period; *ἴστωρ* in *Il.* xviii 501, xxiii 486 means 'judge, arbiter', but here the sense has nothing to do with judging. The schol. (*μεγαλουργόν* and *ἐπὶ μεγάλοις ἔργοις ἱστορούμενον*) do not make clear whether the phrase is pejorative or not: on one hand, recalling the sense of *μέγα* in iii 261, xix 92, *μεγάλων ἐπίστορα ἔργων* might mean that Heracles was 'skilled in' or 'accomplice in' (rather than 'author of') evil deeds; on the other, it might refer to his Labours. The myth is confused and inconsistent: apparently Autolycus, Odysseus' grandfather (cf. the doubtful episode in xix 394-466), stole the mares from Eurytus and entrusted them to Heracles (this perhaps explains the reference to his 'complicity': K. Lehrs, *De Aristarchi studiis Homericis* (Leipzig, 1882³), 109 'in crimine . . . conscium'); Heracles later refused to give them up. Iphitus was perhaps looking for Heracles not in order to reclaim the mares, but to ask for his help, on the grounds that he was to some extent implicated in the crime.

27. **ἐόντα:** concessive. **ᾧ:** reflex. possessive; Heracles murdered Iphitus when he was a guest in 'his own' (i.e. Heracles') house, which made the deed all the more horrible.

28. A direct exclamation by the poet.

28-9. **τράπεζαν:** the sacred table, symbol of the bond of hospitality

COMMENTARY

(S. Laser, *Archaeologia* P, 58), at which the host seated his guest, and on which oaths were sworn, xiv 158, xvii 155 (in xx 230 the variant reading is preferable).   **τήν:** underlines the sacred nature of the table ('that [famous and traditional] one'); the conjecture τὴν δή οἱ of Eustathius and certain MSS is unnecessary. The phrase is ambiguous; the subject might be Iphitus, meaning that he had previously entertained Heracles as a guest, though this is not likely.   **ἔπειτα:** 'even after that, despite that'.

30. 'and besides all this he kept the mares'; the imperf. implies continuity.
31. **τὰς ἐρέων:** 'and while he was seeking for them' (cf. διζήμενος, xxi 22), before meeting Heracles; the phrase takes us back to the narrative from which we digressed in xxi 15. The exchange of gifts is typical (cf. Diomedes and Glaucus in *Il.* vi).
32. This reading, given by P 133 and others (note also γ' in the apparatus), avoids a lengthening in thesis; Grashof's emendation spoils the syntax.   **ἐφόρει:** iterative. Eurytus is described as a great bowman in viii 224–5, where he and Heracles καὶ ἀθανάτοισιν ἐρίζεσκον περὶ τόξων; cf. *Il.* ii 596.
34. **τῷ:** sc. Iphitus.
35–6. They intended to share each other's table, but were forestalled.   **τραπέζῃ:** locative.   **γνώτην ἀλλήλων:** γιγνώσκω with the gen. is rare (Schwyzer, *Grammatik*, ii 106); hence the crop of variant readings, but the construction is paralleled in xxiii 109.   **πρίν:** not 'before', but 'on the contrary, instead'.   **Διὸς υἱὸς:** Heracles.
35. **ἀρχήν:** in apposition; cf. xxi 4.   **ξεινοσύνης:** the only attestation of this word in Greek literature (ξεινίης would require lengthening of the -ι-), xv 343 πλαγκτοσύνη is also a *hapax*.   **προσκηδέος:** only here in Homer, in Herodotus (as a term indicating kinship by marriage), and in Hellenistic Greek, the word is a back-formation from an unattested *προσκήδομαι (cf. περικήδομαι in iii 219, xiv 527); the variant εὐκηδέος in Mon. would also be a *hapax*.
38. **οἱ:** sc. Odysseus.
39. **ἐρχόμενος:** iterative.
40. **αὐτοῦ:** adverbial.   **μνῆμα:** predicative.
41. **κέσκετ':** iterative form of κεῖμαι, either by hyphaeresis of *κεγεσκετο or from the κε- of κέατο through a hypothetical intermediate stage *κέσκοντο; otherwise unattested (but cf. παρεκέσκετο in xiv 521). Odysseus kept the bow for hunting and minor expeditions. Note the lengthening of ἐνί before μεγάροισι, and the variant in P 28.   **ἧς:** reflex. possessive.
42. **τὸν:** this use of the article, and especially its position, has caused remark, but cf. *Il.* xvii 401; it may be demonstrative ('that one' of which we spoke in xxi 8). The variant reading with the possessive is not hopeless, but requires lengthening in thesis; Nauck's conjecture, with its permissible hiatus, may have been the real reading, needlessly 'corrected' by the scribes.
43–4. There are a further four parallel passages on the craft of the carpenter (τέκτονα δούρων, xvii 384): xvii 340–1, identical except for the first hemistich; v 245, almost identical to xxi 44; and the second hemistichs of

152

xxi 121 and xxiii 197 respectively, identical and almost identical to the end of 44. In v 245 and xvii 341 we find ξέσσε(ν), 'smoothed with a plane', as here, and in xxiii 196 ἀμφέξεσα, 'planed all around'. In all five passages the στάθμη is mentioned; the etymology of this word suggests that originally it referred to a tool for testing vertical alignment, like our 'plumb-line', but in Homer this is the function of the στάθμη only in xvii 341, for a pair of cypress door-jambs. Here some sort of 'ruler' for testing straightness is not impossible, but the στάθμη is more likely to be a kind of 'spirit-level' for checking the horizontal alignment of the threshold. It is certainly a linear 'ruler' in v 245 (for the planks of the raft), xxi 121 (the axes), and xxiii 197 (the planks of the bed). The verb ἰθύνω also appears in all five passages, and also in v 255 (the building of the raft), as well as contexts to do with archery, such as xxii 8, and navigation.

43. **δρύϊνον:** 'wooden (not necessarily of oak)', only here in Homer, not attested again before Hippocrates and Euripides. The wooden threshold indicates a humble room; the threshold of the feast-hall, always described as λάϊνος (xvii 30, xx 258, xxiii 88), is made of more valuable material; in xvii 339 μελίνου οὐδοῦ (ξεστοῦ leg. Bérard), 'threshold of ash-wood', raises the thorny question of whether the hall had more than one threshold.

45. A typical example of parataxis, loosely co-ordinated with the preceding relative clause.

46-8. See n. on xxi 6. **θοῶς:** Penelope 'expertly' unties the complicated knot which fastened the door.

47. **ἐν ... ἧκε:** tmesis. **θυρέων:** synizesis; the door has two leaves (θύρετρα). **ἀνέκοπτεν:** here only in Homer; the verb is not attested again before Thucydides. **ὀχῆας:** the 'lock', which also consists of two bolts (cf. xxi 391).

48. **ἄντα τιτυσκομένη:** the phrase is used, for example, of taking aim in archery (cf. xxi 421; and xxi 6n. on its force here).

48-9. **τὰ δ' ἀνέβραχεν ... | ... λειμῶνι:** a fine simile for the loud creaking of a door which has long been unused (cf. xxi 393-5), which is reminiscent of other passages on grazing cows and bulls (see for example Il. ii 480-1); it displays a sharp eye for nature unusual in this type of simile in the Odyssey, raising suspicions as a possible cento of passages from the Iliad (Il. xxi 237 μεμυκὼς ἠΰτε ταῦρος, Il. xvi 151 βοσκομένη λειμῶνι; see Blass, Interpolationen, 201). Furthermore, though there are 'bellowing' doors in Il. v 749 and Il. xii 460, the only other occurrence of ἀνέβραχε (Il. xix 13) refers to the sound of a weapon; ἔβραχε in Il. v 859 denotes the war-cry of Ares, in Il. xvi 468 the whinnying of a horse. These problems, as well as the repetition of the same word in the identical position in two successive lines and the difficulty of the neuter τά, which must be taken as anticipating θύρετρα, are resolved by Nauck's conjecture; but this leaves τόσα unexplained.

51. **ὑψηλῆς σανίδος:** σανίς, 'plank', here has the unparalleled meaning of 'wall-shelf' (cf. xxi 137), or more likely (ἐπί ... βῆ) a raised wooden stage or dais placed at some height above the floor to avoid damp. Perfume was placed in the chest for the same purpose, and to prevent moth (cf. a similar

case with ἐσθής in ii 339, viii 438; and see further S. Laser, *Archaeologia* P, 68–9).

53. ὀρεξαμένη: 'standing on tiptoe'; the peg would have to be high up to hold the huge bow. Pegs were also used to hang clothes (i 440), a lyre (viii 67), and another bow (*Il.* v 209).

54. αὐτῷ γωρυτῷ: on γωρυτός see the Introduction. A fine example lined with gold has been found by Andronikos in Vergina. The pronoun is sociative, 'with its bow-case and all', emphasizing the heavy weight which Penelope has to lift.　ὅς: lengthening before ϝ..

55. ἑζομένη . . . κατ': tmesis; in x 567 κατ' αὖθι should perhaps also be divided thus. Apoll. (καταῦθι, li 1079, xii 528) misunderstood the Homeric usage.

56. ἐκ δ' ᾗρεε: on this tmesis, see the Introduction; Bentley's conjecture, supported by a parallel, preserves the ϝ-. The plural is often used to indicate bow and quiver together, and occasionally for the bow alone (cf. *Il.* i 45).

57. = xix 213, 251.

58. Penelope does not linger over the complicated business of locking the door (cf. xxi 46). Likewise Telemachus forgets to lock the door in xxii 112, confessing in xxii 156 that he left it 'ajar' (ἀγκλίνας).　μετὰ: cf. xxi 17.

60. See the Introduction and apparatus.

61-2. Both lines are indispensable; Bérard's rejection of xxi 62, which he considered an echo of iii 388, xiv 326, xix 295, makes σίδηρος very awkward.

61. The two maidservants (but cf. xxi 66) carry the heavy basket; Penelope is also heavily laden (xxi 54), but carrying the bow is a ceremonial act. ὄγκιον: the noun is difficult (see S. Laser, *Archaeologia* P, 70) for various reasons, including accentuation (see the variants in the apparatus, and Chantraine, *Formation*, 54, who argues that dactylic words should take the paroxytone), the material of which it was made (Pollux x 165 σκεῦος πλεκτόν suggests wickerwork or some other light material), and etymology (probably from ἐν-εγκεῖν, '[something] to carry things in'; less likely is the derivation '[a receptacle] for ὄγκοι, arrow fletchings', the latter being so called from their function as counter-weights; though ὄγκιον might mean 'basket, chest with handles', from the resemblance of the latter to the curved ὄγκοι).

62. ἀέθλια: ἀέθλιον (S. Laser, *LfgrE*, i 148–51) is a suppletive form of ἄεθλον, always used in ∪ − ∪ ∪, particularly convenient before the bucolic caesura; of the fourteen occasions it appears, nine mean 'prize', one means 'contest' (viii 108; cf. xxi 91), and the remaining four mean 'gear, sports equipment' (compare xxi 4 with xxiv 169; in xxi 117, based on *Il.* xxiii 736 ἀέθλια . . . ἀνελόντες and *Il.* xxiii 823 ἀέθλια . . . ἀνελέσθαι, an odd expression which is translated, hardly satisfactorily, as 'be[ing] handy with the gear'). τοῖο: emphatic demonstrative, 'that one [of whom we know]' (cf. xxi 42).

63-6. = i 332–5, xviii 208–11, xvi 414–16 (less the last line). In the three earlier passages a maidservant stands on either side, but only i 331 and xviii 207 state beforehand that Penelope is accompanied by only two maid-servants. In theory we might take this passage to mean that there were four slave-girls, two carrying the ὄγκιον (xxi 61) and two more standing at Penelope's sides; but it is easier to suppose that there are only two girls. At all events xxi 66 is suspect (see apparatus).

64. ῥα: that is, 'as was to be expected from a queen'.

65. κρήδεμνα: Homer uses the poetic word κρήδεμνον (associated with the cult of Hera in Samos according to Leumann, *Wörter*, 296 n. 60) in both singular and plural forms, without distinction in meaning, to indicate a woman's head-dress; this implies some sort of veil with various pins and appurtenances, not a simple hair-net or diadem. Besides, Nausicaa and her friends would not have had to remove anything so flimsy as a hair-net in order to play ball (vi 100). In Penelope's drawing of the veil across her cheeks (on which see further Lorimer, *Monuments*, 385–6; and, on the κρήδεμνον, G. Bielefeld, *Archaeologia* C, 3 n. 10), H. Haakh, 'Der Schleier der Penelope', *Gymnasium* lxvi (1959), 374–80, sees a gesture designed not to cover her face, but rather to give a glimpse, at once polite and alluring, of her eyes.

68-73. Bérard deleted these lines on the grounds that such insults are inconsistent with Penelope's apparently conciliatory mood. The first four and a half feet of xxi 68=xx 292.

69. ἐχράετ': the verb governs both τόδε δῶμα and the two infinitives, which are consecutive or final. ἐμμενὲς αἰεί: cf. ix 386.

71. μύθου ... ἐπισχεσίην: 'excuse expressed in words (that is, lies)', or 'offer of an excuse, pretext'; the noun is otherwise unattested. Homer only once uses the synonym ἐπίσχεσις (xvii 451), later common in prose.

72. ἱέμενοι: the participle must be taken as the equivalent of an abstract noun, as the object of ποιήσασθαι, or we must supply 'but you did [what you have done]' (cf. xxi 323).

73. τόδε ... ἄεθλον: the force of τόδε is either 'this prize of which I am about to speak', or, rather crudely for Penelope's way of speaking, 'the prize you see before you, i.e. this woman as wife' (cf. xxi 106–7, where τόδε ... ἄεθλον is followed by οἵη). ἄγετε: not a mere interjection, but with its original imperative force, 'act now!'

74. γὰρ: the particle refers back to τόδε.

75-9. = xix 577–81; on the significance of the earlier passage see n. on xxi 1–2.

77. κεν ... ἐσποίμην: the sense is close to that of an ordinary future.

79. ποτε: indefinite, here more or less 'always, ever'. περ: 'even'. After this, Penelope does not speak again until 311 (J. L. Myres, 'The Pattern of the *Odyssey*', *JHS* lxxii (1952), 8), but there is no indication that she has left the hall.

80-100. The passage is suspect; a number of deletions based on linguistic anomalies such as those of 91 and 93 have been proposed (see Shipp,

Studies, 352). The possibility that Eumaeus played no part in the original version has been mentioned in the Introduction.

81. = xxi 3.

82-3. On the weeping in these two lines see the Introduction.

82. κατέθηκε: 'laid it on the ground'; cf. xxi 136 θῆκε χαμᾶζε.

83. βουκόλος: the character of Philoetius may have been an invention of poet *B*, as suggested in the Introduction; after a brief mention in xx 185 ff., he reappears here, but is not named again until xxi 240.   **ἄλλοθ':** 'for his part, too'.   **τόξον:** see the apparatus.

84. ἔκ τ' ὀνόμαζε: the original construction with this verb (see, for example, O'Nolan, *Doublets*, 23–37, esp. 30–1) required that, in cases where the line began with the name of the speaker in the nominative, the name of the addressee should follow in the vocative at the beginning of the next line, as in xxi 167–8; otherwise the name of the addressee appeared in both lines, the first time in the accusative, as in xvi 417–18. But the expression ἐκ . . . ὀνόμαζε became fixed as a formula, and we find it used even in cases where the speaker is not in fact required to 'call the addressee by his proper name': for example, where a superior is speaking to an inferior, as in the present lines or in xviii 78, xix 90, xxi 287, addressed respectively to Irus, to a maidservant, and to Odysseus disguised as a (nameless) beggar; when Telemachus addresses his own mother, as in xviii 96; or indeed, in cases such as xxi 248, where the speaker uses no name at all.

85-95. Antinous reproaches the servants for their tears, and at the same time contrives to ingratiate himself with Penelope, even by such flattering and emotional touches as xxi 94–5, and by his false modesty about the suitors' chances of success.

85. The insults in this line are out of tune with δειλώ in the next: a similar case is x 189, athetized by the ancients.   **ἀγροιῶται:** the element of social snobbery in the townsman's disdain for the 'yokels' gives the line a modern, 'almost Theocritean' ring in the view of Finley Jun., *Odyssey*, 191; Stella (*Ulisse*, 375) contrasts the passage with xi 489–91, where Achilles considers the labour of the fields only a minor evil.   **ἐφημέρια φρονέοντες:** schol. τὸ παραυτίκα μόνον φρονοῦντες (cf. *Il.* i 343 οὐδέ τι οἶδε νοῆσαι ἅμα πρόσσω καὶ ὀπίσσω).

86. The following series of duals is addressed to Eumaeus and Philoetius; for the first of them, cf. xviii 389.

87. Cf. xvii 150.   **ἦ τε καὶ ἄλλως:** the relative has causal force; ἄλλως implies 'without your upsetting her further'.

89. ἀλλ' ἀκέων: ἀκέων was already suspect in antiquity (Eust. ὀχλεῖ τινὰς διὰ τὸ καινοφανές), giving rise to various conjectures, of which ἀλλὰ καὶ ὧς is the most ingenious. ἀκέων is used twenty-one times in epic, on nine occasions in the masc. nom. sing., on six in other cases, and on four occasions as an indeclinable adjective (*Il.* iv 22 and viii 459 ἀκέων as fem. nom. sing.; *h. Ap.* 404, as masc. nom. pl.; here as masc. nom. pl. or dual); it is usually explained as the fossilized participle of an unknown *ἀκέω, 'am silent', used indeclinably because of the frequency of its occurrence in the masc. nom. sing. But Leumann (*Wörter*, 166–7) suggests a development from βῆ *τακέων (cf. Lat. *taceo*), corrupted to βῆ τ' ἀκέων; while V. Pisani (*LfgrE*, i 410–11) postulates an adverbial form *ἀκηον which evolved phonetically to both ἀκέων and ἀκήν, 'silently' (the latter is usually explained as a primitive fem. sing. acc.).   **δαίνυσθε:** 'continue eating', durative.

90. κατ' ... λιπόντε: tmesis.

91. ἄεθλον: 'contest' (cf. xxi 62, xxii 5); masc. sing. acc. in apposition. **ἀάατον:** the prosody of this word is difficult: in *Il.* xiv 271 it is scanned ∪ –⁴ – –⁵; in xxi 91, xxii 5, Apoll. ii 77 ∪ –⁴ ∪ ∪. The etymology of the word obviously points to *ἀϝατη > ἄτη, 'harm, deceit', but it is unclear whether the prefix ἀ- is negative (schol. ἀβλαβής), in which case we should expect ἀν, or intensive (schol. ἐπιβλαβής). Apoll. took it to be the latter, applying the adjective to a particularly dangerous boxer; but the three Homeric attestations allow the other interpretation. In *Il.* xiv 271 the waters of Styx cannot be said to be 'deceitful'; here Antinous does not mean that the contest will be 'harmful', since as far as he knows nobody is going to shoot with the bow; and we must translate Odysseus' words at xxii 5 'up to now [it is true] the contest has been harmless [though matters are about to change]'. Antinous' words here are therefore full of dramatic irony; the audience knows that the contest will not in fact turn out to be 'harmless'. But if the audience was also aware of the intensive force of ἀ-, there could be a play on words: the line might either be read with a comma after μνηστήρεσσιν and no pause after λιπόντε in xxi 90, or with a pause after the participle to suggest the meaning 'disastrous for the suitors'; the poet leaves a question mark over the hateful Antinous' remark, which could be seen as an expression of ill omen (van der Valk, *Textual Criticism*, 211 n. 3). The best solution is to leave the phrase without punctuation, as Stanford does in his edition. See further H. Seiler, *LfgrE*, i 2–3 s.v. ἀάατος.

92. Here and in xxi 97 we have asigmatic futures. On the expansion of the formulaic τόξον ἐΰξοον, found again in 281, 286, 326, see Hainsworth, *Flexibility*, 78.

93. μέτα: the only occurrence in Homer of this form for μέτεστι.   **τοίσ-δεσι:** the form with the double ending has caused doubt (see the apparatus), but occurs in x 268; the same form with -σσ- occurs three times in the *Odyssey* and once in the *Iliad*.

94. The first three feet = xix 315.

95. The paratactic construction is concessive in sense.

96. τῷ δ' ἄρα: ἄρα 'as was to be expected from so wily a man', in close conjunction with the dative of possession τῷ.

97–100. On these lines see the Introduction.

98. ἦ τοι: 'and yet', heavily ironic; the irony is increased by the sardonic understatement of γεύεσθαι, 'taste'.

99. ἀτίμα: in xvii 445–80 Antinous not only insulted Odysseus, but threw a stool at him.

100. ἐπὶ δ' ὄρνυε ... ἑταίρους: 'and also egged his companions on [to make like mockery]'; the epexegetic phrase stands in loose paratactical relation to a preceding relative clause, as in xxi 45. **ἥμενος:** the conjecture ἥμενον is based on xxi 425 (ἥμενος in the same metrical position, used by Odysseus of himself), xviii 224, xix 322 (again in the first foot, used by Penelope of Odysseus), xx 262 (Telemachus tells his father to sit, ἧσο); the participle would then be causal in force. However, Focke (*Odyssee*, 351–2) adduces this line precisely in order to prove that in xvii Odysseus was not yet sitting inside the feast-hall, but only on its threshold.

101. = ii 409, xviii 405, and similar to xviii 60, xxi 130; and with different verbs, xvi 476, xxii 354. A transitional stage which points towards this formula is xii 175, where Odysseus' μεγάλη ἴς is almost personified as he warms the wax. For the adj. ἱερός in a similar periphrastic expression cf. xiii 20 ἱερὸν μένος Ἀλκινόοιο; the word means 'strong, mighty' (cf. Skt. isirá-), as also in xxiv 81 ἱερὸς στρατός.

102. Perhaps Telemachus has inadvertently let fall a smile of joy at the thought of his father's imminent triumph; he now tries to divert his listeners' attention from the slip (see Büchner, 'Penelopeszenen', 153, 160). **ὦ πόποι:** an exclamation of surprise; cf. xxi 131, 249.

103. **φίλη:** here not with its usual possessive sense (that is provided by μοι), but 'dear, beloved', which makes the boy's speech sound all the more awkward and silly. **περ:** this particle makes the participle concessive. The line ending = xx 131.

104. Cf. xix 579, xxi 77.

106–10. The crude tone of these lines has caused unease, reflected in the various conjectures recorded in the apparatus (in 106–12, Bérard removes everything from μνηστῆρες to μύνῃσι (111) inclusive, and changes the following παρέλκετε to ἐπέλθετε); but their lively irony is quite Homeric.

106. Cf. xxi 73; τόδε here anticipates γυνή.

107. **Ἀχαιΐδα γαῖαν:** Ἀχαιῒς γῆ, γαῖα, or αἶα, which occurs in xi 166, xiii 249, *Il.* i 254, seems to include only the Peloponnese; hence xxi 109, a combination of xiv 97–8, is out of place here. By the same reasoning, xxi 108 might also be spurious.

108–9. Locative genitives. ἱερῆς alludes to the cult of Poseidon at Pylos, on which see E. T. Vermeule, *Archaeology* V, 125.

110. 'and you yourselves know it'.

111. **ἄγε:** refers back to xxi 106. **μύνῃσι:** back-formation from μύναμαι, only here in Homer, but attested in Alcaeus (fr. 392 L–P); the word shares the same root as ἀμύνω, 'drive off, defend oneself from', with loss of the intensive ἀ-; ἀμεύσασθαι, 'break free from, overcome', and hence 'get away from the truth, make excuses'. **παρέλκετε:** cf. παρέλκετο, xviii 282. **τόξου:** depends on τανυστύος.

112. **ἀποτρωπᾶσθε:** frequentative. **τανυστύος:** only here; the suffix -τυς is twice as common in the *Odyssey* as in the *Iliad* (cf. xxi 306 ἐπητύς, xxiv 229 γραπτύς). **ὄφρα ἴδωμεν:** the hiatus before digamma is normal; 'let's see [what happens]', cf. xxi 336.

113. κεν ... πειρησαίμην: equivalent to a future (cf. xxi 77). τοῦ: demonstr., 'that bow [of which we know]'.

114. ἐντανύσω: of fourteen occurrences of ἐντανύω, only this one and xxi 185 are used intransitively.

115–16. οὔ κέ μοι ἀχνυμένῳ ... λείποι: the thought is oddly phrased, and ambiguous: either 'I would not be sorry if my mother were to leave, so long as I were left ...' (taking ἀχνυμένῳ as an ethic dat. approaching a dat. absolute, and causal ὅτε; alternatively, taking ὅτε temporally, 'while I was left'); or, 'she will not have to leave (for the future sense cf. xxi 113n.) to my sorrow [that is to say, she will remain] as long as I remain'. The contrast between λείποι/λιποίμην fits the first of these two interpretations, which is not inappropriate to Telemachus' sarcastic tone. The second interpretation postulates a change of mood by attraction.

117. Cf. xxi 62. οἷός τ': predicative, and followed by an infin., almost as in Attic; the origin of the construction is clearly seen in xxi 172–3 τοῖον ... | οἷόν τε ... ἔμεναι.

118–19. Normally only the χιτών was worn indoors, but here Telemachus, who has to keep going out to the courtyard, is wearing a χλαῖνα, which he throws back in order to slip his swordbelt off his shoulder, since he needs his sword for digging (cf. xi 24–5 for a similar task carried out with an ἄορ). φοινικόεσσαν: 'cerise, light red', whereas πορφύρεος denoted a deeper colour, 'garnet, dark red' (see S. Marinatos, *Archaeologia* A/B, 3); in Mycenean we have the adj. *po-ni-ki-ja*, 'red', and the neuter noun *po-ni-ki-jo*, 'red dye', perhaps for colouring perfumes. The same word is applied to a χλαῖνα at xiv 500, *Il.* x 133 (at the end of the line, as here); to reins at *Il.* viii 116 (end of line), and to bruises at *Il.* xxiii 717 (–² ∪ ∪ –³), apparently with short -ῐ-, instead of the correct long -ῑ- seen in xxiii 271 φοινικοπαρῇους (end of line); either we must assume synizesis, or postulate an original *φοινικϝεσσαν with L. R. Palmer (*Companion*, 105). ὀρθός: predicative-proleptic.

120–3. Bérard's conjecture is noteworthy; its bearing on the whole question of the setting-up of the axes has been mentioned in the Introduction.

120. πελέκεας: synizesis (cf. xxi 421). διὰ ... ὀρύξας: tmesis. τάφρον: fem., like many words for 'hole, aperture'; Callimachus (*h.* iv 37 βαθύν ... τάφρον) was doubtless misled by *h. Cer.* 383 βαθὺν ἠέρα, where the confusion arises from the common gender of ἀήρ.

122. ἀμφί ... ἔναξε: strictly speaking, this is not tmesis, since there is no such compound of νάσσω, a verb found only here before Hippocrates and Aristophanes. ἰδόντας: the parallel with vii 224, xxiii 47, with substantival ἰδόντα or ἰδοῦσα giving rise to a possibly spurious following line of epexegesis, has led various scholars to delete xxi 123; others accept Ἀχαιούς in xxi 122 on the basis of iii 372, with θάμβος (but there the reference is to the men of Pylos, not the suitors).

123. ὡς: exclamatory, or perhaps equivalent to ὅτι οὕτω. εὐκόσμως: only here in Homer (the adj. is found later in Sol. fr. 4. 32 West; the adv. in Thgn. 242); normally the expression is κατὰ κόσμον (five times in each poem) or εὖ κατὰ κόσμον (Il. x 472, Il. xii 85, Il. xxiv 622). The parataxis is concessive in force. All this, and the excessive repetition of -σ-, have led to widespread condemnation of the verse.

124. The οὐδός and the question of whether Telemachus' attempt belongs to the original poem have been discussed in the Introduction. F. Wehrli opines that 'der poetisch wenig glückliche Auftritt gehört zu den Bemühungen, ihn überall in der Vordergrund zu schieben' ('Penelope u. Telemachos', *MH* xvi (1959), 233). **τόξου πειρήτιζε:** the gen. is normal with verbs of aiming, attempting; the impf. denotes repeated attempts.

125-6. The similarity of 125 (except that Allen prints ἐρύσσασθαι) and the beginning of 126 to Il. xxi 176–7, where Asteropaeus pulls a spear, have aroused suspicion; Jordan's conjecture involves the suppression of xxi 127 in order to avoid the repetition of the verb, but even then ἐτάνυσσε occurs again in xxi 128. **βίης:** both here and in Il. xxi 177 (where the MSS also offer variants) the ablative is preferable, in contrast to the instrumental in xxi 128.

126-7. With this reading of the text ἐπιελπόμενος is concessive, and looks forward to the infinitives in the next line, of which ἐντανύειν is also future (cf. 92). But the reading of P 28 is interesting; its editors have pieced together a syntactically rather clumsy ἀλλ' οὖν τό γ' ἄρ' ἤ]θελε θυμ[ός on the basis of parallels such as xiii 40 ἄ μοι φίλος ἤθελε θυμός, xxi 273; K. Matthiessen adduces three passages where Apollo stops Diomedes or Patroclus at a fourth attempt (Il. v 438, xvi 705, 786), and a fourth, most tellingly, at Il. xxi 177 (see the previous note), which ends τὸ δὲ τέτρατον ἤθελε θυμῷ, followed by an infinitive, where Achilles does the same to Asteropaeus ('Eine Variante zum Odysseevers xxi 126 im Papyrus Rylands 53', *Zeitschr. Pap. Ep.* xxvii (1977), 85–8). But the repetitive phrasing of xxi 128 is still ugly.

128. The crop of variants represent attempts to avoid hiatus. **ἀνέλκων:** the word accurately represents the necessary upward pull on the string (as described in the Introduction).

129. Strictly speaking, we expect an unfulfilled protasis (cf. Il. v 312, 680). **ἀνένευε:** Odysseus only employs this gesture in one other passage, when signalling to his companions not to weep (ix 468 ἀνὰ δ' ὀφρύσι νεῦον ἑκάστῳ); the Greek equivalent of shaking the head to show disapproval, then as now, was to raise the eyebrows with a slight upward nod of the head; the word for 'nod (downwards) in assent' was κατανεύω, found at xxiv 335 and five other places in the *Odyssey*; on two occasions νεύω alone is used to indicate a silent command (xvi 164, 283). The end of the line occurs in iv 284, xvi 430, xxii 409, with the concessive participle (cf. xxi 103) differently inflected; it is very much to the point here, as Telemachus, carried away by his sporting spirit, momentarily forgets himself. Besides, the young hero could not with propriety be shown failing a fourth time (F. Eichhorn, *Homers Odyssee: Ein Führer durch die Dichtung* (Göttingen, 1965), 122 n. 103).

130. Cf. xxi 101.

131-3. Unease has been evinced at these lines (see especially Blass, *Interpolationen*, 202), with their reminiscences of ii 60-2 and xvi 71-2, the latter being identical except for the first hemistich (xvi 72 = *Il.* xxiv 369, which is perfectly in context there, after the preceding οὔτ' αὐτὸς νέος ἐσσί in 368: Hermes tells the aged Priam that his travelling companion is another old man, so that he will be unable to defend himself against attack; in the other passages no attack is foreseen). It has been suggested, therefore, that the last two lines, or at least the third, be deleted. The removal of 133 is certainly possible, but the whole passage from ὦ πόποι nicely carries forward the streak of ironic pretence we have seen in xxi 102 ff. At all events, ἤ is to be preferred to ἦ in xxi 131 (cf. ii 60); καὶ ἔπειτα should be translated 'in the future as well [as now]'; and in xxi 132 νεώτερος is intensive, 'too young'. πέποιθα: cf. xxi 315.

134. ἀλλ' ἄγεθ': on this interjection cf. xxi 106, 111, and also xxi 142.

135. Cf. xxi 179-80n.

136-9. The position in which Telemachus lays down the bow (we have not been told how he picked it up) has been discussed in the Introduction. The last three lines = xxi 164-6.

137. κολλητῇσιν ... σανίδεσσιν: of the thirteen occurrences of σανίς, 'board, plank', seven of them in the *Odyssey*, only one (xxi 51) refers to anything other than the folding wooden leaves of a door; other epithets which refer to the idea of 'close fitting' are πυκινῶς ἀραρυία(ς) (*Il.* xxi 535, *Od.* ii 344; cf. *Od.* xxiii 194, applied to the door as a whole); εὖ ἀραρυῖαι (xxii 128, xxiii 42); ἐπὶ τῆς ἀραρυίαι (*Il.* xviii 275-6, with a reference to the plaster door-frame); μακραί, ἐζευγμέναι, εὔξεστοι (ibid.); here too we have εὐξέστης, 'well planed' (cf. xxi 43-4) and κολλητῇσιν, 'close-fitted' (cf. *Il.* ix 583, *Od.* xxiii 194). The conjectures recorded in the apparatus reflect attempts to eliminate the ending -ης, rare before a consonant (but cf. xxii 288 ἀφραδίης μέγα). For a discussion of which doors are referred to, see the Introduction.

138. ὠκὺ βέλος: this formula, found only here and in 165, is an inversion of βέλος ὠκύ, found at the end of the line in 148 and in the same position in *Il.* xi 397 and six other places (Hainsworth, *Flexibility*, 67). αὐτοῦ: adv.

139. θρόνου: the first mention in the last books of the θρόνος (S. Laser, *Archaeologia* P, 38-41); this is not a royal 'throne' of the Mycenean type, but a very costly chair all the same (cf. the epithets applied to it elsewhere, such as xxii 341 ἀργυρόηλος, xxii 438 περικαλλής), on which a king, among other noble personages, might deign to sit (cf. vi 308). Here it is Telemachus who sits on such a seat; at xxi 166 it is Antinous, and in xxii 87 Eurymachus, whose death-rattle shakes it but does not topple it over (it was a substantial piece of furniture); in xxii 23 all the suitors rise from their θρόνοι. Medon is able to hide underneath a θρόνος in xxii 362, which implies a high chair; that explains why a θρῆνυς, 'stool' is needed to sit down in it (see for example i 131). We find θρόνοι being put to a variety of uses: the chair was portable, and could be put in the place of honour next to a column (viii 65; on xxii 341, cf. xxi 141–2n.), and kept for guests as a sign of honour (for example, i 130); but clothes could also be hung on it (xvii 86, 179, xx 96, but not xxi 118, on which see the n.), and on one occasion a spear is propped up against one (xxi 434; the text of this line is doubtful, however). A curious feature of the construction of the θρόνος may have been the attachment of side-trays or flat arm-rests: Antinous, mortally wounded, leans over to one side (xxii 17 ἐκλίνθη δ' ἑτέρωσε) to vomit before he falls off (xxii 22 πεσόντα). Normally the seats would be ranged down the sides of the walls (vii 95), and were not kept very clean, to judge by the cloths that are spread on the seat to protect the clothes of their occupants (i 130, x 352, xx 150). It is hardly surprising, however, that in xxii 438, 452, after the slaughter, the chairs are washed as well as the tables (the latter being normal practice after meals, i 111). Odysseus, who has several times been shown to a θρόνος as a guest (e.g. v 195, x 233), is now seated as a humble beggar (xxi 177 n.); but if we accept the MSS reading at xxi 434 (Telemachus stands close to his father's chair, πὰρ θρόνον ἑστήκει), even this humble beggar's seat (δίφρος) undergoes the same sort of magical transformation which turns Odysseus from beggar into warrior (G. W. Houston, 'Θρόνος, δίφρος, and Odysseus' Change from Beggar to Avenger', *CPh* lxx (1975), 212–14). And indeed, at xxiii 164 we find Odysseus seated on his throne once more, this time as the lord of the house. Finally, it is noteworthy that in xxiv 385 (where κλισμός, probably a synonym, appears for the only time in the later books) Eumaeus and Philoetius sit down on thrones, doubtless remembering their master's promises in xxi 207 ff. On this point see further S. Laser, *LfgrE*, i 38–41.

141. **ἐπιδέξια:** cf. xvii 365–6, where Odysseus goes begging round the suitors ἐνδέξια. Without, of course, excluding other possible arrangements, it may be helpful to consider Pocock's plan of the feast-hall (Figure 8). *B* represents the σανίδες: *1* the wooden threshold of the door between the vestibule and the courtyard; *3* the stone threshold beside which Odysseus is seated (*4*); *5* the trench and the axes; *6* the position of Telemachus; *7* that of Leodes, who is in the corner (xxi 146) next to the amphora (xxi 145); and *8* that of Antinous. The order in which the suitors are to shoot goes from right to left, as did Odysseus' begging, so that Leodes is the first to try his hand. But if, as some suppose, it was considered unlucky to take turns anti-clockwise, there is no reason why we should not turn the plan around in a mirror image; then ἐπιδέξια will mean 'from left to right', not 'from right to left'.

142. **χώρου:** gen. after a verb of beginning. Commentators have been worried by the meaning of περ, 'exactly', adding precision to the adverb of place (cf. xxi 134, where the particle adds nothing); and by the fact that the verb lacks an expressed subject such as 'the cupbearer', which must be understood (cf. Hdt. ii 47. 3 ἐπεὰν θύσῃ, and οἰνοχόος in xxi 263). Hence the reading of P 28, an acceptable emendation (cf. ἐποινοχοεύω in *h. Ven.* 204); the impossible conjectures of J. Mon and of Fick, and the very doubt-

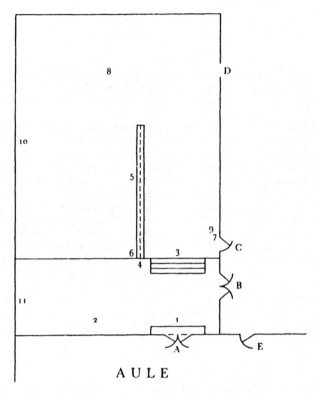

8   D

10

5

9
7   C

6   3
4

B

11

2   1

A   E

A U L E

FIGURE 8. Plan of the feast-hall (Pocock, *Odyssean Essays*, 18, fig. 2)

ful suggestion of Bérard, ὅθεν τ' ἔπι οἰνοχοεύειν (ἔπι = ἔπεστι does appear in ii 58 and xvi 315, though we should expect πάρα; οἰνοχοέω and οἰνοχοεύω are found in eight other places in Homer, but in the *Iliad* always in references to the world of the gods and of fighting; ὅθεν τέ περ comes in the same place in the line in iii 321). Translate: 'starting at the place where [the cupbearer, going to and fro with his ladle to the amphora by Leodes' side,] begins to pour the wine'.

143. = xxi 269.

144. Even von der Mühll, who writes Λειώδης in his edition (as Allen admits Λειώκριτος in ii 242, xxii 294), prefers the form Ληώδης, from *Λᾱϝο-ϝαδης; the confusion is due to itacism. The name of his father is also debated: ἤνοψ, which also seems preferable to the itacistic Οἶνοψ, is found as an adj. applied to bronze in x 360, *Il.* xvi 408, *Il.* xviii

163

349; an etymology based on ἀν- and -οψ, 'dazzling, which cannot be looked at', is impossible because the adj. shows traces of ϝ- in every case (hiatus in two cases, and an unshortened diphthong where we would otherwise expect correption in the second of the passages cited); when used as a proper name Ἠνοψ also occurs in hiatus (*Il.* xvi 401, *Il.* xxiii 634, and the present passage). Stanford comments, however, that these readings spoil a witty pun on Leodes' name: 'Smooth [λεῖος], son of Pink-face [i.e. face like wine], ... in other words, the soft son of a soft father'.

145. ὅ σφι θυοσκόος: σφι dat. of possession; ὁ demonstr. Leodes is an augur (θυο-σκόος, 'one who inspects victims'); Odysseus remarks that he has often prayed for his return to be delayed (xxii 321–2). On the mixing-bowl, which was generally placed on the floor, not on a table (S. Laser, *Archaeologia* P, 57), and on the cupbearer's job, cf. ix 9–10, xxi 142.

146–7. Despite the pred. οἴῳ, Leodes is not the only suitor to be presented in a relatively favourable light; another is Amphinomus, the 'good suitor' in xviii (see Hoekstra, *Epic Verse*, 57, on significant names such as Ἀμφί-νομος, 'temporizer', against Ἀντί-νοος, 'cross-grained'). Leodes is a doublet of Amphinomus, a man of finer feelings but weaker character (Fenik, *Studies*, 192–7); but Amphinomus is no priest, even though he indulges in prophecy at xx 245 and displays his piety in xvi 400–5. The νῦ ἐφελκυστικόν serves merely to lengthen the syllable.

146. μυχοίτατος: adj. used adverbially; here only in Homer, the word is formed from an unattested loc. *μυχοί, 'in the corner', which later gave μυχαίτατος (see the app.) by analogy with forms such as πάλαι.

148. ὅς ῥα: ὅς demonstr.; ῥα picks up the thread of the narrative again after the digression. This time we are told that he took hold of the bow and arrow (cf. xxi 136–9).

149. = xxi 124.

150. πρὶν: cf. xxi 35–6n. ἀνέλκων: cf. xxi 128n.; here too the participle is absolute; χεῖρας is acc. of respect.

151. ἀτρίπτους: 'smooth, unhardened', here only in Homer but later found in prose. The end of the line = xvii 467, xxii 4.

152–62. Leodes' calm and conciliatory words are coherent up to xxi 159: 'I cannot bend it; but let some other suitor take it [concess. imper., slightly condescending] in his turn (καί), for this bow will be the death of us; [sc. yet some will take hold of it for all that,] for death is better than failure, and so each one of us (τις) hopes to win Penelope, although when he fails ...'.

152. The odd intransitive use of τανύω (not fut. as at xxi 92, 97, 127, but durative pres. 'I am not able to draw [it]') would be removed by reading μιν; γάρ, 'since, in view of the fact', is not unattractive, but μέν is also acceptable, meaning 'I for one; to be sure'.

153. The reduplicated and factitive fut. κεκαδήσει, 'will deprive', found again in xxi 170 and appropriate enough on the lips of an augur, is paralleled by *Il.* iv 497, xv 574 ὑπό ... κεκάδοντο, 'they retreated'; Hsch. κεκαδῆσαι· ... στερῆσαι, κεκαδών ... στερήσας, ἐκεκήδει·

ὑπε⟨κε⟩χωρήκει; and above all *Il.* xi 334 θυμοῦ καὶ ψυχῆς κεκαδών (see Wilamowitz, *Heimkehr*, 195). The proposed etymological link with χάζομαι, 'retreat', would require a rare inverse assimilation κεχα- > κεκα-. **ἀριστῆας:** cf xi 333.

154. On the ablatives cf. xxi 153. The end of the line is repeated in *Il.* i 169, *Od.* xii 109, with νῦ ἐφελκυστικόν.

155. The antecedent τούτου is understood before οὗ θ', gen. of the relative ὅς τε, so the conjunction should not be removed, even though ἕνεκα, despite having no trace of ϝ- (cf. Myc. *e-ne-ka*), occurs in hiatus in *Il.* iii 100, vi 356, xxiv 28 (all in the same metrical position), and *Il.* iii 206.

156. **ποτιδέγμενοι ἤματα πάντα:** = ii 205, which probably lies behind the curious reading of P. Gen., which inserts a line (and also has a variant in 157): ἐνθάδ' ὁ]μιλέομεν πωλεύμενοι, οὐδ[ὲ μετ' ἄλλας | ἐρχόμεθ',] ἃς ἐπήοικεν ὀπύειν ἄνδ[ρα ἕκαστον. The logic of this reading is acceptable, though it finds no support in the rest of the tradition: πωλεύμενοι recalls ii 55 and xvii 534 οἱ δ' εἰς ἡμετέρου πωλεύμενοι ἤματα πάντα, an expression used by the suitors by Telemachus and Penelope respectively; the remainder of P. Gen.'s reading parallels Eurymachus' words in ii 205-7 ποτιδέγμενοι ἤματα πάντα | εἵνεκα τῆς ἀρετῆς ἐριδαίνομεν, οὐδε μετ' ἄλλας | ἐρχόμεθ', ἃς ἐπιεικὲς ὀπυιέμεν ἐστὶν ἑκάστῳ, a passage athetized by Aristophanes of Byzantium; ἐπήοικεν may be the result of a series of corruptions due to itacism of ἐπιεικές > ἐπιεικεν > ἐπιοικεν, or alternatively an error for ἐπέοικεν (found in the same position in the line and with following inf. in *Il.* i 126, iv 341; in the same position, *Il.* ix 392; with inf., *Il.* x 146, xxii 71; cf. especially xi 186 ἃς ἐπέοικε δικασπόλον ἄνδρ' ἀλεγύνειν); the vowel and inflection of ὀπυιέμεν will have been contracted due to itacism or Atticism or both; and the line-ending ἄνδρα ἕκαστον is found in five passages in the *Iliad* and four in the *Odyssey* (x 173, 547, xii 207, xxiv 441), though never as the subject of an acc. and inf. construction.

159. Note the aor. subj. with short vowel. Van Herwerden's conjecture is unnecessary: translate 'and sees [that he fails]' (cf. vi 126, with a similar line-ending). Nor is it necessary to punctuate with three dots indicating an ironic ellipse of some such phrase as '... will make a fool of himself'; cf. xxi 160.

160. The end of the line = *Il.* v 424. Here there is evidently some contamination. Leodes ought to have continued: 'let him marry another woman, and Penelope will find no husband', but xxi 161-2, a doublet of xvi 391-2, have somehow crept in (see Blass, *Interpolationen*, 202); the lines fit well at xvi 391-2, where Antinous is proposing that all the suitors should retire while Penelope makes her choice between them. See the apparatus to lines 157-62 here, and note that in xxi 168-74 Antinous makes no reply to these last two lines. The Ionicism of P. Gen.'s reading is an attempt to avoid hiatus.

161. **ἔπειτα:** not temporal, as in 160, but means rather 'in this case'.

162. **γήμαιθ':** conditional by attraction of the mood of the two verbs with κε in the relative clause; the dat. antecedent of ὅς is understood. **ἔλθοι:** not simply equivalent to the copula, but with an idea of motion, closely

dependent on the pred. μόρσιμος, 'may turn up, brought here by fate'. The ἔεδνα for Penelope's hand have been mentioned in the parallel lines at xvi 391–2, and also in i 277, ii 196, xi 117, xiii 378, xv 18, xix 529 (of doubtful authenticity).

163–6. The first of these lines is almost the same as 136; the remainder = 137–9, and are unnecessarily expunged by Blass, *Interpolationen*, 202–3, who considers Leodes a figure of minor importance. P. Gen. 338 (saec. ii A.C., see *MH* xxxvii (1980), 213–15) has 164–5 and a verse replacing 163.

163. P. Gen. 338 reads τόξον μὲ]ν κατέθηκεν ἐπὶ χθο[νὶ πουλυβοτείρῃ (suppl. C. Wehrli), a blend of *Il.* vi 473 κατέθηκεν ἐπὶ χθονί with *Il.* iii 89 etc. ἐπὶ χθονὶ πουλοβοτείρῃ. As restored in the ed. pr. the verse is clearly unacceptable. S. R. West (verbal communication) suggests ὡς εἰπὼ]ν κατέθηκεν ἐπὶ χθο[νὶ καμπύλα τόξα.

166. On θρόνος see xxi 139n.

167. = xxi 84.

168–74. The lines suit Antinous' sarcastic personality, and show his inconsistency, since in 91–2 he pretended to doubt the suitors' ability to bend the bow.

168. This formulaic exclamation, with its double accusative (object and internal), is common (cf. xxiii 70): behind it lies the animistic concept of the words 'imprisoned' in the closed mouth like a cage.

169. The first half of the line is paralleled, for example, by v 175, 367, xii 119; the second phrase is parenthetic, and should be translated as a relative clause.

170–1. The train of thought (the end of xxi 170 repeats that of xxi 153; cf. xxi 333) is somewhat difficult: 'if [you say] this bow . . . [merely] because' (σύ is emphatic; δή, 'of course, as it seems', sarcastic, together with γε, 'at least as far as this bow is concerned (and it is not so terrible as you say)'.

172. γάρ: understand '[and this is the case] because'; the line recalls i 223. The papyrus reading πως is also possible.

173. Cf. xxi 117; the vowel of τε is lengthened before ῥυτῆρα as in xviii 262, *Il.* xvi 475 (cf. βρύτηρ, with barytonesis < *ϝρύτηρ in App. Dysc., and αὐερύω < *ἀν-ϝερυω); the five attestations of the latter word are all explicable assuming a root *ϝρῡ-, parallel to *ϝερυ- (ἐρύω); in the *Iliad* passage ῥυτήρ means 'rein, that pulls [the horse]'; in xvii 187, 223, 'guardian, that pulls out [of danger]'; in xviii 262 ῥυτῆρας ὀϊστῶν is applied to archers who 'pull back' the arrows; here the word is used with two gen. ἀπὸ κοινοῦ, with the arrows and also, less appropriately, with βιοῦ, which is pulled in the opposite direction.

174. τανύουσι: the fut. is here intransitive (cf. xxi 152); Bérard's conjecture (τό γε for τάχα) is unnecessary.

175–85. The appearance of Melanthius, a character who may have been an invention of the later poet(s) *B*, casts suspicion on these lines, and on the action described in them. His name, which is copied from that of a hero in *Il.* vi 36 Μελάνθιον, scanned ∪ –́ ∪ ∪, appears in two forms: Μελανθεύς (end of xvii 212, xx 255, xxi 176, xxii 152; before a bucolic caesura in xxii

159, though this could be emended to Μελάνθιος reading the following word as ὅν, not τόν), and Μελάνθιος (eleven times scanned ∪ –⁴ ∪ ∪, once as ∪ –² ∪ ∪ in xxii 474). The removal of all the lines would involve some excisions and patchwork in xxi 246 and its surrounding lines (as von der Mühll notes in his apparatus); on the other hand, xxi 175 alone could be excised without further consequences.

176. ἄγρει: the variants reflect the fact that this is the only occurrence in the *Odyssey* (found in *Il.* v 765, vii 459, xi 512, xiv 271) of this non-Homeric verb used as a synonym of ἄγε; but the back-formation ἄγρη occurs in xii 330, xxii 306; αὐτάγρετος in xvi 148; ζωάγριον in viii 462, *Il.* xviii 407; μοιχάγριον in viii 332; and παλινάγρετος in *Il.* i 526; and the pl. ἄγρειθ', with an accentuation which shows total loss of the verb root or barytonesis, in xx 149. πῦρ κῆον: the fire is to be lit not on the hearth, which is already burning because of the seasonal cold, but in the λαμπτῆρες (cf. xviii 307, 343, xix 63, and see S. Laser, *Archaeologia* P, 86). On κείον for κῆον, from *ἔκηϝα, see the apparatus and cf. xxi 144.

177. πὰρ δὲ τίθει: tmesis. δίφρον: a number of these 'stools' (see S. Laser, *Archaeologia* P, 36-8) are mentioned in the palace; doubtless they were lighter and more portable than the θρόνοι (cf. xxi 139 n.). Thus in the final books we find the 'humble, lowly' one (ἀεικέλιος, xx 259) which Odysseus is given to sit on (cf. xxi 243, 420); another occupied by Philoetius (xxi 392); a well-polished one occupied by Dolius (or, in another reading, which Dolius offers to Odysseus) in Laertes' house (ἐΰξεστος, xxiv 408); another in the women's quarters which they likewise offer to Odysseus, and which they cover with fleeces, as here (xix 97, with the same line-ending; xix 101, 506; similar fleeces cover the δαιδάλεοι thrones of the suitors in xvii 32); another, described as περικαλλής, on which Penelope sits in her chamber (xxi 387); the one also called ἐΰξεστος (xvii 602) kept for the δαιτρός (see Figure 8), which Eumaeus rather boldly takes for himself (xvii 330; Bérard's conjecture κείμενον for ποικίλον in xvii 331 is uncalled for); and this one, where the attempts to emend μέγαν are unnecessary, since the word does not mean 'large, high', but 'long', suitable for the complicated operation of greasing the bow, which would stain the seat if it were not first covered with the fleeces.

178. Note the tmesis. For the great 'round' or cake of wax or tallow, cf. xii 173, from the episode of the Sirens, which probably inspired this passage (cf. xxi 246). Another point is the purpose of the greasing, and how it was supposed to make the bow easier to string: W. Richter, *Archaeologia* H, 59, n. 339, talks of making wood more supple by this method, but if the bow was made of horn, as we suppose, it is difficult to see how this would help. Presumably, therefore, it was the string which was supposed to be worked upon, to make it more elastic after a long period of stiffening through disuse (cf. xxi 395). The word στέατος, from an original *στάγαρ (στῆρ Pap.) > στέαρ (from the idea of 'consistency, stolidity'), occurs in Homer only here and at 183 below; it must be scanned with synizesis, or we must assume that δὲ is not lengthened before the στ-, as in the case of σκέπαρνον

(v 237, ix 391), Ζάκυνθος (i 246, etc.), Σκάμανδρος (*Il.* v 36, etc.).
ἐόντος: the Papyrus reading ἐόντων is defensible as a partitive gen., like παρεόντων in vii 176, and especially ἔνδον ἐόντων in xv 77.

178-9. The second line is similar to 184 below; the first is identical to 183, except that here ἔνεικε is used as a thematic aor. imper. (instead of the ἔνεικον found in Anac. fr. 51. 2 P), a suspicious and rather forced word-play on the normal 3. sing. indic. of ἔνεικα used in 183 (consequently Wackernagel, *Untersuchungen*, 112, believes that the reading is the work of an Attic editor who has attempted to give ἔνεγκε an epic form).

179-80. νέοι is very odd, especially on the lips of one of the 'youths' (cf. xxi 184, where this is not the case); Hartman's conjecture νέον requires the dubious meaning 'for a short while', adv.; van Leeuwen's is over-bold from the paleographical point of view; Bérard's ἐπιχρίωνται is based on the middle verb in xviii 179, which has a similar ending to this line, and leads him to reject xxi 180 (= xxi 268, and almost identical to xxi 135), which at least frees Antinous from the peccadillo of youthful arrogance. But the suitors were indeed young men: cf. xxi 361, and the biographical detail in xxi 95, xiii 425 (spoken by Athena), xviii 6, xvii 479 (also spoken by Antinous, and scanned ∪ −², as here and in iii 460), xxi 310 (Antinous again), and Eurymachus' use of the word in the voc. at xx 361. The two participles are used intransitively (cf. xxi 174), in asyndeton (the aspect of the verbs excludes any notion of anteriority); θάλπω is found in Homer only here and at xxi 184, 246 (later in Hes. and others; θαλπιόων in xix 319).

182. Tmesis (cf. xxi 177).

183. Cf. xxi 178 and apparatus.

184. Cf. xxi 179.

185. Cf. xxi 114, and also the apparatus at 125-6. **πολλὸν δὲ βίης ἐπιδευέες:** βίης is best taken as abl. 'far too lacking in the force [needed for the task]' (cf. the similar line ending in xxi 253, and xxiv 171, with a similar construction implied in ἐπιδευής); a parallel construction occurs in *Il.* xxiii 670, xxiv 385, where μάχης is used with the verb ἐπιδεύομαι to denote someone who is 'not up to the fight'. The acc. πολλὸν is adverbial; δὲ here serves to give the paratactic clause a causal sense.

186-7. ἐπεῖχε may mean '(they) held back [from attempting the test]' (sing. with pl. subj.); or it may be governed only by the first subject, Antinous, who is to propose a postponement in xxi 257ff., but not to Eurymachus, who tries to bend the bow in xxi 245ff.; but the most likely meaning is '(they) remained [to try]'. I have commented on θεοειδής in the Introduction. The lines = iv 628-9 with the exception of the first verb. Here the two suitors outstanding for their ἀρετή (for the pairing of the two cf. xxi 311-53, and Fenik, *Studies*, 198-205) do not join sport with the small fry.

188-244. On the textual problems of these lines see the Introduction.

188. ὁμαρτήσαντες implies 'at the same time'. The prefix is cognate with ἄμα, 'together'; and the ancient variant with ἀμ- < sṃ- is perhaps preferable, the change to ὀμ- being explained by the analogical tendency of

Attic, and to differentiate the word from ἁμαρτάνω. In xiii 87 ὁμαρτήσειεν, *Il.* xii 400 ὁμαρτήσανθ', *Il.* xxiv 438 ὁμαρτέων, the MS tradition is unanimous; in xxii 81 and three passages in the *Iliad* the editors prefer the reading ἁμαρτή or ἁμαρτῇ, and in *Il.* xiii 584 ὁμαρτήδην, each supported by some MSS. Note the pl. verbs with the duals τώ and ἄμφω; βῆσαν is pluperf. in sense (Antinous has thrown them out in xxi 89–90).

190. Tmesis; μετά has both temporal and local sense.

191. The form θυρέων without synizesis, which does not correspond metrically with the primitive ending in -αων, seems late; it is found also in *Il.* vii 1, xii 340 (cf. xxi 47). The characters are now in the street.

192. This line-ending is found again in xx 165, and a variation of it in xi 552. The reading σφ' ἐπέεσσι disregards the digamma, while the other two readings fail to lengthen the -ι before a semivowel; perhaps we should read σφε ἔπεσσι, the dual σφε being the poet's variation on the usual μιν in formulae such as xix 214 ἐξαῦτίς μιν ἔπεσσιν (cf. xxi 206).

193. τι is indefinite: 'a word (which I have in my mind)'. The scansion points to ϝ- before ἔπος. The line is σπονδειάζων.

194. There is hiatus after ἤ. The subj. is dubitative; αὐτὸς 'to myself'.

195. The end of the line = i 414, ii 351; κε with the opt. after εἴτε is unparalleled in Homer, which has given rise to a throng of variants. The hiatus before the verb, which is consecutive-final in sense, would be avoided in the reading recorded in the apparatus (but cf. ii 60 τοῖοι ἀμυνέμεν in —³ ∪ ∪ —⁴ ∪ ∪).

196. ἐνείκαι: the primary form, as against the secondary form in xxi 178. αὐτὸν has caused surprise; ὧδε, 'just like that'.

197-8. The clumsy test to which Odysseus submits his servants makes these two lines, already doubtful in these surroundings, even more suspicious. Note further the hiatus in xxi 197 εἴπατε, which parallels the sigmatic forms (cf. xxi 196); the synizesis in xxi 198; and ὅπως used to introduce an indirect question. For the final formula cf. xxi 342.

199. βοῶν ἐπιβουκόλος ἀνήρ: the first appearance in these books of this epithet for Philoetius, already used of him in xx 235, and of another character in iii 422. The parallels in xiii 222 (Athena compared to a young ἐπιβώτορι μήλων), xii 131 (ἐπιποιμένες), etc., show that the phrase does not denote 'herdsman in chief', but merely someone who looks after (ἐπί) the oxen. Nevertheless, the formation is somewhat strange; in antiquity a no less unusual ἐπὶ βουκόλος was proffered as a conjecture, and Leumann, *Wörter*, 92–3, comes up with a complicated history for the analogical formation of the word. In *Il.* xiii 450, where Zeus engenders Minos Κρήτῃ ἐπίουρον, the primary idea is Κρήτῃ ἔπι οὖρον; this false analogy will have given rise to xiii 405, xv 39 ὑῶν ἐπίουρος, 'swineherd', and this in turn must lie behind the formation of ἐπιβουκόλος.

200. Ζεῦ πάτερ: the voc., which exactly parallels the Latin *Iuppiter*, occurs elsewhere, for example in v 7. On Philoetius's sentimental remark, which is almost a repetition of his words in xx 236, see the Introduction. Here the protasis is not left, as it usually is, to stand alone as an optative expression

('if you were to do this [I would be glad]', and thence 'if only you would do this'), but is followed by an apodosis of sorts in xxi 202.

201. The line stands in apposition to ἐέλδωρ, and takes the optative by attraction. It repeats xvii 243, where ἑ is also equivalent to αὐτόν, and is probably imitated from that line: Shipp, *Studies*, 353, notes that the expression fits less logically here, since the mention of another god (δαίμων) sits uneasily with the address to Zeus in the same sentence.

202-4. = xx 237-9; in view of what is said in the note to xxi 200, the occurrence of the lines here is suspicious. In the first line of the three we must understand 'what strength I have and [what] hands are at its call' (cf. *Il.* iv 314, where the knees are asked to obey the θυμός); but the ellipsis makes the phrase hard to understand, which explains the variant reading.

203. In principle the parallel with xx 238 favours the reading ἐπεύξατο.

204. Hiatus after νοστῆσαι, probably because the line = xx 329, where the inf. follows ἐώλπει, which perhaps lends credibility to the variant νοστήσειν (cf. Shipp, *Studies*, 353).

205. τῶν γε: 'of these at least'; γε is important in reminding us that Odysseus has as yet no grounds to rely on the fidelity of the other slaves.

206. Cf. xxi 192; ἐξαῦτις because he has already spoken to them there. The end of the line is similar to xix 214.

207-8. Ἔνδον μὲν δὴ ὅδ' αὐτὸς ἐγώ: 'I myself [am] that very man, returned home (that is, here before your eyes)'; ἔνδον < *ἔνδομ retains the force of its etymological connection with δόμος (cf. xvi 462, xix 40). The abrupt manner of Odysseus' surprise revelation recalls ii 40-1 οὐχ ἑκὰς οὗτος ἀνήρ... ὃς λαὸν ἤγειρα; xxiv 321 κεῖνος... ὅδ' αὐτὸς ἐγώ... ὃν σὺ μεταλλᾷς, imitated by Verg. *A.* i 595-6 *coram quem quaeritis adsum, Troius Aeneas*; here, however, there are no relatives, and ὅδε is predicative. It would be preferable, therefore, to punctuate with a colon at the end of 207, with asyndeton in the following line; this would be avoided by the papyrus καί for κακά, but the reading is made less likely by the parallel line-ending in vi 175, xxiii 101, 169.

208. The case for deletion (see the apparatus, and Blass, *Interpolationen*, 203) is based on the parallels in xvi 206, xxiv 322, both preceded by asyndeton as in the present case; in xix 484 and of course xxiii 102 (with the opt.), on the other hand, the line is indispensable. As for the morphology of ἤλυθον, it has been argued that we have an adaptation of the original formula ἤλυθε ϝεικοστῷ to the 1st. pers., with consequent problems with the digamma (Hoekstra, *Modifications*, 52); Allen and von der Mühll print ἤλυθον εἰκοστῷ in xvi 206, xix 484, xxi 208, xxiv 322 (cf. ἔλθοι ἐεικοστῷ, xxiii 102), but von der Mühll prefers the reading ἤλθον ἐεικοστῷ in xvi 206, xix 484, xxi 208, xxiv 322. Note, however, the three cases of hiatus in the following ἔτεϊ, the first due to digamma, the second to the loss of -σ-, the third accompanied by lengthening in thesis.

209. The alternative form γι(γ)νώσκω appears here for the first time in our MSS and editions. ἐελδομένοισιν: ethic dat., οἵοις pred., δμώων partitive.

210-16. In the context of this whole dubious episode (cf. xxi 197–8n.), Odysseus' grand promises make this passage even more objectionable.

210. τῶν δ' ἄλλων: τῶν is of course demonstrative ('these others'); the gen. is partitive, after the indef. τευ.

211. Nauck's conjecture does not resolve the hiatus before and after ἐμέ. ὑπότροπος, which later almost disappears except in the late cognate verb ὑποτρέπομαι, is attested elsewhere in archaic verse at h.Ap. 476 (with ἔσεσθε) and four times in Homer (here, and in Il. vi 367, 501, Od. xx 332) used predicatively with ἰκνέομαι. The similar ending of xxii 35 supports the reading οἴκαδ' ἰκέσθαι, as against οἴκαδε νεῖσθαι; but neither these readings nor xxii 35 take account of digamma in the adv. (cf. xxi 332). ἐνθάδ' is unjustifiable, as Chantraine has pointed out (Grammaire, i 145). The other suggestion, ἀπότροπος, is found only at xiv 372, meaning 'retired, remote'.

212. ὡς ἔσεταί περ is in apposition to ἀληθείην (cf. xix 312, correlative with ὧδε). The end of the line = xvi 226, xvii 108, xxii 420.

213-16. The offer corresponds with Eumaeus' own assertion of what Odysseus would have done for him if he had come home in xiv 56–71; on the legal problems posed by such a mock 'adoption' see further Ramming, Dienerschaft, 70–2 and 112 n. 1, and the note on xxi 139 about xxiv 385.

213. = xix 488, and cf. xix 496.   δαμάσῃ: potential subj.

214. ἄξομαι: the middle is used in iv 10 to refer to Menelaus marrying a girl to his son; in vi 28 of the supposed suitors for Nausicaa's hand; in xv 238 of Melampus giving his brother a bride.   ἀμφοτέροις: i.e. ὑμῖν.

216. The hiatus before ἑτάρῳ (the reading Τηλεμάχῳ, possess. dat., in the preceding position is also possible) and before ἔσεσθον (avoidable with Fick's conjecture) is suspicious, as are the three duals, since the two characters do not form a pair in the structure. To call them 'brothers' of Telemachus also seems odd, given the large disparity in age; Eumaeus elsewhere claims (xv 352–79) to have been brought up as a brother to Ctimene, Odysseus' sister.

217-21. The story of the scar makes four appearances: in xix 386 ff., the long passage about its discovery by Eurycleia (393, the original formula which gave rise to the remaining occurrences according to Hoekstra, Modifications, 111 = xxi 219, with the logical exception of μιν, which fits the 3rd. pers. narrative at that point, here changed to με with consequent metrical lengthening; the first half of xix 394 = xxi 220, but is there followed by μετ' Αὐτόλυκόν τε καὶ υἶας, also read here in some witnesses); this passage; xxiii 73–7 (Eurycleia's explanation to Penelope; 73 is similar to xxi 217 and also to xi 126; there is no line corresponding to xxi 218, which has led to its athetization; 74 = xxi 219, but with μιν again; no line corresponding to xxi 220); and xxiv 330–5 (Odysseus' explanation to Laertes; the end of 332 = xxi 219). There has been endless debate as to whether these lines, with all the critical oddities of xxi 219–20, are not perhaps even later than xxiv. At all events, the whole passage is late, as I have said; one must add that the servants had no way of knowing much about the scar, whereas Eurycleia did.

COMMENTARY

217. δείξω: subj. of volition after the interj. εἰ δ' ἄγε, 'come now' (cf. xxiv 336). καί: adv. σῆμα: pred., with following hiatus which shows that this is adapted from xxiii 225 σήματ' ἀριφραδέα. ἄλλο: 'something else, besides'.

218. The duals continue (this time in contracted subj. forms, another possible sign of late composition), mixed with plurals in xxi 222 ff. On εὖ cf. xxi 369.

219–20. The fact that these lines are lacking in P 28 and Mon. may be significant; von der Mühll brackets them (see Blass, *Interpretationen*, 203). Note what has been said above about the end of xxi 220 compared to xix 394, and the absence of any parallel after xxiii 74; further suspicions are aroused by the end of xxi 219, found in the 3rd. pers. narrative of the episode in question at xix 465, and by xxi 220, identical to xix 466.

221. The fact that Odysseus' scar is hidden by his long tunic is taken by Lorimer to indicate that the χιτών was of the plebeian type, perhaps of wool (*Monuments*, 372 n. 7), whereas a similar wound borne by the aristocratic Menelaus (*Il.* iv 146) is perfectly visible.

222. Similar to x 453, xxiv 391. The verbs have the sense of our pluperfect. Even if ἄνακτα is read, with von der Mühll, this cannot clinch the question of the authenticity of xxi 217–21.

224–5. Slaves kiss their master on the head, shoulders, and hands (like the serving-girls and Odysseus in xxii 499–500), or on the head and shoulders only (like the slave-girls and Telemachus in xvii 35); Penelope kisses her son on the head and eyes (xvii 39); Eumaeus kisses Telemachus on the head, eyes, and hands (xvi 15–16), a sign of his important position in the household; Penelope thinks of kissing the head and hands of Odysseus in xxiii 87; Odysseus himself kisses Dolius' hand in xxiv 398. Note the emotional effect of the servants' continuous imperf. κύνεον, 'began to kiss', in contrast to the sober and single ἔκυσσε of their master.

226. = xvi 220. ὀδυρομένοισιν: cf. xxi 209 n. on ἐελδομένοισιν.

227. αὐτός: reflects Odysseus' forceful character; he is the first to pull himself together.

228. The line is similar to iv 801, xvii 8, xxiv 323 (see O'Nolan, *Doublets*, 32). ἴδηται: intrans.

229. The variants attempt to correct the hiatus after μεγάροιο. ἀτὰρ εἴπῃσι καὶ εἴσω: ἀτάρ, 'and then', is asyndetic; εἴπῃσι, 'tell', intrans., like ἴδηται in 228; καί, adv.; on εἴσω cf. iii 427, iv 775 n.

230. 'Stop crying and go in, not all together but one by one (that is, me first and then you)'. The etymology of προμνηστῖνοι, 'one by one', paralleled only by προμνηστῖναι in xi 233 (the suffix is found in ἀγχιστῖνοι, xxii 118, xxiv 181, 449, and two Iliadic examples), has been debated: B. Forssman, 'Gr. πρύμνη, ai. nimna- u. Verwandtes', *Zeitschr. Vergl. Sprachf.* lxxxix (1964), 11–28 has found little acceptance; the word must originally have been fem., referring to the women who 'filed' past the suitor before the appearance of the bride-to-be during the *προμνηστις, 'asking ceremony' (Frisk, *GEW*).

231. ἀτὰρ τόδε σῆμα τετύχθω: 'let this be the sign'; σῆμα is pred., ἀτάρ marks the transition to a new topic.

232. γὰρ carries forward from τόδε (cf. xxi 74, for example): the sign will be that, when Odysseus asks for the bow (he does not explain this detail here, but it takes place in xxi 275 ff.), the suitors will be angry (as they are, in xxi 285); that will be the moment for Eumaeus to hand him the bow (xxi 359 ff.) and give the word to the women (xxi 381 ff.).   ἄλλοι . . . πάντες ὅσοι μνηστῆρες: the whole phrase means 'all the rest, that is as many suitors (as there are)'. The beginning of the line is repeated in *Il.* v 877.

233. ἐάσουσιν: synizesis (cf. *Il.* v 256 ἐᾷ, x 344 ἐῶμεν). The apparatus gives a possible alternative; in theory the -a- may not have been lengthened. The phrase means 'they will not allow it to be given to me' (cf. xix 25).

234. It is noteworthy that here, as on every other occurrence of δῖ' Εὔμαιε (xvi 461, xvii 508, xxii 157), some MSS read δή.   ἀλλὰ: 'well then', looking back to the earlier phrase: 'when the rest . . . then you'. φέρων: has as much weight as θέμεναι, 'fetch and place before me'. ἀνά: here means 'the length of, all along' (since Odysseus takes his seat at the far end of the hall).

235. The two infinitives θέμεναι and εἰπεῖν have imper. force, according to the regular conditions for this usage: namely, that they refer to a future which is still some way off, that they are preceded by a voc., Εὔμαιε, and by a true imperative, τετύχθω. εἰπεῖν, 'ask' (so that κλῆῖσαι is not past in meaning). In the second half of the line, which is almost identical to xv 76 and similar to xxii 431, δὲ is a better reading than τε.

236-9. = xxi 382-5, where the command is repeated word for word.

236. On several occasions we have been shown the women sitting in their private μέγαρον (xviii 316, xix 16), or leaving it (xix 60, xx 6, xxii 497); and in xix 30 Eurycleia closes the θύρας μεγάρων εὐναιεταόντων, a formula which reminds us of this one. Doubtless the doors between the main hall and the women's μέγαρον are meant; and it is these that Odysseus wants locked from the women's side, so that they can be kept out of the fight and so that the suitors, who are unaware that the doors are locked (xxii 76, 91 probably refer to them too), will be unable to escape through them.

237-9. These lines imply the existence of another door between the women's quarters and the courtyard; this is not to be locked, but the women are not to go out through it into the open, even if they are frightened by the sound of the battle.

237. τις: 'any one (of the women)'. The genitives are normal after a verb of hearing. On ἔνδον cf. xxi 178, 183, 207; it is not clear whether the word here means 'inside', with ἀκούσῃ, or anticipates ἐν ἕρκεσι.

238. ἀνδρῶν depends on στοναχῆς ἠὲ κτύπου.   ἕρκεσι has been interpreted, perhaps fancifully, as a bloodthirsty irony (the hall will become a huge net; cf. xxii 469).   μή τι: 'not at all, in no way'.

239. προβλώσκειν recalls προβλωσκέμεν, xix 25 (cf. xxi 233); it has the slightly familiar tone of 'show their faces, peep out'. Both this infin. and ἔμεναι might in theory be taken as 3rd. pers. imperatives (cf. xxi 235 n.), but

COMMENTARY

it is more likely that they are governed by εἰπεῖν. Note the hiatus between
αὐτοῦ and ἀκήν (cf. xxi 89n., and Frisk, *GEW*, on the digamma), as well as
the usual one in παρὰ ἔργῳ, 'at their own business'.
240. **δῖε**: cf. xxi 234n. **θύρας ... αὐλῆς**: regardless of whether the
contest takes place in the hall or in the courtyard, these doors must be
those of the gate of the courtyard into the street (cf. xxi 389, where the order
is carried out, with Bethe's comment, *Odyssee*, 75; xxii 137 αὐλῆς καλὰ
θύρετρα; and xviii 239, where some read ἐπ' αὐλείῃσι θύρῃσιν).
241. **κληῖσαι κληῖδι**: schema etymologicum, with the instrum. The line-
ending, with its tmesis, is almost identical to viii 443, 447; supply the dat.
'to the doors'. **θοῶς**: 'skilfully, dexterously', as in xxi 46. The
procedure is quite different from that described in xxi 6, 47, but identical to
that in i 422: Philoetius is to close the doors from inside with a simple bolt
(κληῖδι); in addition, at xxi 390, he ties it fast with the first thing that comes
to hand in the courtyard (as a slave, he does not have a very good
knowledge of arrangements inside the palace), to prevent it being easily
opened by panic-stricken men trying to get out.
242. = xvii 324; acc. of direction. Both lines refer to someone entering from
the street, not from the courtyard (cf. xxi 191). On εὖ cf. xxi 369.
243. = xxi 392; the ending is also found in xxi 139, 166 (see the nn. on xxi 139,
177). **ἔπειτ'**: to our way of thinking the word is asyndetic, as so often.
ἰών is emphatic: 'he went and sat down'. περ underlines the fact that this is
the same seat as before, and ἀνέστη is equivalent to a pluperfect.
244. **ἐς δ' ἄρα καὶ ... ἴτην**: ἄρα, 'as they had agreed'; καὶ, 'as well, in their
turn'; note the tmesis, and the variants recorded in the apparatus in
response to the hiatus before ἴτην. There is a further case of hiatus before
Ὀδυσῆος.
245. **ἤδη**: 'at last', looks back to ἐπεῖχε in xxi 186. The end of the line is
repeated at xxii 10; here the bewildered Eurymachus turns the bow from
side to side in his attempts to make it bend.
246. On the heating of the bow over the λαμπτῆρες cf. xxi 176 and the Introduction. **ἔνθα καὶ ἔνθα**: 'this way and that'. The contracted long
vowel of the instrumental σέλᾳ (cf. x 316 δέπᾳ, xi 136 γήρᾳ, in contrast to
Il. xvii 739 σέλαϊ) is a late form which shows that this passage is derivative.
μιν refers to the bowl.
247. **μέγα δ' ἔστενε κυδάλιμον κῆρ**: in this phrase, which also appears as
the end of *Il.* x 16, we must take κῆρ as an acc. of respect, as in *Il.* xviii 33 ὅ
δ' ἔστενε κυδάλιμον κῆρ (but cf. *Il.* xx 169 ἐν δέ τέ οἱ κραδίη στένει ἄλκιμον
ἦτορ); the initial nasal of μέγα, which may be translated 'aloud', causes
metrical lengthening of the preceding vowel.
248. A remarkable line: the first hemistich, ὀχθήσας δ' ἄρα εἶπε(ν), appears
seven times in the *Iliad* followed by πρὸς ὃν μεγαλήτορα θυμόν, and in *Il.*
xxiii 143 followed by another formulaic line-ending, and in v 298, 355, 407,
464, always with πρὸς ὃν μεγαλήτορα θυμόν; but this is the only occurrence
in Homer of the formula ὀχθήσας δ' ἄρα εἶπε followed by ἔπος τ' ἔφατ' ἔκ τ'
ὀνόμαζεν—a formula which, as pointed out in xxi 84n., should properly be

174

followed by a proper name. But this is the reading (with loss of digamma if εἶπεν is accepted) of the papyrus and some MSS; it represents an attempt on the part of these witnesses, using the model of vii 330 εὐχόμενος δ' ἄρα εἶπεν ἔπος κτλ., to resolve the problem created by the commoner MS reading πρὸς ὅν κτλ., of Eurymachus here speaking to his own θυμός, but being answered below by Antinous. This, however, does not seem to van der Valk a strong enough reason to reject the consensus of the majority of witnesses (*Textual Criticism*, 93).

249. The syntax is difficult, no doubt reflecting Eurymachus' strong feelings. The first hemistich is identical to *Il.* xx 293: ὦ πόποι is an exclamation of indignant incredulity, and ἐστί must be supplied with ἄχος.   **αὐτοῦ:** i.e. ἐμαυτοῦ; it is less emphatic than πάντων; according to Eurymachus, he is concerned not so much with his own honour as the criticism which will be levelled at the suitors as a whole.

250-3. **τοσσοῦτον:** the gemination of -σ- is for metrical reasons; we expect an answering correlative such as ὅσσον, but in xxi 253 (after a parenthesis of two lines) we find ἀλλά, as at xiv 142-4 οὐδέ νυ τῶν ἔτι τόσσον ὀδύρομαι . . . ἀλλά, and xxii 50-1, similar to this passage, οὔ τι γάμου τόσσον κεχρημένος . . . ἀλλά; cf. also iv 104-5 τῶν πάντων οὐ τόσσον ὀδύρομαι . . . ὡς.

250. **γάμου:** ablative gen. after a verb of emotion.   **ἀχνύμενός περ:** concess., 'although [to a certain extent, it is true,] I do grieve [for this failure too]'; cf. iv 104 and xiv 142 ἱέμενός περ, both mentioned above.

251-2. It is impossible to judge how far Eurymachus' sudden disdain for Penelope may be sincere; cf. Leodes' words at xxi 160ff.

252. There is no need to supply ἐν with the loc. ἄλλῃσιν πολίεσσιν. The reference is of course to the neighbouring islands.

253-5. The syntax is still loose: either εἰ must be taken causally rather than conditionally ('I grieve because'), or the phrase in xxi 255 must be seen as a sort of apodosis, despite the colon.

253. **τοσσόνδε:** supply 'as we see here'.   **βίης:** governs ἀντιθέου Ὀδυσῆος; on this gen. see xxi 125-6n. and 185n.

254. **ὅ τ':** a form equivalent to the later causal conjunction ὅτι. Here too we expect a correlative of τοσσόνδε.

255. **ἐλεγχείη κτλ.:** again, we must supply '[that will be] a shame'. καί, 'even'; the inf. is consecutive and final in implication. For this preoccupation with the judgement of posterity (Eurymachus always speaks with an outward show of decency, cf. i 402-4, xvi 435-47), compare the well known ἐσσομένοισιν ἀοιδήν of iii 204, and *Il.* ii 119 αἰσχρὸν γὰρ τόδε γ' ἐστὶ καὶ ἐσσομένοισι πυθέσθαι (Agamemnon speaking of defeat at Troy); likewise xxiv 433-5, the first line of which has the same ending, λώβη . . . τάδε γ' ἐστὶ καὶ ἐσσομένοισι πυθέσθαι, and which is followed by a conditional protasis, and then a second apodosis in asyndeton, οὐκ ἂν ἐμοί . . . γένοιτο, which shows the close dependence of that passage on this one; a similarly ironic apodosis is found in xiv 406, after a relative clause with conditional force.

256. = i 383, iv 641, xvii 477, xviii 284.

257–62. The passage has been adjudged an interpolation, probably wrongly. It is true that Antinous' excuse is specious, no more than an attempt to win time or, better still, save face if the contest is forgotten; if his objection were valid, it would be absurd that no one should have thought of it before. But the festival of Apollo, which is somehow related to the new moon (see Bona, *Studi*, 127), has been mentioned before in xix 306–7 (Odysseus 'will return this very month, τοῦδ' αὐτοῦ λυκάβαντος, on the new moon), xx 156 (Eurycleia says the suitors will soon be back because of the festival, ἐπεὶ καὶ πᾶσιν ἑορτή), xx 276–8 (heralds announce a sacred hecatomb). The argument that a festival sacred to the archer god (cf. the epithet in xxi 267) would be just the occasion for a contest with bow and arrow is based on an anachronism; but it does not follow that any such exercise would be incompatible with the festivities—indeed, the idea of rendering homage to Apollo fits well with some later remarks by Odysseus (xxi 280, xxii 7) and Penelope (xxi 338), to the effect that it will be Apollo who grants victory to the winner (in addition, note the favourable omen in xv 525–6, and Apollo's tutelary interest in Telemachus at xix 86; these mentions of Apollo may be clues to an earlier version of the poem in which he, not Athena, was Odysseus' protector). Furthermore, there is a grim and appropriate irony in the suitor's using as his excuse a god from whom he is to receive nothing but harm.

257. νοέεις δὲ καὶ αὐτός: Antinous' phrase may be a form of courtesy, or conceal an accusation of insincerity on Eurymachus' part; it is clearly dependent on *Il.* xxiv 560, but νοέω there means 'propose, intend' and governs an inf.; here it is absolute, 'as you know very well'.

258. Once again, ellipsis of the verb 'is', as in xx 156 (see n.). τοῖο: emphatic, as in xxi 62.

259. ἀγνή: postponed for emphasis; the rhetorical question follows closely (no one would even think of drawing a bow on such a holy day). ἀλλὰ is effectively 'no; on the contrary . . .'; ἔκηλοι is more or less adverbial.

260. κάτθετ': i.e. the bow. εἴ κ' εἰῶμεν κτλ.: as usual in this type of aposiopesis (cf. *Il.* i 580–1, xxiii 556–9, 567), the conditional implies some unspoken apodosis such as 'that would be a good idea'; or, if we take εἰ concessively, 'there would be no harm'. However, the last conjectures in the apparatus would do away altogether with the conditional in the protasis. πελέκεας: synizesis; the word is placed early for emphasis: 'as for the axes (if anyone thinks they may be stolen)'. εἰῶμεν: contraction of the original pres. subj. *ἐάωμεν to ἐῶμεν lies behind this rare metrical lengthening of the first syllable, which Eustathius' conjecture is designed to eliminate.

260–1. εἰῶμεν . . . ἐστάμεν: 'let be, i.e. leave alone, in their place'. The passage has a bearing on where the contest is supposed to take place, in the feast-hall or the courtyard: the ironic ὀΐω (cf. ὀΐομαι, xxii 140) perhaps refers to the impossibility of entering the μέγαρον. But this argument is weakened if, as some have proposed, xxi 262 be removed as superfluous (but note that the almost identical line xvi 104 has been condemned precisely on the grounds that it appears to be an echo of this one—unless both are dependent on the very similar xviii 24). In this case, the meaning would be that no one would steal the axes, either in the feast-hall or the courtyard, because the culprit would be immediately detected.

261. The object of ἀναιρήσεσθαι must be the axes; naturally, the bow would be taken away by the competitors.

262. Λαερτιάδεω: the synizesis and hiatus is perhaps imitated from original formulae such as *Il.* i 1 Πηληϊάδεω Ἀχιλῆος, where the primitive form would have been Πηληϊάδᾱ' Ἀχιλῆος.

263. = xviii 418. ἄγετ': von der Mühll gives enthusiastic praise (*optime*) to Bentley's conjecture ἄγε with following digamma. The word οἰνοχόος is found only once in the *Iliad* (ii 128), in connection with the rules of war; in *Od.* ix 10 the word is used in a general sense; the cup-bearer in Odysseus' palace (cf. xxi 142, 145) has been mentioned in xviii 418-19 where, having apparently recovered from a blow struck at him by Eurymachus (xviii 396), he is given the same order as here; in the identical line xviii 418 we should also read ἄγε, which indeed is supported by one witness.   ἐπαρξάσθω δεπάεσσιν: the verb refers to the *ἐπαρχή, or action of emptying a libation of a few drops from each cup before filling it, as the servants pour ἐπαρξάμενοι δεπάεσσιν in iii 339-40, xxi 271-2 (passages dependent in turn on *Il.* ix 175-6), or as Eumaeus offers a cup to Odysseus σπείσας in xiv 447.

264. The first hemistich is also paralleled at xviii 419; σπείσαντες is emphatic: '(only) after pouring a libation'. Bérard's καταπαύσομεν is arbitrary, despite xxi 279. On ἀγκύλα see the Introduction.

265-6. The repetitive wording, pointed by hammering alliterations down to αἰπολίοισιν ('amongst all flocks', partitive dat.; cf. i 71, xv 227, the latter also with ἔξοχα), is immediately noticeable. The lines are almost identical to xvii 213, xx 173-4. ἠῶθεν: the suffix is abl.; translate 'at daybreak'.

266. μέγα: adv., 'much the finest'.

267. ἐπί ... θέντες: tmesis, as in iii 179 πόλλ' ἐπὶ μῆρ' ἔθεμεν; cf. i 140 ἐπιθεῖσα. There is a similar tmesis with μηρία and ἐπί ... ἔκηαν or ἔκηε in iii 9, xvii 241, xxii 336. κλυτοτόξῳ: cf. xxi 257-62 n.

268. = xxi 180.

269. = xxi 143.

270-3. For the repetitions (xxi 271-2 = iii 339-40; xxi 273, almost identical to iii 342; xxi 270 = i 146, iii 338, etc.) and the practice of libations see xxi 263 n. The lines have been needlessly condemned on the grounds that they slow up the pace of the narrative.

273. Both here and at iii 342 von der Mühll, following Aristarchus, prefers πίον without the augment. ὅσον: 'all'.

276. This line has no MS authority whatever, and is an editorial addition; it should be excised (see further Blass, *Interpolationen*, 204). Both xvii 469 and xviii 352, on which it is based (cf. xxi 342), are followed by asyndeton, whereas here we have δέ in xxi 277.

277. The papyrus' inversion of the names, which may well be correct, has been discussed in the Introduction; the suggestion that θεοειδέα (with synizesis, as in such models for this line as *Il.* iii 27) is to be taken with both names is unacceptable.

278. Odysseus singles out the two heroes in his request, and especially the second, who, since he spoke with restraint and good sense in xxi 257–68 (note the usual hiatus before ἔπος; the line-ending is similar to that of viii 141, 397), will likewise (καί) listen with sense to his supplications now. The substance of the request implied in λίσσομαι follows in xxi 281.

279. The infinitives παῦσαι τόξον and ἐπιτρέψαι have been taken as imperatives, but in view of what has been said in the note on xxi 235 it is perhaps preferable to take them as epexegetic, in apposition to ἔπος. τόξον here means 'the archery contest', and this must be understood also as the object of ἐπιτρέψαι.

280. Although the phrase is paratactic, it loosely reproduces Antinous' thought in xxi 267. **ἠῶθεν:** cf. xxi 265 n.

281. Voss's conjecture is excellent; the beginning of the line is identical to ii 212, iv 669, but here greater emphasis falls on the pronoun. **μεθ' ὑμῖν:** 'among you'; Odysseus modestly asks only to be allowed to try his strength with the bow, not to take part in the contest as a competitor.

282. χειρῶν καὶ σθένεος πειρήσομαι: the aor. subj. πειρήσομαι implies an open question, '(to see) whether', which can be followed equally well either by εἰ or ἤ (see the apparatus, and xxi 284). For χειρῶν καὶ σθένεος cf. δύναμις καὶ χεῖρες in xxi 202, xx 237.

283. γναμπτοῖσι: the word has been interpreted here as 'flexible, pliant', but all of the eleven occurrences of the word in Homer allow the meaning 'bent', not only when applied to curved objects (*Il.* xviii 401, *Od.* iv 369, xii 332), a jaw-bone (*Il.* xi 416), or a tortuous mind (*Il.* xxiv 41), but also in the five occurrences of the line-ending ἐνὶ γναμπτοῖσι μέλεσσι(ν): in *Il.* xxiv 359 Priam's limbs are naturally bent with age; in *Il.* xi 669 (with a first hemistich similar to the present line) Nestor speaks of the strength having gone out of 'my (now) bent limbs'; in *Od.* xi 394 Agamemnon talks of a body becoming 'bent' in Hades; in xiii 398, 430 the word is used proleptically (Athena withers Odysseus' skin over his 'now bent' limbs); here Odysseus talks like his old fighting-companions.

284. The line is suspect for various reasons, and its removal would support the reading εἰ in xxi 282: the hiatus in the first foot (which could be avoided by reading ἤ', that is elided ἠέ); the fact that we must supply 'for me' or 'my strength' with ὄλεσσεν; and the rarity of ἀκομιστίη, 'neglect' (ἄλη, however, which is used only three times and always in the *Odyssey*, at x 464, xv 342, 345, need not be questioned). ἀκομιστίη, which naturally requires long -ῑ- to avoid the cretic like ἀτιμίῃσιν in xiii 142, is found only here in archaic texts; it is related to the Homeric words κομίζω and κομιδή, but apart from ὀλιγιστία in Democritus, the only parallel forms are in

Xenophon (ἀχαριστία) or later authors (ἀοριστία, Aristotle; ἀνελπιστία, ἀφροντιστία, ἀχωριστία).

285. = xvii 481. Note the mixture of anger, pride (cf. xxi 289), and fear; ἄρα has its common meaning, 'as was to be expected'.

286. Deletion is not called for (cf. the apparatus on xxi 285).

287. = xxi 84, 167; see the notes on the text of those lines and on xxi 248. The papyrus has no νύ ἐφελκυστικόν after ἐνένιπε on this occasion; the editors disagree on this point.

288. The initial apostrophe is copied from xiv 361, but here it has an insulting tone (cf. xxi 86) which is lacking there; ξείνων is a partitive gen. **ἔνι τοι φρένες οὐδ᾽ ἠβαιαί:** ἔνι is the ancient adv., here used with a plural subj.; τοι, possess. dat. A similar line ending is found in xviii 355 and *Il.* xiv 141; of the remaining Homeric examples, six (five in the *Iliad* and *Od.* iii 14) have οὐδ᾽ ἠβαιόν, while ix 462 has ἠβαιόν without the negative. The existence later of βαιός, 'small', led Leumann to posit a ghost form derived from οὐ δὴ βαιόν (*Wörter*, 50), but this is difficult here, where οὐδέ, 'not even', gives good sense.

289. Although this reading is supported by no lesser authority than Aristarchus, and has a close parallel in ii 310–11 (Telemachus says οὔ πως ἔστιν ὑπερφιάλοισι μεθ᾽ ὑμῖν | δαίνυσθαί τ᾽ ἀκέοντα καὶ εὐφραίνεσθαι ἔκηλον), it is odd that the word ὑπερφίαλος should be used in the good sense of 'person of quality' here (see van der Valk, *Textual Criticism*, 54), after having been used in such a different sense in xxi 285 ὑπερφιάλως. The former meaning (for which see also *Il.* v 881, where Ares applies the word to Diomedes) is consistent with either of the two possible etymologies, from φιάλη or from φυ- with dissimilation of the vowel. The papyrus reading does not entirely support Schwartz's conjecture, which attempts to get round this problem; the second of our two readings would be acceptable in the text too. **ἀγαπᾷς:** ἀγαπάω, 'be contented with', with internal acc. implied as the antecedent of δ, is found only here and in xxiii 214, against various attestations of ἀγαπάζω in both active and middle; and the meaning 'be contented with, resigned to', as opposed to 'love', is unique to this passage. **ἔκηλος:** 'at ease, unmolested', in contrast to the troubles of the previous day; the preceding hiatus implies digamma, perhaps indicating a common root with ἑκάεργος, etc.: 'keeping apart, aloof', 'undisturbed' (cf. Hesychius' gloss γέκαλον· ἥσυχον).

290. **δαιτὸς:** '(your share) of the banquet'; cf. xx 293–4 n. **αὐτάρ:** 'and even', asyndeton. **ἀκούεις:** 'you can listen'.

291. **καὶ ῥήσιος:** seems superfluous after μύθων ἡμετέρων (skilfully inverted in the next verse); and ῥῆσις, otherwise unattested in Homer, is next found in lyric poetry (cf. ῥήτρη in xiv 393, a prosaic word used by Tyrtaeus to refer specifically to the laws of Lycurgus; ῥητήρ in *Il.* ix 443, also with μύθων, found only in inscriptions; ῥητός in *Il.* xxi 445, found in Hesiod). **οὐδέ τις ἄλλος:** 'and yet no one else'.

292. **καὶ** marks a climax: '(not merely) a stranger, but a beggar to boot'.

293-310. Antinous' moralizing digression sits ill on the lips of a wastrel like him, and has therefore attracted frequent condemnation; but the editors are unsure as to the extent of the passage to be excised. The most extreme position is that of van Leeuwen, whose suggestion would bring together the two occurrences of ἔκηλος (xxi 289, 309) in a concise phrase. Other editors begin the excision in 295, or remove only the descriptive passages in 297–8, 299–304, 303–4, or 303 alone; others confine their attentions to 305–9, or even to 308 alone. There are, it is true, several oddities, but the style of the whole digression is really rather good; its structure bears a remarkable affinity to the *Iliad*'s favourite threefold scheme for sententious passages, with exposition (293–4) followed by *exemplum* (295–304) and moral (305–10) (see Heubeck, *Dichter*, 25).

293. **μελιηδής:** this epithet is applied to οἶνος on four occasions in the *Iliad* and seven in the *Odyssey*; doubtless it looks back to the time when μέθη had the meaning 'mead'. Antinous' accusation of drunkenness recalls Odysseus' words to Eumaeus in xiv 463–6, and above all his fear of being thought drunk in xix 122 βεβαρηότα ... φρένας οἴνῳ; compare also the well-known οἰνοβαρής of *Il.* i 225, paralleled by οἰνοβαρείων at the end of xxi 304, which in turn recalls ix 374, x 555. This is the only Homeric occurrence of τρώει; the present tense of this verb was later substituted by τιτρώσκω, a correlative of the sigmatic forms in xvi 293, xix 12, *Il.* xii 66, xxiii 341 (τρωτός already in *Il.* xxiii 568).

294. The sing. ὅς after pl. antecedent ἄλλους is common in such *ad sensum* constructions; a similar case, but in reverse, is seen in xix 40 θεὸς ... οἵ. **χανδὸν:** the word is formed on the analogy of, for example, ἐξαναφανδόν in xiii 48, from a root χαν- (χάσκω is not found until Anacr., χαίνω even later) attested in eight places in the *Iliad* (with ἀμφέχανε, xxiii 79), and in xii 350, where it describes a person who swallows mouthfuls of sea water; this fits well with the meaning 'at a mouthful, at one gulp' > 'greedily' (cf. ἄμυστις, 'a long draught taken at a single gulp', also attested from Anacr. onwards). **αἴσιμα:** adverbial; its sense 'reasonable, (intellectually) sensible' makes it an apt adv. with οἶδα (ii 231, v 9, xiv 433), but not with πίνῃ, so that Leumann may be correct in seeing this line ending as an adaptation of *Il.* xv 207 αἴσιμα εἰδῇ (*Wörter*, 166).

295–304. The story of Peirithoüs and the Centaurs is alluded to in passing in *Il.* i 267–8 φηρσὶν ὀρεσκῴοισι (on the formulaic features of this passage see the interesting remarks of Hoekstra, *Modifications*, 152); *Il.* ii 743–4 φῆρας ... λαχνήεντας; in *Il.* xi 832 Cheiron is already described as δικαιότατος Κενταύρων. There is no idea as yet of the Centaurs as creatures half man, half horse; but xxi 303 ἀνδράσι implies that they are thought of as not quite human.

296–302. The repeated word-play (ἄασ' ... ἄασεν ... ἀασθείς ... ἄτην ... ἀεσίφρονι) emphasizes the destructive moral blindness caused by ἄτη (see xxi 91 n. on ἀάατος). In the *Iliad* the verb usually occurs in the middle or passive, and is applied, as it is here in 301, to someone (who may even be Zeus, as in *Il.* xix 95, 113) who misleads himself or is misled by some unknown impulse, like Agamemnon, Oeneus, Diomedes, and

Patroclus; the same is the case in *Od.* iv 503, 509, on Ajax, son of Oileus; in *Il.* xix 91, 129 Ἄτη herself πάντας ἀᾶται; the sigmatic aor. is used of Zeus misleading mankind in *Il.* viii 237. But the *Odyssey* tends increasingly to use the word in a more modern sense (see H. Seiler, *LfgrE* i 9–12 s.v. ἀάω), in which the cause of the moral blindness or madness is, at least in part, some more or less physical agent, such as sleep and friends (Odysseus in x 68), wine and fate (Elpenor in xi 61), or wine alone as here in 296 (cf. μαινόμενος, xxi 298), and also perhaps in 297 if Duentzer's intelligent conjecture is accepted (the corruption in this case being psychological, due to the late placing of the word; otherwise we are presented with the odd notion of the Centaur, ὁ, misleading his own understanding, φρένας).

298. δόμον: Eustathius' γάμον, an attempt to work in a reference to the well-known story of Eurytion's kidnapping of Peirithoüs' bride Hippodameia, is ingenious, but worthless.

299-304. ἥρωας: i.e. the Lapiths.   **ἄχος:** 'anger'. The end of 299 is identical to xviii 386; the geography of the palace is similar to that of Odysseus' (see the Introduction on θύραζε, and xx 355n. on πρόθυρον and αὐλή). ἀναΐξαντες is emphatic. Antinous himself and the rest of the suitors have already spoken in xviii 83–7 and 115–16 of the cruelty of Echetus, who was probably tyrant in Epirus across the straits from Ithaca (cf. 84, 115 ἤπειρόνδε) and whose name, 'he who holds prisoner', looks like a reminiscence of some cave troll or underground demon (according to Apoll. iv 1092–5, he tortured his own daughter, called Metope in other sources). In the earlier passage Antinous threatens Irus (xviii 85, 116 = xxi 308; end of xviii 86 = xxi 300) with the same frightful punishment at Echetus' hands as he here darkly intimates (xxi 305) may await Odysseus if he is not careful (cf. xx 382–3, where they also wanted to send him ἐς Σικελούς); here we are told that the punishment was actually administered to Eurytion, and later we see it inflicted on Melanthius (xxii 473–7; the end of 475 = xxi 300).

300-1. ἀπ' ... ἀμήσαντες: we must distinguish between three similar verbs (see J. Irigoin, *LfgrE* i 606–7, s.v. ἀμάομαι): first, ἀμάομαι with short first vowel, which means 'collect' (*Il.* xxiv 165 καταμήσατο, of dung; v 482 ἐπαμήσατο, of leaves; ix 247 ἀμησάμενος, of milk); second, ἀμάω, also with short initial vowel, which means 'tear, rend' (*Il.* iii 359, vii 253 διάμησε, of clothes); and last, ἀμάω, with long initial vowel, 'reap, mow, cut'. It is to this last verb that the present compound with ἀπό (in tmesis) belongs, as do ἀμήσαντες (*Il.* xxiv 451, of foliage), ἀμῶεν (*Od.* ix 135, of harvest corn), and ἧμων (*Il.* xviii 551, used intransitively). The use of ἀπάμήσειε in *Il.* xviii 34 to refer to so noble a hero as Achilles cutting his own throat indicates that in these contexts the word carried no ironic or bathetic overtones from its root meaning of 'mow'.   **ἀασθείς:** causal.

302. ἤϊεν: continuous, 'went about (making an exhibition of himself)'; the -ν, like that of φρεσίν in xxi 301, is due to loss of digamma in the following possessive.   **ὀχέων:** a frequentative form of *Ϝεχω, 'carry', emphasizes the continuous aspect; the six Homeric examples of the word in the middle voice show the usual development from 'carry oneself' > 'ride', while

three out of four examples in the active show a parallel development from
'carry' > 'bear, put up with' (xi 619 μόρον; vii 211 ὀϊζύν; and the present
example, where the object is to be understood not as the ἄτη itself, but its
consequences); the fourth (i 297 νηπιάας ὀχέειν, 'behave childishly') could
be due to contamination with *σεχω, 'have', as in viii 529 πόνον τ' ἐχέμεν
καὶ ὀϊζύν. The well-attested reading ἀχέων is unsatisfactory, even though
ἦν ἄτην ἀχέων (as opposed to the ὀχέων of most witnesses) is also found in
various texts of Ps.-Hes. *Sc.* 93, including Stobaeus'. The parallel is coincid-
ental; here the corruption is due to the alliteration in a-, in the Hesiodic
passage it is caused by μετεστοναχίζετ' in the previous line.   ἀεσίφρονι θυμῷ: von der Mühll's conjecture ἀασίφρονι is based on Hesych.
ἀασίφρονι· βλαψίφρονι, φρενοβλαβεῖ· ἀᾶσαι γὰρ τὸ βλάψαι, and
supported by Apollonius the Sophist; some grammarians propose reading
ἀασιφροσύνῃσιν in Hes. *Th.* 502, and Wilamowitz would also read ἀασί-
φρονα in *Op.* 315, 335, 646; Hesychius also offers ἀασιφόρος· βλάβην
φέρων, and Apollonius ἀασιφρονία. The remaining Homeric parallels (*Il.*
xx 183, xxiii 603 ἀεσίφρων; *Od.* xv 470 ἀεσιφροσύνῃσι, and the whole of the
rest of the epic tradition; Hesych. ἄεσις· πόνος, βλάβη) certainly betray a
derivative vowel-change, due either to dissimilation, or to contamination
by ἄεσα, 'I passed (the night)', 'I slept' (ἀεσίφρων thus meaning 'with
slumbering mind; thoughtless') or by ἄημι, 'blow (of wind)' ('with the
mind wandering on the breeze'), or finally to the analogy of ἀλφεσίβοιος,
ἑλκεσίπεπλος, etc.; but at any event no less genuinely Homeric than
ἀασίφρων (see H. J. Mette, *LfgrE*, i 4–5, 182, s.v. ἀασιφροσύνη, ἀασίφρων,
and ἀεσιφροσύνη, ἀεσίφρων).

303. οὖ: either masc. (referring to θυμός) or neut. ('because of all this'); there
is a similar ambiguity in i 74, but in ii 27 the expression is clearly neut. The
end of the line appears also in *Il.* xi 671. The excision of the line (see the
apparatus) leaves the syntax clearer.

304. οἱ δ' αὐτῷ πρώτῳ: οἱ ... αὐτῷ, emphatic reflexive, a rare usage;
πρώτῳ, predicative.   εὕρετο οἰνοβαρείων: causal part.; εὕρετο,
middle, underlines the self-destructive nature of his madness.

305. αἴ κε remote; τό demonstrative, 'this bow (of which we all know)', as in
xxi 113.

306. γάρ: 'in fact, indeed', referring back to πιφαύσκομαι. τευ is another
case where gender is hard to determine (cf. xxi 303 n.); either fem., 'you will
not get any kindness', or masc., 'you will not get kindness from anyone',
with the usual gen. after such verbs. ἐπητύς is a hapax; parallel forms (cf.
xxi 112) are confined to the *Odyssey* (ἐλεητύς, xiv 82, xvii 451; βοητύς, i 369;
ἀγορητύς, viii 168), with the single exception of ἐδητύς, which is attested
twenty-nine times, twenty-one of them in the formulaic line ἐπεὶ πόσιος καὶ
ἐδητύος ἐξ ἔρον ἕντο (fourteen occurrences in the *Iliad*, seven in the
Odyssey), five of them in the line ending ἐδητύος ἠδὲ ποτῆτος (four in the
Iliad, one in the *Odyssey*), two in the phrase πόσιος καὶ ἐδητύος (*Il.* xix 231,
320), and one on its own (*Od.* vi 250), but still in ∪ –‿ ∪ ∪; this has led to
some witnesses reading ἐδητύος in the present line, with fem. τευ. A less

probable solution is the reading ἐπητέος, 'anything friendly', with masc. τευ, neut. gen. of ἐπητής, 'caring, careful', possibly a psilotic form related to ἔπω, 'look after, care for', which appears in xiii 332, xviii 128.

308. The line has been condemned as an interpolation dependent on xviii 85, 116 (cf. xxi 299–304 n., and see the testimony of the MSS and the general remark in von der Mühll's apparatus, as well as Blass, *Interpolationen*, 204); but the mention of deportation in πέμψομεν (see D. Gray, *Archaeologia* G, 117) requires a lative complement (generally with ἔπι or ἐς; see for example *Il.* xxi 454, xx 383). The use of εἰς or ἐς with a person, unusual in Attic, is common in Homer (cf. iii 317, vi 176, 327, xiv 127, xx 372, xxii 202, xxiv 334; and similarly xxii 99, 112, with εἰσαφίκανεν); the origin of this usage may be found in such expressions as ἔς τε Πύλον καὶ Νέστορα, xvii 109.

309. σαώσεαι: 'you will escape unhurt', with abl. complement ἔνθεν.

309–10. ἀλλὰ ἔκηλος | πῖνε: a sort of ring-composition, ending the speech where it began (see xxi 293–310 n.; for the enjambment cf. xiv 167–8 ἔκηλος | πῖνε); ἀλλά, '(do not run this risk,) but instead'.

310. πῖνέ τε μηδ' ἐρίδαινε: the collocation of τε μηδέ is remarkable (Denniston, *Particles*, 514; cf. cases such as *Il.* v 359 κόμισαί τέ με δὸς δέ μοι); the most promising of the conjectures is σύ, which supplies the necessary emphasis and has parallels such as *Il.* xiv 5 ἀλλὰ σὺ μὲν νῦν πῖνε. The concessive imper. πῖνε nicely picks up the fact that they have just finished eating; ἐρίδαινε is durative, 'don't keep on quarrelling'. κουροτέροισι: as in *Il.* iv 316, the word is not simply comparative, 'with men who are younger than you' (cf. xxi 179–80; the final example of Antinous' youthful petulance, since these are his last words), but also intensive, 'with men who are still (comparatively) young'; for similar absolute uses cf. ἀγρότερος (vi 133, xi 611, xvii 295) and θηλύτεραι (viii 324, xi 386, 434, xv 422, xxiii 166, xxiv 202).

311–53. This passage has aroused heated discussion. First of all Penelope intervenes (311–19, 321) to tell Antinous that it is wrong to insult one of Telemachus' guests (the argument is rather weak); not even the beggar can be thinking, in his lowly estate, of winning her as his wife, and so his motive must be, at most, to test his strength *hors concours*, as it were. To this Eurymachus replies—and that he should do so, rather than Antinous, is in itself strange (cf. xxi 186–7), though the same thing has already happened before in xvi 434—with the reasonable point that victory for the beggar would reflect badly on the suitors (320–9). Penelope then repeats her request, with a speech whose ending is suspicious, for reasons to be discussed below (330–42); to which Telemachus unexpectedly retorts, with surprising rudeness, that the final decision about the bow lies with him, and openly humiliates his mother by telling her to take herself off to some task more fitting for a woman (343–53). It is difficult to resolve the difficulties of all this by piecemeal deletions (see the notes and apparatus on 334–5, 335, 343–55, 347, 350–3). Consequently, a number of scholars (most recently Merkelbach, *Untersuchungen*, 115; Ph. W. Harsh, 'Penelope and Odysseus in *Odyssey* xix', *AJP* lxxi (1950), 1–21; Page, *Odyssey*, 128; for opposing views see, for example, Erbse, *Beiträge*, 55–109; Eisenberger, *Studien*, 252–72 n. 49) have concluded that the passage is the work of a late editor who was here faced with conflating two different versions of the story: one in which Odysseus was recognized by Penelope after the death of the suitors, and another in which the recognition took place before. The version we now possess presents us with the recognition scene in xxiii 1–296, a fine passage in which the only discordant notes are the late interpolations in 96–165, and perhaps in the last lines; in this account, Penelope is portrayed as finally learning the truth at the end of a story in which she has played, up to that moment, only a marginal part. But in the hypothetical second version, of later date than xxiii, the recognition scene would have taken place earlier, during the bathing of the wound in xix 53 ff., at the point in the text of our MSS where Odysseus asks for an old woman such as Eurycleia to attend him (xix 343–8); and this would have been followed by husband and wife together hatching the plot for vengeance. This would explain passages like xviii 158–305, which would originally have come after Book xix; there the queen behaves like a strumpet, as one critic has described it, with her alluring make-up, demand for gifts, and so on (and her no less surprising dream, which is little less than magical). Such behaviour would be explained as part of the same clever plan as the proposal of the contest; so would Telemachus' public show of hardness towards his mother (reproaches in xx 129–33; plans for her remarriage in xx 341–2; the 'auction' in xxi 106–10, on which see n. ad loc.; etc.). All this would also fit the account given by Amphimedon in Hades (xxiv 167–9), who claims that the trial of the bow was all a cunning plan suggested to Penelope by Odysseus. In that case xxi 312–13 would be subtly ironic, in the best manner of the original poet; the irony would be heightened by the intentional juxtaposition with ὁ ξεῖνος Ὀδυσσῆος in 314, and then in 334–6; 314–19 would be an attempt to calm the fears of the suitors, lest they oppose the beggar's taking part in the contest; in 331–3 Penelope, imprudently emboldened by the approach of her moment of triumph, would give free rein to her bitterness. Lines 337–42 must be a clumsy and extremely derivative interpolation, equally irrelevant in either version of the story (for the problems of these lines see the Introduction). As for Telemachus' remark in 343–9, Merkelbach has even suggested emending the first words to Ἀντίνο', ἡ μὲν τόξον (*Untersuchungen*, 9 n. 1): in the version which has Penelope ignorant of the real situation, they may be addressed to the suitors, who still oppose giving the bow to Odysseus. Telemachus' further rudeness to his mother in 350–3 would be designed both to trick his enemies and to get her out of the way before the bloody denouement (see Büchner, 'Penelopeszenen', 154–5). Wehrli, however, sees in these lines further evidence of the tendency to give prominence to Telemachus ('Penelope', 234–5; cf. 124 n.).

312–13. The end of the first and beginning of the second lines = xx 294–5 (Ctesippus' sarcastic remark before throwing the cow's trotter).   μὲν: 'certainly', as often.   ἀτέμβειν: the etymology of the word is obscure;

but the primary meaning seems to be trans., as here, 'disappoint, frustrate'; cf. ii 90 and the five occurrences of the middle, 'be frustrated, deprived of' (the doublet ix 42/549 and *Il.* xi 705, xxiii 445, 834 ἀτεμβό-μενος . . . ἴσης), where the active voice must probably be taken to mean 'deprive of', as it does in xx 294, cited as a parallel above, where ἴσης has been subsumed in the preceding μοῖραν . . . ξεῖνος ἔχει. | ἴσην. A mis-understanding of this passage lies behind Apollonius' use of the middle to mean 'reproach' (ii 566, 1199, iii 99, 938; and cf. *EM* ἀτέμβιος· μεμψί-μοιρος, as against the correct ἀτεμβόμενος· στεριοκόμενος of Hesych.). On the *ad sensum* agreement of ὅς with a pl. antecedent, cf. xxi 294 n.

314. The question is rhetorical; the sense of ἔλπομαι neutral, as always ('expect', not 'hope'). The ending is almost identical to xxiv 172.

315. The alliteration of φ/π denotes, ironically in Penelope's case (on the juxtaposition ὁ ξεῖνος Ὀδυσσῆος see the Introduction), a vehement and triumphant state of mind; note the inversion of the formula ἧφι βίηφι, *Il.* xxii 107, with τε introduced between the two (Hainsworth, *Flexibility*, 101). It is difficult to decide between the readings πεποιθώς and πιθήσας. The perfect appears fourteen times in the *Iliad* and thirteen in the *Odyssey*; of the latter, eight are trisyllabic, five of them at the end of the line (cf. the line endings χερσὶ πέποιθα, xvi 71, xxi 132; ἀλκὶ πεποιθώς, vi 130; and ὄφρ' ἥβη τε πεποίθεα χερσί τ' ἐμῇσι, viii 181). The aor. appears seven times in the *Iliad*, always at the end of the line (χειρὶ πιθήσας, *Il.* xi 235, xvii 48) except in one case, which is precisely *Il.* xxii 107 ἧφι βίηφι πιθήσας, and this one example from the *Odyssey*, also at the end of the line (cf. πιθήσεις, xxi 369; βίῃ καὶ κάρτεϊ εἴκων, xiii 143). On the hiatus before ἧφι, which is not repeated in xxi 316, cf. xxi 302 n.

316. Cf. xxi 72.

317. Penelope loads her speech with all the tones of deliberate sarcasm: οὐδέ, 'not even'; που, 'I suppose'; γε, 'at least'. The line-ending is almost identical to xx 328.

318. ὑμείων: partitive. γε is sarcastic again, ἀχεύων emphatic ('let no one be angry at the dinner table'). The line-ending is identical to *Il.* v 869, xviii 461, xxiii 566.

319. The Homeric examples of ἔοικε (with its double hiatus due to digamma) all occur in precepts to do with ethical and social duties (dowries, i 278, etc.; obeying one's elders, iii 357; political life, vi 60; hospitality, xxii 196; ἐπέοικε in vi 193, xi 186, xiv 511, etc.) and prohibitions (rude table-manners, iii 335, vii 159; setting oneself up against the gods, v 212; argumentative behaviour, viii 358).   **οὐδὲ μὲν οὐδέ:** there are a good number of examples of the double negative, from *Il.* xii 212, an exact parallel to this case, 'nor is it in any way fitting', and the related expression in v 212, 'in no way at all is it fitting', to other variations, all of them curiously enough found in viii, such as 32 οὐδὲ γὰρ οὐδέ τις ('nor anyone either'), 176–7 οὐδέ κεν ἄλλως | οὐδὲ θεός ('nor otherwise nor even a god'), and 280 οὔ κέ τις οὐδὲ ἴδοιτο | οὐδὲ θεῶν ('no one could even see it, not even one of the gods'). The expression here looks two ways: it is not fitting

COMMENTARY

that the beggar should marry a queen, but neither is it fitting that anyone should show his bad temper at table.

320–9. Cf. xxi 311–53 n.

321. Not counting various datives (cf. xxi 2), the formula περίφρων Πηνελόπεια, doubtless based on the περίφρων Ἀδρηστίνη of *Il.* v 412, appears forty-one times (including xxi 311, 330), besides the βασίλεια περίφρων of xi 345 and two examples of περίφρων Εὐρύκλεια in xx 134, xxi 381. In the voc., the name of the nurse naturally forces the use of the nom. for voc. περίφρων (xix 357), whereas with the queen's name περίφρων and περίφρον are metrically interchangeable. The MSS mostly give the latter, which led Allen to regularize its use in xvi 435, xviii 245, 285, and here; but the papyrus and other witnesses to this passage do not support his reading. Von der Mühll therefore prefers to read περίφρων in every case.

322. τι: adv., '(not) at all'. ὀϊόμεθ': volitive; σε and τόνδε are object and subject respectively of ἄξεσθαι. οὐδὲ ἔοικεν: these words may either be taken parenthetically, as an affirmation of xxi 319; or with the immediately preceding idea, 'nor is it fitting (that we should think so)'.

323. The apparent anacoluthon, which van der Valk sees as colloquial (*Textual Criticism*, 58; cf. Chantraine, *Grammaire*, ii 328), may be construed *ad sensum*: 'we do not act like this because we think . . . but because we fear the shame' (cf. xxi 72, somewhat similar). Barnes' conjecture would remove the problem altogether. In either case the pl. part. makes the papyrus' reading in xxi 322, with ὀῖομαι in the sing., impossible.

324. μή ποτέ τις: 'lest it happen that someone', a construction dependent on the idea of fear which underlies the notion of shame (see my rendering of αἰσχυνόμενοι in the preceding note); the vowel in τις is metrically lengthened by following digamma. κακώτερος ... Ἀχαιῶν: Ἀχαιῶν partitive, κακώτερος probably comparative in sense (the shame being that someone 'worse than oneself' should criticize), as it is in Hector's words in *Il.* xxii 106, on which this line is clearly based (cf. also *Il.* xxii 105, which is closely paralleled by 323); the only other occurrence of the word, in Nausicaa's speech at vi 275, requires the intensive sense ('someone very wicked').

325. ἦ πολὺ χείρονες: ἦ is sarcastic, 'so it seems'; πολύ, adverbial. The gen. ἀνδρός functions both as a term of comparison after χείρονες and as a possessive after ἄκοιτιν. Both Menelaus (iv 333–4) and Penelope (xx 82) break out with similar laments on this situation.

326. μνῶνται: this rare contracted form with following hiatus is due to diectasis of original μνάοντ' to μνώοντ', from a verb in *βν- > μν-, 'be a suitor (for the hand of a woman)'. οὐδέ: this reading involves taking the parataxis as what we should regard as a subordinate clause, throwing χείρονες into sharp relief: 'they are worse . . . because they do not . . .'; the two unacceptable variants given in the apparatus represent subsequent attempts to normalize the syntax. τι is used in the same sense as in xxi 322; ἐντανύουσιν is present ('are able to draw'), unlike the form in xxi 92.

327. A series of insulting epithets; the end of the line, identical to xiii 333 and

186

xiv 122, shows the normal meaning of the perfect ('who has arrived after having wandered'; cf. *h. Cer.* 133 ἱκόμην ἀλαλημένη), whereas in xi 167 ἀλάλημαι, xx 340 ἀλάληται have intensive force ('I (or 'he') am on my wanderings'), as do the infs. in ii 370, xii 284; this has caused the accentuation of the pres. to spread not only to these forms, ἀλάλησθαι, but also to the three masculine participles mentioned above, although Ptolemy of Ascalon preferred the MS reading with the paroxytone accent.

328. Almost identical to xxiv 177, which also has tmesis; and similar to xxi 97, 114, 127 διοϊστεύσειν or διοϊστεύσω τε σιδήρου.

329. ἡμῖν: emphatic, 'for persons so important as us'. Eurymachus himself showed his preoccupation about bequeathing ἐλεγχείη, 'shame', to posterity in xxi 255 (see n.). The optative implies an unspoken protasis: 'if they were to speak of it'. The late reading δέ κ' is acceptable (see the apparatus, and Nausicaa's words in vi 285, ὥς ἐρέουσιν, ἐμοὶ δέ κ' ὀνείδεα ταῦτα γένοιτο; the beginning of this line is identical to *Il.* xxii 108).

330. Cf. xxi 321n.

331. ἐϋκλείας: original *ἐϋκλέϝεσας ought to have given ἐϋκλεέας, but the primitive representation of this as ΕΥΚΛΑΕΑϹ gave rise to this spelling with 'metrical lengthening' (see Chantraine, *Grammaire*, i 10, 30–1). κατά carries the implication 'the length and breadth of the city'.

332. The subject of ἔμμεναι is the unspoken antecedent of οἵ; δή, with synaloepha (ignoring the digamma in οἶκος, cf. xxi 211), reinforces the causal sense of the relative. οἶκος here means 'patrimony, estate'; with ἀτιμάζοντες we must supply the object ('it').

333. The beginning of the line is identical to xxiv 460, *Il.* xv 489, xvii 203; the epithet is applied to Odysseus only in these two lines of the *Odyssey* (xiv 218 refers to imaginary warriors; xxiv 86, to the Achaean heroes at Troy; vi 34, xxi 153, 170, to the suitors; xv 28 μνηστήρων ... ἀριστῆες, to some of them). In the rest of the line there is a clear reference back to xxi 329; ταῦτα is heavily emphatic, while ἐλέγχεα is predicative ('precisely *these* criticisms', when you have already incurred shame for other reasons); τί δ', 'so why, why then?'.

334–5. These lines, in which Penelope tries to justify Odysseus' participation in the contest by adducing the noble lineage which he himself claimed in xix 180–1, are certainly unnecessary; they are lacking in one MS, and inverted in another. Further doubt is cast on them by the unusual εὐπηγής, 'well-built', found only here in Homer, and furthermore in a sentence with no main verb. The adj. is later attested in Hippocrates and Apollonius; there are only four further instances of compounds with the second element—πηγής, of which only καινοπηγής (A. *Th.* 642) and περιπηγής (Nicander) are found in poetry.

334. On μέν, see xxi 312–13n.

335. The oddity in this line is neither εὔχεται, 'boasts of', typical in genealogies, nor the internal acc. γένος (cf. iv 63, xiv 199), but υἱός at the end of the line, which is redundant after πατρός at the beginning (hence the papyrus reads ἀνδρός). It seems to derive from *Il.* xiv 113, which has the

same beginning but ends καὶ ἐγὼ γένος εὔχομαι εἶναι; here there has been a clumsy attempt to adapt the phrase to the third person, involving the insertion of a word unnecessary to the sense, whereas in the line from the *Iliad* εἶναι fits well with πατρός ... ἐξ ἀγαθοῦ. Similarly, in the other parallels, we find xiv 199 ἐκ Κρητάων ... εὔχομαι, 'I boast of being a Cretan' (with no need for another verb), and iv 63 ἀνδρῶν ... ἐστέ; note, however, i 207 ἐξ αὐτοῖο ... πάϊς εἰς Ὀδυσῆος.

336–42. Only the first of these lines, which is identical to xxi 281 and repeats the ending of xxi 112, is necessary; of the remainder Stanford remarks, amusingly though a trifle simplistically, that 'Homer is resting before he soars to the height of his climax', since they are simply a patchwork of shreds from other contexts: 337 = *Il.* i 212, and is almost identical to xvi 440, xix 487; 338, similar to ix 317, *Il.* vii 154, with an ending identical to xxi 7, *Il.* vii 81, xvi 725; 339, similar to xiv 341, 516, xv 338, and is a doublet of xvi 79 (Telemachus, speaking of Odysseus), xvii 550 (Penelope, of the same); the end of 340 = xiv 531; 341 copies xvi 80; and 342 = xvi 81, and recalls xv 395.

336. Cf. xxi 112 n.

338. On the festival of Apollo cf. xxi 257–62 n.

339. Double acc. after a verb of dressing; note the hiatus before the digamma of εἵματα.

340. The anaphora of δώσω in this line and the next may reflect the fact that the poet is trying to cram an extra reward, the ἄκων, into the passage from which this one is imitated, xvi 79–80. As the text makes clear, the ἄκων, here and in xiv 531 (cf. 336–42 n.), is a peacetime weapon useful for country living; cf. xiii 225, where Athena disguises herself as a shepherd with πέδιλα (cf. xxi 341) and ἄκων, 'javelin'. In xiv 225, however, ἄκοντες are weapons of war.   ἀλκτῆρα: applied to persons in the *Iliad* (*Il.* xiv 485, Acamas; xvii 100, Achilles; xviii 213, warriors in general), the word is applied to weapons here and in Ps.-Hes. *Sc.* 128 (but in *Sc.* 29 it applies to Heracles, and in Hes. *Th.* 657 to Zeus).

341. ἄμφηκες: the epithet, which occurs in three other places in Homer (xvi 80, *Il.* x 256, *Il.* xxi 118), belongs to the period when the sword ceased to be used solely as a thrusting, piercing weapon, and began to be used as a cutting, slashing one, a development which made the double edge necessary (see Lorimer, *Monuments*, 275 n. 2).   ὑπὸ ποσσὶ πέδιλα: four passages in the *Iliad* on sandals read ποσσὶ δ' ὑπὸ λιπαροῖσιν ἐδήσατο καλὰ πέδιλα, which implies some sort of fastening in which the lace passed under the foot, perhaps through a slit in the sole (cf. xv 369, xviii 361 ποσίν ... ὑποδήματα δοῦσα or δοῖεν; and later ὑποδέω), and something similar is seen in *Il.* xxiv 340 ὑπὸ ποσσὶν ἑ. κ. π. The *Odyssey* has various formulas: those in xvi 80 δώσω ... ποσσὶ πέδιλα, and xiv 23 ἀμφὶ πόδεσσιν ἑοῖς ἀράρισκε πέδιλα, which do not mention any fastening, are perfectly logical, and xvi 154–5 εἵλετο χερσὶ πέδιλα, | δησάμενος δ' ὑπὸ ποσσὶ κτλ. also corresponds with the Iliadic examples; but this passage, which shows confusion in the poet's mind between xvi 80 (cf. xxi 336–42 n.) and the

mentions of fastenings, is illogical. Even more so is xiii 225, where Athena
ποσσί... ὑπὸ λιπαροῖσι πέδιλ' ἔχε.
342. The ending of this line (cf. xxi 276) is found six times in the *Odyssey*; viii
204–5 τῶν δ' ἄλλων ὅτινα κ. θ. τε κ. | ... πειρηθήτω must be translated
'whomsoever his feelings incite (to fight), let him ...' (the same beginning
of the line is combined with κραδίη καὶ θυμὸς ἀνώγει in xv 395, which
O'Nolan, *Doublets*, 28 singles out as a rare and unnecessary metrical
equivalent of the more usual formula); xxi 198 εἴπαθ' ὅπως ὑμέας κτλ. is
equivalent to 'tell me the way your feelings drive you'; the remaining four
examples, xiv 517, xv 339, xvi 81, and this passage, are combined with
πέμπει or πέμπω followed by σε or μιν, meaning 'I will send (him) whichever way his feelings drive him'.
343–53. See the general note on xxi 311–53.
344. After τόξον μὲν we expect σὺ δέ, but in xxi 350 we have another
anacoluthon with ἀλλά. Ἀχαιῶν, partitive (cf. xxi 324); ἐμεῖο, gen. of comparison.
345. κρείσσων: '(is) better qualified'; the following infinitives are
consecutive-final, governing τόξον, which is placed at the beginning for
emphasis.
346–7. The two ὅσσοι follow τις in xxi 344, with agreement *ad sensum* (cf. xxi
294 n.). The lines are unnecessary and one MS omits them, but this is
unsufficient reason to expunge them. This and other passages pose the
famous problem of the four islands: the catalogue of ships in *Il.* ii 625–37
mentions troops from Dulichium and the Echinae or Echinades, which are
Ἤλιδος ἄντα and whose leader is Meges, in contrast to the troops of
Odysseus, lord of the Cephallenians who rule in Ithaca, Zacynthus, and
Samos. The doublets i 245–8/xvi 122–5 mention the inhabitants of the
islands of Dulichium, Same, Zacynthus, and Ithaca; in xiii 237–49 it is
stated that the last of these is well known both to those who live πρὸς ἠῶ τ'
ἠέλιόν τε and also to those who dwell μετόπισθε ποτὶ ζόφον ἠερόεντα; in ix
21–7 we read that Ithaca is πανυπερτάτη and πρὸς ζόφον, while the
remaining islands are situated ἄνευθε πρὸς ἠῶ τ' ἠέλιόν τε; and finally, the
poet here refers to the lords of Ithaca (xxi 346 = i 247, xvi 124; xxi 347 is
similar to i 245, xvi 122; κάτα is anastrophic) in contrast to the lords of the
isles which face Elis (πρός, 'facing towards'); the loc. νήσοισι requires some
verb such as κοιρανέουσι to be supplied; the ellipse would be removed by
the reading ναίουσι, which recalls xiii 240, *Il.* ii 626, and the ναιετάουσι of
ix 23). The modern place-names of the region, as well as certain geographical features, suggest that Ithaca is present-day *Thiaki* or *Ithaki*;
Samos or Same is *Kephallenia* (where there was once a city called *Same*);
Zacynthus is obviously present-day *Zakynthos*, which is indeed the only
one of the islands which can clearly be said to 'face' Elis; and Dulichium, if
its name is connected with δολιχός, 'long', may be one of the Echinades
now called *Makri*. There is, however, another well-known theory which
locates Ithaca in *Leukas*, the most northerly of the islands (considered as
part of the chain which runs NW–SE parallel to the coast of Acarnania: see

COMMENTARY

Cauer, *Homerkritik*, 243); this theory tentatively identifies Samos or Same as present-day *Ithaki*; and Dulichium—which is described as πολύπυρος (xiv 335, xvi 396, xix 292) and ποιήεις (xvi 396) and accounts for fifty-two of the suitors (xvi 247–51, against twenty-four from Same, twenty from Zacynthus, and twelve from Ithaca), and which must therefore have been quite large—as modern *Kephallenia*. There is even a third theory, based on the Iliadic allusion to Odysseus as leader of the Cephallenians, which proposes *Kephallenia*, which is indeed the most westerly of the isles, as the homeland of the hero, at least in a primitive stage of the legend.

347. In addition to the previous note, it may be relevant that the adj. ἱππόβοτος is always applied to Argos except in iv 606 (Ithaca is suitable for rearing goats, not colts), *Il.* iv 202 (Thessalian Trice), and this passage, which may be compared with *Il.* xi 680–1, where Nestor talks of the horses reared in his homeland. Hoekstra makes the interesting observation that although Ἧλις appears to be a clear case of original initial digamma, nine of the eleven Homeric occurrences of the name ignore digamma completely and the other two do not definitely respect it: in this case the original may have read προτί, not πρός (*Modifications*, 46–7).

348. μ' ἀέκοντα βιήσεται: 'will prevent me'; the idea is phrased similarly in several passages, such as *Il.* xv 186 (βίη and ἀέκοντα); i 403 (βίηφι (cf. xxi 315) and ἀέκοντα); *Il.* vii 197 (βίη with ἑκὼν ἀέκοντα); *Il.* xiii 572 (βίη and οὐκ ἐθέλοντα); and here, with a cognate verb and conditional ἀέκοντα.

349. καθάπαξ: only here in archaic poetry, the word produces an ugly and unparalleled sound-clash with the following ξείνῳ; the uncompounded form ἅπαξ only appears twice (xii 22, 350), in each case signifying 'once and for all', with reference to death. Taken together with the middle φέρεσθαι (consecutive-final inf.), the words imply that the gift would be permanent.

350–3. The lines are a well-known triplet, found also in *Il.* vi and *Od.* i: xxi 350 = *Il.* vi 490/*Od.* i 356; 351 = *Il.* vi 491/*Od.* i 357; 352 = *Il.* vi 492/*Od.* i 358 as far as the caesura, followed by πόλεμος, μῦθος respectively for xxi 352 τόξον, and the remainder of the line identical in both of the *Odyssey* passages. Hector's words to Andromache in the *Iliad* are obviously the most ancient occurrence; from it the others derive, even though εἰς οἶκον is more modern than οἴκαδε (see Hoekstra, *Modifications*, 58); in the present passage, therefore, οἶκον must be taken metaphorically, not literally. τόξον is striking, since what is referred to is not the bow or its handling, but a decision about the contest; and the latter was, precisely, Penelope's idea. μελήσει must have ironic undertones, half hinting that the 'men' will indeed have to 'watch out for' the bow before long, in quite another sense. The passage in *Od.* i, on the other hand, was athetized long ago by Aristarchus; its connection with the preceding passage, where Odysseus is included among the fallen at Troy, is very weak, and μῦθος is a sign of its derivative nature, since it would presuppose that Penelope was unable even to speak; in xxi, however, even this word would be admissible (see the papyrus reading, and von der Mühll's suggestion), given that the speaker is in league with his mother, or that he is attempting to bamboozle the suitors and needs to get the heroine out of the way before the slaughter begins.

350. ἰοῦσα: emphatic. σ' αὐτῆς: i.e. σὰ αὐτῆς, reflexive; the reference is to the loom and the distaff, typical emblems of women's work.

352. ἔργον ἐποίχεσθαι: cf. xvii 227, xviii 363.

353. The beginning of the line appears in xi 353; here and in other passages in the *Odyssey*, the demonstrative τοῦ for ἐμοῦ is noteworthy (see Schwyzer, *Grammatik*, ii 208); on the other hand, the hiatus before the digamma of οἴκῳ is regular. This line is followed in some MSS by a different line, called xxi 353a by von der Mühll, which perhaps deserves consideration; it would make a good substitute for 354, though the two cannot both stand. In the *Iliad* the inceptive aor. ῥίγησε(ν) is usually applied to shuddering at disagreeable or important scenes, but it is used twice (*Il.* iii 259, Priam before the herald; xv 34, Hera before Zeus) of a character's reaction to an unnerving piece of news, as it is in the passages of the *Odyssey* where it occurs (v 116, 171, Circe before Hermes, and Odysseus before Circe).

354-8. On Penelope's sleep here, see the Introduction; in i, xvi, and xix her slumbers seem less necessary, and her laments less fitting, than they do here. οἰκόνδε, this time with hiatus, fits well with xxi 350 (on its meaning, and the expression ἐς . . . ὑπερῷα, cf. xxi 5n.), as does πεπνυμένον with xxi 343.

354. The same θάμβος is experienced (the verb is inceptive once again) in the face of the supernatural (Telemachus and the omens, i 323; before Athena, iii 372), of stunning news (the suitors, at Telemachus' departure, iv 638), or at meeting someone unexpectedly, especially Odysseus himself (the Aeolidae, x 63; Telemachus, xvi 178; the suitors, xvii 367; the dead, xxiv 101; Dolius, xxiv 394). βεβήκει: the pluperfect marks the rapidity of Penelope's reaction; she is gone before they realize it.

355. ἔνθετο: aor. for pluperf.; Penelope stores away her son's words to think about later. Telemachus' masterful way of speaking, which reminds her of Odysseus, is one of the causes of her tears.

357. ἔπειτ': 'for a while afterwards'. φίλον: here half way between its proper meaning and a possessive. ὄφρα: 'until'; with hiatus before οἱ. It seems unrealistic for Penelope to fall asleep at such a climactic moment, of course, but her slumber is more than justified artistically by the opportunity is gives for the beautiful scene of her awakening at the beginning of xxiii; Fenik has pointed out the parallel with xiii 79–80, where Odysseus falls into a no less unrealistic sleep, which cleverly prepares the scene for his feigned drowsiness in 282, and his disbelief on waking in 324–6, which is paralleled by Penelope's (*Studies*, 162).

359-91. Suspicions about the authenticity of this passage are expressed in the Introduction, apparatus, and note on xxi 360–78; Telemachus' bold and peremptory words, for example, contrast with the lack of respect for him and his men shown in xxi 361–4. It is assumed that the poet of the original version presented the vengeance taking place without the help of the servants; but it looks as if the later poet found the idea of Telemachus having to give the bow to Odysseus with his own hands unworthy. At all events, the passage fits well with xxi 234–5, where the disguised Odysseus orders Eumaeus to bring him the bow, which was still lying where Eurymachus put it down (xxi 246–7).

359. On the papyrus reading see the Introduction; this line breaks up the usual formula καμπύλα τόξα (−² ∪ ∪ −³ ∪, as in 362), and inverts it, giving −² ∪ . . . −⁴ ∪ ∪ (see Hainsworth, *Flexibility*, 95).

360. The beginning of the line = xx 373; the end = xxi 367, xxii 211. **ὁμόκλεον:** Amphimedon uses the same verb of the scene in xxiv 173; although the verb and its noun are almost always aspirated, the variant κέκλητ' ὁμοκλήσας at *Il.* xx 365 and the unanimous reading ὑπ' ὁμοκλῆς at Ps. Hes. *Sc.* 341 show that the rough breathing is derivative (see Frisk, *GEW*, on a possible etymological link with Skt. *áma-*, 'strength'), by analogy with ὁμο-, originally in cases where the booing and hissing was done by a crowd (note also the reading ἄμα; on the other hand ἄρα, 'consequently', as in other passages, is irreproachable). Nevertheless, the clamour is not always collective: against this passage and xix 155 (the suitors chide Penelope on discovering the trick of the tapestry), set xiv 35 (Eumaeus scolds his dogs) and xvii 189 (a master scolds his servants).

361. = ii 324, iv 769, xvii 482, xx 375; the same ending in ii 331, vi 5 (describing the Cyclops, the only occasion when the derogatory epithet is not applied to the suitors); xvii 581, xxi 401; and almost the same ending in ii 266 κακῶς ὑπερηνορέοντες), iv 766 (κ. ὑπερηνορέοντας), xxiii 31, and *Il.* iv 176. For the lengthening of τις (here 'each one') cf. xxi 324 n. For the youthfulness of the suitors, cf. xxi 179 n.

362. **πῆ δή:** sarcastic, 'but where on earth'; cf. x 281 (Hermes to Odysseus, ὦ δύστηνε, asking him where he is going), xvii 219 (with identical beginning and end, ἀμέγαρτε συβῶτα, where Melanthius asks Eumaeus where he is taking the beggar). **ἀμέγαρτε:** the adj. is related to μεγαίρω, which is close in meaning to φθονέω, 'envy' > 'deny (out of envy)'; the suffix is passive in sense, 'unenviable' > 'miserable, awful' in *Il.* ii 420 (a task, punishment), xi 400, 407 (a wind), Hes. *Th.* 666 (battle); here and in xvii the sense is cruelly ironic ('unenviable' > 'pitiful', like mankind in *h.Merc.* 543); though one could also take it, in the case of the swineherd, in an active sense, 'unsparing' > 'prodigal, mad', and in the other Homeric instances as 'prodigal' > 'unending, intense' (cf. sch. *Il.* ii 420 ἀμέγαρτον· ἄφθονον, πολύν).

363. **πλαγκτέ:** this verbal adj. from πλάζω is found only here; in xii 61, xxiii 327 (absurdly) we read of the Πλαγκταί, rocks which it is not certain are 'wandering'; in xv 343, of the πλαγκτοσύνη or 'wanderings' of Odysseus (another *hapax* which is not found again until Nonnus). Here there are various possible translations: 'trickster, one who confuses (others)' (for this active sense, cf. ii 396, where Athena πλάζε, 'confuses' the minds of the suitors); 'vagabond' (and hence, as when applied to the floating corpses in A. *Pers.* 277, 'wretched'); 'with wandering wits' > 'mad' (thus Clytaemestra, of herself in A. *Ag.* 593; cf. *Il.* iii 108 φρένες ἠερέθονται; xviii 215 φρένες ... (οὐκ) ἔμπεδοι; 327, Melantho considers Odysseus φρένας ἐκπεπαταγμένος). τάχ' αὖ: τάχα, 'soon', not 'perhaps' (cf. xxi 174); αὖ, 'in your turn', that is, 'in return', in payment for your effrontery (more effective than the reading ἂν with fut. κατέδομαι as an old subj., despite τάχ' ἄν with opt. in Il. i 205, Od. ii 76). ἐφ' ὕεσσι: not merely locative, but indicating Eumaeus' lowly post (cf. Philoetius ἐπὶ βουσίν, xx 209); his own dogs will devour him, not alive like Actaeon, but after his death, when his corpse lies unburied (cf. a similar remark, this time about vultures, in xxii 30; and about dogs, Il. i 4, etc.).

364. Pathos is evoked by the loneliness of his body (cf. Il. ix 437–8 ἀπὸ σεῖο ... | οἶος; xix 329 οἶον ... ἀπ' "Ἀργεος; xxii 39 οἶος ἄνευθ' ἄλλων; ix 192 οἶον ἀπ' ἄλλων; xiv 450–1, the swineherd buys Mesaulius out of his own resources, οἷος ἀποιχομένοιο ἄνακτος, where the gen. is not yet absolute, νόσφιν δεσποίνης καὶ Λαέρταο); and also by the ingratitude of his dogs (Priam fears the same ingratitude in Il. xxii 66–71 κύνες ... οὓς τρέφον). For Apollo's role, cf. xxi 338 n.

365. ἱλήκῃσι: a unique form, perf. subj. with -κ- and ending in -σι on a root inflexion, which corresponds to ἱλήκοι in h.Ap. 165, both with long initial vowel, as in the imper. ἵληθι in iii 30, xvi 184, and various Homeric forms such as ἱλάσκομαι (a secondary form with short vowel, however, is seen in ἵλαμαι, h.Hom. xix 48, xxi 5; ἱλάσσεαι, Il. i 147; ἱλάονται, Il. ii 550, etc.). The aspect of the verb is quite clear: 'be favoured by us'; the initial vowel, perhaps merely in spelling, has replaced a false diphthong *σε-σλᾶ- > εἰλη- (though the emendation εἰλήκῃσι in Hesychius s.v. εἴληος εἰ· ἵλεως εἰ is no longer acceptable, pace Wackernagel, Untersuchungen, 81); in contrast, ἵληθι may derive from *σε-σλᾶ- (cf. Hesych., εἴληθι· ἵλεως γίνου; Aeol. ἐλλᾶθι) or from *σι-σλᾶ- (cf. Il. i 583 ἵλαος < *σι-σλᾶ-ϝ-ος). ἀθάνατοι: note the metrical lengthening of the first syllable, which is not represented by η- in order to highlight the negative prefix; this licence is due to the fact that almost all cases of the primitive pl. paradigm require a long final syllable, giving ∪ ∪ ∪ –, which makes the usual lengthening of the second syllable found in the sing., ∪ – ∪ ∪, impossible.

366. θῆκε φέρων αὐτῇ ἐνὶ χώρῃ: each verb has equal emphasis, 'he picked up (the bow) and then set it down in the same place'; αὐτῇ can be used to mean 'same' with or without the article in Homer: cf. vii 55 τῶν αὐτῶν, and compare Il. vi 391 τὴν αὐτὴν ὁδόν with xvi 138 αὐτὴν ὁδόν. χώρη may mean 'land' as opposed to sea (xvi 352, Il. xvi 68); '(geographical) place, site' (only in viii 573); or 'place, position', as here (cf. Il. vi 516; and Il. xvii 394, xxiii 349, Od. xxiii 186, all at the end of the line).

367. If this line is not an interpolation derived from xxi 360 (see the apparatus), it describes accurately the slave's fear (cf. xvii 322–3).

368. The beginning of the line is identical to xvi 43; the end reappears in xx 272, but with ἀγορεύει. ἑτέρωθεν: 'for his part' (cf. vii 130, xi 83, xvi 43, xxii 211). ἐγεγώνει: pluperf.; the word is usually linked to a verb of uttering, to which it adds the notion of intelligibility (cf. γιγνώσκω), as in the well-known idiom peculiar to the Odyssey, ὅσσον τε γέγωνε βοήσας

COMMENTARY

(v 400, vi 294, ix 473, xii 181), or *Il.* xxiv 703 (with κώκυσεν) and viii 305 (with ἐβόησε). The present passage is an exception, as is another example of the pluperf. in the final position in the line in *Il.* xxiii 425, and the unusual ἐγέγωνεν in *Il.* xiv 469; while *Il.* xxii 34, in the same position, follows οἰμώξας. Syntactically, the pluperf. cannot be justified by the explanation given for βεβήκει in xxi 354 n.; morphologically, the three occurrences in -ει have been assimilated by some scholars to the form ἐγέγωνε(ν) mentioned above; but it may be that this latter should in fact be read without the augment, αὖτε γέγωνεν, in which case the three examples with the diphthongized ending are once again left unexplained.

369-75. Telemachus' renewed rudeness will not surprise Eumaeus after xxi 344 ff.; in the light of what he knows of the situation, the slave must realize that his master's implicit confession of impotence is designed to lull the suitors into a sense of security. Ramming's comments about the 'insecure labour conditions' of slaves are therefore quite beside the point (*Diener-schaft*, 71).

369. The hypocoristic voc. ἄττα, 'dad; old boy' (misunderstood by some MSS; see the app.) is used by Achilles and Menelaus to address Phoenix (*Il.* ix 607, xvii 561 ἄττα γεραιέ), and six times including the present occasion by Telemachus as a pet-name for a fatherly old servant. πρόσω φέρε τόξα: 'carry on bringing up the bow (now you have started)'. τάχ' οὐκ εὖ πᾶσι πιθήσεις: τάχα (cf. xxi 363) introduces a complicated construction, 'soon (you will find that) you will not do well to obey everyone [sc. if you pay attention to these others]'. Von der Mühll and Allen differ in their treatment of εὖ when it occurs in arsis: here and in xxi 242, 387, xxii 399, xxiv 362, where the adv. precedes the partic. of ναιετάω in the fourth foot, von der Mühll writes ἐῦ with hiatus, while Allen prefers the diphthong; but in xxiv 271, in the same position before ἐξείνισσα, both editors print the form with hiatus. The alliteration recalls xvii 21 πάντα πιθέσθαι and xxi 315, where the common intrans. use of the aor. πιθήσας provides a model for this unique intrans. use of the fut. πιθήσεις, otherwise unattested in Greek; the usage parallels factitive πεπιθήσω (*Il.* xxii 223) and ἀπιθήσω (*Il.* x 129, xxiv 300), which occurs alongside numerous examples of ἀπίθησε(ν) such as xxii 492, and one example of ἀπίθησαν (xxiii 369).

370. μή with the subj. often introduces a threat (cf. *Il.* i 26, etc.). καὶ ὁπλότερος περ ἐών: καί ... περ makes the partic. concessive; ὁπλότερος is the result of a semantic evolution, from an originally intensive use of the comparative suffix, of a word meaning 'armed man' > 'young man' (compare *Il.* iii 108 αἰεὶ δ' ὁπλοτέρων ἀνδρῶν φρένες ἠερέθονται, where the comparative suffix is still intensive in force, with *Il.* iv 324-5 αἰχμὰς δ' αἰχμάσσουσι νεώτεροι, οἵ περ ἐμεῖο | ὁπλότεροι γεγάασι, where it is already almost comparative); the masc. comparat. is found in xix 184, *Il.* ii 707, the masc. superl. in *Il.* ix 58, but the clearest evidence of the loss of any semantic connection with ὅπλον is its use in the fem. superl. in *Il.* xiv 267, 275, *Od.* iii 465, vii 58, xi 283, xv 364; and its use in this passage, where Telemachus means that he will prove stronger than Eumaeus *despite* being

younger than he.   **δίωμαι:** the verb usually takes the ablative gen. with ἐξ (ἀποδίωμαι, *Il.* v 763), ἀπό (xvii 398, xx 343, *Il.* xvi 246, xvii 110), or without a prep. (*Il.* xii 304); less commonly it takes the lative acc. of direction in which the object is driven or place to which it is chased, as in *Il.* xii 276, xv 681 (with προτί); both constructions are combined in *Il.* xxii 456 πόλιος πεδίονδε.

371. **χερμαδίοισι:** instr., '(pelting) with stones'.   **βίηφι:** cf. xxi 315n.; the endings of xxi 371, 373 are similar to those of vi 6, xii 246, the suffix carrying its proper comparative force, 'I am better (than you); that is, I can beat you'.

372-5. On Telemachus' astute ploy in these lines (which some have been bold enough to condemn) see the note above on xxi 369-75; the general laughter with which they are greeted—the last laugh these frivolous young men are destined to enjoy—serves to relax the tension, as in similar situations in *Il.* i 599, ii 270. The lines are full of echoes, as we shall see.

372-3. A remote or unfulfilled desire may be expressed by ὄφελον, or by an optative introduced by εἴθε (*Il.* iv 313, vii 157, xi 670), αἴθε (*Il.* xvi 722 αἴθ' ὅσον ἥσσων εἰμί, τόσον σέο φέρτερος εἴην, cf. *infra*), αἲ γάρ (here, and in *Il.* xiii 825), or without a conjunction (xviii 79).   **πάντων . . . μνηστήρων:** the hyperbaton is deliberate; the gen. depends on φέρτερος, which goes with τόσσον; we must supply 'as much stronger (as I am compared to you)'.

374. Here too (cf. xxi 369n.) von der Mühll and Allen differ, the former printing τῶ (primitive instrumental) and the latter τῷ; either way, the word is demonstr., 'in that case', used to introduce an unfulfilled apodosis (xxiii 23, xxiv 285) or the counterpoint to a remote wish, as in *Il.* vii 158, xvi 723; here with κε followed by a conditional opt.; cf. xxiv 30-2 ὡς ὄφελες . . . | . . . ἐπισπεῖν· | τῶ, and xxiv 376-81, with an unfulfilled volitive inf., αἲ γάρ . . . | . . . ἐφεστάμεναι καὶ ἀμύνειν | . . . τῶ. τάχα (cf. xxi 363) expresses the speed with which Telemachus would act if he were more robust.   **στυγερῶς:** the word appears twice elsewhere in Homer, at xxiii 23 and *Il.* xvi 723, both cited above; in every case it means 'wretchedly' (cf. Soph. *Phil.* 166 στυγερὸν στυγερῶς; Apoll. ii 244 στυγερώτερον; the respective editors Brunck and Ruhnken restore the forms with σμ- in both these two cases, on the analogy of ἐπισμυγερῶς at *Od.* iii 195, iv 672, Apoll. i 616, iv 1267, 1651; ἐπισμυγερός, in Ps.-Hes. *Sc.* 264, Apoll. iv 1065; σμυγερῶς, in Apoll. iv 380; and σμυγερώτατος, Apoll. ii 374). In *Il.* xvi 723, the disguised Apollo tells Hector that if he were only stronger he would make him pay dearly for his faintheartedness, τῶ κε τάχα στυγερῶς πολέμου ἀπερωήσειας.   **τιν':** sarcastic and threatening, 'someone (not far away)'; cf. xiii 394, 427, xxii 67.   **πέμψαιμι νέεσθαι:** the phrase usually (but not always: in iv 8 Menelaus escorts Hermione to her wedding, and in xiii 206 some king might have sent Odysseus home) implies ordering someone to leave against their will (in *Il.* xviii 240 Hera orders the sun to set ἀέκοντα, and again in xxiii 23-4 Penelope would have sent the supposedly indiscreet

slave girl packing ἔσω μέγαρον); here the suitors would have to leave ἡμετέρου ἐξ οἴκου.

375-6. The end of the first line is similar to xvi 134, and identical to xvii 499; the end of the second = xx 358.

377. μέθιεν: μεθίημι occurs six times in the *Odyssey*: in the intrans. sense of 'letting onself go' (iv 372); of a physical state 'leaving' a person in the acc. (v 471); of 'throwing' an object in the acc. (v 460); or of 'relaxing, giving up' one's anger, also in the acc. (i 77–8 μεθήσει | . . . χόλον; cf. *Il.* i 283, xv 138 μεθέμεν χόλον); or, as here, the same expression with the ablative gen. (cf. xxi 126n. on βίης).

378. Τηλεμάχῳ: dat. of interest, 'against (the suggestion of) T'. **τὰ:** demonstr. (cf. xxi 305). **φέρων:** continuous pres.; the aspect of the verb emphasizes the notion of his progress up the great hall (ἀνά, 'the length of').

379. θῆκε παραστάς: both verbs are emphasized: 'offered him (the bow) and placed it in his hands'. The beginning of the line appears also in *Il.* x 529.

380. = xix 15; similar line-openings in xxii 436, *Il.* v 427. The tmesis emphasizes the idea of calling the person 'out from within' present in the prefix; cf. x 471, xxiv 1, *Il.* xxiv 582, ii 400 (ἐκπρο-). The swineherd, under cover of the suitor's laughter, carries out the order given at xxi 235–6 through Eurycleia; unaware that she has already recognized their master, he mentions only Telemachus.

381. On the final words see xxi 321n.

382-5. = xxi 236–9 (see the nn. ad loc.). The repetition of ἡμετέροισιν ἐν ἔρκεσι assumes an irony of which Eumaeus is probably unaware.

386. ἄπτερος ἔπλετο μῦθος: this expression has been much discussed (see J. Latacz, *LfgrE*, i 1116–17, s.v. ἄπτερος), but the solution seems to be quite simple: whereas ἔπεα πτερόεντα, 'winged words', are words which are spoken and then reach the interlocutor, an ἄπτερος μῦθος is a thought or emotion which is not openly articulated. In the four attestations of the word in the *Odyssey* (in A. *Ag.* 276 ἄπτερος φάτις is better understood, as here, as 'an unspoken rumour', rather than 'a sound of beating wings'), it is always a woman who thus registers wordless surprise: Penelope, at her son's speech, in xvii 57; Eurycleia, at Telemachus' rudeness, at xix 29 (see below); the nurse again in xxii 398, when Telemachus informs her that Odysseus is calling for her, showing that there is no longer any need for secrecy; and again here, where she realizes that despite Odysseus' order that she should not disclose his identity to anyone (xix 486), Telemachus is in full possession of the facts. We are not told what Eumaeus did after speaking to the nurse. Some MSS replace this line by another made up of the beginning of xix 100 (which, together with *Il.* iii 260, xix 317, offers ὀτραλέως) and the ending of viii 272, xvii 574.

387. = xix 30, and parallels in xxii 399 (with ὤιξεν for κλήϊσσεν) and ii 400, xx 371 (ending only). Cf. xxi 369n. on εὖ.

388-91. It is still not clear (cf. xxi 386n.) why the swineherd does not accompany Philoetius here; in order to close the door between the court-yard and the street (cf. xxi 240–1) the cowherd has not had to leave the house as he did in xxi 188–91.

388. There is a strong reminiscence of *Il.* xxiv 572, where Achilles οἴκοιο (without a prep.) λέων ὣς ἆλτο θύραζε; ἆλτο there represents Achilles' anger, but here it corresponds to Philoetius' discreet but rapid diligence. On θύραζε see the Introduction.

389. εὐερκέος αὐλῆς: this line-ending is also found in xxii 449, *Il.* ix 472, both in conjunction with ὑπ' αἰθούσῃ; cf. also xviii 102, *Il.* ix 476 ἑρκίον αὐλῆς, and the description of Odysseus' palace at xvii 266–8 ἐξ ἑτέρων ἕτερ' ἐστίν, ἐπήσκηται δέ οἱ αὐλή | τοίχῳ καὶ θριγκοῖσι, θύραι δ' εὐερκέες εἰσὶ | δικλίδες.

390. In the courtyard, as one might expect in a seafaring town, there lay a rope from a ship 'curved at prow and poop' (the epithet ἀμφιελίσσης is found twelve times in the *Odyssey*, always at the end of the line; with νεός in vii 252, x 156, xii 368, xv 283, and always of Odysseus' ships except in xv 283, where it refers to Telemachus' vessel, and vi 264, vii 9, where it refers to the Phaeacians'). In xiv 346, the companions of Odysseus tie him up ὅπλῳ ἐϋστρεφέϊ, the only other occurrence of ὅπλον in this sense in the sing. in Homer; in Hes. *Op.* 627 the word designates any piece of nautical equipment. The rope is made of papyrus fibre; the adj. βύβλινος is also used in Hdt. vii 25, 36, viii 20, ix 115, 121, to describe the cables used for the Persian bridges across the Hellespont, which were βύβλινά τε (four each, and made in Egypt according to vii 34) καὶ λευκολίνου (two each, made in Phoenicia); Hdt. mentions the use of papyrus in the manufacture of ropes (ii 38), sailcloth (ii 96), shoes (ii 37), and for calking (ii 96); on the Egyptian plant βύβλος cf. Hdt. ii 92 (as a food), A. *Suppl.* 761; for its use in rolls for writing, Hdt. ii 100; in codex form, A. *Supp.* 947; books are mentioned twenty-one times in Hdt. Although all these passages have an explicit or implicit connection with Egypt, and A. *Pr.* 811 describes the Nile flowing down Βυβλίνων ὀρῶν ἄπο (the word πάπυρος, probably of Egyptian origin, is not found until the Hellenistic period), Hdt. already talks of books as something imported from Phoenicia (v 58), and the usual explanation of this family of words is that they derive from Βύβλος, a Phoenician city originally called Gubla, later Gebal (Ezek. 27: 9), which must have been the intermediate trading post for imports and exports of papyrus between Egypt and Greece, either in its raw or processed state for both chandlery and writing, from remote antiquity; see further L. J. Jeffrey, *Companion*, 556–7; F. Eckstein, *Archaeologia* L 1, 42. This etymology would explain the spelling βυβλ- normally found in ancient texts, except in the MS of A. *Pr.* 811 and some Hdt. witnesses, which already employ the common later spelling βιβλίον. Another important textual question is raised by the variant provided by P 120, an *ostracon* which has traces of an Homeric glossary of the third century BC; next to this passage, which unfortunately is damaged at the crucial point, appear the words σοῦσα σχοινία, followed immediately by a fr. from Antimachus concerning Athena's fitting-out of the

COMMENTARY

Argo: λαίφεσι δὲ λινέοις | σοῦσα ἐτίθει παντοία. The passage must be related to Athen. 513f. (*Susa* is so called because in Greek σοῦσον is another name for τὸ κρίνον, 'lily'); to the obscure fr. 121 w of Antimachus (with Hesych. οἶσον· . . . σχοινίον); to Alex. Et. fr. 3, 21 Pow. (the touch of a barrel breaks the rope of a well which is in bad condition διά . . . κακὸν ἤρικεν οὖσον); and Lycophr. 21 (οὖσα, 'hawsers'). All this very strongly suggests that the *ostracon* reading, despite being a *lectio difficilior* which avoids hiatus (and this latter point is weak, in view of the wide consensus in favour of ὅπλον), is really no more than a ghost-word invented by the glossator and accepted, as far as we know, by no one except him; it receives no support from Athenaeus' passage, since lily-stalks are too fragile to be used in rope-making (van der Valk, *Textual Criticism*, 82; Leumann, *Wörter*, 45). The origin of the corruption, according to Frisk in *GEW*, must have been two *scriptiones continuae* in Hom.: ΑΙΘΟΥΧΙΟΠΛΟΝ by dittography > ΑΙΘΟΥΧCΟΥCΟΝ, wrongly divided ΑΙΘΟΥΧ COYCON, with the dat. subsequently restored; and in Antimachus: ΛΙΝΕΟΙCΟΥCΑ > ΛΙΝΕΟΙCCΟΥCΑ. Wyss already gives οὖσα in fr. 57 as a form which would have been incorrectly imitated by the Alexandrians.

391. **ἐπέδησε:** the word corresponds to ἐπὶ . . . ἰῆλαι in the orders given in xxi 241; it seems likely, therefore, that it comes from the compound verb ἐπιδέω, otherwise unattested in Homer (it is not likely to be in tmesis at *Il.* v 729–30) but found in Hdt., rather than from the verb πεδάω used, for example, in iii 269, xiii 168, xxiii 17. **ἐς δ' ἤϊεν αὐτός:** apart from the variant ἤλυθεν (frequent in the fifth foot), a peculiar alternative reading of this line-ending is preserved in Galen 767, 10 κ, who was perhaps quoting from memory, καὶ μακρὸν ὀχῆα (see F. Kudlien, 'Ein unbekannter Versschluß für φ 391', *Philologus* ci (1957), 324–5). καὶ μακρὸν ὀχῆα is found at the end of *Il.* xii 121, 291, xiii 124 applied to the great bar which closes the Achaean stockade, described in *Il.* xii 455–6 δοιοὶ δ' ἔντοσθεν ὀχῆες | εἶχον ἐπημοιβοί, μία δὲ κληῗς ἐπαρήρει, which Hector smashes with a rock at *Il.* xii 460. We find similar bars or bolts in *Il.* xxiv 446, 566, closing Achilles' camp, and *Il.* xxi 537, on one of the gates of Troy; but these arrangements have nothing to do with the one described in xxi 47, though they do with the order given in xxi 241, where mention is made of a κληῗς which is none other than this bolt. We also find the expression ἐκλήϊσεν ὀχῆας in xxiv 166, where it refers, as in xxi 47, to a store-room which should have been locked from the outside, but which Telemachus (despite Amphimedon's account of the matter) forgot to lock.

392. = xxi 243; cf. xxi 177 n.

393–5. Odysseus more or less repeats the procedure used by Eurymachus (cf. xxi 245 ἐνώμα; xxi 246 ἔνθα καὶ ἔνθα); but whereas the latter turned the bow round and round to see if he could figure out its secret, and even tried heating it, Odysseus' examination is that of the skilled professional checking for damage caused by long disuse.

393. The variant attempts to eliminate the hiatus; the demonstr. refers, of course, to Odysseus himself.

394. ἀναστρωφῶν: another *hapax*; στρωφάω is used several times (vi 53, 306, vii 105, xvii 97) of women working with the distaff; cf. ἐπιστρωφάω, 'haunt, range about' in xvii 486, and ἀμφιπεριστρωφάω, 'drive back and forth', of horses, in *Il.* viii 348.

395. μὴ: 'lest', introducing a subordinate clause of fearing after πειρώμενος (cf. xxi 282), with oblique opt.; the pres. ἔδοιεν implies 'were eating it (still)'. The line-ending appears in xiv 8, 450, xvii 296 (something similar in i 135, iii 77, xix 19, xxi 70); but the gen., which is grammatically dependent in the first and last of the passages and 'quasi-absolute' in the other (cf. xxi 364), is here absolute, used temporally; and ἄνακτος, preceded by hiatus, refers somewhat awkwardly to the subject of the sentence. **κέρα:** acc., here only (nom. pl. in *Il.* iv 109, xix 211); in every case it forms a Pyrrhic, for which there are various explanations; either an archaic form without the suffix -σ-; shortening before following vowel (since this is the case in all three attestations, unless ἴψ, a *hapax* which is not found again until Theophrastus, had digamma, which seems unlikely: see L. Gil, *Nombres de insectos en griego antiguo* (Madrid, 1959), 116); or elision of pl. κέρα(α) or dual κέρα(ε). The juxtaposition of these two rare words has caused problems of transmission, as can be seen from the apparatus. It is not clear what sort of worm is meant, or whether there is a species which attacks horn; F. Eckstein is inclined to suppose that the bow was made of wood, with κέρας used metaphorically (*Archaeologia* L 1, 41 n. 287).

396. = viii 328, x 37, xiii 167, xviii 72, 400. **εἴπεσκεν:** for the metrical lengthening of the last syllable and the -ν see respectively xxi 361 n. and xxi 248 n.

397-400. An excellent passage, full of delicate sarcasm: ἦ τις, 'certainly some sort of'; ῥά νύ που; τοιαῦτα, 'things as fine as this'; καί, 'even'; ὅ γ', 'this chap at least'; and the two final words, heavily emphatic. All this will become bitterly ironic in a moment, when it turns out that Odysseus is indeed an expert connoisseur.

397. θηητὴρ: 'one who looks, knows how to look; connoisseur', here only in antiquity; some prefer the more banal reading θηρητήρ, used five times in the *Iliad* of 'hunters' (H.-G. Buchholz, G. Jöhrens, and I. Mauhl, *Archaeologia* J, 7 n. 43). **ἐπίκλοπος ἔπλετο τόξων:** this line-ending recalls *Il.* xxii 281, of Achilles ἐπίκλοπος ἔπλεο μύθων; ἐπίκλοπος, 'wily, sly', appears also in xi 364 (of Odysseus) and xiii 291; it is perhaps worth noticing the conjecture ἐπίσκοπος, not in the sense it is used four times in the *Iliad*, but like viii 163-4 (Odysseus looks like a merchant ἐπίσκοπος . . . ὁδαίων | κερδέων θ' ἁρπαλέων) and Hdt. iii 35 (ἐπίσκοπα τοξεύοντα).

398. αὐτῷ: possess. dat., followed by hiatus.

399. ἐφορμᾶται: not with the meaning it has in i 275, but 'desires', governing the fut. inf. after a verb of wishing as in *Il.* xii 199, xiv 89. **ποιησέμεν:** 'to make (himself one)'; on ποιέω as a term for craftmanship see F. Eckstein, *Archaeologia* L 1, 6. If the line is punctuated by a question mark or colon after ποιησέμεν, the phrase beginning with ὥς, which is a shortened version of xxi 393-4, will be an exclamation (cf. *Il.* xxi 441, for example); if we punctuate with a comma, ὡς must be taken as roughly equivalent to ὅτι οὕτως (cf. i 227, ii 233, xxiv 194).

400. ἔμπαιος: the word is found only twice in the *Odyssey*, and next in Lycoph. 1321. In the other Odyssean example, xx 379–80, the word is scanned as a dactyl and used negatively; the positive sense which we can deduce from the context, 'conversant with, expert in deeds and endowed with strength', is what we would expect from the etymological link with ἔμπης, 'completely, altogether': 'completely in control of'. Here the word is used sarcastically; the only thing Odysseus has mastered is 'evil', as Melanthius has already said (xvii 226 ἔργα κάκ᾽ ἔμμαθεν) and Eurymachus has echoed (xviii 362).

401. ὑπερηνορεόντων: the lines which end with this word have already been listed in xxi 361 n. This line is identical to ii 331, but there is a strange inconsistency in the editors' treatment of the two: von der Mühll here retains the MS reading αὐτ᾽, relegating Bentley's ingenious conjecture αὐ (τ- replacing digamma) to the app., whereas Allen accepts αὐ; but in ii 331 von der Mühll remarks *rectius foret* αὐ, whereas Allen reads αὐτ᾽.

402–3. 'May this fellow be as successful (i.e. unsuccessful) henceforth as he is about to be with the bow', an unkind expression similar to such examples as *Il.* iv 178–81, xxi 428–31, xxii 41–43; *Od.* ix 523–5, xviii 235–42 (the latter no longer sarcastic), which is here deeply ironic, since Odysseus is going to be successful. ὄνησις, here only in Homer, is later common in poetry; the gen., whose form is paralleled in Homer only by λύσιος in *Il.* xxiv 655, is normal after verbs of obtaining. The postponement of οὗτος would disappear in Agar's conjecture, giving better syntax; but cf. xxii 169.

404. The beginning of the line = xvii 488, similar to xx 384. The line-ending ἀτὰρ πολύμητις Ὀδυσσεύς, occurs in *Il.* x 488; but this epithet for the hero, which is so common in the *Odyssey*, has only occurred in this position in the line once before in the *Odyssey*, in xxi 274. It occurs regularly from here onwards in the last three books.

405. This is the third mention of Odysseus' careful scrutiny of the bow (cf. xxi 393–4, 400); since we have already been told that the bow is in good condition, the emphasis seems largely pointless, and Woodhouse acutely suggests that the repetition probably betrays traces of the ancient legend of the Wanderer's Homecoming (*Composition*, 100). βαστάζω occurs in Homer only here and in xi 594 (Sisyphus lifts his rock); the hiatus before ἴδε is due to digamma.

406–9. The poet introduces a simile from his own profession with the typical ὡς ὅτε, 'as when' (cf. xxii 468, thrushes; xxiii 159, goldsmith; xxiii 233, landfall dear to the sailor; xxiv 6, bats) followed by ὣς ἄρ᾽ (cf. xxiii 162, 239; cf. ὣς in xxii 471, xxiv 9).

406. This is the only occurrence of ἐπιστάμενος with the gen., as if it were a substantive (cf. εἰδώς in *Il.* ii 718, xi 710, xii 100); in other places it is used absolutely ('competent, expert', iv 231, xiii 313, xiv 359, xxiii 185) or with the inf. (ix 49, *Il.* ii 611) or with something understood (iv 730). **φόρμιγγος:** primitive φόρμιγξ (common in Hom. and *h.Hom.*: see for example xxi 430, xxii 332, 340, xxiii 133, 144) is more or less synonymous with κίθαρις (also common: see i 153, 159, viii 248; note *Il.* xviii 569–70 φόρμιγγι ... | κιθάριζε), λύρη (*h.Merc.* 423), and χέλυς (*h.Merc.* 25, 153, 242). The instrument consisted of the ζυγόν, or top cross-piece to which the strings were fastened (ἀργύρεον, *Il.* ix 187); the πῆχυς, lit. 'elbow, crook of the arm', that is, two curved horns fastened to either end of the ζυγόν at the top and joined together at the bottom in the shape of an elbow by a sound-box to which the other end of the strings was fastened (eight occurrences in Hom. and two in the *h.Hom.*, but six of these in the anatomical sense; applied to the χέλυς in *h.Merc.* 50; to a bow (see the Introduction to this book), in xxi 419, *Il.* xi 375, xiii 583, a connection which probably suggested this simile to the mind of the poet); the strings, each called χορδή (only here; cf. *h.Merc.* 51: the etymology is doubtful, but if the word came from *χορνή, related to Lat. *hernia* or *haru-spex*, it would fit in with the fact (cf. xxi 419) that the strings were made of animal gut); and finally the κόλλοψ, another *hapax* of debatable etymology in which the meaning 'peg' (which is turned to tighten the string, as with a modern stringed instrument) has probably supplanted an older meaning found in certain passages, 'hump, fatty bulge on the neck of cattle' (cf. perhaps Lat. *callum*); this might suggest two possibilities for the semantic shift to 'peg', namely 'rim of the ζυγόν to which the strings are fixed' (the bovine metaphor), or alternatively 'resin, glue (cf. κόλλα) used to hold the strings firm on the stretcher'.

407. ἐτάνυσσε: gnomic aor. The beginning of the line occurs in xxi 328. νέῳ is difficult; Tyrrell suggests ἑῷ, Duentzer νέην (corruption due to confusion with the dat. κόλλοπι), Agar νόῳ (cf. vi 320, xvi 197). The MS reading is defensible, however, if we assume that the instrument itself is a new one (so Ameis–Hentze–Cauer); or that the peg is new in the sense that it is 'new' to the string being fitted to it (D. S. Barrett, 'Homer *Odyssey* xxi 406–9', *CPh* lxv (1970), 38–9); or, if we stick with the idea of 'glue' (though this is difficult with περί), that the glue has had to be replaced to fit the new string ἀμφοτέρωθεν, i.e. top and bottom, to stretcher and bridge. ῥηϊδίως ('nonchalantly', as Stanford puts it) is the point of the comparison (W. Richter, *Archaeologia* H, 59): there is a considerable difference between tightening the fine string on a lyre and stretching, with equal ease, the thick, tough bowstring (νεῦρα βόεια) of a huge bow.

409–11. The bow is readied for action in two stages. First it is braced, for which the verb is τανύω or ἐκτανύω (23 times in this book); then the tension of the bowstring is checked. At 410 Odysseus takes hold of the πῆχυς with his left hand and lightly twangs the νευρή with his right to feel the tension; the note produced by the vibration in 411 is satisfying high and sweet. The effort of the draw does not come until 419.

411. ἥ: demonstr., referring to the νευρή. καλὸν: adv.; used thus four times in the *Odyssey*, always of a musical note (i 155, viii 266, x 277, xix 519); in *Il.* i 473, xviii 570 the usage is less clear, since καλόν may be an adj. with παιήονα and λίπον; in the latter passage we read ὑπὸ καλὸν ἄειδε, but the syntax of ὑπό (tmesis, or adv. 'with (musical accompaniment)') differs from

that of the present phrase, where the word means 'under (his hand)'.
χελιδόνι εἰκέλη αὐδήν: the line-ending is almost identical to xxii 240, but the ἄντην of that passage, '(to look at) before one', read by some witnesses here, does not fit. It seems excessively fanciful to see a connection, as Austin, *Archery*, does, between this simile of the swallow and passages about the spring (xviii 367, xxii 301, the nightingale of xix 518), and to argue on that basis that Odysseus' return symbolizes the end of winter's gloom and melancholy; we may say, simply, that the simile implies the same animistic tendency to endow inanimate objects with life as we saw in the simile in xxi 48. The false diphthong in εἰκέλη is probably due (Leumann, *Wörter*, 306 n. 76) to a metrical lengthening of ἴκελος, which appears elsewhere with short initial vowel in the zero grade *ϝικ- (on *Il*. xi 282 and *Od*. xi 207, where there is no hiatus as there is here, see Chantraine, *Grammaire*, i 129).

412–15. Von der Mühll considers these lines spurious, on the grounds that the suitors' fear is premature; even in xxii 31–2 they continue to think that Antinous may have been killed by accident (P. von der Mühll, 'Einige Interpretationen in berühmten Stellen der *Odyssee*', *Philologus* lxxxix (1934), 391–6). The second author (see the Introduction to this book) is fond of these divine interventions.

412. We find ἄχος combined with γένετο in the same position in the line in *Il*. xii 392, xvi 508, 581. The word's range of meanings is very wide (see E.-M. Voigt, *LfgrE*, i 1774–8, s.v. ἄχος): it denotes any unpleasant state of mind, from fear (as here; cf. Goth. *agis*), shame (*Il*. ix 249) to anger (*Il*. xx 298), nostalgia (iv 108), sadness (iv 716), remorse (xxii 345), or Laertes' misery when he thinks that Odysseus is dead (xxiv 315).

412–13. For the suitors' sudden pallor cf. xxii 42 χλωρὸν δέος (the same expression appears in xii 243, xxiv 450, 533, *Il*. xvii 67, 143, 633), and *Il*. xii 284, xvii 733 τρέπεται or τράπετο χρώς; the same idea is expressed by the otherwise unparalleled words ὦχρος in *Il*. iii 35, and ὠχρήσαντα χρόα in *Od*. xi 529.

413. ἔκτυπε: the only occurrence in the *Odyssey* of this aor., which appears four times in the *Iliad*, together with three examples of κτυπέω (amongst the latter, *Il*. vii 479, also in conjunction with χλωρὸν δέος); of the Iliadic occurrences of ἔκτυπε, *Il*. viii 75 is followed two lines later by χλ. δ., *Il*. xvii 595 has μεγάλ' ἔκτυπε, and *Il*. xv 377 μέγα δ' ἔκτυπε, which may have been the origin of the variant reading recorded in the app. (*ἀνακτυπέω does not exist, but ἀναβροντάω does, used strangely enough to refer to Odysseus' way of speaking in Triphiodorus 118). The line-ending occurs in *Il*. ii 353, ix 236 (both with ἀστράπτων), and *Il*. iv 381 (cf. another thunderbolt from Zeus in xx 103, 113).

414. = xiii 353. The very common final formula is found preceded by γήθησεν δέ in vii 329, viii 199, xiii 250, xviii 281, xxiv 504.

415. ὅττι ῥά οἱ: the same phrase is found at the beginning of xiv 527; ῥα, 'as he expected'. Note the description of Zeus as son of Cronos 'of the twisted counsels' (cf. Κρονίων, xxi 102, xxii 51, xxiv 472); the gen. ἀγκυλομήτεω, always at the end of the line and scanned with synizesis, occurs seven times in the *Iliad*; ποικιλομήτης, in the same position, in *Il.* xi 482 and five occasions in the *Odyssey* (cf. xxii 115, 202, 281); the voc., used of Zeus by Athena, in xiii 293. The diaeresis in πάϊς (see xxi 95, 320; in contrast, παῖς occurs fourteen times) is due to original *παϝις, Att. παῦς, without the suffix, and Lat. *pau-cus*, with a different one.

416. On fifteen occasions in the *Odyssey* the editors write ὅ for the nom. of the relative pronoun, which could only have replaced ὅς in viii 271 (before σφ') and xxi 145 (before σφι; see the app.); in i 300, xiv 3, and in the present line, the MSS (and, in the case of xiv 3, secondary witnesses) read ὅς, which gives rise to an impossible cretic. It was Aristarchus who restored the correct form in i 300, with hiatus before original *ϝϝ-; and Bentley who emended the present line. The following οἱ is an ethic dat.: the arrow is the one laid aside by Eurymachus, but the table is not necessarily the one which was placed at Odysseus' side in xx 259.

417. The use of τοί for οἱ is due to metrical considerations. On the quiver see the Introduction to this book.

418. The narrator's biting hostility to the suitors recalls the remarks made in xx 392–4.

419–23. For remarks on πῆχυς, νευρή, γλυφίδες, the stance taken up on the δίφρον, and the difficult phrase πελέκεων ... στειλειῆς see the Introduction to this book.

419. ἕλκεν: there is constant fluctuation between augmented and unaugmented forms of this verb.

421. The beginning of the line = xxiv 181; similar phrases in xxi 48 (see the n.), xxii 118, 266.

422. διαμπερές is split in this way on two other occasions, *Il.* xi 377, xvii 309; the unusual tmesis of an adv. may here be explained by its derivation from the verb πείρω, 'pierce', but this explanation will not do for the other two occurrences.

423. ἰὸς χαλκοβαρής: the same line-opening is found in *Il.* xv 465; χαλκοβαρής, 'heavy bronze(-tipped)', is applied to a spear in xi 532, xxii 259, 276, *Il.* xxii 328; to a helmet in *Il.* xi 96. This is the first occurrence in this book of ἰός, which will appear seven times in xxii; ὀϊστός has been used up to this moment in xxi 12, 60, 98, 173, 416, 420, and reappears three times in xxii, and once again for the last time in xxiv 178.

424. ὁ: clearly demonstr., 'this stranger'; the conjecture recorded in the app. is therefore unnecessary. ἐνί has the usual lengthening of -ι before μ-. ἐλέγχει: the verb is attested only twice in Homer, with a slightly different but related meaning in each case: in *Il.* ix 522 Phoenix opines that Achilles is going to 'insult' the messengers, whereas here Odysseus is not going to 'shame' his protector.   οὐ: its position makes this word emphatic.

425. ἥμενος: the nom. part. appears eleven times in the *Odyssey*, always in the first position in the line. In *Od.* xv 392 it refers to Odysseus sitting in the animal fold; in Ithaca, xvii 158; in the palace, xviii 224, xix 322 (cf. xxi 100); the implication is either 'sitting idle' (which would shame Telemachus) or

'seated here (in the place which befits him)'. It is followed by a verb in the
1. pers. sing., and by another demonstr. τοῦ, 'this target (which is so
difficult)', which gives an acceptable text (cf. app.).

426. The adv. δήν goes with τανύων: 'I did not tire myself out trying to draw
the bow for a long time', i.e. 'I drew it straight away' (cf. κάμε in xxi 150).
The line-ending is identical to Il. v 254, and similar to phrases in xix 493,
xxii 226; it recalls Odysseus' words in xxi 281–4.

427. The line has been thought to be an interpolation corresponding to the
insults of xx 376–9, but there is no reason to excise it: the syntax is elliptical,
but can be paralleled by such lines as xxiv 199, 'they will celebrate
Penelope in song, not like Clytaemestra (of whom they will sing that she)
behaved evilly'. Here the sense is: 'I still have my strength, not as (they
say when) they insult me'. Both cases are signs of late composition.

ὄνονται: ὄνομαι occurs on only three other occasions in the *Odyssey*
(which has led to a variant here), each time with a different construction:
'complain about something' with the gen. (v 379), 'criticize something'
with the acc. (viii 239), and 'complain that' with ὅτι (xvii 378). The preceding part. recalls xxi 99 (Antinous humiliates Odysseus) and xxi 332 (the
suitors dishonour the hero's table).

428–30. Excellent lines, full of sarcasm (cf. xxiii 133–6, 143–7): 'next comes
the entertainment'. The meals of the last two days can be traced back quite
satisfactorily: on the previous day Melanthius took goats to the palace for
the δεῖπνον, 'lunch' (xvii 214), which is seen taking place in xvii 170
(δείπνηστος), 176, 269 (δαῖτα); Odysseus partakes twice, when Telemachus gives him food in xvii 359 (δεδειπνήκειν) and then when the others
give him a share in xvii 506 (ἐδείπνει); nightfall overtakes them as they
enjoy the entertainments after the meal (xvii 606), by which time meat is
already being roasted for supper (xviii 44 ἐπὶ δόρπῳ). The dishes which
reward Odysseus' discomfiture of Irus (xviii 118–21) are clearly part of this
supper; the suitors rise from the table in xviii 428. Penelope is concerned
that Odysseus lunches next day with Telemachus (xix 321 δείπνοιο); the
dawn rises in xx 91, and the woman who grinds the corn expresses the wish
that this lunch be the suitors' last (xx 119 ὕστατα δειπνήσειαν. Melanthius
brings fresh goats (xx 174–5 = xvii 213–14) and the δεῖπνον begins (xx 390),
but is soon followed by the ironic remark that the δόρπον is to be a grim
one (xx 392–4). All this fits the scheme proposed by G. Bruns (*Archaeologia*
Q, 57–9), in which ἄριστον (xvi 2, Il. xxiv 124) is equivalent to 'breakfast',
δόρπον (iv 786, vii 166, viii 395, Il. viii 503, ix 88, xxiv 2, 444, 601) is 'supper',
the last meal of the day, and δεῖπνον is either 'lunch (taken a few hours after
breakfast)', as in these passages and Il. x 578, xxiii 158, or a large breakfast
taken early before a heavy task (battle in Il. ii 381, woodcutting in Il. xi 86).
In *Od.* xvii 599 Telemachus allows Eumaeus to leave, but only δειελιήσας:
this has been taken to refer to an afternoon snack taken between δεῖπνον
and δόρπον, but a more likely meaning is 'having passed the afternoon
(here)', since the swineherd shortly afterwards joins the others for the entertainment after δεῖπνον (602).

428. Cf. xiv 407 νῦν δ' ὥρη δόρποιο; but this construction is more primitive: '(this is) an opportunity to (prepare)', καί 'also'. The reduplicated aor. inf. τετυκέσθαι from τεύχω has an unexplained unaspirated consonant (cf. xxi 48, 421 τιτύσκομαι, compared to τυγχάνω, if this word is derived from *τι-τυκ-σκ-ομαι). In the act. the word is applied to serving-girls and governs δεῖπνον in xv 77, 94; in the middle we find twelve examples, governing δόρπον (xii 283, 307, xiv 408, and here), δαῖτα, or δεῖπνον (xx 390). It seems likely that warriors of travellers would prepare their own meals (middle of interest), but in the last of the passages quoted the suitors would order others to cook the food for them (factitive middle), and that is a possible interpretation here ('it is time for the Achaeans to order their dinner, i.e. to dine'; see Hoekstra, *Epic Verse*, 71–2); an alternative and ironic interpretation might be 'it is time for you and I to prepare dinner for the Achaeans', but this active use of the middle would be unprecedented.

429. ἐν φάει: possibly 'while there is still light', but more probably oxymoron is intended: this is to be an extraordinary dinner, taking place as it does 'in the daytime'. ἐψιάασθαι: distension of this verb is found, also at the end of the line, in xvii 530 ἐψιάασθων; and the verb is found in compounds with ἐφ- (xix 331, 370) and καθ- (xix 372). Its etymology is unclear: Hesych. ψιά·χαρά, γελοίασμα, παίγνια and ψιάδδειν·παίζειν are no help at all. For the aspirate, not found in Attic, see Wackernagel, *Untersuchungen*, 46–7.

430. The beginning and end of the line is almost identical to i 152 (see K. Lehrs, *De Aristarchi*, 139). For music at banquets see viii 99, xvii 270–1.

431-4. There are some problems, but they do not amount to a case for the excision of these beautiful closing lines, whose high proportion of dactyls (five, four, five, four) hurry us swiftly on to the stunning effect of xxii 1.

431. For ἦ cf. xxi 118; on the gesture of 'nodding with the eyebrows', xxi 129n. The tmesis ἐπ'... νεῦσεν appears also in xvii 330, the compound verb in *Il.* xv 75, xxii 314. ἀμφέθετο: ἀμφιτεθεῖσα (of a helmet) in *Il.* x 271 is the only other attestation of the compound, but ἀμφιτίθημι in tmesis is used of a hero girding on a swordbelt over the right shoulder (viii 416; cf. περί... θέτο in ii 3, iv 308, xx 125), or the strap of his shield (xxii 122, *Il.* x 149, xv 479). In xxi 118 Telemachus ἀπό... θέτο, 'threw back' (not 'off': see the note ad loc.) his χλαῖνα, the same verb in tmesis being used in xxi 119 to denote his unbuckling of the sword which he now girds on again (cf. xiv 528, where Odysseus ξίφος ὀξὺ περί... βάλετ' ὤμοις).

432. = xv 63, 554, xx 283, etc.; the line-ending also in xxi 74, 189, and the whole line apart from the first proper name in xxiv 151. All these similarities have led to the line being declared spurious, the demonstr. ὁ δέ, 'and the other', of the previous line being sufficient on its own.

433. This appears to be the only example of ἀμφιβάλλω used to mean grasping a spear with the hand (φίλην, possessive); the verb is found, without tmesis, in four passages of the *Odyssey* (xvii 344, xxiii 192; middle, vii 178, xxii 103, see note ad loc., and two of the *Iliad*. Telemachus leaves his spear leaning against a column in xvii 29, picks it up in xx 127, carries it out with him into the street in xx 145, and has it by him when he returns (as he has done in xx 257) in xx 306. ἔγκει has hiatus before and after the final -ι. The line-ending is paralleled in *Il.* xvii 10 and ii 417, which does not support the conjecture mentioned in the next note.

434. The book ends with a grave textual problem: according to the text, Telemachus is standing (on the presence or absence of an augment in ἑστήκει see the app. and cf. xxi 418; the papyrus reading is doubtful) by his seat (see xxi 139n.) at his father's side (αὐτοῦ). But κεκορυθμένος αἴθοπι χαλκῷ (a formula applied to warriors nine times in the *Iliad*) is difficult: not until xxii 101–3 does the boy announce that he is going to fetch a shield, two spears and a helmet πάγχαλκον to put on (ἀμφιβαλεῦμαι), and only in xxii 113 does he actually do so. Yet the phrase cannot refer to Odysseus, who remains near the door, not πὰρ θρόνον, until xxii 99. A good solution is provided by Protodikos' suggestion κεκορυθμένον (cf. *Il.* xvi 802 ἔγχος κ., xxii 125, *Il.* iii 18, xi 43 δοῦρε δύω κεκορυθμένα χαλκῷ). The whole phrase would then explain the preceding one: Telemachus was able to grasp his bronze-tipped spear (xxi 433) because it was 'standing next to him (αὐτοῦ) by his chair'; it is not necessary to change δ' ἄρ' in 433, supported by the parallels in *Il.* xvii 10 and ii 417, to γάρ, since the causal link can just as well be expressed by simple juxtaposition. Otherwise we must accept Hoekstra's theory of an 'involuntary metonomy' due to the clumsy adaptation of an ancient formula to a modern passage (*Modifications*, 113–14).

BOOK XXII: INTRODUCTION

The more ancient passages of the book are not lacking in literary quality, but its overall structure is unsatisfactory. This is because the primitive version of the myth presupposed a much simpler denouement: the shooting down by arrows of the defenceless suitors in the *megaron*. Once the poet (doubtless *A*) decided to round off Odysseus' home-coming with an Iliadic-style spear battle, however, the plot ran into numerous contradictions. Nor was the poet able to give the story the twist of suspense, partly because the narrow stage on which his characters fight leaves little room for an exciting battle.

The storyline is further muddied by an attempt, this time attributable to poet *B*, to make a place in the plot for secondary characters who had no part in the original action: Eumaeus and Philoetius on one side and Melanthius on the other.

The taut and intense beauty of the opening lines on the death of Antinous, who fails to guess the true identity of Odysseus, is maintained more or less down to 98. Even so, there is a first problem in 23–5, which may be interpolated (with or without 22): the terror of the suitors at this killing is premature, if they really believe it to be an accident. But it could be argued that they have, nevertheless, an instinctive foreboding of impending danger. Or the passage might be a 'late' addition like 99–125, connected to xvi 281–98 and xix 1–52, and intended, like these, to introduce an interesting subplot. As for 31–3, they may be authentic (despite Aristarchus' censorious frown, and the strange ἴσκεν), precisely because they portray the suitors overcoming the panic of 23–5 by convincing themselves that the beggar is not, after all, as dangerous as they supposed.

The narrative continues skilfully as far as 98, although with occasional signs of possible interpolation (37 may be a sign of the later poet's constant obsession with the sexual conduct of the slavegirls; 43, a line taken from the *Iliad*, again overplays the suitors' fears, when they still think a deal is on the cards). The deaths of Eurymachus and Amphinomus, the first killed by an arrow from Odysseus and the second by a spearthrust from Telemachus, are as good as anything in Homer; the objection which has been raised against Telemachus' exultant leap in 80 is irrelevant.

However, the text becomes more problematic in 99–125, a passage full of oddities. It is natural that Telemachus should be worried about getting another spear for himself; less so that he should also think about doing so for the slaves. It may be, therefore, that 103–4 are late. Nor are we told whether or not he closed the door of the storeroom. Since it is Telemachus himself who has taken the initiative, line 108 (a doublet of xix 14) is out of place here. In 109, κεῖτο is an odd word for arms hidden only the day before. There is a further allusion to the slaves, again with the stamp of later composition, in 114–15. And finally, the sordid content hardly lends much glamour to Odysseus' warlike shaking of his crest in 124.

Meanwhile, the pace of the narrative has accelerated alarmingly: even before arming, the hero has killed a large but unspecified number of suitors (118), in order to reduce their enormous numerical superiority of one hundred (xvi 247–51) to the more manageable number of twelve (see the note on xxii 241).

Next follows the long and difficult digression on Melanthius (126–202). Although pedantically fussy in topographical details, 126–30 are necessary for the sense of the passage; 134, however, is an unnecessary repetition of 78. Melanthius, besides being very evil, would have to be extraordinarily clever to guess that the men who had taken away the weapons were Odysseus and Telemachus (140–1), and then to work out where they had taken them. Besides, how could a single man carry twelve complete suits of armour, each consisting of shield, spear, and helmet (144–5)? Why did the crafty goatherd distribute his load so unevenly, leaving only one helmet and a rusty old shield for his second trip (184–5)? Simply, we must suppose, to give his enemies a chance to capture him.

No less incredible is Telemachus' feat of detection in 157–9, when he immediately suspects Melanthius. Furthermore, he orders Eumaeus to lock the door, which is by then quite beside the point.

We meet fresh improbabilities in 171–7. The punishment of the goatherd is necessary, perhaps, but hardly urgent; here it becomes a pressing obsession. Odysseus' instructions, though rather disjointed (there is no need, however, to expunge 175–7 in face of 192–3), leave no doubt how the punishment—and, more importantly, immobilization—of Melanthius is to be carried out. There is no need to condemn 174, if we take σανίς to mean an ordinary 'plank', not the leaf of a door.

It seems admissible to remove the unnecessary 191; 192–3, however, look like genuine formulaic repetition. On the other hand, 195–9 have attracted suspicion by their high literary style, which makes them stand out in an otherwise mediocre passage. All this brings to an end the episodes of the arming of the hero and his party, the counter-arming of his opponents, and the coda of Melanthius' punishment: together, they occupy no less than 102 lines, a disproportionate length in terms of the scale of the book.

In 205–40, the author of the later reworking of the poem shows himself to have been a fluent but somewhat incoherent storyteller. The intervention of Athena–Mentor, and the simile (or metamorphosis?) of the swallow, call for a number of comments, most of which are discussed in the notes on the passage. Line 223 slightly disturbs the syntax, and 238 has the anomalous υἱοῦ.

By contrast, 241–96 are a good example of Iliadic poetry. The only difficulties are to be found in the opening lines (I favour the solution of reordering 244–5 between 241 and 242), and the obviously spurious doublet 257–9. There is no reason to condemn the beautiful verses at 285–91; nor should suspicion fall upon 296 because Leocritus falls forward. However, the late poet's hand is evident in the two similes in 297–309; the first (299–301) is pretty enough, but imitated from xviii 367; the second (302–6) is frankly a mess. Furthermore, it is illogical for Athena to brandish the aegis against a couple of almost defenceless warriors, Leodes, and perhaps Eurynomus: such overkill seems to suit the late poet's fondness for magical interventions by the goddess.

The remainder of the book, as remarked in the notes, deals with the suitors' subordinates and accomplices: the priest (who is allowed no reprieve because he prayed for Odysseus' death), the bard and the herald (one saved by his craft, the other made sympathetic by his comic terror), the maidservants (constant preoccupation of the late poet, they suffer an awful death), and of course Melanthius, whose cruel mutilation is inspired by religious superstitions (474–7 may, indeed, be due to an even later interpolation).

This whole section falls clearly into two parts. The first (310–408) is of fairly high literary quality. However, 319 is an almost exact repetition of iv 695; it is absurd for Odysseus to suppose that Leodes, too, entertained the idea of slipping between the sheets with Penelope (324). Line 329 comes from *Iliad* x; 341 upset Blass; and Telemachus' joke in 395–6 has been supposed to be unsuitable to the tragedy of the situation. The accumulation of similes such as the fishes and the lion (384–8, 402–5), unparalleled in any other book of the *Odyssey*, has also occasioned unfavourable remarks.

The second section (409–77) cannot be said to be of the same calibre. The execution of the slavegirls, with the clumsy simile of the birds in 468–70, presents the commentator with several knotty problems. For instance, the humanitarian phrase in 414–16 is evidently out of tune with the ethical views of poet *A*; 422–3 present textual difficulties which are hardly resolved even by the suggestion adopted in the note; the memory of Telemachus' youth in 425–7 (lines omitted by a papyrus) sounds out of place in the mouth of the over-talkative Eurycleia; and 442, repeated in 459, is clearly spurious. The close of the book (478–501) may be counted amongst the most perfect passages in the *Odyssey*, and prepares us for the beautiful opening of the following book.

To conclude, I add some notes on the layout of Odysseus' palace which may help to clarify the setting of the action in this book, and of the last four books in general. In its main lines, the following explanation is based on Figure 9 (taken from Lorimer's *Monuments*). In relation to the sketch already given in xxi 141 n. above, the chief differences are the position of the ὀρσοθύρη and ῥῶγες (*C* and *D* in Pocock (Figure 8 above), *A* and *B* in Lorimer's more convincing reconstruction, next to the store-rooms).

1. In xxii 2 we first encounter the οὐδός which separates the feast-hall from the courtyard (*1* in Pocock, *D* in Lorimer). By this threshold Odysseus stands through almost the entire end of the poems. Its epithet μέγας does not mean that it was either particularly high or narrow. There are further οὐδοί: one leads to the two store-rooms mentioned (which may, in fact, be one and the same room), others are used by Penelope (xxi 43) and Melanthius (xxii 182) to enter, and yet another leads to the apartments of the queen and her slavewomen (*B* in Pocock, *E–G* in Lorimer; xvii 575, xx 128, xxiii 88). Odysseus' threshold is λάϊνος, 'stone' in xvii 575, xx 258; ξεστός in xviii 33, xxii 72 (in xvii 339 Bérard conjectures ξεστοῦ for μελίνου), all of which could refer to 'polished (stone)'. The threshold of the store-room is a simpler, wooden affair (xxi 43 δρύϊνος, see n.), while Penelope's is again described as λάϊνος (xxiii 88).

2. In xxii 109 Telemachus makes for the θάλαμος (compare nn. on xxi 5, 8–9), a term which signifies any room with a door: the ruler's own bedroom (i 425), Penelope's bedroom (iv 718) or that of the slavegirls (xxiii 41), and various allusions to store-rooms which may or may not all refer, as noted above, to the same room—that is, Odysseus' great treasury (ii 337 ὑψόροφον), the room where the weapons are stored (xvi 285 ὑψηλοῦ, xix 17, xxiv 166, and the present line), the room where Penelope's robes are kept (xix 256), and the room from which she brings out the axes (xxi 8, 42).

3. In xxii 120–1 Odysseus lays down the bow πρὸς σταθμὸν

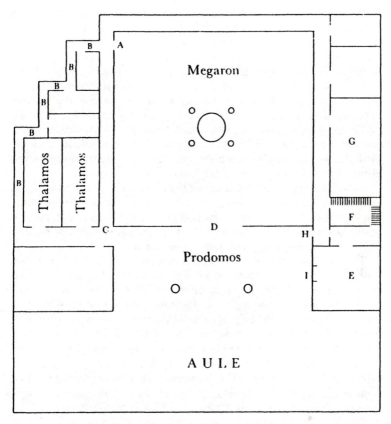

FIGURE 9. Plan of the palace (Lorimer, *Odyssean Essays*, 18, fig. 2)

ἐϋσταθέος μεγάροιο and πρὸς ἐνώπια παμφανόωντα. The word σταθμός has various meanings: in i 333 and xxi 64 it refers to the central 'pillar' of the hall, but in iv 838, xxi 45, xxii 181 to the 'door-post' of, respectively, Penelope's bedroom, the store-room where the axes are kept, and the store-room where Odysseus hid the weapons. Here it refers to the door-post of the main entrance into the hall from the courtyard; in xvii 340 this is described as σταθμῷ κυπαρισσίνῳ. In xxi 137 and 164 σανίδεσσιν must refer to one or other of the two leaves of the door against which Telemachus and Leodes lean the bow; in xxii 257-8 and 274-5 one spear lands in the door while another hits the door-post. In the passage under discussion here,

Odysseus could have stood the bow upright in the crack between the door-post and the inturned door, but he prefers to leave it further out of reach of the suitors, leaning it against the brick-built outside wall in the courtyard. In *Il.* viii 435 (Olympus) and *Od.* iv 42 (the palace of Menelaus), chariots are parked πρὸς ἐνώπια παμφανόωντα; in *Il.* xiii 261 the same location is presented as an inappropriate place for Idomeneus to display his Trojan trophies. As for the epithet παμφανόωτα, this is the only phrase where it is applied to part of a building. It has been suggested that it refers to walls whitewashed against the weather, which in sunlight would form a brilliant contrast with the μέγαρα σκιόεντα indoors (the latter phrase is attested seven times in the *Odyssey*, for instance in xxiii 299).

4. For xxii 126 ff. one may consult the diagram in Lorimer, where *A* is the ὀρσοθύρη, *B* the ῥῶγες, *A–C* the λαύρη, and *C* the way which leads to the latter from the great hall door into the courtyard. It was important that the doorways of the store-rooms should not overlap the λαύρη, which was much used by servants.

The diagram assumes that the whole house was built on one level with the exception of Penelope's bedroom with its ὑπερώϊον reached by the steps at *F* (recall our n. on xxi 5). The words ἀναβαίη (xxii 132), ἀνὰ ῥῶγας (xxii 143), and ἀνέβαινε (xxii 142) do not imply a climb upwards, but simply movement from the end of the great hall towards the street, perhaps at most up a gentle slope.

The ὀρσοθύρη is an opening in the wall separating the great hall from the λαύρη. The word appears three times in the book, and elsewhere only in the doubtful fragment 17 W of Semonides. The commonly accepted etymology (related to οὐρά 'tail', ὄρρος 'rump', ἄψορρος, παλίνορσος, etc.) clearly indicates a 'back door'. Less convincing etymologies, in our view, are those which connect the word with the root of ὄρνυμι and with other words such as ὀρσόλοπος (an epithet of Ares in Anacreon fr. 48 P which may carry some idea of 'exultation': cf. ὀρσολοπεῖται· διαπολεμεῖται, ταράσσεται, Hesych.); or with οὖρος 'guardian' (four times in the *Iliad*, and at *Odyssey* iii 411, xv 89), an hypothesis influenced by the well-known sentry on the roof at the beginning of Aeschylus' *Agamemnon*. The latter, however, was posted on the roof only as a special measure, to watch for the distant signal-beacon. Both these etymologies would lead us back to a palace built on several floors, and would make Melanthius' task even harder, with dangerous acrobatics up and down steps.

Agelaus proposes that someone escape through the ὀρσοθύρη into the λαύρη, and thence into the courtyard to shout for help. But it is impossible to use this route, because Odysseus has ordered Eumaeus to take up position as close as he can to the exit from the λαύρη at the end of the ῥῶγες, at a spot which also sports a pair of σανίδες (xxii 128; cf. xxi 137 n.); though these, unbeknown to the suitor, are open so that Eumaeus can spy through them to keep watch.

For his part, Melanthius guesses that Odysseus and Telemachus have carried off the weapons which he spots missing from their usual hanging-place on the walls of the great hall, and plans to get through the ὀρσοθύρη, not to the λαύρη, but into the ῥῶγες. Here he finds the open store-room which Telemachus has forgotten to lock, and returns through the ῥῶγες again with the weapons.

Odysseus, who has missed Melanthius' exit in the darkness and confusion of the crowded hall, is disheartened to see the suitors arming themselves, and jumps to the conclusion that some traitor has given the key to the goatherd, until Telemachus confesses his mistake. Eumaeus then enters by the λαύρη or the ῥῶγες and catches Melanthius by surprise on his second sally; he returns to Odysseus for orders, and then goes back to the store-room with Philoetius.

5. The two examples of λαύρη in xxii 128 and 137 are unique in Homer. The word is fairly common later (and compare Mount Λαύρειον, with its mine-shafts; Hesych. διάλαυρος· οἰκία μεγάλη πανταχόθεν λαύραις διειλημμένη, and so on).

6. In xxii 143 we find the hapax ῥώξ 'opening, crack, narrow passage', related to ῥήγνυμι; compare ἀπορρώξ 'steep, abrupt' (ix 359, x 514, xiii 98); διαρρώξ 'broken' (E. *IT* 262); Mod. Gr. ρουγα 'corridor'. It seems impossible to interpret the word as 'skylights' or high windows (later called ὀπή, see Ar. *V.* 317 etc.); this would take us back to the theory of a palace on several floors.

7. In xxii 180 ff. Melanthius finds the store-room stripped almost bare by his own and Telemachus' incursions, and has to spend some time searching about in its far corners. This gives Eumaeus and Philoetius, who have crept in through the λαύρη and ῥῶγες, to take up their position on the threshold of the store-room, where they are to pounce upon him.

8. In xxii 239, Athena's flight upwards as a swallow calls for some comment. The preposition ἀνά neatly captures the sudden upward movement (cf. xxii 176 n., and ἀναΐξασα in 240) towards her perch in the topmost nook of the roof-beam (compare viii 279, where Hephaestus hangs his net from a roof-beam, μελαθρόφιν; or xi 273, where Epicasta hangs herself from one; the eagle in Penelope's dream at xix 544 perches just like the swallow here), just under the

ceiling, which in 298 is referred to by the word ὀροφή, here only in Homer but found later in Herodotus (cf. ὄροφος, of a 'thatch' of reeds in *Il.* xxiv 451). On the epithet αἰθαλόεις, see xxii 120–1 n. on the smoke-shadowy darkness of the feast hall, which made it necessary to light λαμπτῆρες (see the introduction to Book xxi, and xxi 176–246 n.); hence Deroy deduced an original form *νέγαρον, related to Latin *niger*, which later changed to μέγαρον by analogy with μέγας; and original *μελεθρον, meaning 'skylight' (from the same root as *μλωθρος > βλωθρός 'high'; the first letter of κμέλεθρον 'beam' would be derivative) which later changed to μέλαθρον by analogy with μέλας, because of the blackening of the beams by smoke (in this connection, note that in xix 7–9 it is feared that weapons left in the hall may become oxidized). To all this we may add that the original and primary meaning of αἰθαλόεις is connected to the flash (cf. αἴθω) of lightning (Hes. *Th.* 72, 504, 854), and then to the blackened soot of carbonization (*Il.* xviii 23, *Od.* xxiv 316); only later, and by transference, at *Il.* ii 415 and in this line, to a smoke-blackened roof.

9. The door mentioned in xxii 394 is the one which leads, directly or not, from the hall to the women's quarters. This door has been closed in xxi 387 following the orders given in xxi 236, as Eurycleia relates in xxiii 42. It is unlikely that this is one of the doors alluded to in xxii 76, 91; the suitors never think of trying to escape through it. On the contrary, it is quite clear that in xxi 237–9 another exit from the women's quarters is referred to, one which leads to the courtyard and which they are not to use; this, too, would lead only to another locked door (xxi 391), the one to the street.

The location of this door in 394 is unclear; it may be in the wall opposite the ὀρσοθύρη. It is locked from the inside; Telemachus does not have the key and cannot open it using the leather thong (see xxi 6 n.), so that he must knock at it—not by beating on it with the knuckles as we would today (compare κρούειν or κόπτειν τὴν θύραν in Attic texts), but by shaking the door-knob, exactly as in *Il.* ix 583 σείων κολλητὰς σανίδας. Eurycleia slips out quietly so as not to raise the suspicions of the slavegirls and send them running through the door into the courtyard; the two of them then lash the door shut by tying the thong to the door-knob to prevent the women from following them, and go back out into the great hall.

10. On ἡγεμόνευεν in xxii 400, it has been suggested that what is meant is that Telemachus 'guides' Eurycleia in the sense of leading her a roundabout way through the λαύρη. But the verb is used in all sorts of ways in the *Odyssey*: of guiding a person who genuinely does

not know the way, certainly (iii 386, vi 261, viii 4, 421, xxiv 225), and of the supernatural guidance of a god (vii 30, ix 142, x 141),but also of Eurynome lighting the couple to their own bed with a torch (xxiii 293), and of Telemachus marching at the head of a party while his father brings up the rear (xxiv 155, with a line-ending identical to that of xxii 400).

11. The etymology of θόλος, 'roundhouse, vaulted rotunda' in xxii 442 is obscure; it is probably related to θολία, 'a lady's round-brimmed (perhaps conical) hat' (Theoc. xv 39). The word was feminine in Classical Greek (Pl. *Ap.* 32c), masculine in Hellenistic; here in xxii 442, 458 the gender cannot be deduced, while in 466 is is uncertain whether μεγάλης agrees with θόλοιο or with κίονος (κίων in the *Odyssey* is sometimes masc., viii 66, 473, xix 38, but more often fem., i 53, xxii 176, 193; i 127, xvii 29, xiii 90 are doubtful, since μακρήν is in the final foot). However, κίων is nowhere else qualified by the epithet μεγάλη, but always by μακρός or μακρή. At all events, κίων (which does not occur in the *Iliad*) is never used of colonnades, but only of the pillar of a store-room (xxii 176, 193), or of the tall columns of the house in general (xix 38), or of two of the columns in the great hall in particular: the one by the entrance where the visitor courteously leaves his spear as a sign of peace (Telemachus, at xvii 29; cf. also xv 282, xvi 40; in i 127 Athena stands her weapon in the spear-rack or δουροδόκη, where, incidentally, it remains forgotten when the goddess changes into a bird and disappears at i 320), and the great central pillar by which Odysseus seats himself in silence facing Penelope (xxiii 90).

If we accept, therefore, that in 466 μεγάλης agrees with θόλοιο, the latter will have been a large, well-built orifice; this raises several difficulties in the execution of the slavegirls. The roundhouse will have been very close to the perimeter wall of the courtyard, since the girls huddle close (see 441–7 n.) between the two (xxii 460). The rope must have been tied, then, to one of the columns of the πρόδομος or πρόθυρον, or less probably of the αἴθουσα. The only other explanation is Robert's: that the rope was not lashed over the top of a conical roof, but wound round the entire θόλος some six feet above ground level and secured by a knot, hitched up at intervals over the projecting capitals, and then decorated with the grim frieze of girls hung by the neck in the gaps between each column.

If we imagine a gap of a yard and a half between each column, the circumference of eighteen yards would give us a diameter of roughly six yards; and this would require an uncommonly high dome. It would be anachronistic to adduce the parallel of the twenty-column θόλος of Delphi, or the roundhouse of the *prytaneis* in the Athenian agora, each some 18 metres in diameter. But some light is shed on our problem by archaeological finds whose use was more enigmatic, such as the strange circular buildings in Smyrna, the small conical models of roundhouses in Attic tombs, some Corinthian terracotta figurines, and others from Egypt, for example: were these storehouses for precious objects such as ceramics (as the scholia suggest), or dovecotes, or ovens, or granaries?

12. The αὐλή in xxii 442 (cf. xxi 191, 240, 389; xxii 137, 376, 442, 449, 459, 474, 494) is the great courtyard in which the θόλος and other outbuildings are situated. The οὐδὸς αὔλειος of i 104 is the one between this courtyard and the street outside; the αὐλή is surrounded by a perimeter wall called, in the description of Amyntor's palace, ἑρκίον αὐλῆς (*Il.* ix 476), whereas in *Od.* xxii 442, 459 the word used is ἕρκος αὐλῆς. The general description of the palace in xvii mentions some θύραι . . . εὐερκέες, 'firm safe doors' (xvii 267), and the same adjective is applied to an αὐλή with the meaning 'well-enclosed' in *Il.* ix 472, *Od.* xxi 389, xxii 449.

13. There is some doubt about the etymology of αἴθουσα in xxii 449; related to αἴθω, it was probably 'a place where fire could be lit' rather than, as the scholia have it, 'a place lit by the rays of the sun'. Its distinguishing feature is a sort of colonnaded verandah or porch; running along two sides of the courtyard wall, or perhaps on either side of the street gate, it provided a shelter from sun and rain.

There is an αἴθουσα at Pherae (iii 493, probably spurious, and xv 191, where the chariot which has been parked in the courtyard for the night drives out by the street gate past, or through, the porch). In Sparta (iv 297, xv 146), Pylos (iii 399), and Scheria (vii 336, 345, and less strikingly viii 57), the αἴθουσα is used as a place for distinguished guests to sleep—a somewhat uncomfortable one, to judge by the epithet ἐρίδουπος, 'echoing' (iii 493, vii 345), so called no doubt because it was opposite the *megaron*, on the wall adjacent to the noisy street.

There is also one mention of the αἴθουσα in Amyntor's palace (*Il.* ix 472 ὑπ' αἰθούσῃ εὐερκέος αὐλῆς), and five of the one in Odysseus' (xviii 101–2, where Irus is dragged from the πρόθυρον to the αὐλή and αἰθούσης . . . θύρας, the latter presumably the great street-gates flanked by the porch; xx 175, 189, where the goats and the ox are left tied up ὑπ' αἰθούσῃ ἐριδούπῳ—another passage incompatible with the old interpretation of the word as 'guest-room'; xxi 390, as a store for old tackle; and xxii 449, where it is used as a place to pile the corpses, as being the place furthest from the great hall and therefore least likely to stink the place out). Note that in xxiii 49 Eurycleia speaks of the corpses being piled ἐπ' αὐλείῃσι θύρῃσιν, next to the main street gate.

In this connection, we should recall what was said about the ἐνώπια: their presence excludes the possibility of an αἴθουσα running along the outside of the front wall of the *megaron*. That is correct; chariots should not have to negotiate the whole courtyard before being parked. Besides, in all the mentions of the threshold by which Odysseus spends so much time, there is never a word about a porch overhead.

14. The πρόθυρον in xxii 474 must be a synonym for the πρόδρομος, a word not used at all in these two books, but which forms part of Menelaus' palace (iv 302, xv 5), of Eumaeus' sheepfold (xiv 5), and of an imaginary building (xv 466). This πρόδρομος may be identified in xx 1, 143 with the vestibule shown in Lorimer's diagram more or less adjoining the threshold which separates hall and courtyard, where Odysseus spends the night. In xxii 474 Melanthius is dragged along the λαύρη just like Irus to the πρόθυρον, and thence to the αὐλή. But πρόθυρον may also be used in another sense, of the space by the street-gate, as in i 103–4, 119 (recall the οὐδὸς αὔλειος quoted above). Lastly, it is worth noting that in xviii 385–6 Odysseus threatens Eurymachus that if, when the master of the house returns, he tries to escape out of the palace (θύραζε) through the πρόθυρον, he will find the θύρετρα 'which now are so fine and broad' all of a sudden too narrow.

BOOK XXII: COMMENTARY

1. **ῥακέων:** ablatival gen. without preposition. In the description of Odysseus' clothes from xiii 434 onwards the poet constantly uses the doublet ῥάκος ἄλλο κακόν . . . ἠδὲ χιτῶνα, a sort of hendiadys for his beggar's costume ('a poor, ragged tunic'; cf. xiv 342, in the course of a false story). In vi 178, too, the hero asks Nausicaa for a ῥάκος (cf. the synonym λαῖφος in xiii 399, xx 206). The description of the rags is expressed in various ways: by ῥάκος (xiv 349, in the course of the same story), ῥάκεα (xiv 512, xviii 67, 74, xix 507, xxi 221, on which see n.), λυγρά . . . εἵματα (xvi 457, xvii 203, 338, 573), or, from xiv 132 and when referring to the decent clothes which the hero asks for and obtains, χλαῖνάν τε χιτῶνά τε εἵματα (cf. the probably spurious xiv 154 and xxi 39 χλ. τ. χ. τ., εἵματα καλά); so xiv 320, etc. (except in xvi 173 φᾶρος - - - ἐϋπλυνὲς ἠδὲ χιτῶνα). Here Odysseus takes off his ῥάκεα for the fight, but in 488 he has put them on again, ῥάκεσιν πεπυκασμένος; the scholiast explains this as meaning that the hero does not strip completely, thereby preserving decency as well as the coherence of the text (van der Valk, *Textual Criticism*, 121). The formulaic epithet πολύμητις appeared in xxi 274, 404, and is to be found again in xxii 34, 60, 320, 371, 390, xxiii 247, as well as in the formula in xxii 105 (see n. below).

2. The final vowel of ἐπί is lengthened before following μ-; the first word may also be read as an unaugmented form, ἄλτο.

3. On ἰός see the n. on xxi 423. **ἐμπλείην:** note the variant εὐπλείην, on the analogy of the metrically secure *hapax* ἐϋπλείην in xvii 467; a similar emendation could be suggested for the ἐμπλείην in xviii 119, xx 26, but there are four examples of ἐνίπλειος, amongst them xxi 78. Odysseus drops the arrows from his quiver (cf. xxi 417–18, and the Introduction to Book xxi) so as to be free to make his shot more comfortably. ὀϊστός appears six times in the preceding book (cf. xxi 423n.), once with the epithet ὠκύς (cf. 83; *Il.* v 395, xi 478 ὠκὺν ὀϊστόν; on ὠκὺ βέλος and βέλος ὠκύ see n. on xxi 138, 148, 165), which corresponds to ταχύς here and in xxiv 178, the ending of which repeats these lines, as well as *Il.* xxi 492 ταχέες . . . ὀϊστοί on Artemis' arrows spilling from her quiver onto the ground. This is the first of many Iliadic reminiscences which fill this book.

4. First hemistich = *Il.* xvi 472. **αὐτοῦ:** adv. (cf. xxi 40, 239, 385). The second hemistich is related to xxi 151, which betrays the routine formulaic use of μετά, since Odysseus is not properly speaking 'amongst them'.

5-7. A large part of the effectiveness of these lines (cf. *infra*) lies in the fact that the suitors cannot be aware of what is really going forward (Erbse, *Beiträge*, 38 n. 94).

5. On ἄεθλος (which is preceded by hiatus and shortening of the vowel of δή)

218

and the irony of ἀάατος on Odysseus' lips see xxi 91 n.; the perf. ἐκτετέλεσται is here full of significance (the game is well and truly over), but has a different sense in xxiii 54.

6-7. The syntax of these lines is open to various interpretations: (a) 'I will know, i.e. hit another target, if my aim is true and Apollo grants my prayer' (see n. on 7); (b) 'I shall know, with regard to another target, whether I shall hit the mark and whether Apollo will grant . . .' (acc. of respect; cf. the similar construction in xiv 365-6, 'I know, with regard to my return, that . . .'; indirect questions, but cf. 7n. below); (c) 'I shall look for (ἔπειμι) another target, to see if by chance I hit and Apollo grants . . .' (for this meaning of εἴσομαι cf. Il. xxi 335, xxiv 462; xv 504 ἀγροὺς ἐπιείσομαι ἠδὲ βοτῆρας, xv 213 δεῦρ' εἴσεται; this usage implies a following acc. of direction, but cf. ἐείσατο with gen. in xxii 89, and εἴσατο in xxiv 524; for the implied indirect question in αἴ κε τύχωμι '(to see) if I can hit', cf. Il. vii 243).

6. For βάλεν, 'shot at', with the acc. see the passage at Il. vii 242-3 alluded to in the preceding note (σ' ἐθέλω βαλέειν).

7. τύχωμι, πόρῃ: for this ending of the subj. cf. xxi 348; τύχωμι is supported by a papyrus against the commoner τύχοιμι. Rarer still is the itacistic πόροι. The line is a close echo of Penelope's prophetic words in xxi 338 (see the notes on xxi 257-62 and 336-42); this parallel supports the first of the alternative interpretations given in the note on 6-7 above.

8. For ἦ, 'he said', from *ἄg-t, see xxi 118 and 431. The word is commonly used in this type of phrase with another verb: 'He spoke, and (accordingly; or, nevertheless) did (something)' (cf. ii 321, xxi 118, 431, xxii 236, xxiii 366); variations of the scheme are frequently found ('he spoke, and then did . . .', for example in v 28, vi 198, xv 539, xvii 396, xviii 356, xix 96; or with a change of subject, 'he spoke, and then someone or something else did . . .', for example in Il. xiv 475, Ajax/the fear of the others, Il. xxiv 643, Priam/Achilles; similarly, with a change to a previously mentioned subject, for example in iii 337 ἦ ῥα Διὸς θυγάτηρ, οἱ δ' ἔκλυον, xxii 292, Il. vi 390 ἦ ῥα γυνὴ ταμίη, ὁ δ' . . . Ἕκτωρ). ἰθύνετο: the verb ἰθύνομαι occurs in Homer only here and in v 270 (Odysseus steers the raft with the rudder); for the metrical constraints which confine the word to − −⁴ ∪ ∪ see Hoekstra, Modifications, 106. The line-ending πικρὸν ὀϊστόν occurs ten times in the Iliad, besides πικρὰ βέλεμνα in xxii 206.

9. The demonstrative use of ὁ has already been seen in xxii 1. It is perfectly logical that Antinous should be drinking, since, although we have been told nothing of this, the suitors are now embarked on the δόρπον announced in xxi 428 (see n. ad loc.). ἔμελλε: 'was on the point of', pointing the ironic contrast between Antinous' easy nonchalance and his imminent fate. Many commentators adduce the proverb πολλὰ μεταξὺ πέλει κύλικος καὶ χείλεος ἄκρου, 'there's many a slip betwixt cup and lip'. ἀναιρήσεσθαι: 'raise to his lips'; cf. xxi 261, Il. xi 637 (Nestor easily raises, ἄειρεν, the great cup), and Il. xvi 8, 10 (ἀνελέσθαι, 'pick up a child in one's arms'). The future is normal after μέλλω in Homer (see K. Lehrs, De

Aristarchi studiis Homericis (Leipzig, 1882³, 120–1). **ἄλεισον:** etymologically, probably a substrate word for a small cup, usually of delicately-crafted gold as here and in the two Iliadic and seven Odyssean occurrences (see further G. Micknat, *LfgrE*, i 465–6, and Frisk, *GEW*).

10. ἄμφωτον: the adj. is a *hapax*, of a relatively late kind of formation (see A. di Luzio, *LfgrE*, i 703, and the n. on 475 below). It clearly means a two-handled cup of a well-known Mycenean type, but its synonyms are complex: iii 63 δέπας ἀμφικύπελλον is described ten lines earlier as χρύσειον ἄλεισον, but as χρυσείῳ δέπαϊ in 41, and δέπας in 46 and 51. The same is true here: ἄλεισον in 9 is the same cup as δέπας in 17. As for the adj. ἀμφικύπελλον, which appears eight times in the *Iliad* and seven in the *Odyssey*, including the passage mentioned above and also xxii 86 (Eurymachus' δέπας ἀμφικ.), it is clearly related etymologically to the noun κύπελλον (Lat. *cúpa*, etc., perhaps Myc. *ku-pe-ra* in Ue 611, 1; see Frisk, *GEW*, A. di Luzio, *LfgrE*, i 679), which occurs five times in each of the two poems, again with a number of synonyms (the δέπα ἀμφικύπελλα of xx 153 are called κύπελλα in xx 253; *Il.* xxiv 285 χρυσείῳ δέπαϊ is the same as the κύπελλον in 305); again, the prefix ἀμφι- may indicate a two-handled cup, though some scholars believe it refers to a kind of double cup formed of two bowls joined on a single base, and whose use is a mystery; see further Hoekstra's comments on the metrical constraints operating on its formulaic use (*Modifications*, 94 n. 2). **μετὰ χερσὶν ἐνώμα:** = ending of xxi 245 (see n. ad loc.). The verb occurs in xxi 400, and also in xxi 272, but there with the very different meaning of 'share out (the wine)'; here it describes Antinous' action as he appreciatively swirls the wine round the brimming cup before drinking. As remarked in the Introduction to xxi, the hero's calm behaviour hardly accords with the tense atmosphere of the dangerous competition taking place in the feast-hall around him.

11–12. ὄφρα πίοι οἴνοιο: optative of indirect speech, and partitive gen. There is hiatus due to *digamma* before both οἴνοιο and οἱ. The juxtaposition of οἴνοιο and φόνος, 'a (possible) violent death', is purposely ironic. The pluperf. μέμβλετο < *με-μλ-ε-το, here meaning 'worried', is found in *Il.* xxi 516; the perf. μέμβλετ' in *Il.* xix 343, μέμηλε(ν) five times in the *Iliad* and three in the *Odyssey*.

12–14. Rhetorical questions expecting negative answers are very rare in Homer's narrative; compare *Il.* xxii 202–4 (whereas the example of Nestor's speech in iii 113–14 is different). The meaning, demanded by the emphatic reflex, οἱ, is: 'Who at a banquet with many friends would ever expect a single adversary, however strong he might be, to court his own death (by taking them all on single-handed, to his own certain defeat)?' There are similar expressions in xvi 88–9 πρῆξαι ... ἀργαλέον ... μετὰ πλεόνεσσιν ἐόντα | ἄνδρα καὶ ἴφθιμον, xx 313 χαλεπὸν γὰρ ἐρυκακέειν ἕνα πολλούς, and above all ii 244–5 ἀργαλέον δέ | ἀνδράσι καὶ πλεόνεσσι μαχέσσασθαι περὶ δαιτί (compare, however, xxii 138). The ending of 13 is very similar to viii 139. Underlying the lines is the still implicit idea that the suitors have failed to grasp the true import of Odysseus' words in 5–7 (see n.).

14. **θάνατόν τε κακὸν καὶ κῆρα μέλαιναν:** the phrase, which is paralleled in *Il.* xxi 66, is an adaptation of the common line-ending θάνατον καὶ κῆρα μέλαιναν, of which there are four examples in the *Odyssey* (for example, xxiv 127), by the insertion of the epithet κακόν (O'Nolan, *Doublets*, 23–37, esp. 29). On other occasions the formula is varied by substituting μέλαιναν with a verb (xxii 66, xxiv 414); the variant φυτεῦσαι is due to psychological confusion with lines such as ii 165 φόνου καὶ κῆρα φυτεύει and *Il.* xv 134 κακὸν μέγα πᾶσι φυτεῦσαι.

15. **δ':** strongly adversative. **κατὰ λαιμὸν ἐπισχόμενος:** 'after taking aim at his throat'; λαιμός occurs four times in the *Iliad*, once (xviii 34) in the same metrical position in the line; the meaning of ἐπέχω, 'have a go at, attack' (note the occurrence in tmesis in xxii 75), in the middle voice extends to 'aim at', like τιτύσκομαι (cf. xxi 421, and the Introduction to that Book). **βάλεν ἰῷ:** also in *Il.* viii 303, xiii 586.

16. This line is omitted in a secondary witness (Ps.-Plu. *Vit. Hom.* ii 82), and is directly modelled on *Il.* xvii 49 (death of Euphorbus), *Il.* xxii 327 (death of Hector); the ending ἦλυθ' ἀκωκή occurs in *Il.* v 16, 67, xvi 478, and the noun ἀκωκή itself is found thirteen times in the *Iliad* and once more in the *Odyssey* (xix 453), always at the end of the line except in *Il.* xxi 60. In all these passages except *Il.* xiii 251 (an imaginary arrow), the word refers to the heavy tip of a spear; here, therefore, its use emphasizes the violent impact of the hit.

17. **ἑτέρωσε:** generally 'to one side', without specifying the direction, as of the lolling of a wounded head (*Il.* xiii 543, with the same opening to the line as here), the drooping of a poppy (*Il.* viii 306), or the toppling of a basin (xix 470); conversely, οὐδετέρωσε is used of something that inclines 'neither to one side nor the other' in *Il.* xiv 18. However, it should be recalled that though kicking away the table (20) might seem a normal reflex for someone falling backwards, the fact that Antinous does not collapse (22) until after he has vomited implies that he is propped up for a moment by the side-rest of the θρόνος (see n. on xxi 139; S. Laser, *Archaeologia* P, 40). **δέπας δέ οἱ ἔκπεσε χειρός:** on δέπας see nn. above on 9–10; οἱ, ethic dative; the gen. χειρός depends on the prefix ἐκ- in ἔκπεσε.

18. For gen. βλημένου despite dat. οἱ in the previous line (note the *lectio facilior* βλημένῳ in the app.), compare vi 155–7 σφίσι . . . λευσσόντων and ix 256–7 ἡμῖν . . . δεισάντων. αὐλός signifies 'flute' in *Il.* x 13 and xviii 495; 'tube' in *Il.* xvii 297, *Od.* xix 227 (Lorimer, *Monuments*, 244 n. 2, and 512 n. 1); here it has the metaphoric sense 'jet, stream' (M. Wegner, *Archaeologia* U, 20 notes that this usage in fact indicates that the original meaning was 'pipe', which only later acquired the musical sense). ἀνά, 'through'; παχύς, predicative.

19. **ἀνδρομέοιο:** of the eight occurrences of the adj. in Homer, on three occasions in the Cyclops episode it refers to human flesh, on three others to skin, and on another to a crowd; only here and in the almost identical

line-opening of ps.-Hes. *Sc.* 256 is it used of blood (K. Strunck, *LfgrE*, i 806–7); *Il.* xvii 572 has αἷμ' ἀνθρώπου instead. Note the reflexive εἷο, and the Homeric custom by which each banqueter had his own table (S. Laser, *Archaeologia* P, 58).

20. **ἀπὸ δ' εἴδατα χεῦεν ἔραζε:** tmesis; ἔραζε is derived from old neuter ἔρας, 'earth' (possibly, therefore, we should read ἔρας· γῆ in Hesychius, instead of the reading γῆς printed in Latte's ed.), with the lative suffix -δε. It occurs nine times in Homer, four of them in the *Odyssey*, of which this and two others (85, with identical second hemistich, and 280) are found in this book. The adverb is always placed at the end of the line, and is practically synonymous with χαμᾶζε, which is also found in line-endings, for example in xxi 136, xxii 327, 340 (but not xxii 84); Hoekstra notes that, while χεῦεν or κατέχευεν precedes ἔραζε in eleven passages, there is not a single example of *χεῦε χαμᾶζε, and surmises that there may have been a doublet of this formula in *Χεῦαν ἔραζε which was simplified as soon as it became possible to avoid hiatus after the 3. sing. by the addition of νῦ ἐφελκυστικόν (*Modifications*, 90).

21. The original long final vowel of κρέα, from *κρεασα, is shortened by analogy. φορύνετο agrees with the nearest of the two subjects, as for example in iv 79, xiv 291, xxii 68; the etymology of the verb, which is attested only here in archaic poetry, is unclear; the word is related to the participle φορύξας, xviii 336, which is also not attested again until much later (compare Hesych. φορύνει· φυρᾷ, μολύνει, συγχεῖ), and combines the ideas of dirtying and mixing (cf. φύρω, which occurs five times in the *Odyssey*). This line is probably the source of the late passage in xx referring to the nightmarish omen interpreted by Theoclymenus, in which the suitors believe they are eating flesh mixed with blood; that passage contains the suspect *hapax* αἱμοφόρυκτα (xx 348). ὁμάδησαν occurs in five line-endings in the *Odyssey*, but never in the *Iliad*.

22–5. The textual difficulties of the lines are multiple. First, there is the strange repetition of κατὰ δώμαθ' (22; note the variant δῶμα, the pl. perhaps having been introduced to avoid hiatus) and κατὰ δῶμα (23). Second, the temporal use of ὅπως in 22 is not normally found before Herodotus; in the three parallel passages in Homer with ὅπως ἴδον or ὅπως ἴδεν in the same metrical position in the line, there are variants with ἐπεί in papyri (*Od.* iii 373, *Il.* xi 459) and MSS (*Il.* xii 208, which is besides the famous 'tapering' or 'curtal line', στίχος μείουρος, ending with a short syllable in the thesis of the last foot, αἰόλον ὄφιν); on the other hand, *Od.* ii 155, x 152, 219, 414 have ἐπεί in the same position before ἴδον, and preceded by regular hiatus; and note that in xx 331 the identical opening μνηστῆρας κατὰ δώματ' is followed by ἐπεί (causal in this case). Third, ὀρινθέντες, 'shocked' (23), is otherwise unattested. Last, the construction of παπταίνω with ποτί (or κατά; see app.) in 24 is almost unparalleled save for xii 233, with πρός (for first hemistichs very similar to this one see xxii 380, *Il.* xiii 649, xvii 674; on xxii 43, see n. and app. below). For these reasons and others besides (to which one might add the omission in some MSS of

23), editors have been prodigal with deletions: Agar condemns 22 and 24–5 Duentzer and Kirchhoff reject 23–5 (*recentiora esse vidit Kirchhoff*, notes von der Mühll), while Blass expunges 24–5 (*Interpolationen*, 204), alleging the dependence of 24 on xxii 380, and of ἐϋδμήτους ποτὶ τοίχους in the same line on xxii 126; on the latter see my n. ad loc.). It is generally held, though without any adequate explanation of the motive for the interpolation, that at least 24–5, and probably 23 as well, must be spurious because it is premature for the suitors, who after all carry swords (cf. 74 ff.), to start looking for arms hanging on the walls. Their words in 27–30 impute only clumsiness to the beggar, not evil intentions, since in 31–3 we are explicitly told that the suitors are still under the misapprehension that the killing of Antinous has been an accident. As commented in the note on 5–7 above, they still have not grasped the meaning of Odysseus' words. What seems to have happened is that some interpolator who wished to introduce an element of further complexity into the plot of the slaughter has here tried to work in a reference to the well-known episode of the hiding of the arms (see 101–25, 140–1 and nn.). Nevertheless, though the weight of opinion since the last century has been to condemn the lines outright (thus Monro in his edition, and even more recently Lorimer, *Monuments*, 432; Page, *Odyssey*, 99–100, n. 15; Merkelbach, *Untersuchungen*, 108; and others), there has been a growing tendency to defend them, beginning as long ago as E. Kammer, *Die Echtheit der Odyssee* (Leipzig, 1873), 593, and in our day W. Büchner, 'Die Waffenbergung in der *Odyssee*', *Hermes* lxvii (1932), 438–45; Focke, *Odyssee*, 357–8; Stanford's edition, ad loc.; L. G. Pocock, *Odyssean Essays* (Oxford, 1965), 25; Bona, *Studi*, 132 n. 4; Besslich, *Schweigen*, 25–8; Erbse, *Beiträge*, 5, 38–9, etc. In every case the arguments are the same: the suitors are acting nervously, instinctively, at the prompting of an unease which causes them to look for arms as a sort of mechanical reflex; besides, they realize that swords would be useless against a strategically positioned bowman supported by Telemachus.

26. There are only two other occurrences of νεικείω, with its required metrical lengthening, in the *Odyssey* (xvii 189, xviii 9). The verbal adj. χολωτός occurs four times, always in the same formulaic phrase with ἐπέεσσι and νεικέω (apart from this line and 225 later in the same book, also preceded by δ᾽ Ὀδυσῆα, the passages are *Il.* iv 241, xv 210). The meaning of the suffix -τος is not active, as Ameis says in his edn., but passive: 'enraged, angry words' (Schwyzer, *Grammatik*, i 503).

27–30. Even if 31–3 are removed below, these four lines already suggest that the suitors believe the killing to be an accident (Erbse, *Beiträge*, 38 n. 95). Stanford remarks: 'just how, it is not easy to see, especially in view of O.'s words in 6–7 above. But they would be reluctant to face the terrible real truth.'

27. κακῶς and ἀνδρῶν (gen. after verbs of aiming) are emphatic: 'it is to your own harm to go shooting men (who are nobler than you)'; as usual, the judgement stresses profit and loss, not moral considerations (cf. xxi 369 ff. and n.; but contrast xvii 483 οὐ μὲν κάλ᾽ ἔβαλες δύστηνον ἀλήτην). There

follow two asyndeta, reflecting the speakers' excitement, and linked to each other by a sort of indirect causal relation: 'you have made a mistake, (and I say this because) you will not use a bow again, (and I say this because) you are going to die'. The allusion to 5 in ἀέθλων is compatible with the suitors still not having understood the real situation; they regard Odysseus as a bad marksman, as well as a presumptuous one (cf. xxi 397–400).

28. ἀντιάσεις: this choriambic fut. is unique, amongst the complex of forms associated with ἀντάω, ἀντιάω, ἀντιάσω, followed by the usual gen. after verbs of touching, trying, etc. (E. M. Voigt, LfgrE, i 918–22); besides the rhythm, unparalleled in Homer, the form implies a pres. in ἀντιάζω, something not found until Hdt. (note Cobet's conjecture in the app.). Syntactically, the fut. is a so-called 'prospective', implying obligation rather than volition on the part of the subject. νῦν τοι σῶς αἰπὺς ὄλεθρος: σῶς is difficult (hence Schulze's suggestion, recorded in von der Mühll's app., of a σάος related to σεύομαι, 'hurled upon one'), unless of course we take it as a deliberate oxymoron (σῶς 'safe and sound' > 'entire' > 'wholly accessible' . . . ὄλεθρος), an ironic reference to suicide being the 'safe' way out. This interpretation would fit the identical hemistich in Il. xiii 773 (Hector speaking to Paris), but not Od. v 305 (with μοι for τοι, the hero's monologue during his shipwreck). αἰπὺς ὄλεθρος is a very common line-ending; the adj. is extremely ancient (Fr. Scholz, LfgrE, i 334–6; compare the place-name Aἰπύ in Myc. a-pu₂-we, An 427, 1, etc.; Il. ii 592, Mimn. fr. 3, 1 G.-Pr.), and is probably connected to αἶψα (Frisk, GEW), the meaning developing from 'swift' to 'steep, headlong', and thence to 'violent, fatal'; it occurs with ὄλεθρος twelve times in the Odyssey, seven of them in conjunction with φεύγω and its compounds with the idea of escaping death (including the possibly spurious xxii 43; see n. ad loc. below); the remaining five examples are the present line, v 305, i 37 (not at the end of the line), ix 303, and Odysseus' sarcastic remark to the suitors in xvi 280, where one variant offers αἰπὺς ὄλεθρος after παρίσταται instead of αἴσιμον ἦμαρ.

29–30. There is a striking parallel with xxiii 121–2 ἕρμα πόληος ἀπέκταμεν, οἳ μέγ' ἄριστοι | κούρων εἰν Ἰθάκῃ.

30. κοῦρος is frequently used to refer to the Phaeacian youths (six times), to Telemachus and Peisistratus (xv 151), or as a synonym for 'son, boy' (xix 523, xxiv 54) or 'servant' (i 148, iii 339, xxi 271; in vii 100 the word refers to statues), but it is used in ten passages of the suitors (on their youthfulness see xxi 179, 361), as here and in xxiii 122 (as a voc., on Penelope's lips, ii 96, xix 141, xxiv 131, and on Medon's, xvii 174). In prose, we should expect the idea in the gen. κούρων to be expressed by something such as τῶν ἐν Ἰθάκῃ κούρων. τῷ: cf. xxi 374 n. The second half of the line alludes to the common theme of a condemned man's unburied body being eaten by vultures (as, for example, in the myth of Polyneices); vultures appear seven times in Homer, besides the οἰωνοὶ | ὠμησταί of Il. xi 453–4 (cf. 302 n.): Il. xi 162 (unburied warriors again), Od. xi 578 (punishment of Tityus), and five parallels to the present line, namely Il. xvi 836 σὲ δέ τ' ἐνθάδε γῦπες ἔδονται (Hector to Patroclus), Il. iv 237 (also ending γῦπες ἔδονται), and

two others, *Il.* xviii 271 and xxii 42 (Priam wishing Achilles' death), which end γ. ἔδονται and γ. ἔδοιεν but where the vultures are joined by scavenging dogs (cf. xxi 363 n.). On vultures see further H.-G. Buchholz, G. Jöhrens, and I. Maull, *Archaeologia* J, 117.

31-3. The lines are not as intrinsically objectionable as 22–5, the only obstacles being the asyndeton with ἴσκε in 31, the repetition of the singular metaphor in 33 and 41, the similarity of 32 to ix 442, and the fact that the formula in 34 is normally used to introduce a response which immediately follows the event which has provoked it. The other objections which have been raised to the lines, such as Faesi's fustigations of their lameness, or his and others' allegations of their irrelevance, are largely subjective; such arguments, even if true, do not mean that the lines are spurious. Nevertheless, the ancients on the whole condemned them, in particular Aristarchus (see Lehrs, *De Aristarchi*, 97–8, Cauer, *Homerkritik*, 56) and Eustathius (νοθεύεται ὑπὸ τῶν παλαιῶν τὸ χωρίον τοῦτο). Modern editors, with the exception of those such as Knight and Roemer who cut out the good wood with the bad by athetizing the whole passage 26–33, are divided in equal measure over these lines and 22–5, though not necessarily on the assumption that the genuineness of the former presupposes that of the latter, or vice-versa. Those who argue that 22–5 indicate the suitors' bewilderment and instinctive reflex action, are quite able to accept that they should nevertheless try to convince themselves that the killing was an accident and that all is well. Alternatively, one could argue that the suitors merely pretend to think the killing was involuntary, in order to gain time by humouring their powerful opponent. Focke, *Odyssee*, 357–8, Stanford ad loc., Pocock, *Odyssean Essays*, 25, Besslich, *Schweigen*, 25–8, and Erbse, *Beiträge*, 5 and 38, all accept both passages; Blass, *Interpolationen*, 204–5 naturally condemns both; while Büchner, 'Waffenbergung', quite consistently accepts the first and condemns the second. For those who condemn 22–5 but deliver an open verdict on 31–3, such as Monro ad loc. and von der Mühll ad loc. (who also condemns xxi 412–15; see n. ad loc.), the decision depends on the interpretation given to ἴσκεν in 31.

31. Ἴσκεν: as one sch. comments, οὐδέποτε Ὅμηρος ἐπὶ τοῦ ἔλεγε τὸ ἴσκε, though one must distinguish (as, for example, Gehring does in his index) between the participles ἴσκουσα (iv 279, Helen imitating voices) and ἴσκοντες (*Il.* xi 799, where Allen prints εἴσκοντες, 'imitating', as at *Il.* xvi 41), which certainly derive from *ϝικ-σκ-ω (cf. ἔοικα, etc.), and two non-participial forms. In xix 203 ἴσκε ψεύδεα πολλὰ λέγων ἐτύμοισιν ὁμοῖα, the verb doubtless means 'made up, invented' (hence the sch. comment on this passage, ἠπάτηται ὁ διασκευαστὴς ἐκ τοῦ ἴσκε ψεύδεα [τ 203]). It must be accepted, therefore, that we are dealing with a late passage, and that with ἴσκω 'say' the διασκευαστής has been responsible for the invention of one of those 'Homeric glosses' studied by Leumann and later imitated by the Alexandrians (Apoll. ii 240, Theoc. xxii 167, etc.); Aristarchus had every reason to condemn the passage, despite von der Mühll's *vix recte*. The other interpretations which have been suggested, such as the translation 'each tried to conjecture (what was going to happen, or what had happened)', or van der Valk's (*Textual Criticism*, 116 n. 7) impossible connection with ἐνίσπω, related to ἐννέπω, with a labial derived from an original labio-velar, are unconvincing. The asyndeton may be explained as an attempt at analogy between the made-up word ἴσκω 'say' and the parallel ἦ '(so) he said' (see 8 n. above) in the same position. The adv. ἦ in this line means 'indeed, in truth', emphasizing the striking fact that the suitors have not yet grasped the situation; φάσαν, 'they said (to themselves), they persuaded themselves'; οὐκ ἐθέλοντα is adverbial in sense (eleven of the twenty-two occurrences of ἐθέλων have the negative, five of these being placed at the end of the line and three being identical to this example, v 99, x 573, xxiv 307).

32. **τὸ**: anticipates the phrase introduced by ὡς. The poet speaks in his own person, expressing with the half predicative, half exclamative adj. νήπιοι a view of the suitors' foolishness which carries, as the word often does, a trace of compassion (though not in the apostrophe of Antinous to Eumaeus and Philoetius in xxi 85; see n. ad loc.). As noted above, the close imitation of the second hemistich of ix 442 (the poet's pitying remark on the Cyclops) has been used to call the authenticity of this line into question.

33. **σφιν καὶ πᾶσιν**: 'to one and all, every single one of them' (cf. xx 156). **ὀλέθρου πείρατ' ἐφῆπτο**: yet another objection to the authenticity of these lines is the close proximity of two such similar line-endings as this one and 41 below (and note the possible variant ἐφῆπται); the formula is paralleled also in *Il.* vii 402, xii 79 (and note ὀλέθρου πείρατα in *Il.* vi 14). The metaphor is complex; πεῖραρ means 'end, boundary' (iv 563, ix 284), 'limit, bounds' (v 289), but also 'end of a (ship's) cable, binding line' (xii 51, 162, 179). This causal, defining sense ('that which binds') is crossed with the idea of 'the boundary of death' (τέλος θανάτοιο, as Odysseus puts it in his prediction to Antinous, xvii 476) to give a play on words: each suitor is already bound (ἐφῆπτο) by the cable-end which ties him to his end in death. Büchner also suggests an allusion to the tying of the two ends of the rope from which the suitors will be (metaphorically) hung ('Waffenbergung', 444).

34. As remarked in the n. on 31–3, the distance between the response denoted by this phrase and the event which provoked it is a further argument against authenticity. The same line, with different pronouns, appears in xix 70, xxii 60, 320, each time with ὑπόδρα < *ὑπο-δρακ 'looking askance, grimly', an attitude which fits Odysseus' situation well; note the following hiatus before the digamma of ἰδών. **πολύμητις**: see 1 n.

35. **ὦ κύνες**: the insulting voc., which von der Mühll thought lively enough for *A* ('Odyssee', 757), has parallels in the κύον of *Il.* xi 362, xx 449 (one warrior addressing another) and *Il.* xxii 345 (Achilles to Hector). **ἐφάσκεθ'**: the only Homeric example of the 2nd pl. of this iterative form, as xi 512 νικάσκομεν is the only example of the 1st pl.; the sense is similar to that of φάσαν in 31. **ὑπότροπον οἴκαδ' ἱκέσθαι**: the first problem is metrical, the lack of lengthening before the digamma in οἴκαδε (see xxi 211 n.), which Bérard and others try to mend by conjecturing ὑπότροπα,

ἐνθάδε, and so on. But the papyrus and some MSS also offer a critical problem: against the majority reading, which is supported by Eustathius and accepted by Allen, the *lectio difficilior* οἴκαδε νείσθαι, despite the unanimous testimony against it in the parallel line xxi 211 (see n. ad loc.) and the fact that νείσθαι is only otherwise attested in xv 88 (and not at the end of the line), is accepted by von der Mühll, and supported on syntactical grounds by Chantraine, who argues that the future sense of νέεσθαι with φημί is paralleled in *Il.* xiv 221, *Od.* ii 238, xi 176, xxiv 460, and (with ἰέναι) *Od.* xv 214 (*Grammaire*, ii 307). In cases where the aorist depends on a verb of volition it is normal (see Schwyzer, *Grammatik*, ii 296) for the emphasis to fall on the aspect, not the tense, as in the two parallel passages with final οἴκαδ' ἱκέσθαι, both without hiatus before digamma, ix 530 (governed by δός) and xv 66 (with ἐέλδεται), and xv 210, where the phrase appears in a different position in the line after πρίν and preceded by hiatus after ἐμέ; but this is not usually the case with verbs of understanding, saying, or feeling, as here.

36. δήμου ἄπο Τρώων: another peculiarity of these lines is this initial formula, in contrast to nearly a dozen examples of δήμῳ ἔνι Τρώων (amongst them xxiv 27, 31). **ὅτι ... κατεκείρετε:** on the indirect causal sense of ὅτι ('and I say this because') see n. on 27-30, and Schwyzer, *Grammatik*, ii 646, with other examples such as v 340, xiv 367, xviii 392. κατακείρω originally referred to the scything or shearing down of corn-fields; it can be used metaphorically with βίοτον (iv 686), or, rather far-fetchedly, with μῆλα (xxiii 356), or, as here, with οἶκον (note the observance of digamma; compare κατέδω, also applied to the suitors and governing οἶκον (ii 237), κτῆσιν (xix 534), and βίοτον (six examples, one of them being the spurious xiii 396).

37-8. The majority of MSS invert the order of these two lines, probably because 37, athetized by various scholars, was originally omitted; when inserted, it seemed more logical to place the wife (38) before the maid-servants (37).

37. The arguments against the authenticity of this line (see previous note) are, leaving aside the unimportant textual variant between δέ (Allen's preference) and the papyrus's τε (daringly accepted by von der Mühll): the unparalleled παρευννάζομαι (but cf. v 119 παρ' ἀνδράσιν εὐνάζεσθαι), and the false assertion that the female slaves were forcibly violated (cf. xx 6–8, xxii 424, 445). The latter is considered by von der Mühll to be a melodramatic touch typical of B ('Odyssee', 757).

38. αὐτοῦ: emphatic, for ἐμοῦ; the gen. is on the way to being absolute, as in xiv 8, xxi 395 (see n.). **ὑπεμνάασθε:** hapax, with an underlying idea of stealth in ὑπό (Schwyzer, *Grammatik*, ii 524).

39. δείσαντες: probably governs both θεούς and the following acc. and inf. construction (thus Schwyzer, *Grammatik*, ii 357); alternatively, we may take νέμεσιν as the second object, and ἔσεσθαι as an epexegetic inf. The line-ending is paralleled in iv 378, and (with τοί) in *Il.* xx 299, xxi 267, *Od.* i 67, iv 378, 479, etc.

COMMENTARY

40. As far as I know, this is the only occasion in Homer where νέμεσις means 'vengeance' ('desire for revenge', *Il.* vi 335; 'fear of vengeance', *Il.* vi 351, xiii 122; weaker meanings in *Il.* iii 156, xiv 80; *Od.* i 350, ii 136, xx 330). For κατόπισθεν, 'in the future', see xxi 116, xxiv 546, but compare the different sense in xxii 92. Note the variants in the appendix criticus.

41. In this and other passages, Allen prints ὑμῖν whereas von der Mühll prefers the different reading ὕμιν. On the final phrase see 33 n.

42. χλωρὸν δέος: 'fear which makes one turn pale' (Greek colour-words are notoriously vague; Stanford's fanciful explanation that sallow Mediterranean complexions turn 'sickly green' when alarmed, whereas Nordic types turn chalk white and blacks turn ash grey, is therefore hardly convincing). The phrase occurs nine times in Homer (and cf. xxi 412–13 n.), always in the same metrical position − −ˢ ∪ ∪ and followed by a similar verb in various forms: αἱρεῖ (*Il.* xvii 67), ᾕρει (xi 43, 633, xii 243, 479, xxiv 450), εἷλε(ν) (here and *Il.* viii 77, *Od.* xxiv 533). Here, at xxiv 450, and at *Il.* viii 77 (which is identical to this line, and perhaps its source), the phrase is preceded by πάντας ὕπο or ὑπό (tmesis); the prefix implies something 'creeping stealthily up' on its victim (cf. 38 n. above; xvii 564 ὑποδείδια; *Il.* xx 28 and xxii 241 ὑποτρομέω; *Il.* xvii 533 ὑποταρβέω, with ὑποκλοπέομαι in 382 in a different sense; and, for the whole phrase, the many variations of the common Iliadic formula of τρόμος 'possessing' or 'stealing over' someone: with ἔχε, vi 137, x 25, xviii 247; ἕλε, xix 14, xxii 136; ὑπό ... εἷλεν, v 862; ὑπό ... ἱκάνει, xi 117; ὑπήλυθε γυῖα ('over his limbs', with double acc.), vii 215, xx 44; ὑπό ... ἔλλαβε γυῖα, iii 34; with double acc., xiv 506; without ὑπό, xxiv 170; with dat., viii 452; and also two further parallels in the *Odyssey*, xviii 88 τῷ ... ὑπὸ τρόμος ἔλλαβε (*var.* ἤλυθε) γυῖα, xxiv 49 ὑπὸ δὲ τρόμος ἔλλαβε (*var.* ἤλυθε) πάντας Ἀχαιούς).

43. As will be seen in the apparatus, this line is omitted in MSS and papyri, while one MS adds a further line (43a) taken from viii 234; it is deleted by Blass (*Interpolationen*, 205) and von der Mühll. In addition, xxii 43 = *Il.* xvi 283 and xiv 507 (immediately following a line which has already been cited as a parallel to the previous line in the preceding note); and its opening recalls *Il.* xii 333, *Il.* xvii 84, and *Od.* xxii 381. The suitors' terror is, besides, somewhat premature at this juncture (see n. on 22–5); though van der Valk considers the fact that they now look for an opening to run away, rather than for their arms as in 24, as an excellent stroke of psychological detail (*Textual Criticism*, 270). For the implications for dating of the formulaic preservation of digamma in ἕκαστος, here and in *Il.* xiv 507, xvi 283, see Hoekstra, *Modifications*, 74 n. 2. ὅπη ... φύγοι: cf. 28 n.; ὅπη introduces an indirect question, φύγοι oblique opt. equivalent to a deliberative subj.

45–59. This speech combines toadying flattery, a rapid calculation of practical cost, and the ill-natured calumny by which the dead Antinous is blamed for the greater part of the wrongs committed (but see on this point the nn. to 52–3). As such, it is typical of Eurymachus, whom Fenik defines as a dangerous hypocrite (*Studies*, 199; and see xxi 186–7 n.).

45. Ἰθακήσιος: the adj. appears, always in the same metrical position, in *Il.*

228

ii 184, in five previous books of the *Odyssey* (the closest parallel being ii 246), and in four passages in xxiv. Its use here, however, is significant: Odysseus has regained his full rights as a citizen (Bowra, *Companion*, 31). δή: 'as you say', preceding hiatus in thesis. εἰλήλουθας: with metrical lengthening, gives a σπονδειάζων ending, underlining the sense of something finally and forever consummated.

46. αἴσιμα εἶπας: cf. xxi 294 n. on αἴσιμα πίνῃ; the word occurs in the fifth foot with forms of οἶδα in ii 231, v 9, xiv 433; it is used in the context of indemnities or honours in viii 348, xiv 84 (Fr. Scholz, *LfgrE*, i 374-5). Here the adj. is predicative: 'this you have said in accordance with justice'. Note the hiatus before εἶπας. Here and here only (cf. iii 227, iv 204, xvi 243), unlike von der Mühll, Allen writes εἶπας against the general testimony in favour of εἶπες (except in papyri and some MSS at iii 227; but see the app. to xxii 46), following the precedent of εἴπατε shared by all at iii 427 (though Erotian has εἴπετε) and xxi 198 (except the MSS mentioned in the apparatus; see n.), and also the lead of Aristarchus and Eustathius, who defend εἶπας in *Il.* i 106, 108 (where Allen also accepts it): see Schwyzer, *Grammatik*, i 745. ὅσα: close to the exclamatory sense usually paraphrased as ὅτι τοιαῦτα; ῥέζεσκον, which occurs again in 209, is an iterative form of ῥέζω (cf. xviii 15), from a primitive *ϝρεγιο > *ῥαζω (Myc. *wo-zo*), with the vowel affected by analogy with cognate ἔρδω (see 218 n.).

47. Of the fourteen occurrences of ἀτάσθαλος (see H. W. Nordheider, *LfgrE*, i 1485-8) in the *Odyssey* (if we include the variant at xx 170), all except xviii 139 in ∪ −⁴ ∪ ∪, the majority (for example, xviii 143, xx 170, 370; xxii 314, where Leodes denies such actions; xxiv 282, 352) have to do with the suitors. We have been told nothing of their misdeeds in the countryside, however.

48. ὁ is demonstrative and predicative: '(behold) this man (who) already lies dead'. We have already seen ἔπλετο in this position in the line in xxi 386, 397.

49. οὗτος: emphatic and pejorative, 'this (was the fellow who)'; note the lengthening of the preceding syllable in thesis. ἐπίηλεν: strictly speaking a *hapax* (but note the forms in tmesis in ix 288, xv 475), and the only example with this metrical lengthening of the stem in ∪ −⁴ − −³ (it is short in *Il.* xv 19 ἴηλα, *Od.* viii 447 ἴηλε, *Il.* xi 628 ἐπιπροΐηλε). None of this, however, justifies excision.

50. γάμου: i.e. to Penelope; ablatival gen. χατίζων: this doublet of χατέω, found six times in Homer (amongst them ii 249, iii 48, xiii 280, xv 396), always occurs at the end of the line where the alternative verb is metrically excluded (three examples in the *Iliad*, two of them in the pres. indic., the third in the pres. part. as here; four participles in viii 156, xi 350, xxii 50, 351).

51. On the slight syntactical inconcinnity, see the n. on xxi 250-3; τά is relative, and followed by hiatus. Similar lines occur in iii 119, iv 699, xx 236 (and see the variant reading in xv 536, xxi 415 n.).

52-3. In i 384-7 Antinous treats Telemachus as a child, in an attempt to

COMMENTARY

convince him that although in theory he should succeed his father as king of Ithaca he is still too young to do so (see V. Bartoletti, 'Aristocrazia e monarchia nell'*Odissea*', *St. It. Filol. Cl.* xiii (1936), 213–65; and Eisenberger, *Studien*, 44 n. 28, who thinks there is here an ominous allusion to the conspiracy against the prince, especially in the parallel between 53 and iv 670, and that both this passage and that in i are the handiwork of the late poet, who wanted to dovetail them with the *Telemachy*; cf. also Erbse, *Beiträge*, 125–6). In i 389–98 Telemachus replied by pointing out the political ambitions of various suitors (βασιλῆες Ἀχαιῶν εἰσὶ καὶ ἄλλοι | πολλοὶ ἐν ἀμφιάλῳ Ἰθάκῃ, 394–5); in i 400–4, Eurymachus diplomatically left unanswered the question touched upon in these lines, which Bergk wished to suppress (see 53 n.).

52. The line-ending is more or less in apposition to ἄλλα; compare *Il.* v 564 φρονέων, ἵνα; *Il.* x 491 φρονέων . . . ὅπως; and, to an extent, *Od.* xxiii 117 φραζώμεθ', ὅπως and even *Il.* iv 465 λελιημένος ὄφρα.

53. αὐτός: 'himself, on his own', emphatic (this is a grave problem, for the many editors who would delete the line as a late interpolation on the grounds stated in the note on 52–3; see also Focke, *Odyssee*, 359), since the suitors have already appeared as βασιλῆες in the plural not only in i 394 but also, for example, in viii 41 and, referring to Eurymachus and Antinous, in xviii 64. The second half of the line, with a second oblique optat. after ὄφρα, is a kind of ὕστερον πρότερον common in Homer (Pocock, *Odyssean Essays*, 124).

54–5. The two balanced phrases are not of equal emphasis: '(since) he is dead, (therefore) spare these people as your own' (note the strong predicative force of σῶν; cf. Eisenberger, *Studien*, 52).

54. νῦν δ': normally follows an unfulfilled conditional, which reflects the unreality of Antinous' suggestion. ἐν μοίρῃ: 'according to his just desserts ordained by destiny' (cf. *Il.* xix 186 'justly'; contrast κατὰ μοῖραν in *Od.* xxi 278 and n., xxii 486). πέφαται: the well-known perfect, from the same root as θείνω, ἔπεφνον, and φόνος, which (besides πέφανται, πεφάσθαι, πεφήσεται, and πεφήσεαι in *Il.* xiii 829, *Od.* xxii 217) occurs here and four times in the *Iliad*, in *Il.* xvii 164 at the same place in the line. Except for πέφνῃ in *Od.* xi 135, the verb is always applied to violent deaths.

55. ὄπισθεν: 'later, in the future', compare κατόπισθεν in 40. ἀρεσσάμενοι: the aorists and futures collected by H. Neitzel, *LfgrE*, i 1227–8 s.v. ἀρέσαι are related to ἀραρίσκω, ἀρετή, etc., and share the root-meaning 'order, fit, fix', hence 'compensate' (a crime), or 'conciliate, give satisfaction' (the injured party) by offering compensation. Of the nine other occurrences in Homer, five take acc. of the person satisfied (viii 396, 402, 415, all referring to the compensation received by Odysseus from Euryalus; *Il.* ix 112 ἀρεσσάμενοι in the same position as here, *Il.* xix 179), and four acc. of the thing compensated (the pair *Il.* ix 120 = xix 138 ἀρέσαι, and similar *Il.* iv 362, vi 526 ἀρεσσόμεθα with ὄπισθεν). Here the sense has been much debated: what Eurymachus seems to be offering is first a collective compensation for the victuals consumed, and second a collective fine or

230

indemnity for the insult committed. There are various parallel passages in the *Odyssey*: ii 77-8 (Telemachus would go κατὰ ἄστυ demanding compensation for the food which has been eaten at his expense), xiii 14-15 (on making a gift to Odysseus, Alcinous explains that he will seek compensation for his expense—τισόμεθα—by a public collection, ἀγειρόμενοι κατὰ δῆμον, at the end of the line), xix 197-8 (the 'beggar' tells how he served Odysseus δημόθεν ἄλφιτα δῶκα καὶ αἴθοπα οἶνον ἀγείρας | καὶ βοῦς), xxiii 356-8 (the victorious hero will seize cattle in compensation for the beasts stolen from him, and the Achaeans will give him others εἰς ὅ κε πάντας ἐνιπλήσωσιν ἐπαύλους). In view of the syntactical problems in the passage, it is not surprising that some have proposed reading ἀγειράμενοι.

56. ὅσσα: of the four parallels of ἀρέσαι with acc. of 'thing compensated' just cited from the *Iliad*, two have direct objects expressed by ταῦτα (*Il.* iv 362) and τά (vi 526) meaning 'this (complaint)', and the other two have some such complement understood. Here the verb must be understood not as 'having settled (the complaint)', but as 'having replaced (in settlement of the complaint)', governing unexpressed τοσαῦτα before ὅσσα. τοι, dative of disadvantage, is followed by two verbs, both of which must be understood as sharing the force of the perfective ἐκ- prefixed to the first (see Schwyzer, *Grammatik*, ii 237, on the development of the passive sense 'it has been drunk up and eaten' from this type of expression, 'it is all drunk up and eaten'). **ἐδήδοται:** poses a problem which is not merely textual; the MSS reading is corrected by Aristarchus and others, unintelligibly, to ἐδήδαται, apparently plural (impossible according to Schwyzer, *Grammatik*, i 766 n. 5); Herodian prefers ἐδήδεται, which von der Mühll does not reject, with parallels later in Aristotle's ἀπεδήδεμαι, and which later either acquired (cf. Schwyzer, *Grammatik*, i 775) an intrusive -σ- (κατεδήδεσμαι, Plato) by analogy with hypothetical forms such as *ἔσθηναι and *ἔστεος, or became assimilated by rhyme to ἐκπέποται (cf. ἐδηδώς, *Il.* xvii 542), whence came Aristophanes' ἐδήδοκα.

57-9. The main verb is ἀποδώσομεν (ἀπο- carries the idea of expiation), with two participles, ἄγοντες being modal (it is wrong, therefore, to punctuate after 57) and ἀρεσσάμενοι temporal. **ἀμφὶς ... ἕκαστος:** 'each on his own account, in turn', with the common *ad sensum* singular for plural; cf. xix 46 'each thing in its turn' (where Bekker's proposal to restore the hiatus before digamma by reading ἀμφὶ ἔκαστα is inadmissible; in answer to Fick's condemnation of this line because of the lack of the necessary hiatus, Bekker likewise restores it, reading neut. pl. ἐεικοσάβοια, a form paralleled in i 431). **τιμὴν ... ἐεικοσάβοιον:** probably predicative in apposition to the nouns χαλκόν τε χρυσόν τ'. In τιμή the concrete sense of 'compensation for a misdeed' takes first place over that of 'honour, (act of) respect' (cf. xiv 70 and 117, 'the compensation owed to Agamemnon', and *Il.* iii 286, 288, where the Trojans ought to return Helen and the treasures stolen with her and then τιμήν ... ἀποτινέμεν ἥν τιν' ἔοικεν, followed by τιμήν ... τίνειν and ποινῆς). Each suitor must contribute gold and bronze to the value of twenty oxen; various editors give pecuniary—the term is

COMMENTARY

particularly appropriate—equivalents, such as four oxen for a skilled female slave (*Il.* xxiii 705), nine for a suit of armour (*Il.* vi 236), twelve for a large tripod (*Il.* xxiii 703), twenty for Eurycleia (*Od.* i 431, and see above), and one hundred for a male prisoner (*Il.* xxi 79). The following phrase cannot, therefore, be an invitation for Odysseus to fix the price of the compensation; although εἰς ὅ is temporal, 'until', it must be taken here as meaning that the hero will indeed be satisfied by the deal proposed, but that meanwhile, until the money is paid (πρίν is adverbial), his anger is not blameworthy (νεμεσσητός is found only here and at xxii 489 in the *Odyssey*; the end of the line comes from *Il.* ix 523, on the wrath of Achilles; see Lorimer, *Monuments*, 484; similar is *Od.* xviii 227, where Telemachus speaks to Penelope). **ἰανθῇ:** the long initial vowel is probably due to the augment; cf. the examples in *Il.* xv 103, xxiii 598; *Od.* x 359, and Hoekstra, *Modifications*, 122 n. 1, and the corresponding lengthening of the initial vowel in ἀείδῃ, xvii 519.

60. Cf. 34 nn.

61–3. ἀποδοῖτε picks up ἀποδώσομεν in 58, concessive optative. The construction οὐδ᾽ εἰ . . . οὐδέ . . . ὥς (cf. xxi 246 n.) occurs, for example, in Achilles' similar rejection of Agamemnon's offer in *Il.* ix 379–86; there, the following lines (388–91) continue with expressions of contempt for the proposals related by Odysseus, apparently balancing a negative in οὐ with οὐδ᾽ εἰ and then with οὐδέ . . . ὥς; likewise in *Il.* xxii 348–52 Achilles rejects Priam's offer with οὐκ . . . οὐδ᾽ εἰ . . . οὐδ᾽ ὥς; a simpler case is *Il.* viii 482–3 οὐδ᾽ ἤν . . . οὐ; also οὐ . . . οὐδ᾽ εἰ 'not . . . even if' (i 203–4, xiv 138–40). In iii 113–16 οὐδ᾽ εἰ implies a negative main clause in reply to a rhetorical question (see the n. on 12–14). The construction runs: 'not even if you were to pay me all your father's wealth which you now have as your inheritance (τόσσα understood before ὅσσα, with possessive dat.), nor even if you were to add more (ἄλλα) from elsewhere'; cf. *Il.* ix 379–80 'not even if he offered me twentyfold his present wealth (τόσα . . . ὅσσα τέ οἱ νῦν ἐστι), nor even if his offer were to be raised somehow (καὶ εἰ πόθεν ἄλλα γένοιτο)'. Alternatively, we might translate: 'all that you have and other goods too, if you were to add them'.

63. οὐδέ κεν ὥς: after countless examples of ὥς 'thus' in xxi and xxii, and with many more to come, usually in initial position and apparently derived from *só (alternating with τώς five times in Homer, amongst them *Od.* xviii 271, xix 234), it is a surprise to find this appearance in xxii (but see already xxi 246) of οὐδέ . . . ὥς 'even so . . . not', found eleven times in the *Odyssey* and parallel to καὶ ὥς 'even so', found eight times. Von der Mühll accentuates both with the circumflex, following Herodian (see Schwyzer, *Grammatik*, ii 577); Allen does the same in his edition of the *Iliad*, but regularizes the accent with an acute in his *Odyssey*. ἔτι: 'now, at this stage of the game'. λήξαιμι: the syntax of λήγω has been found difficult; normally it takes the part. (*Il.* ix 191, xxi 224) or gen. (ἔριδος, *Il.* i 210, 319, ix 257, xxi 359; φόνοιο in *Il.* vi 107). Here we must translate: 'make my hands cease from slaughter' (cf. *Il.* xiii 424, xxi 305, with acc. μένος).

232

64. This phrase, an exact parallel of xiii 193 and xxii 168, is often cited as the origin of the construction of πρίν with inf. (Schwyzer, *Grammatik*, ii 654). In *Il.* xxii 354 the clause introduced by 'even so . . . not' is followed by 'but on the contrary'; in *Od.* iii 117 'who . . . would tell?' and the unspoken answer '(nobody), even if' is followed by adv. πρίν 'before that happens . . .; before, unless so many years pass'. Here the inf. is probably imperative in sense: 'before that, rather than that, let them pay . . .'; somewhat similar is *Il.* ix 387, with ἀπό . . . δόμεναι 'rather let him give back', or *Il.* xix 423, with λήξω, 'I shall not cease; rather let me sate . . . (ἄδην ἐλάσαι)'. But at *Od.* xvii 597 we already find πρίν with inf. after an affirmative clause. πᾶσαν: almost adv., 'completely'. ἀποτῖσαι: the subj. is μνηστῆρας, the direct obj. ὑπερβασίην. The verb appears twenty-seven times in Homer, sixteen of them in the *Odyssey*; the pres. ἀποτίνω is only found in ii 132, xxii 235, the aorist here and in five other passages (i 43, iii 195, xiii 193, xxii 168, and xxiii 312).

65. ὑμῖν: cf. 41. παράκειται ἐναντίον: παράκειται is synonymous with the παρίσταται quoted at the end of n. on 28; ἐναντίον, adv. 'face to face', with the same military sense as ἄντην in *Il.* xxii 109, found several times in the *Iliad* (iii 433, ix 559, xv 304, etc.).

66. φεύγειν: both 'flee' and 'escape', the latter being the one which connects with the succeeding relative clause, which requires us to supply a τοῦτον as subj. of the inf. θάνατον καὶ κῆρας ἀλύξῃ = *Il.* xxi 565 (with ἀλύξαι); κήρ in the sing. is found at 14 (see n.), and again in 330, 363, 382; the plur. does not occur again until xxiii 332, once again in a line ending with ἄλυξεν. The pres. part. ἀλύσκων precedes κῆρα μέλαιναν in 363, 382 (cf. xxiv 127); trisyllabic parts of the same verb are common at the end of the line (e.g. ἀλύξαι in xxii 460, without a complement; Χάρυβδιν | Σκύλλην θ' . . . ἄλυξαν, xxiii 328, κακὰς ὑπὸ κῆρας ἄλυξεν, xxiii 332).

67. φεύξεσθαι: the sense of the future again implies 'escape' rather than 'flee'. αἰπὺν ὄλεθρον: cf. 28, 43. The sense of τινα in the negative clause is ominous and ironic (cf. xxi 374 and n., xiii 394, 427); 'I do not believe any will escape' is equivalent to 'I believe none will escape', a semantic shift similar to οὐκ ἔφη 'he said no', or *Od.* xvi 446 οὐδέ . . . ἄνωγα 'and I do not exhort you to fear' > 'and I exhort you not to fear'; xii 227 οὐ . . . ἀνώγει 'she did not advise me to arm myself' > 'she advised me not to arm myself'.

68. αὐτοῦ: adv., as in 4 (see n.), but here emphasizing less the place than the time, 'then and there, immediately', referring to the sudden slackening of the limbs and courage in shock. The same line-ending is applied to the description of these symptoms in Odysseus himself in v 297, 406, xxii 147; the same line, with the substitution of τῆς or τοῦ, based on for example *Il.* xxi 114, appears in *Od.* iv 703, xxiii 205, xxiv 345; cf. also xviii 212 λύτο γούνατα, xviii 238 λελύτο γυῖα, and, with the possess. φίλος also used here, xviii 242 φίλα γυῖα λέλυνται.

COMMENTARY

69. δεύτερον αὖτις: pleonastic, based on *Il.* i 513, and found also in iii 161, ix 354, xix 65; cf. xiv 356 πάλιν αὖτις, xviii 157 ἄψ . . . αὖτις, etc.

70–8. Eurymachus accepts the situation with style, and rapidly thinks up a makeshift strategy.

70. γὰρ: we must either supply some unspoken antecedent such as '(and I speak in this tone) because' (cf. for example xxiii 248), or take the clause introduced by γάρ as a causal anticipating the main clause with μνησώμεθα. The line is almost identical to 248, where Agelaus expresses his pious hopes of defeating Odysseus.   **ἀνὴρ ὅδε:** represents a last and childishly half-hearted attempt (compare the εἰ of 45) to deny the evidence of the hero's identity.   **σχήσει:** against straightforward ἕξει 'he will hold, keep', σχήσω (see Chantraine, *Grammaire*, ii 203–4) carries the nuances 'uphold' (*Il.* xiv 100), 'hold in, contain' (*Od.* xxii 172), 'hold back, stay, restrain' (an enemy, *Il.* xi 80, xiii 151; a ship, by grappling, *Od.* xi 70; one's own hands, here and in 248).   **ἀάπτους:** the epithet, found several times in the *Iliad*, is always applied to hands and, with only one exception, always at the end of the line (H. Erbse and S. Laser, *LfgrE*, i 3–4); there are three further examples in the *Odyssey* (xi 502, Achilles, of his own hands; xx 237, in the variant reading, of Odysseus; and xxii 248, also of the protagonist). There was already disagreement about the correct spelling in antiquity: Zenodotus and Aristarchus wrote ἀάπτους, but Aristophanes of Byzantium preferred, perhaps correctly, ἀέπτους (cf. Hsch. ἄεπτον· ἰσχυρόν, ἄθικτον, a conjecture for ἀοίκητον, which Latte however retains). The same word seems to lie behind the corruptions in A. *Ag.* 141 (where, however, the meaning 'which cannot follow' is acceptable, speaking of a whelp) and *Supp.* 908 ἄεπτα . . . πάσχομεν, spoken by the Danaids. The primitive form is probably related to εἰπεῖν, or ἕπεσθαι, 'hands (so large) that cannot be described, or which a description cannot follow'; original ἄεπτος will have contracted to *ἅπτος with subsequent diectasis to ἄαπτος, on the analogy of frequent formulas such as χειρὸς ἅπτεσθαι, which would then have been understood as 'untouchable, unapproachable'. The same problem attends the hapax ἀπτοεπές in *Il.* viii 209 (see E.-M. Voigt, *LfgrE*, i 1117–18), where ἀπτο- was probably originally *ἀεπτο- (Poseidon tells Hera that her words have been 'indescribable, unheard of').

71. ἐπεί: a cross between temporal ('now that') and causal ('since'); the word expresses Eurymachus' rueful realization that he and the others have been responsible for allowing what they ought to have prevented all through xxi. The form ἔλλαβε is found not only in the two passages cited in the note on 42, but also in i 298 and xviii 394; the gemination of the λ is a scribal graph designed to indicate the lengthening of the vowel before -λ- reduced from -σλ-.   **ἐΰξοον:** cf. xxi 92n., 281, 286, 326, 336.

72. ἄπο: ἐπὶ of many MSS is a dittography of ἐπεί in 71. The line-ending is almost the same as that of such lines as *Il.* xxi 133. The future is clearly prospective, of something which is inevitable (cf. 28n.).

73. χάρμη: the only occurrence in the *Odyssey*; the word, which is probably related to χαίρω ('joy of battle'), frequently occurs in the *Iliad* at line-end in the gen. after some part of the verb μιμνήσκομαι or cognate words (μνησώμεθα χάρμης itself in *Il.* xv 477, xix 148).

74. Asyndeton, with a strong link between the previous exhortation and this detailed explanation of the strategy proposed (see the Introduction to xxi and note on 70–8; on the swords, see also xxii 22–5 n.). **φάσγανα:** the first occurrence in this or the preceding book of this word (Myc. *pa-ka-na*), which reappears in 79, 84, 90, 98, and then disappears once again, replaced by ξίφος in 326 (the word already used in xxi 34, 119, 341, 431 n.). **ἀντίσχεσθε:** this prefixed verb is unique in Homer, transitive in meaning and implying action taken by the subject for his own safety, governing as a gen. after the ἀντι- element ('place the tables in front of, opposite'). On the individual τραπέζας see 19 n.; from this passage it would appear that they were light and easily handled (S. Laser, *Archaeologia* P, 58; but cf. 84–8 n.).

75. **ὠκυμόρων:** the usual meaning is 'destined to die soon' (of Achilles in *Il.* i 417, xviii 95, 458; of the suitors in *Od.* i 266, iv 346, xvii 137), but here and in *Il.* xv 441 the epithet is applied to duels, with the sense 'which brings sudden death'. **ἐπὶ ... ἔχωμεν:** tmesis (cf. 15 n.).

76. **εἴ κε:** 'in case, in the event that', and aor. subj. with shortened thematic vowel.

77. Behind ἀνά (with the usual hiatus before the digamma of ἄστυ) lies the idea that the suitors will disperse once out of the place. The three subjunctives are not precisely parallel, since one would expect rather 'in the event that we get out and, once dispersed, raise the hue and cry'. **γένοιτο:** for the optative offered by the MSS and accepted by Allen here (though not by von der Mühll), cf. the optat. in 133; the mood would indicate less hopefulness on Eurymachus' part, but there is another possible interpretation, volitive ἔλθωμεν (Schwyzer, *Grammatik*, ii 315) and condit. γένοιτο without ἄν. Eisenberg sees evidence in this passage for the existence of a faction in the city favourable to the suitors (*Studien*, 308 n. 15; cf. xxiv 412–37).

78. =134. **τῷ:** cf. xxi 374 n. **τάχ':** 'soon' (the meaning 'perhaps' is in general later), as in xxi 174, 363, 369, 374 n., 418; here it affects the meaning of ὕστατα τοξάσσαιτο, 'would stop shooting'. **οὗτος ἀνήρ:** here with the usual contemptuous or pejorative undertone (cf. 70 and n.).

79–80. **εἰρύσσατο:** see 372 n. **φάσγανον:** the φάσγανα are for the moment the only arms available to the suitors. 79 = *Il.* xxii 306; the line-ending, with the epithet ὀξύ, is found in *Od.* x 145, xi 95, and reappears below in 90. The sword is made of bronze, as usual in Homer. **ἀμφο-τέρωθεν ἀκαχμένον:** the interpretation of ἀκαχμένος, a participle probably derived from *ἀκ-ακ-σ-μενος (see Frisk, *GEW*, and E.-M. Voigt, *LfgrE*, i 407), is unclear, though its etymological connection with words of sharpening or whetting is clear; in many passages (i 99, xv 551, xx 127), where it is applied to a spear it seems to mean 'fitted with a tip of bronze', ἀκαχμένος ὀξέϊ χαλκῷ (cf. 122–5 n.), but here and in v 235, where it refers to an axe with the same first hemistich, the interpretation 'two-edged' is

COMMENTARY

preferable (cf. ἄμφηκες of a ξίφος in *Il.* xxi 118, *Od.* xvi 80, xxi 341 n.; and of a φάσγανον in *Il.* x 256). Lehrs' deletion is worth a glance (Blass, *Interpolationen*, 205): it is odd that Eurymachus leaps up to attack (on ἄλτο see xxi 388, xxii 2), after having himself just suggested taking shelter behind the tables. This is doubtless the difficulty which prompted the variant versions of the end of 80, ἐπταβόειον (five occurrences in the *Iliad*: see 57–9 n.) and ὀξέϊ χαλκῷ (out of place here, but suggested by the formula quoted above). The received text can be defended by adducing the Iliadic examples of σμερδαλέα ἰάχων [(see next note), which always portray the warrior in the act of hurling himself into the attack.

81. **σμερδαλέα ἰάχων**: the only occurrence of this participle in the *Odyssey*, which is here used to lend a certain valour to Eurymachus' last moments; it occurs in this form eleven times in the *Iliad*, usually preceded by hiatus and a vowel lengthened in thesis (e.g. *Il.* xvii 213, xviii 160) and most commonly of all, in seven cases, after σμερδαλέα in the first foot. We also find σμερδαλέα κτυπέων at the beginning of the line in *Il.* vii 479, which may have been the original pattern for this metrical oddity; σμερδαλέον is found eleven times at the beginning of the line in the *Iliad* and six in the *Odyssey* (e.g. *Od.* xxiv 537) with verbs similar in meaning to ἰάχω. But the digamma in this verb, theoretically from *ϝι-ϝαχ-ω (see the apparatus for a quibble on the accentuation; but ἰαχῶ is not found before the *h.Hom.* and later), is obscure: examples such as μεγάλ' ἴαχε in ∪∪–⁴∪∪ (*Il.* i 482 etc.) or the compound ἐπίαχον in ∪–⁴∪∪ (*Il.* v 860 etc.) argue against it (Chantraine, *Grammaire*, i 139–40) despite the hiatus here; on the other hand, we find ἄϊεν ἰάχοντος in ∪∪–²∪∪–³∪ (*Il.* xi 463), where the digamma causes lengthening of -εν, which leads one to wonder whether σμερδαλέον ought not always to be replaced by σμερδαλέα (nevertheless, we would still be left with examples such as *Il.* xvii 213 μέγα ἰάχων in ∪–²∪∪–³); the hapax αὐίαχος in *Il.* xiii 41 might be explained as a formation with intensive ἀ- (M. Schmidt, *LfgrE*, i 1458). **ὁ δ' ἁμαρτῇ δῖος Ὀδυσσεύς**: the demonstr. ὁ is brought forward to the start of the sentence, as usual; ἁμαρτῇ (von der Mühll ἁμαρτή), adv. 'simultaneously' (see xxi 188 n.).

82. The well-attested variant ἀποπροϊείς (cf. *Il.* xvi 669 ἀποπρό 'far away') induced van Leeuwen's conjecture with double acc., which provides a remedy for the lack of augment and of an object pronoun referring to Eurymachus. The line-ending occurs elsewhere, for example in *Il.* iv 480.

83. **θοὸν βέλος** is unparalleled (cf. 3 n.).   **ἄρα**: 'consequently'. The line-ending =*Il.* xi 239.

84. The subj. of ἧκε, from ἵημι, is Eurymachus; ἧκε χαμᾶζε is a formula (cf. 20 n.) not used at the end of the line (cf. xvi 191), where we find instead θῆκε or κατέθηκε χαμᾶζε (xxi 136, xxii 340), ἀποπροέηκε χ. (xxii 327); the lative adv. χαμᾶζε, which should be thus accented in Homeric texts (χαμᾶζε is peculiar to Attic: see von der Mühll ad loc.), cannot be derived from a non-existent plural as in the case of Ἀθήναζε etc., but is probably formed by analogy with it and other words and also ἔραζε (Schwyzer, *Grammatik*, i 625, nn. 2 and 20).   **περιρρηδής**: *hapax* of unknown meaning and

236

etymology, formed like adjectives such as περικαλλής < κάλλος but without a corresponding neuter noun *ρῆδος with which to connect it. If it is correct to relate it to words such as ῥαδινός 'pliable' (applied to a whip in Il. xxiii 583), βράδινος 'soft' (in Sappho, indicating the presence of digamma to explain the -ρρ-), ῥοδανός 'bending, swaying' (with variant readings such as ῥαδαλός, of a reedbed in Il. xviii 576), βραδανίζει (glossed by Hesych. ῥιπίζει, τινάσσει; note the initial βρ- again), we might translate 'crumpled up, limp' (Eustathius gives as synonym ἀμφιρρηδής). The word's occurrence in this passage may well have influenced Hippocrates, who sometimes uses it with στῆθος (Leumann, Wörter, 314–15; Frisk, GEW, is doubtful of the suggestion), and also the adv. περιρρηδην 'bending down' (Apoll. iv 1581; note Hesychius' enigmatic gloss ῥαδές· τὸ ἀμφοτέρως ἐγκεκλιμένον).

84-8. The hero is on his feet when he is hit by the arrow; he drops his sword and falls forward, but without knocking his table over (which must therefore be a sturdy piece of furniture: S. Laser, Archaeologia P, 40, and see the note on 74), though he does tip everything on the table onto the floor. There he lies bent double, head on the ground (the table must be low) and feet kicking the still-standing chair in his death-agony, a pathetic and spectacular sight. The end of 85 repeats that of 20; on the beginning of 86 see the n. on 10. Van Herwerden needlessly removes the punctuation after ἀμφικύπελλον and replaces ὁ δέ by ἠδέ, thereby eliminating the necessary demonstrative ('as for him ...'). Bérard also changes ὁ δέ to ἰδέ.

85. κάππεσεν: from καταπίπτω. ἰδνωθείς: the verb appears three times in the Iliad (ii 266 ἰδνώθη, of Thersites cowering down under a blow; xiii 618, Pisander doubles up as he falls; xii 205 ἰδνωθείς, of a serpent coiling ready to strike an eagle which is carrying it off, but there bending ὀπίσω, 'backwards', in the opposite sense to this passage; cf. the n. on ἑτέρωσε in 17), and in one other passage of the Odyssey (viii 375 ἰδνωθείς ὀπίσω, of a ball-player bending over backwards to make a catch). Amongst the variants recorded in the apparatus note δινηθείς, which, as van der Valk reminds us (Textual Criticism, 48), was Aristarchus' reading.

87. θυμῷ ἀνιάζων: the expression appears also in Il. xxi 270, with shortening of -ῳ in hiatus and long -ῐ- (as in ἀνίη, and in eleven of the fourteen occurrences of ἀνιάζω in Homer, the exceptions being Il. xviii 300, xxiii 721, Od. iv 460), meaning 'in the throes of death'.

88. λακτίζων ἐτίνασσε: λακτίζω, normally reserved like the cognate adv. λάξ for heroic gestures such as planting one's foot on a dead foe's corpse, either to pull the spear from it (Il. v 620, vi 65, xvi 503, 863) or as a sign of triumph (Il. xiii 618), undergoes a process of vulgarization, first of rousing a sleeping man with one's foot (Il. x 158, and thence Od. xv 45), and then of Melanthius kicking Odysseus (Od. xvii 233), and finally of the vanquished Irus' clownish gestures (Od. xviii 99). ἐτίνασσε, imperf. to underscore the long-drawn and painful nature of the death. The end of the line has many parallels, not all of the dark night of death, as here and in Il. v 696, xvi 344; in Il. xx 421 ἀχλύς refers to Hector's swoon at the sight of Patroclus' death,

in *Od.* xx 357 to a rising mist seen by the prophet Theoclymenus, and in five further cases (*Il.* v 127, xv 668, xx 321, 341, *Od.* vii 41) to supernatural mists called up or dissolved by the gods.

89. ἐείσατο: see 6–7 n. for another example of this supposed cognate of εἰμί, which is better understood as a derivation from *ϝίεμαι 'rush, launch oneself', which later became confused with the middle of ἵημι (Frisk, *GEW*). Besides the various examples of εἴσατο we find ἐεισάσθην (once, at *Il.* xv 544) and compounds with ἐπι-, κατα-, and μετα- (amongst them, ἐπιείσομαι with acc., *Il.* xi 367, xx 454); examples governing the usual gen. of 'object aimed at' occur in *Il.* xv 415 (with the same line-ending), *Il.* iv 138, xiii 191. Nevertheless, it is debatable whether Ὀδυσῆος depends directly on the verb (for a parallel construction, cf. *Il.* xiv 488 ὡρμήθη δ' Ἀκάμαντος) or on the following ἀντίος (cf. *Il.* xv 415 Ἕκτωρ ... ἀντ' Αἴαντος ἐείσατο κυδαλίμοιο).

90. ἀντίος ἀΐξας: a common initial formula (cf. *Il.* xv 694; with ἀΐσσουσι, *Il.* xi 553, xvii 662), but this construction with a verb of motion governing a gen. of the person approached or encountered, whether in friendly or hostile manner, occurs elsewhere only in *Od.* xvi 14 ἀντίος ἦλθεν ἄνακτος, where the approach is respectful (E.-M. Voigt, *LfgrE*, i 944–9).

91. εἴ πως: see n. on εἴ κε in 76. **εἴξειε:** the verb εἴκω, originally with digamma (itacistic γίξαι· χωρῆσαι in Hsch.) on its own means 'give way' (*Il.* xxii 321 εἴξειε; for the opt. here see 77 n.); 'give up (one's place)' (*Od.* ii 14). With the dat. it means 'yield to, be less strong than' (xiv 221 εἴξειε); 'give way' to one's own θυμός (v 126), to a worthy impulse such as shame (*Il.* x 238) or an unworthy one such as fear (*Il.* xiii 225), overbearing violence (*Od.* xiii 143, xviii 139 βίῃ καὶ κάρτεϊ), or imprudence (xxii 288 ἀφραδίῃς; in *Il.* x 122 the indulgent Agamemnon describes his brother Menelaus as οὔτ' ὄκνῳ εἴκων οὔτ' ἀφραδίῃσι νόοιο, cf. Hes. *Op.* 330); 'give in' to a circumstance such as poverty (xiv 157), or to a person (*Il.* xiii 321 εἴξειε, *Od.* xi 515, where the verb also governs an abl. of place from which one retreats, from battle in *Il.* v 348, from the πρόθυρον in *Od.* xviii 10). **φθῆ:** this verb is usually accompanied by a participle which completes the sense (xi 58, xvi 383, xxiv 437); it can also govern the acc. of the person anticipated (*Il.* xi 451, xxi 262), so that here μιν (Amphinomus) is governed both by φθῆ and by βαλών. **ἄρα:** 'as expected', expressing the active loyalty of Telemachus.

92. Telemachus is no longer standing by his father as at xxi 433, but is more or less in his original seat (see xxi 141 n.). Now, after hesitating for a moment whether or not to retrieve the valuable spear from Amphinomus' dead body, he chooses the better part of valour and returns to Odysseus' side (ἀπόρουσε, 95; εἰσαφίκανεν, 99). It is the shortage of arms which leads to his suggestion in 101 ff.

93. = *Il.* v 41, 57, viii 259, xi 448. The line-ending is also paralleled in *Il.* xxii 284. ἔλασσε has the spear as its unexpressed direct object. On διά with a word formed with -φιν see Schwyzer, *Grammatik*, ii 172.

94. The first hemistich occurs again in xxiv 525; it is a common Iliadic formula, usually followed by ἀράβησε δὲ τεύχε' ἐπ' αὐτῷ (*Il.* iv 504, v 42, 540, 617, etc.); here the second hemistich is identical to that of 296, and similar to that of 86. ἤλασε: the striking image of the crash as a stricken warrior falls to the ground (ἐλαύνω, 'strike, thrash') better fits contexts where the fighters are in heavy battle-armour (xxiv 525, and the Iliadic passages) than here, where the combatants are unarmed.

95. ἀπόρουσε: ingressive, 'began to run', a frequent sense in the *Iliad* (v 20, 297, etc.). δολιχόσκιον: this epithet for a spear, which occurs a further four times in the *Odyssey* (xix 438, xxii 97, xxiv 519, 522), has been much discussed: 'long-shadowing' strikes some as too far-fetched a notion for archaic ways of thought; but 'with long beechwood shaft', which postulates an etymological link with later ὀξύη 'beech' (cf. μελίη 'ash' 'spear' in Homer; ὀξύη, 'spear' in Archilochus, fr. 229w; ὀξυόεις 'beechen (spear)' twice in *Od.*, nine times in *Il.*), would require a most improbable metathesis and other highly dubious special pleading (Frisk, *GEW*, s.v. σκιά, ὀξύα).

96-8. αὐτοῦ: 'there' (see 4n.). περί ... δίε: 'he was greatly afraid', followed by μή as in *Il.* xvii 666 (cf. *Il.* v 566, ix 433, xi 557, with dat.). Ἀχαιῶν: partitive gen., in final position as in *Il.* xii 390, xxiv 650. The syntax is confused, which has provoked editorial meddling. The best solution seems to be to accept Doederlein's conjecture τύψαι (oblique opt., like ἐλάσειε; if τύψας is retained, it must be by attraction from ἀΐξας): '... lest one of the Achaeans should leap on him while he (Telemachus) was pulling the spear (from Amphinomus' body) and transfix him with a thrust of the sword (on φασγάνῳ ἀΐξας see 90n., and *Il.* v 81, x 456) or slash him with a downward cut while he (Telemachus) was stooping down (προπρηνέα, wrestling with the stuck spear)'. This skirts the unintelligible, though genuinely Alexandrian (van der Valk, *Textual Criticism*, 48), variant προπρηνέϊ; as for the lack of a direct object for ἐλάσειε, there is no need to suppose the usual loss of an original ϝ in ἤ(ϝ') ἐλάσειε. However, the difference between τύπτω and ἐλαύνω is not clear-cut, nor are they restricted in use to sword or spear respectively; we find, for example, ἐρύσσατο ... ξίφος ... | τῷ ... τύψε (*Il.* iv 530-1) besides ξίφει ἤλασε (*Il.* v 584), and δουρὶ τυπείς (*Il.* xi 191) besides ἤλασεν ... ἔγχος (*Il.* xx 259). For cutting v. thrusting see J. Bérard's discussion of the passage.

99. βῆ δὲ θέειν: ingressive aor. with consecutive-final inf., 'he started to run', a very common construction (ii 298, xxii 109 βῆ ... ἴμεναι; iii 176 ὦρτο ... οὖρος ἀήμεναι; iv 260, etc., τέτραπτο νέεσθαι); the phrase occurs seven times in the *Iliad*, and once more in *Od.* (xiv 501). The variant θέων is inadmissible; this participle is never used in conjunction with βῆ, although it occurs seven times (including *Od.* iii 288, viii 193, xxii 106) in the same position in the line. φίλον: possessive (see 68n.). εἰσαφίκανεν: on the formation of this word, which occurs also in 112 and in *Il.* xiv 230 (with the island Λῆμνον as complement of the εἰσ-: see xxi 308n.) see Schwyzer, *Grammatik*, ii 429.

100. = *Il.* iv 203, xiii 462, xiv 356, xvi 537, *Od.* iv 25, xvii 552; a heavily

formulaic line. Initial ἀγχοῦ is frequent (vi 5, xvii 526, xix 271); so too is initial ἀ. δ' ἱστάμενος (*Il.* xiii 768, xv 243, xvii 684) or ἱσταμένη (for example, *Od.* v 159, xv 9); the whole line is found in the feminine (for example, at *Il.* iv 92, v 123), or in the masc. but with ἀγόρευε at the end of the line (*Od.* xvii 349). The formulaic ἔπεα πτερόεντα προσηύδα (which causes lengthening of the usual preceding participle in -ος due to digamma) is immensely common: there are six occurrences in this book alone, all except one (150) preceded by a participle. Neither ἀγχοῦ . . . ἱστάμενος nor προσηύδα contains any reference to the person approached or spoken to, Odysseus.

101-25. In xvi 281–98 (a passage athetized by Zenodotus and Aristarchus), Odysseus, though he had not yet stepped inside the palace and was ignorant of the state of play within, told Telemachus to collect the arms from the hall at a signal, and carry them to a store-room (285 ἐς μυχὸν ὑψηλοῦ θαλάμου); if the suitors missed them, Telemachus was to tell them that he had removed the weapons to prevent them getting sooty or being used in some squabble. He was to leave in the *megaron* two φάσγανα, two δοῦρε, and δοιὰ βόαγρια, 'oxhide shields', νῶϊν . . . οἷοισιν (295–6; note the dual—there is no talk here of the servants). In xix 1–52, a passage likewise much athetized in antiquity (von der Mühll: 'ab ult. Odyss. poeta inserti esse vid.'), Odysseus, by now inside the palace, repeated the order to his son (xix 5–13 = xvi 286–94), and the two of them, lighted on their way by Athena's strange lamp amidst supernatural visions—all this typical of the *B* poet—carry a number of κόρυθάς τε καὶ ἀσπίδας ὀμφαλοέσσας | ἔγχεά τ' ὀξυόεντα to the θάλαμον (17), without so much as a word about any reserve of weapons left in the *megaron*; and in xxii 25 we are specifically told that not an ἀσπίς nor an ἔγχος is left hanging on the walls of the feast-hall (see n. ad loc.). And yet here, in yet another suspicious passage with signs of lateness (89 n. *et infra*), we have Telemachus fetching arms for four men (τέσσαρα . . . σάκεα . . . δούρατα . . . ὀκτώ . . . πίσυρας κυνέας). The swords mentioned in xvi 295–6 are forgotten (here, instead, we have some helmets not mentioned there); and there is no suggestion whatever that Telemachus has opened or closed the store-room, despite what is said in xxiv 165–6 or admitted by Telemachus himself in 154–9 below. A further problem is the closing of the door of the store-room: in xxiv 165–6 Amphimedon on his way to Hades recounts how Odysseus and Telemachus took the weapons to the θάλαμον and then locked it, ἐκλήϊσσαν ὀχῆας, whereas in xix 47 nothing is said of either father or son locking the room, doubtless because the poet had his mind on the business of the magic lamp. They must have done so, though, by pulling the cord. In this case, in xxii 109 Telemachus would have needed a bulky key like the one used by Penelope in xxi 6 (see n. ad loc.); like her, he would have needed to fetch it from the bedchamber. Furthermore, once laden with the heavy weapons (110–11), Telemachus would have had his hands too full to lock the door after him; the door must have been left ajar, and the key placed on the floor, on a shelf in the store-room, or in the lock.

101. ἤδη: 'immediately, without delay'.   τοι: dat. of the 2. sing. personal pronoun. **οἴσω**: straightforward future of volition. **δοῦρε**: the dual is quite natural, since it was normal to carry two spears in battle, the second as a spare (so Athena imagines Odysseus ἔχων πήληκα καὶ ἀσπίδα καὶ δύο δοῦρε in i 256; the hero arms himself to meet Scylla καταδὺς κλυτὰ τεύχεα καὶ δύο δοῦρε in xii 228; he longs for the same arms in xviii 377–8, almost a replica of these lines 101–2; on xvi 295 see the note on 101–25 above).

102. ἐπὶ κροτάφοις ἀραρυῖαν: very similar phrases in xviii 378, *Il.* xiii 188 (agreeing with κόρυθα), *Il.* xviii 611. Von der Mühll prints κροτάφοισ', Allen κροτάφοις, a discrepancy which is not simply orthographic. **κυνέην**: on the different types of Homeric helmet see, for example, Lorimer, *Monuments*, 238 n. 1, 244 n. 4, 509 n. 1. The various different words used (not including κράνος, which is later) are naturally commoner in the *Iliad* than the *Odyssey*: κόρυς (*Od.* xix 32, xxiv 523), fem. πήληξ (*Od.* i 256), στεφάνη (Iliadic only), τρυφάλεια (*Od.* xxii 183, see below), and κυνέη (*Od.* x 206, xiv 276, xviii 378; in this book, here and at 111, 123, 145; and xxiv 231, where the noun's decline from 'helmet' to 'cap' is clearly seen in αἰγείην κυνέην 'goatskin hat'). The etymology of κυνέη from κύων indicates a headpiece originally made of dogskin; further examples of leather caps are the κυνέην . . . ταυρείην of bullhide, 'also known as καταῖτυξ' as the text informs us, in *Il.* x 258; the κτιδέη of weasel-skin, from ἰκτίς 'weasel', in *Il.* x 335; and the famous description of the κυνέην . . . ῥινοῦ ποιητήν adorned with boar's teeth in *Il.* x 261–5. But there are many passages where κυνέη is qualified by epithets, such as πάγχαλκος (only here and at *Od.* xviii 378), which indicate a helmet made of metal: χαλκήρης (*Od.* x 206, xxii 111, 145), χαλκοπάρῃος (*Il.* xii 183, *Od.* xxiv 523), even χρυσείη (*Il.* v 744). So too the synonyms mentioned above are found with epithets such as λαμπρή (*Il.* xvii 269), λαμπρὸν γανόωσα (*Il.* xix 359), πάναιθος (*Il.* xv 372), χαλκείη (*Il.* xii 184), χαλκοβάρεια (*Il.* xi 96), καλή (*Il.* xviii 597, *Od.* xxii 183), φαεινή (*Il.* xiii 527); a helmet as it falls κονάβησε (*Il.* xv 648) or καναχὴν ἔχε (*Il.* xvi 105); cf. *Il.* xiii 340–1 ὄσσε δ' ἄμερδεν | αὐγὴ χαλκείη κορύθων ἄπο λαμπομενάων, *Il.* xvi 70–1 ἐμῆς κόρυθος . . . μέτωπον | . . . λαμπομένης.

103–4. Here and in 114–15 we may suspect a late interpolation intended to incorporate the two servants in the battle.

103. 'I for my part will go and arm myself'; but ἰών is semantically weak, the idea of the trip to the store-room being already present in οἴσω.

104. καὶ τῷ βουκόλῳ ἄλλα: 'and the same to the other, the cattle-herd'. **τετευχῆσθαι**: a unique and problematic word, from a denominative *τευχέω 'put on armour' < τεύχεα 'armour'; Wackernagel notes that the correct formation from hypothetical *τευχεσ-y-ω would be *τε-τευχεσ-σθαι > τετευχέσθαι (*Untersuchungen*, 249). For ἄμεινον without the copula see vii 310, xv 71.

105. A formulaic line (cf. 1 n.) found also at 170, 430, 490, xxiii 129, 263, xxiv 302, 330, 356, 406.

106. 'Run and bring me them quickly while I still have some arrows left, not

COMMENTARY

when they have run out'. Schwyzer attempts to bring out the volitive force of the imperative οἶσε, formed from the fut. οἴσω, by translating 'wolle bringen' (*Grammatik*, i 788). On θέων 'running' see 99 n. **ἦος**: the spelling of the conj. in the papyri will have been *EOC*, which makes it difficult, before a consonant or in some cases such as this (cf. *Od.* iii 126, iv 800, v 429, vi 80, ix 376, xii 327, xiii 321, xvii 390), to choose between the εἵως preferred by the MSS (which alternate throughout between this spelling and ἕως, regardless of metrical quantity) and von der Mühll's normalized εἵος or Allen's ἦος, supposedly the original form (cf. Skt. *yāvat*). When followed by a vowel, as in iv 90, 120, v 365, 424, vii 280, ix 233, xiii 315, xv 109, 153, xix 367, only the last two spellings are possible; in v 386, xviii 358, xix 530, where the transmitted text presupposes synizesis, both editors allow the correction to εἵος or ἦος; in ii 148 and v 123, Allen also emends, while von der Mühll prefers ἕως with synizesis; finally, there is an iambic scansion in ii 78 where both editors accept ἕως (see Chantraine, *Grammaire*, i 11–12). **ἀμύνεσθαι**: consecutive-final (see 22–5 n., and Schwyzer, *Grammatik*, ii 363). **πάρ'**: the well-known adverbial use of πάρα without the copula, which has been considered to be a rough equivalent of πάρεστι, as in *Il.* i 174; from 'at my side (there are) arrows' comes the sense 'I have arrows to hand'.

107. Epexegetic after θέων: 'lest (if you dawdle) . . .' (cf. xv 278). **ἀποκινήσωσι**: only here and at *Il.* xi 636. **μοῦνον ἐόντα**: the participle is causal; the servants, as yet unarmed, do not count.

108. = xix 14, in the scene of the hiding of the arms, where the line is more appropriate, since Telemachus is obeying an order, whereas here it is he who has taken the initiative. **φίλῳ**: possessive once again.

109. **βῆ δ' ἴμεναι**: on this restricted use of the inf. see 99 n.; the line-opening is identical to xxi 8. The line has been suspected (Blass, *Interpolationen*, 232–3) on the grounds that κεῖτο implies a lengthy duration and is inappropriate to describe something put there only the day before; the reflex. dative of possession οἱ, preceded by hiatus, is also objectionable, attributing as it does the father's weapons to his son.

110. The papyrus reading εἵλετο supports von der Mühll against Allen's ἔξελε, which is found in the suspiciously similar line 144; the 3rd pl. is found in three other passages in this position, amongst them *Od.* vii 10. The compound occurs in *Il.* xxiv 229–31, in a passage very similar to this one: ἔνθεν δώδεκα μὲν περικαλλέας ἔξελε πέπλους, | δώδεκα δ' ἀπλοΐδας χλαίνας, τόσσους δὲ τάπητας, | τόσσα δὲ φάρεα λευκά, τόσσους δ' ἐπὶ τοῖσι χιτῶνας. εἵλετο is also common (cf. xxi 6, 416, xxii 125).

111. **πίσυρας**: a well-known Aeol. form which here replaces the metrically-excluded τέσσαρας. For χαλκήρης in formulae see 102 n. and Hoekstra, *Modifications*, 98 n. 5.

112. **βῆ δὲ φέρων**: 'he came back carrying (them)'; this line-opening occurs in *Il.* xi 247. The line-ending repeats that of 99.

113. In parallel with the aor. δύσετο here, the imperf. dual δυέσθην in the next line indicates simultaneous action ('while they both . . .'). The verb

242

strictly applies only to the helmet (χαλκόν referring back to πάγχαλκον in 102), not to the shield and spears.

114. ὡς δ' αὔτως: 'likewise'. δμῶε: the dual has been used already at xxi 244; here it is preceded by τώ which is almost equivalent to an article, but which it seems unnecessary to emend.

115. ἔσταν: 'took their stand, went and stood', perfective. ποικιλομήτην: cf. ἀγκυλομήτεω in xxi 415 and n. ad loc., with the impossibly corrupt ἀγκυλόμητις; here too Nauck defends ποικιλόμητιν against ποικιλομήτην (acc. once in the *Iliad*, five times in the *Odyssey*, three of them in this book).

116. αὐτὰρ ὅ γ': 'He for his part'. The line-ending repeats 106, but the situation is different: there Odysseus spoke of defending himself if he was attacked while Telemachus was away, but here he uses up his last arrows killing unnamed suitors without any mention of them having attacked him.

117. μνηστήρων: partitive gen. αἰεί: indicates a succession, 'one by one'. The line-ending, with its two hiatus in front of digamma and a further one in thesis, occurs in xxiii 57; it magnificently underscores the justice of the hero's bloody vengeance. There is no reason to emend this supposedly 'jejune' line.

118. τιτυσκόμενος: except in xxi 48 (see n. ad loc., and also on xxi 6) and viii 556, this verb is always used (in the same position in the line) to describe the shooting of arrows (cf. xxi 421 n., xxii 266, xxiv 181, Amphimedon's speech in Hades). The two imperf. main verbs nicely capture the repeated action. τοὶ δ' ἀγχιστῖνοι ἔπιπτον: the phrase occurs in *Il.* xvii 361, *Od.* xxiv 181, xxiv 449 (the dubious line *Il.* v 141 refers to a heap of dead sheep). ἀγχιστῖνοι is an exact parallel of the semantically-related προμνηστῖνοι in xxi 230 (see n. ad loc.); the suffix of that word has probably been taken and joined to ἄγχι 'near', or it is derived from the superl. ἄγχιστα, seen for example in *Il.* xx 18 (E.-M. Voigt, *LfgrE*, i 110–11). At any rate, the idea is of a pathetic pile-up of bodies, 'one on top of another'.

119. λίπον: 'ran out, failed, were used up' (with acc. of the person concerned). ἄνακτα: of the five cases of this word in xxi, three respect the digamma as here (9, 62, 395) while two (56, 83) ignore it, leaving a preceding short vowel followed by a consonant.

120-1. There is a splendid calmness in this careful resting of the now no longer required bow. ἔκλιν': the aor. appears twice meaning 'defeat, win' (*Il.* v 37, *Od.* ix 59) and once meaning 'tilt a battle one way or the other (of a god)' (*Il.* xiv 510); in the literal sense, apart from *Il.* viii 435 and *Od.* iv 42 (leaning chariots against the ἐνώπια), compare *Il.* xxiii 510 (leaning a whip against the handrail of the chariot); προσέκλινε occurs in *Od.* xxi 138, 165. For the force of perf. ἑστάμεναι, which in three passages of the *Iliad* means to 'resist (in war)' and at *Il.* x 480 'to keep still', compare *Il.* xiii 261 ἑσταότα, and above all *Il.* xviii 373–4, where Hephaestus made (ἔτευχεν) tripods ἑστάμεναι (consecutive-final, as here) περὶ τοῖχον ἐϋσταθέος μεγάροιο.

122-5. Scenes of arming take at least three forms. The longest type is that such as Agamemnon's in *Il.* xi 16–46; a second relatively full type is that such as Paris' in *Il.* iii 328–38 or Patroclus' in *Il.* xvi 130–9 where the greaves, breastplate, sword, shield, helmet, and spear(s) are described; the third and simplest type is that such as Ajax's in *Il.* xv 479–82 and Odysseus' here where only the shield, helmet, and spears are mentioned. Line 122 on the shield is identical except for the beginning to *Il.* iii 334, xvi 135. The two lines on the helmet are identical in all four passages. Line 125 on the two spears copies the first hemistich of *Il.* xvi 139 and the second hemistich of *Il.* iii 18 (Paris) and xi 43 (Agamemnon; and see also *Od.* xxi 434 n.), which replaces the ὅ (or τά) οἱ παλάμηφιν ἀρήρει of *Il.* iii 338, xvi 139, and the ἀκαχμένον ὀξέϊ χαλκῷ of *Il.* xv 482 (cf. 79–80 n.). **τετραθέλυμνον:** 'made of four layers of hide' (cf. 186); this and *Il.* xv 479 (for the formula see Hoekstra, *Modifications*, 94–5) are the only attestations of this adj. Eustathius has τριθέλυμνος, and there are three occurrences in the *Iliad* of the word προθέλυμνος: two of these presuppose a stem θέλυμνον (the neut. pl. θέλυμνα has been proposed as a conjectural emendation for θελεμνά in Empedocles fr. 21, 6 D; cf. θέμεθλον) meaning 'root, underlay' (of trees or hair 'pulled out by the root', *Il.* ix 541, x 15), while the prefix προ- of the third, which is applied to shields (*Il.* xiii 130), is probably (see Wackernagel, *Untersuchungen*, 241, and Lorimer, *Monuments*, 183) the Aeolic equivalent of τρα- as in τράπεζα '(four-legged) table', or τρυ- in τρυφάλεια (see n. on 102). **δεινόν:** adv. **καθύπερθεν:** 'hanging downwards'. Note the common agreement of a dual δοῦρε, followed by the primary form δύω (cf. the secondary δύο in 101), with plural adjective. Line 124, paralleled as we have seen in several of the Iliadic passages, has been emended by some editors, who find the mention of a gallant plume irrelevant in this sordid scene (see von der Mühll's contemptuous opinion of the late poet).

126–202. This problematic passage, several lines of which are suspicious (126–30, 134, 140–1, 144–5, etc.), has been endlessly discussed. Evidently, straightforward slaughter by bow and arrows offered less possibilities for dramatic treatment than an Iliadic duel of spears, which serves to cast a heroic glow over the grim episode we have just witnessed and also over the following one, obviously attributable to the later poet, where the swineherd and neat-herd join forces with Odysseus against the suitors and their ally Melanthius.

126. **ἔσκεν:** the iter. form of εἰμί has already appeared in xxi 94, 145, 283.

127. The best translation is 'hard by the edge of the threshold', taking ἀκρότατον as predicative; this superlative occurs twice more in the *Odyssey*, xii 11 and 15, but there are sixteen cases in the *Iliad*, frequently in the same position in the line (see *Il.* i 499, iv 139, v 754, etc.). The final hemistich is repeated from 120.

128. 'There was a passage from the courtyard to the street'. We should translate the loose paratactic phrase in the second hemistich by a relative ('which was closed by a pair of close-fitting doors': cf. vii 88 θύραι . . . δόμον ἐντὸς ἔεργον); compare xxi 236, 382, and later xxii 155, 258, 275, xxiii 42,

which repeats this hemistich). λαύρη occurs only here and at 137 in Homer; the word is common in later texts (Hsch. διάλαυρος· οἰκία μεγάλη πανταχόθεν λαύραις διειλημμένη; Mount Λαύρειον with its mining galleries, etc.).

129. The two readings adopted by von der Mühll (τὴν) and Allen (τὴν δ') are both demonstrative, and refer not to ὀροσοθύρη but to ὁδός or λαύρη. ἀνώγει: the pluperf. does not specify when Odysseus gave the order. φράζεσθαι: 'look to, take care of', with acc. δῖον ὑφορβόν: Eumaeus' epithet has already occurred in xxi 80, 234 (see n. ad loc.), 359; it is applied to Philoetius in xxi 240 (see n.).

130. ἑσταότ': see n. on 120-1; the participle occurs eight times in the *Odyssey*, five of them like this one in initial position (viii 380, xi 583, xiii 187, xxiii 46, xxiv 204) and the other two in a second-foot dactyl (ix 442, xi 571). The spelling vacillates between forms with and without synizesis (-αο-/-εο-/ -εω-/-ω-); Aristarchus preferred the Ionic form with metathesis of quantities ἑστεώτ' in *Il.* xxiv 701, which is also found in papyri for *Od.* xxii 130, xxiii 46, xxiv 204 (against ἑσταότ' here), and suggested for this line by Wackernagel, *Untersuchungen*, 72, and Chantraine, *Grammaire*, i 430. ἄγχ' αὐτῆς: the papyrus reading ἀγχοῦ τῆς would have the advantage of removing an αὐτῆς used in the post-Homeric sense *eius* (Cauer, *Homerkritik*, 31; Stanford's note ad loc. and on xxiv 241); but ἀγκοῦ is found only nine times in the *Odyssey*, against numerous examples of ἄγχι (xxi 433, xxii 136, 333, xxiv 368), always in initial position and always, except in vi 5 and xvii 526, as part of the formula used in 100 above. μία δ' οἴη γίγνετ' ἐφορμή: another paratactic phrase, this time causal, '(because) it was the only avenue (by which the suitors might attack)'. ἐφορμή is found only here in Homer; we find it used later by Thucydides and Apoll. iv 148, 204. The MSS tend to dissimilate the second gamma in γίγνομαι and γιγνώσκω (see 306, and xxi 209n., xx 501), writing γίνομαι, γινώσκω with compensatory lengthening of the iota; von der Mühll opts for this spelling, Allen normalizes to -γν- (Chantraine, *Grammaire*, i 12-13 leaves the question undecided).

131. Ἀγέλεως: unlike Πηνέλεως in *Il.* ii 494 etc., where the quantitative metathesis is metrically indispensable since *Πηνέλᾱος is impossible, this name has the same prosody as Μενέλᾱος, and appears thus as the name of a different warrior in *Il.* xx 321, 339, xxii 136, 212, 241, 327. Here and in 247, unless we emend, we must admit the metathetized form (on the formulaic implications see Hoekstra, *Modifications*, 9 nn. 4-5, 39-40, 137); this calls attention to the fact that μετέειπεν only occurs in this position in two doublets, this line = 247 and xiv 459 = xv 304, where synizesis is also in play (τοῖς δ' Ὀδυσεὺς μετέειπε, συβώτεω πειρητίζων). The νῦ ἐφελκυστικόν masks the hiatus which would be caused by following digamma. πιφαύσκων: 'bringing to light > manifest', derives from *φαϝος 'light'; there are seven examples of the middle in the *Odyssey* (see xxi 305, xxiii 202) and four of the active (xi 442, xii 165, xxii 131, 247), but all of them have short iota, whereas in *Il.* x 478, 502, xviii 500 the active lengthens the vowel (not in x 202, however).

132–4. Agelaus' proposal is made in the same courteous tone of enquiry as, for example, *Il.* iii 52, *Od.* vi 57–9.

132. The first hemistich = xviii 414, xx 322, xxi 152, xxii 70, etc. Note the repetition of the prefix in ἀνά.

133. See 77 n. on the second hemistich. The suitors are unaware that, though the door to the λαύρη may be open, since Eumaeus comes and goes through it, the gate of the courtyard has been locked (xxi 391 n.). As usual, the parataxis conceals a syntactical relation, this time of purpose, 'and tell the folk (so that) . . .'.

134. There is very general consensus that this line is spurious, copied here from 78 (see the note on τῷ ad loc.) because of the similarity of the previous line to 77. It is out of place here, since Odysseus is no longer shooting his bow (Blass, *Interpolationen*, 205–6).

135. = xvii 247. The goat-herd Melanthius, whom we met in xxi 175–85 (see n. ad loc.) and 265, here steps into the scene again. His role as a symbol of cunning and evil in the later layers of the myth was briefly touched upon in the Introduction to xxi; it is revealed by his name, 'he of black designs', and by those of his family (Melantho, his sister in xviii 321, xix 65; his father Dolius 'the crooked', xviii 322, xxii 159, xxiv 222, etc.). αἰπόλος 'one who comes and goes about the goats' > 'goat-herd' appears in two similes in the *Iliad* (ii 474, iv 275), and nine times in the *Odyssey* (from xvii 247 onwards), always in the nom. or acc. and at the end of the line with the pleonastic and alliterative αἰγῶν (H. Geiss, *LfgrE*, i 338; on the alliteration see xxi 265–6n.).

136. οὔ πως ἔστ': 'That is quite impossible'. διοτρεφές: it is hardly surprising that this common epithet for Menelaus (twelve examples) in ∪ –́ ∪ ∪ should be used for the metrically equivalent name Agelaus; it is twice applied also to Odysseus (x 266, 419), once to Peisistratus (xv 199), and once to Agamemnon (xxiv 122), always in the same position in the line. ἄγχι . . . αἰνῶς: 'very close'; αἰνῶς is here simply 'very' (cf. Engl. 'terribly good'), without any residual connection with the idea of terror or anger, as in *Il.* iii 158, where Helen is 'terribly like a goddess', αἰνῶς . . . ἔοικεν, or *Od.* xvii 24, 'terribly badly dressed', αἰνῶς . . . εἵματα . . . κακά (V. Pisani, *LfgrE*, i 320–3; cf. vi 168, xviii 80, xix 324, xxiv 353, where the etymological meaning still subsists).

137. The entrance of the passage is dangerous, impassable (E.-M. Voigt, *LfgrE*, i 1185–91). This means either that it is dangerously near the door of the feast-hall (the paratactic link with the preceding clause would be causal, 'and therefore'), or that besides being close it is also dangerously narrow (in which case the link would be with the following asyndetic clause in 138, 'and (I say it is dangerous because) . . .').

138. εἴη is opt. by attraction from the main clause, with a suggestion of conditional force. On ἐρύκοι see 409 n.

139. ἀλλ' ἄγεθ': 'well then', interj. (E.-M. Voigt, *LfgrE*, i 129–34; Schwyzer,

Grammatik, ii 245, 314, 583–4; Palmer, *Companion*, 150); there are numerous parallels, for example with following imper. in iv 294, x 460, xii 23, xxi 134, 263, xxii 252 (on xxi 73 and 106, see nn. ad loc.); with subj., as here, in xiii 179, and, with ἀλλ' ἄγε, in xxii 428, 487; ἀλλ' ἄγε with imper. in xxi 281, 336, xxii 233, 417; with neg. imper., xxi 111.   ὑμῖν: see 41 and 65 n.; von der Mühll does not go so far as to write ὕμιν here. θωρηχθῆναι is a consecutive-final inf.

140–1. As noted in the comment on 22–5, these lines have been suspected of being an interpolation designed to link this passage with the episode of the hiding of the arms: Melanthius, it is argued, had no way of knowing anything about it (Blass, *Interpolationen*, 206–7, 233; cf. Focke, *Odyssee*, 358). But Page and others defend the lines on the grounds that the goat-herd is an unusually cunning and resolute character, who as we see puts his plan into action without waiting to discuss it (Page, *Odyssey*, 99 n. 15). There is little to choose between the two interpretations which have been proposed: 'for (the arms are) inside (the house) and they have not put them anywhere outside', or, deleting 141 alone with Kirchhoff, 'for (the arms) are inside and nowhere else'; or even 'for they have put them in the store-room and not anywhere else'.   **ὄΐομαι**: parenthetic ὀΐω is common (e.g. ii 255, xvi 309), but ὀΐομαι used in the same way occurs only here and in xiv 363 (Schwyzer, *Grammatik*, ii 584; xxi 79, xxii 67 are not comparable).   **κατθέσθην**: the dual form repeats that of xix 20; the second hemistich of 141 is identical to that of xix 31.

142–3. The juxtaposition of the two proper names in adjacent lines is deliberate: a vulgar and bare-faced goat-herd dares to enter Odysseus' store-room. Bérard's ingenious conjecture requires lengthening in thesis.

144–5. It has been remarked how absurd it is to portray one man carrying so many weapons: the lines (so similar to 110–11) were already condemned by Aristarchus, who, according to Eustathius, athetized them with a χ and the comment ἀδύνατον εἶναι ... τοσαῦτα βαστάσαι ἄνθρωπον. In truth, Melanthius could have divided his burden better, seeing that only one suit of armour was left after his first trip to the store-room. But the fact remains that the narrative requires both that there should be two trips to the store-room, and that as many as possible of the suitors should be armed as quickly as possible. 'Aristarchus', remarks van der Valk (*Textual Criticism*, 189), 'failed to bear in mind the mythical and fantastic atmosphere of the *Odyssey*' (see also Blass, *Interpolationen*, 206).   **ἔξελε**: see the apparatus, and compare 110 n.

146. Cf. 109 n.

147–9. By a fine touch, Odysseus does not realize what is happening until he sees the suitors arming themselves (τεύχεα means shield and helmet) in the shadows at the other end of the hall, after Melanthius' return through the ὀρσοθύρη, and when some of them are already starting to threaten him with their great spears. The hero's momentary loss of heart (note the formula in 147, paralleled in 68, see n. ad loc.) introduces an interesting element of suspense.   **περιβαλλομένους** is a variation on the ἀμφιβάλλομαι 'put on (clothes)' of 103, also used in vi 178; this compound with περι- is found elsewhere only in tmesis (v 231, xiv 528; the active, in 466, is used in a different sense). **μέγα . . . ἔργον**: the lexical meaning is 'exploit, deed (of war)', here used to mean a great deed yet to be accomplished (as in *Il.* xi 734, xii 416, xvi 208), not, as elsewhere in the *Odyssey*, one already undertaken or accomplished (*Od.* xvi 346, xxii 408), or a blameworthy one (xix 92).

150. = xvii 591, xix 3, xxiii 112. Cf. 100n.

151-2. ἦ μάλα δή τις: 'someone, so it seems'. The final vowel of ἐνί is lengthened before the following μ-. **νῶϊν**: dual, because Odysseus and Telemachus are the only ones who count. After speculating whether one of his women-slaves has betrayed him to the suitors by opening the door, Odysseus makes a second and more well-founded guess: 'unless it be Melanthius' (but see the apparatus).

153. A heavily formulaic line, with Telemachus' typical epithet πεπνυμένος (from i 213, with τήν, and i 388, with τόν; cf. xxi 343, πεπνυμένος qualifying μῦθος in xxi 355, and ἀντίον ηὔδα at the end of the line in xxi 320, on which see n. on 90 above).

154. ὦ πάτερ: see 101 n. **αὐτὸς ἐγὼ τόδε γ' ἤμβροτον**: αὐτὸς ἐγώ., 'it was I and no one else', heavily emphatic; τόδε is internal acc. of the mistake committed, qualified by γ' in slight mitigation: 'I have erred, in this at any rate (though I am more careful otherwise)'; ἤμβροτον is an Aeolic form, as the psilosis and the reflex -ρο- of the *r* show, useful for feet in dactyls, as we have seen in xxi 421, 425 (cf. vii 292). The line-ending, with enjambment of the following αἴτιος, is found again in xi 558–9.

155. The relative is causal in sense. On the final formula see n. on 128, and the variant in the apparatus (singular here and in 258, 275; plural in xxi 236, 382).

156. ἀγκλίνας: aor. part. with apocope of the prefix ἀνα- (cf. κάλλιπον, from κατ(α)-λείπω), found in *Il.* iv 113 with the very meaning 'leaning (something on something else)' (see the Introduction to xxi on xxi 138, 165). At *Il.* v 751, viii 395 (of which *Od.* xi 525 is a probably spurious imitation), the Hours are said to be in charge of 'opening and shutting' the clouds as if they were doors, ἀνακλῖναι and ἐπιθεῖναι (cf. 157 ἐπίθες). ἀνακλίνω probably originally referred to the latch being lifted 'upwards', as at Hdt. v 16, and then came to mean 'swing the door away from the doorpost', leaving it ajar; ἐπιτίθημι, on the other hand, meant 'put the door back against the doorpost', leaving it closed. On Telemachus' carelessness see n. on 101–25. σκοπός: the word is applied to Eurycleia as 'superintendent' of the servants in 396, to the 'guards and sentries' posted by Aegisthus in iv 524 and by the suitors in xvi 365 (cf. *Il.* xviii 523), and to Dolon as the 'guide' of a scouting party in *Il.* x 324, etc. The poet wished to say that Melanthius had proved a better 'spy' than Eumaeus; but the latter has taken no part in this, being in no position to observe the goat-herd's comings and goings through the ῥῶγες; as it stands, the phrase means something like 'someone has summed up this situation more cleverly (than us)'. This is to overestimate the cunning of Melanthius, who could not have been sure of finding the locked store-room so providentially open when he made his suggestion.

157–9. Telemachus' instructions are somewhat incoherent: first he asks Eumaeus to close the door (see the notes to xxi 6, 241), a detail which would be of little significance at this juncture except that some suitors have yet to arm themselves, causing the goat-herd to make a second sally (whose failure to secure further weapons could not be foreseen by Telemachus); and second, to seek out the identity of the traitor, which would have been impossible if the swine-herd had found the store-room empty. Nevertheless, if we suppress these lines (see the apparatus) we shall have to suppose that Eumaeus sees Melanthius from his vantage-point by the threshold, and that is impossible.

157. ἀλλ': 'come now!' (cf. 139). δῖ' Εὔμαιε: see n. on xxi 234.

158–9. φράσαι: 'consider, think' followed by two indirect questions; cf. xvi 260–1. Telemachus picks up his father's suggestion about the women-slaves (ἄρα, 'perhaps'), but instinctively prefers to believe, like him, that the culprit is Melanthius (note περ with the rel., and see n. and app. crit. on xxi 175–85).

160. = xxiii 288, xxiv 98, 203, 383, a very common formula, with its unaugmented verb.

161. The aor. may be translated as pluperf.; meanwhile, the goatherd had already entered again.

162. οἴσων: fut. part. with final sense 'in order to bring', as in iv 532, viii 257. The second hemistich is similar to xvi 5.

163. The second hemistich is repeated in 355 and, with προσηύδων, in xiv 484; it derives from such lines as *Il.* ix 201, xi 464.

164. = v 203, x 401, xxiv 542, etc.; similar to xxiv 192.

165. 'You are right (δή), there he is (κεῖνος predicative, cf. for example *Il.* xiv 344) coming into the hall again, that loathsome man, just as we thought'. δὴ αὖτε has synaloepha (cf. ix 311, in the same position in the line). ἀΐδηλος: 'that cannot even be looked at' > 'loathsome' (R. Philipp, *LfgrE*, i 265–7; cf. viii 309, xvi 29, xxiii 303); the word nicely captures the psychological detail of the faithful servant's impatient indignation at a faithless one. ὃν ὀϊόμεθ' αὐτοί: after ὀϊόμεθα we seem to have an ellipsis in the acc. and inf. construction (ὅν . . . ἐλθεῖν; the verb appears to be an unaugmented imperf. here and in the only other passage where the form ὀϊόμεθα occurs, xxi 322 (see n. ad loc.), 'as we already thought (before you said it, in xxi 322; before it was proved by the evidence, here)'; for the form cf. ὀΐσατο in i 323, ix 213, xix 390, as against ὠΐετο, x 248, xx 349; but the etymology of the verb is obscure (in principle, it should be from *ὀϝισγομαι, but the question of quantity is important: alongside examples of ὀΐω with short -ῐ- such as *Il.* i 558, xiii 153, xxiii 467, the remainder offer the etymologically inexplicable long -ῑ-; cf. xxi 79, 91, 261, xxii 67, 140 and n., 159, 210, 215, xxiii 261, xxiv 401, beside contracted οἶοιτο in xxii 12; see Chantraine, *Grammaire*, i 371–2).

COMMENTARY

166. The second hemistich is identical to *Il.* xiv 470, *Od.* iii 101, xxiii 35, etc.; the variant ἀληθὲς ἐνίσπες is found in iii 247. The aor. imperative ἐνίσπες in the same position occurs also in *Il.* xi 186, *Od.* xi 492, *Od.* xiv 185, etc.; it is an old injunctive form, like θές, σχές, etc., from a pres. ἐνέπω or ἐννέπω < *inseq*ᵘō, with locatival prefix ἐνι-; the unfamiliarity of the ending has led in the *Odyssey* to a secondary ἔνισπε (iv 642; see Chantraine, *Grammaire*, i 467), and a large number of variant readings without the final -ς.

167–8. The double indirect question is parallel to the construction in 158–9, but here ἦε < *ἦϝε is not contracted to ἦ; ἀποκτείνω is aor. subj., deliberative. At the end of the line, the expression κρείσσων γένωμαι or γένηται indicating victory in combat appears in *Il.* iii 71, 92, *Od.* xviii 46, 83 (with κρείσσων in another sense, xxi 345, xxii 353).

168. ὑπερβασίας: the word is always found at the same place in the line except in *Il.* iii 107.   ἀποτίσῃ: the verb takes the same construction here as in 64 (see n.), xiii 193; cf. iii 206 τείσασθαι μνηστῆρας ὑπερβασίης, 'avenge myself *on* the suitors *for* their outrage'.

169. οὗτος: contemptuous, as in xxi 334, 403, xxii 5, 49, 78 (see nn.), 134. The final phrase, with its double hiatus (the first in thesis, the second caused by digamma) heightens the gravity of Melanthius' evil deeds.

170. Cf. 105 n.

171–2. As Eumaeus is incapable of overcoming Melanthius single-handed, Odysseus gives Philoetius leave to accompany him.   ἦ τοι ἐγὼ καὶ Τ: 'for our part Telemachus and I'; in Greek the first person is not put last for politeness.   μνηστῆρας ἀγαυούς: the usual formula for the suitors in nom. (xxi 174, 232) and acc. (xxi 58, 213 n., xxiii 63).

172. σχήσομεν: 'we will contain them' (cf. 70 n.; the chief danger is that the suitors will escape from the hall, robbing Odysseus of his tactical advantage). For the concessive force of περ with part. cf. xxi 103, 129, 250, 370 nn., xxii 409.

173–93. To understand these lines without recourse to unnecessary deletions (see the apparatus, and G. Pasquali, 'Versi spuri in χ', *SIFC* vi (1928), 225–9, who condemns 175–7, 192–3), we must distinguish between Odysseus' orders and their execution (187–93). Melanthius finds the store-room almost bare after Telemachus' and his own incursions, and has to poke about in the corners a while before finding not a complete suit of armour, but a decent helmet and a broken-down old shield of Laertes'; meanwhile, unbeknownst to him, Eumaeus and Philoetius reach the doorway of the store-room through the λαύρη and the ῥῶγες. They lie in wait while he takes up his load, which puts him at a disadvantage. They put down shield and spear by the door; when the goat-herd puts his foot out of the door they attack him, overpower him, drag him by his hair back into the store-room and throw him to the floor; then they find a plank (probably a shelf: see 174 n.), lash him with his back to it and his hands and feet tightly bound behind it, leaving him entirely helpless, and then tie a stout rope to one end of the plank, throw it over one of the roof-beams close to the central pillar where it is free of the ceiling and haul the plank up until Melanthius is suspended high on the column, hitching the free end of the rope to a nail or boss on the wall. After a few taunts to the prisoner, they then pick up the weapons and lock the door behind them (201) as they have been ordered, though this is no longer necessary. We see, therefore, that Odysseus' orders (tie his hands and feet behind him, throw him to the ground, lash him up) are not in logical order, while the plank is not mentioned at all in the narrative of their execution.

173. **σφῶϊ δ' ἀποστρέψαντε:** 'you two'; van Leeuwen notes the lack of a pronoun complement with the double acc. after ἀποστρέψαντε, which Bérard attempts to resolve with his δέ ἑ στρέψαντε, bearing in mind that none of the seven examples of ἀποστρέφω in Homer (of which this and the cases in 190, iii 162, xi 597 are Odyssean) bears the meaning 'twist back' in the context of torture or punishments which is found in Sophocles, Herodotus, and Aristophanes. As for the second hemistich, there are abundant examples of ὕπερθε(ν) at the end of the line (v 184, xvi 47, xx 2, xxiv 230, 344; χείρας ὕ., viii 135), and of πόδας καὶ χείρας.

174. Von der Mühll and others bracket this line, on the ground that it is omitted by one papyrus. In my view it is a mistake to take σανίδας here as 'doors' and connect it with the order in 157, which as we have seen is incoherent, an interpretation which has given rise to conjectures such as ἐπιθεῖναι and variants such as ἱμάντι (cf. i 442, iv 802, xxi 46n.); the leather thong is indeed used by Eumaeus and Philoetius in the end, but without tying it to the κορώνη, since there is no danger of anybody opening the door from inside (see xxi 241n.); this excludes such an interpretation. As for ὄπισθε (always at the end of the line in the *Odyssey* except at xvii 201, xxii 55, xxiii 249, 261), there is no parallel for the translation '(closing) after one-self', of a door. It is therefore better to take σανίς, a word of uncertain etymology but with a suffix common in technical terms, as 'board, (unshaped) plank', a meaning we have already encountered in the 'shelf' in Penelope's store-room (xxi 51n.); this may indeed be the same piece of timber. Indeed, since xxi 51 is the only occurrence of the word in the singular, the text here would be improved by accepting Nauck's conjecture σανίδος, with ἐκδῆσαι (inf. for imper. like ἐρύσαι and πελάσαι in 176) taking Melanthius as unexpressed direct object and the gen. dependent on the prefix ἐκ-; on the other hand, σανίδας 'doors' would require us to take the inf. as perfective.

175-7. These lines have been subject to a deluge of condemnation, not only because of the mistaken interpretation of σανίδας above but also because 175, repeated in 192, is ὁλοσπόνδειος (Blass, *Interpolationen*, 207). Once again, deletion seems unnecessary; *pace* Pasquali ('Versi spuri'), the lines describe a torture well-known from Herodotus, a type of crucifixion or ἀπο-τυμπανισμός (ix 120 πρὸς σανίδα προσπασσαλεύσαντες ἀνεκρέμασαν). It is also referred to by Aristophanes, using the same word σανίς (*Thesm.* 931–40; in *Pl.* 309–12 there is a direct reference to Melanthius, though it is falsely asserted that he was suspended by the genitals). The text itself refers to the torture in unequivocal terms: the agony of the victim is mentioned in

188–9 (θυμαλγέϊ δεσμῷ), whether because the ropes are painfully tight or because the body is squeezed by the plank, and the cruelly sarcastic taunts (εὐνῇ ἔνι μαλακῇ, 196; ταθεὶς ὀλοῷ ἐνὶ δεσμῷ, 200) are paralleled in similar scenes in Homer, if not during Hera's punishment in *Il.* xv 18–21 (where the goddess does not know what she is hanging from, with two anvils tied to her feet and her hands bound with a golden chain) at least during Achilles' torture of his prisoners by tying their hands behind their backs (ὀπίσσω) in *Il.* xxi 30.

175. On this στίχος ὀλοσπόνδειος see the note on xxi 15 and the possible solution to the objections of Eustathius and others (see app.). σειρή is a rare word in Homer (*Il.* viii 19, 25, on the famous golden rope which Zeus defies the other gods to pull; *Il.* xxiii 115, ropes to tie bundles of firewood). πειρήναντε: for περαίνω 'tie', related to πεῖραρ 'cable, rope', see 33 n.; cf. *Od.* xii 37 πεπείρανται 'is accomplished'. **ἐξ αὐτοῦ**: 'attached to, around his body'.

176. **ἀν'**: 'up on, at the top of (the column)' (Schwyzer, *Grammatik*, ii 441). On δοκοὶ καὶ κίονες ὑψόσ' ἔχοντες see the n. on xix 38. On the two infinitives used as imper. see 174 n.

177. Final clause, which in Homer may take either κεν or ἄν. **δηθά**: 'for a long time', with the same suffix as ἔνθα, appears seven times in the *Iliad* and thirteen in the *Odyssey*; it is not used with a preceding short vowel metrically lengthened by the original δϝ-.

178. = iii 477, xv 220, xxiii 141; very similar are vi 247, xx 157.

179. **βὰν δ' ἴμεν**: cf. 109 n., 146. They take their weapons with them (see 114, 173–93 n.). The two servants do not actually enter the store-room, but stop at the door; Classen's conjecture is therefore inadmissible. **λαθέτην**: λανθάνειν with a part. normally means 'to do something without being noticed' (cf. 198); cases such as this one where the verb takes an acc. personal object, meaning 'to escape someone's notice, not to have one's presence observed by someone', are much rarer (cf. xi 102, xiii 393, xvii 305; xi 126 οὐδέ σε λήσει is rather different, '(something) will not escape your notice'; so is ix 281, where λάθεν means something like 'deceived').

180–1. While Melanthius (ὁ) is busy rummaging (ἐρεύνα, imperf.) for arms in the corners (μυχὸν κάτα) of the almost bare store-room, the two servants (note the duals with pl. verb ἔσταν, and see the app.) halt one at either side of the door; so too the two Phaeacian serving-girls stood πάρ ... | σταθμοῖϊν ἑκάτερθε, vi 18–19.

182. **εὖθ'**: '(and) when'; asyndeton with εὖτε at the beginning of a line is relatively common (iii 9, xiii 78, 93, xvii 359, xx 56, 73, xxiv 147). The temporal clause stretches down to the parenthetical line 186; the simultaneity of Melanthius' action and that of his two opponents is reinforced by the contrast between the imperf. ἔβαινε and the aorists in 187.

183–4. **τῇ ἑτέρῃ μέν ... | τῇ δ' ἑτέρῃ**: cf. v 265–6 (one skin of wine, the other of water), *Il.* xxi 164–6 ('to one ... to the other', of a pair of warriors), and especially *Il.* xiv 272–3, xxi 71–2, on a person's two hands.

183. On the τρυφάλεια see n. on 102 and 122–5; this is the only occasion the word is qualified by καλή.

184. γέρον: the unique use of this adj. for a thing rather than a person has provoked corrupt readings, though later we find Simon. fr. 145, 3D χαλκός . . . γέρων; S. El. 25 ἵππος . . . γέρων; E. Or. 529 γέροντ' ὀφθαλμόν; S. fr. 794 R γέροντα βουλεύεις (cited by Eustathius as a parallel on this line); also A. Ch. 314 τριγέρων μῦθος, and fr. 651 M γέρον γράμμα (Schwyzer, Grammatik, ii 176). ἄζη or ἄζα is hapax, of uncertain meaning; its etymological cognates imply some kind of dry deterioration such as rusting (V. Pisani, LfgrE, i 183; cf. ἀζαλέος 'dry', as in ix 234; καταζαίνω 'dry out, shrivel', xi 587; Hellen. ἄζα 'drought', ἀζαίνω; Hsch. ἀζαυτός· παλαιότης καὶ κόνις; in xix 18 the excuse for hiding the arms is that they will otherwise be spoilt by the smoke from the hearth), but the verb παλάσσω (especially if one prefers some sort of etymological connection with Hesychius' παλκός· πηλός, rather than with πάλη 'fine flour') implies some kind of spattering by liquids (with blood, αἵματι, λύθρῳ, αἵματι καὶ λύθρῳ in Il. v 100, vi 268, xi 169, xx 503; Od. xxii 402, 406, and the dubious xxiii 48; with brains, Il. xi 98; with blood and brains, Od. xiii 395; with sweat, Il. xvii 387). See Hoekstra, Modifications, 92 n. 7.

185. The variant derives from line-endings such as xiv 9, 451. κουρίζω 'be a young man' in the temporal sense is a hapax (see the conjecture in the app.) which reappears in Hellenistic texts. **φορέεσκε:** 'used to carry', the only example in the Odyssey of this doubly marked iterative form with vowel-change and suffix.

186. The whole line is parenthetical. **δὴ τότε γ' ἤδη:** 'but by that time' (cf. Il. xi 107, Od. xvii 296), but γε, despite Il. xiii 441, has caused difficulties: for example, the papyrus reading τότ' ἄρ' ἤδη. Van Herwerden's conjecture is based on parallels such as xxiv 187, and one might add vi 26, which like this passage offer κεῖμαι 'be laid up' (cf. 109 n.). The second phrase is paratactic; we should translate with a causal conjunction. **ῥαφαί:** 'seams', here only in Homer; the sense is that the leather laces (on ἱμάντων cf. 174 n., and note the hiatus) used to sew together the shield's layers of hide were coming apart (see 122–5 n.; for the process, see Il. xii 296–7, where a craftsman βοείας ῥάψε θαμειὰς | χρυσείης ῥάβδοισι διηνεκέσιν περὶ κύκλον). The variant reading with unaugmented verb requires an impossible caesura after a trochee in the fourth foot.

187. Apodotic δέ (see 182 n.), as for example in xx 57. The piling-up of aorists (mixing plurals with duals, as usual) strikingly portrays the swiftness of the action. **εἴσω:** 'inside'.

188. **κουρίξ:** 'by the hair', another of this book's unique forms, imitated by Apoll. iv 18; it is formed from κουρή, a word not found in that form in Homer which later meant 'tonsure, haircut' as well as 'hair clippings' (Hdt. iii 8), from κείρομαι (iv 198, xxiv 46; see n. on 36 for a metaphorical use, and for another, the pecking of vultures, xi 578), with a suffix like that of γνύξ (six examples in the Iliad), λάξ (twice in the Odyssey), ὀδάξ (see 269 n.), πύξ (four times in the Odyssey; cf. later ἀπρίξ). Melanthius, in contrast to the normal custom of slaves, wears his hair long (see the sch. in the papyrus quoted in the apparatus), a habit which arouses the ill-feeling of his fellows (S. Marinatos, *Archaeologia* B, 3; and see the notes on 192–9 and 196 below). ἐν δαπέδῳ δὲ χαμαί: the pleonastic expression is deliberate, underlining Melanthius' helplessness; the line-ending, with parallels in x 67, xii 153, 250, 270, xxiv 420, is a fine psychological detail.

189. σὺν ... δέον: tmesis. On the painful bonds see 175–7 n.

190. We should translate aor. ἐκέλευσεν by a pluperf.; compare similar expressions in ii 415 (orders by Odysseus) and vi 212 (Nausicaa).

191. This superfluous line, whose first hemistich is similar to viii 18, is omitted by various MSS and papyri; it is condemned by von der Mühll, and by Blass, *Interpolationen*, 207.

192–9. The repetition of 175–6 in 192–3 and the high-flown tone of 195–9 have prompted critics to delete these lines; the latter are, however, perfectly defensible as a cruel sarcasm directed at one who has got above himself (see 188 n.).

194. It is a striking fact that, whereas in the *Iliad* Homer frequently addresses a character directly, in the *Odyssey* he only ever does so to Eumaeus, and always when introducing a speech. There are fifteen examples of the line-ending προσέφης Εὔμαιε συβῶτα from xiv 55 (cf. Εὔμαιε συβῶτα in a speech by another character in xv 381). ἐπικερτομέων: elsewhere only at *Il.* xvi 744, xxiv 649, in the same position in the line, the first in a similar apostrophe to Patroclus (cf. *Il.* xvi 20, etc., and *Il.* iv 27 and others addressed to Menelaus; xv 365, to Phoebus; xv 582, to Melanippus; xx 2, to Achilles). On all this see Hoekstra, *Modifications*, 138–40.

195. πάγχυ: 'undoubtedly', as in 236 below, and also in ironic sense at xv 327 and xvii 217, which has the same opening as this line. νύκτα φυλάξεις: 'you will spend the night awake, on watch' (see *Il.* x 312, *Od.* v 466, with the same construction; cf. the different construction in *Od.* xx 52–3 φυλάσσειν | πάννυχον ἐγρήσσοντα); an unkind understatement, in view of Melanthius' somewhat uncomfortable position.

196–8. The opening of 196, with lengthening before μ-, is repeated in *Il.* ix 618, x 75, xxii 504, and similar to *Od.* xxiii 349. καταλέγμενος: there are eight Odyssean examples of the stem λεγ- 'lie down' with the prefix κατα- from which this pass. part. derives (the same form, in the same position in the line, at xi 62). ὥς σε ἔοικεν: this ending (cf. xxi 319 n., 322 n.) has caused textual problems, even though the hiatus (*ϝεϝοικεν) is irreproachable. The sarcasm of the phrase is more biting if one recalls Eumaeus' previous mockery of Melanthius' airs and graces in xvii 244–5. A minor problem in 197 was raised by Eustathius, who pointed out that this is the only occasion when Eos is connected with Ocean by a character, not by the poet (Blass, *Interpolationen*, 207–8; see Lorimer, *Monuments*, 82 n. 2, and Pocock, *Odyssean Essays*, 2, 66; for analogical παρά with a proper name see Schwyzer, *Grammatik*, ii 497). A more significant point is that 197 and xxiii 347 (which may have been copied from it) are the only occasions where ἠριγένεια is used as a noun to mean 'dawn', against ii 1 and so many other examples where it is an adjective (the attempt by Eisenberger, *Studien*, 314 n. 1, to defend the authenticity of xxiii 347 by arguing that in every case Ἠριγένεια can be taken as a noun, just like Τριτογένεια in iii 378, is unconvincing; Erbse, *Beiträge*, 191–2). Blass proposes solving the problem by fusing 196–7 into one line, ending in καταλέγμενος, οὐδέ σέ γ' Ἠώς. **σέ γ':** heavily emphatic, 'you at any rate (who in your "elevated" position will be the first to glimpse the light of dawn over the horizon)'. **λήσει:** on the uses of λανθάνω see 179 n. **ἐπερχομένη:** against the doubtful reading ἀνερχομένη (see the variants in the apparatus) must be placed the fact that Homer nowhere else uses ἀνέρχομαι for the coming of the dawn, the sun, etc. (cf., however, Aesch. *Ag.* 658), whereas ἐπέρχομαι is used for the seasons (ii 107), the night (xiv 457). **χρυσόθρονος:** this epithet of Dawn is used ten times in the *Odyssey*, all of them except xiv 502 (in the fifth foot) in the same position in the line and frequently followed by ἦλυθεν Ἠώς. On Ocean conceived as a river flowing round the earth and bounding it on the east, as here and at xxiii 244, and on the south (x 508), west (xi 156), and north (v 275), see D. Gray, *Archaeologia* G, 5. **ἡνίκ' ἀγινεῖς:** attempts have been made to correct ἡνίκα, significantly found only here in Homer (and not an Ionic form, despite τηνικαῦτα in Hdt., Schwyzer, *Grammatik*, ii 652; nor is τηνίκα found in the poems, Chantraine, *Grammaire*, ii 255) by the conjecture ὁππότ'. In either case the meaning is 'at that time of day when normally . . .'; this sense requires the unaugmented imperf. ἀγίνεις rather than pres. ἀγινεῖς, which would also lend added point to Eumaeus' taunt. ἀγινέω has been used in xiv 105 of bringing animals to slaughter for the suitors.

199. **κάτα** is used in anastrophe. **πένεσθαι:** consecutive-final; the line-ending is used for the preparation of meals by servants in iii 428, iv 683, or by soldiers and sailors in iv 531, xiv 251; the variant formula περὶ δεῖπνον . . . πένοντο is applied to slaves in iv 624, xxiv 412; interestingly enough, only here and at ii 322 (δαῖτα πένοντο) is the meal prepared by the suitors themselves (see xxi 428 n.).

200. **ὁ:** demonstrative again; Melanthius 'had been left there', the pluperf. λέλειπτο signalling the swift progress of the action; this is the only example of this passive in the *Odyssey*, but it occurs three times in the *Iliad*, twice in conjunction with the pathetic ταθείς, of warriors 'stretched out' on the ground (Harpalion, 'like a worm', at *Il.* xiii 655, and Lycaon at xxi 119).

201. See the nn. on 157–9, 173–93 and 179; for variations on this phraseology, compare this passage with xxiv 498 ἐς τεύχε' ἔδυνον; xxiv 496 with *Il.* xxiii 131 ἐν τεύχεσσιν ἔδυνον; xxii 114.

202. The end of the line is identical to that of 115 (see also the apparatus here). The two servants naturally return by way of the λαύρη. On this type of line, and the relation between the dual βήτην and the older βάτην (xxiv 361), see Hoekstra, *Modifications*, 134–5. For ἐς with personal names (a usage which has nothing to do with ἐς πατρός in ii 195) see xxi 308 n., xxii 99 n.

203. **μένος πνείοντες:** cf. xxiv 520 ἔμπνευσε μένος; the phrase, with sing.

μένος, is an Odyssean variation on μένεα πνείοντες/-ras (*Il.* ii 536, iii 8, xi 508, xxiv 364). ἐφέστασαν: pluperf., used in the same way as λέλειπτο in 200; it is used five times in the *Iliad*, always in the same position in the line.

204. Predicative, 'four in number', emphasizing the contrast (οἱ μέν ... οἱ δέ) between the small group on the threshold and the crowd of strong warriors facing them (the line-ending occurs also in vi 284, and a similar one in xxiv 427).

205-40. A well-written episode, with some fine and lively dialogue, but full of the inconsistencies and touches of fancy characteristic of the later poet. Opinions are divided: Kirchhoff and Duentzer as usual condemn them (Duentzer includes 203–4), whereas Blass (*Interpolationen*, 240–3), van der Valk (*Textual Criticism*, 241–2), and Besslich (*Schweigen*, 97–8) are more lenient. In fact, three elements of the myth are uneasily combined here: first, the character of Mentor, who is oddly described in ii 226–7 as having been entrusted by the absent Odysseus with the government of his house, who supports Telemachus in the assembly in ii 224–56, and who briefly reappears in iv 655, xvii 68; secondly, the disguised Athena (for her ability to change herself at will into various persons see xiii 312–13, as well as xvi 208–10 on her limitless power to so change Odysseus himself), who appears to Telemachus in Mentor's shape from ii 267 onwards to act as his guide throughout the remainder of ii and iii; and third, the goddess' continued part in the action, as she directs the hero at every step, disguised as a shepherd (xiii 221) or a woman (xvi 157, xx 30) and clothing and unclothing him (xvi 173, 457), helping him against Irus (xviii 69), lighting his way in the strange scene of the lamp (xix 33); or as she inspires Penelope to show herself before the suitors (xviii 158), hides the truth from her (xix 479), draws sleep down over her eyes (xix 604, xxi 358), or suggests the test of the bow (xxi 1); or again, as she incites the suitors to their insults (xviii 346, xx 284) or to morbid laughter (xx 345). The presence of the goddess was not necessary during the brief battle with bow and arrow, but this poet sees her help (promised in xiii 393, xx 47, and expected by the hero in xvi 260–1) as indispensable, in Iliadic fashion, to the spear-fighting. Nevertheless, he has recourse to the old expedient of making her appear disguised as Mentor (205–6). Odysseus is heartened, suspecting the truth (208–10). Agelaus, however, shows in his speech (213–23) that the suitors are not surprised at the unexpected, and unexplained, appearance of a further ally of Odysseus: they must suppose he has come in through the door from the courtyard, and this mode of entry will have encouraged them to think that news of what is happening has got abroad in Ithaca, and that the hoped-for βοή (77, 133) is on the way. Agelaus says nothing of this, but confines himself to threatening Mentor with a suitor's usual boastfulness, emboldened by the weapons they have already obtained, and (since he and the others are still ignorant of Melanthius' fate) by the confident expectation of obtaining more. Athena, for her part, adopts a strange attitude: angry with we know not whom (224), she reproaches Odysseus with words which, though they may hearten him in part, unjustly accuse him of weakness of spirit (225–35). We are, besides, immediately aware that the goddess is not playing a decisive role for the moment, but is rather submitting father and son to a typically Homeric test, just as Odysseus himself did to Eumaeus in xiv 459, xv 304, also with the word πειρητίζω (the meaning of xxi 124, 149 is, however, quite different). She subsequently disappears, flying up to the carved ceiling of the feast-hall 'like a swallow' or 'as a swallow', we are not quite sure which. Immediately her plans change again: without Odysseus having responded to the test in one way or the other, the goddess begins to deflect the spears of the suitors (256, 273), until at last she allows herself to be seen, brandishing the aegis in rather grotesque fashion from the roof. As for the suitors, they do not ask how Mentor, after his fiery speech, disappears into thin air; Agelaus, on noting his disappearance, exults at the vain effect of Mentor's threats (248–54), and assuming effective leadership of the suitors now that their three chiefs Antinous, Eurymachus, and Amphinomus have fallen, comes up with a simple but intelligent strategy to avoid losing their twelve precious spears in ineffectual casts: the attack is to be made in two waves of six throws each, in the hope that the most dangerous opponent, Odysseus himself, will be killed in either the first or the second assault. Both assaults are frustrated, however, as we have seen, by Athena. It remains to consider Medon's words at xxiv 445–59, evidently the work of the late poet: he claims to have seen a god, whom he does not name, helping Odysseus and disguised as Mentor. This can be explained as a realization which the herald has reached *a posteriori*, on thinking back over the remarkable series of events.

205. = xxiv 502, and a similar text in ii 267. ἐπ' ... ἦλθεν: tmesis. ἀγχί-μολον, adv., found thirteen times in the *Odyssey*, five of them in xxiv, but only three times in the *Iliad*.
206. = ii 268, 401, xxiv 503, 548. εἰδομένη: the other occurrences of the verb, with its obvious initial digamma, refer, with the single exception of xi 241 (Poseidon changes into the river Enipeus), to Athena's metamorphoses (i 105, into Mentes; iii 372, into a vulture; vi 22, 24, into the daughter of Dimas; viii 8, into a herald, as at *Il.* ii 280).
207. This line is similar, but not identical, to xxiv 504; the opening is identical to xiii 226. γήθησεν is used of joy at a god's intervention also in xiii 250 (Athena), xx 104, xxi 414 (Zeus; see n. ad loc.).
208. ἀρήν: a clear distinction must be made between *ἀρϝά > ἀρή 'prayer, curse' (iv 767, xvii 496), and ἀρή 'evil, ruin', of unknown etymology but related to ἀρημένος (once in the *Iliad*, six in the *Odyssey*, amongst them xxiii 283) and also to Hesychius' ἄρος· βλάβος ἀκούσιον and ἀπαρές· ὑγιές (A. Ebner, *LfgrE*, i 1232–3; R. Mader, ibid., 1233–5). The latter word is found six times in the *Iliad* and at *Od.* ii 59, xvii 538 ἀρὴν ἀπὸ οἴκου ἀμῦναι, but never in the position in the line it occupies here. ἑτάροιο φίλοιο: 'your dear friend'; the adjective is more than possessive here.
209. ὅς σ' ἀγαθὰ ῥέζεσκον: the relative clause is causal in meaning. There is an important double meaning implicit in the iterative ῥέζεσκον (cf.

46 n., 314 n., and notice the lengthening of the preceding vowel; ῥέζω here takes a double acc.), with its alternative sense of 'sacrifice, worship' (*Il.* viii 250 ῥέζεσκον, *Od.* xvii 211 ἐπιρρέζεσκον; cf. 'do (evil) deeds' in 46). Odysseus uses a well-known formula for invoking Mentor's help, accompanying the two imperatives (one active, the other middle) with a mention of past favours and their shared age and class; but since ὀϊόμενος in 210 reveals that the shrewd hero has already surmised the identity of the goddess, we may interpret Odysseus' words in two ways: to the suitors he appears to say 'remember the honours I have bestowed upon you', to the goddess the same words mean 'remember the worship I have offered up to you'. **ὁμηλικίη:** related to ὀμῆλιξ 'of the same age' (once in the *Iliad*, four times in the *Odyssey*, including xxiv 107), this noun has undergone a curious shift of meaning, from 'sameness of age' (*Il.* xx 465) to 'age-group' (three times in the *Iliad*, and at *Od.* ii 158, iii 364) and thence to something between the two (e.g. *Il.* xiii 485, where Idomeneus, Aeneas' senior, says εἰ ... ὁμηλικίη ... γενοίμεθα, with a clear semantic shift from 'if we were an age-group together' to 'if we were of the same age-group, of an age'), and finally, with the usual change from abstract to concrete (cf. our use of the words 'an acquaintance', 'a relation'), to 'a peer, contemporary' (*Od.* iii 49, vi 23), which is the meaning here, where it appears in the same position in the line as in five other attestations.

210. 'Suspecting (his ally) was Athena'. **λαοσσόον:** always found in the same position, is a rare epithet; in the *Iliad* it is applied to three different gods, at *Il.* xiii 128 to Athena; in the *Odyssey* it is found only at xv 244, of Amphiaraus, and here, where it is extremely apt.

211. The end of the line is similar to xxi 360 (see n.) and 367.

212. After predicative πρῶτος and a pronoun reinforced by γε we find a re-duplicated aorist ἐν-ένιπον (cf. xxi 84, 167, 287), which like ἠνίπ-απ-ον (xx 17, with a different type of reduplication) derives from the pres. stem ἐνίσσω (xxiv 161, 163) or ἐνίπτω (*Il.* iii 438; the original root was probably a labio-velar), and from the noun ἐνιπή (v 446, x 448, xx 266), etc. On Agelaus' name see 131 n.; the formula with his patronymic is used also in xx 321, xxii 241 (Hoekstra, *Modifications*, 39.

213. For the doubt between von der Mühll's σ' ἐπέεσσι and Allen's σε ἔπεσσι cf. xxi 192 n., 206. **παραιπεπίθησιν:** for παραί-, a doublet of παρά with the old locatival ending which occurs twelve times in Homer, including xxiv 411, compare παραιβάτης (*Il.* xxiii 312) and παραίφασις (*Il.* xi 793, xv 404); in compounds of πείθω with factitive reduplication (e.g. πεπιθεῖν, *Il.* ix 484), we also find παραιπεπιθοῦσα at *Il.* xiv 208 (cf. *Od.* xiv 290 παρπεπιθών, *Od.* xxiv 119 παρπεπιθόντες). The prefix here expresses the idea of persuading 'by hook or by crook, by trickery', through Odysseus' typical arts of bamboozlement (see xxi 111 n., and compare παρφάσθαι in xix 6).

215. **ὧδε:** refers forward to the futures. In contrast to similar phrases at *Il.* i 204, *Od.* i 201, iii 226, xv 173, this is the only occasion on which the subject of the future passive τελέεσθαι is ἡμέτερον ... νόον, 'our plan'; γε points to the obstacles to the fulfilment of plans in general.

216. Agelaus' boastfulness makes him use the temporal conjunction instead of the conditional. **κτέωμεν**: this rare form with synizesis (cf. θέωμεν, xxiv 485) may represent an ancient *κτάομεν; cf. ἔκτα (i 300), ἀπέκταμεν (xxiii 121), κταμένοισι(ν) (xxii 401, 412, xxiii 45), where -ᾰ- represents the -ν- of the non-thematic aor. of κτείνω.

217. ἐν is part locative, part comitative ('amongst', as in *Il.* xiii 829, xxiv 62). δέ is apodotic (cf. 187n.); σύ, emphatic, 'you too'. ἔπειτα, 'immediately'; on πεφήσεαι, see 54n., and for a parallel to οἷα here see the n. on ὅσα in 46, and cf., for example, iv 611, xviii 338.

218. ἔρδειν: from ancient *ϝερδω (cf. Cret. βέρδη), which corresponds (see n. on ῥέζω in 46) to ἐργάζομαι, etc., through *ϝεργγω > *ϝερzdω; cf. aor. ἔρξε, xxiii 312; ἔρζον, xxiv 481; ἔρξανθ', xxiii 277.   ἐν μεγάροις: 'in this house', with an insolently proprietary tone.   κράατι: a unique form of the dative (instrumental, of price, with verbs of paying) of κάρ (*Il.* xvi 392) or κάρη (329), which may be compared with κράατος (*Il.* xiv 177) and κράατα (*Il.* xix 93); it corresponds to *krs-n-t-i (cf. Skt. abl. sĩrṣa-tás > κράατι, which contracts to the κρᾱτί of 123).   αὐτοῦ makes the pronoun reflexive (cf. 64n.).

219. ὑμέων γε βίας ἀφελώμεθα: ὑμέων γε is odd: the plural will have to be understood as 'when we have rid you (and your friends) of your urge to dominate'; the foolishness of Agelaus' remark is clear when we recall that he is speaking to a god. Bérard's conjecture βίον is ingenious (cf. *h.Hom.* xxx 6 βίον . . . ἀφελέσθαι); it will have been replaced by βίας to avoid the lengthening in thesis.

220. τοι: possessive. Two types of goods are mentioned in apposition to κτήματα, those kept inside the palace and those held in lands and cattle.

221. τοῖσιν: neut. pronoun, here close in function to the article (Schwyzer, *Grammatik*, ii 21; cf. *Il.* ix 342 τὴν αὐτοῦ 'his wife'). Von der Mühll's μεταμείξομεν and Allen's μεταμίξομεν (cf. xxiv 314), 'we will combine with' (that is, confiscate together), are merely orthographic variants (see 218n.). τοι: ethic dat.

222-3. Whether or not one deletes 223, it is far from clear whether he means to kill the menfolk and banish the women, or banish both men and women; if 223 is retained, however, there is a slight anacoluthon.

223. 'Nor even (your) wife'; the formulaic epithet κεδνήν has already occurred in xxi 66 (but cf. xxi 63-6n.; the word is applied also to women slaves in i 335, xviii 211; to a wife in i 432; to a mother in x 8.   πολεύειν: 'come and go', apposite for the idea of freedom; this is the only occurrence of the simple verb, against five examples of the compound ἀμφιπολεύω, including xxiv 244, 257.

224. The beginning of the line is the same in *Il.* xxi 423; the end, in *Il.* xxi 136 (Scamander), *Od.* ix 480 (Cyclops), xvii 458 (Antinous), xviii 387 (Eurymachus); a similar formula is v 284 (Poseidon), and of other emotions, xv 370 (love), xi 208 (sadness), *Il.* ix 300 (hate). μᾶλλον: 'much, greatly', without any comparative force. χολώσατο: there is a deliberate ambiguity, Athena's real anger being directed towards the suitors but her angry words being apparently directed at Odysseus. Her pretence of wrath towards the latter is designed to test his faith and courage, if he knows that it is indeed Athena; if he still thinks it is Mentor, however, the purpose will be to strike fear into the suitors by a show of high mettle by the new ally.

225. Almost exactly the same line was used in 26 to describe the suitors' angry words to Odysseus.

226. οὐκέτι σοί γ': 'not even in *you* any longer'; strong reproach is conveyed by οὐκέτι and the possessive dative σοι. ἔμπεδον: 'steadfast, still remaining' (nineteen occasions in the *Odyssey*, eleven of them in this position in the line; with νοῦς in x 240, φρένες in x 493, xviii 215, ἴς in xi 393, βίη in xiv 468, 503, and, like here, with μένος in xix 493, xxi 426); supply ἐστί. ἀλκή: the word occurs regularly henceforth and in the following Books (237, 305, perhaps xxiii 128, xxiv 509). Athena makes a clever pun which involves the whole semantic range of the word and its cognates, from 'help, succour' to 'capacity to help, warlike strength': 'you no longer have ἀλκή, you refuse to be ἄλκιμος, but luckily here is Mentor Ἀλκιμίδης ("Son of the Brave" the only time he is given this patronymic in the poem)'.

227. ἀμφ' Ἑλένῃ: the phrase is taken from *Il.* iii 70, 91 (in the same position in the line); cf. 254 ἀμφὶ γυναικί. λευκωλένῳ also has the flavour of Iliadic imitation; we find it used with Ἑλένη in the same position in the line, and with the same shortening of the vowel, in *Il.* iii 121; elsewhere in the *Iliad* it is applied to Hera and Andromache, in the *Odyssey* to Nausicaa, Arete, and the maidservants (vi 239, xviii 198, xix 60). εὐπατερείη, 'of a good father', a rare and much-discussed formation which is used of Helen in *Il.* vi 292 and of Tyro in *Od.* xi 235 (later in Euripides and Hellenistic writers); cf. Athena's epithet ὀβριμοπάτρη in i 101, iii 135, xxiv 540. Comparison with regularly formed feminine personal names in -άνειρα, etc., and with δμήτειρα, *Il.* xiv 259 (which Zenodotus wanted to correct to μήτειρα, cf. Hsch. μήτειρα· φρονίμη· καὶ ἡ μήτηρ); δρήστειρα, x 349, xix 345; ὀλέτειρα, *Batr.*; δώτειρα, Hes.; ἐλάτειρα, Pindar, have led to the correction *ἠϋπατείρη, postulating an original spelling *ΕΥΠΑΤΕΡΕ* > *ΕΥΠΑ-ΤΕΡΕΕ*, and paralleled by ἠϋγένειος (iv 456), ἠΰκομος (viii 452), etc.

228. εἰνάετες: the adv., used at *Il.* xviii 400 in another context, is commonly used in the *Odyssey* to describe the duration of the Trojan war (at the beginning of the line, iii 118, v 107; xiv 240); ἐμάρνατο occurs at *Il.* xii 40, and in the imper. μάρναο a further twice, once (xv 475) in conjunction with Τρώεσσι. νωλεμές: adv., with no corresponding adj. form, possibly derived from the privative prefix νη- and a neuter noun *ἄλεμος 'interruption'; it appears nine times (five of them in the *Odyssey*) in the form νωλεμέως, and eight (six in the *Odyssey*) in the present form, six of those examples being in this position in the line and followed by αἰεί (e.g. xvi 191), a formula similar to the ἄφθιτον or ἄφθιτα αἰεί found at the end of four lines in the *Iliad*.

229-30. The verbs are still dependent on ὅτε; but we might paraphrase the parataxis of the second with the conjunction 'until'. ἥλω: this form (which could easily be substituted by ἑάλω: Schwyzer, *Grammatik*, i 654) is the only Homeric example with the contracted augment from what would in post-Homeric Greek become ἁλίσκομαι; cf. *Od.* xiv 183 ἁλώῃ, xviii 265 ἁλώω, xxiv 34 ἁλῶναι. σῇ ... βουλῇ, 'by your strategy'. The Iliadic epithet of Troy εὐρυάγυια is found in the same position in the line at *Od.* iv 246; and, applied to Athens, at vii 80, and another city, xv 384.

231. Rhetorical question ('and that being so, how is that ...?'); ὅτε is both temporal and causal, 'now and at this important moment when'; γε reinforces the possessive.   ἱκάνεις: equivalent to a perfect, 'have reached' (cf. xxi 201), with acc. of direction.

232. ἄντα: for this preposition see xxi 48, 65, 421 and nn.   ὀλοφύρεαι: this verb is very common (e.g. xxii 447, xxiv 59), but nowhere else takes an inf.; translation is difficult, versions which suggest themselves running from an impossible 'you lament that you are brave' to 'you lament that you have to be brave' or 'you regard with pain the necessity of being brave'; or it may mean 'you sadly refuse to be brave', or even 'you are painfully keen to be brave' (cf. *Il.* ii 290 ὀδύρονται οἰκόνδε νέεσθαι 'they desire painfully, i.e. ardently, to go home'). There are approximate parallels in such lines as xx 202-3 οὐκ ἐλεαίρεις ἄνδρας ... | μισγέμεναι κακότητι 'you show no compassion at men being overwhelmed by misfortune'; ii 52 ἀπερρίγασι νέεσθαι 'they view the return with horror'. Be this as it may, ὀλοφύρεαι must have an emphatic ring, in the context of the aggressive tone which Athena puts on for her double-faced game with Odysseus (cf. xiii 291-2): in general terms her remark must mean something like 'it is ridiculous of you to bewail the need for bravery'. Van Leeuwen's reservations about this line are understandable, but Bérard's solution, based above all on *Il.* xvi 450, xxii 169, is facile.

233. The exhortation ἀλλ' ἄγε (cf. 139n.) is both emotional and brisk; δεῦρο, adv. of place with lative force, is here used almost as an imperative '(come) here!' (cf. plur. δεῦτε, used four times in the *Odyssey*); the vocative πέπον, apparently from an adj. whose original meaning was 'cooked' (cf. πέσσω), hence 'ripe, mature' > 'soft' > 'sweet', indicates a cordial but somewhat mocking relationship between speakers; in the *Iliad* it is put in the mouth of a friend who is also in some sort a superior (Agamemnon to Menelaus, Nestor to Patroclus, Sarpedon to Glaucus, Ajax to Teucer, etc.; also Poseidon haranguing the Greeks, xiii 120). Occasionally it crosses the boundaries of friendly banter, and becomes insulting (Thersites, *Il.* ii 235). In the *Odyssey* we find the word used as a term of affection by Zeus to Poseidon (xiii 154) or Cyclops to his ram (ix 447). The first four feet of the present line are taken from *Il.* xi 314 (Allen prefers to print ἵστασο in such passages, while von der Mühll chooses the analogical form ἵστασο); the whole line repeats xvii 179 (ἐμ' = ἐμοί).

234. The MSS waver between ὄφρ' εἰδῇς (from οἶδα, accepted by von der Mühll though it ignores digamma) and ὄφρα ἴδῃς (read ἴδῃς, from ὁράω, preferred by Allen here and in ix 348).   οἷος: sc. ἐστί, followed by an ethic dat. τοι (also governed by δυσμενέεσσιν) and a consecutive-final inf. similar to that in xxi 195 with ποῖοι (see n. ad loc.).

235. **εὐεργεσίας ἀποτίνειν**: εὐεργεσίη is found only in this book (cf. 319 n., 374, in the same position in the line); the verb is also rare (four examples in the *Iliad*; on iii 286 see 57–9 n.; *Od.* ii 132, Telemachus' supposed compensation to Icarius if he expels Penelope).

236. **Ἦ ῥα, καί**: cf. 8 n.; the sense is not '(so) he said and . . .', but '(so) he spoke, but . . .'. **οὔ πω** 'not yet' is important with the imperf., 'began to give' (this delay is part of the test). **πάγχυ**: see 195 n.; with neg. 'not altogether' (ii 279, iv 755, 825, xiii 133). **ἑτεραλκέα**: the epithet is used in the *Iliad* (with the exception of *Il.* xv 738, always with νίκην and in this position in the line; and note the hiatus in thesis here) to refer to a reverse in the fortune of battle which switches the advantage to the side which has been losing up to that moment (*Il.* vii 26, Athena intervenes to protect the hard-pressed Greeks; viii 171, Zeus does likewise for the Trojans; xv 738, Ajax speaks of the Hellenes being able to turn defeat into victory; xvi 362, the same hero sees the balance tip in favour of the Trojans; xvii 627, Zeus saves the Trojans from imminent defeat). Here, Athena puts off the moment for coming to the aid of Odysseus, though his numerically inferior force is obviously in the weaker position.

237. **ἄρα**: 'as one would expect from a goddess'. On the 'testing' implied by πειρητίζω with the gen. (Schwyzer, *Grammatik*, ii 105) see 205–40 n.; it is used at xvi 313 of Odysseus testing his servants to see how they have behaved, and at xxiv 221 of examining his orchards.

238. **υἱοῦ**: the only Homeric example of this form of the gen., has aroused suspicions of 'late composition', like the υἱοῖσι of xix 418 (Chantraine, *Grammaire*, i 228).

239–40. The episode of the swallow has been much discussed (for example, by Focke, *Odyssee*, 361–2). There is argument as to whether Athena really changes into a bird, or whether this is merely a further example of the epic simile: in i 319 and iii 371 she disappears suddenly 'like a bird' (ὄρνις . . . ὥς) or 'like a vulture' (φήνῃ εἰδομένη; note also the φήνη at xvi 217). The latter word εἰδομένη is also used, however, to refer to actual metamorphoses, though it is not the only word: in xiii 222 Athena's transformation into a shepherd is described by the part. εἰκυῖα, and the same word is used in v 353 of Ino's transformation into a seagull; in xvi 157, xx 31 ἤϊκτο is used of a transformation into a woman; other technical terms are ἔϊσκω in xix 313 (though not in other occurrences of the word in the *Odyssey*, where it refers simply to facial or other resemblance), ἐναλίγκιος in xvi 209, 273, xvii 202, xxiv 157, and εἰκέλη, common in this poem, with its digamma and preceded by hiatus, in x 304, xi 207, xix 384, xx 88; see xxi 411 n., which is also about a swallow.

240. **εἰκέλη ἄντην**: 'alike to look at (face to face)'; ἄντην, found only at the end or (in four cases) at the beginning of the line, appears coupled with ἐναλίγκιος in similes, where it has the same meaning (ii 5, iv 310, xxiv 371;

G. Lohse, *LfgrE*, i 924–6), comparable to such phrases as εἰσάντα ἰδέσθαι (v 217) or εἰς ὦπα ἰδέσθαι (xxii 405).

241–329. It is not difficult to calculate the number of suitors. Dispensing with the absurd figure of 110 given in xvi 247–51, which would not fit in the *megaron* (see xxi 346–7 n.), we may take it that the poet began by thinking of a relatively large number, but that he drastically reduced the figure in xxii 118 in order to concentrate on the deaths of the most important ones. Antinous son of Eupeithes has been killed in 16, Eurymachus son of Polybus in 82, and Amphinomus son of Nisus in 93; these three were the spokesmen of the group. Now the poet names six others (241–3): Agelaus son of Damastor who has just spoken, Eurynomus son of Aegyptius (cf. ii 22), Amphimedon son of Melaneus (cf. xxiv 103), Demoptolemus, Peisander son of Polyctor (cf. xviii 299), and Polybus. To these we may add Ctesippus son of Polytherses (mentioned in xx 288, he wounds Eumaeus at 279 below), two further suitors mentioned elsewhere called Leocritus son of Euenor and Eurydamas (ii 242, xviii 297), another two who are not named until the moment of their deaths, Euryades and Elatus (267), and finally the priest Leodes (cf. xxi 144). This makes a total of fifteen; besides the three principals, already killed, the deaths of Demoptolemus (266), Euryades and Elatus (267), Peisander (268), Eurydamas (283), Amphimedon and Polybus (284), Ctesippus (285), Agelaus (293), Leocritus (294), and Leodes (328) are individually recounted. It is noticeable, as Bérard observed, that the death of Eurynomus is not given separate mention. The author is careful to apportion the fourteen killings he describes according to a strict order of precedence: six to Odysseus, four to Telemachus, and two each to Eumaeus and Philoetius. Furthermore, adding Eurynomus to the fourteen warriors slain, and deducting the three victims of the arrows and Telemachus' first spear, we are left with twelve men, the same number as the sets of armour carried in by Melanthius, who on his last trip intended to find further sets for himself, the herald, and the minstrel. Finally, it may be noted that many of these names are borrowed from the *Iliad*; all of them except Polybus (the Trojan of xi 59; there are a further three characters with this name in the *Odyssey*, Eurymachus' father in i 399, an Egyptian in iv 126, and an artist in viii 373: see F. Eckstein, *Archaeologia* L, 1, 18–19) and Eurydamas (*Il.* v 149), killed in combat (cf. Trojan Elatus in vi 33; the Trojan Agelaus in viii 257, the Greek in xi 302; two Trojans and a Greek named Peisander in xi 122, xiii 601, xvi 193; the Greek Leocritus in xvii 344). The development of the battle is fairly clear: Agelaus sees Odysseus as the only serious threat, and in view of the impossibility of a simultaneous charge in the oblong *megaron* divides his forces into two ranks; the first rank of six warriors will cast their spears against the hero while the others line up against the walls, and then, if they are unsuccessful, they will retire to allow the second rank to make their assault. In the first rank Demoptolemus, Peisander, Euryades, Elatus, Eurynomus, and Leodes (whose assertion that he has taken no part in the proceedings at

313–14 is not to be believed) throw their spears, but all of them miss the target (256; on 257–9 see below). Odysseus' ensuing tactic is the opposite of Agelaus': he orders each of his men to aim, as far as possible, at a different suitor; though, to be sure, it must have been difficult in the heat of battle to be sure of choosing a target not aimed at by anyone else. And, since the cowardly Leodes has hidden by the wall and the poet has forgotten about Eurynomus, each of Odysseus' men manages to fell one of the remaining four suitors who have thrown their spears (265–8). Eight suitors are thus left, not all of them armed; and they now (270) commit the tactical blunder of retreating to the corner of the *megaron*, allowing Odysseus both to retrieve the spears stuck in the bodies of the fallen, including Amphinomus (though the pulling out of this one was, as we have seen at 95–6, a difficult and dangerous feat: see 271 n.), and to pick up the spears dropped by the dead. Next the remaining six suitors, Agelaus, Polybus, Eurydamas, Leocritus, Amphimedon, and Ctesippus, make their spear-cast (272): three spears miss, a fourth is not described, and the fifth and sixth cause slight wounds (273–80), leaving the suitors unarmed. A scene of butchery ensues; following the same stratagem (282 = 263), Odysseus and his companions each slaughter a different opponent, Eurydamas, Amphimedon, Polybus, and Ctesippus (281–91). The two survivors of the second wave, Agelaus and Leocritus, draw their swords for a desperate charge and launch themselves against Odysseus in hand-to-hand battle, αὐτοσχεδόν (293), and are speared by the hero and his son (292–5). It only remains (since Eurynomus has faded out of sight) for Odysseus to kill Leodes with the sword dropped by the dying Agelaus (310–29); this scene is illogically preceded, however, by the passage where Athena unnecessarily brandishes the aegis (297) against the one or two almost defenceless warriors left alive, who are inappropriately compared to a herd of cattle (299–306).

241–6. Von der Mühll's edition prints augments on the forms with double consonants or diphthongs, whereas Allen prints all the verbs without augment (cf. xxi 100, xxii 261, 308, 461, xxiii 19, 86, 310, 370, xxiv 9, 184, 225, 413, 487, 490, 496, 501). ὄτρυνε is picked up by μετέειπεν in 247 (cf. 212 n.), but the ines are syntactically unsatisfactory. Various solutions are possible: to suppress 242–4, with Bérard; to take all the nominatives of 242–3 as subjects of the verb in 241, in which case the best of the survivors would all encourage the rest (but it is doubtful if τε καί in 242 will bear this explanation); to interpret the lines as a nominative absolute (see Chantraine, *Grammaire*, ii 15–17; xxi 323 is a different case, see n. ad loc.); or finally, to transpose 242–3, placing them after 245, with a strong stop after 241, and postulate a bold ellipsis: 'Agelaus exhorted the suitors, (of whom) these (οἵ) were the most distinguished of all those (τοσούτων) who were still alive, namely Eurynomus, etc., whereas the real champions (τοὺς δέ) Antinous, Eurymachus, and Amphinomus had been killed by the arrows.' At any rate, 244 is almost a replica of iv 629, xxi 187 (see n. on 186–7), which refer indeed to Antinous and Eurymachus.

246. ταρφέες: the adj. is related to τρέφω ('well tended' > 'thick, abundant' > 'massed, close, thick-falling'), and occurs six times in the *Iliad*, three of them in this position in the line; ταρφέα, adverbial neut. pl., refers to the rapid steps of dancers beating on the ground at viii 379 (cf. *Il.* v 555, xv 606, where τάρφεα means 'thickets'); the identical line-ending is used to describe bow and arrows in *Il.* xi 387, xv 472, but here ταρφέες is inappropriate, since Odysseus on his own cannot be said to shoot a shower of 'massed' arrows.

247. Cf. 131 n.

248. The line is almost identical to 70 (see n. ad loc.), with ἤδη, 'shortly, in a moment'.

249. The parataxis is causal in sense; καὶ δή, 'in fact'. οἱ, ethic dat., is sarcastic in tone, like κενά; the latter adj. exhibits the forms κεινός (four times in the *Iliad*, always in the material sense) and κενεός (*Il.* ii 298, *Od.* xv 214 'empty-handed', of a man; *Od.* x 42 'empty', of the hand itself), but never κενός, which long ago provoked Bentley's conjecture; εὔγμα is a *hapax*, later taken up by Aeschylus.

250. οἱ δ' οἷοι: 'and so they (the four there were before) are the only ones left ...'.

251. On τῷ see xxi 374 n.; the word is out of place here, since the plan of battle has nothing to do with the disappearance of Mentor.

252. ἀλλ' ἄγεθ': cf. 139 n.   οἱ ἕξ: the article with the numeral as usual denotes a fraction, 'six of you' (cf. *Il.* v 270-2, Anchises keeps four of his six colts, τοὺς μὲν τέσσαρας, and gives two of them to Aeneas, τώ ... δύο; *Il.* x 252-3, πλέων νύξ | τῶν δύο μοιράων has passed; *Il.* xi 174, of the herd one cow, τῇ ἰῇ, is to die); there is no call for Naber and Bérard's emendation (ἀλλ' ἄγε, οἱ ἐξ πρῶτοι, where οἱ is 'against him alone'), nor for Bérard's effort in 255 (ὣς φάτο· ἐξ δ' ἄρα πρῶτοι).   ἀκοντίσατ': the first of six occasions on which ἀκοντίζω is used in this book (see also viii 229); though related to ἄκων (cf. xxi 340 n.) and ἀκόντιον 'javelin, hunting spear' (*h.Merc.* 460), the verb is normally used with αἰχμή, δόρυ, ἔγχος, μελίη, and the more general βέλος. The same enjambment of the phrase or αἴ κέ ποθι Ζεὺς | δώῃ, meaning 'to see if by any chance ...', occurs at *Il.* vi 526-7, *Od.* xii 215-16; a similar device occurs in *Il.* i 128-9.

253. βλῆσθαι: only here and at *Il.* iv 115 do we find this passive inf.; cf. 18, and xvii 472 βλήεται.   καὶ κῦδος ἀρέσθαι: the change of subj. is rare, but not unparalleled; cf. the much-discussed line in ii 227, 'so that the rest obey and he take care'; xx 316-17, 'it would be better for him to die than this to be seen'; *Il.* ix 230-1, etc. We find eight Iliadic examples of the formula κῦδος ἀρέσθαι, seven of them at the end of the line; ἀρέσθαι ends the line also at i 390 and in three places in the *Iliad*.

254. 'The others are nothing to worry about, they are no danger'; the echo of κῦδος/κῆδος is probably unintentional. It is surprising that Allen, inconsistently (cf. xxi 159, xxii 219, 440), prints ἐπεί χ' οὗτος here (cf. the somewhat similar case of xxiv 140). οὗτος is contemptuous (cf. 169 n.).

255. ἄρα: 'in obedience to his order'. The textual problem is the inverse of 190 (see the apparatus), but the choice between the aor. or imperf. of κελεύω does not affect the sense. At all events, this line-ending taken together with xv 437, xviii 58, xxiv 492 tends to support the deletion of 191 (see n. ad loc.).

256. ἱέμενοι: we have already seen ἱέμενοι in –²∪∪–³ and preceded by hiatus at xxi 72; and the concessive formula ἱέμενόν περ at the end of the line and preceded by the euphonic -ν of xxi 129 is paralleled in six other lines in the *Odyssey* (including xxii 409, with preceding ἔσχεθεν, as in iv 284, xvi 430; x 246, xiv 142 ignore the digamma); the placing of the párticiple at the beginning of the line, as here, is paralleled by fourteen cases, including xxii 273, xxiii 353 (note the compound ἐσιέμεναι in xxii 470), always with the idea of a physical or emotional effort directed to some end. The word is probably derived from an ancient *ϝίεμαι related to Skt. *vēti*, etc., which has been influenced by contamination from the middle ἵεμαι, probably from *si-se- or *yi-ye-, though in Attic tragedy the ῑ- is short. It is impossible, therefore, to say whether the word means 'putting all their effort into it', or 'aiming well', or something of the kind.   τὰ πάντα: sc. δούρατα or ἀκοντίσματα, a word unattested before the classical period but easily supplied.   ἐτώσια: predicative; its use at xxiv 283, of useless gifts, placed in ∪–²∪∪ and without digamma, is unusual, all the remaining examples (six in the *Iliad*, and *Od.* xxii 256, 273) appearing in the same position in the line as here with preceding hiatus or -ν, and only one of them (*Il.* xviii 104) referring to anything other than a weapon failing to hit the target. The word may go back to Skt. *svatá-*, despite the smooth breathing born both by this word and by the Attic idiom οὐκ ἐτός which is supposed, though not without posing several difficulties, to derive from it; but if this etymology is correct, it poses a problem of semantics.

257-9. The lines are evidently interpolated here: the account of the results of the spear-casts, which did not all miss (τὰ δὲ πολλά, 273) properly belongs at 274-6. Despite this, Blass believed that 274-6 should be expunged, not these lines, because Eustathius' comment on 257-9 uses the word ἐκείνους, not τούτους (*Interpolationen*, 208). That proves only that the ancients habitually condemned repetitions on their second occurrence, not on their first.

260. ἀλεύαντο: translate with pluperf.; this form is found only here; cf. ἀλεύατο in xvii 67, xx 300, 305, against non-Aeolic forms such as ἀλέασθε (iv 774), ἀλέασθαι (ix 274), ἀλέαιτο (xx 368).

261. = xxiv 490.   μύθων ἦρχε: 'he began to speak', is a common formula (see 241-6 n.).

262. ἤδη: sc. 'in the circumstances, in view of this'. The echo of the opening of 248 has a certain ironic pointedness; καὶ ἄμμι, 'to us too' (as Agelaus said to his men). ἐγώ followed by hiatus is perhaps preferable to ἐγών; κεν with the optative is the usual way of framing a polite request, 'I should advise'.

263. ἐς ὅμιλον ἀκοντίσαι: 'to shoot at the throng indiscriminately'. The relative clause is causal in sense.

264. ἐπὶ προτέροισι κακοῖσιν: 'besides the wrongs they have done me earlier'; cf. iii 113 ἄλλατε τε πόλλ' ἐπὶ τοῖς πάθομεν κακά.

265. The variant line-endings given in the apparatus, based on 255 and 368 respectively, may be due to the rarity of the ending ὀξέα δοῦρα, attested only in 265, 272, and 282; the same formula or something like it, but differently placed in the line, can be found in Il. v 495, 619, vi 104, xi 44, 212.

266. ἄντα τιτυσκόμενοι: cf. xxi 48, 421 and nn.

268. βοῶν ἐπιβουκόλος ἀνήρ: for this formula of the end of the line, structurally parallel to αἰπόλος αἰγῶν (135n.), see the n. on xxi 199; it appears again in 285, 292.

269. ἔπειθ': 'as a consequence'; ἅμα stresses the simultaneity of the deaths, which strikes terror into the hearts of the enemy. **ὀδάξ:** the etymology of this word is unclear (Frisk, *GEW*; cf. 188n.); it is doubtless influenced by verbs, attested in later texts, such as ὀδακτάζω, ὀδάξω, ὀδαξάω, and their corresponding middles, 'feel pain; scratch, bite' (cf. Hsch. ὀδάξει· τοῖς ὀδοῦσι δάκνει), and by popular etymology from ὀδών 'tooth' and δάκνω 'bite'. The cruel expression 'bite the dust' need not refer to the gnashing of the death-rattle (cf. W. Richter, *Archaeologia* H, 95); it appears in five Iliadic passages, of which two offer variations (ii 418 λαζοίατο γαῖαν, xxii 17 γαῖαν . . . εἷλον), one is very similar (xi 749), and two others (xix 61, xxiv 738) have the same line-ending with ἄσπετον οὖδας. ἄσπετον 'which cannot be followed' (cf. ἕπομαι) > 'enormous', qualifies οὖδας only in these two Iliadic passages, *Od.* xiii 395, and the present line, always in connection with the dying; it is naturally metaphorical, suggesting the width of the battlefield. The word ἄσπετον occurs again in 407.

271. τοί refers to Odysseus and his companions, as again, more clearly, in 281; ἄρα, 'as a result of this error'. Depending on whether we take ἐξ with νεκύων or as a prefix in tmesis, it is arguable which arms are here being retrieved (see n. on 241); one is inclined to think they are trying to strip the suitors' bodies, not pick the weapons up off the floor (cf. Il. x 343, 387 for someone intending to strip arms, συλήσων, off corpses, νεκύων).

273–6. Cf. 256, and see the n. on 257–9. Each succeeding spear is deliberately made to fall further short of the mark.

275. βεβλήκει: this unusual pluperf. (βέβληκα does not exist in Homer; βεβλήκοι, only at Il. viii 270) has caused remark (Schwyzer, *Grammatik*, ii 288–9; Chantraine, *Grammaire*, ii 200), not only because it is 'resultative' (putting the emphasis on the effect on the object, not on the subject), but also because of the tense. In general, such usages signal the rapidity of the action described by the verb, as if the event were seen from a perspective which sent it some distance back into the past: before the thrower could follow the throw with his eyes, the spear had landed. This interpretation will do for eleven of the Homeric examples (258, 275, 286 in this book, and eight cases in the *Iliad*), but not so well for Il. xvii 606. A further problem (see Schwyzer, *Grammatik*, i 405) is the presence of the νῦ ἐφελκυστικόν on these 3rd pers. pluperf. forms (which are always placed in the first foot and a half except at Il. xiv 412, where it is in the second and first half of the third). It is everywhere allowed in the papyri and by the three great Alexandrian grammarians (see the app. here and at 258); von der Mühll always retains it before a vowel (cf. also v 112 ἠνώγειν, xvii 359 δεδειπνήκειν, xviii 344 ἑστήκειν); but Allen sometimes omits it even in this situation (xxii 275, *Il.* xiv 412 βεβλήκει, a reading accepted also by Mazon).

276. μελίη: the 'ash-wood spear', mentioned thirteen times in the *Iliad* (and μέλινον ἔγχος, as many again), makes its appearance in the *Odyssey* only here, at 259, and at xiv 281 (Odysseus' fantastic tale); for the fem. χαλκοβάρεια at the end of the line, as an epithet for a spear (above, 259), and *Il.* xxii 328), or a helmet (*Il.* xi 96) see xxi 423n.

277. ἄρα looks back to τά ... πολλά in 273; this normal usage may explain the odd case of 267–8. ἐπὶ καρπῷ: καρπός 'wrist', from *κϝαρπος (cf. Skt. *hwerban*), quite distinct from καρπός 'fruit', occurs three times in the *Odyssey* and seven in the *Iliad*, four of them in this line-ending χεῖρ' ἐπὶ καρπῷ, and two besides the present example (*Il.* v 458, 883) describing wounds.

278. λίγδην: 'slightly', another *hapax* of uncertain etymology (cf., with the same meaning, ἐπιλίγδην, *Il.* xvii 599, and ἐπιγράβδην, *Il.* xxi 166; see n. on ἐπέγραψεν in 280). ἄκρον ... ῥινόν: Eustathius already noted the double gender of ῥινός 'skin, hide', which occurs twelve times in the *Iliad* and seven in the *Odyssey* (Schwyzer, *Grammatik*, ii 34); von der Mühll prefers the *lectio difficilior* of predicative ἄκρην, supported by fem. adjectives in *Il.* vii 248, xx 276; the word is also fem. in the *Scut.* and *Rhesus*, while the Alexandrians use both genders. δέ is lengthened before digamma, which is assured by Hsch. γρῖνος· δέρμα and γρίντης· βυρσεύς, and by the form ταλαύρινος (four examples in the *Iliad*).

279. The shield is not of the type which protects the whole body, τερμιόεις (*Il.* xvi 804, *Od.* xix 242) or ποδηνεκής (*Il.* xv 646), but a round or oval targe which leaves the shoulder vulnerable.

280. ἐπέγραψεν: of the five occurrences of ἐπιγράφω, three (*Il.* iv 139, xi 388, xiii 553) refer, as this one does, to grazes caused by weapons; *Il.* vii 187 shows the semantic shift 'graze, scratch' > 'engrave', of writing on a shard used for casting lots. A similar development operates on the simple verb γράφω (of a wound, *Il.* xvii 599; γραπτύς 'scratch, graze', *Od.* xxiv 229; of writing, the famous σήματα λυγρά, *Il.* vi 169). τὸ δ' refers to ἔγχος. πῖπτε: the circumflex accent is correct, despite the variants in some papyri, for this imperf. of πίπτω, which owes its long -ι- to the analogy with ῥίπή; the tense elegantly catches the way in which the spear first flies too high (ὑπέρπτατο; cf. ἔπτατο, xxiv 534, from πέτομαι), and then starts to drop towards the floor. The line-ending is of a type very similar to those of 20, 85 (see nn.), and, specifically with πίπτω, of *Il.* xii 156 (falling snow), xviii 552 (corn falling before the sickle), and above all xvii 633 (arrows falling ἐτώσια to the ground: see Hoekstra, *Modifications*, 90, and n. on xxii 256 above).

281. τοί: the pronoun is not used as an article here, nor in iii 162–3 οἱ μέν ... ἔβαν ... ἀμφ' Ὀδυσῆα, and viii 502–3 τοί ... ἀμφ' Ὀδυσῆα εἴατο, but the postponement of the verb in this last example and the present line point the way to the later development (perhaps already complete in *Il.* iii 146-9: Schwyzer, *Grammatik*, ii 416) by which such sentences could come to mean 'a man's companions including himself', with the preposition and its complement as a substantival phrase. **δαΐφρονα:** the epithet occurs in xxi 16; of Odysseus, in xxi 223; in similar line-endings, at xxii 115 (see n. and app. ad loc.), 202.

282. A combination of 263 and 265 which marks the fulfilment of Odysseus' order in 262-4.

285-91. Though these lines have been condemned by some, they can be linked (Eisenberger, *Studien*, 279) to the well-known (though disputed) anticlimactic 'sequence' of three missiles thrown at Odysseus: Antinous' θρῆνυς, which hits him on the shoulder (xvii 462), Eurymachus' σφέλας, which hits a nearby cup-bearer (xviii 396), and Ctesippus' ox-foot, which misses altogether (xx 299). Ctesippus is a loud-mouthed upstart (xx 287, xxii 287), and his fate here is a sort of poetic justice, as Stanford notes and Philoetius' own words emphasize, since he suffers vengeance at the hands of the very herdsman whose products he abused when he hurled the foot of one of his oxen at a guest.

285. For the formula βοῶν ἐπιβουκόλος ἀνήρ cf. xxi 199 n., xxii 268, and see W. Richter, *Archaeologia* H, 20; we find a variation, without ἀνήρ, in 292.

286. The first hemistich = *Il.* iv 108 (cf. 275 n.). **ἐπευχόμενος:** 'exulting (over a fallen enemy)'; the only Odyssean example of this typically Iliadic meaning (cf. *Il.* xi 431, xiii 373) of the ancient verb εὔχομαι (cf. Myc. *e-u-ke-to*) 'vow, pray' (cf. xxi 203 n., which is also relevant to the variant reading in this passage; also x 533, xi 46, xiv 423, 436, xx 60, 238); this use of the word is related to the meaning 'boast of' (v 119, x 368, xvii 46), and is close to the sense of ἐπεύχεο in xxiii 59, where Eurycleia displays an exultant and hostile joy: see J. H. Finley Jun., *Homer's Odyssey*, 197. Philoetius' attitude is profoundly sarcastic: despite ποτε in 287, it is too late for Ctesippus to mend his ways.

287. Ctesippus' patronymic, 'son of Much Boldness', is of course significant; it recalls the name Θερσίτης (*Il.* ii 212, etc.; note the curious variant reading), whereas in Ἀλιθέρσης in *Od.* ii 157 (also with Aeolic metaphony) there is no intended insult. **φιλοκέρτομε:** here only, which has caused textual doubts (but cf. κερτομέω, six times in the *Odyssey*; ἐπικερτομέω, 194 n.; κερτομίη, xx 263; κερτόμιος, xxiv 240 and ix 474, xx 177, where it functions almost as a neuter noun; κέρτομος is not found until Hes.).

288. On εἴκω see 91 n. ἀφραδίη is used in the *Odyssey* for senseless behaviour (ix 361, Cyclops), simple foolishness (x 27, the sailors before Aeolus; xix 523, Aedon), or real wickedness (xvii 233, Melanthius). **μέγα εἰπεῖν:** 'boast, speak proudly', with hiatus, is unique in the *Odyssey* (cf. the less impolite λίην μέγα εἶπες with which Telemachus addresses Athena and Odysseus, iii 227, xvi 243); the inf. is used for the imperative, as in the following line.

288-9. θεοῖσι | μῦθον ἐπιτρέψαι: 'let the gods have the last say' (cf. xix 502 ἐπίτρεψον ... θεοῖσιν, without a direct obj.). The end of the line is also found in *Il.* x 557, xx 368, *Od.* xvi 89; πολύ, adv.; the term of comparison in φέρτεροι is mankind.

290. τοῦτο: sc. 'this spear', or 'death'. ξεινήϊον: 'guest-gift', given in return for the 'conviviality' of Ctesippus' insult, is deeply sarcastic; the word occurs six times in the *Odyssey*, including xxiv 273; τοι is a possessive dat., ποδός refers to the infamous ox-foot. ποτε can refer to events which have happened the same day, as here. Eustathius noted that the phrase τοῦτο ἀντὶ ποδὸς ξεινήϊον 'became proverbial for being paid back in one's own coin' (Stanford, ad loc.).

291. ἀντιθέῳ: the epithet is often used in the *Odyssey* at the beginning of the line to refer to the hero, here with hiatus in thesis (cf. xxi 254). ἀλητεύοντι: ἀλητεύω, unattested in the *Iliad*, occurs six times in the *Odyssey* and always in connection with the vagrant wanderings of the hero except in xiv 126 (various travellers) and xviii 114 (Irus).

292. Ἦ ῥα: cf. 8 n. ἑλίκων: there are eight examples of the adj. ἕλιξ in the *Odyssey*, and six in the *Iliad*; it is always applied to oxen or cows, once with καλαί (xii 355), seven times on its own or with other epithets not relevant here (including xi 289, xii 136, and this passage), and six times in the end-of-line formula εἰλίποδας ἕλικας βοῦς (three Iliadic examples, and *Od.* i 92, iv 320, ix 46). Its meaning is not clear: εἰλίπους is generally translated 'with trailing feet, shambling', more strictly 'with circling feet' (εἰλέω < *ϝελ-νε-ω, cf. Lat. *uoluo*; but Chantraine notes that digamma is never observed in this word, *Grammaire*, i 132), which describes the characteristic rolling gait of oxen very well (see Hsch. εἰλίπους· διὰ τὸ εἰλίσσειν τοὺς πόδας κατὰ τὴν πορείαν; and compare ἀερσίπους 'high-stepping, lifting its feet', an Iliadic epithet for horses). ἕλιξ may, then, be an abbreviated form of *ἑλικο-πους (Risch, *Wortbildung*, 149); but there is also a word κραῖρα, glossed by Hsch. as ἡ κεφαλή, together with various compounds in -κραιρα (*κρᾶσργα, rel. to κέρας 'horn') such as ὀρθόκραιρα (of oxen, *Il.* viii 231, xviii 573, *Od.* xii 348, *h. Merc.* 220; of ships with pointed, horn-like prow and stern, *Il.* xviii 3, xix 344) which, in conjunction with *h. Merc.* 192 βοῦς κεράεσσιν ἑλικτάς, suggests the alternative interpretation, from an abbreviation of *ἑλικο-κραιρα, 'with twisted horns' (Risch, ibid.). Presumably various distinct breeds of straight-horn and twisted-horn cattle became confused as both epithets later became general (W. Richter, *Archaeologia* H, 47–8).

293. οὖτα: an athematic verb of uncertain etymology, with the short vowel probably derived by analogy from the passive οὐτάμενοι (xi 40) passing to the active infinitive οὐτάμεναι (ix 301, xix 449) or οὐτάμεν (*Il.* v 132, 821) and to the 3rd sing. aor. οὖτα found in these two lines and in the *Iliad*; the iterative οὔτασκε (*Il.* xv 745) is more doubtful, and οὖταε (356) is clearly derivative, whence come the conj. in οὐτάω (οὔτησε, xix 452) and οὐτάζω (οὐτασμένος, xi 536), and also ἀνούτατος (*Il.* iv 540). αὐτοσχεδόν: see n. on 241–329; the adv. is found here and in seven Iliadic passages, in all but one case in the same position in the line; there is a parallel adv. αὐτοσχεδά (*Il.* xvi 319) and a noun αὐτοσχεδίη 'hand-to-hand fighting' (*Il.* xv 510), used also adverbially in the acc. (*Il.* xii 192, xvii 294).

294. On Leocritus' name see xxi 144 n.; here and in ii 242 Allen writes -η-; von der Mühll prints -ει- but expresses a preference for -η- in his apparatus (the two editors treat Leodes' name in the same way; see 310); in the case of *Il.* xvii 344, for which see the n. on 241–329, both Allen and Mazon regularize to -ει-.

295. κενεῶνα: with predicative μέσον, here and in four places in the *Iliad* designates the soft underbelly (around which Ares would gird his armoured belt, ὅθι ζωννύσκετο μίτρην, *Il.* v 857); hence the weapon passes right out through the body (διαπρό). **διαπρὸ . . . ἔλασσεν:** the same line-end is found in *Il.* xiii 388, xv 342, xvi 309, 821, xvii 579; there is a similar expression in 93, and cf. also xxiv 524 διαπρὸ δὲ εἴσατο χαλκός.

296. The second hemistich is identical to 94 and similar to 86 (see n. on 84–8); the first hemistich = *Il.* v 58. **πρηνής:** this adj. (cf. Lat. *pronus*) is common in the *Iliad*, and occurs in *Od.* v 374, of Odysseus falling headlong into the water. Aristarchus seems to have taken objection to this line, and he is followed by Blass, who adduces the case of Amphinomus in 94 (*Interpolationen*, 208–9); but both he and Eurymachus in 86 fall head first.

297–309. The episode of the aegis is typical of the late reviser's penchant for fantasy (see n. on 241–329), and the two following similes present problems, amongst them their high proportion of very unusual diction. The lines have therefore been subject to a series of deletions.

297. δὴ τότ': 'then and only then', after a prudent allowance of time for father and son to show their prowess. **φθισίμβροτον:** 'man-slaying' (φθίνω, βροτός; the epithet is used only here, of the aegis, and in *Il.* xiii 339, of battle; its long first -ῑ- is curious, however, since it cannot come from φθίνω < *φθινϝω (cf. φθίσις, etc.); hence von der Mühll and others' suggestion of a possible itacistic corruption of φθεισίμβροτος, with e-grade (φθεισήνωρ is found in better MSS instead of φθῑσήνωρ in five places in the *Iliad*).

298. ἐπτοίηθεν: the only occurrence in Homer of πτοιέω, which later became so common (cf. trans. διεπτοίησε, again a unique instance, in xviii 340). This is probably the moment mentioned by Amphimedon in his retelling of the tale at xxiv 182, γνωτὸν δ' ἦν, ὅ ῥά τίς σφι θεῶν ἐπιτάρροθος ἦεν.

299–308. Epic similes are naturally less frequent in the *Odyssey* than in the *Iliad*, its plot being less monotonous and consequently less in need of the spice and relief of variety; there are, nevertheless, a number of examples, some of them suspicious, such as xii 251–4 (see n. on 384–8), xiii 81–3 (a ship 'runs' like a horse), xvi 216–18 (birds of prey, φῆναι or αἰγυπιοί, deprived of their clutch of nestlings; cf. 239–40 n.), xvii 126–30 (a lion devouring fawns; cf. 402–5); xix 205–7 (laments rushing down like the spates of snow-melt), xix 518–23 (the nightingale's song; cf. 288 n.). In the following lines we have a noteworthy series of such similes (299–301; 302–6; 384–8; 402–5; 468–70).

299. ὥς is placed in so-called anastrophe, an order which originated in syntactical juxtaposition of the type seen in *Il.* iii 2 Τρῶες . . . ἴσαν ὄρνιθες ὥς 'the Trojans went, birds (go) thus' > 'the Trojans went like birds' (Schwyzer, *Grammatik*, ii 667); there are twenty-four examples of the usage in the *Odyssey*, including this one and xxiii 339. An etymology such as *ϝωός* or *ϝϝος* (see 63n.) is suggested by the fact that the word often behaves as if it has digamma, producing hiatus (iv 160, viii 453, 467, xv 181, xviii 323) or lengthening of short vowels before consonants (iv 32, v 36, vii 71, viii 173, xi 413, xiv 205, xviii 29, xix 280, xxiii 339); but there are eight cases of elision before ὥς, and in the present case the preceding word must be scanned as a dactyl despite its -ς. ἀγελαῖαι: 'in a herd', from ἀγέλη; we find it again, always at the end of the line and applied to cows, in *Il.* xi 729, xxiii 846, *Od.* x 410, xvii 181, xx 251.

300. τὰς μὲν: it is better to take τάς here as demonstrative than relative. αἰόλος οἶστρος: the adj., only here in the *Odyssey*, is used of arms 'glinting' in the sun (*Il.* v 295, vii 222, xvi 107), but also of fast-moving, agile animals 'darting' or 'swarming' (wasps, *Il.* xii 167; a snake, *Il.* xii 208; a horse, *Il.* xix 404; worms 'writhing all over', *Il.* xxii 509); this is also the first appearance of οἶστρος 'gadfly', which was later used so often in the literal, not the metaphorical sense, especially in the legend of Io: see T. Krischer, *Formale Konventionen der homerischen Epik* (Munich, 1971), 58–9. ἐδόνησεν: gnomic aor.; the verb appears only three times in Homer, the other two being references to the wind shaking a tree (*Il.* xvii 55) or blowing up clouds (*Il.* xii 157).

301. =xviii 367, the beautiful passage in which Odysseus talks of challenging Eurymachus to a contest mowing the spring hay (see Austin, *Archery*, 247, and xxi 411n.). εἰαρινῆ: the adj. occurs four times in the *Iliad*, two of them in the line-opening ὥρῃ ἐν εἰαρινῇ (*Il.* ii 471, xvi 643); ἔαρ, ἔαρος 'spring', in *Il.* vi 148, *Od.* xix 519 (see 288n.). Digamma is guaranteed by Lat. *uer*, Hesych. γέαρ· ἔαρ, and various prosodic features such as hiatus in *Il.* viii 307, euphonic -ν in *Il.* ii 89, lengthening of a short vowel followed by a cons. in xix 519 (Chantraine, *Grammaire*, i 128); Bentley's deletion of ἐν (cf. ὥρῃ χειμερίη v 148) eliminates the problem of the unlengthened ἐν.

302. οἱ δ': sc. Odysseus and his men, switching attention to the new subject of the next simile; ὥς looks forward to ὡς ἄρα τοί in 307. On ὥς τε in similes, see Schwyzer, *Grammatik*, ii 669. αἰγυπιός 'vulture, lammergeier' is used as a synonym of γύψ (cf. 30n.), though there are problems in identifying the precise species meant by both these words and by φήνη (see nn. to 239–40 and 299–308), and even by αἰετός (see W. K. Kraal, *LfgrE*, i 259–60); αἰγυπιός is used in similes in *Il.* xvi 428 (identical to this line, on Patroclus and Sarpedon fighting), *Il.* xiii 531, xvii 460 (Meriones and Automedon in combat) and in divine metamorphoses in *Il.* vii 59 (Athena and Apollo), as well as at *Od.* xvi 217 (cf. 299–308n.). Its etymology would seem to imply an *ἀργιπιος, Skt. *ṛji-pyá-*, epithet for a bird of prey (Frisk, *GEW*) modified by popular etymology from γύψ and αἴξ 'goat', either as thought of as the bird's prey or because of the slight resemblance between the faces of the two animals. γαμψώνυχες, 'with crooked talons', occurs in the two parallel passages and in xvi 217; the second element ἀγκυλοχείλαι, found in this position in the same passages and also, of an eagle, xix 538 (see below), must be χείλος 'lip' > 'beak', with the sense 'hook-beaked', rather than χήλη 'claw', which would here make for an irritating tautology.

303. Cf. xix 538, where an eagle descends from the mountains. The iterative subj. without ἄν is a Homeric construction seen also, for example, in viii 524 (relative clause) and in xix 519 (simile with ὥς . . . ὅτε; see n. on 299–308).

304-6. A difficult passage which has been variously explained: (*a*) 'the birds (used to flying low and not in the mountains) scatter (note the shortening of the previous syllable before the short ῑ- of ἵημι; see 256n.) over the plain in terror of the clouds (the predators come from the open sky, cf. xx 104), but the lammergeiers swoop down (ἐπιάλμενος, xxiv 320; ἐπάλ-μενος, xiv 220) and kill them (ὀλέκω, x 125) without quarter (the phrase οὐδέ τις ἀλκή, which appears as a line-ending in 226, and, followed by γίγνετο in *Il.* xxi 528–9, is causal), while the spectators—sportsmen who 'enjoy watching . . . as nowadays one watches the manoeuvres of fighter aircraft', comments Stanford ad loc.—enjoy the hunt'; this will involve taking ὄρνις as fem., as in *Il.* ix 323, xiv 290, although it appears always to be masc. in the *Odyssey* (ii 181, xv 160, 525, 531, xx 242, xxiv 311, and probably v 51, xix 548), and also taking πτώσσω as a trans. verb with the object of which one is afraid in the acc., as at *Il.* xx 427, although the two Odyssean examples are intrans. (*Od.* xvii 227, xviii 363); or alternatively, (*b*) 'the terrified birds of the plain (a construction similar to later Att. αἱ ἐν τῇ πεδίῳ) launch themselves upwards towards the clouds (νέφεα, acc. of direction) in a vain attempt to outfly the predators, which nevertheless soar above them with one glide' (van Leeuwen ad loc., and, more or less, Krischer, op. cit. (300n.), 59, 'diese flattern ängstlich auf zu den Wolken, um sich zu verstecken, aber . . .'), though such an attempt to escape powerful fliers by climbing above them seems futile, and besides would provide scant spectacle for the spectators below; or (*c*) either of these interpretations as far as the first hemistich of 306, but taking the last hemistich to mean that the huntsmen set the chase up in some way in order to catch the birds: see H.-G. Buchholz, G. Jöhrens and I. Maull, *Archaeologia J*, 116, who cite Schadewaldt's translation and W. J. W. Koster's argument against P. Chantraine, *Études sur le vocabulaire grec* (Paris, 1956), 41 in his review, *Mnemosyne* xi (1958), 54, according to whom ἄγρη nowhere refers to the depredations of birds of prey, but only to hunting by men or gods, as in xii 330, where Odysseus and his men catch fish and birds; cf. *h. Hom.* xix 15, Pan returns from the hunt, *h. Hom.* xxvii 5, Artemis enjoys the hunt, τερπομένη); or finally (*d*) in the same sense as *c*, but more precisely, '(the birds) terrorized (by the lammergeiers) launch themselves towards the nets on the plain and the men (not the lammergeiers) throw themselves upon them and kill them, taking pleasure in the hunt'; this scenario for bird-catching (which, rather improbably, depends on there being some lammergeiers roaming about to do the chasing), requires us to take νέφεα as some sort of hunting-tackle (see sch. νέφεα· τὰ λίνα; cf. νεφέλη in Aristophanes, *Av.* 194, 528), and to construe the phrase τ' ἐν πεδίῳ νέφεα as a reduction of Att. τὰ ἐν τῷ πεδίῳ νέφη, with the same omission of the article observable in reductions such as ἀμφιπόλων ἐνὶ οἴκῳ (xix 514), αἱ ἄλλαι δμῳαὶ κατὰ δώματα (xx 122), μνηστῆρας κατὰ δώματα (xx 331), γυναικῶν ἐν μεγάροισιν (xxii 313). The final solution, an all-too-easy resort to emendation (for example, Bérard's νέφος ὥς, 'they launch themselves across the plain in, like a cloud', adducing 299, *Il.* iv 274, xxiii 133 νέφος . . . πεζῶν, xvi 66 Τρώων νέφος), is to be frowned upon. For ἀλκή 'refuge, possibility of escape' cf. 226 and *Il.* xxii 270 ὑπάλυξις, 301 ἀλέη.

307. **ἐπεσσύμενοι** picks up and repeats ἐπάλμενοι. **κατὰ δῶμα** indicates that they now control the hall.

308–9. **τύπτον:** iterative imperf., shows that they are no longer using spears, but have begun to fight with swords, probably the ones dropped by the dead suitors (cf. 328). **ἐπιστροφάδην:** 'rushing to and fro', is inappropriate in the narrow confines of the hall, though it reappears in Amphimedon's account (xxiv 184–5 = xxii 308–9, with κτεῖνον for τύπτον); the first line of *Il.* x 483–4 = 308, with κτεῖνε, the second with initial ἄορι θεινομένων, where Diomedes deals indiscriminate blows in all directions (it is doubtful, *pace* Lorimer, *Monuments*, 485, that the *Odyssey* is the source here); the same in *Il.* xxi 20–1, with τύπτε, of Achilles' ἀριστεία (in 12–14 his enemies flee like trapped locusts, in 22–4 they dash away like fish pursued by a dolphin; see Krischer, op. cit. (300n.), 59). **τῶν δὲ:** sc. of the suitors, possessive gen. dependent on κράτων or στόνος, or possible ablatival gen. after ὄρνυτο (on which see the note above on 241–6); the four parallels mentioned are the only places where ἀεικής 'ugly, unbecoming' > 'horrible' qualifies στόνος (see 432n.). **κράτων τυπτομένων:** here as on other occasions (see 38n.) we have a gen. on the way to becoming absolute, with causal sense; the verb, like the ἄορι θεινομένων cited in the parallel adduced above, refers to sword-fighting again (Merkelbach, *Untersuchungen*, 127 n. 2; we may thus reject Blass' conjecture κράτων πιπτόντων, based on *Il.* xi 158, 500 πῖπτε κάρηνα); κράτων may be added to the forms mentioned in the n. on 218, along with κρᾶτα (viii 92), κρᾱτός (v 323), κρᾱσίν (*Il.* x 152), κρᾱτεσφι (*Il.* x 156), and noting the accent, which is correct since according to Herodian the regular oxytone accentuation of the gen. does not apply to contracted disyllables. The second hemistich of 309 is repeated not only in xxiv 185 but also in xi 420; the Aeol. spelling θυίω is often found for θύω 'rage, be furious', related to θυμός 'spirit, temper' and not with θύω 'sacrifice', found four times in the *Odyssey* (Chantraine, *Grammaire*, i 51, 372; θυίω in *h.Merc.* 560; cf. also θύνω, xxiv 449); we find the verb applied to the wind in xii 400, 408, 426, to the sea in xiii 85 (in the *Iliad* it is always applied to warriors, among them the personified Scamander).

310–80. There remains one last score to be settled, that of the suitors' 'hirelings', as we may call them, who aided and abetted the wrongdoers. Leodes the priest, though he has taken little part in the fight against Odysseus and has always kept himself disapprovingly apart from the suitors (see xxi 146–7), nevertheless as one of their number cannot escape his companions' fate. The minstrel Phemius, on the other hand, is protected by innocence, and the holiness of his calling; for him Telemachus pleads pardon, and likewise for Medon in his grotesque hiding-place, a lackey who merely obeyed orders. The two survivors' anguish at the uncertainty of their fate in 379–80 is a delightful touch.

310. On Leodes' name see 294 n. ἐπεσσύμενος jars by its close proximity to the identically-placed ἐπεσσύμενοι of 307 (cf. v 428, 431). Ὀδυσῆος may depend on γούνων, or be a gen. of that towards which one leaps (the emendation Ὀδυσῆα, based on 342, is not necessary; cf. *Il.* xii 388, xvi 511–12 ἐπεσσύμενον . . . τείχεος, against *Il.* xii 143–4, xv 395–6 τεῖχος ἐπεσσυμένους . . . | Τρῶας; *Il.* xxii 26, of a horse which runs ἐπεσσύμενον πεδίοιο, is however a different construction). λάβε γούνων at the end of the line, with the gen. of contact and the ritual act of suppliancy or begging for pardon, is found at x 323 (Circe to Odysseus), xxii 342 (Phemius to Odysseus), xxii 365 (Medon to Telemachus); with λαβών, vi 142 (Odysseus to Nausicaa), x 264 (Eurylochus to Odysseus); and similar expressions in vi 169, x 481, xxii 337, 339.

311. = 343, 366 (the petitions of Phemius and Medon).

312. = 344; the line is taken from *Il.* xxi 74 (with Ἀχιλεῦ for Ὀδυσεῦ). γουνοῦμαι is found at the beginning of the line in vi 149 (Odysseus before Nausicaa); and at x 521, xi 29. σὺ δέ μ' αἴδεο καί μ' ἐλέησον: Hecuba beseeches Hector τάδε (her own breast) τ' αἴδεο καί μ' ἐλέησον (*Il.* xxii 82); ἐλέησον at the end of the line in *Il.* xxii 59 (Priam to Hector) and *Il.* xxiv 503 (Priam to Achilles, with αἰδεῖο θεούς); αἴδεο is from αἴδομαι, not from the αἰδέομαι seen at xxi 28.

313-19. Compare the poet's statements to the same effect in xxi 144–7, with the echoes of ἀτασθαλίαι (314, 317) in xxi 146, of νεμέσσα (314–15) in 147, and of θυοσκόος (318) in 145.

313-14. Leodes is not only confident of not having insulted Penelope, but also proclaims (φημι) that he has never said or done anything improper, double acc., to any of the women-slaves (see 304–6 n.), who as we know from xvi 108–9, xx 318–19 were ceaselessly molested by the other suitors. The first hemistich of 313 is repeated in iv 141, and similar to xix 380. ῥέξαι: although the initial digamma of ῥέζω (see 46 n.) ought to lengthen a preceding vowel (and does so in iv 690, v 102, viii 148, xiv 251, xxii 46, 209; preceded by -ν in iv 649), there are cases, like this one, where it fails to do so (note the conjecture ἔρξαι). ἀτάσθαλον: on this adj. see 47 n.; on the suitors' wanton behaviour, ἀτασθαλίαι, see n. on 313–19, and cf. also xxiii 67, xxiv 416, 458; ἀτασθάλλω, xviii 57, xix 88 (the women-slaves).

316. οὐ πείθοντο . . . ἔχεσθαι: 'they paid no attention to me as far as keeping their hands out of (ἄπο, anastrophe) mischief was concerned'; πείθω in the act. takes acc. of person and acc. or inf. of the object of the persuasion, in the pass. the inf. remains unchanged; on ἔχεσθαι see 423 n.

317. = 416. τῷ: cf. xxi 374n. ἐπέσπον: aor. of ἐφέπω 'look to, meet' (the pres. inf. is attested at *Il.* xx 357), from *sep-, and quite distinct both from ἕπομαι < *seqᵘ- (Chantraine, *Grammaire*, i 308–9), and from the non-Homeric ἐπι-σπάω; see 416 and xxiv 22, and ii 250, iv 196, xxiv 31 for other moods of the verb.

318–19. Leodes' pessimistic resignation recalls that of Lycaon before his death at the hands of Achilles in *Il.* xxi 92–3 (Fenik, *Studies*, 197).

318. θυοσκόος: 'augur, examiner of victims', prominently highlighting the sacrilege of Leodes' coming death, is the word used at xxi 145 (see n. ad loc., and 321, *Il.* xxiv 221, both in the same metrical position); the second element *-σκοϝος (cf. Lat. *haru-spex*) is a derivative with mobile σ- of later κοέω 'observe, inspect'. οὐδὲν ἐοργώς: cf. 46, 218, 314nn.; of eight Iliadic examples, seven respect hiatus and xxi 399 can, like the present line (see apparatus), be emended to do so (see Chantraine, *Grammaire*, i 115, Hoekstra, *Modifications*, 54, and cf. iv 693 ἄνδρα ἐώργει, *Il.* ix 320 πολλὰ ἐοργώς at the end of the line).

319. κείσομαι: 'I shall lie', obviously a prospective rather than a volitive fut.; cf. 48. Prophecies with the same fut. at the beginning of the line occur in *Il.* viii 537, xviii 121, xxi 318, xxii 71. Unless we write κείσομαι· ὥς, 'then, so', we must take ὥς as exclamatory, 'how (I see) there is no . . . (in the world)!' (see Schwyzer, *Grammatik*, ii 668; cf. for example iii 196, xxiv 194–5). The line is repeated, with the exception of the first word, in Penelope's complaint to Medon at iv 695; on this basis Pasquali (*Versi Spuri*, 228–9), who does not accept that Leodes is pessimistic (see n. on 318–19 above), affirms that 319 is an interpolation. **μετόπισθ':** 'in the future' (cf. 40, 55n., 345, xxiv 84). **εὐεργέων:** εὐεργής appears four times in the *Iliad* and sixteen in the *Odyssey* (see xxiii 234, xxiv 274; cf. fem. εὐεργός 'virtuous' in xi 434, xv 422, xxiv 202), but only here and in its parallel at iv 695 is it used in the neut. as a noun meaning 'good deed, favour', dependent on χάρις, 'thanks, gratitude for'. On Odysseus' εὐεργεσίη, see 235n.; the hero gives Leodes' words the lie in 374.

320. = 60 (see n., and cf. 1n.).

321. 'If you really boast of being the augur amongst them'; εὔχομαι is here rather more emphatic than it is when used in genealogies (xxi 335n., xxiv 269).

322. πολλάκι που μέλλεις ἀρήμεναι: 'you must often have prayed, no doubt'; μέλλω with inf. indicating a probability is a common construction, but the inf. is not made to show tense (see Chantraine, *Grammaire*, ii 307–9; cf. *Il.* xi 364 = xx 451 ᾧ μέλλεις εὔχεσθαι 'to whom you must *have* prayed'; *Il.* xxi 83 μέλλω που ἀπεχθέσθαι Διὶ πατρί 'I must *have* become hateful'— note the reinforcing που, 'no doubt', which supports the majority reading here; *Od.* xiv 133–4 ἤδη μέλλουσι κύνες . . . | ῥινὸν ἀπ' ὀστεόφιν ἐρύσαι 'the dogs must already *have* torn off'); thus ἀρήμεναι (for its long initial vowel see 208n.) is an intrans. active pres. inf. of the so-called Aeolic athematic type, with -η- for -ᾱ- in contracted verbs (see C. Calame, *LfgrE*, i 1168–76, Chantraine, *Grammaire*, i 305–6; and cf. xii 110 ποθήμεναι, xviii 174 πενθήμεναι, xx 137 πεινήμεναι). On the ritual see E. T. Vermeule, *Archaeologia* V, 100.

323. ἀρήμεναι: like ἀράομαι, takes acc. with inf.: '(you must have prayed) for the accomplishment of my sweet return home to be long delayed'; τέλος is therefore the subj. of γενέσθαι. For parallels see xx 74 τέλος . . . γάμοιο 'the taking-place of the marriage', xxiv 124 ἡμετέρου θανάτοιο . . . τέλος 'the accomplishment of our death'.

324. Despite the claim made in 313, Odysseus supposes that Leodes used to pray to take his place in the bedchamber, once the hero was dead; the two infinitives parallel γενέσθαι; ἄλοχον φίλην, 'my wife', is the subj. both of σπέσθαι (aor. of ἕπομαι; see 317n., and cf. *Il.* v 423, *Od.* iv 38) and of τεκέσθαι (the four examples of the aor. middle of τίκτω in the *Odyssey* refer to the father 'begetting' children, in iv 387, xv 249, or to the two parents together, xxiii 61, xxiv 293, but in the *Iliad* it is used of the mother 'conceiving', as at *Il.* ii 742).

325. This τῷ is sarcastic, 'precisely for this monstrous ambition'; cf. 317. The opt. with ἄν is a polite form, here used with menacing coolness (cf. *Il.* i 301, ix 375–6); γε, 'at least as far as I am concerned'. δυσηλεγέα: δυσηλεγής, 'which brings fatal cares, doleful', applied here to θάνατος and at *Il.* xx 154 to πόλεμος, is related to an alleged neuter *ἄλεγος from which derive ἀλέγω '(take) care' and the common ἀλεγεινός 'causing care, toilsome'; cf. also ἀπηλεγέως 'carelessly, without scruple', *Il.* ix 309, *Od.* i 373; conjecture νηλεγής in Alcm. fr. 26, 4 P, and the late ἀνηλεγής 'carefree, careless'. προφύγοισθα: προφεύγω appears in *Il.* vi 502, xi 340, xiv 81, *Od.* xi 107; for the middle ending -σθα cf. *Il.* xv 571 βάλοισθα, *Il.* xxiv 619 κλαίοισθα).

326. ξίφος: (cf. Myc. dual qi-si-pe-e) reappears instead of φάσγανον (see 74 n.); again in 443, xxiv 527. On Odysseus' 'sturdy' hand see xxi 6 n.

327. κείμενον: 'which was lying on the floor'; ὅ, rel. The dying Agelaus (κτεινόμενος, in the next line) had thrown his sword forward on the floor as he fell (ἀποπροέηκε, aor. for pluperf.; for the meaning cf. xiv 26, of sending a man on ahead, xxii 82, of letting fly an arrow; Odysseus now picks it up.

328–9. μέσσον ἔλασσε: the verb, with predicative μέσσον (cf. 295), is used of spears (93, 295) as well as swords (97); as explained in the n. on 96–8, it is not always easy, when swords are used, to know whether thrusting or cutting is meant, but here the macabre detail of severing the head by one tremendous swing to the neck puts it beyond doubt that cutting is meant (cf. the similar expression in *Il.* xx 455). For further decapitation, see 349 below (though it is not certain that δειροτομέω and its compound in ἀπο- always imply beheading; it does so in *Od.* xi 35, of sheep, and *Il.* xxiii 174, of dogs, and even in *Il.* xviii 336, and xxiii 22, of human victims, but *Il.* xxi 555 is less clear-cut, and in *Il.* xxi 89 Lycaon fears that, with him dead, Achilles will have 'cut the throats', δειροτομήσεις, of both himself and his brother, though we know that he has killed Polydorus by a spear-thrust to the belly). In *Il.* x 455–7 Diomedes first wounds Dolon, ὁ δ' αὐχένα μέσσον ἔλασσε | φασγάνῳ ἀΐξας, and then cuts the two tendons of the neck, ἀπὸ δ' ἄμφω κέρσε τένοντε; this is followed by a line identical to 329 (which has

277

given rise to the deletion of the latter); in *Il.* xiv 496–9 Penelaus topples Ilioneus with a spear-thrust to the eye, unsheaths his ξίφος and aims a cut at the neck, αὐχένα μέσσον ἔλασσεν, slicing the head to ground with helmet and all, ἀπήραξε . . . χαμάζε, and then raises the head aloft, still stuck on the spear like a blood-red poppy. **φθεγγομένου:** despite the pronoun τοῦ dependent on κάρη, the part. is here almost absolute (see n. on 308–9; Eustathius' variant for the parallel line at *Il.* x 457 presents the curious picture of a disembodied head talking); ἄρα points to the inevitability of the result of such a blow. **κονίῃσιν ἐμίχθη:** for the significance of this mention of dust, see 383 below and the Introduction to xxi; for the oscillation in the spelling of ἐμίχθη, see n. on 221; and for the relation of this passive formation to formulaic parallels, Hoekstra, *Modifications*, 136.

330–80. It has been well said that this passage, where Phemius' honourable treatment contrasts with the ridiculous role of Medon and the cruel fate of Leodes, constitutes the Bard's own tribute to the immortal gift of poetry (see, for example, Besslich, *Schweigen*, 101–4, M. Wegner, *Archaeologia* U, 31).

330. Phemius, who is mentioned in i 154, 337, xvii 263, has another of the *Odyssey*'s significant names, 'Fame-giver' or 'Rich in lays' (cf. πολύφημος in 376; at ii 150 it has another meaning; Stanford ad loc. cites Euphorion fr. 67, 1 c. φῆμις ἀοιδῶν); here reinforced for the first time by the significant patronymic 'son of Terpis or Terpius, Giver of delight' (for τέρπειν of the minstrel's gift, cf. i 347). For further examples of significant patronymics see 235, 287. **ἀλύσκανε:** 'tried to escape', otherwise unattested in Homer, a conative form related to ἀλέομαι < *ἀλέϝομαι (cf. 260n.); xvii 23 ἀλέῃ 'escape', xxiv 229 ἀλεείνω 'run away, shun'; see n. on 66 for ἀλύσκω 'run away', and n. on 38 for ὑπαλύσκω 'run stealthily away, creep off' (cf. iv 512, v 430, viii 355, xix 189), ἀλυσκάζω, xvii 581. **κῆρα μέλαιναν:** cf. 66n.

331. Against the μετά of certain MSS, preferred by Allen, the exact parallel with i 154 inclines the balance in favour of παρά, read by other MSS and preferred by von der Mühll. **ἀνάγκη:** expresses here, as in many other passages, the poet's benign attitude towards his fellow artist (Hoekstra, *Modifications*, 121–2).

332. **ἔστη:** probably indicates a sudden movement on Phemius' part. The rest of the line is paralleled in viii 394–5, xxiii 268 (μετὰ χερσίν, v 49, xxii 497, xxiii 294); the line-ending φόρμιγγα λίγειαν occurs seven times.

333. The end of the line is similar to xvi 73 μητρὶ δ' ἐμῇ δίχα θυμὸς ἐνὶ φρεσὶ μερμηρίζει; only in these two cases, of the seven occurrences in the *Odyssey*, does δίχα introduce a choice expressed by a double indirect question expressed by ἤ . . . ἤ < ἤϝε, 'whether . . . or', which we also find after the verb μερμηρίζω in vi 142–3, xvi 74–6 (cf. ἤ . . . ἠέ 'either . . . or' in xxi 97–8, xxii 468; in iv 118–19, x 51–2, xvii 236–7, xx 11–12 we have instead ἠέ . . . ἤ, and in xviii 91–2 ἤ . . . ἠέ).

334–5. **ἐκδὺς:** implying stealth. **ἵζοιτο:** pres. opt. (oblique, like λίσσοιτο (337), corresponding to a deliberative subj. in *oratio recta*); the aspect has caused remark, since the meaning requires a single action, 'whether to sit down ...'. **τετυγμένον**: 'solidly made', from τεύχω; cf. xxi 215, and xxiv 206, a field well-cultivated, or well-fenced with solid walls.

336. The son assists his father in the ceremony. The tmesis emphasizes the root-meaning of ἐπί, 'burnt on (the altar)'.

337. On this and the following lines see nn. on 310–12. **προσαΐξας** recalls the ἐπεσσύμενος of Leodes; it occurs in 342, 365 in the same formula.

338. δοάσσατο: 'seemed', found only once elsewhere in Homer (xxiv 239; cf. *Il.* xxiii 339 δοάσσεται), appears to be modified by analogy with ἔδοξε from an assumed *δεασσατο, akin to δέατο (vi 242), to Hsch. δεάμην· ἐδοκίμαζον, ἐδόξαζον, and δέαται· φαίνεται, δοκεῖ, and to *δεαλος > δῆλος.

339. On the patronymic see xxi 262 n.

340-1. ἤ τοι: 'and so, in fact'. The ritualistic care with which the minstrel handles his instrument is deliberate (cf. viii 67–8); it is quite wrong to comment, as do Blass (*Interpolationen*, 209), Duentzer, and others in favour of deleting 341 (a line untouched by Eustathius, by the way), that the detail of where Phemius puts it down is 'irrelevant'. It is however true that ἰδέ (a conj. formed from the pronoun *ἱ- and δέ) generally causes preceding hiatus, for reasons which are not clear (Schwyzer, *Grammatik*, ii 566–7; see for example i 112, where however the editors prefer Aristarchus' πρότιθεν, τοὶ δέ to Herodian's προτίθεντο ἰδέ; iii 10; or, with preceding τε, iv 604, xi 337, xviii 249, xxiii 289), except where it is masked by euphonic -ν (ix 186, xi 431, 626); this has been taken to indicate that passages which ignore hiatus, like this one and *Il.* ii 511, v 171, vi 4, xxiv 166, are of later date (Hoekstra, *Modifications*, 144–5). **χαμάζε**: cf. 327. **ἀργυροήλου**: for this epithet of θρόνος see xxi 139, and Lorimer, *Monuments*, 274 n. 1.

342. αὐτὸς δ' αὖτ': 'he for his part'. The same first hemistich is found in xx 165.

345. αὐτῷ τοι: 'to yourself'; the same line-opening at *Il.* ix 249, where Odysseus prophesies similar remorse in Achilles' case if he does not yield. **μετόπισθε**: cf. 319 n. **ἄχος**: 'remorse' (cf. the nom. in xxi 249, 299 n., 412; gen., xxiv 315). **ἀοιδόν**: in connection with ἀείδω in the next line, may be translated 'the singer (that I am)'.

346. πέφνῃς: cf. xxi 29, 36, xxii 54 n., 217, 229, 268, 359; the verb occurs in the subj. in two other passages of the poem (xi 135, xxiii 282). **θεοῖσι καὶ ἀνθρώποισιν**: sc. at religious solemnities and civic festivals; for the dat. of advantage of persons for whom one sings, cf. i 154, 325. The word ἀείδω deliberately picks up ἀοιδὸν in the previous line.

347-9. The lines have attracted endless comment, particularly on the word αὐτοδίδακτος, which is not found elsewhere in Homer. It is often supposed that Phemius' claim is connected with the well-known debate between natural gifts and acquired skills, 'nature' and 'nurture', which is so important, for example, in the poetry of Pindar and the disputes of the sophists and their enemies. But there would be little sense in Phemius thus boasting of being self-taught to Odysseus, a man who himself owes none of his skills to teachers; and this remains true despite Plato and the Platonists' use of the lines to support their theory of anamnesis (for example, *Ion* 533e; cf. M. Schmidt, *LfgrE*, i 1619–20, and amongst others Bowra, *Companion*, 73, or, to somewhat different effect, M. Wegner, *Archaeologia* U, 31, 35). On the contrary, his patronymic (see 330n.) places Phemius firmly within a family tradition or school like that of the Homeridae, of whom we hear so much from Pindar (*N.* ii 1) and Plato himself. What he seems to be trying to say, in his desperate plea for life (and remember that Odysseus' drawn sword is still at his throat), is that he has an innate capacity to *apply* the traditional repertory of inherited poetic craft to the particular case relevant to the audience of the moment. Thus Telemachus reproaches Penelope in front of Phemius in i 346–9 for not allowing the singer to choose the subject of his songs, τέρπειν ὅππῃ οἱ νόος ὄρνυται; likewise, in viii 43–5, Alcinous calls Demodocus θεῖον ἀοιδόν and explains the epithet by saying that the god has endowed him in especial measure (πέρι) with the gift of song (ἀοιδήν), to give pleasure (τέρπειν) in whatever way his spirit dictates, ὅππῃ θυμὸς ἐποτρύνῃσιν ἀείδειν (cf. the echo of this line in *Ag.* 991–2 αὐτο-δίδακτος . . . θυμός). Indeed, this ability springs from and relies on the singer's immense traditional repertory; Telemachus congratulates Phemius in i 337–8 on his wide knowledge of βροτῶν θελκτήρια . . . | ἔργ' ἀνδρῶν τε θεῶν τε, τά τε κλείουσιν ἀοιδοί. Thus one of the singer's powers is, for example, to celebrate the deeds of Odysseus himself, as Demodocus does at viii 499–520, and this is one sense in which it would be a mistake on the hero's part to kill him, thereby depriving himself (αὐτῷ τοι, 345) of so powerful an advocate. Besides, Phemius enjoys that divine protection which is so clearly revealed by the legends of inspired poets of later times such as Hesiod (*Th.* 23–4), Stesichorus (Pliny, *NH* x 82), Pindar (Paus. ix 23. 2), Callimachus (fr. 2 Pf.), and Horace (*C.* iii 4. 9–20). Demodocus was much loved by the Muse, who gave him blindness, it is true, but gave ἡδεῖαν ἀοιδήν in recompense (viii 63–4 πέρι . . . ἐφίλησε). Odysseus affirms in viii 479–81 that singers are worthy of all honour and respect, for σφέας | οἴμας Μοῦσ' ἐδίδαξε, φίλησε δὲ φῦλον ἀοιδῶν. With this affirmation Phemius' claim agrees, when he uses the *hapax* ἐμφύω (note the rare repetition ἐν- and ἐν; the word is used of love, for instance, in X. *Mem.* i 4. 7; the simple verb φύω occurs as trans. in Homer only at *Od.* x 393, of the bristles which Circe made grow on the sailors, and *Il.* i 235, of the leaves which will not grow on the sceptre) to describe his inspiration: 'the god has *implanted* in my mind all kinds of song (lit. "all ways, paths"; οἴμη occurs in viii 74, 481, both times in reference to Demodocus' songs; like οἶμος at *Il.* xi 24, the word is cognate with εἶμι "go"; cf. παντοίος in xxiii 161, xxiv 343)'. The more usual word for divine mental 'implantation' is the aor. of τίθημι, used six times in the *Odyssey* for Athena's suggestions (e.g. *Od.* v 427 ἐπὶ φρεσὶ θῆκε; cf. xxi 1), or for suggestions by the θεός in general (xiv 227), by Zeus (xvi 291), by the Erinys (xv 234), by Teiresias in Hades (xi 146); only once do we find the expression ἐνέπνευσε φρεσὶ δαίμων, of a god suggesting the ruse of Penelope's weaving in xix 138 (see Bona, *Studi*, 133 n. 9).

348-9. These lines also present difficulties. ἔοικα δέ τοι παραείδειν | ὥς τε θεῷ is often loosely translated 'and you seem a very god when I sing by your side', lit. 'and I seem to sing by your side as if by the side of a god'; θεῷ bears heavy emphasis in this rendering, and the present inf. would have to refer to a time before Odysseus' journeying, which scarcely fits with the perf. ἔοικα. παραείδω with dat. of person governed by the prefix, and implying the idea of having the seat of honour next to a superior, is unattested elsewhere (cf. later expressions such as πάρεδρος). This personal construction with ἔοικα is also unique in Homer, though we have a parallel in *Il.* vii 192 δοκέω νικησέμεν Ἕκτορα 'it seems that I shall defeat Hector'. But the gravest objection is that, phrased like this, Phemius' rather blatant piece of flattery (cf. Telemachus' compliment to the effect that Nestor looks to him like a god, iii 246; the people listen to Alcinous θεοῦ . . . ὥς, vii 11; the Ithacans look on Eurymachus ἶσα θεῷ, xv 520) cannot constitute a convincing logical argument for sparing the minstrel's life (cf. following τῷ, like that of 325 and so many other passages). For this reason Monro and Stanford prefer the no less tentative translation 'I am fit to sing before you . . ., I am the right person to be your poet (if you spare me, and therefore you ought not to kill me)'. ἔοικε 'be fitting' is very common: cf. xxi 319, 322, xxii 196; also xxiv 254, with Bentley's conjecture ἔοικεν); but I can find no parallel for the construction used personally in Homer (the use of the part. ἐοικώς 'fitting' at i 46, iii 124-5, iv 239 is not strictly parallel, though it does later occur in the tragedians (S. *El.* 516, *Tr.* 1241; E. *Hel.* 497). λιλαίεο: λιλαίομαι 'yearn, desire earnestly' (cf. xxiii 334, xxiv 536) captures the fierce look of glee and menace in Odysseus' face, as does the terrifying δειροτομῆσαι (on the exact meaning of which see 329n.).

351. The line provides the apposition to τάδε in the previous clause. The first hemistich, with shortening of ἐγώ and the expected hiatus before ἑκών (cf. Locr. ϝεκών), is repeated in iv 377. οὐδὲ χατίζων: 'nor much less in hopes (of any gain)'; the conj. is used in a different sense in the two direct parallels, *Il.* xvii 221 (without a complement) and 50 (see n.).

352. πωλεύμην: 'frequent, go repeatedly'; this form with long vowel and Ionic semi-contraction occurs seven times in the *Odyssey* and eight in the *Iliad*, and is close in meaning to πολεύω in 223 (see n.). It is uncertain whether μετά should be taken closely with the inf., 'to associate with, take part in (the suitors' feasts)' (thus Chantraine, *Grammaire*, ii 118), or translated 'after (dinner)', in close conjunction with δεισόμενος, final fut. part. (thus Schwyzer, *Grammatik*, ii 486 n. 2; cf. i 152, and iv 194 ὀδυρόμενος μεταδόρπιος, 'to lament during supper', something which is not usual).

353. On πλέονες see 12-14n.; for the line-ending, 331.

354. The first hemistich is repeated in 361 and xix 89; the second, with its periphrasis and hiatus before .ἷς (cf. Lat. *uis*), in xxi 101 (see n.) and 130.

355. The possessive ἑός < *σεϝος has occurred already in xxi 316, and appears again in 381, xxiii 223, xxiv 162, 236, 295; it is less common than ὅς

COMMENTARY

(see xxi 5, 27, 41, 204, 301–2, 315, and nn.). The line-ending is the same as that of 163.

356. ἴσχεο: 'contain yourself, hold your hand'; on ἴσχω < *σισχω, related to ἔχω, see nn. on 70 and 172, and cf. 248; later it occurs also in 367, 411, xxiv 54, 323, 531, 543. ἀναίτιον: only here, at xx 135 (Penelope, according to Eurycleia), and in three places in the *Iliad*. οὕταε: cf. 293 n.

357. 'And Medon too': Telemachus cannot see the hiding herald, but thinks that if none of his three companions has yet killed him, they should spare him too. σαώσομεν, aor. subj. with short thematic vowel.

358. οἴκῳ ἐν ἡμετέρῳ: this line-opening, with shortening of the final syllable of οἴκῳ before the following vowel, is paralleled in i 258, *Il.* iii 233. κηδέσκετο: 'used to look after me', iterative of κήδομαι (cf. xxiii 9 κήδεσκον). Medon proved an affectionate ally to Penelope in iv 677–715, xvi 412, but also behaved politely towards the suitors in xvii 172–6. He repays Odysseus' clemency in xxiv 439–49. παιδὸς ἐόντος agrees with μευ, but the part. here borders on the gen. absol. (see 328–9 n.).

359. The sing. ἔπεφνε agrees with the nearest of its two subjects, Φιλοίτιος. For examples of εἰ δή at the beginning of the line see xxi 170, xxiv 434.

360. In some cases ἀντιβολέω does not indicate a casual encounter (thus Athena, Hermes, and Poseidon 'appear' to various characters in vii 19, x 277, *Il.* xiii 210); when it does, however, the subj. of the verb is the less important character, the one who is 'bumped into' by the person who is the main character from the point of view of the narrative (thus Eurypylus is encountered by Patroclus in *Il.* xi 809, Meriones by Idomeneus in xiii 246; the usages in xxi 306, xxiv 87 are distinct). Only here, however, does the verb have hostile undertones. ὀρινομένῳ: temporal, equivalent to an imperf., 'while you were prowling angrily about'; compare the pass. in 23 (see n.); it is active in xxi 87, xxiv 448, and middle, here and in xxiv 318.

361. The line begins in the same way as 354; poor, trembling Medon has his ears pricked to catch the smallest sound. τοῦ: sc. Telemachus. The line-ending, with its hiatus, is applied to Medon himself in iv 696, 711, xxiv 442, but also to Peisenor in ii 38; the part. has already occurred in xxi 343, 355 (see n.), xxii 153.

362–3. A comic episode which slightly relaxes the tension. πεπτηώς: it is difficult to sort out the various forms related to the root of this verb; besides πίπτω 'fall' (cf. 280 n.) and πέτομαι 'fly' (πέτεσθαι, ii 147; ὑπέρπτατο, 280 n.), we have a group of forms with intrusive *-κ in the stem which mean 'crouch, cower' related to post-Homeric πτήσσω < *πτάκyω (viii 190 κατά . . . ἔπτηξαν, 'they crouched cowering'; hence trans. πτῆξε 'alarmed, gave a fright to', *Il.* xiv 40) and πτώσσω < *πτωκyω ('crouch', *Il.* xxi 26; 'flee in alarm', *Il.* xxi 14; 'cower', 304 n.; cf. πτώξ 'hare', *Il.* xvii 676; with affective aspiration, πτωχός 'crouching' > 'beggar', for example in xxi 292, 327, xxiv 157, πτωχεύω 'beg', xvii 11). In the perfect it is important to distinguish the 'falling' verbs (πεπτεῶτ', *Il.* xxi 503, *Od.* xxii 384; πέπτωκα is un-Homeric) from the 'crouching' ones (ὑποπεπτηῶτες,

282

Il. ii 312—note the prefix, cf. 38n.; xiii 98, of rocks which 'lower' over the harbour entrance, with textual variants undecided between λιμένος πότι πεπτηυῖαι and λιμένος ποτιπεπτηυῖαι; xiv 354, 474, xxii 362); the long -η- corresponding to the disyllabic stem is always maintained except in the πεπτεῶτα(ς) of *Il.* xxi 503, *Od.* xxii 384, which display quantitative metathesis of -ηο- and subsequent synizesis (Chantraine, *Grammaire*, i 71–2, 428, 430 postulates -εο- or even -ω- here; see 130n.).   ὑπὸ θρόνον: lative after πεπτηώς; on the sort of chair intended see xxi 139n. ἀμφὶ δὲ δέρμα | ἕστο: 'he had wrapped himself up in a cowhide', from head to foot (cf. iv 436–40, where Eidothea likewise completely shrouds the crouching Menelaus and his companions in seal-skins which are likewise νεόδαρτα); ἀμφί. . . ἕστο, aor. for pluperf., with tmesis (cf. xxiv 158, 227; the fut. ἕσσω in xxi 339 and n.; aor. in -σσ-, xxiv 59, 250, 467, 500; in -σ-, xxiii 131, 142; perf. εἵμαι < *ϝεσμαι, xxiii 115). On the presence in the palace of recently skinned oxen, Stanford remarks (n. on 362): 'Van Leeuwen is pained to find a newly flayed hide lying about in a palace like this; but sadly compares i 108; xx 2 and 299–300'.   ἀλύσκων: conative; for the line-ending see n. on 330.

364. Medon can no longer stand the stench of the new-flayed skin (cf. Menelaus' similar predicament, iv 441–3).   ὑπὸ: 'from underneath' (cf. for example vi 127 θάμνων ὑπεδύσετο; Bérard's ὑπέκ is unnecessary).   ἀπέδυνε: with acc. of the garment taken off; see i 437 ἔκδυνε, v 372 ἐξαπέδυνε, and cf. the contrary ἐς τεύχε᾽ ἔδυνον, 'they put their armour on' (xxiv 498).   βοὸς ... βοείην: a grossly pleonastic phrase, obviously derivative from such lines as *Il.* xvii 389, xviii 582 βοὸς μεγάλοιο βοείην, where the adj. makes the phrase justifiable, in contrast to the present case; cf. *Il.* xxii 159, *Od.* xx 96 (cf. 375n.), where βοείη, which as a subst. presupposes some noun such as later δορά, has no such complement (note the sch. and the ingenious conjecture inspired by xxi 46, 241, xxii 19 in the app.).

365-6. = 342–3, with the exception of the first hemistich of 365.

367. ἐγὼ μὲν ὅδ᾽ εἰμί: 'here I am!'; cf. xxi 207n. on punctuation.   σὺ δ᾽ ἴσχεο· εἰπὲ δὲ πατρί: 'stay your hand, and tell your father (to do so too)' (cf. xv 150–1 χαίρετον . . . καὶ Νέστορι . . . εἰπεῖν, 'fare you well, and tell Nestor (to fare well too)'). Medon harps back to the imper. ἴσχεο of 356, showing that despite 357 he does not yet trust Telemachus not to strike him.

368. περισθενέων: 'in his moment of triumph', only here in Homer; cf. ἐρισθενής in viii 289.   δηλήσεται: subj. with short thematic vowel, governs με. The final formula has already occurred ten times in i–xx.

369. κεχολωμένος: takes an ablatival gen., '(angry) because of them'; χολόομαι has already appeared in xxii 59, 224n.   ἀνδρῶν μνηστήρων: identical line-opening in xxiii 138, 303, 363, xxiv 2; ἀνδρῶν is unemphatic, as in many similar formulaic expressions (cf. vi 3 Φαιήκων ἀνδρῶν, *Il.* xxi 574 ἀνδρὸς θηρητῆρος, and similarly vii 347 γυνὴ δέσποινα, xx 105 γυνὴ . . . ἀλητρίς; see n. on 395–6). The following rel. is causal; the

COMMENTARY

ethic dat. οἱ produces an ugly repetition, with hiatus in thesis and shortening. On ἔκειρον see 36n.

370. There is little to choose between von der Mühll's μεγάροις and Allen's
μεγάρῳ. νήπιοι: cf. 32n. The paratactic clause with ἔτιον should
logically be subordinate to the preceding one ('without paying him any
respect').

371. = Il. x 400. ἐπιμειδήσας: Stanford notes that, 'except for his
sardonic humourless grimace' in xx 301, the comedy of Medon's terror has
provoked Odysseus' very first smile (cf. the smiles of Menelaus, iv 609;
Calypso, v 180; Athena, xiii 287; Telemachus, xvi 476); later he smiles once
more, at Penelope (xxiii 111). The compound ἐπιμειδάω appears here and
in three identical line-openings in the Iliad (x 400; iv 356, Agamemnon
smiling at Odysseus; viii 38, with initial τήν, of Zeus smiling at Athena).
πολύμητις: cf. 1n.

372. θάρσει: imper., found in seven other places in the Odyssey, all except
one of them in the same position at the beginning of the line, and all except
two (xix 546, Penelope's dream, xxiv 357) in the mouths of characters other
than Odysseus. οὗτος: sc. Telemachus. ἐρύσατο: the verbs
*ἔρυμαι, ἐρύω, ῥύομαι, representatives of various developments from a
semantic cluster 'pull towards oneself' > 'rescue' > 'protect', present an
inextricable puzzle. It is generally thought that the whole group has initial
digamma (cf. Delph. ϝερυσάτω, and see xxi 173n. on ῥυτήρ); nevertheless,
digamma is ignored in the ἐρύσατο of this line, in contrast to the many
cases of *ϝερυ- stems where it is respected (Il. xvii 287, ἐρύειν with
lengthening of a preceding short vowel-consonant cluster; iii 65, iii 470, xx
279, aor. ἐρύσαντο preceded by hiatus; xxii 79, aor. εἰρύσσατο) with long
-ῡ- and doubled -σ- from *ἐϝερ-; xxi 125, fut. ἐρύσσεσθαι similarly formed
(preceded by euphonic -ν), and to cases where it is impossible to tell
whether digamma is respected or not (xxii 176 ἐρύσαι, xxii 187, 193
ἔρυσαν, xxii 386, 476 ἐξέρυσαν). In the case of *ϝρυ- stems, digamma is
clear in aor. ἐρρύσατο < *ἐϝρύσατο (Il. xv 290, where it is followed by καὶ
ἐσάωσεν with hiatus in thesis, a near parallel to the tautological formula of
the present line), in pf. εἴρυσθαι < *ϝε-ϝρυ-σθαι (xxiii 82, 151; note the
accentuation), in plupf. εἴρῡτο < *ἐ-ϝε-ϝρῡ-το (xxii 90, xxiii 229). See
Chantraine, Grammaire, i 136–7.

373. Unlike Ctesippus (cf. 286n.), Medon will be permitted to learn from his
mistake. ὄφρα is loosely constructed not with θάρσει, but with the idea of
pardon implied by that word; the contraction γνῷς is paralleled only by
γνῷ in Il. i 411 (see the apparatus). Asyndetic ἀτάρ has appeared inxxi 229
(see n. ad loc.), the ending of which is very similar to this line, and also in
xxi 231, 260, 404, xxii 53, 55; for the ending of εἴπησθα, the digamma of
which causes lengthening of the previous syllable, see 325; καὶ ἄλλῳ, 'to
others too'.

374. A rather banal apophthegm. κακοεργίη, with lengthening of the -ι- to
avoid the cretic, is unique in Homer (κακοεργία is found later in Plato, and
κακουργία in Attic prose; see κακοεργός in xviii 64, later common,

284

especially in the contracted form κακοῦργος; cf., xxiv 251 ἀεργίη with the same scansion, which is paralleled in examples such as ἀτιμίῃσιν in xiii 142, compared to ἀεργός in *Il.* ix 320, *Od.* xix 27; on εὐεργεσίη see 235 n., 319 n. on εὐεργής, etc.).

375. ἀλλ': 'so, to end with'. **ἕζεσθε:** imper.; cf. 335 n., but here the idea is a cross between 'sit down' and 'remain seated'.

375-6. θύραζε |... εἰς αὐλήν: see Introduction to xxi, and cf. xx 97, where Odysseus takes his stinking βοείη out into the courtyard.

376. 'Leave this hall with its bloody slaughter'; cf. the similar phraseology of *Il.* x 298 ἄμ φόνον, ἄν νέκυας, *Il.* xxiv 610 κέατ' ἐν φόνῳ. **σύ τε καὶ πολύφημος ἀοιδός:** 'you and the minstrel together'; on πολύφημος see 330 n.; it is used in a very different sense as the name of the Cyclops in i 70, etc.

377. ὄφρ' ἄν: 'while', temporal consecutive, with πονήσομαι, subj. with short thematic vowel, from πονέομαι, trans. 'work hard at, labour over' (cf. *Il.* xxiii 245, *Od.* ix 250, xi 9). **χρή:** the origin of this word, which on the face of it is used as a verb, was in fact an ancient noun with stem-vowel in -ā (cf. original acc. such as δήν, xxi 426, xxii 473; λίην, xxiii 175; πλήν, viii 207) meaning 'necessity', used originally with a plain infin., and then with an acc. and inf. (without acc., xxiv 324 χρὴ σπευδέμεν 'hurrying is a necessity' > 'it is necessary to hurry'; with acc., xxiv 407 τί σε χρὴ ταῦτα πένεσθαι; 'what necessity is it that you labour?' > 'why is it necessary for you to labour?'; cf. xxiii 250). A similar development takes place with the noun χρεώ or χρειώ, invariably in the nom. except in *Il.* viii 57, where uses in which its true function as a substantive is quite clear (iv 312 τίπτε δέ σε χρειὼ δεῦρ' ἤγαγε;) occur side by side with constructions with the plain inf. (*Il.* xxiii 308 καί σε διδασκέμεν οὔ τι μάλα χρεώ) and acc. and inf. (xv 201 ἐμὲ δὲ χρεώ... ἱκέσθαι). It is nevertheless troubling to find the word 'governing' an acc. in cases where we should expect a dat., as here, even in cases where the latter is not excluded by the metre (Chantraine, *Grammaire*, ii 40); thus xxi 110, 'what need have I of praising my mother?', with ablatival gen. of the obj. μητέρος αἴνου; iv 463 τέο σε χρή; iii 14 οὐ μέν σε χρὴ ἔτ' αἰδοῦς. The line-ending ὅττεό με χρή is paralleled in i 124, with μυθήσεαι, which may be understood as an indirect question, 'tell me what you need'; but here we must construe 'while I busy myself with what(ever) I need' (for the gen. of ὅτις see 315 n.); cf. *Il.* xi 606 τί δέ σε χρεὼ ἐμεῖο, iv 634 ἐμὲ δὲ χρεὼ γίνεται αὐτῆς. Usages such as v 189 ὅτε με χρειώ... ἵκοι, vi 136 χρειὼ γὰρ ἵκανε have led some to suppose that one of these verbs should always be supplied with χρή also, the acc. being an acc. of direction; at all events, the construction here is parallel to later uses of δεῖ (only once in Homer with acc. and inf., *Il.* ix 337; cf. A. *Pr.* 86 αὐτὸν γάρ σε δεῖ προμηθέως).

378. ἔξω βήτην... κιόντε: 'they went out' (Schwyzer, *Grammatik*, ii 538; on the dual, cf. 202 n.); κίω (the pres. in -ω is derivative, as the accent on the part. shows) appears again in 479, xxiii 228, 295, and seven times in xxiv; it is used in much the same way as εἶμι in xxi 243, 392, xxii 103 (see nn.), and it looks as if only hiatus has prevented the poet from using ἰόντε (compare line-endings such as iii 276, iv 478).

379. ἐξέσθην: cf. 375 n. ἄρα, 'as they had been told to'; τώ γε, 'the two of them', sc. Phemius and Medon. The beginning of the line is identical in xv 134, the end of it in 334.

380. παπταίνοντε: with its expressive reduplication, is a graphic verb, related to Hsch. ἱμπάταον· ἔμβλεψον and καπατάς· καθορῶν; it describes the haunted look of a frightened man gazing wildly about him, as here and in the disputed 24 and 43 (cf. xii 233, Odysseus looking out for Scylla); the concentrated scanning from side to side of a man searching for something, as in xvii 330 where Telemachus looks for a seat; the ecstatic stare of the dreamer (Penelope in xix 552), or the fixed watchfulness of the warrior (Heracles in xi 608, Odysseus during the slaughter according to Amphimedon's account in xxiv 179, and the next line). The repetition in 381 is deliberate: 'as for the hero, he too had his eyes staring wide (but for a quite different reason, not the unnerved panic of these two)'. The line-ending, with metrical shortening of the dual ending of ποτιδεγμένω, is almost the same as ix 545, xxiv 396, Il. xix 336; it captures the nervousness of the two men, who are still not entirely reassured; ποτιδεγμένω, causal pres. part. from an Aeol. athematic form of προσδέχομαι (cf. δέγμενος in xx 385, ὑποδέγμενος in xiii 310); αἰεί 'at any moment'. Notice the line's effective use of alliteration to underscore the comic tone.

381. κατά captures the comprehensive ranging of his glance up and down the room; ἑόν marks the look as the victor's solemn act of repossession. εἰ may be taken as introducing an indirect question, 'to see if any of the suitors was left alive', or prospectively, 'in case any suitor . . .'.

382. ὑποκλεπέοιτο: opt. in indirect speech; the word is an otherwise unattested form related to κλέπτω (Il. i 132), κλέπτης (Il. iii 11), κλεπτοσύνη (Od. xix 396), κλόπιος 'shifty, deceitful' (Od. xiii 295); for the prefix, see nn. on 38, 330, 362–3. The end of the line = 363.

383. δὲ: 'but'; note the hiatus before ἴδεν. **μάλα πάντας:** 'every one of them'. The second hemistich is almost identical to the endings of Il. xv 118, xvi 639, and the beginning of Il. xvi 796; on the dust, see 328–9 n. and Introduction to xxi.

384. πεπτεῶτας: cf. 362–3 n. **πολλούς:** predic., 'in great heaps'.

384–8. Another simile, this time from fishing, with ὡς . . . ὥς; it was doubtless these lines which inspired the famous metaphor in A. *Pers.* 424–6. Fishing was generally considered by the Greeks, who by preference ate meat, as a humble occupation (H.-G. Buchholz, G. Jöhrens, and I. Maull, *Archaeologia* J, 103, 132, 169, 175); elsewhere in the *Odyssey* fish is only eaten in the last resort, for instance by Menelaus' starving companions, who 'began to fish with curved hooks', ἰχθυάασκον . . . γναμπτοῖσ᾽ ἀγκίστροισιν, in iv 368–9; the same verb is used of Scylla fishing for dolphins, seals (κύνας), and whales in xii 95–6; Odysseus and his men fish and catch birds when their provisions run out in xii 330–2 (the last line of which, with its inapposite mention of fish-hooks in the context of bird-catching, is suspect); the strong thread of such mentions which runs through xii is maintained in the simile at xii 251-4, where we are shown a fisherman (ἁλιεύς, unattested in the *Iliad*, derived from ἅλιος < ἅλς; ἁλιεύω, in NT and in Plutarch; in xvi 349, xxiv 419 means simply 'sailor') with a long rod (περιμήκεϊ ῥάβδῳ) provided with a tube of horn, προῆσι βοὸς κέρας ἀγραύλοιο, and at the end of it (besides a lead weight, μολύβδαινα, cited in *Il.* xxiv 80), a tasty bait probably of meat, δόλον κατὰ εἴδατα βάλλων. There is a further allusion to fishing in xix 113-14. Here the fishermen, ἁλιῆες, drag up the fish from (ἔκτοσθε) the deep sea in a net and empty them out onto the beach, where they die (we miss here the typical ἀσπαίρω 'gasp', cf. xii 254-5, and 473n.) in heaps under the pitiless sun, pathetically yearning their hearts out for the sea.   κοῖλον ἐς αἰγιαλόν: αἰγιαλός is used only here in the *Odyssey*; cf. *Il.* ii 210, iv 422 in the same position, xiv 34; κοῖλος, to judge for example by x 92 λιμένος κοίλοιο, indicates a 'curved' beach or bay; the adj. is common (thirty-one occurrences in the *Odyssey*, among them xxi 417, xxiv 50) but invariably occurs in situations where it can be scanned trisyllabically (cf. Lat. *cauus* and Hsch. κόοι· τὰ χάσματα τῆς γῆς καὶ τὰ κοιλώματα, which suggest *κοϝιλος > κόϊλος: Chantraine, *Grammaire*, i 28); hence the question mark placed over the text here, where κοῖλος must be disyllabic, by Meister, *Kunstsprache*, 50, van Leeuwen, and Nauck.   πολιῆς ... θαλάσσης: 'hoar-grey, white-flecked', a well-known epithet for the streaked appearance of the billowing sea, used thirteen times in the *Odyssey* with ἅλς, including xxiii 236, and a doublet in which the word is used as a two-termination adj., ἁλὸς πολιοῖο, v 410, ix 132 (cf. xxi 3n. and 81 for 'hoar-grey' iron; of a grey-haired or hoary head, xxiv 317); the same formula occurs in this position in the line in a similar phrase at vi 272.   δικτύῳ ... πολυωπῷ: δίκτυον, from *dik- 'throw', is found only here in Homer, as is πολυωπός (cf. Hellenistic πολυωπής, and post-classical ὀπή 'hole'); this is the only Homeric mention of fishing with nets except the doubtful one, in a metaphor of a military encirclement in *Il.* v 487, ἀψῖσι λίνου ἀλόντε πανάγρου, where ἀψίς is 'knot' and λίνον indicates the 'yarn' from which the net is woven; this may have been a hunting-net, however (cf. 304n.).   ἐπὶ ψαμάθοισι κέχυνται: 'they are poured out on the sand'; for the verb in final position cf. 389; ἐκέχυντο, of the geese in Penelope's dream, xix 539, ἐξεκέχυντο of ropes in viii 279; cf. κέχυτο in ix 330, and of dung in xvii 298; ψάμαθος occurs nine times in the *Odyssey*, in the same formulaic position in xiii 284, iii 38 ἐπὶ ψαμάθοισ' ἁλίησι.   τῶν μέν τ' Ἥλιος ... ἐξείλετο θυμόν: τῶν, pron., sc. 'of the fish', dependent on θυμόν; the line-ending is similar to *Il.* xv 460, xvii 678, *Od.* xi 201, with gnomic aor.; φαέθων, from the root of *φαϝος > φῶς, with intrusive -θ, is used as an epithet of the sun at the same position in the line in *Il.* xi 735, *Od.* v 479, xix 41; it occurs also in xi 16.

391. εἰ δ' ἄγε: 'come now', cf. xxi 217, xxii 233, etc. μοι, ethic dat. For the formulaic τροφὸν Εὐρύκλειαν see 480n.

392. Note the hiatus before ἔπος, and the lengthening of its final syllable

before digamma. εἴπωμι, aor. thematic subj. with -μι (see app.); τό relative. For καταθύμιος 'preoccupying, on one's mind' cf. *Il.* x 383, xvii 201 (Lehrs, op. cit. (9n.), 146 n. 86).

393. = 108 (see n.).

395-6. The repetition of δεῦρο δὴ ὄρσο by ἔρχεο in 397, in asyndeton, is curious (hence the deletion recorded in the app.); δεῦρο ... ὄρσο is an elliptical expression for 'get up (and come) here' (ὄρσο in vii 342; here and in *Il.* v 109 we have a variant reading ὄρσεο, a thematic form with -σ-parallel to λέξεο, xix 598; ὧρτο is very common, cf. 364, xxiii 348). γρηῦ παλαιγενές: inspired by *Il.* xvii 561 ἄττα γεραιὲ παλαιγενές, Menelaus' tender address to Phoenix, which occurs in the same metrical position (imitated also in *h.Merc.* 199 γεραιὲ παλαιγενές, in the same position again; and cf. *Il.* iii 386, *h.Cer.* 101, 113, of the aged Demeter); its use by Telemachus here is a piece of humorous banter which shows his elation at the triumph (cf. xix 346, where Odysseus enquires of Penelope whether there is some γρηῦς ... παλαιή about). The contrast between the disyllabic form of the voc. γρηῦ here and in 481 (see also the dat. in xxiii 33, and nom. in 433, 495, xxiii 1, 292, xxiv 211), and the diphthongized γρηῦ· of 411 (theoretically, a possible disyllable too) and γρηῦς of xxiv 389, shows that a metrical licence is in play (Chantraine, *Grammaire,* i 224), but it is not clear which of the two scansions represents the original form; the uncontracted one seems more likely if the word is indeed related to γέρων, γῆρας by an ancient noun *grāyús 'old age' > 'old woman', paralleled by *suyús > υἱύς 'birth' > 'son'. γυναικῶν | δμῳάων ... ἡμετεράων: for the construction see 369n. and, for example, xiii 66. The whole question of the women-slaves and their conduct has been well treated by Ramming, *Dienerschaft,* 34–41, and W. Beringer, 'Die ursprüngliche Bedeutung von δουλοσύνην, -ς ἀνέχεσθαι in *Odyssee* xxii 423', *Athenaeum* xxxviii (1960), 65–97. Twelve of them are judged to have sinned (424), a number which approximately corresponds to that of the suitors (see n. on 241). σκοπός: fem. (see 156n.).

397. κικλήσκει: a near-synonym of καλέω, appears in iv 355, ix 366, xv 403, xviii 6. Telemachus at last solemnly reveals the great secret to the old woman; compare this line with xxi 381–5 (see n. on xxi 380, and Focke, *Odyssee,* 362). The line-ending, with the usual hiatus before digamma, is found in the first person in vi 239, xviii 43, xx 292.

398. Cf. xxi 386n.

399. The line, which describes the opening of the doors which were closed in xxi 387, is identical to that one except for the first word, where ὤϊξεν replaces κλήϊσεν. ὤϊξεν derives from the dialect. inf. ὀείγην < *ὀϜειγην, according to Frisk, *GEW*; cf. *Il.* xxiv 455 *ἀνϜοίγεσκον, which hides a supposed *ἀνοειγεσκον < *ἀνοϜειγεσκον, and *Il.* xxiv 228 ἀνέῳγεν, hiding a presumed *ανοϜειγεν, as well as Hesychius' gloss ἴγνυντο· ἠνοίγοντο, from an original *Ϝιγνυντο without prothesis. Fick and others, tentatively supported by von der Mühll, would substitute ὤϊξα etc. for ὤειξα etc. in i 436, xxiii 370, xxiv 501, all in initial position in the line and followed by δέ or ῥα and θύρας. The formula of the second hemistich occurs in ii 400, xix 30, xxi 387; and with δόμων, in xx 371; cf. also xxi 242 and its parallel at xxiv 362, and see n. on xxi 369 on εὖ.

400. Cf. 179n.

401. = xxiii 45 except for a change of person (Eurycleia's tale). The beginning of the line is the same in *Il.* ii 169, xi 473 μετά, 'among'. The middle of the part. κταμένοισι here has possessive force (cf. 412, and κατακτάμενος in xvi 106); νέκυς should be rendered 'body', not 'corpse' (the formula νεκύων κατατεθνηώτων occurs five times in x and xi, νέκυας κατατεθνηῶτας in 448, νεκύεσσι καταφθιμένοισιν in xi 491). The dat. plur. νεκύεσσι is attested four times, νέκυσσιν at the end of xi 569, here, and in xxiii 45; but since this latter form never occurs in the *Iliad*, whereas the nom. and acc. sing. νέκυς, νέκυν, which are never found in the *Odyssey*, occur there twice and six times respectively scanned as iambs (not counting *Il.* xvii 277 νέκυν ἐρύοντο, where the digamma of ἐρύοντο interferes with the scansion: see 372n.), von der Mühll thinks the reading νέκῦσιν offered by some witnesses in these three cases is perhaps preferable to νεκύεσσιν.

402. αἵματι καὶ λύθρῳ πεπαλαγμένον: the same formula occurs in *Il.* vi 268, *Od.* xxiii 48; on παλάσσω see 184n.; λύθρον, 'clotted blood', besides the three passages cited, appears in *Il.* xi 169, xx 503. The formula at the end of the line is paralleled in *Il.* v 136, which also introduces a simile.

403. ὅς ῥα: reinforced pronoun (cf. xi 414, xv 319). βεβρωκὼς: from later βιβρώσκω we find in Homer only this trans. part. βεβρωκώς 'having eaten' (cf. also *Il.* xxii 94, of a serpent), an enigmatic pf. opt. βεβρώθοις (*Il.* iv 35; the -θ- is variously explained by Chantraine, *Grammaire*, i 429, Schwyzer, *Grammatik*, i 662), and fut. pf. βεβρώσεται (*Od.* ii 203, used metaphorically of one who is going to use up all his money); it governs the part. gen. βοός. ἔρχεται, 'comes away (after eating)'; ἄγραυλος implies, not 'wild', but rather 'which lives or grazes in the open countryside', thus making it an easy prey for the lion (cf. x 410, of calves; xii 253, with n. on 384-8 above).

404. ἄρα, sc. as a result of its feeding. οἱ, possessive dat.; στῆθος and the neut. pl. παρήϊα are terms which are more naturally applied to human beings (thus the latter in xix 208; but in *Il.* xvi 159 it applies to wolves). ἀμφοτέρωθεν (cf. xxi 408, xxii 80) is just right here for the two jowls.

405-6. αἱματόεντα πέλει: 'are covered in blood', agreeing with the nearest subject; cf. *Il.* xvii 541-2, Automedon πόδας καὶ χεῖρας ὕπερθεν | αἱματόεις ὥς τίς τε λέων κατὰ ταῦρον ἐδηδώς. δεινὸς δ' εἰς ὦπα ἰδέσθαι: the phrase seems to be the result of a cross between δεινὸς (ἐστὶ) ἰδέσθαι 'terrible to see' (cf. a similar consecutive-final use of the middle aor. inf. ἰδέσθαι preceded by hiatus; at the end of the line, for example, in xxiv 369 πάσσονα θῆκεν ἰδέσθαι) and δεινὸς εἰς ὦπα ἔοικε 'he seems terrible for the face (which is looking at him)' (i 411 οὐ . . . κακῷ εἰς ὦπα ἐῴκει, *Il.* iii 158 θεῇς εἰς ὦπα ἔοικεν); the hybrid formula means something like 'terrible to see face to face', and is found in xxiii 107 εἰς ὦπα ἰδέσθαι ἐναντίον, *Il.* ix

373, xv 147 (cf. 240n., and the *hapax* ἐνωπαδίως 'face to face' in xxiii 94). πεπάλακτο: cf. 402n.

407. 'And she, when indeed she saw ...' ἄσπετον: 'abundant, immeasurable' (cf. 269 and n. for a quite different meaning). ἔσιδεν: codd. invariably write εἴσιδεν: ἔσιδεν, i.e. ἔσφιδεν, in Bekker's conjecture which is regularly accepted by Allen in the *Odyssey* except (presumably by inadvertence) at i 118 and v 392.

408. ἴθυσέν ῥ' ὀλολύξαι: 'launched into her ululations', aor. with augment; the same form is used with the inf. in *Il.* xvii 353, but in the more physical sense 'launched into battle (μάχεσθαι)'. The force of ῥα is not clear; von der Mühll judges its omission, displayed in some MSS, admissible. ὀλολύξαι: ὀλυλυγή (with the long -υ- which led Cobet to suggest accentuating this word with the circumflex, ὀλολῦξαι) refers to the ritual ululation of women, as of the Trojan women in the temple in *Il.* vi 301, whereas the deeper male equivalent, used as a war cry in xxiv 463, was called ἀλαλητός; the verb ὀλολύζω occurs here, in 411, and in iii 450 (Nestor's womenfolk at a sacrifice), iv 767 (Penelope sacrificing to Athena and entreating her help against the suitors). ἔσιδεν requires an unusual initial hiatus; this, and the close repetition of the verb in the previous line which might theoretically have been due to scribal dittography, has prompted Monro's conjectural correction εἴσατο, with initial hiatus (ἐείσατο or εἴσατο 'appeared, seemed', twelve times in the *Odyssey*; on the verb cf. 206n., not to be confused with the different εἴσατο adduced in the n. on 6–7 above). μέγα ... ἔργον: 'great achievement' (cf. the very different meaning in 149; note the neglect of hiatus before ἔργον).

409. κατέρυκε: the verb is related to the forms cited in 372n., though the semantic connection is unclear (the idea of 'saving' seems to have gone hand in hand with 'containing' the attacker); to these cognates may be added ἐρύκω (with long υ and expressive reinforcement of the stem; cf. 138), and this compound κατερύκω (xxiii 334, xxiv 51), as well as the redupl. aor. ἐρύκακε (xxi 227), ἐρυκάνω (x 429), κατερυκάνω (*Il.* xxiv 218), and ἐρυκανάω (i 199). The second hemistich is repeated in xxi 129; the whole line is almost identical to iv 284, xvi 430; ἔσχεθεν, 'held back, restrained' (cf. 172n.), aor. of ἔχω reinforced with -θ- (cf. xxiii 243, xxiv 530), the aspect of the verb strongly emphasizing the energetic action (which is therefore not merely tautological with imperfective κατέρυκε). ἱεμένην περ: 'although she was set upon it'; see Hoekstra, *Modifications*, 49–50, and nn. on 172, 256.

410. Cf. 366.

411–16. The authenticity of Odysseus' humane and compassionate speech, apparently so out of tune with the archaic ferocity of the rest of the Book, has been much disputed: see, for example, Heubeck, *Dichter*, 83, Erbse, *Beiträge*, 130–1, Eisenberger, *Studien*, 142. The deluge of deletions has been swollen, in addition, by the fact that this is a cento of Homeric passages from elsewhere: 414–15 = xxiii 65–6, a speech by Penelope; the beginning of 415 = *Il.* vi 489, and is similar to *Od.* viii 553; its ending, almost identical to xx 188; 416, a calque of 317 with an opening similar to that of xxiii 67. To the general condemnation, Blass adds his vote, somewhat irrelevantly alleging in reference to 414–16 that Odysseus' speeches to Eurycleia are otherwise (431–2, 481–4, 491) short and to the point (*Interpolationen*, 209–10). But Odysseus' sentiments can be paralleled elsewhere in Homer, in passages which condemn *hybris* and warn of its consequences: thus ii 168–9, Halitherses' prophecy and warning to the suitors to moderate their actions; ix 270–1, Odysseus calls to mind Zeus' protection of suppliants and strangers; xiv 83–4, Eumaeus states that the gods dislike σχέτλια ἔργα, honouring justice and αἴσιμ' ἔργα; xviii 141–2, Odysseus demands that no one be ἀθεμίστιος, and that all enjoy in silence the δῶρα θεῶν . . . ὅττι διδοῖεν; xxi 28–9, the poet comments on Iphitus, σχέτλιος, and his lack of respect for the θεῶν ὄπιν and the table of hospitality; and so on. On the lofty tolerance and respect for the dead shown, for example, in 412, it has been objected (E. T. Vermeule, *Archaeologia* V, 125) that the adj. ὅσιος is nowhere used in Homer, and that there is only one other occurrence of the noun ὁσίη, formed from the adj. with the abstract suffix -ια *ὁσιά, and preceded by οὐχ in a parallel to the Lat. *non fas est* (xvi 423, where Penelope reproaches Antinous for the plot against Telemachus, οὐδ' ὁσίη κακὰ ῥάπτειν ἀλλήλοισιν). Scholars have often adduced the parallel of Archilochus fr. 134 w οὐ γὰρ ἐσθλὰ κατθανοῦσι κερτομεῖν ἐπ' ἀνδράσιν cited by the sch. on 412 (see also the apophthegm of Cheilon τὸν τεθνηκότα μὴ κακολογεῖν, and Cratinus fr. 102 φοβερὸν ἀνθρώποις τόδ' αὖ | κταμένοις ἐπ' αἰζηοῖσι καυχᾶσθαι μέγα); the Archilochean passage has even been proposed as the source of the supposed interpolation here (whereas Merkelbach, *Untersuchungen*, 129 n. 2 and 231, argues the exact contrary, asserting that the Archilochean passage is derivative and hence provides a *terminus ante quem* for these lines). The most illuminating parallel, however, is to be found in Odysseus' humane and sympathetic words on Socus, whom he has just killed, in *Il.* xi 450–5. It may be noted, finally, that van Leeuwen's interpretation of εὐχετάασθαι in 412 as 'pray', as if Odysseus meant to prohibit an act of religious worship in the polluted vicinity of the slaughter, has found no favour.

411. ἐν θυμῷ: 'in your heart', not outwardly; on this use of the locative dat. with a preposition (cf. for example viii 450 ἴδε θυμῷ) see Schwyzer, *Grammatik*, ii 170. χαῖρε: concessive imper.; for ἴσχεο see 356, 367.

412. εὐχετάασθαι: εὐχετάομαι, with amplification of the stem of εὔχομαι and with the same meanings of 'boast, exult' as well as 'pray' (cf. 286 n.), occurs on nine other occasions in the *Odyssey*: see Chantraine, *Grammaire*, i 358.

413. Odysseus emphasizes μοῖρα θεῶν rather more than ἔργα (the latter with the usual hiatus): 'it was destiny, not I, who brought death upon them, and their own wickedness'; for the expression μοῖρα θεῶν cf. iii 269. In xx 75–6 Athena says that Zeus knows everything, the μοῖρα and the ἀμμορίη of men. To the examples of σχέτλιος cited in the n. on 411–16, one could add (from the total of eighteen occurrences in the *Odyssey*) xxiii 150, said by the people of Penelope when they think she has re-married.

415. οὐ κακὸν οὐδὲ μὲν ἐσθλόν: this sort of paired negative, where in prose we should expect οὔτε . . . οὔτε, is not uncommon; cf. an identically phrased clause in the same metrical position in a passage similar to this one, *Il.* vi 488–9 μοῖραν δ' οὔ τινά φημι πεφυγμένον ἔμμεναι ἀνδρῶν, | οὐ κακόν, οὐδὲ μὲν ἐσθλόν, and another identically placed parallel in *Od.* viii 552–3 οὐ μὲν γάρ τις πάμπαν ἀνώνυμός ἐστ' ἀνθρώπων, | οὐ κακὸς οὐδὲ μὲν ἐσθλός. This is a clear example of the 'polar expression', with apparent co-ordination masking the emphatic opposition between the terms ('they honoured neither the good nor the bad', i.e. they did not even honour the good); for further examples see *Il.* ix 35–6 ('this is known even to young Argives'), *Od.* ii 345–6 (Eurycleia was awake even at night), x 93–4 (not even the smallest sea-swell got up).   ὅτις σφέας εἰσαφίκοιτο: 'who-ever might unluckily happen (iterative opt.) to run into them'; σφέας, indir. refl., is correctly given the tonic accent by Allen,but not by von der Mühll; similar line-endings occur in xii 40, xvi 228, and xx 188.

417–18. The cento continues: 417 is similar to xix 497 (and Merkelbach, *Untersuchungen*, 130 n. 1, proposes a text which is an even closer copy of that line; see Krischer, op. cit. (300n.), 155–8), while 418 is almost identical to xvi 317/xix 498. In the first of these passages Telemachus exhorts his father to find out which of the women are innocent; in the second, Eurycleia promises to give him a list of the guilty, but Odysseus replies (500–1) that there is no need to do so as he will investigate the matter himself, despite the fact that in xvi 235 he has asked Telemachus for a list of the suitors; all this poses problems discussed by, amongst others, Erbse, *Beiträge*, 20–1.   νηλίτιδές: there is a real textual confusion between the νηλείτιδες read by von der Mühll, and by Bekker in three passages, and the νηλίτιδες pre-ferred by Allen (there is, however, little to recommend the νηλιτεῖς of van der Valk, *Textual Criticism*, 50); von der Mühll's reading would give us a derivative of ἀλείτης 'sinner' (*Il.* iii 28, *Od.* xx 121) with the neg. prefix νη-, in support of which Herodian cites ἀλεῖτις '(female) sinner' (cf. *Suda* ἀλειτεία· ἡ ἁμαρτία; Hsch. ἀλοῖται· κοιναὶ ἁμαρτωλαί, ποιναί); Allen's νηλίτιδες, if it is not simply an itacistic corruption (against which must be placed the long -ῐ-), would lead us instead in the direction of ἀλιταίνω 'sin, transgress', with zero grade (the full grade is not attested, however, against the four forms recorded in the *Iliad* and the three in the *Odyssey*), ἀλιτήμων (*Il.* xxiv 157, 186), ἀλιτρός (*Il.* viii 361, xxiii 595, *Od.* v 182).

419. = xix 21, xxii 485; almost identical to iv 742, xxiii 25, 39; the same line-ending in ii 361, xxii 492, xxiii 69.

420. = xvi 226; the line-ending is the same as that of xxi 212.   τοιγὰρ: 'well then'.   καταλέγω: 'disclose, relate'.

421–2. On the γυναῖκες δμῳαί see n. on 395–6. The number of fifty is notional and symbolic (Ramming, *Dienerschaft*, 111 n. 3); Alcinous too has the same number of women-servants (vii 103, with the same line-opening and ending). The figure may seem high, but tablets from the

palace at Pylos reveal the presence of 347 women, 240 girls, and 159 boys in
the royal household alone, besides the 322, 152, and 122 respectively mentioned for the region as a whole (Webster, *Companion*, 460; W. Richter,
Archaeologia H, 21).

422. διδάξαμεν: διδάσκω is used for the training of poets by the Muses,
viii 481, 488 (cf. 347–8 n.); for the training in horsemanship given by Zeus
and Poseidon in *Il.* xxiii 307–8, and in archery given by Artemis in *Il.* v
51; and for Phoenix and Cheiron's tutoring in *Il.* ix 442, xi 831–2). On
the maidservants' professional training see Webster, *Companion*, 459.
ἔγρα . . . ἐργάζεσθαι: for further examples of the etymological internal
acc., cf. the fine iii 66 μοίρας δασσάμενοι δαίνυντ' ἐρικυδέα δαῖτα; vi 61
βουλὰς βουλεύειν. For this phrase, cf. *Il.* xxiv 733, *Od.* xx 72 (on both of
which see F. Eckstein, *Archaeologia* L, 5 n. 24); the traditional text here,
unlike those lines, inserts τ' before ἔργα, so that the initial digamma is
observed in neither word. This is accepted in Hoekstra (*Modifications*, 79
n. 7) as an adaptation of a traditional formula. The τ' was removed by
Bentley.

423. The infinitives ξαίνειν and ἀνέχεσθαι are in apposition to ἔργα in the
preceding line. The women's tasks include, in the first place, the typical
spinning and weaving of wool: εἴρια, prob. < *ϝερϝος, cf. Lat. *ueruex*
'wether' (εἶρος, in iv 135, ix 426, εἴριον, here and at *Il.* iii 388, xii 434, *Od.*
xviii 316, ἔριον in iv 124, εἰροπόκος in *Il.* v 137, *Od.* ix 443, εἰροκόμος in *Il.*
iii 387; only in iv 124, xviii 316, and perhaps *Il.* iii 388 is hiatus duly
observed); ξαίνω, 'card, comb', only here in Homer (cf. xviii 316 πείκω
'comb', with metrical lengthening; *Il.* iii 388 ἀσκεῖν, in a broader sense).
καὶ δουλοσύνην ἀνέχεσθαι: καί, 'and in general', introducing a phrase
which is not strictly a counterpart of the first term. The disputed *lectio
facilior* δουλοσύνην ἀνέχεσθαι, has been taken to mean simply 'resign themselves to their slavery'; but Beringer (op. cit. (395–6 n.)) has convincingly
argued that ἀνέχεσθαι (thirty-four occurrences) cannot bear this meaning
(cf. Ramming, *Dienerschaft*, 129–30, and W. Richter, *Archaeologia* H, 20),
and that δουλοσύνη, which is nowhere else attested before Pindar and
Aeschylus, has the special meaning 'sexual bondage, concubinage',
besides the sense of the related δμώς 'house-slave, maidservant' (xxi 210,
224, xxii 114, xxiv 210, 213, 219, 223, 257; see also above on δμωή; significantly the masc. δοῦλος is never found in Homer, despite Myc. do-e-ro;
but note δούλη, Myc. do-e-ra, *Il.* iii 409, *Od.* iv 12, δούλιος, *Il.* vi 463, *Od.* xiv
340, xvii 323). This δουλοσύνη would therefore indicate concubinage such
as that of the twelve women guilty of having entered the suitors' beds (note
the absence in this passage of Melantho, who is not mentioned again after
xix 65; see 135 n.). If this is so (Schwyzer, *Grammatik*, ii 134 is not decisive),
the *lectio facilior* must be rejected in favour of δουλοσύνης ἀνέχεσθαι, a rare
construction meaning 'to abstain from bed-slavery'; subsequent to
Beringer's article, the publication of a new papyrus by V. Bartoletti has
brought to light yet another *lectio difficilior*, δουλοσύνης ἀπέχεσθαι (for this
verb with the gen., cf. xii 321, xix 489, xxii 316 *in tmesi*), which may be

COMMENTARY

tentatively accepted as the definitive reading; see Bartoletti, 'Un papiro prealessandrino dell' *Odissea*', *St. Cl. Or.* xxvi (1977), 251–5.

424. τάων δώδεκα πᾶσαι: τάων, pron., partitive gen.; πᾶσαι is predicative, 'twelve in all' (cf. for example xviii 293 ἐν δ' ἄρ' ἔσαν περόναι δυοκαίδεκα πᾶσαι). **ἀναιδείης ἐπέβησαν:** the same verb is found at the end of the line, after a gen. of the path or conduct on which one embarks or finds oneself upon, in xxiii 13 (σαοφροσύνης), *Il.* viii 285 ἐϋκλείης; and, in a different position in the line, at *Il.* ii 234 (κακῶν). ἀναίδεια occurs in *Il.* i 149, ix 372, both times used by Achilles of Agamemnon's behaviour.

425–9. Lines condemned by Duentzer and by van Herwerden, and missing in the papyrus mentioned in the n. on 423 above. Bartoletti approves the omission, commenting that the passage portrays Eurycleia as a garrulous busy-body, and Telemachus as an immature boy ('Un papiro prealessandrino', 253–4).

425. 'Respecting neither me (as their superintendent) nor Penelope (as their mistress, αὐτήν)'. The hiatus in thesis after τίουσαι has been mended by three conjectures, but at the cost, in the case of Bérard's two suggestions, of a violent asyndeton (see app.). The quantity of the first vowel of τίω, long in the first of the conjectures and short in the other two, offers no decisive criterion; the pres. generally (e.g. 370, 414, xxiii 65, xxiv 78), but not always (cf. i 432, xiii 129, 144, xvi 306, xix 247, xx 132), has -ῑ-.

426. 'Whereas Telemachus (I do not mention because he, δέ) had only just started growing up'. (νέον, 'lately, recently' with verbs in the punctual or durative aspect (viii 13, xvi 181; xvi 199); 'recently, for a short time now, only just' with verbs in the durative aspect (i 175 'you have only been a visitor for a short time', iii 318 'he has only been here a short time'.) **ἀέξετο:** in four other passages of the *Odyssey* the pres. or impf. middle of ἀέξω is used of excitement growing within one (ii 315), the day advancing (ix 56), waves swelling (x 93), or work increasing (xiv 66); but we do find it of young gods 'growing up' in the *h. Hom.* (*Cer.* 235, *Merc.* 408, xxvi 5). The line-ending, with non-reflexive ἑ preceded by the required hiatus (cf. xxi 201, and the refl. ἑ in 436) occurs again in xxiv 292.

427. εἴασκεν: the only iterative from ἐάω in the *Odyssey*, is followed by an acc. and inf. clause, the subject of which is ἑ; σημαίνειν, 'give orders', in the *Iliad* generally of a military kind, with dat. (*Il.* i 289, ii 805, x 58, xvii 250; cf. xiv 85, with gen. by analogy with ἀνάσσω, etc.) or without a complement, as here (*Il.* xvi 172, xxi 445 of Laomedon's instructions to Apollo and Poseidon, *Od.* xxii 450 of Odysseus' commands to the women-slaves; cf. a different sense in xii 26); ἐπί here has a function similar to that in *Il.* vi 25, xi 106 ἐπ' ὄεσσι '(to be shepherd) over the sheep', *Od.* xx 209 ἐπὶ βουσίν '(to be made cowherd) over the oxen' (later ἐπί was used more or less in this sense with τῷ στρατῷ, τοῖς πράγμασι, etc.): cf. xxi 199 n., Schwyzer, *Grammatik*, ii 467. For the phrase δμῳῇσι γυναιξίν see 420–1 n.

428. Eurycleia tries to make a suggestion, well-intentioned but clumsy. **ἀλλ' ἄγ':** 'but come now', cf. xxii 139 n.; ἀλλά, as often, marks a new subject or idea (cf. xxi 134, 263, xxii 139, 417, 487). **ἐγών:** 'I for my part'.

294

429. ἄλοχος has not so far been used of Penelope as Odysseus' wife in these last books (cf. xxi 214, xxii 223, 324), but after this discovery of the truth it is so used no less than eight times in xxiii–xxiv. On Penelope's divinely induced slumber see xxi 357 n. ἐπῶρσε: contrary to the opinion of van der Valk (*Textual Criticism*, 50), the principle of *lectio difficilior* is not decisive here; the word ἐπῶρσε, attested in several papyri, is used of divine actions in v 109, vii 271, ix 67, but the imperf. of χέω with ὕπνον referring to sleep inspired by gods is no less common (ii 395, Athena puts the suitors to sleep, v 492, xx 54, Athena puts Odysseus to sleep; vii 286, a god sends sleep to Odysseus; xviii 188, Athena sends sleep to Penelope; in xxi 357 the formula is different, and xi 245 is spurious).

430. For the final formula, see 105 n.

431-2. Odysseus is tenderly anxious to spare Penelope the gruesome sight of slaughter; she is therefore allowed to sleep on until xxiii 5.   σὺ δ' ἐνθάδε εἰπὲ ... | ἐλθέμεν: 'instead, you tell the women to come'; ἐνθάδε, lative, depends on ἐλθέμεν as in 168, 483, and is equivalent to δεῦρο (cf. 233, 395), in contrast to the normal usage (cf. xxi 156, 319, xxii 30). Both here and in 491 Odysseus rejects Eurycleia's suggestion (Fenik, *Studies*, 239).   αἵ περ: περ lends precision, 'just the ones who behaved badly'. πρόσθεν: 'during all this time'.   ἀεικέα μηχανόωντο: this line ending occurs in xx 394 (of the suitors; see also xx 317) and xx 170. ἀεικής has already occurred in this Book applied to a well-deserved bad end (317, 416); in xxiii 222 it describes Helen's conduct, in xxiv 250 ἀεικέα ἔσσαι Odysseus uses it of Laertes' rags.

433-4. = xviii 185-6. The first line is a calque of xix 503. On the implication of the tense ('hardly had he spoken, when she was already on her way') see 275 n. The two fut. participles are final in sense; after ἀγγελέουσα suppl. 'what had happened'.   ὀτρυνέουσα: ὀτρυνέων in the same sense, xxiv 116; without inf., 241, xxiii 264, xxiv 405, 487; with consecutive-final inf., as here, ii 244 ἡμέας ὀτρύνων καταπαυέμεν, xix 158-9 ὀτρύνουσι τοκῆες | γήμασθαι. In 484, Odysseus repeats the order (434 = 496), this time for the faithful maidservants.

436. For direct refl. ἓ see 426 n.; cf. xvii 330, 342 ἐπὶ οἷ καλέσας; and in general, *Il.* iv 400 υἱὸν γείνατο εἷο χέρηα; for indirect refl., vii 39-40 οὐκ ἐνόησαν ἐρχόμενον κατὰ ἄστυ διὰ σφέας, vii 217 ἕο μνήσασθαι '(the belly demands) that one remember it'; see further Schwyzer, *Grammatik*, ii 194-5. For the beginning of the line, which is similar to *Il.* v 427, *Od.* xix 15, see xxi 380 n., and Hoekstra, *Modifications*, 134.

437. ἄρχετε νῦν: the men are to get started 'immediately' on the heavy business of dragging out the bodies, which the faithless women-slaves will then complete.   φορέειν: iterative, 'clear away (one by one)', a different sense from the 'carry (habitually)' of xxi 32 (see n.), 41, and the suffixed form in xxii 185 n.; later the verb reappears in 448, 451 (ἐκφόρεον), 456, xxiv 417.   ἄνωχθε: 2nd pl. perf. imper. from ἄνωγα 'order', representing *ἄνωκτε but influenced, here and in the 3rd sing. ἀνώχθω (*Il.* xi 189), by analogy with the 2nd sing. ἄνωχθι (six times each in *Iliad* and *Odyssey*, including *Od.* xxii 483): see Schwyzer, *Grammatik*, i 800. Thematic forms of the pres. tense are seen in xxi 194, xxiii 267, 368, xxiv 167, and above all xxiii 132 δμωάς ... ἀνώγετε εἴμαθ' ἐλέσθαι. With ἄνωχθε here we must of course supply φορέειν, 'order them to carry too'.

438–9. = 452–3 (with κάθαιρον), where the order is carried out. The cleaning of the hall is not merely hygienic, but also a ritual cleansing of pollution (S. Laser, *Archaeologia* P, 58); καθαίρω is used in the religious context in xxiv 44 (washing of Achilles' corpse), and in a semi-religious sense in xviii 192 (Penelope's *toilette* overseen by Athena); it is used of ordinary household cleaning in vi 87, 93 (Nausicaa's laundry), xx 152 (brushing out the hall). This latter passage is the only passage besides i 111 and the present lines (439/453) where sponges (σπόγγοισι) are mentioned in the *Odyssey* (cf. *Il.* xviii 414, where Hephaestus wipes off his sweat with a sponge: see further Stubbings, *Companion*, 527); πολύτρητος 'full of holes', only here and in i 111 (cf. τρητός 'perforated', five times in the *Odyssey* and twice in the *Iliad*). On the θρόνοι, their daily cleaning, and the epithet περικαλλής, see xxi 139n. and Laser, ibid., 40. The way in which the master gives the order through a third party (καθαίρειν depends on ἄνωχθε) is reminiscent of xxi 235–9 (imper. εἰπεῖν addressed to Eumaeus, with three following infinitives of commands for the women).

440. κατακοσμήσησθε: the middle is not entirely factitive, since Telemachus and his companions also take a hand in the clearing-up (see 437 ἄρχετε). Von der Mühll's choice of διακοσμήσησθε is more persuasive than κατακοσμήσησθε, preferred by Allen. Also worthy of consideration is Barnes' suggestion, κάτα κοσμήσησθε, where the direct complement of the verb would be πάντα and the prep., in anastrophe, would go with δόμον; κοσμέω appears in vii 13, ix 57, and various Iliadic passages, whereas the compound κατακοσμέω occurs only in *Il.* iv 118, and διακοσμέω only in *Il.* ii 126, 476.

441–73. This passage, besides the strange and unwarranted cruelty it describes (the women's illicit intercourse with the suitors having played no significant part in the events of the story), is problematic for a number of reasons. Odysseus' plan, perfectly coherent, seems to be to have the guilty women brought from their rooms (where the servants have all been locked up, 394–400n.) to clean the hall of the debris of battle as part of their punishment, and then to lead them out one by one to execution (441 = 458) by swords (443), probably indeed the suitors' swords. In this interpretation 442 (= 459) is clearly spurious. Eurycleia, who has crossed and left the *megaron* (433), opens the women's chamber with her key, picks out the twelve unfaithful slaves and leads them in a group back to the hall (446), leaving the rest of the women in confinement. The twelve do the cleaning (448–57), then they are hurried (Odysseus is impatient, 451, and in haste lest the alarm is raised outside: cf. 77n., and note the precautions which he is still to take in xxiii 133–9) out of the hall (457–9; 440–1 = 457–8) and into the courtyard by Telemachus, who is not inclined to obey his father's instructions to the letter. He pens them up in a corner (460), and then, judging that death by the sword is too good for such sinners (461-4), thinks up another form of execution which is here described in an imprecise and probably fanciful way. It is clear that he picks up a ship's cable from the αἴθουσα (cf. xxi 390-1), and ties it firmly by both ends. But the details of what happens next present a series of practical problems. First, if the twelve women are not to touch each other, making the execution more difficult, we must suppose a gap of at least a yard and a half between them; this would require a rope eighteen yards long, probably too long for the narrow Homeric courtyard, longer than the usual ship's cable, and certainly too long to tighten up to a tension sufficient to bear the weight of six or seven desperately twitching bodies. Second, if one end of the rope were hitched over the conical roof of the θόλος (see below), and the other tied with a knot to one of the columns of the portico, which must have been fairly low, the angle of the rope would be impossibly steep. Third, the rope lashed around the column would tend to slide down it under the weight. Fourth, they would need a further rope, thinner and about twelve yards long, for the twelve separate nooses (βρόχοι, 472). And last, since it is improbable in the extreme that the hangmen could have been strong enough to hoist the women-slaves aloft from ground level simply by hauling on the free end of the rope and using the conical roof as a sort of pulley, we must imagine them dropping the victims from standing position off twelve stools from the hall. As can be seen, all this would be quite impossible to accomplish for two men on their own (Odysseus, and probably Telemachus too, being excluded from such a degrading task); and even if they could, it would take several hours, an impossible delay in the urgent circumstances. Besides, what would be the point of this mass execution, apart from the exemplary spectacle? It would surely be simpler to string the women up one by one. Further difficulties of detail will be considered below. There is a useful discussion of the minutiae of the execution in the paper by F. Robert, 'Le Supplice d'Antigone et celui des servantes d'Ulysse', *Bull. Corr. Hell.* lxx (1946), 501-5, though its bold general thesis may not convince: it proposes that the whole passage is an interpolation intended to provide an αἴτιον for an ancient myth similar to that of Antigone's hanging in a θόλος or bee-hive tomb, in which both aspects of the punishment would be related to the killing of a scapegoat, φαρμακός, designed to cleanse the miasma of a crime; the suspended corpses would, in this theory, recall the *oscilla* of Verg. *G.* ii 389, which were hung from trees to ensure fertility; and the women-slaves themselves would be a distant memory of ancient rituals, since Autonoe and Eurynome (xviii 182, xvii 495, though both, to be sure, belong to the number of the innocent maidservants) bear the same names as a goddess worshipped in a θόλος at Mantinea (Paus. viii 9. 5) and a sea-goddess mentioned in *Il.* xviii 398 who had a sanctuary in Arcadia (Paus. viii 41. 4).

422. The line is an interpolation here (see n. on 441-3).

443-4. **θεινέμεναι**: inf. for imper., 'kill (sc. the women)'; θείνω, from the same root as φόνος (see 54 n.) is used three times in the *Odyssey*, with

COMMENTARY

different meanings: ix 459 (to smash a head against the ground, with fatal results); xviii 63 (to strike, without killing); and here (to kill with a sword). **τανυήκεσιν**: 'long-bladed', or perhaps 'broad-bladed', of a slashing cutlass (Lorimer, *Monuments*, 275 n. 2; cf. xxi 341, xxii 79–80nn. on ἀμφήκης); the word is found as an epithet of ἄορ 'sword' (eight examples in the *Odyssey*) in the *Iliad* (twice) and *Od.* x 439, xi 231. **πασέων**: van Leeuwen's conjecture *πάσας*, sc. the women, is designed to eliminate the synizesis at the end of the line, which occurs nineteen times in the *Odyssey* (Chantraine, *Grammaire*, i 65, 69, 201; cf. θυρέων, xxi 47, and ψυχέων, xxii 245n.); if it is accepted, then the construction with double acc. of part and whole enjoins the further change of ψυχάς to distrib. sing. ψυχήν in the next line, 'take the life of every one of them'. **ἐξαφέλησθε**: cf. *Il.* xx 436 ἀπὸ θυμὸν ἕλωμαι, *Il.* xv 460, xvii 678 ἐξείλετο θυμόν (of a single life in each case); the compound with double prefix is unique in Homer. **καὶ ἐκλελάθωντ' Ἀφροδίτης**: 'and thus may they fully (ἐκ-; cf. x 557 ἐκλάθετο, iii 224 ἐκλελάθοιτο γάμοιο) forget the delights of love', heavily ironic; Ἀφροδίτη is here used more or less by antonomasia for carnal intercourse, like 'Ares' for war (xx 50), 'Muse' for poetry (xxiv 62), 'Hephaestus' for fire (xxiv 71).

445. **τὴν**: rel.   **ἄρ'**: 'as we may surmise'.   **ὑπὸ**: both 'under the orders of' (iii 304, vii 68) and also (physically) 'under, on their backs beneath' (in this sexual sense, *Il.* ii 714, 728, 724). The rather vague ἔχον may be variously rendered as 'dedicated themselves to, worshipped' or, taking Ἀφροδίτην in its figurative sense, 'practised, performed' (cf. i 368, viii 285, xxiv 516). Despite the rather loose paratactical structure (in Greek, such links with a parallel relative clause where the antecedent is lost sight of are not impossible), the emphasis in the clause falls on the second verb, μίσγοντο, 'in the service of which goddess they copulated ...' (the common sexual sense; cf. i 73, xxiii 219, etc.).

446. **ἀολλέες**: predicative, 'huddling together'; used in the fem. in four other places in the *Odyssey* (iv 448, a flock of seals; xi 228, the dead women in Hades; iii 165, x 132, a fleet of ships), the adj. here graphically captures the sight of the women clinging to each other in terror.

447. **αἶν'**: adv., here in its root sense of 'horribly, dreadfully' (cf. 136n.); the same form in *Il.* i 414, *Od.* xvi 255.   **θαλερὸν κατὰ δάκρυ χέουσαι**: *Il.* vi 496, *Od.* iv 556, x 201, 409, 570, xi 5, 466, xii 12, and a pair of examples where the metre imposed δάκρυον εἴβων (xi 391) or εἴβεν (*Il.* xxiv 9, cf. *Od.* xxiv 234); there are an extraordinary number of verbs for 'shedding' tears (ii 81 ἀναπρήσας, viii 86 λείβων, xvii 490, xxi 362 βάλεν, ἔκβαλε, xxi 86 κατείβετον, xxiii 33 ἀπό ... ἧκε; in xix 122, however, δακρυπλώειν is preferable to δάκρυ πλώειν); καταχέω is here used in tmesis. θαλερός, 'flowering, lush' > 'abundant, flowing'; δάκρυ, collective, 'weeping'.

450. **ἀλλήλοισιν ἐρείδουσαι**: cf. xxiii 46–7 κραταίπεδον οὖδας ἔχοντες | κείατ' ἐπ' ἀλλήλοισιν. The women are told to pile up the bodies (suppl. αὐτούς) under the roof of the portico, 'a grim touch' as Stanford remarks; it would be a necessary one, if we accepted the traditional number of over

298

one hundred suitors (see nn. on 241–329, 308–9). The editors unanimously prefer this reading to the ἀλλήλῃσιν of a number of MSS, which would require an intrans. use of ἐρείδω, 'leaning against one another (sc. the women)', in terror of instant death (cf. *Il.* xvi 108, and Schwyzer, *Grammatik*, ii 230 n. 1).

451. αὐτὸς ἐπισπέρχων: 'limiting himself (as the master) to chivvying them along'; the active of σπέρχω appears in *Il.* xiii 334, *Od.* iii 283, but used intransitively; the same is true of ἐπισπέρχω in v 304, the only parallel for which is *Il.* xxiii 430, of spurring on a horse, which fits nicely with the imperious treatment of the women-slaves here. On the end of the line see nn. on 331, 353; ἀνάγκη occurs in the final position in nineteen places in the *Odyssey*; the more forceful καὶ ἀνάγκη is found in v 154, x 434, xiii 307.

453. See 438–9n.

454–6. In view of the urgency of the situation Telemachus joins with the servants in carrying out these servile tasks. The need to sweep or rake the floor of the hall was discussed in the Introduction to xxi. λίστρον: 'shovel', is found nowhere else (cf. the dimin. λίστριον in Hsch., and λείστριον in a later inscription); it displays an obvious affinity with λιστρεύω 'dig' (xxiv 227), and with a series of related adj. meaning 'even, smooth, polished' such as λίς (of πέτρη, xii 64, 79), λισσός (iii 293, v 412, x 4), λεῖος (v 443, vii 282, ix 134, x 103); cf. Myc. *ri-ta*, of cloths, and later λῖτός 'simple', as well as acc. and dat. λῖτα, λιτί (*Il.* xviii 352, xxiii 254, *Od.* i 130, x 353) from an unattested *λίς 'linen'. πύκα ποιητοῖο, 'solidly built', elsewhere in the *Odyssey* always with τέγεος (i 333, viii 458, xvi 415, xviii 209, xxi 64) or θαλάμου (i 436); the adv. πύκα is from the same root as πυκνός and πυκάζω 'cover' (cf. 488). On δάπεδον see 188n. and 309, xxiv 185.

456. ξῦον: this unique expression for 'scraping, raking' the floor belongs to a family of technical terms for 'smoothing, polishing, planing,shaving down'; cf. ξέω and ἀμφιξέω (xxi 44n., with the note on ἰθύνω, xxiii 199; see F. Eckstein, *Archaeologia* L 1, 9) as well as ξεστός (2n., 72n.), ἐΰξεστος (xxi 137n., xxi 164, xxiv 408), ἐΰξοος (of a bow in five places in xxi, and xxii 71n.); the noun ξυστόν 'well-trimmed and polished stave, shaft' > 'spear' (*Il.* iv 469, xi 260, 565, xiii 497, xv 388) or 'boat-hook' (*Il.* xv 677); ξαίνω, used of combing or carding (423n.); and the incompletely-explained ξύω of *Il.* 179 (which remains unclear, despite his efforts, for S. Marinatos, *Archaeologia* A, 3). ἀποξύσας in *Il.* ix 446 is used in a vague general sense (a god 'brushes' the old age from a man to make him young again); ξυρέω 'shave' is post-Homeric, but in *Il.* x 173 we find the proverbial expression ἐπὶ ξυροῦ . . . ἀκμῆς 'on the razor's edge' (S. Marinatos, *Archaeologia* B, 24). The imperfects stress the repetitive nature of the long, heavy task (see 437n.); the direct obj. of τίθεσαν must be supplied, 'the debris from the hall'. On θύραζε see Introduction to xxi.

458–9. δμῳὰς δ': the δέ is 'apodotic'. The connective particle commonly introduces the principal clause of a sentence after αὐτὰρ ἐπεί . . . e.g. iii 473–4, viii 24, etc. αὐτὰρ ἐπεί . . . τοῖσι δέ. The particle is here omitted by

P. 28 and some codd. **μεσσηγύς** has appeared in 93 and 341, in the latter at the beginning of the line; the whole of 459 is in effect equivalent to a lative acc., '(having taken them out) to a place between . . .'. For τε . . . καί cf. 324, xxiv 67. **ἀμύμων:** a formulaic epithet meaning 'blameless', is not often used of inanimate objects, but cf. xii 261 (the island of the Sun), xxiii 145 (the dance), xxiv 80 (a tomb), xxiv 278 (women-servants' handiwork); there is a slight lack of stylistic control in the way the agreement of this adj. is left havering between ἔρκεος or αὐλῆς.

460. εἴλεον ἐν στείνει: the verb εἰλέω (cf. 292 n.) appears in only three other places in the *Odyssey*, always appositely: xi 573 (Orion rounding up wild beasts), xii 210 (Cyclops trapping Odysseus), xix 200 (Boreas blowing ships off course); in contrast to later στένος Homer offers, here and in two places in the *Iliad* (xii 66, likewise followed by hiatus in thesis, with ὅθι, and xxiii 419) the lengthened στεῖνος < *στενϝος 'narrow, confined space'; the figurative sense 'anguish, dire strait' is seen in *Il.* viii 476, xv 426. **ἀλύξαι:** cf. 66 n.; three examples in the *Iliad*, and at *Od.* iv 416, v 345, xii 216, always at the end of the line.

461. The formulaic line, with its τοῖσι 'amongst them', is more appropriate to meetings and assemblies (ii 15, Aegyptius to his compatriots) or social gatherings (xvi 345, xviii 349, xx 359, Eurymachus and the suitors) than to the present situation.

462. Telemachus expresses his opposition to his father's more decent proposal for dealing with the execution of the women-slaves (443) with a strongly asseverative opt. (ἀπὸ . . . ἑλοίμην, tmesis) which almost amounts to an oath to the effect that he at least (μὲν δή) will not be responsible for doing something of which he cannot approve; cf. the opt. of strong desire in xiv 405, and with the neg., vii 316, xx 344. The closest parallel to this particular case are three disputed passages in the *Iliad* where the opt. is introduced by μὴ μὰν ἀσπουδί (*Il.* viii 512, xv 476, xxii 304; see Denniston, *Particles*, 332). the variant ἔλησθε is feeble and insipid. καθαρῷ is in an emphatic position; its meaning, however, is not quite certain. None of the other eight Homeric examples of the word authorize us to interpret it in the religious sense which it later acquired; in iv 750, 759, vi 61, xvii 48, 58 it refers merely to clean clothing, in *Il.* viii 491, x 199, xxiii 61 to a clear and unencumbered space. Nor can Telemachus mean a 'clean' death in the sense of one free from ritual pollution, since the spilling of blood by decapitation would in turn require further purification. Furthermore, the fact that so many tragic heroes choose to commit suicide by hanging themselves excludes the possibility that he means an 'honourable and heroic' death by the sword, as against a shameful and dirty death by the rope. We are left with the idea of a 'clean', in the sense of 'quick and easy', death. Be that as it may, the speech is out of character for the mild Telemachus, and Odysseus' easy acceptance of the change in plan is surprising.

463. τάων, αἳ δή: 'of these women who, as is well known'. **ἐμῇ κεφαλῇ:** that Telemachus should here present the serving-women's behaviour as a slight to his own self-esteem is a sign of his youthful immaturity. The phrase is Iliadic (cf. *Il.* xi 55, xviii 82, where Achilles, who prized Patroclus *ἴσον ἐμῇ κεφαλῇ*, goes in search of Hector to avenge the death of 'his beloved head', xviii 114; see also, in anticipation of a phrase much used in later times, viii 281 *φίλη κεφαλή*, xxiii 94 *ἠθείη κεφαλή*), and is paralleled also in *Od.* i 343-4, where Odysseus misses Penelope *τοίην . . . κεφαλὴν | ἀνδρός, τοῦ κλέος κτλ.* The existence of the verb *καταχεύω* is guaranteed, against the *lectio facilior κάκ'* for *κατ'*, by xiv 38 *ἐλεγχείην κατέχευας. ὄνειδος* appears only twice elsewhere in the *Odyssey*, at vi 285 and xvii 461.

464. ἡμετέρῃ: the use of pl. for sing., so common in later times, is not adequately explained by the example of i 176, where Telemachus speaks of 'our house' collectively; a more telling parallel is xix 344, where Odysseus asserts that no woman will touch 'our foot'. **ἴαυον:** there are thirteen attestations of the verb in Homer, eight of them in the *Odyssey*; it is probably a reduplicated *ἴ-αυ-ω* (cf. Hellenistic *αὔω*) related to *αὖλις* (cf. 470), *αὐλή*, etc., meaning 'spend successive nights, pernoctate' in a place (cf. also xxiv 209; of animals, ix 184, xiv 16, 21); it sometimes governs *νύκτας* (*pace* Chantraine, *Grammaire*, i 313; see *Il.* ix 470, *Od.* v 154, xix 340), and very occasionally has the sexual sense it clearly has here (*Il.* xiv 213, of Hera and Zeus; *Od.* v 154, Odysseus and Calypso; xi 261, Antiope and Zeus). We also find compounds such as *ἐνιαύω* 'dwell' (ix 187, xv 557; perhaps the origin of *ἐν-ιαυ-τός* 'resting-place of the sun' > 'solstice' > 'year', eighteen examples in the *Odyssey*) and *παριαύω* (*Il.* ix 336, Agamemnon with the daughter of Chryses). It is not certain that the aor. *ἄεσα* belongs to the same root (six occurrences in the *Odyssey*, always with *νύκτα(ς)*, never sexual; a contracted form, *ἄσαμεν*, in xvi 367), besides which the *ἰαῦσαι* of xi 261 would clearly be secondary.

465. πεῖσμα: 'hawser, cable' (always for mooring, for instance to a stone bollard, x 96, xiii 77; cf. also ix 136, x 127, where Odysseus cuts the *πείσματα . . . νεὸς κυανοπρώροιο*; the only exceptions are vi 269, where the Phaeacians busy themselves with *πείσματα καὶ σπείρας*, 'nets and cables' in a general sense, and x 167, nothing to do with ships, where Odysseus makes a rope from some reeds to tie up a dead deer); this is, then, another piece of nautical equipment which happens to be lying about in the *αἴθουσα* (cf. xxi 390). The word derives from an assumed **πενθσμα*, from the same root meaning 'to tie' as *πενθερός* 'relative by marriage', *φάτνη* < *πάθνη* < **bhṇdhnā* 'cradle, manger', etc. (Schwyzer, *Grammatik*, i 287). Such a hawser would have to be quite long, though not perhaps as long as the eighteen yards which were postulated as necessary to hang all twelve women at a time. The problematic final formula occurs in two forms, with *νεός* (*Il.* xv 693, *Od.* ix 482, 539, x 127, xi 6, xii 100, 148, 354) and with *νηός* (*Il.* xxiii 852, 878, *Od.* xiv 311); the variant *νεώς* is impossible, though we find nom. *Ἀκρόνεως* (viii 111) and *Ἀναβησίνεως* (viii 113) as significant names for Phaeacians, with quantitative metathesis, against primitive *νηός* and *νεός* with shortening of the first long vowel in hiatus: see Chantraine, *Grammaire*, i 72, Hoekstra, *Modifications*, 125-6. Alongside the form *νέας* κυανοπρωρείους (iii 299), considered correct by Risch (*Wortbildung*, 130–1), may be set the tradition represented by Herodian and the *Etymologicum Magnum* through Schulze and Schwartz; this induced von der Mühll not only to read κυανοπρῳείρους in that passage, but also to suggest tentatively that κυανοπρωείρου or -πρωίρου should be read in every case for -πρῴροιο (see his app. crit. on ix 482, x 127), basing the suggestion on a hypothetical pairing of *πρωϝαργα > πρῷρα (cf. χίμαιρα/γέραιρα) and *-πρωϝεργα > πρώειρα (cf. πίειρα, πέπειρα). He would thus eliminate the two-termination adj. κυανόπρωρος, from κύανος 'lapis lazuli' and πρῷρα 'prow'. He cites Simonides fr. 120 P, in which κυανοπρώειραν seems preferable to the probably itacistic -πρώϊραν.

467. The aor. participle does not signify successive action: Telemachus first of all ties one end of the cable and then with the help of his servants hauls it up into the air (ὑψόσε) by heaving on the other end. τανύω has been used, unless I am mistaken, nine times in xxi to refer to the drawing of the bow, and ἐντανύω fourteen times. The meaning of this unique double prefix in ἐπεντανόω seems to be that this rope cannot be tightened and slackened at will like a bowstring by bending the arms on which it is strung, but is braced hard on (ἐπὶ) two fixed arms (the same, incidentally, could have been said of the lyre-string in xxi 407); for another example of this double prefix cf. ἐπεμβεβαώς in *Il.* ix 582. μή τις introduces a final clause, 'so that none of them'; the MSS are divided on the following oblique opt. ἵκοιτο (Chantraine, *Grammaire*, ii 269). οὖδας, acc. of direction. The line is curiously reminiscent of viii 375–6, quite different in subject, on a player who catches a high ball by leaping up, ὑψόσ' ἀερθείς, and taking it on the wing πάρος ποσὶν οὖδας ἱκέσθαι.

468–73. The final simile of xxii. The poet tiptoes over the intricate (and perhaps the impracticable) details of the execution, jumping from the hauling up of the rope to the tableau of the hanging women. We are not fully informed about the construction of the bird-catching nets referred to here, but it is difficult to imagine one designed to catch a *row* of birds by the neck; the simile is probably less exact in its application, picturing just one bird, a thrush or dove returning to its roost in the woods, which fails in the twilight to notice the snare hidden among the leaves, flies into it, and is strangled by its own momentum. Or the poet may be thinking of some sort of spring-loaded snare which whips upward and breaks the bird's neck. The image of the single bird is then applied to the whole row of executed women. See further H.-G. Buchholz, G. Jöhrens, and I. Maull, *Archaeologia* J, 106, 116–18; and cf. *Od.* xxii 304 n.

468. ὡς δ' ὅτ' ἄν: in contrast to the simple 'as . . . so' scheme for similes (see 299–308 n., and xix 205–7 ὡς δέ with indic., *Il.* v 161–2 ὡς δέ with subj., *Od.* xiii 81–3 ὥς τε with indic.), there is a commoner scheme, introduced by 'as [happens] when'; thus xix 518–23 ὡς δ' ὅτε with subj., xii 251–4 ὡς δ' ὅτε with indic., *Il.* xi 305–8 ὡς ὁπότε with subj., *Od.* xvii 126–30 ὡς δ' ὁπότε with subj., *Il.* xi 492–5 ὡς δ' ὁπότε with indic., and the present passage with ὡς δ' ὅτ' ἄν with the subj. κίχλη, a word familiar in later

comedy, is found only here in Homer; τανυσίπτερος, of birds in general, v 65; πέλεια occurs five times in the *Iliad* and four in the *Odyssey*.

469. This is the only pre-classical occurrence of the word ἕρκος 'net' (cf. xxi 238n.). ἐνιπλήξωσι: 'batter, dash into'; here and in *Il.* xii 72 ἐνιπλήξωμεν we have the intrans. sense; cf. the adv. ἐμπλήγδην 'madly', applied to Penelope by Telemachus in xx 132, a unique form which presupposes a latent ἔμπληκτος 'struck' > 'stunned, reeling' > 'mad' found in Sophocles and later. ἑστήκῃ: 'has been placed', subj. of intrans. ἕστηκα, only paralleled by *Il.* xvii 435 (of a funeral stele); the subj. would take the 'generalizing' ἄν in Attic.

470. αὖλιν: 'roosting place'; cf. *Il.* ix 232 the Trojans αὖλιν ἔθεντο 'established a camp'. ἐσιέμεναι, here in the physical sense which later became common, 'launching themselves towards' with acc. of direction (cf. 256n.) is not paralleled in Homer, but Herodotus has three examples of ἐσίημι; there is no need to emend. The parataxis of the second hemistich is adversative in meaning ('they launch themselves, but . . .'). στυγερὸς δ' ὑπεδέξατο κοῖτος: the phrase contains a double oxymoron; first, because the verb ὑπεδέξατο, sc. αὐτήν, gnomic aor. (cf. 388, another simile), is usually used of a kindly reception (cf. ii 387, xiv 52, 54, xvi 70, xix 257, xx 372, xxiii 314); a distinct meaning is seen in xiii 310, xvi 189 'support', and a different kind of sarcasm in xiv 275 ἔτι γάρ νύ με πῆμ' ὑπέδεκτο; for the irony of *Il.* vi 136, xviii 398, where Thetis welcomes Dionysus and Hephaestus into her watery bosom, see Bowra, *Companion*, 32); and second, because κοῖτος 'bed, sleeping place', which suggests ideas of safety and comfort (ten examples, all in the *Odyssey*; see S. Laser, *Archaeologia* P, 4), is qualified by στυγερός (cf. xxiv 126, xxiv 200).

471. 'So they held their heads in a row'; again, the emphasis falls on the second element in the paratactical structure, 'with their necks in the noose'. πάσαις 'each one of them'; double dat. of person and part of the body (the word does not agree with δειρῇσι), where our stylistic feeling would make us expect πασέων (van der Valk, *Textual Criticism*, 58); the apparent Atticism of the ending -αις (Chantraine, *Grammaire*, i 202) has given rise to a bundle of variants; cf. *Il.* xii 284 ἀκταῖς at the end of the line (in *Od.* v 119 either θεαῖσ' or θεῇς is possible before ἀγάασθε; in *Il.* i 238 Mazon prints παλάμαις against Allen's παλάμης before a consonant).

472. βρόχοι: βρόχος, 'noose', appears elsewhere only in xi 278, on the suicide of Epicasta. οἴκτιστα is unemphatic; they had put the nooses around their necks so that they should die, and in addition their deaths were miserable; this is the only Homeric example of the superl. οἴκτιστα used as an adv. (cf. *Il.* xxii 76, *Od.* xxiii 79, xxiv 34, and two further passages; *Od.* xi 421 οἰκτροτάτην; xi 381 οἰκτρότερα, acc. pl.); οἰκτρά as an adv. occurs four times in the *Odyssey*, including xxiv 59 (cf. 447n.).

473. ἀσπαίρω is used of the convulsions, gasping, and panting of the dying, for instance of a stricken warrior (viii 526, *Il.* x 521, xiii 573); in *Il.* xiii 443 the subj. is the heart of the dying man, implying a reference to cardiac symptoms; here it indicates the twitching and kicking of the suffocating women, which recalls its use in a number of images from the animal world: of fishes (xii 254–5; cf. 384–8 n.), deer (xix 229, 231, also with kicking of the feet), lambs (*Il.* iii 293), snakes (*Il.* xii 203), and oxen (*Il.* xiii 571). The line recalls two passages in the *Iliad*: i 416, where Thetis says to Achilles ἐπεί νύ τοι αἶσα μίνυνθά περ, οὔ τι μάλα δήν, and above all *Il.* xiii 573, where Adamas is compared to a dying ox, ἤσπαιρε μίνυνθά περ, οὔτι μάλα δήν. δήν is an ancient acc. (cf. 377 n.) related to δηρός 'long' (of time, *Il.* xiv 206, 305), often used in the acc. δηρόν as an adv. 'for a long time' (i 203, xxi 112, xxiv 395), and to the adv. δηθά 'for a long time' (cf. 177 n.); it derives from *δϜην, which accounts for the lengthening of a preceding vowel here and in xxiv 125, *Il.* i 416, xiii 573 (as also with δηρόν at *Od.* i 203; but this is not always the case, cf. Chantraine, *Grammaire*, i 163).

474–7. Another terrible punishment, of Melanthius, which offers various puzzles. Odysseus gives no orders for this savage act, and it is not made clear who carries it out—Stanford hopes, piously, that Telemachus is not among their number. Nor are we told exactly at what moment the unfortunate Melanthius dies. The four lines have the look of an interpolation; even if they were absent, the goatherd's unpleasant death by ἀποτυμπανισμός might have been surmised. Merkelbach, for whom 473 is also the work of the *B* poet, points out some interesting ritual elements in the execution: the cutting off of parts of the body as in the μασχαλισμός of the tragedians, which parallels the ritual ὠμοθετεῖν carried out on sacrificial animals (iii 458, xii 361); and the throwing of the genitals to be eaten by dogs, as was done with the animal's entrails during sacrifice. Such practices were apotropaic, designed to ward off the posthumous vengeance of the victim; see further K. Meuli, 'Griechische Opferbräuche', in *Phyllobolia für P. von der Mühll zum 60. Geburtstag* (Basle, 1946), 185–8; Merkelbach, *Untersuchungen*, 130 n. 2. The passage in xviii 86–7, where Antinous threatens Irus (cf. xxi 308 n.) with sending him, if he is defeated, to the abominable King Echetus, there to have his ῥῖνα . . . καὶ οὔατα cut off νηλέϊ χαλκῷ (xviii 86; almost identical to xxii 475), and his genitals thrown to the dogs (μήδεά τ' ἐξερύσας . . . κυσὶν ὠμὰ δάσασθαι, xviii 87, similar to xxii 476), is derived from the present passage (and cf. xxi 300–1, and n. on xxi 299–304, for a similar punishment meted out to Eurytion). Apart from Eisenberger's objections (*Studien*, 243 n. 21), the passage shows traces of the later poet's hand: they drag Melanthius from the store-room (ἐκ . . . ἦγον, tmesis) into the courtyard; the execution, like that of the maids, may take place there, unseen from the street outside (although screams can be heard outside; note the precautions taken in xxi 133–6 to ensure that the neighbours hear only so much as may raise, but cannot answer, speculation), and the gate to the street remains shut until xxiii 370 (cf. xxi 389–91). The syntax of 475–7 is confused; after ἀπὸ μὲν we wait for δέ, but are disappointed. The intrusion of ἐξέρυσαν prevents us from taking the attractive solution of ἀπό in double tmesis, with both ἀποτάμνω and ἀποκόπτω (Faesi ad loc.; Blass counters by proposing the elimination of 476, *Interpolationen*, 210); both these compound verbs are commonly paired as close synonyms, though the first strictly means to 'slice off' and the second to 'knock off': cf. *Il.* viii 87 παρηορίας ἀπέταμνε 'he cut the traces off the horse' with *Il.* xvi 474 ἀπέκοψε παρήορον 'he cut the horse free from the traces'; ἀποκόπτω in the sense 'cut off' is found several times (*Il.* ix 241, xi 261, *Od.* iii 449, ix 325, xxiii 195; in tmesis, *Il.* xi 146, *Od.* x 127), though simple κόπτω almost always means simply 'to strike, hit' a person (viii 528, ix 290, xviii 28, 335; of boxing, *Il.* xxiii 690, 726; a solitary exception in *Il.* xiii 203 'separate the head from the body with a blow'); or to 'hit' an animal (xiv 425) or 'forge something with blows, hammer' (*Il.* xviii 379, *Od.* viii 274), or in the middle to 'beat one's head' (*Il.* xxii 33). At all events, the semantic distinction between the two verbs is slight; cf., as etymological correlates, Lith. *kariù* 'fell, cut down a tree' and *tinù* 'sharpen a scythe against a whetstone'.

475. ῥῖνας: oblique cases of later ῥίς 'nose' have already occurred in xxi 301, xxii 18, and do so again in xxiv 318; there are a further three attestations in the *Odyssey*, and eight in the *Iliad*.   οὔατα: neut. οὖς 'ear', from *ousos*, occurs in the acc. in *Il.* xi 109, xx 473; gen. οὔατος < *ous-ṇ-tos*, whence comes later ὠτός, in *Od.* xviii 96, etc.; this neut. pl. nom.acc., in xii 47, 177, xvii 291, 302, xviii 86, xx 365, xxi 300; the problematic dat. pl. ὠσίν in xii 200 has been emended to οὔασ'. In *Il.* xi 633, xviii 378 οὔατα is used figuratively of the 'handles' of a cup and tripods respectively; hence of bowls without handles. Myc. *a-no-wo-to* < *an-ousṇtos* (K 875), *a-no-we* < *an-óus-ēs* (Ta 641), ἀνούατος (Theo. *Ep.* iv 3); of one-handled cups, perhaps *o-wo-we* from οἶος (Ta 641); of two-handled cups, ἄμφωτος in xxii 10, which may be from *ωϝατος (the lengthening of the first vowel of the second element being paralleled in ἀμφώης, Theoc. i 28, though the disparity with ἀνούατος has prompted emendation from Fick); and of three and four-handled vessels, dual *ti-ri-o-we-e* and *qe-to-ro-we*, also in the famous Tablet of the Tripods from Pylos (Ta 641). The formula νηλέϊ χαλκῷ occurs at the end of the line in *Od.* iv 743, viii 507, x 532, xi 45, xiv 418, xviii 86, xxi 300; it is this passage, however, that most vividly preserves the original sense of νηλής, 'pitiless'.

476. μήδεα: 'pudenda', a word of uncertain derivation (perhaps a euphemism, related to μήδομαι and μῆδος, 'that which one should be careful to cover') and whose relation to the synonyms μέζεα (Hes. *Op.* 512, cf. μήδεα in *Th.* 180, 188, 200) and μέδεα (Archil. fr. 222 w) is imperfectly understood, is found in xviii 87 (cited above), vi 129 (Odysseus covers himself in the presence of Nausicaa), and xviii 67.   ἐξέρυσαν: cf. 386 (see nn. on 372, 384–8), and see ix 397 (the Cyclops pulls the stake from his eye), xviii 87.   κυσὶν ὠμὰ δάσασθαι: the end of the line repeats *Il.* xxiii 21, where Achilles swears to the shade of Patroclus that he will feed Hector's corpse to the dogs; the fact that this latter line and *Od.* xviii 87 both have the necessary δώσειν and δώῃ, missing here, further indicates the derivativeness of the formula's use here. ὠμά, predicative, is found also in *Il.* iv 35, xxii 347 (eating a person raw), *Od.* xii 396 (raw meat), and in a metaphorical sense at xv 357 (Laertes' cruel old age). δάσασθαι, consecutive-final.

477. κεκοτηότι θυμῷ: the phrase seems somewhat exaggerated, especially after they have already subjected Melanthius to ἀποτυμπανισμός, as if the slaves were aping their masters in their servile parody of his noble wrath; κότος appears in the *Odyssey* only of Poseidon's anger against the hero, xi 102, xiii 342; κοτέω, of the rancour of gods—Athena in i 101, Zeus against Calypso in v 147—except in xix 83 (Penelope, against Melantho); the end-of-line formula κεκοτηότι θυμῷ is probably imitated from *Il.* xxi 456 (Apollo and Poseidon, against Laomedon), as also probably in *Od.* ix 501 (Odysseus against the Cyclops) and xix 71 (Melantho against her master).

478. Οἱ μὲν: sc. Telemachus and the servants (cf. 454). The phraseology is again unusual; the various examples of the middle of νίζω or ἀπονίζω take an internal acc. (vi 224, and with ἀπο- xviii 172, 179, 'wash oneself all over (χρόα); ii 261, x 182, xii 336, *Il.* xvi 230, 'wash one's hands'; *Il.* x 572, with ἀπο-, 'to wash off sweat'); in the active we find it used of washing the feet (xix 356, 376; 387, ἐξαπο-) and similar cases (ἀπονίζω of another person, xix 317, xxiii 75, *Il.* vii 425 in tmesis; washing of blood, *Od.* xxiv 189); but only here do we find the verb used with the derivative formula χεῖράς τε πόδας τε (for parallels, cf. xi 497, age has taken hold of Peleus' hands and feet; xii 50, 178, Odysseus is tied hand and foot to the mast). But it is hardly surprising that after such slaughter they should need, and be required by ritual, to wash both hands and feet, or indeed their whole bodies.

479. At an unspecified moment during the two executions, Odysseus has gone into the hall. κίον, aor. (cf. 378 n.), is qualified both by δόμονδε and by εἰς with the proper noun (cf. 202 n.). The line-ending, with its regular hiatus, also occurs in *Il.* xix 242; in *Il.* vii 465 it is placed ∪ ∪ –⁴ ∪ ∪ –⁵ ∪; the paratactical clause is causal ('they went to find Odysseus because their work was done').

480. The end-of-line formula, here amplified by the addition of φίλην, occurs in xxi 380, xxii 391, 394; in the nom., xxii 419, 485, 492, xxiii 25, 39, 69; Eurycleia's name takes the epithet περίφρων in xxi 381 (see n.), and occurs in the voc. in xxiii 177; τροφός alone, without a proper name, in xxiii 289 (see Ramming, *Dienerschaft*, 51–3).

481. οἶσε: cf. 106. There follows a cleansing of the blood-stained house, both practical and ritual (κακῶν ἄκος, the latter word used only here and in *Il.* ix 250, where Odysseus urges Achilles to come to the aid of the Achaeans, warning him that the consequences if he fails to do so will have no remedy, ἄκος; cf. however, the ἀκέσματα which Patroclus sprinkles on Eurypylus' wound in *Il.* xv 394). The cleansing is carried out with θέειον 'sulphur', which appears six times in Homer, four of them referring to the smell left in the atmosphere by a bolt of lightning (*Il.* viii 135, xiv 415, *Od.* xii 417, xiv 307), once in connection with the cleaning of a cup by Achilles (*Il.* xvi 228), and the remainder in this passage; θεειόω 'fumigate by burning sulphur on a fire (πῦρ, here and at 491, 493)' occurs in xxiii 50, and in the unique compound διαθειόω in 494 below. The origin of the word seems to be neut. *θϝεσος 'smoke' (related to *θϝεσος > θεός 'god'; cf. θύω 'offer smoke' > 'sacrifice', and θῦμός 'spirit') from which came *θϝεσειον >

θέειον (cf. Lith. *dvasià* 'spirit'), simplified by hyphaeresis in post-Homeric times to θεῖον (and in διεθείωσεν in 494), which in turn produced θήϊον, the form in 493, by lengthening of the first vowel. Sulphur may have been imported from Melos, or alternatively the Aeolian islands (R. J. Forbes, *Archaeologia* K, 10; Pocock, *Odyssean Essays*, 10).

482. σὺ δὲ: 'and (while I fumigate the μέγαρον—not just the hall, but the courtyard and the rest of the palace, 494), you . . .'.

483. ἐνθάδ᾽: cf. 431 n.   ἄνωχθι: cf. 437 n., in the transferred sense 'give (my) orders to Penelope' (Eurycleia cannot herself give orders to the mistress); cf. xvii 569, where Odysseus tells Eumaeus in the same way to 'give an order' to Penelope (J. Grimm, *LfgrE*, i 960–70), whereas in xxii 437 Telemachus may himself give orders. The ἀμφίπολοι Myc. *a-pi-qo-ro*; cf. xxi 8, 61, 66, 351, 356) are distinct from mere δμωαί (not mentioned in xxi; xxii 37, 396, 422, 427, 441, 456, 458, 484), being the hand-picked attendants on the mistress' person, whose duties of serving at table, spinning, and weaving were lighter than those of the ordinary house-servants; thus it is that Penelope is to descend σὺν ἀμφιπόλοισι γυναιξί, 'with her handmaidens', while Eurycleia is to fetch the other servants, those of them who have remained faithful and whose job is to attend about the house (δμωὰς κατὰ δῶμα is equivalent to Attic τὰς κατὰ τὸ δῶμα δμωάς, cf. 304–6 n., 313–14 n., though at this time they are probably hiding in a room somewhere (cf. xxi 235–9, 381–5).

485–91. On the significance of this passage, where Odysseus proposes appearing before Penelope in his beggar's rags in order to put off the anagnorisis (xxiii 95 ἄλλοτε δ᾽ ἀγνώσασκε κακὰ χροΐ εἵματ᾽ ἔχοντα), see Erbse, *Beiträge*, 64, and Eisenberger, *Studien*, 307.

486. Old Eurycleia's noticeably familiar tone (τέκνον ἐμόν; see also xix 492, and xxiii 70 to Penelope) strikes a pleasant note here; all the other examples of this form of address are of parents speaking to their children (Zeus to Athena, i 64, v 22, xxiv 478; Anticleia to Odysseus, xi 216; Penelope to Telemachus, xxiii 105) except the venerable Tiresias' address to the hero in xi 155.   κατὰ μοῖραν: 'suitably, to the point'; μοῖρα here has nothing to do with the 'destiny' of xxi 24, xxii 413; see 54 n., and compare the numerous examples of this common line-ending in ii 251, iv 266, viii 141, xiii 385, xviii 170, xx 37, which also occurs with ἔειπε (with or without -ν) in vii 227, viii 397, xiii 48, xxi 278 n.; and with the aor. of καταλέγω, iii 331, viii 496, x 16, xii 35; cf. also xiv 509 οὐδέ τί πω παρὰ μοῖραν ἔπος νηκερδὲς ἔειπες.

487. ἀλλ᾽ ἄγε: cf. 1 n., and for the following subj., 139 n.   εἵματ(α) is always placed in the fifth foot and preceded by the requisite hiatus (cf. Lat. *uestis* etc.) in the last four books; the same line-ending is found in xxi 339 (cf. also xxi 52, xxiii 95, 132, xxiv 156, and for εἵματα followed by a further hiatus before the cognate verb εἷμαι, ἔσσαν, ἔστο, xxiii 115, xxiv 59, 158).

488. ῥάκεσιν: cf. 1 n.   πεπυκασμένος: cf. 455 n. on πυκάζω; we find two forms of the act. in the *Odyssey*; here and in three places in the *Iliad* the pf. part. shows analogical assimilation, in contrast to the πεπυκάδμενον

COMMENTARY

of Sappho fr. 166L–P (Schwyzer, *Grammatik*, i 773). **ὤμους**: internal acc.

489. ἔσταθ': the only Homeric example of the 2nd sing. imper. of ἔστηκα (cf. *Il.* xxiii 443 ἔστατον, *Il.* xx 354 ἔστατε; none of the variants is satisfactory (though inf. ἦσθαι, which would here be imper. in sense, occurs in initial position in x 507, 536, xix 120, xxiii 365; cf. xxiii 91, 93 ἦστο). Eurycleia observes Odysseus' shabby appearance (cf. xxiii 115 ῥυπόω, κακὰ δὲ χροῖ εἵματα εἶμαι), though doubtless he has washed himself of blood (402) with the others at 478. The conditional which follows requires some protasis such as 'if you did'; νεμεσσητόν occurs in the same position in 59 (see n.), *Il.* xix 182; without gemination, *Il.* xi 649; the same line-ending in *Il.* iii 410, xiv 336, xxiv 463.

491. πῦρ: see 481 n., and cf. xxiii 50–1 ὁ δῶμα θεειοῦται περικαλλές, | πῦρ μέγα κηάμενος. πρώτιστον, adv. 'immediately, first of all'; cf. x 462, xx 60, and perhaps *Il.* ii 702; πρώτιστα occurs in the same sense eight times in the *Odyssey* (see 113) and four times in the *Iliad*.

492. ἀπίθησε: independently of the fut. πιθήσεις (xxi 369 n.) and aor. part. πιθήσας (xxi 315, and seven examples in the *Iliad*) we find two examples of the fut. ἀπιθήσω (*Il.* xxiv 300, *Il.* x 129) and thirty-two of the aor., formed on the base of *ἀπίθης which was supplanted in the classical language by ἀπειθής 'disobedient' in contrast to ἀπειθέω 'disobey'. The verb is always used with the neg. in litotes, 'did not disobey' = 'obeyed'; only four of the examples belong to the *Odyssey*, applied elsewhere to Hermes (v 43), Eteoneus (xv 98), and Eumaeus and Philoetius (xxiii 369, the only pl.).

494. διεθείωσεν: the prefix (cf. 481 n.) emphasizes the fact that the fumigation was carried out right through the palace.

495. On the contrast of the aor. ἀπέβη with the series of six imperfects which close xxii see Schwyzer, *Grammatik*, ii 277, Chantraine, *Grammaire*, ii 194.

496. = 434.

497. = *Il.* xxiv 647, *Od.* iv 300, vii 339 (see S. Laser, *Archaeologia* P, 85–6). In these latter passages it is natural that the women-slaves should leave the hall carrying torches, in order to set up the bed in the αἴθουσα; similar is xxiii 294, which is also easily explained, since Eurynome is lighting the wedded couple to their nuptial chamber. Here, however, the line may well be spurious; even if we accept that μέγαρον here denotes the women's quarters (cf. xviii 185, 198, 316), the presence of torches lacks point since, if it is not still daylight (cf. xxi 429 n.), the recently kindled fire and the λαμπτῆρες will be quite sufficient to light the men's hall. Alternatively, we must imagine the women coming forth from the *megaron* into the courtyard, in which inappropriate place they must awkwardly embrace their master in joyous reunion while at the same time clutching the inconvenient torches in their hands (for further examples of μετὰ χερσίν, see for example xxi 245, xxii 10, with νωμάω; cf. ἐν χείρεσσιν ἔχων, xxii 332 n.). Besides all this, Blass would like to see some reference hereabouts to Odysseus taking a bath; the ablutions of xxiii 154, which take place after the hero's reunion with Penelope, come a good deal too late for his taste (*Interpolationen*, 224;

cf., however, 489n.). **δάος:** as names for torches we find ten examples of δαΐς in the *Odyssey* (of which xxiii 290 comes very close to δάος in 294, indicating synonymy) and five of δάος (also related to δαίω), as well as δεταί (from δέω, a 'bundle' of branches or straw) in *Il.* xi 554, xvii 663. Here and in iv 300 the variant may conceal, as von der Mühll suggests, a correct reading μεγάρου δᾳδας (contracted form of δαΐδας).

498. **ἀμφεχέοντο:** the closest parallel to this use of the verb is xvi 214, where Telemachus weeps ἀμφιχυθεὶς πατέρα; elsewhere it is used of sleep or pain gripping someone (*Il.* ii 41 ἀμφέχυτο, *Il.* xiv 253, xxiii 63 ἀμφιχυθείς; *Od.* iv 716 ἀμφεχύθη), or in the act. in tmesis and with a very different meaning (viii 278). In *Il.* xxiii 764, ἀμφιχυθῆναι refers to dust settling over some tracks. **ἠσπάζοντ':** the verb occurs only four times in Homer, and elsewhere always with δεξιῇ (*Il.* x 542, Nestor and his retainers greet Odysseus and Diomedes) or χερσίν (iii 35, Nestor's sons greet Telemachus, xix 415, Autolycus and his sons greet Odysseus), which indicate an embrace. ἀσπάσιος and ἀσπαστός, however, which occur frequently in xxiii (60, 233, 238–9, 296), are less physical in meaning, denoting the happiness with which one greets an unexpected arrival.

499-501. This beautiful scene marks a deliberate coda after the brutality of the preceding action.

499. **κύνεον:** the verb, which is found only three times in the *Iliad* (vi 474, Hector kisses Astyanax; viii 371, Thetis kisses the cheeks of Zeus; xxiv 478, Priam kisses the killer's hands of Achilles), is, by contrast, of frequent occurrence in the *Odyssey*. To the examples already cited in the n. on xxi 224–5 may be added, quite apart from the lines in which Agamemnon and Odysseus kiss the ground after a narrow escape (iv 522, v 463,xiii 354) and the fantastic passage in which the hero kisses the knees of the King of Egypt (xiv 279), the following: xvi 21 (Eumaeus kisses Telemachus), 190 (Odysseus kisses Telemachus), xix 417 (Amphithea kisses Odysseus), xxiii 208 (Penelope kisses Odysseus), and xxiv 236, 320 (Odysseus kisses Laertes). As can be seen, only xxiii 87 and 208 carry any erotic overtone. **ἀγαπαζόμεναι:** this middle is attested only in the part. (cf. also ἀμφαγαπαζόμενος, *Il.* xvi 192), in vii 33 (men kiss each other) and in three closely parallel passages, xxi 224 (Eumaeus and Philoetius kiss Odysseus), xvii 35, and here, the latter being the only times it is applied to women kissing, of the women-slaves kissing Telemachus and Odysseus respectively. In all three of the latter passages the final vowel of κύνεον is lengthened; van Leeuwen has suggested, as elsewhere, that this may be due to a lost pronoun ϝ'.

500. **αἰνύμεναι:** the only other occasion on which αἴνυμαι means 'touch, lay hold of' is *Il.* xv 459, where Teucer grasps an arrow; here it contributes to the emotional force of the moving scene, τε indicating that the physical contact signified by αἰνύμεναι applies to all the previous nouns, head, shoulders, and hands. **τὸν:** sc. Odysseus. **ἵμερος:** the evolution of the noun, with its cognates ἱμείρω, ἱμερτός (*Il.* ii 751) and ἱμερόεις (five examples in each poem), is interesting; whether or not they be related to

Skt. *iccháti* 'desire', this group of words evidently describe the 'longing' one feels for something one does not have, an emotional need which can be fulfilled, and even sated, by simple possession and satisfaction of the object of desire, whether it be food (*Il.* xi 89), music and dance (*Od.* xxiii 144), the coolness of the night air (*Od.* x 555), or home-coming (*Od.* i 41). Sometimes the desire is destructive (death, *Od.* i 59), or mistaken (x 431); and an early restriction of meaning reduces ἵμερος to the passion of love, whether of a general kind (for husband, city, and parents, *Il.* iii 139) or a specific one (*Il.* iii 446, xiv 328 ὥς σεο νῦν ἔραμαι καί με γλυκὺς ἵμερος αἱρεῖ, obvious sources of the present passage; similarly *Od.* v 209–10 ἱμειρόμενός περ ἰδέσθαι | σὴν ἄλοχον, *Il.* xiv 163–4 εἴ πως ἱμείροιτο παραδραθέειν φιλότητι | ᾗ χροιῇ), and also to 'sexual desire' (*Il.* xiv 198, 216). In the present case, κλαυθμοῦ καὶ στοναχῆς (unique, but cf. γόοιο and γόου, *Il.* xxiii 14, 108, 153, xxiv 507, 514; *Od.* iv 113, 183, xvi 215, xix 249, xxiii 231) shows a further shift, from the longing passion of desire to the emotional longing for release after a climax of suffering, a release whose melancholy comfort of the spirit may rightly be called 'sweet' (cf. *Il.* xxiv 513 γόοιο τετάρπετο).

501. For the two spellings of γινώσκω see xxi 209n. φρεσί: not merely formulaic here, but a touch of psychological realism; Odysseus had forgotten the names after all this time, but now, as he runs his eyes over the crowd of faces, he brings to mind each individual's name.

BOOKS XXIII–XXIV

Alfred Heubeck

The late Alfred Heubeck's Introductions *and* Commentary *on Books xxiii and xxiv were translated for this volume after his death by Jennifer Brooker and Stephanie West.*

BOOK XXIII: INTRODUCTION

The scene at the heart of this book is the reunion of Odysseus with his wife. It is framed by the conversation between Penelope and Eurycleia (1–84) and the account of Odysseus' actions on the following day (344–72). The reunion is a climax to which the two main lines of the story, which begin in i (Ithaca) and v (Ogygia) respectively and are brought together in the second half of the poem (from xiii), have been leading. The meticulous preparation of the scene is, however, most apparent in the several instances on which the couple are brought together but Penelope's recognition of Odysseus is postponed or prevented (xviii, xix, xxi).

Higher criticism of xxiii has concentrated on two main questions. First the so-called 'digression' during the recognition scene, i.e. 117–72 (following Wilamowitz, Finsler, Focke, and Schadewaldt: but there is some disagreement as to the extent of the passage concerned: thus von der Mühll and Merkelbach give 96–195, Page takes 115–70, and Kirk 111–76). From Kirchhoff onwards the passage has been widely regarded as the work of another hand, whether that of an editor or of the so-called 'last poet'.

The second critical question arises from the information recorded in the ancient scholia on 296, that Aristophanes and Aristarchus set the τέλος (πέρας) of the *Od.* here. This report, combined with numerous other observations on the final section of the poem (xxiii 297–xxiv 548), has been regarded by many scholars (and not only those of the analytical school) as proof that the *Odyssey* did in fact originally end at 296, and that the rest of the poem is a late addition to the text, possibly by the author of 117–72. (This is the majority view; Focke, Schadewaldt, and M. Müller, on the other hand, take the original text to end at 343.)

By its nature a commentary which concentrates on those aspects which argue for the authenticity of the lines in question cannot deal systematically with the views put forward by these analytical critics. It is neither possible nor desirable to give a complete list of the extensive secondary literature on the subject. The following list is intended only as an indication of the most important recent work on the 'digression'. (The older literature is given in Ameis–Hentze, *Anhang* iv[3] (Leipzig, 1900), 90; and Heubeck, *Frage*, 128, see below.) The most extensive, and original, modern exposition of the analytical

313

approach is by W. Schadewaldt, 'Neue Kriterien zur Odyssee-Analyse: Die Wiedererkennung des Odysseus und der Penelope', *SHAW* ii (1959). In defence of this passage see:

J. I. Armstrong, 'The Marriage Song. Odyssey xxiii', *TAPhA* lxxxix (1958), 38–43.

G. Bona, *Studi*, 167–8.

Allione, *Telemaco*, 99–111.

A. Ortega, 'El baño de Ulises en el canto XXIII de la Odisea', *Emerita* xxxi (1963), 11–19.

A. Amory, 'The Reunion of Odysseus and Penelope', in C. H. Taylor (ed.), *Essays on the Odyssey* (Bloomington, 1963).

K. Matthiessen, *Elektra, Taurische Iphigenie und Helena: Untersuchungen zur Chronologie und dramatischen Form im Spätwerk des Euripides*, Hypomnemata, iv (Göttingen, 1964), 99–107.

F. Eichhorn, *Homers Odyssee* (Göttingen, 1965), 148–53.

Lesky, *Homeros*, coll. 121 ff.

Besslich, *Schweigen*, 83–96.

Thornton, *People*, 104 ff.

Erbse, *Beiträge*, 55–72.

U. Hölscher, 'Die Erkennungsszene im 23. Buch der Odyssee', in E. Römisch (ed.), *Griechische in der Schule* (Frankfurt-on-Main, 1972), 156–65.

Eisenberger, *Studien*, 303–13.

Fenik, *Studies*, 64 ff.

The most important discussions of the authenticity of the final section of the *Odyssey* are given in the introduction to xxiv. Two editions and commentary on xxiii deserve mention:

R. Strömberg, *Odyssé, Tjugotredji sången* (Götteborg, 1962).

G. Maina, *Odissea, canto XXIII* (Torino, 1969).

Works listed here that do not appear also in the List of Bibliographical Abbreviations are cited in the commentary by author's name and the abbreviation 'op. cit. (Introd.)'.

BOOK XXIII: COMMENTARY

1-84. This conversation between Eurycleia and Penelope has been well prepared: before the contest with the bow Telemachus had sent his mother to her own apartment upstairs (xxi 343 ff.), where Athena had closed her eyes in refreshing sleep (357–9). Thus Penelope was not a witness to the contest and subsequent slaughter of the suitors; and the poet has managed by this somewhat unsubtle device to remove the queen from the scene of action and separate Odysseus' recognition by his wife from his recognition by the suitors; cf. U. Hölscher, in B. Fenik (ed.), *Homer. Tradition and Innovation* (Leiden, 1978), 64–7. The opening scene is further prepared by xxii 428–31, where Odysseus forbids Eurycleia to waken her mistress until the main hall is cleansed, and punishment meted out to the unfaithful servants. Only then does Odysseus bid the nurse call the faithful servants and Penelope herself (480–4). The structure of 1–84 is clear and tightly controlled: the conversation between Penelope and Eurycleia falls into four exchanges which prepare for the moment of recognition, but which also express the ambivalence of the wife's feelings and attitude towards her long-absent husband. Twenty years of sorrow and disappointment have made Penelope distrustful of any promise of relief from her sufferings. This suspicion is difficult to allay; on the other hand she is still sustained by a hope and trust which have defied the passing years; cf. van der Valk, *Textual Criticism*, 252 ff.; Besslich, *Schweigen*, 95 n. 20.

1. Eurycleia (γρηῦς) carries out Odysseus' command of xxii 482–3, and gives way now to the expression of joy (καγχαλάω *hapax* in the *Odyssey*; cf. Bechtel, *Lexilogus*, 185) which Odysseus had shortly before forbidden her in the presence of the suitors' corpses (xxii 411).   ὑπερῷ(α): cf. xxi 356.

2. 2ᵇ = xix 477ᵇ.

3. ἐρρώσαντο: (cf. xx 107) 'moved swiftly'.   ὑπερικταίνοντο (*hapax*) may be related to adv. ἴκταρ ('close to'); cf. Chantraine, *Dictionnaire*, and Frisk, *GEW* s.v. 1. ἴκταρ. The exact sense is unclear, but must be related to ἐρρώσαντο, perhaps 'she stumbled' (Aristarchus: ἄγαν ἐπάλλοντο). Van der Valk well defends the unanimous reading of the MSS (*Textual Criticism*, 83–4) against Hesychius' gloss ὑποακταίνοντο· ἔτρεμον preferred by Bechtel (*Lexilogus*, 175) and others.

4. = xx 32.

5. ἴδηαι: the middle indicates strong emotional involvement (cf. Ameis–Hentze–Cauer, ad loc.); cf. J. Bechert, *Die Diathesen von ἰδεῖν und ὁρᾶν bei Homer* (Munich, 1964), i 62.

6. 6ᵇ = v 210ᵇ. The use of τ' is irregular, possibly influenced by the model v 210; cf. Ruijgh, *te épique*, 414.

7. Note the threefold statement of the main idea, ἦλθ'-ἱκάνεται (meaning pf.) -ἐλθών (concessive).

315

COMMENTARY

9. **κήδεσκον:** (iterat. from κήδω) 'kept troubling'.

11-24. Penelope scolds the nurse for being a fool, reprimands her for waking and mocking her mistress, and orders her back to the μέγαρον. She does not spare a single word for the content of Eurycleia's news.

11. **μάργην:** only here and xvi 421 and xviii 2. **θέσαν:** τιθέναι takes a double accusative: σε (object) and μάργην (complement). The meaning and construction are exactly the same as for ποιεῖν (12): καὶ ... ἐόντα (object: 'even one who ...')—ἄφρονα (complement). On the function and meaning of the 'epic' τε see Ruijgh, τε épique, 359, 372.

13. **χαλιφρονέοντα:** (hapax; cf. χαλιφροσύνη, xvi 310; χαλίφρων, iv 371, xix 530; Risch, Wortbildung, 219) 'simple'. Döderlein's conjecture χαλίφρον' ἐόντα should not be adopted; cf. Leumann, Wörter, 116. **σαοφρο- σύνη:** (only here and 30) an abstract in -σύνη from σα(ϝ)όφρων (elsewhere only iv 158; Il. xxi 462; later σώφρων); 'of sound mind'. **ἐπέβησαν:** (gnomic aorist) here from ἐπέβησα, causative from ἐπέβην, i.e. 'they have (often before now) led one on the way out (ἐπ-) to σαοφροσύνη'; cf. J. Latacz, Zum Wortfeld 'Freude' in der Sprache Homers (Heidelberg, 1966), 164.

14. The first half of the line rounds off the line of thought from 11-13 (μάργην ... θέσαν: ἔβλαψαν). **πρὶν:** adv. here. **αἰσίμη:** here applied to a person; elsewhere it is always neuter (e.g. αἴσιμα ῥέζειν); it also governs φρένας (acc. of respect).

15. **λωβεύεις:** (only here and 26 and ii 323) + acc., 'mock, ridicule'.

16. **παρὲξ:** 'out beside (the truth), wide of the mark'. **καὶ ... | ἠδέος** amplifies λωβεύεις; hence the fut. part. (expressing purpose) ἐρέουσα (cf. Stanford, ad loc.). 16-17 recall xxi 357-8.

17. **ἐπέδησε:** from πεδάω.

18. **τοιόνδε:** sc. ὕπνον: acc. of the 'internal object'. **κατέδραθον:** aor. of δαρθάνω; cf. v 471.

19. = xix 260. 18-19 recall Penelope's lament of xix 515 ff. There is no reason to suspect their authenticity (questioned by von der Mühll, Philologus lxxxix (1934), 393-4; Odyssee, col. 761).

20-4. These lines cannot be an interpolation (as von der Mühll, loc. cit., suggests): the order to Eurycleia to withdraw to the μέγαρον (here as at 24 probably 'women's quarters') at 20 is an essential element of the passage, and 21-4 serve to mitigate the harshness of the rebuke.

21-4ᵃ. The construction is similar to that of xxi 372-5ᵃ (cf. esp. 23 and xxi 374); on the construction εἰ γάρ, 'for if', see D. Tabachovitz, Homerische εἰ-Sätze (Lund, 1951), 48, 64 ff. **μ':** μοι.

23. In contrast with the simple demand at 20 the emphasis here is on στυγερῶς, 'miserably, with insult and ignominy'.

24. **τοῦτό γε:** (adv.) 'in this at least'. **γῆρας ὀνήσει:** 'will help'; i.e. Penelope is not sending her away στυγερῶς.

26-31. Eurycleia denies the accusation made by Penelope (οὔ τί σε λωβεύω: λωβεύεις, 15). She repeats her news (27ᵃ = 7ᵃ), insisting that it is true (ἔτυμον). Now she adds the further information that Odysseus is actually

316

that (ὁ) stranger who was subjected to such indignity by the company in the hall (28: the authenticity of the line is rightly defended by Focke, *Odyssee*, 364 n. 1, against Wilamowitz, *Untersuchungen*, 82–3, and *Heimkehr*, 68, and von der Mühll, *Odyssee*, col. 761), and that Telemachus had been privy to his father's plans.

29–30. The reference is to the agreement made between father and son to keep Odysseus' identity a secret; cf. Focke, loc. cit. **σαοφροσύνῃσι:** cf. 18n.

31. βίη: here collective, 'violence'. **ὑπερηνορεόντων:** cf. i 266n.

32–8. Eurycleia's insistence prompts the first alteration in Penelope's feelings, as disbelief turns to joy. Doubts, however, rise again: how could Odysseus have overcome the suitors single-handed?

33. περιπλέχθη: from -πλέκω; here aor. pass. with middle sense, 'embraced'. **ἧκε:** like βάλε, iv 114.

34. = i 122 etc.

35. ~ xii 112.

36. The line refers back to 7 and 27. **εἰ ἐτεὸν δή:** cf. xix 216.

37. ~ xx 29; 37–8 ~ xx 39–40. Penelope is beset by the same doubts as Odysseus in xx.

40–57. The nurse answers Penelope with an account of the action of xxii, a little of which she had experienced as an eye-witness, and the rest of which she had heard (40–51). She invites Penelope to come with her and assure herself of the truth of the story; and finally she proclaims that all her mistress' wishes have been realized (52–7). Von der Mühll, *Odyssee*, col. 761, considers the passage to have been revised by a later hand (i.e. by his *B*-poet). But it is precisely the numerous similarities between the language and content of these lines and xxi–xxii which argue that the lines are genuine. 52–7, rejected by Payne Knight and others, should also be retained.

40. πυθόμην: sc. from others. For the sake of euphony G. Scheibner, in *Miscellanea Critica* i (Leipzig, 1965), 256, argues for the *v.l.* ἄκουον.

41–2. 42ᵇ = xxii 128ᵇ. The lines pick up the action from xxi 235–9, 380–7; θάλαμος is the μέγαρον (women's quarters) of xxi 236, 382. **ἀτυζό-μεναι:** cf. xi 606.

43–4. Here the reference is to the action of xxii 393–400. **πρίν γ' ὅτε δή:** (+ ind.) 'before the time when . . .; until at last . . .'; cf. Palmer, *Companion*, 172. **καλέσσαι:** inf. expressing purpose sc. με.

45. = xxii 401.

46. 46ᵃ ~ xi 370ᵃ. **ἐσταόθ'** (-ότα): only this form is possible; cf. M. Leumann, *Kleine Schriften* (Zurich, 1959), 253 n. 5. The variant ἐστεῶθ', the form preferred by Aristarchus (cf. sch. on *Il.* xxiv 701), is a pseudo-Ionism. **οἱ δέ** (sc. μνηστῆρες) **μιν ἀμφὶ** (~ ἀμφὶ αὐτόν). **κραταί-πεδον οὖδας:** 'floor made with hard-pressed earth' (κραται-(κρατερός) + πέδον); a *hapax*, perhaps a possessive compound (or determinative?); cf. E. Risch, *IF* lix (1944), 14–15 (= *Kleine Schriften* (Berlin, 1981), 14–15); *Wortbildung*, 214, 219. **ἔχω:** here 'cover'.

COMMENTARY

47. cf. xxii 389. **κείατ':** cf. xxi 418. 47ᵇ: 'at the sight you would be moved to joy in your heart (θυμόν)'; on the meaning of ἰαίνω/-ομαι see the explanation given by Latacz, op. cit. (13n.), 226–30.

48. = xxii 402. This line, omitted in many MSS, is considered by a number of editors and critics (among them Ameis–Hentze–Cauer; von der Mühll, *Odyssee*, col. 761; W. Schadewaldt, op. cit. (Introd.), 15 n. 9) to be a late interpolation, largely on account of its 'unseemliness', which may already have led to its athetesis by the Alexandrian critics (which then influenced the MS tradition). Such purely subjective arguments can, however, lead to false conclusions. Here it must be borne in mind that the speaker is Eurycleia who earlier had herself been moved to jubilation by the sight of the dead suitors (xxii 407 ff.: ἴθυσέν ῥ' ὀλολύξαι). For the authenticity of the line cf. Stanford, ad loc.; van der Valk, *Textual Criticism*, 271; G. Scheibner, *DLZ* lxxxii (1961), col. 622 ('xxiii 48 recalls once again the description of xxii 204 ff.).

49–51. The most important events after the slaughter of the suitors are briefly summarized. 49: cf. xxii 448–51. 50–1ᵃ: cf. xxii 480–94. 51ᵇ: cf. xxii 482–3. **ἐπ' αὐλείῃσι θύρῃσι:** (= xviii 239ᵇ) recalls the similar expression ὑπ' αἰθούσῃ . . . ἐυέρκεος αὐλῆς xxii 449; on the architectural conception see St. Hiller, *WS* N.F. iv (1970), 14–27. **ἀθρόοι:** sc. εἰσίν (cf. ἀλλήλοισιν ἐρείδουσαι, xxii 450); cf. Penelope's dream of xix 536–51 (οἱ δὲ κέχυντο | ἀθρόοι, 539–40); cf. H. Stockinger, *Die Vorzeichen im homerischen Epos* (diss. Munich, 1959), 74. On **κηάμενος/κειάμενος** cf. xi 74 n. on κακκῆαι. **σε:** object of καλέσσαι.

52–3. ὄφρα . . . ἦτορ: 'so that you may set foot on (ἐπι-) the path to bliss (εὐφροσύνη) both in your dear hearts (acc. of respect)'; cf. Latacz, op. cit. (13n.), 164; cf. the similar construction at 13 (with causative ἐπέβησαν). σφῶϊν is here second person nom. dual (in contrast to the more usual nom. σφῶϊ; cf. xxii 173 etc.; for gen./dat. σφῶϊν cf. xvi 171 etc.), like the first person nom. dual νῶϊν, *Il.* xvi 99; cf. Shipp, *Studies*, 357. ἐπιβῆτον (< *-βήετον) is second person dual aor. subj. 53ᵇ = *Il.* iii 99ᵇ ~ *Od.* x 465; on πέποσθε see x 465 n.

54. νῦν δ' ἤδη: 'now at last'. τόδε is prospective: the content of the long-cherished (μακρὸν) wish is given at 55–7.

55. ἦλθε . . . ἐφέστιος: ἐφέστιος predicative with the verb: 'came home to his hearth'; cf. vii 248. καὶ σὲ: sc. ζωήν.

56. κακῶς: with ἔρεζον.

59–68. Eurycleia's words have failed to dispel the doubts that already at 37–8 were once more forming in Penelope's mind. She rebukes the old woman for her jubilation (καγχαλόωσα, 59, as at 1) and refuses to believe her report (ὅδε μῦθος, 62). The stranger whom Eurycleia had identified as Odysseus (27–8) must, she thinks, be a god. The reasoning behind this statement has to be supplied from Penelope's question of 37–8: her assumption is that only a god could, μοῦνος ἐών, have overcome all the suitors. The real Odysseus, on the other hand, must, in her view, be dead.

318

59. μή πω: (temporal) 'not yet, not prematurely'. ἐπεύχεο: (ἐπ-εύχομαι) 'rejoice over (the events)'.

61. 61ᵃ = i 359ᵃ etc.

63-7. Penelope's surmise, that divine power lay behind the victory over the suitors, is in fact not so far off the mark, since Athena gave active assistance to Odysseus (xxii 205-40, 297-8). It also accords with the interpretation of events given by Odysseus to Eurycleia: τις ἀθανάτων κτεῖνε, 63 ~ μοῖρ' ἐδάμασσε θεῶν, xxii 413. The correspondence is further underlined by the repetition of xxii 414-15 at 65-6 (67ᵃ ~ xxii 416). The crucial factor, however, is the agreement in the explanation given for the divine intervention: the gods are outraged (cf. ἀγασσάμενος, 64) by the ὕβρις of the suitors, their κακὰ ἔργα (σχέτλια ἔργα, xxii 410) and their ἀτασθαλίαι (67)— identified by both husband and wife as offences against the law of hospitality (65-6 = xxii 414-15)—and so divine justice is unleashed against the suitors. Similar thoughts had been expressed earlier by Telemachus (confronting the suitors, ii 67) and by some of the suitors themselves (xv 483-7); cf. D. Kaufmann-Bühler, *Hermes* lxxxiv (1956), 267-95, esp. 290-1; Bowra, *Companion*, 64 ff.; A. Dihle, *Homerprobleme* (Opladen, 1970), 167 ff. The view that men themselves call down divine retribution by their own sinful actions (σφετέρῃσιν ἀτασθαλίῃσιν) represents a significant shift away from the ethical and theological conceptions of the *Iliad*.

68. ὤλεσε ... ὤλετο: on the emphatic expression cf. vii 60. It is not clear whether τηλοῦ is to be construed as a preposition + gen. (Ἀχαιΐδος sc. γαίης) as at xiii 249 (cf. Ameis-Hentze-Cauer ad loc.) or as an adverb (taking Ἀχαιΐδος as dependent on νόστον).

70-9. Eurycleia is disconcerted by her mistress's continued refusal to believe that the stranger is in fact Odysseus. Now she offers further proof of the stranger's identity, a σῆμα ἀριφραδές, Odysseus' scar (cf. xix 386 ff.). Once more she invites Penelope to come with her (78 : 52), and seeks to overcome her mistress's doubts by offering to stake her life for the truth of her tale. U. Hölscher, op. cit. (Introd.), 158, has drawn attention to the parallel with Odysseus' assurance to Eumaeus (xiv 391-400). On that occasion the still unrecognized Odysseus had failed to convince the herdsman (xxiii 72 ~ xiv 390) and had offered a wager (xxiii 78-9 ~ xiv 393-400); cf. also von der Mühll, *Odyssee*, col. 761.

69-70. = xix 491-2; 70 = i 64 etc.

70-2. This streak of mistrustfulness noted by Eurycleia is a feature of Penelope's character which she shares with her husband. These lines recall Calypso's words to Odysseus, v 182-3, and Athena's observation at xiii 330 ff. Cf. Allione, *Telemaco*, 104.

71-2. 'You thought that your husband would never return, although he is at this very moment in the house'; cf. xiv 149-50. παρ' ἐσχάρῃ (cf. ἐφέστιος, 55) strengthens ἔνδον.

72ᵃ. = ii 176ᵃ etc.; 72 ~ xiv 150.

73-7. These lines, rejected as an interpolation by Payne Knight (and later by Wilamowitz, *Heimkehr*, 68; von der Mühll, *Odyssee*, col. 761), are quite indispensable; cf. Focke, *Odyssee*, 364–5; H. Erbse, *Beiträge*, 56. The allusions to (and verbal echoes of) xix are intentional: 74 = xix 393 (= xxi 219); cf. also the correspondence between 73 and xxi 217); for 75ᵃ cf. xix 392; for 75ᵇ cf. xix 476–7; for 76–7 cf. (with slight alteration of content) xix 480–90.

76. ἐλὼν ἐπὶ μάστακα χερσὶν: 'placing his hands over my mouth'; cf. iv 287.

77. A firm decision here, between the variants πολυκερδείῃσι (on the formation see Risch, *Wortbildung*, 129–30) and πολυϊδρείῃσι is impossible. Support for the first reading is to be found at xxiv 167, where the same trait is attributed to Odysseus, and at xiii 255 (*νόον πολυκερδέα νωμῶν* sc. Odysseus). On the other hand πολυϊδρείῃσιν is used at ii 346 of Eurycleia, who is herself described as πολύιδρις by Penelope at 82. Cf. van Leeuwen, ad loc.; Focke, *Odyssee*, 365 n. 1, who prefers the latter reading.

78. ἐμέθεν περιδώσομαι αὐτῆς: 'I'll stake my life on it'. περιδίδομαι only here and *Il.* xxiii 485. ἐμέθεν αὐτῆς = ἐμαυτῆς.

79. ἐξαπάφω: aor. subj. from -απαφίσκω; cf. *LfgrE* s.v. **κτεῖναι:** the infinitive is loosely dependent (consecutive or explanatory) on περιδώσομαι: 'that you can kill me'; less likely is the suggestion by Ameis–Hentze–Cauer and Stanford, ad loc., that it is used as an imperative.

81–4. Penelope replies with a generalization (possibly proverbial) about human helplessness in the face of the gods' δήνεα (81–2), and tells the nurse to accompany her to the hall (83–4); ἀλλ'... ἴομεν (subj.) represents a positive response to Eurycleia's ἀλλ' ἔπεο (78), but Penelope does not refer at all to the main theme of the nurse's speech, the σῆμα. This does not, however, mean (as Wilamowitz, *Heimkehr*, 68, and von der Mühll, *Odyssee*, col. 761, suppose) that the lines are spurious. On the contrary: the very evasiveness of 81–2 demonstrates the effect on Penelope of 73–8. She deliberately avoids the subject of the σῆμα, for the confident words of the nurse, although not entirely without effect, have not served to banish mistrust and suspicion. These inner conflicts, between hope and doubt, prevent her from directly addressing the nurse's argument; cf. Focke, *Odyssee*, 364–5; Allione, *Telemaco*, 104; Besslich, *Schweigen*, 18–20; Eisenberger, *Studien*, 304.

81–2. Understanding of this gnomic-looking expression depends on the interpretation of the problematic εἴρυσθαι, which ancient scholars also found perplexing (cf. Eust., ad loc.; Stanford, ad loc.). What is clear is that Penelope's somewhat vague words refer back to 63–4, and that those lines must be our starting point in elucidating εἴρυσθαι. Certainly it would be wise to avoid a solution based on conjectures such as εἴρεσθαι, 'explore, penetrate' (Schulze, *Quaestiones*, 100) and ἀνευρέσθαι (Agar), or isolated readings such as ἱδρύσασθαι (cf. G. Scheibner, op. cit. (40 n.))—particularly in view of the similar phrase at 82, ἀνὴρ δέ κεν οὔτι Διὸς νόον (~ δήνεα) εἰρύσσαιτο, οὐδὲ μάλ' ἴφθιμος. Suggestions made by earlier scholars include 'durchschauen' (Besslich), 'ergründen' (Schadewaldt), 'decouvrir' (P. Wathelet, in A. Bartoněk, ed., *Studia Mycenaea* (Brno, 1968),

108); 'sich hüten vor' (Ameis–Hentze–Cauer; Erbse). The right approach is surely that indicated by Chantraine, *Grammaire* i 295 n. 1: 'surveiller > épier, connaître, découvrir'. F. Bader, *Bulletin de la Société Linguistique* lxvi (1971), 139–211, esp. 146, has established a firmer basis for this interpretation. On the form (pres. inf.) cf. Bader, 174–6. χαλεπὸν: sc. ἐστιν. δήνεα (attested elsewhere only x 289 and *Il.* iv 361): 'plans, counsels'; cf. Bechtel, *Lexilogus*, 99; Chantraine, *Dictionnaire* s.v. πολύϊδριν: an epithet applied earlier to Eurycleia, ii 346.

83. ἔμπης: 'be that as it may'. ἴδωμαι: J. Bechert, op. cit. (above, 5 n.), 71, has demonstrated that the reading ἴδωμεν is untenable.

84. ἠδ᾽ ὃς ἔπεφνεν: shows Penelope's reserve; cf. Besslich, *Schweigen*, 88.

85–95. Penelope descends to the main hall, and sits opposite Odysseus, unable to bring herself to speak.

85ᵃ. Ὣς ... ὑπερώϊα: = xviii 206ᵃ; on the construction see van der Valk, *Textual Criticism*, 54. 85ᵇ = vii 82ᵇ.

86–7. ὅρμαιν᾽, ἤ ... ἤ ...: the schema familiar from the *Iliad* for a hero choosing between alternative courses of action is modified here by the selection of a third possibility (88 ff.). The poet is concerned here not so much with the act of decision, as with the heroine's mood, her indecision and confused emotions; cf. C. Voigt, *Überlegung und Entscheidung* (Meisenheim, 1972), 79. The expression φίλον πόσιν clearly shows that she thinks there is a distinct possibility that Eurycleia's news may indeed be true. ἀπάνευθε: 'from a respectable distance'. ἐξερεείνοι: 'question'; the reference is to the right and duty of a host to enquire of a visitor his name, origin, and the purpose of his journey.

87. Cf. xvii 35 = xxii 499.

88. = xvi 41, xvii 30. In xx (258) Telemachus offers Odysseus a place παρὰ λάϊνον οὐδόν, whereas at xvii 339 Odysseus sits down ἐπὶ μελίνου οὐδοῦ; the problems thus produced are hardly soluble; cf. Ameis–Hentze–Cauer, ad xvii 339, xx 258; Stanford, ad xxiii 88.

89. ἐν πυρὸς αὐγῇ: Penelope also sits παρὰ πυρὶ at xix 55; similarly Arete, vi 305, ἐπ᾽ ἐσχάρῃ ἐν πυρὸς αὐγῇ.

90. τοίχου τοῦ ἑτέρου: (= *Il.* xxiv 598) 'against (in the area of) the other wall opposite the door'. πρὸς κίονα μακρὴν: (= i 127ᵇ) sc. 'leaning'. Unlike i 127 and xvii 29, what is meant here is a κίων inside the μέγαρον, whether by the door or by the hearth.

91–3. Odysseus waits (ποτιδέγμενος) for his wife to begin the conversation, and so holds his peace (92ᵇ = xi 615ᵇ). Penelope too, however, remains silent (ἄνεω: used adv. only here): τάφος ('wonder, bewilderment, numbness') has overcome her; cf. her own admission at 105, θυμός μοι ἐνὶ στήθεσσι τέθηπεν. The situation is now a stalemate, to be broken only by a third party, Telemachus.

94–5. The purpose of these obscure lines ('depravati esse videntur', von der Mühll, ad loc.) must be to explain and illustrate Penelope's attitude, which has already been indicated by the word τάφος: her inner conflict and doubt (ἄλλοτε μὲν ... ἄλλοτε δ᾽). ἐσίδεσκεν: in place of the reading given

COMMENTARY

by all our MSS ('sine sensu', van Leeuwen), Didymus cites as a variant the more immediately intelligible ἤϊσκεν. This alternative is preferred by some modern scholars, notably Düntzer, Payne Knight, van Leeuwen, Ameis–Hentze–Cauer, Stanford, and Bérard; cf. Ameis–Hentze, *Anhang*, iv 88–90, where however ἤϊσκεν is ultimately rejected. ἤϊσκεν must be merely an ancient conjecture. ἐσίδεσκεν is supported by the evidence of: the contrasting ἀγνώσασκε, the form in -σκ- being created by analogy; Penelope's words at 107 (οὐδ' εἰς ὦπα ἰδέσθαι ἐναντίον sc. δύναμαι), which refer back to 94; and *Il.* xx 205 (ὄψει δ' οὔτ' ἄρ πω σὺ ἐμοὺς ἴδες), where ὄψει (!) ἰδεῖν 'meet face to face (and so come to know)', is contrasted with ἴδμεν ἀκούοντες (203–4). ἐσιδεῖν implies the recognition linked with seeing: 'ein ἰδεῖν ohne "Erkennen" muß ausdrücklich im Kontext vorbereitet werden: xiii 197 ff.' (J. Bechert, op. cit. (5 n.), 337). This yields a meaning on the lines of 'she saw, and at one moment thought she recognized him' (ὄψει: 'by sight'); G. Finsler, *Homer* ii² (Leipzig/Berlin, 1918), 432; Focke, *Odyssee*, 366. ἐνωπαδίως: formed with adjectival suffix -άδιος from the adverb ἐνωπαδόν from (κατ')ἐνῶπα (*Il.* xv 320); cf. Risch, *Wortbildung*, 123, 355, 365; A. Heubeck, *ŽA* xxiv (1974), 37; literally '(looking) into his face', weakened perhaps to 'clearly, distinctly' (Hölscher, Risch). On the iterative (or rather intensive) -σκ- forms ἐσίδεσκε (ἴδεσκε is found only here and *Il.* iii 217) and ἀγνώσασκε (*hapax*; cf. Shipp, *Studies*, 357) see the full discussion by P. Wathelet, *AC* xlii (1973), 379–405, esp. 393–5, who notes the common device of using two or more -σκ- forms in conjunction. κακὰ χροῒ εἵματ' ἔχοντα: (causal) Eurycleia had offered to fetch Odysseus clean clothes, xxii 487, but he had refused; the poet obviously wishes to emphasize that Odysseus is still dressed as a beggar (cf. 115; Focke, *Odyssee*, 365–6), and so prepares indirectly for 155.

96. xxi 84.

97–103. Telemachus seizes the initiative, and breaks the long silence held by his parents. He reproaches his mother for her apparent lack of feeling, and her hard-heartedness. It is also interesting to note that in the exchanges which follow both Odysseus and Penelope avoid addressing each other directly: their comments are made via their son as mediator, although of course meant for each other; cf. Schadewaldt, op. cit. (ψ), 16.

97. μῆτερ ... δύσμητερ: (*hapax*) the word is formed like Δύσπαρις (*Il.* iii 39, xiii 769), (μήτηρ). δυσαριστοτόκεια (*Il.* xviii 54, also used only once); cf. also Ἶρος, Ἄϊρος (xviii 73). ἀπηνέα: a possessive compound (ἀπηνής) cf. xix 329) from ἀπο- and *ἄνος, ἤνος, 'face', i.e. originally 'with one's face turned away > unapproachable, cold, and unfriendly'; cf. Frisk, *GEW*, Chantraine, *Dictionnaire*, *LfgrE* s.v.; Risch *Wortbildung*, 81; Allione, *Telemaco*, 107 n. 70 (following Benfey). The Mycenaean name *pu-wa-ne/Purwanēs*/PY 832. 5 is formed along similar lines; A. Heubeck, *Beiträge zur Namenforschung*, xi (1960), 3–4. Bechtel's discussion, *Lexilogus*, 69 (following A. Fick) is unsatisfactory.

98–9. The words are spoken with obvious reference to 89 (ἔζετ'... Ὀδυσῆος ἐναντίη), 86 (ἐξερεείνοι), and 91 (εἴποι) above; 99ᵇ = xix 171ᵇ.

322

100-1. τετληότι θυμῷ: a variation on ἀπηνέα θυμὸν (97).   ἀφεσταίη
similarly picks up νοσφίζεαι (98).
102. = xix 484 (cf. xvi 206).
103. Telemachus concludes by repeating, in the form of an unfair generalization (αἰεὶ) his initial reproach (cf. 72); this is the climax and summary of his
reproof.
105-10. Penelope justifies to her son her behaviour towards the man whose
identity she will be able to establish beyond doubt by σήματα.
105-7. Her θυμός is neither ἀπηνής (97) nor 'constantly hard' (αἰεὶ στερεωτέρη, 103): but for the moment it is stunned by surprise (τέθηπεν: cf. τάφος
93 and 91-3n.). Thus she is unable to react in the way that is expected of
her; for προσφάσθαι cf. εἴποι (91); for ἐρέεσθαι cf. ἀνείρεαι and μεταλλᾷς
(99); for εἰς ὦπα ἰδέσθαι ἐναντίον (on the meaning of middle ἰδέσθαι see
J. Bechert, op. cit. (5n.), 174-5) cf. ὄψει . . . ἐνωπαδίως ἐσίδεσκεν, 94.
107-8. Cf. 36.   ἦ μάλα: 'for quite certainly'.
109. γνωσόμεθ' ἀλλήλων: cf. xxi 36.   καὶ λώϊον: 'even better' (than by
the ἀνείρεσθαι and μεταλλᾶν which Telemachus expects).
110. σήμαθ': picks up a keyword in Eurycleia's report (73); but these
σήματα are a surer sign than that cited by the nurse. The signs which
Penelope has in mind are known only to her and her husband (κεκρυμμένα
ἀπ' ἄλλων: 'hidden from others'). Specifically the reference is to the λέχος
which will later play such a significant part in the development of the story,
when it is mentioned—apparently ingenuously—by Odysseus (170).
Penelope's self-defence recalls her resolve at xix 215-19 to put the stranger
(unrecognized as Odysseus) to the test (πειρήσεσθαι, 215) by means of a
σῆμα (cf. xix 250).   καὶ: was first criticized by Bothe as inappropriate;
and numerous emendations have been suggested since (cf. van Leeuwen,
ad loc.). The word may, however, be allowed to stand: 'we also (like other
married couples)'. The use of νῶϊ (108, 110) and ἡμῖν (109) shows that
already Penelope has subconsciously abandoned many of her doubts and
reservations.
111. Odysseus' attitude is in complete contrast to the emotional outburst of
his son: he smiles, with self-assurance, but also with understanding and
sympathy—like Athena, xiii 287, and Calypso, v 180; cf. Focke, Odyssee,
366 n. 3; Allione, Telemaco, 106. So he accepts his wife's behaviour. Once
again (cf. xviii 281) he is given proof that his wife shares his characteristic
qualities: extreme caution and extraordinary cunning. Penelope is worthy
of her epithet περίφρων.
112. = xix 3.
113-22. Odysseus reassures Telemachus as to the behaviour of his mother,
and counsels patience. Then he asks him to join in considering what
measures should be taken after the suitors' death.
113. ἦ τοι: ἦτοι is to be preferred; cf. Ruijgh, τε épique, 197-200; in its
'preparatory' function it is similar to the particle μέν; it points to a later δέ-
clause; cf. Kühner–Gerth, Grammatik, 146ff.; Ruijgh, loc. cit. This fact, as
Hölscher, op. cit. (Introd.), 163 n. 13, Eisenberger, Studien, 306, and

Besslich, *Schweigen*, 85–6, have rightly emphasized, is incontrovertible proof of the essential unity of 113–22, against all attempts to regard 117 ff. as a 'digression' added subsequently. The ἤ τοι passage (113–16) is clearly contrasted with the δέ-clause, 117–22 (cf. Ameis–Hentze–Cauer). The contrast ἤ τοι μητέρ': ἡμεῖς δέ is further elaborated: at ἐνὶ μεγάροισιν Odysseus refers to matters in the home, whereas at ἡμεῖς δέ his thoughts turn to the situation outside it.

114. Odysseus correctly guesses that Penelope intends to make use of the σήματα she has mentioned (109–10) as a means of identification (πειράζειν; cf. the similar situation in xix, where the same ideas appear, σήματα at 250 and πειρήσεσθαι at 215). He has every confidence that she will achieve greater certainty by this πεῖρα (note the absolute use of φράσεται; cf. γνωσόμεθ' at 109); and with καὶ ἄρειον (adv.) deliberately echoes her own expression, καὶ λώϊον (109).

115-16. At the same time Odysseus also recognizes, however, the reason why his wife is not yet (νῦν δ') quite free from reservations. She denies him the customary honour due (ἀτιμάζει) and indeed refuses to recognize him as her long-lost husband because he is still dirty and dressed in rags (115 = xix 72). The lines recall the description of Odysseus' horrific appearance after the battle with the suitors (xxii 401–6) as well as the fact that he had for the time being ignored Eurycleia's offer to bring him fresh clothes (xxii 485–91). The passage also points forward: Odysseus evidently assumes that nothing will hinder Penelope's acknowledgment of his identity once his outward appearance is changed. (So the scene is set for the bathing episode at 153 ff.; cf. Besslich, *Schweigen*, 90; Lesky, *Homeros*, coll. 121–2.) Odysseus puts to one side the idea of σήματα, and deliberately delays the moment of recognition (cf. Eisenberger, *Studien*, 305); his conversation with Penelope, which has only been indirect (via Telemachus), is now broken off altogether. Penelope briefly drops out of the epic narrative (until 163); for poet and audience alike she simply ceases to exist. This need not cause any great surprise: there are numerous comparable examples of the epic poet turning his audience's attention away from a character in this way; cf. Fenik, *Studies*, 64–6. Odysseus is freed for a moment to turn his attention to mastering the 'political' crisis precipitated by the slaughter of the suitors.

117-22. Odysseus invites his son to join in his deliberations, and illustrates his anxieties with a general example of the consequences of an action much smaller in scale. Someone who has killed just one fellow-member of his δῆμος (on φῶτα ἐνὶ δήμῳ cf. ἄνδρα ἔμφυλον in a similar context at xv 272–3), who may have few friends or relatives to aid him (ἔωσιν ἀοσσητῆρες ὀπίσσω, 119; cf. iv 165), would have to leave behind his kinsmen (πηούς, 120, is used in its generalized meaning; cf. Shipp, *Studies*, 358) and home. If such a man has to flee into exile, what fate awaits those who have killed the noblest young men in Ithaca, the support of the state (ἕρμα πόληος, 121; cf. *Il.* xvi 549), who—we must supplement—of necessity must have many ready to avenge their deaths? With τὰ δέ σε φράζεσθαι ἄνωγα (122ᵇ = xvii

324

279ᵇ) Odysseus recurs by way of conclusion to ἡμεῖς δὲ φραζώμεθ' (117). The passage also recalls the occasion on which he had expressed similar fears to Athena (xx 41–3; here 122ᵇ = xx 43ᵇ). Indeed the suitors themselves had hoped to be able to summon help from the town (132–4 ~ xxii 77–8). Odysseus' fears in fact prove to be well grounded at xxiv 413ff.; and this passage prepares for those events; cf. W. Theiler, *MH* xix (1962), 18.

119. On the use of μή with indefinite relative and subj. cf. Chantraine, *Grammaire*, ii 332; Shipp, *Studies*, 145.

121. ἕρμα: see W. Bergold, *Der Zweikampf des Paris und Menelaos* (Bonn, 1977), 204.

124–9. Telemachus leaves the planning to Odysseus, and promises his father every support from himself and the two herdsmen.

124–5. αὐτὸς ταῦτά γε λεύσσε: 'These things (the considerations you have indicated) you must see to!' λεύσσω (cf. vi 157 etc.) is used here in its transferred meaning. σὴν μῆτιν ἀρίστην (predicative) ἔμμεναι ἐπ' ἀνθρώπους; cf. i 299.

126. ἐρίσειε: here 'rival'.

127–8. = *Il.* xiii 785–6. These two lines are found only in a very few MSS, and so are regarded by most editors as a late interpolation (modelled on the Iliadic passage). They are, however, found in one third-century papyrus, and fulfil an important function within the framework of Telemachus' response: his passing of responsibility for planning back to Odysseus (αὐτὸς . . . λεύσσε) is immediately tempered by the offer of practical help as required (ἡμεῖς δ'). The passage also foreshadows the battle at xxiv 463ff.; cf. W. Diehl, *Die wörtlichen Beziehungen zwischen Ilias und Odyssee* (diss. Greifswald, 1931), 121–4; van der Valk, *Textual Criticism*, 269. **δ' ἐμμεμαῶτες:** to be preferred to δὲ μεμαῶτες; cf. Aristarchus' comment on *Il.* xiii 785; cf. xxii 172. ⟨ἡμᾶς⟩ ἀλκῆς δευήσεσθαι (cf. for example vi 192): 'that we will lack the strength for combat'. **ὅση δύναμίς γε πάρεστιν:** 'as far as we can'.

130–40. Odysseus now gives his orders: they are to celebrate in the palace in order to give outsiders the impression that a wedding is taking place—it would of course be assumed that it was the marriage of Penelope with one of the suitors. At all events the news of the suitors' death should not be allowed to reach the outside world until Odysseus and his supporters have retreated to his country property. Odysseus' plan does not, however, merely determine the action to follow (with the description of the festivities cf. 141–52; with the withdrawal to the farm, 350–72, esp. 359–60, cf.xxiv 205ff.; with the programme indicated at 139–40 cf. the divine intervention at xxiv 472ff.). Odysseus is also revealing (in Penelope's presence) his μῆτις, and thus presents himself as lord of the house, in possession of his rights; cf. Besslich, *Schweigen*, 88–9ff.

130. 130ᵃ = xvi 259ᵃ, *Il.* i 76ᵃ; 130ᵇ ~ xiii 154ᵇ, *Il.* ix 103ᵇ.

131. The three men involved in the fighting are to bathe and change into fresh clothes (and so prepare for the planned celebration). They had

COMMENTARY

already washed their hands and feet immediately after the battle, xxii 478. On χιτών cf. S. Marinatos, *Archaeologia* A, 7–9.

132. εἵμαθ' [καθαρὰ] ἐλέσθαι: (cf. xvii 48, 58) 'to put on [clean] clothes'.

133–4. 133ᵇ = xxii 332ᵇ. θεῖος ἀοιδὸς: is of course Phemius, whom Odysseus had rightly spared during the fighting; cf.xxii 330–80. His task now is to provide with his φόρμιγξ the music for the dancing at the coming celebration, to act as 'leader' in the dance (ἡγεῖσθαι here with dat. ὑμῖν).

φιλοπαίγμονος: (*hapax*) with παίγμα ('play, sport') or *παίγμων (from παίζω) as its second element; on the formation see Risch, *Wortbildung*, 52, 193; on παιγ- (rather than the expected παιδ-) cf. Frisk, *GEW*, and Chantraine, *Dictionnaire* s.v. παῖς. Literally: 'loving the play (of dance)'.

135. 135ᵃ ~ xviii 218ᵃ. γάμος: here 'wedding feast'.

136. ἤ οἵ περιναιετάουσι: (cf. ii 66) 'or one of those living near'.

137–8. μὴ ... μνηστήρων: κλέος εὐρὺ (as at xix 333) φόνου, with dependent ἀνδρῶν μνηστήρων: 'the news of the slaughter of the suitors must not be allowed to spread before . . .'

139. ἀγρὸν ... πολυδένδρεον: the fact that the ἀγρός where Laertes lives has already been mentioned several times in the course of the poem (e.g. xi 188) establishes that the farm meant here is that of Odysseus' father. Note the pointed use of the epithet πολυδένδρεος (cf. 359–60): the δένδρεα will later play a significant role; cf. besides xxiv 246–7, esp. 336–44.

140. φρασσόμεθ': 'we will be able to establish (by our deliberations)'. **ἐγγυαλίξῃ:** 'give into someone's hands, grant'; used with κέρδος only here, elsewhere combined usually with κῦδος or κράτος.

141–52. Odysseus' directions are followed in every detail; his hopes and expectations (135–8) are exactly fulfilled. The improvised wedding celebration is the formal background to the imminent reunion of Odysseus and Penelope, and not only meets the immediate need of postponing the reckoning with the suitors' aggrieved families but also represents the solemn re-enactment of the marriage ceremony celebrated twenty years before by Odysseus and Penelope; cf. Hölscher, op. cit. (Introd.), 162; Eisenberger, *Studien*, 308; Besslich, *Schweigen*, 89. That the room where this pseudo-wedding takes place is also that in which Odysseus and Penelope once more sit opposite each other (164 ff.) is not as strange as Kirchhoff, *Odyssee*, 557 supposes (cf. also Focke, *Odyssee*, 369). 'Noise and disturbance can disrupt, but they can also create an intimate situation by shielding the participants from the main action' (Besslich, *Schweigen*, 89–90; who well compares the similar situation at i 152 ff., 325). Finally it should be noted that Telemachus is naturally allowed to disappear from view among the revelry of Odysseus' household; he must not be present at the recognition of Odysseus by his wife (cf. Penelope's words at 109–10); cf. Erbse, *Beiträge*, 67; Eichhorn, op. cit. (Introd.), 148 ff.

142. Cf. 131.

143. ὅπλισθεν: cf. εἵμαθ' ἐλέσθαι, 132; here then 'they got ready, dressed up'. ὅπλον/-α, ὁπλίζειν, -εσθαι are not restricted in Homer to military contexts.

143ᵇ-5. Cf. 133-4. ἵμερος + gen.: 'longing, desire for'. 145 = *Il.* xiii 637.
μολπή: in origin 'singing and dancing (by a chorus)'; cf. K. Bielohlawek,
WS xliv (1924/5), 1-18, 125-43; xlv (1926/7), 1-11; M. Wegner, *Archaeologia* U, 42-3.

146. τοῖσιν: literally 'for them', i.e. 'as they danced'.   περιστενα-
χίζετο: cf. x 10.

147. παιζόντων: here 'dancing'; cf. viii 251 and the inscription on the Attic
dipylon jug IG iᶻ 919 (8th century): *hός νυν ὀρχἐστόν πάντόν ἀταλότατα
παίζει*...; details and bibliography are given in A. Heubeck, *Archaeologia* x
116-18.   καλλίζωνος: (*hapax* in the *Odyssey*; *Il.* vii 139, xxiv 698): 'with
beautiful girdle'; on the formation of the word see Risch, *Wortbildung*, 183,
219. On the girdles used by women, particularly with the πέπλος, see
S. Marinatos, *Archaeologia* A, 11-12.

148. 148ᵃ = xx 375ᵃ; on 148ᵇ cf. 135ᵇ. Odysseus' expectations (135-6) are
fulfilled at 148-51.

149. ἦ μάλα δή: 'now quite certainly'.   πολυμνήστην: cf. iv 770, xiv 64.

150. σχέτλιος: meant originally one 'who once having laid hold on something, does not relax his grip (ἔχει), whether in a good or a bad sense'
(Ameis–Hentze–Cauer, ad xiii 293, xx 45). Here it is almost untranslat-
able, but means approx. 'wicked'.   οὐδ' ἔτλη: 'she did not hold out'.
κουριδίοιο: cf. xi 430n.

151. εἴρυσθαι: (cf. 82n.) here 'keep (for him, i.e. her husband)'.   ἦος
ἵκοιτο: 'until the time when ...'. ὄφρ' ἂν ἵκοιτο is in fact better attested
though grammatically strange; cf. Chantraine, *Grammaire*, ii 263.

152. ἴσαν: (cf. iv 772) 3rd pl. preterite (strictly speaking plpf.) from οἶδα; cf.
Chantraine, *Grammaire*, i 437. The plural form is hardly remarkable after
the iterative τις εἴπεσκε.

153-63. Odysseus' bath. The description of the bath itself and Odysseus'
change of clothing is carefully prepared and firmly rooted in the wider
context (cf. 115-16n.). First there is Penelope's order to the servants to offer
the as yet unrecognized Odysseus a bath in the morning (xix 317-22). The
second indication is the description of Odysseus' appearance after the
battle (xxii 401-6). This is followed by his ignoring Eurycleia's offer at that
point to bring him fresh clothes (xxii 485-91). Fourth there is the explanation given by Odysseus to his son for his wife's failure to honour, or even
recognize him: in his present state (νῦν) he is unidentifiable (115-16). Also
significant here is the account of the bath and change of clothing by
Odysseus' companions who had taken part in the fighting (131, 142); but of
course the continuation of the action, particularly the exchange of 165-80,
would be impossible, certainly incomprehensible, without 153-63. Finally,
was Odysseus to share Penelope's bed without bathing? Discussion of this
scene has tended to concentrate on the fact that after the 'transformation' of
Odysseus into a beggar (xiii 429-38), the reversal of this process in
Telemachus' presence (xvi 172-6), and its subsequent repetition (xvi
454-7)—in all three cases through Athena's use of her ῥάβδος—nothing is
actually said about the restoration of Odysseus' proper form. However

what is related in xiii is not magic or sorcery in the strict sense, such as Circe exercises on Odysseus' companions. Athena merely alters or disguises Odysseus' appearance in order to conceal his true nature; gradually it reverts to its original condition, in the wrestling match with Irus (xviii 67–9, 74), as Odysseus' feet are washed' (xix 358–9, 379–81), when he is recognized by the herdsmen (xxi 221–2), during the trial of the bow and the battle with the suitors (xxi 393 ff., xxii 1 ff.), and after the battle in which Odysseus has shown himself in all his greatness as a hero, far removed from the beggar whose guise he had assumed (xxii 401–6). After the battle the hero must cleanse himself of the blood and dirt (xxii 402) and don fresh clothes not least for the sake of Penelope, who, as he rightly supposed (115–16), found it difficult to recognize him as her husband on account of his dirty appearance and wretched clothes. Viewed in this light 153–63 appear less closely related to the situation of xvi 172–6 than to that of vi, where the naked and filthy hero is transformed by bathing in the river and receiving new clothes, so that he again appears an imposing figure, attractive to Nausicaa (cf. esp. vi 209–37). Moreover both here and at vi 229–35 Athena adds a touch of beauty or distinction (κάλλος or χάρις) to Odysseus' head and shoulders—an action which appears in xxiii to imply also removal of the most obvious signs of old age (cf. xiii 430–4). For interpretations of the scene see, among others: Schadewaldt, op. cit. (Introd.), 21–2; G. Scheibner, *DLZ* lxxxii (1961), col. 619; Allione, *Telemaco*, 107 n. 69; A. Ortega, *Émerita* xxxi (1963), 11–19; Besslich, *Schweigen*, 91; Lesky, *Homeros*, col. 129; M. Müller, *Athene als göttliche Helferin in der Odyssee* (Heidelberg, 1968), 146–7 (who includes some important reflections on the parallel between the scenes of vi and xxiii); Hölscher, op. cit. (Introd.), 164 n. 14; Erbse, *Beiträge*, 59–65; Eisenberger, *Studien*, 308–9; H. Kilb, *Strukturen epischen Gestaltens im 7. und 23. Gesang der Odyssee* (Munich, 1973), 159 ff.

153. ~ xxiv 365.   ᾧ ἐνὶ οἴκῳ: 'in his own house' is emphatic; cf. xxii 117, xxiii 57.

154. ~ iii 466. Eurynome is described here, as on her first appearance (xv 496) and elsewhere occasionally, as ταμίη (as is Eurycleia at ii 347); she is also once called θαλαμηπόλος. On the poetic reasons for the coexistence of two 'housekeepers' see G. Ramming, *Die Dienerschaft in der Odyssee* (diss. Erlangen/Nuremberg, 1973), 103–4, 155–7; Fenik, *Studies*, 189–92. On the interpretation of these Homeric bathing scenes cf. H. Lütz, *Beiträge zur Frage der Leibeserziehung und zur Erklärung einzelner Stellen in Homers Odyssee* (diss. Erlangen, 1927), 10–33.

155. = iii 467; *Il.* xxiv 588; ~ *Od.* x 365. An exact definition of the meaning of Homeric φᾶρος and χιτών is difficult, and not in fact aided greatly by comparison with Myc. *pa-we-a* /pharweha/, pl., and *ki-to* /khitōn/, *e-pi-ki-to-ni-ja* /epikhitōnija/; cf. J. Chadwick, L. Baumach, *Glotta* xvi (1963), 253, 257. Cf. further H. P. and A. J. B. Wace, in *Companion*, 498–503, and the explanation given by S. Marinatos, *Archaeologia* A, 6–11, which seems to throw most light on the subject: φᾶρος was a square shaped wrapper like a cloak, usually made of linen, in contrast to the χλαῖνα which was generally smaller and woollen; it was held in place with a brooch (περόνη) and worn over the χιτών as an ornamental garment by the nobility; whereas the χιτών was worn by all. This was the only piece of clothing that was sewn together; it was usually fashioned of wool, and was probably a short tunic worn with a belt. It is less likely that φᾶρος means here 'bath towel' as Lutz suggests, op. cit. (154 n.), 29–30.

156. κὰκ = καὶ ἐκ.

157-62. These lines are often regarded as a late interpolation, borrowed by rhapsodes from vi 230–5 (the encounter with Nausicaa). This is the view taken by Ernesti, Payne Knight, Düntzer, Bekker, Kirchhoff, Wilamowitz, van Leeuwen, Ameis–Hentze–Cauer, Schwartz, von der Mühll (*Odyssee*, col. 761), Marzullo (*Problema*, 422), and Erbse (*Beiträge*, 65). There is however also a substantial body of opinion in favour of the authenticity of these lines: see for example van der Valk, *Textual Criticism*, 217 n. 2; Schadewaldt, op. cit. (Introd.), 21 n. 19 ('*B*-poet'); J. Bechert, op. cit. (4 n.), 155–6; Besslich, *Schweigen*, 91; M. Müller, op. cit. (153–63 n.), 147 n. 29. The grammatical link between 156 and 157 is in fact weak: at vi 230 the infinitives are dependent on θῆκεν, 229; at xxiii 157 they are left hanging in the air. Moreover the resumption of κὰκ κεφαλῆς, 156, by κὰδ δὲ κάρητος, 157 (which causes no problem at vi 230), is very awkward. On the other hand there is little cause to doubt the authenticity of 159–62 (= vi 232–5); cf. Monro and Stanford, ad loc.; Hölscher, op. cit. (Introd.), 164 n. 17; Friedrich, *Stilwandel*, 72. On the appositeness of using the same image (drawn from the sphere of craftsmanship) in these two parallel scenes cf. particularly M. Müller, op. cit., 147 n. 29, and R. Friedrich, op. cit., 72–3. If we assume that 159–62 were intended to follow directly on 156, we can see that the ὥς-clause of 162 picks up 156, which immediately precedes the comparison; and that thus the word κάλλος is taken up, with significant variation, with χάρις. χάρις can be understood as 'a kind of glittering, clinging covering that gave the wearer an air of distinction' (Latacz, op. cit. (13 n.), 81–2). Bestowal of χάρις is the climax to the restoration of Odysseus' former appearance. On the language of 157–62 see Hainsworth, vi 230–5 n.

163. = iii 468 (163ᵃ = xxiv 370ᵃ; 163ᵇ = viii 14ᵇ).   δέμας: acc. of respect.

164. = v 195, xviii 157, xxi 139, 166.

165. Odysseus sits down in his former place, opposite his wife, and at once addresses her. This is obviously in contrast to the normal development of this form of typical scene; in such circumstances it is usual to mention the effect of the transformation of appearance on the other person (θηεῖτο δὲ κούρη, vi 237; θάμβησε δὲ . . . υἱός, xvi 178; μνηστῆρες δ' . . . ἀγάσαντο, xviii 71; cf. also ii 13, viii 17) and then for the other party to make some comment on the change: Nausicaa, vi 239 ff., Telemachus, xvi 181 ff., and one of the suitors, xviii 73 ff. Here, however, there is no mention of Odysseus' transformed appearance having any visible effect on Penelope. Odysseus, obviously bitterly disappointed by the apparent lack of feeling on the part of his wife, is obliged to take the initiative himself. Note that he

COMMENTARY

addresses her directly for the first time: previously they had spoken indirectly, addressing their remarks to the intermediary Telemachus; as a result of Odysseus' bath the situation has altered sufficiently for both partners to speak directly to each other; cf. Bona, *Studi*, 167–8. Indeed Telemachus is no longer on the scene: the final recognition is an essentially private affair between Odysseus and Penelope.

166–72. Odysseus speaks.

166–7. Odysseus' disappointment at the unexpected behaviour of his wife is shown by his use of δαιμονίη, approx. 'you strange creature'; cf. x 472 n. περὶ: + gen. 'beyond, more than . . .'; cf. Chantraine, *Grammaire*, ii 129. γυναικῶν θηλυτεράων: cf. xi 386. ἀτέραμνον: (*hapax*) predicative with κῆρ; the obvious similarity to the words of Telemachus at 97, ἀπηνέα θυμὸν ἔχουσα, and 103, κραδίη στερεωτέρη . . . λίθοιο, suggests the meaning 'hard, unyielding, implacable'. The morphology (apart from the alpha privative) is uncertain: cf. Bechtel, *Lexilogus*, 73, Frisk, *GEW*, Chantraine, *Dictionnaire*, *LfgrE* s.v. Risch, *Wortbildung*, 54. It is an attractive idea that a deliberate note of ambiguity was intended by the use of δαιμονίη and ἀτέραμνον: Odysseus may be as much taken aback·by admiration for the exceptional cunning of his wife as disappointed by her reaction; cf. Allione, *Telemaco*, 107–9; Besslich, *Schweigen*, 92; Erbse, *Beiträge*, 68–9.

168–72. Odysseus repeats the dejected words of his son (168–70 = 100–2). Although there may be in this quotation a note of recognition, and even admiration, of his wife's position—lacking in Telemachus' utterance—Odysseus here expresses a disappointment which is in marked contrast to his self-assured optimism before bathing (cf. μείδησεν, 111). Line 172 is in any event a critical moment in the development of the story: Odysseus has reached the end of the road which he had hitherto followed; the situation is now extremely critical. For this reason he turns abruptly, in mid-speech, to Eurycleia (μαῖα must refer to her; cf. 177), and bids her prepare a bed, so that he, καὶ αὐτός, may rest. καὶ αὐτός is usually understood to mean 'even if alone (sc. without Penelope)'. This interpretation is rejected in the extensive discussion of αὐτός by C. Sperlich and E.-M. Voigt, *LfgrE* i, col. 1661, 14–19, who stress a lack of parallels for such a usage, and suggest instead 'so that I too may lie down to rest (sc. like all others)'. The action which follows does suggest, however, that the conventional interpretation, 'albeit alone', may well be correct; and moreover there are other instances of αὐτός being used in this way, namely i 53, xiv 8, xv 311, xxiii 332, *Il.* viii 99 (Ameis–Hentze–Cauer, 171 n.). στόρεσον: cf. 177–80 n. At 172ᵇ Odysseus finishes with a return to his reproachful manner (cf. κῆρ ἀτέραμνον, 167). His words also recall the end of Telemachus' speech quoted at 168–70 (103: κραδίη στερεωτέρη . . . λίθοιο). The variation on his words is in conscious imitation of *Il.* xxii 357 (Hector's words to Achilles; cf. also xxiv 205, 521); cf. K. Reinhardt, *Der Dichter der Ilias* (Göttingen, 1961), 504. With the change of direction, ἀλλ' ἄγε, 171, Odysseus has to a certain extent restored the momentum of the relationship that had threatened earlier to stall. He also, surely unconsciously, offers his wife the opportunity she needs by the introduction of the

key word λέχος and provokes her into taking the initiative herself and
finally putting into operation the plan she had indicated at 108–10 (where
the keyword is σῆμαθ'), and which Odysseus had recognized, and
approved, as a πεῖρα (113–14).

174–80. Penelope replies.

174–6. Penelope first addresses the earlier part of Odysseus' speech (166–
70), and then (177–80) continues from Odysseus' instructions to the maid
(171–2), turning the situation to her advantage, so that she now provokes
him. Addressing him as δαιμόνι' she throws back at him the very reproach
he had made against her (166): he is no less δαιμόνιος than herself. Then
she rebuts the interpretation he had placed on her attitude at 115–16, and
which she had originally endured in silence: she had not denied him due
welcome and respect on account of his dirty appearance and ragged
clothes. She vigorously denies the charge ἀτιμάζει με of 116 with two asser-
tions: οὔτ' . . . μεγαλίζομαι (only here and Il. x 69), 'I am not acting
proudly', and οὔτ' ἀθερίζω 'I do not undervalue, make light of' (attested
elsewhere only viii 212 and Il. i 261; on the uncertain derivation cf. Bechtel,
Lexilogus, 15; Frisk, GEW (on *ἀθερο-, 'lower'); and for a different view
M. Grošelj, ŽA i (1951), 253–4; Chantraine, Dictionnaire s.v.; F. Sieveking,
LfgrE s.v. (on ἀθήρ). After this vehement defence of her behaviour she goes
one step further in the argument with οὐδ' ἄγαμαι. The original meaning
behind the verb is 'to have an impression of someone/something over-
stepping the limits of what is usual/expected/normal human behaviour'
(H. J. Mette, LfgrE i, col. 33, 6–8). This suggests the meaning here 'on the
other hand I am not unduly impressed or surprised'. This interpretation
also calls for the reading οὔτ' ἄρ'. . . οὔτ'. . . | οὐδὲ (not as OCT); it relates
these words to the outward change in Odysseus (153–6, 159–60). In other
words, Penelope's words (in contrast to the usual interpretation, put
forward latterly by Schadewaldt) can only be understood if the 'digression'
of 117–72 is retained as an integral part of the outward action and the
psychological reactions of the characters. The bath and change of clothing
may not have evoked any visible response from Penelope (cf. 165 n.);
certainly they are not mentioned by her in as many words. They have
nevertheless had some effect on her: previously she had been hindered by
τάφος (93) from addressing Odysseus directly (cf. 105–7); now, however,
she does feel in a position to speak to him and defend her conduct. Indeed
she has already taken the decisive step in accepting Odysseus back as her
husband, by addressing him as she does for the first time in 175–6,
although the exact sense of 175ᵇ–6 is not easy to determine; cf. Ameis–
Hentze–Cauer and Stanford, ad loc. Perhaps 'I know very well that you
looked the same then, when you left Ithaca'. On ἔησθα (cf. xvi 420; Il. xxii
435) as an artificial form for the end of a line see Shipp, Studies, 358,
177ᵇ = xix 339ᵇ. For interpretation of 174–6 in the wider context cf. among
others G. Scheibner, DLZ lxxxii (1961), coll. 619–25; A. Heubeck,
Gymnasium lxxi (1964), 54; M. Müller, op. cit. (153–63 n.), 148; Besslich,
Schweigen, 93–4; Erbse, Beiträge, 71.

177-80. In spite of her change of mind Penelope is not prepared to forgo her plan to put the identity of the stranger beyond all doubt. She takes up her husband's words of 170-2 (177 ~ 170) and in elaborating the instructions to Eurycleia (178-81) takes the initiative in advancing the πεῖρα (114, 181) which she had first aired at 108-10, and which depends on a sure and certain σῆμα, the λέχος (171, 177). Her hope lies in the fact that she knows that her detailed instructions on the preparation of the λέχος must surely provoke an outburst of protest from her husband which will finally remove any lingering doubts in her mind that this really is Odysseus. Unfortunately it is impossible to reconstruct exactly what is meant by the details of her instructions. If we follow the reading given in all sources, we see that Penelope orders the λέχος to be prepared outside the θάλαμος. The orders are given twice: στόρεσον λέχος ἐκτὸς θαλάμου and ἔνθα ἐκθεῖσαι λέχος... ἐμβάλετ᾽ εὐνήν. But this would appear not to be consistent with the question which Odysseus then asks: τίς δέ μοι ἄλλοσ᾽ ἔθηκε λέχος; (184). This clearly implies that the λέχος has already been moved, and has some time before been placed elsewhere (outside the θάλαμος?); cf. Merkelbach, *Untersuchungen*, 134 n. 2. To avoid this difficulty J. H. Quincey, *Philologus* cviii (1964), 288-90, has suggested (and his view is supported by Eisenberger, *Studien*, 310 n. 20) that 179-80 should be rejected as interpolation, and that 177-8 should be read as meaning that Eurycleia should make up the bed which is already standing outside the θάλαμος (cf. 184). No explanation is given as to how a passage which evidently confuses rather than elucidates the meaning of the text could have come to be inserted. An alternative solution is to emend the transmitted text: to alter ἐκτὸς, 178, to ἐντὸς (as in the *editio Florentina*) and ἐκθεῖσαι, 179, to ἐνθεῖσαι—a bold move which would not, however, contradict ἄλλοσ᾽ ἔθηκε, 184. It has found support from, among others, Wecklein, van Leeuwen, and V. Bérard; cf. also van der Valk, *Textual Criticism*, 37-8, and, for a slightly different view, L. G. Pocock, *Philologus* cvii (1963), 309-11 (who suggests ἐντὸς, 178, and ἐκθεῖσαι, 179, an emendation rightly rejected by Quincey, loc. cit.). G. Scheibner, loc. cit., also notes the superior sound-effects produced by such emendation. If we reject both hypotheses, of interpolation and textual conjecture, we must take Odysseus to mean that he assumed from Penelope's words that in his absence someone had cut the bed from its place (built round the growing trunk of an olive tree) in the θάλαμος (204) and moved it to another position in the room (ἄλλοσ᾽ ἔθηκεν, 184, 204), from which it could now be easily moved elsewhere.

177. στόρεσον πυκινὸν λέχος: (cf. esp. vii 335-41) 'make up the bed'; this abbreviated instruction is to spread the bedclothes (στορέσαι) over the strongly constructed bed (πυκινὸν λέχος).

178. ἐϋσταθέος: cf. xx 258 etc. **αὐτὸς:** 'with his own hands', but here also implying 'alone, without help from others' (cf. αὐτὸς, 171 n.); cf. Eichhorn, op. cit. (Introd.), 135 n. 120. The πεῖρα depends on the fact that only Penelope and Odysseus know the secret of the construction of the bed in the θάλαμος. ἐποίει: on the strange imperfect cf. the common signature on pots, ὁ δεῖνα ἐποίει.

179–80. The instruction given at 177–8 is elaborated: Eurynome and the other servants are to move the bed to its new position (ἔνθα, i.e. ἐκτὸς θαλάμου) and lay on it the bedclothes. On ἐμβάλετ' cf. στόρεσον, 177; the use of εὐνή to mean 'bedclothes' is unusual, but guaranteed by the context, with three words in 180 (~ xix 318) explaining what comprises εὐνή. It consists of three layers: the undermost κώεα, 'fleeces'; χλαῖναι, 'blankets' (cf. iv 299); and ῥήγεα, 'sheets' made of linen (σιγαλόεντα is normally used of clothing woven from linen), which presumably covered the fleeces. On the detail of this passage see the comprehensive explanation offered by S. Laser, *Archaeologia* P, 1–15.

181–2. πειρωμένη: confirms again that Penelope's words are intended as a πεῖρα (cf. πειράζειν, 114). Like Odysseus' test of his father, this πεῖρα consists of a κερτομίοισ' ἐπέεσσιν πειρηθῆναι (xxiv 240 ~ ἐρεθιζέμεν κερτομίοισ' ἐπέεσσι, *Il.* iv 5–6), and does not fail in its effect. Odysseus, who just a short while before was unruffled by his wife's announcement of her intention to test his identity (μείδησεν, 111), is now very angry (ὀχθήσας). This is of course the object of Penelope's carefully worked out plan to be absolutely sure of Odysseus' identity; cf. F. Müller, *Darstellung und poetische Funktion der Gegenstände in der Odyssee* (diss. Marburg, 1968), 37. κεδνὰ ἰδυῖαν: cf. xix 346.

182–204. Odysseus replies, obviously taken in by his wife's deliberate mistake in describing the arrangement of the bed. He has failed to recognize her provocative words as the promised πεῖρα (177–80). In this sense the speech represents a climax to the exchange between Odysseus and his wife: at last he has found his match in wisdom and cunning; and in the construction of elaborate πεῖραι they are both equal; cf. Besslich, *Schweigen*, 96; Erbse, *Beiträge*, 70. In his anger (ὀχθήσας, 182) Odysseus cannot imagine how the bed he made could have been moved; he gives vent to his perplexity in a detailed description of the bed's design and construction. It is characteristic of the poet that this lengthy description of the bed, like the detail given of other objects in the story, is not introduced for its own sake, as a showpiece of descriptive power, but as an integral element in plot development. It has an important function to fulfil in the story, and moreover the poet's aim is not so much simply to describe the object's appearance, but by means of description of its construction to conjure up a general picture of the λέχος in the reader's mind (even if some of the details are obscure); cf. F. Müller, op. cit. (181–2 n.), 39–40. The symbolic significance attached to the details given is overestimated by G. Dietz, 'Das Bett des Odysseus', *Symbolon* vii (1971), 9–32.

183. = xix 39. θυμαλγὲς: (cf. viii 272+) is predicative with τοῦτο ἔπος.

184. ἄλλοσε: cf. 177–80n. 184^b = xiii 141^b.

185–6. 185^a = xiii 313^a, 185^b, 186^a = xvi 197^b, 198^a. ὅτε μὴ θεὸς ...: 'unless/even if a god came and ...'. αὐτὸς: 'personally'. ἐθέλων: 'according to his will'.

187–9. ἀνδρῶν (part. gen.) οὔ τις ζωὸς βροτός (similarly ζωοὶ βροτοί, *Il.* xviii 539) is the counterpart to θεός, 185. 'Not even a man in the full strength of youth could have (with the aid of a lever, ὀχλεύς) moved it away (cf. θείη ἄλλῃ ἐνὶ χώρῃ, 186).' There are two models for this passage in the *Iliad.* In both cases similar thoughts are expressed of entirely hypothetical situations: xii 380–2 and xxiv 565–7. All three passages include the phrase οὐδὲ μάλ' ἡβῶν (188ᵇ = *Il.* xii 381ᵇ = *Il.* xxiv 565ᵇ), which is best suited to the context of *Il.* xxiv, where Achilles has in mind the aged Priam. ῥεῖα μετοχλίσσειε(ν) is found in Homer only at 189ᵃ = *Il.* xxiv 565ᵃ (cf. οὐκ ἄν . . . ὀχλίσσειαν, ix 241–2; for ῥεῖα cf. ῥέα, *Il.* xii 381). The unusual expression ἀνδρῶν οὔ . . . τις ζωὸς βροτός, 188 (cf. βροτὸς, *Il.* xxiv 565) is also reminiscent of ἀνήρ . . . οἷοι νῦν βροτοί εἰσιν, *Il.* xii 381–2. Cf. K. Reinhardt, op. cit. (168–72 n.), 483–4; M. J. Apthorp, *The Manuscript Evidence for Interpolation in Homer* (Heidelberg, 1980), 58 and 110 n. 68. σῆμα τέτυκται ἐν λέχει ἀσκητῷ: Odysseus obviously means by σῆμα the special distinguishing mark, the unique feature involved in his construction of the bed rather than the token of his identity which Penelope seeks (cf. σήματα, 110; cf. also 202), for he is quite unaware that his response to his wife's orders to the maid (177–80) supplies the very σῆμα which Penelope presumably had in mind at 108–10. Cf. Stanford, ad loc.; Besslich, *Schweigen*, 96; Eisenberger, *Studien*, 310 n. 21. ἀσκέω: 'fashion artfully'. For 189ᵇ cf. αὐτὸς ἐποίει, 178.

190–201. In the course of his account of the construction of the bed Odysseus explains the unusual feature of its design (the σῆμα). Not all the details of his account can be fully understood. Ethnological parallels to the bed 'rooted' in the earth are given in Germain, *Genèse*, 211–12.

190. θάμνος: (cf. v. 467 etc.) 'bush', here probably 'trunk'. τανύφυλλος: 'cf. xiii 102) possessive cpd., with *τάνυς, 'long, thin' as first element; cf. Risch, *Wortbildung*, 190–1. ἕρκεος ἐντός: 'within the (enclosed) property (of Odysseus/his father)'.

191. ἀκμηνὸς: (*hapax*) probably a denominative -no- derivative from ἀκμή, meaning then approx. 'fully grown' (similarly θαλέθων, 'flourishing'); cf. Bechtel, *Lexilogus*, 26; Chantraine, *Dictionnaire*, 44 s.v. ἀκ-; Risch, *Wortbildung*, 99. πάχετος: (cf. viii 187) ~ παχύς; cf. Risch, op. cit., 26.

192. τῷ (sc. θάμνῳ) . . . ἀμφιβαλὼν θάλαμον δέμον: 'I built the θάλαμος round it'.

193. πυκνῇσιν: 'close-packed'. λιθάδεσσι: λιθάς, -άδος (only here and xiv 36) ~ λίθος; the variant λιθάκεσσι must be rejected; cf. van der Valk, *Textual Criticism*, 40. καθύπερθεν ἔρεψα: cf. *Il.* xxiv 450; ἐρέφω, 'cover with a roof' (cf. ὄροφος).

194. κολλητὰς: (cf. xxi 137) 'closely joined'. ἐπέθηκα θύρας: (sc. θαλάμῳ) cf. xxi 45. ἀραρυίας: 'fitting tightly'; attested in Myc., a-ra-ru-ja /ararujja/, 'provided with'; cf. J. Chadwick, L. Baumbach, *Glotta* xli (1963), 174.

195. Odysseus did not begin construction of the bed itself until the θάλαμος was finished. In this way no one could observe his work. **κόμην:** 'leaves (and branches)'.

196. **κορμὸν:** (*hapax*) deverbative *-mo-* derivative from κείρω (Risch, *Wortbildung*, 44): 'trunk stripped of branches and foliage; stump'. **ἐκ ρίζης:** 'from the roots up (sc. to the top)'. **προταμὼν:** (προτάμνω) here probably 'cut'. **ἀμφέξεσα:** 'smoothed round'. **χαλκῷ:** here 'bronze adze' (σκέπαρνον, v 237).

197. ~ xvii 341, xxi 44. 197ᵃ = xx 161ᵃ; 197ᵇ = v 245ᵇ etc. **ἐπισταμένως:** 'skilfully'. **ἐπὶ στάθμην:** 'along the line'.

198. **ἑρμῖν' ἀσκήσας:** 'by skilfully working it [κορμὸν] as a bedpost [one of four]'. ἑρμίς, -ῖνος (elsewhere only viii 278) 'bedpost'; cf. ἕρμα; on the form see Risch, *Wortbildung*, 53. **τέτρηνα ... τερέτρῳ:** 'I bored through with the drill.' τετραίνω, cf. v 247. τερέτρῳ only here and v 246; instrumental formation in -τρον; cf. τρητός; Risch, *Wortbildung*, 41–4. πάντα probably refers to the planks of the bed itself (and the other three ἑρμῖνες); on the use of drill-holes see 201 n.

199. **ἐκ δὲ τοῦ:** sc. κόρμου. **ἔξεον:** ξέω here, 'I work everything smooth'. 199ᵇ = 192ᵇ.

200. **δαιδάλλων:** (cf. δαίδαλος) 'skilfully embellishing'. δαιδάλλω probably refers to the same technique as δινόω: cf. xix 56 κλισίην ... δινωτὴν ἐλέφαντι καὶ ἀργύρῳ, which may be either overlay or inlaid work. The technique may have been known to the poet from Cypriot products of the eighth century; cf. S. Marinatos, *Archaeologia* P, 99–103, on the so-called ivory thrones from Salamis in Cyprus. It is most unlikely that the passage refers to the highly developed Mycenaean inlay work (on which see Ventris–Chadwick, *Documents*, 332–48, 498–508), despite the use of similar terminology in the Pylos tablets; cf. A. Heubeck, *SMEA* xx (1979), 240–2 (incl. bibl.).

201. **ἐν δ' ἐτάνυσσ(α):** 'I stretched [in the finished bedframe]'. **ἱμάντα:** here poetic sing. for ἱμάντας; cf. K. Witte, *RE* viii, col. 2231. The ἱμὰς βοὸς is φοίνικι φαεινόν, 'shining with purple (colour)', i.e. 'stained red' as at *Il.* vi 219 and vii 305 (a ζωστήρ) and xv 538 (a λόφος). Cf. further Myc. *po-ni-ki-ja* /phoinikija, -ai/, used of the Cnossian war-chariot (in the S-tablets), prob. 'coloured purple'; see Ventris–Chadwick, *Documents*, 573. Odysseus mounts criss-cross straps across the frame, using the holes drilled; the bedding rests on this (cf. 179–80 n.). For further details of the Homeric bed and beds in the geometric period see S. Laser, *Archaeologia* P, 1–34; on Odysseus' bed, 6–7, and on the τρητὸν λέχος, 31.

202–4. 202ᵃ rounds off the description of the bed (190–201): οὕτω τοι τόδε σῆμα πιφαύσκομαι. With σῆμα Odysseus refers back to 188 (μέγα σῆμα), except that here he obviously means the whole bed, which by reason of its peculiar form is a sure token (as at 110) for both partners, and only for them (cf. 110, 189). Odysseus sees that he has proved his identity; cf. Besslich, *Schweigen*, 96. At 203ᵇ–4 (ἠέ τις ἤδη ἀνδρῶν ἄλλοσε θῆκε) he concludes with a clear reference to his opening question, τίς δέ μοι ἄλλοσε θῆκε; (184). **ἔμπεδόν:** 'firmly planted in the ground'.

COMMENTARY

204. ταμὼν ὕπο: ~ ὑποταμὼν, 'cutting at the base'. πυθμέν: 'foot, base [of an object]'.

205. = iv 703, xxii 68, xxiv 345, *Il.* xxi 114. The formulaic phrase expresses the collapse of physical and emotional resistance in Penelope. Outwardly calm and in control she is in fact overcome not only by the content of Odysseus' reply, but also by his indignant manner (ὀχθήσας); cf. Eisenberger, *Studien*, 310 n. 22; J. T. Kakridis, *Homer Revisited* (Lund, 1971), 159. τῆς: sc. Πηνελοπείης. αὐτοῦ: 'on the spot'.

206. = xix 250 (also Penelope), xxiv 346. σήματ': as at 110, 202. ἀναγνούσῃ: (ethic. dat.) is to be preferred to the variant -ης, in spite of preceding τῆς; cf. Ameis–Hentze, *Anhang*, iv 92. ἔμπεδα: (cf. 203) here 'incontrovertible', predicative with (rel.) τά.

207–8. 207ᵃ = xvii 33ᵃ, 207ᵇ = iv 454ᵇ. δακρύσασα: (ingress.) 'bursting into tears'. ἰθὺς: 'straight (towards him)'. ἀμφὶ: with βάλλ' (tmesis).

209–30. Penelope begs forgiveness from Odysseus for her earlier behaviour. Besslich, *Schweigen*, 96, has shown that this speech can only be fully understood by reference to 117–72, i.e. retaining the so-called digression.

209. μή ... σκύζευ: (pres. imper.) 'do not be angry any more!' the only other instance of the verb in the *Odyssey* is ἐπισκύσσαιτο, vii 306 (etym. unknown; cf. Chantraine, *Dictionnaire* s.v.); Penelope refers to the vehement indignation behind her husband's words (ὀχθήσας, 182). τά περ ἄλλα: (cf. v 29) 'otherwise'.

210. ὀϊζύν: 'sorrow, affliction'; the suffering lies in the heavy fate described at 211–12.

211. νῶϊν: (with ῐ!), dat., 'us both'. ἀγάσαντο: (cf. 64, 175 n.) here 'they begrudged us ...'; cf. iv 181. 211ᵇ = v 227ᵇ; *Il.* v 572ᵇ, xvii 721ᵇ.

212. ταρπῆναι: 'enjoy, experience to the full'; cf. Latacz, op. cit. (13 n.), 189. γήραος οὐδός: here, as at xv 246, 'threshold between the prime of life and old age'; used in a quite different sense in the *Il.* (xxii 60, xxiv 487).

213. Cf. v 215. With μή ... χώεο μηδὲ νεμέσσα Penelope repeats what she said at 209, μὴ σκύζευ. She acknowledges the behaviour which has, not unreasonably, so angered her husband: 'do not be angry with me for (τόδε) ...'

214. τὸ πρῶτον, ἐπεί: 'the first moment when'. ὧδ': sc. as now. ἀγάπησα: here 'lovingly greet'.

215. 215ᵇ = viii 178ᵇ etc.

216. ἀπάφοιτο: from ἀπαφίσκω (the simple form is attested elsewhere only xi 217, xiv 428; cf. also ἐξαπάφω 79): here 'beguile, deceive'.

217. κέρδεα: here 'plots, designs'.

218–24. At first sight these lines seem a superfluous and pointless excursus, easily removable and inappropriate to context; they were regarded as spurious in antiquity, probably by Aristarchus (ἀθετοῦνται, schol. Vind. 133), and most modern scholars have agreed; cf. Kirchhoff, *Odyssee*, 531–2; Wilamowitz, *Untersuchungen*, 84 n. 8; *Heimkehr*, 7; van Leeuwen, ad loc.; Finsler, *Homer*, ii 434 ('Unsinn'); Schwartz, *Odyssee*, 332; von der Mühll,

Odyssee, col. 763 (*B*-poet or rhapsodic addition), ed. ad loc.; Schadewaldt, op. cit. (Introd.), 24 ('unlogisch'). Very few have defended the lines as authentic: Ameis–Hentze–Cauer, ad loc.; Stanford, ad loc.; van der Valk, *Textual Criticism*, 194–6; Besslich, *Schweigen*, 95 n. 20. Of course the fact that the lines are not necessary to the context does not prove that they are inauthentic.

Penelope uses this apparent digression from the point to explain and justify her own conduct (215–17): had Helen known the terrible consequences of her fateful act, and that the Achaeans would bring her back to Greece, she would surely have withstood the suggestions of Paris; in fact she was not in a position to resist his charm, because she was driven to her shameful deed by the prompting of a god; by the time she recognized the awful consequences of her actions, it was too late.

Penelope's analysis of the actions of Helen is calculated to draw the listener's (Odysseus') attention to a comparison with her own behaviour, although this is not directly stated. For many years Penelope had withstood all temptation (215–17). Until she was sure beyond all reasonable, and perhaps unreasonable, doubt of her husband's return she has exercised a self-control, which others had found difficult to understand. This self-control, which was in fact rooted in her incomparable prudence and intelligence, was bound to be viewed by other people as stubbornness and obstinacy. It is significant that she does not claim any credit for her steadfastness, but rather seeks to justify it. Equally she attempts to win sympathy for Helen by showing that her actions were the result of divine influence: she could not have recognized her infatuation for what it was until the consequences of her action were visible. In this sense 218–24 do have an important role in the context, and should therefore be retained.

218. Ἀργείη ... ἐκγεγαυῖα: as at iv 184.

219. ἀνδρὶ ... ἀλλοδαπῷ: (cf. iii 74 etc.) 'from a foreign people' (cf. Chantraine, *Dictionnaire* s.v.); a periphrasis for Paris. 219ᵇ = v 126ᵇ.

220. ὅ: = ὅτι. ἀρήϊοι υἷες Ἀχαιῶν: used only once in the *Odyssey*, but frequently in the *Iliad* (iv 114 etc.).

221. ἀξέμεναι: fut. or aor. inf.; cf. Chantraine, *Grammaire*, i 418; ii 309. οἴκόνδε ... πατρίδ': = v 204 etc.

222. θεὸς: Aphrodite; cf. iv 261. ὦρορεν: redupl. aor. from ὄρνυμι with trans. meaning; cf. further xxiv 62 n.

223. The meaning is explained by the scholion οὐ πρὸ τοῦ παθεῖν ἔγνω τὴν φρενοβλάβειαν. ἄτην: 'infatuation, intellectual blindness'; the word refers to the act of divine intervention, the delusion caused, and the folly that results (cf. 202!); cf. G. Müller, in *Navicula Chilonensis* (Leiden, 1956), 1–15; J. Gruber, *Über einige abstrakte Begriffe des frühen Griechischen* (Meisenheim, 1963), 56–61. οὐ ... ἑῷ ἐγκάτθετο θυμῷ: 'she did not consider, she did not realize'; similarly οὐδ'... ἐνὶ φρεσὶ θέσθε (iv 729), 'it did not occur to you'.

224. πρῶτα: here 'from the start'. καὶ ἡμέας: 'for us too'.

225. νῦν δ': Penelope now resumes the train of thought introduced with αἰεί (215–17): 'always before ...; but now ...'. σήματ': cf. 110, 202, 206.

ἀριφραδέα: cf. σῆμα . . . ἀριφραδές, xi 126. On the unusual lengthening of -έᾱ cf. E. Crespo, 'Elementos antiguos y modernos en la prosodia homerica', suppl. to *Minos* vii (Salamanca, 1977), 39–40. On καταλέγειν see T. Krischer, *Formale Konventionen der homerischen Epik (Zetemata* lvi, Munich, 1971), 146–58.

226. Cf. 178ᵇ, 189. ὀπώπει: plpf. with simple preterite meaning.

227. 227ᵃ = xvi 304ᵃ.

228. ~ iv 736, where Penelope mentions the old δμώς Dolius. This reference to ἀμφίπολος Ἀκτορίς not mentioned elsewhere in the poem is strange. Are we to think that she has died and been replaced by the θαλαμηπόλος Eurynome (cf. 154, 289, 293)? (As Ameis–Hentze–Cauer and Stanford, ad loc., suppose.) Or perhaps the reference is to Eurynome herself, naming her by her patronymic as daughter of Actor (J. A. Scott, *CQ* xii (1918), 75–9; cf. also Fenik, *Studies*, 191 n. 98). ἔτι δεῦρο κιούσῃ: 'at that time when I moved here' (to Ithaca; evidently Penelope's father Icarius was not an Ithacan himself: cf. ii 53–4).

229. νῶϊν: cf. 211. εἴρυτο: cf. εἴρυσθαι, 151 n.

230. πείθεις δή: introduces the main clause after ἐπεὶ ἤδη, 225. With ἀπηνέα θυμὸν Penelope turns to answering the vehement accusation of Telemachus (97).

231. The line is modelled on xix 249, with τῷ for τῇ. The words fit the context of xix somewhat better, with ἔτι μᾶλλον referring to γόοιο, 213, whereas here there has been no mention of γόος on the part of Odysseus.

232. θυμαρέα: similarly *Il.* ix 336 (v.l. -ηρέα); cf. also θυμαρὲς, *Od.* xvii 199 (v.l. -ῆρες) and θυμῆρες, x 362 (v.l. -αρές). In terms of morphology and etymology forms with -ᾱ- and -η- are identical, being based on the root *αρ- (cf. ἀραρίσκω) like other composites formed with suffix -ήρης (cf. χαλκήρης, εὐήρης, Περιήρης). Meaning: 'fitting, suiting the θυμός (cf. iv 777), gladdening the heart'; cf. Bechtel, *Lexilogus*, 169; Leumann, *Wörter*, 66; Chantraine, *Dictionnaire* s.v. -ήρης; Risch, *Wortbildung*, 81. κεδνὰ ἰδυῖαν: as at 182.

233–9. The subject and mood of the comparison are clearly determined by its obvious frame: ὡς δ' ὅτ' ἂν ἀσπάσιος, 233, and ὡς ἄρα τῇ ἀσπαστὸς, 239. The key word is ἀσπάσιος/ἀσπαστός (repeated again at 238, ἀσπάσιοι) for the whole passage is dominated by the concept of the joyful welcome home. But the development of the idea is strange. 232 suggests that the comparison refers in the first instance to the position of Odysseus, and this view seems to be reinforced by 233 ff., which give a picture of shipwrecked seamen, whose ship has been destroyed by Poseidon: a few reach the shore, and full of joy (ἀσπάσιοι) feel solid ground beneath their feet. The parallel, and occasional verbal echo, of Odysseus' arrival, worn out with fatigue and caked with sea salt, on the longed-for shore of Scheria after Poseidon had shattered his σχεδίη is clear. However, the simile then develops in quite another direction: the following ὡς- clause compares the joy of the sailor in the sight of the shore with the welcome sight of the homecoming Odysseus to his wife. Similar shifts of emphasis are to be found in other comparisons which draw on the basic theme of rescue or safe homecoming: cf. xvi 17–21, also x 415–21, and above all v 394–9. This latter example is particularly closely related to the comparison of xxiii both in choice of comparison (Odysseus catching sight of the saving coast of Scheria) and in diction. Cf. Fränkel, *Gleichnisse*, 94–5; van der Valk, *Textual Criticism*, 254; Eisenberger, *Studien*, 311 n. 25; R. Friedrich, *Stilwandel*, 73–4; D. N. Maronitis, *EEThess.* ix (1965), 269–93.

233. ~ v 394. *νήχομαι*: 'swim'.

234. *ὤν . . . εὐεργέα νῆ* '[*a*]/*ἐνὶ πόντῳ* should be taken together: 'on the high seas'.

235. *κύματι πηγῷ*: as at v 388; *πηγός* must be related to *πήγνυμι*, i.e. 'strong, powerful'; on later changes of meaning see Leumann, *Wörter*, 214 n. 8; Chantraine, *Dictionnaire*, 894.

236. *ἐξέφυγον* (i.e. *ἔφυγον ἐξ*) *πολιῆς ἁλὸς*: 'they escaped the grey salt waters'.

237. *πολλὴ*: predicative with *ἅλμη*, 'seawater, salt'.   *τέτροφεν*: intr. pf. from *τρέφω*: 'has grown, has congealed'.

238. *ἀσπάσιοι*: unlike *ἀσπάσιος*, 233 (~ *ἀσπαστὸς*, 239) it here has an active meaning, 'rejoicing'.   *κακότητα φυγόντες*: cf. iii 175 etc.

240. *οὔ πω πάμπαν*: 'not yet completely, still not'.

241-6. These lines have been considered a late addition to the text by many scholars, following Payne Knight, Bergk, and Duentzer: among others Wilamowitz, *Heimkehr*, 68; Finsler, *Homer*, ii 435; Focke, *Odyssee*, 370. Others take the additional material to extend from 241 as far as 288: von der Mühll, *Odyssee*, col. 764; W. Theiler, *MH* vii (1950), 108; Schadewaldt, op. cit. (Introd.), 24 (*B*-poet). But the arguments advanced against the lines do not carry as much weight as certain observations in favour of their authenticity. The most telling point is that the passages describing the recognition of Odysseus by Telemachus and the two herdsmen have a similar structure. In xvi Telemachus embraces his father in tears (213–14 ~ xxiii 207); both succumb to *ἵμερος γόοιο* (215 ~ xxiii 231); their mood is illustrated by a simile (216–19 ~ xxiii 233–40); and then, *καί νύ κ' ὀδυρομένοισιν ἔδυ φάος ἠελίοιο, εἰ μὴ Τηλέμαχος . . .* (200–1 ~ xxiii 241–2). This pattern is somewhat compressed in xxi, where the herdsmen recognize and tearfully embrace their master; Odysseus returns the gesture (222–5); and then follows the concluding 226 (= xvi 220), *εἰ μὴ Ὀδυσσεὺς . . .* In xxiii xvi 220 (= xxi 226) is adapted ('seltsam': Schwartz, *Odyssee*, 136): *καί νύ κ' ὀδυρομένοισι φάνη ῥοδοδάκτυλος Ἠώς*, 241. This is followed by *εἰ μὴ ἄρ' ἀλλ' ἐνόησε θεὰ γλαυκῶπις Ἀθήνη* ('both partners would have wept till dawn, had not . . .'). This alteration, however, matches the different situation. The day had begun at xx 91, and the wealth of incident had evidently lasted until the evening (the poet does not give here any indication of the time). The divergence from the established pattern also arises from the desire to heighten the effect by making a goddess postpone the dawn—a miracle which does not so much set an end to weeping as provide time for the many other things which Odysseus and Penelope have on their minds before sleep (342–3), and which the poet wishes to introduce into his story: the conversation of 247–88, their lovemaking (289–301) and their exchange of news about their experiences (301–4). 'The joy of reunion is augmented by divine grace' (Eisenberger, *Studien*, 311). It is also interesting to note that all three passages compared, from xvi, xxi and xxiii, are modelled on *Il.* xxiii 153 ff.: *Il.* xxiii 153ᵇ ~ *Od.* xvi 215ᵇ, xxiii 231ᵇ; *Il.* xxiii 154 = *Od.* xvi 220, xxi 226 ~ xxiii 241; *Il.* xxiii 155ᵃ ~ *Od.* xvi 221ᵃ, xxi 227ᵃ, xxiii 242ᵃ. The idea of divine influence over the course of day and night is by no means foreign to Homeric thought; cf. *Il.* xviii 239–41. Athena's later actions, in prompting the couple to rise after their sleep (344–8) and stirring Eos into action, after she had been bidden to stay her work, does not in fact contradict 241–6 (as Müller, op. cit. (153–65 n.) supposes). On the contrary: 241–6 and 344–8 should be read in close conjunction as a frame for what is related in 247–343; cf. Eisenberger, *Studien*, 314 n. 2.

241. 241ᵃ = xvi 220ᵃ, xxi 226ᵃ; 241ᵇ = xix 428ᵇ etc. **ὀδύρομαι:** cf. γόοιο, 231.

242. ii 382 etc.

243-6. περάτῃ: from πείραρ, -ατος. According to Chantraine, *Dictionnaire*, 871, ἐν περάτῃ means approx. 'at the furthest end (of the sky), on the horizon'. It may be better understood here in a temporal sense: 'at the end of the course of night'; cf. the κέλευθοι of night and day at x 86, and Hesiod's description, *Th.* 748–57. This is how it is taken in the scholion, ⟨νύκτα⟩ πρὸς τέλει οὖσαν; cf. Stanford, ad loc. **δολιχὴν** is predicative: 'she restrained night, so that it was long (longer than usual)'. The essential counterpart to this act is the holding in check of Eos: ῥύσατ'(ο) here 'held back'. ἐπ' Ὠκεανῷ: 'at the encircling stream'—if we compare xii 2–3 at Aeaea, where Ἠοῦς ἠριγενείης | οἰκία καὶ χοροί εἰσι καὶ ἀντολαὶ Ἠελίοιο. Eos is not normally credited in Homer with a team of two horses. This detail is almost certainly borrowed from the usual depiction of Helius with a pair of horses. The (speaking) names, Lampus and Phaethon, correspond to those given to the nymphs watching over Helius' cattle on Thrinacia, Φαέθουσα and Λαμπετίη, xii 132. πῶλοι is in apposition to οἵ: 'as foals'; cf. Ruijgh, τε épique, 372.

247-88. This section of the conversation between Odysseus and Penelope is thought by some scholars, following La Roche, to be an interpolation: Wilamowitz, *Untersuchungen*, 68 ff.; Bethe, *Homer*, ii 115 (cf. also 241–6 n.). Compelling counter-arguments have been advanced by F. Dornseiff, *Hermes* lxxii (1937), 351, and Focke, *Odyssee*, 270–3. And it is true that the transition directly from 240 or 246 to 289 ff. would be very abrupt. Moreover this is the best point at which to introduce an account of Tiresias' prophecy: if Penelope is to be told something of the future fate of her husband (which can hardly be avoided), then it is fitting that this should happen before the couple retire to bed.

248-55. In the middle of a highly emotional scene Odysseus abruptly breaks the atmosphere of joy by mentioning, albeit in general terms until pressed, the πόνος foretold by Tiresias. However he then abandons this line of thought as well, and suggests to Penelope that they retire to bed (254-5).

248. οὐ γάρ πω: at the beginning of a speech is unusual, and suggests a continuation from an unspoken thought such as, 'Let us put aside all thoughts of the past and future trials!' Cf. Ameis–Hentze–Cauer, ad loc., and the different view taken by Stanford. πείρατ' ἀέθλων: 'end of labours'.

249. ὄπισθεν: here 'later, hereafter'. ἀμέτρητος: attested only here and xix 512.

250. πάντα: predicative with (rel.) τὸν.

251-3. The reference is to the underworld scene, xi 90–151. νόστον ... διζήμενος: cf. x 539 and xi 100 (νόστον δίζηαι).

254. ἀλλ' ἔρχευ: (~ ἀλλ' ἄγε) with this phrase Odysseus breaks off his brief indication of what the future holds in store. λέκτρονδ' ἴομεν: (short vowel subj.). 254ᵇ-5 = iv 294ᵇ-5 = Il. xxiv 635ᵇ-6. καὶ ἤδη: 'now too'.

255. '(that we) may find comfort and satisfaction in sweet enveloping sleep'; cf. Latacz, op. cit. (13n.), 187. There is a difference here from iv 295 and Il. xxiv 636 determined by the context. Here we have a long-separated married couple repairing to bed.

257-62. In 257-9 Penelope picks up the keyword εὐνή (λέκτρον), but then she turns to other matters with ἀλλ'. . . εἴπ' ἄγε. Her reply concentrates on the earlier words of Odysseus; her ἄεθλον (261) takes up his ἀέθλων (248). Her wish—and her psychological need at this point is quite understandable—is to know more about the vague hints of 248-53 before they enjoy the comfort of εὐνή.

257. δή: 'surely', i.e. 'exactly as you wish'. τότ' ... ὁππότε: 'whenever'.

258. ποίησαν: 'they have brought it about'; on which depends acc. + inf. σε ἱκέσθαι.

259. = iv 476 etc.

260. = xix 485, although here ἐφράσθης has a different meaning: 'since your thoughts have turned to them' (sc. the ἄεθλα).

261. καὶ ὄπισθεν: 'anyway at a later time'. ὀΐω: (parenthetic) 'I think'.

262. αὐτίκα ... χέρειον: is also a part of the ἐπεί-clause; αὐτίκα should be taken with δαήμεναι. οὔ τι χέρειον [ἐστιν]: litotes, 'since it is certainly better'.

264-84. Odysseus complies with his wife's request and elaborates on the vague indications given at 248-53.

264. δαιμονίη: cf. 166, 174n. Odysseus cannot understand his wife's insistence. τί τ' ἄρ' αὖ: 'why this again'.

265. εἰπέμεν: 'to tell' (all in detail); 265ᵇ = xix 269ᵇ. The repeated assurance is to signal that his account will closely follow what he learned, and has already reported to the Phaeacians.

266. κεχαρήσεται: redupl. middle fut.: 'your heart will not rejoice (while I tell you)'; cf. Latacz, op. cit. (13n.), 64.

267. πολλὰ βροτῶν ἐπὶ ἄστε': as at xv 492 etc.

268. ~ xi 121.

COMMENTARY

269-84. = xi 122-37 (with minor alterations arising largely from transposition from 2nd to 1st person; first xi 123 > xxiii 268, and finally xi 129 > xxiii 276). On the content and language see xi 122-37 nn.

286-7. Penelope's reply is short and to the point: Odysseus' words have not so much caused her anxiety as inspired her with confidence in the future. She had been right at 260-3 to insist on hearing the news now.　**εἰ μὲν ... ἄρειον:** 'if the gods really do so grant old age to be better'; ἄρειον is predicative with γῆρας (cf. 281-4 n.). 287ᵇ = ii 280 etc.　**ὑπάλυξιν:** (only here and *Il.* xxii 270) with dependent κακῶν, 'escape from'; on the word formation (ἀλύσκω) see H. Jones, *Glotta* li (1973), 7-29, esp. 10.

289-99. Eurynome and Eurycleia prepare the bed, and the couple retire. Meanwhile Telemachus and the herdsmen bring the dancing to an end; then they and the other servants also go to bed.

289. τόφρα: 'meanwhile'. On Eurynome cf. 154 n.　**τροφὸς:** (like γρηῦς, 292) refers of course to Eurycleia. For the first (and last) time the two maids appear together.　**ἐντύω:** 'prepare'. The bed needs to be made because Penelope had slept in the ὑπερώϊον while Odysseus was away (cf. xvii 101).

289-90. εὐνὴν | ἐσθῆτος μαλακῆς: '(bed) of soft coverings'; ἐσθής is used to mean 'bedclothes' only here; cf. Laser, *Archaeologia* P, 11. This unusual usage may be related to the fact that ἔννυσθαι, from which ἐσθής is derived, can also mean 'to dress, cover oneself'; cf. xi 191, where Laertes is described as covering himself with rags, κακὰ δὲ χροΐ εἵματα εἶται. Cf. besides the double meaning of χλαῖνα, 'clothing' and 'blanket' (cf. 155, 179-80nn.). 290ᵇ = xix 48ᵇ; *Il.* xviii 492ᵇ.

291. = vii 340. Cf. 177 n.　**ἐγκονέουσαι:** (elsewhere only vii 340; *Il.* xxiv 648, in the same form as here): 'hasten eagerly'; cf. Chantraine, *Dictionnaire*, 310.

292. κείουσα: 'to go to bed'. κείω (cf. i 424 etc.): 'I want to sleep'; 292ᵇ = i 360ᵇ, xxi 354ᵇ.　**πάλιν οἶκόνδε:** 'back to the οἶκος (the living quarters of the palace?)'; according to Odysseus' description at 189-94 the θάλαμος is separated from the μέγαρον.　**βεβήκει:** cf. ὀπώπει, 226 (and n.). There is no reason to regard the line as a late interpolation (as do Kirchhoff, van Leeuwen, and others).

293. τοῖσιν: the couple.　**θαλαμηπόλος:** cf. 154 n.

294. 294ᵇ = xx 497ᵇ.

295. πάλιν κίεν: '(like Eurycleia) she too retired to her bedchamber'.

296. ἀσπάσιοι: (as at 238) recalls the subject-matter of the comparison at 233-9.　**θεσμὸν:** (*hapax*) is used later to mean 'rule, convention'; here, however, it is perhaps used in its earlier sense, 'place, location'; Ameis-Hentze-Cauer, *Anhang*, iv 94, following L. Döderlein, *Homerisches Glossar* (Erlangen, 1850/8), § 2498; cf. also Stanford, ad loc.; Chantraine, *Dictionnaire* s.v. On the solution to this line see below 297 ~ xxiv 548 n.

297. (~ xxiv 548). A quite indigestible mass of material has arisen round the Alexandrian critics' comment on 296, which is transmitted in two almost identical notes in the scholia: 1. Ἀριστοφάνης δὲ καὶ Ἀρίσταρχος πέρας

342

τῆς Ὀδυσσείας τοῦτο ποιοῦνται (M, V, Vind. 133), 2. τοῦτο τέλος τῆς Ὀδυσσείας φησὶν Ἀρίσταρχος καὶ Ἀριστοφάνης (H, M, Q). In addition there is Eustathius' lengthy note on 296, which responds to the discussion that had clearly developed at an early date round the Alexandrian comment. The only part based on a scholion along the lines of those quoted above is the section [ἰστέον δὲ ὅτι κατὰ τὴν τῶν παλαιῶν ἱστορίαν] Ἀρίσταρχος καὶ Ἀριστοφάνης [οἱ κορυφαῖοι τῶν τότε γραμματικῶν] εἰς τὸ—ὡς ἐρρέθη—"ἀσπάσιοι . . . ἵκοντο" περατοῦσι τὴν Ὀδύσσειαν. What follows is Eustathius' own interpretation of the scholion: τὰ ἐφεξῆς ἕως τέλους τοῦ βιβλίου νοθεύοντες (as is convincingly argued by Erbse, Beiträge, 167–8). A number of different questions arise from the scholiasts' observations. First, in what sense did the Alexandrian scholars use τέλος (or πέρας)? Second, if they really did mean by τέλος the 'end', and so interpreted 296 as the last line of the 'genuine, original' poem, what was the basis for this analytical judgement? Did they detect peculiarities in language, style and content significant enough to lead them to the conclusion that the final section was the work of some other author? Or did the manuscripts available to them offer two distinct versions of which the shorter (i 1–xxiii 296) seemed to them, for whatever reason, preferable to the longer (i 1–xxiv 548)? Third, to what extent can the resources of modern philology help us to settle the disputed authenticity of the final part of the poem as we now know it? It would be impossible in the present context to discuss all the various arguments advanced. This commentary will therefore confine itself to mentioning some of the more important views expressed and a selection of the modern literature on the subject (on the older literature see Ameis–Hentze, Anhang iv, 94–5), and discussing individual points of interest regarding language, style, composition and content as they arise in the text. The underlying assumption is that the scholion itself does not say that the Alexandrians themselves considered the 'end' of the poem to be un-Homeric; and moreover the arguments advanced against the authenticity of the present ending do not justify excluding 297 ff., besides which considerations of both the internal and the overall structure of the epic, and the close interconnection between the ending and the material of i 1–xxiii 296, point to the authenticity of the section. The most important linguistic arguments are to be found in Page, Odyssey, 102–13; K. A. Garbrah, Glotta xlvii (1970), 144–70 (passim); Shipp, Studies, 358–64; and the unitarian responses of Erbse, Beiträge, 189–229; C. Moulton, Greek, Roman and Byzantine Studies xv (1974), 157–61; H.-A. Stössel, Der letzte Gesang der Odyssee (diss. Erlangen/Nuremberg, 1975), 153–72.

No 'original' Odyssey could simply have ended at xxiii 296: οἱ μὲν, 295, calls for a continuation, which in our text appears at 297, αὐτὰρ Τηλέμαχος; cf. latterly Hölscher, op. cit. (Introd.), 165 n. 29. As P. Friedländer, Hermes lxiv (1929), 376, has conclusively shown, we must rule out the theory that a poet adding a final section to a shorter text of the poem altered an original οἱ δ' ἄρ' ἔπειτα to οἱ μὲν. To attribute the 'end' of the

COMMENTARY

poem to another hand necessarily involves assuming either, as von der Mühll does (*Odyssee*, col. 763), that this redactor (his '*B*-poet') made a wholesale revision of the text from at least 289, or that the poem originally ended at some other point. Thus F. L. Kay, *CR* vii (1957), 106, argues that the final line was originally 299; while Focke, *Odyssee*, 372, Schadewaldt, op. cit. (ψ), 25, and Müller, op. cit. (at 153–63n.), 153, argue for 343. Nevertheless there are many scholars, following Kirchhoff and others, prepared to accept the old theory that the poem concluded at 296: Wilamowitz, *Untersuchungen*, 67 ff.; *Heimkehr*, 72 ff.; Schwartz, *Odyssee*, 150 ff.; Finsler, *Homer*, ii 435 ff.; R. V. Scheliha, *Patroklos* (Basle, 1943), 18 ff.; Merkelbach, *Untersuchungen*, 143; Page, *Odyssey*, 101 ff.; L. A. Stella, *Il poema di Ulisse* (Florence, 1955), 245; Kirk, *Songs*, 248; A. Dihle, *Homer-Probleme* (Opladen, 1970), 152; K. A. Garbrah, *Würzburger Jahrbücher für die Altertumswissenschaft* NF iii (1977), 7–16.

It is most unlikely that the Alexandrians, in addition to full-length manuscripts containing all 24 books, also had copies used by the rhapsodes which ended instead at xxiii 296 (as suggested first by Schwartz, *Odyssee*, 150 ff.; similarly Merkelbach, *Untersuchungen*, 143; Stössel, op. cit., 11, and others). It is equally improbable that the Alexandrians had preserved a memory that an original (Homeric) *Odyssey* had once ended at xxiii 296. There is no support for these theories to be found in the notion that Apollonius Rhodius (some time before Aristophanes and Aristarchus) had paid a tribute to the supposed ending of the *Odyssey* by quoting the last line of the (shorter) poem known to him in the final line of his own *Argonautica*: ἀσπασίως ἀκτὰς Παγασηΐδας εἰσαπέβητε, iv 1781. (As suggested by E. Meyer, *Hermes* xxix (1894), 478–9; and after him Merkelbach, *Untersuchungen*, 144 n. 1; L. E. Rossi, *Rivista di filologia e istruzione classica* xcvi (1968), 151–63. This suggestion has been refuted by E. Bethe, *Hermes* liii (1918), 444–6.) If, as seems wholly unlikely, the Alexandrians had known a shorter version of the epic, and considered this to be a superior text, regarding xxiii 297–xxiv 548 as spurious, then this would have been expressed in a form quite different from that reflected in the scholia; cf. among others Erbse, *Beiträge*, 170; latterly Apthorp, op. cit. (at 187–9n.), 62.

In contrast to the very unclear scholion on xxiii 296, there are besides two other scholia which present the views of Aristarchus quite unambiguously: schol. QV on xxiii 310–43, οὐ καλῶς ἠθέτησεν Ἀρίσταρχος τοὺς τρεῖς καὶ τριάκοντα, and schol. MV on xxiv 1, Ἀρίσταρχος ἀθετεῖ ⟨ταύτην⟩ τὴν Νέκυιαν (xxiv 1–204) κεφαλαίοις τοῖς συνεκτικωτάτοις τοῖσδε. Denying the authenticity of these two passages would make little sense if Aristarchus had already (on xxiii 296) dismissed the whole of xxiii 297–xxiv 548 as spurious; convincingly Erbse, *Beiträge*, 169–70 (but cf. Stössel, op. cit., 11; Garbrah, op. cit., 9–10). All this suggests that the Alexandrians must have understood by τέλος/πέρας something other than simply 'the end'.

In considering what, in these circumstances, the Alexandrians meant by τέλος/πέρας, Erbse's comprehensive contribution to the discussion, *Beiträge*, 166–77, deserves particular attention, despite the objections of

344

C. Moulton, op. cit., 154–7, Stössel, op. cit., 10–14, 183–5, and Garbrah, op. cit., 8 *et passim*. Erbse starts from the assumption that the verdict of the Alexandrians on the *Odyssey*'s τέλος reflects Aristotelian literary theory, and was therefore intended only to express the view that in the plan (λόγος) of the poem the reunion of Odysseus and Penelope represents the τέλος. (Aristotle himself had interpreted the λόγος of the poem differently, making the Mnesterophonia its end, *Poet.* 1455b17–24.) Even if Aristarchus had indeed athetized the whole of xxiii 297 ff., his judgement would be no more binding on subsequent generations than, for example, his atheteses of xxiii 310–43 and xxiv 1–204. The deciding factor must be how well the linguistic and stylistic features of the passage under question, as well as its subject matter, fit into the framework of the poem as established up to xxiii 296, and whether the conclusion (xxiii 297–xxiv 548) fulfils a necessary and important function in the structure of the poem as a whole. The answer to both these questions must be positive: Stanford, on xxiii 296 ff.; Heubeck, *Dichter*, 36–40; K. Fiedler, *Der Schluss der Odyssee* (diss. Marburg, 1957), with a review of earlier discussions, 1–16; F. Eichhorn, op. cit. (Introd.), 147–8; Erbse, *Beiträge*, 166–244; Moulton, op. cit., 153–69; Stössel, loc. cit.; R. Friedrich, *Stilwandel*, 164–8; D. Wender, *The Last Scenes of the Odyssey* (Leiden, 1978).

297–9. While Odysseus and Penelope retire to bed (μέν), Telemachus and the herdsmen (αὐτάρ) are calling a halt to the feast held at the behest of Odysseus (131–48). This celebration which they had organized had been more than simply a manœuvre to deceive people outside the palace: it had been held 'als festliche Wiederholung ihres (Odysseus and Penelope's) ersten Hochzeitstages' (as a celebration re-enacting their original wedding) (Hölscher, op. cit. (Introd.), 162). παῦσαν ... πόδας: 'they rested their feet from dancing; they stopped dancing'. παῦσαν δὲ γυναῖκας: sc. ὀρχουμένας.

299. εὐνάζοντο: (cf. xx 1) 'laid down to rest'. 299b = x 479b etc. Here there is a temporary pause in the action.

300–43. After a time for love Odysseus and Penelope find a time to talk, sharing the experiences each had undergone while they were apart.

300. Τὼ δ' ἐπεὶ οὖν: refers back to 295; cf. H. Reynen, *Glotta* xxxvi (1958), 42–4. ταρπῆναι here with (partitive) gen.; cf. xix 213. Literally: 'after they were satisfied by the enjoyment of longed-for love'; cf. Latacz, op. cit. (13n.), 186.

301. = *Il.* xi 643. 'They took pleasure in stories (telling each other their news)'; cf. Latacz, op. cit., 212–13.

302. ἡ μὲν: sc. ἔλεγε.

303. = xvi 29. ἐσορῶσ' ἀΐδηλον ὅμιλον: involves a deliberate play on words (oxymoron). ἀΐδηλος: 'not to be looked at, loathsome'.

304. βόας καὶ ἴφια μῆλα: = xx 51b. In apposition to πολλά; cf. *Il.* ix 446.

305. At πολλὸς δὲ the construction shifts into the passive. πίθων: 'out of the large storage jars'. ἠφύσσετο: ἀφύσσω is used only here with (ablatival) gen., but this is hardly 'linguistically objectionable' (Schwartz,

COMMENTARY

Odyssee, 137); cf. the construction πιεῖν ποτηρίου on the so-called Nestor's cup from Ischia (cf. A. Heubeck, *Archaeologia* x, 109–16, esp. 110). For πίθοι cf. ii 340–1.

307. ὀϊζύσας: (elsewhere in the *Od.* only in a similar context at iv 152) 'enduring suffering, hardship'.

308–9. ἢ δ' ἄρ' ἐτέρπετ' ἀκούουσ': 'she had pleasure in listening'; cf. Latacz, op. cit., 211. 308ᵇ–309ᵃ ~ v 271.   καταλέξαι ἅπαντα: recalling πάντ' ἔλεγ' (ὅσα . . . ὅσα τ'. ., 206–7), refers to the thoroughness and completeness of the accounts; cf. T. Krischer, op. cit. (225 n.), 156.

310–43. Here Odysseus gives the account of his adventures promised at 306–9. His tale is in the form of a recapitulation (ἀνακεφαλαίωσις) of the most important points in the series of afflictions which had befallen him (κήδεα, 306). The literary merit of these lines was already disputed in antiquity: Aristotle, *Rh.* 1417a13–15, considered the passage exemplary (παράδειγμα) (the fact that he speaks of sixty lines indicates that he had before him a somewhat more extensive version). Aristarchus, on the other hand, regarded it as un-Homeric, as can be seen from the note of a scholiast, who distances himself from the opinion expressed: οὐ καλῶς ἠθέτησεν sc. Ἀρίσταρχος. Opinion among modern scholars is also divided (for a bibliography see Ameis–Hentze, *Anhang*, iv 95). Those who regard the passage as authentic include Focke, *Odyssee*, 372 ff.; van der Valk, *Textual Criticism*, 256; J. A. Notopoulos, *TAPhA* lxxxii (1951), 91–5; Schadewaldt, op. cit. (Introd.), 25; Stanford, *Hermathena* vi (1965), 15; Lesky, *Homeros*, col. 131; M. Lang, *Hesperia* xxxviii (1969), 166–7; Erbse, *Beiträge*, 231–2; Eisenberger, *Studien*, 189; Wender, op. cit. (297 ff.n.), 15–18. Contrary views have been expressed by Wilamowitz, *Untersuchungen*, 68; *Heimkehr*, 72–3; Finsler, *Homer*, ii 436; Schwartz, *Odyssee*, 332; von der Mühll, *Odyssee*, col. 764 (*B*-poet); W. Theiler, *Mus. Helv.* vii (1950), 107 ('Interpolation in der grossen Interpolation des jetzigen Odysseeschlusses'); Marzullo, *Problema*, 120; Kirk, *Songs*, 249. On the whole the analytical critics restrict themselves to negative judgements based on aesthetic considerations which by their nature cannot be binding. There are however weighty arguments to be advanced in favour of accepting the lines as genuine. Most important is the fact that retrospection is a thoroughly Homeric technique; most obviously comparable to this passage is the (psychologically well motivated) ἀνακεφαλαίωσις of Achilles to his mother (*Il.* i 365–92). The fact that Odysseus' account, unlike that of Achilles, is given in indirect speech, does not militate against the authenticity of the passage. The timing—after Odysseus has overcome his rivals and been reunited with his wife—is entirely appropriate. And the poet has also carefully constructed parallels between Odysseus' eventful return to his own home (xiii–xxiii) and his arrival in the land of the Phaeacians, where after enduring so many trials and tribulations he had recovered his sense of identity; cf. M. Lang, loc. cit. In this respect his victory over the suitors corresponds to his success in the sporting contest with the Phaeacians; the bath to restore his looks after the slaughter of the suitors parallels the effect of his bath in viii 433–69; and finally the improvised pseudo-wedding celebrations on the reunion of Odysseus and Penelope echo the evening festivities in the palace of Alcinous, which had led to the ἀπόλογοι of ix–xii. Here the reunion with Penelope leads to an account of his wanderings which summarizes the ἀπόλογοι.

310. Odysseus tells of the Ciconian episode (ix 39–66), omitting any mention of defeat.

311. The Lotus-eaters (ix 82–104). 311ᵇ = ii 328ᵇ, Il. xviii 541ᵇ.

312-13. The Cyclopes (ix 105–566). ἔρξε: aor. of ἔρδω. ἀπετίσατο ποινήν: ~ Il. xvi 389; 'he (Odysseus) made them pay a penalty, took revenge'. 313ᵃ ~ xx 20ᵃ. ἤσθιεν: the subject is again Κύκλωψ. οὐδ' ἐλέαιρεν: =Il. xxi 147ᵇ.

314-17. Aeolus (x 1–79). 314ᵇ = ii 387ᵇ, xx 372ᵇ, Il. ix 480ᵇ. πέμπ': (imperf.!) 'he gave me safe conduct'; 315ᵇ = xi 359ᵇ. ἤην: (for ἤεν) appears elsewhere only xix 283, xxiv 343, Il. xi 808 (in every instance with enjambment); cf. Chantraine, Grammaire, i 289; Hoekstra, Modifications, 122–3. 316ᵇ–7 = iv 515ᵇ–6, v 419ᵇ–20. Odysseus does not mention the misconduct of his comrades.

318-19. The Laestrygonians (x 80–132). On 318 cf. x 82ᵃ. οἵ: refers to the name of the people (-όνες) from which the adjective Λαιστρυγονίην is derived. 319ᵇ = x 203ᵇ (nominative at ii 402ᵇ and elsewhere).

320. This line, missing from most manuscripts, and which according to the scholion was unknown to Aristarchus, is generally considered to be a late interpolation; cf. Ameis–Hentze, Anhang, iv 95; van Leeuwen, Stanford, von der Mühll, ad loc.; Schadewaldt, op. cit. (Introd.), 25 n. 26; Eisenberger, Studien, 313 n. 29; Apthorp, op. cit. (187–9 n.), 114 n. 87. Only van der Valk, Textual Criticism, 271, argues for the line's authenticity. It would appear that 320 is in fact a late addition to the text, possibly modelled on 332. πάντας: (in contrast to its counterpart πάντες, 332) is at best used very inaccurately (cf. x 128–32); and the speaker's reference to himself by name (as opposed to αὐτός, 332) seems out of place.

321. Circe (x 133–574; xii 1–143). κατέλεξε: cf. 225 n. πολυμηχανίην: (hapax) is a regular formation from -μήχανος on the same lines as ἀμηχανίη (hapax, ix 295) from ἀμήχανος; cf. Erbse, Beiträge, 189 (against Page, Odyssey, 103).

322-5. The descent to Hades (xi). 322 ~ x 512; 323 = x 492, xi 165. πάντας ἑταίρους: (those mentioned in xi 385–567) 'all his comrades-in-arms' (cf. xi 371). 325ᵃ = Il. xxii 328ᵃ; 325ᵇ = i 435ᵇ; cf. xi 152–225. νηὶ πολυκληῒδι: as at xx 382.

326. The Sirens (x 144–200). ἀδινάων: ἀδινός in loc. sense, 'close-packed, crowding round', temp. 'unceasing' (as for example of γόος); cf. V. Pisani, LfgrE s.v. Its application to people (Σειρήνων) is unusual; for older explanations see Ameis–Hentze, Anhang, iv 95–6; for a defence of the expression against the criticism of von der Mühll (Odyssee, col. 764), Page (Odyssey, 102–3) and Shipp (Studies, 359) cf. particularly Erbse, Beiträge, 189–91, and Eisenberger, Studien, 313 n. 29. The meaning is clearly

'singing unceasingly' (as observed by C. Ameis; the closest analogous usage is perhaps xvi 216); possibly to be explained as *enallage* (for Σειρήνων ἁδινὸν φθόγγον. 326ᵇ = xii 41ᵇ.

327–8. The Planctae, Scylla and Charybdis (xii 201–61, 426–46). The Planctae are described by Circe, xii 59–72, and mentioned again at xii 201– 22 as a grave danger; on the details see A. Heubeck, *WS* NF x (1976), 31–5. ἀκήριοι: (predicative with ἄνδρες) is used only here and (in a similar context) xii 98 to mean 'safe, unharmed'; elsewhere (only *Il.*) always 'lifeless; spiritless'; on the difficult questions of formation and meaning cf. Risch, *Wortbildung*, 113 n. 100 (includes bibliography).

329. The cattle of Helius (xii 361–402).

330–2. The ensuing storm and the death of Odysseus' companions (xii 403– 46). 330 ~ v 131. ψολόεντι: (only here and xxiv 539; Hes. *Th.* 515), an epithet of lightning (otherwise ἀργής) from ψόλος, 'smoke', meaning then 'smoking'; see Erbse, *Beiträge*, 191 (arguing against Page, *Odyssey*, 102). 331ᵃ = v 4ᵇ; 331ᵇ = v 133ᵇ. ἀπὸ ... ἔφθιθεν: (tmesis) has the original -εν ending (later -ησαν). πάντες ὁμῶς: as at iv 775. αὐτὸς: (contrasted with πάντες) here almost 'I alone'; cf. 168–72 n. 332ᵇ = *Il.* xii 113ᵇ; cf. also ii 316, xix 558.

333–7. Calypso (v *et passim*). Ὠγυγίην νῆσον: cf. i 85 etc. Καλυψώ: acc. (cf. Πηρώ, xi 287, Τυρώ, xi 235) see Chantraine, *Grammaire*, i 55. On 334 cf. i 14–15, 55; 334ᵇ = i 15ᵇ, ix 32ᵇ; 335ᵃ = i 15ᵃ; 335ᵇ–6 = v 135ᵇ–6, vii 256ᵇ–7. 337 ~ vii 258, lx 33.

338–41. The Phaeacians (v 382–xiii 187). 338ᵇ = xv 489ᵇ; 339–41 = v 36–8. τιμήσαντο: middle (v 36: τιμήσουσι) only here and xix 280 (= xxiii 339), xx 129, *Il.* xxii 235.

342. δεύτατον: (elsewhere only i 286, *Il.* xix 51) predicative with τοῦτ'... ἔπος. On the etymology cf. Chantraine, *Dictionnaire*, 267; and (probably better) C. J. Ruijgh, in *Acta Mycenaea* (Salamanca, 1972), i 441–50, esp. 450, who gives the derivation *δεῦ ('here') > δεύτερος > δεύτατος.

343. λυσιμελὴς: (only here and xx 57) literally 'loosing the limbs' (Risch, *Wortbildung*, 192)—a wordplay with λύων μελεδήματα (as at xx 56ᵇ = xxiii 343ᵇ); cf. Risch, *Kleine Schriften* (Berlin, 1981), 87–8. Besides 'relaxing the limbs' a secondary meaning is suggested, 'soothing away cares' (μελεδήματα (iv 650 etc.): 'worries, cares'). The phrase οἱ ... ὕπνος ... ἐπόρουσε, 'sleep took him in a surprise attack, pounced on him', criticized by Kirk, *Songs*, 207, is certainly unusual, but deserves praise rather than censure as a lively and vivid expression.

344–8. Athena causes the dawn to rise, and so restores the diurnal pattern which she has disturbed at 241–6. The connection between 241–6 and 344–8 is emphasized by the extensive similarity between 242 and 344. ἀλλ', 344, refers to 243ff. Cf. also the similarities between 347 and 244, 348ᵃ and 245ᵇ. The doubts expressed about 344–72 by Kirk, *Songs*, 249, and Schadewaldt, op. cit. (Introd.), 25 (*B*-poet), are unfounded.

345–6. 'When Athena supposed that Odysseus had had his fill of (ταρπήμεναι) both love and sleep ...'; cf. Latacz, op. cit. (13n.), 186. εὐνῆς and

ὕπνου refer back to 300 and 342-3 respectively. 345ᵇ = *Il.* xiii 8ᵇ. **ἧς**
ἀλόχου: objective gen.

347. **ἠριγένειαν:** here as at xxii 197, without Ἠώ; the epithet is used in
place of the goddess's name in the same way that κυανοχαίτης can be used
to stand for Ποσειδῶν (ix 536 etc.), ἀργεϊφόντης for Ἑρμῆς (v 49, 148 etc.),
τριτογένεια for Ἀθήνη (iii 378). There is therefore no basis for the criticism
expressed by Page, *Odyssey*, 102; cf. Erbse, *Beiträge*, 191–2; Eisenberger,
Studien, 314 n. 1.

348. **ὦρσεν:** 'prompted to rise'.

349. **ἐπὶ μῦθον ἔτελλεν:** tmesis; cf. *Il.* i 25 and other examples. Odysseus'
exact instructions to Penelope are not given until 361–5.

350-65. Odysseus reveals to Penelope his plans for the day which has just
dawned. His exposition is divided into two sections: in the first, which is
just 4 lines long (introduced by ἤδη μέν), he reviews once more the trials
they have already undergone; in the second (νῦν δ') he is more expansive,
in keeping with the situation they now face, and he outlines the measures
he proposes (354–65).

350-3. The first section of the speech is clearly distinguished from the main
part: ἀμφοτέρῳ, σὺ μέν . . . · αὐτὰρ ἐμέ. The word ἀμφοτέρῳ, here placed
so prominently at the beginning, is repeated for emphasis at the opening of
the second section (354).

350. **κεκορήμεθ'(α):** 'we have had our fill'.   **ἀέθλων:** 'troubles, sorrows'
(as at 248).

351. **ἐνθάδ'(ε):** prepares for the counterpart at 353, ἐμῆς ἀπὸ πατρίδος αἴης,
'far from . . .'.   **πολυκηδέα νόστον:** as at ix 37. νόστον | κλαίουσα is
surely not 'linguistically objectionable' as judged by Schwartz, *Odyssee*,
137.

352-3. At αὐτὰρ ἐμέ the poet abandons the participial construction, and
continues with a main clause.   **ἱέμενον:** sc. πατρίδα γαῖαν ἱκέσθαι.
πεδάασκον: (πεδάω (cf. 17), 'bind'), iterat. imperf.; probably from
*πεδάεσκον; cf. P. Wathelet, *AC* xlii (1973), 387, 393: 'persistently held me
back (far from . . .)'.

354-65. Like the first section, the second part of the speech is further divided
into two parts: first (354–8) addressing the problem of regaining and
retaining the wealth formerly theirs; then (359–65, introduced by ἀλλ')
turning to the action that needs to be taken immediately. This half is also
subdivided into two sets of instructions, balanced against each other, first
the particular responsibility of Penelope (κτήματα μέν, 355) and that of
Odysseus (μῆλα δ', 356), followed by ἥ τοι μὲν ἐγώ, 359, contrasted with
σοὶ δέ, γύναι, 361. The chiastic arrangement is striking.

354. **ἀμφοτέρῳ:** as at 351, is emphasized by being placed at the beginning:
both have suffered, and both have a part to play in the joint venture to
come.   **πολυήρατον . . . εὐνήν:** (cf. πολυήρατος γάμος, xv 126) 'to a
union both have longed for'.

355. **τά μοί ἐστι:** 'which I still own'.   **κομιζέμεν:** (inf. with imper. force
for the instructions to Penelope) 'you must care for'.

COMMENTARY

356–8. While it is Penelope's responsibility to look after the possessions (still remaining) in the palace, Odysseus will take on the task of making good their losses outside. He will restore the flocks (μῆλα), a large portion of which the suitors have 'wasted' (κατέκειραν; cf. κατεκείρετε οἶκον, xx 36). Most (πολλὰ μὲν) is to be recovered by raids (ληΐζομαι only here and i 398 and *Il.* xviii 28) and the rest (ἄλλα δ᾽) by contributions from his people (Ἀχαιοί here 'the inhabitants of Odysseus' kingdom' as at i 272, ii 77, etc.) 'until they have filled up again all the stalls' (on ἐπαύλους see below). The concept of the collective guilt of the Ithacan people is here clearly stated: responsibility for allowing the suitors to behave as they did implies responsibility for making good the damage. The idea had already been introduced in the assembly scene of ii, in the section of Telemachus' first speech addressed to the δῆμος as a whole (60–79; cf. esp. 74–8), and in the speeches of Halitherses (161–76, esp. 166–7) and Mentor (229–41, esp. 239–41); cf. W. Krehmer, *ZA* xxvi (1976), 11–22. The concept of collective responsibility does not, however, detract from the primary obligation of the suitors to make reparation, and indeed to pay further damages. The remarks of Eurymachus, xxii 55–9, are of particular interest in this context, as he refers back to the points made in the speech of ii 178–207, esp. 203–7. On the legal concepts see A. G. Tsopanakis, *EEThess.* xi (1971), 333–52.

ἐνιπλήσωσιν: cf. ἐνιπλήσῃς, xix 117.　ἐπαύλους: (*hapax*) the meaning cannot be exactly determined; the reasons lie as much in the multiplicity of meanings surrounding αὐλή (cf. H. W. Nordheider, *LfgrE* s.v.; W. Richter, *Archaeologia* H, 23–32) as in the obscurity of the compound. For details see E. Risch, *Kleine Schriften* (Berlin, 1981), 19–20, who suggests 'animal-shed (supplementary sheds?)'; id., *Wortbildung*, 214; Richter, op. cit., 30 ('stabling?'). The meaning must be approximately 'pen, fold'.

359. ἀλλ᾽(α): Odysseus interrupts his first train of thought, and turns instead to the needs of the moment.　ἦ τοι: which has the same function as μὲν (cf. 113 n.), is reinforced here with an additional μὲν.　πολυδένδρεον ἀγρὸν: as at 139, where Odysseus speaks for the first time (to Telemachus) of his plan to go to the farm. On that occasion he had given a different reason: his motive was to see Laertes again. The passages preparing for the Laertes-scene of xxiv become more frequent.

360. ὅ: = ὅς (rel.).　πυκινῶς ἀκάχηται: as at xix 95 (-ηαι), 'is weighed down by sorrow and cares'. On the difficult morphological questions surrounding this verb see M. Schmidt, *LfgrE* s.v. ἄχνυμαι, ἀκαχίζω, ἄχομαι.

361. τάδ᾽: prepares for 364–5.　ἐπιτέλλω: the extraordinary anomaly presented by the lengthening of ι here required by the metre has led some to adopt the reading ἐπιστέλλω (given only in one papyrus and the *editio Florentina*); among them, following the example of others before them (cf. Ameis–Hentze, *Anhang*, iv 96) van Leeuwen, J. Bérard, von der Mühll. Others believe that the unusual form reflects later expansion, the work of the final redactor, e.g. Schwartz, *Odyssee*, 137; Page, *Odyssey*, 102; Kirk, *Songs*, 249; Shipp, *Studies*, 359. There are, however, good reasons to retain the form unanimously given in the MS tradition: the fact that ἐπιτέλλω is a clear reference back to ἐπὶ μῦθον ἔτελλεν, 349; while ἐπιστέλλω appears to be foreign to the language of epic, and attested in the meaning 'order' only after Aeschylus. Thus Hentze, Cauer, and Stanford accept the reading ἐπιτέλλω; cf. also Erbse, Beiträge, 192–3; Eisenberger, Studien, 314 n. 1. Erbse, loc. cit., gives a convincing explanation, based on a suggestion by Stanford, for the lengthening: ἐπῑτέλλω may be supposed to have been modelled on forms such as ἐπ-ῑθύουσι, Il. xviii 172, and ἐπ-ῑθύσαντες, Od. xvi 297, which could easily have been understood as ἐπῑ-θ-. 361ᵇ = xx 131ᵇ, xxi 103ᵇ. With a concessive colouring (περ) of the participial construction Odysseus does to a certain extent excuse his giving orders to a wife whose wit would undoubtedly have ensured that she would have taken the correct measures unbidden.

362-3. This is the only instance in the Homeric poems of γὰρ used in an anticipatory sense (cf. Denniston, Particles, 69), so that the γὰρ-clause justifies a statement (here a command) that follows (364–5). This unusual use of the particle is, however, mitigated by the preparation for the order provided by τάδ᾽, at 361. The comment from Ameis–Hentze–Cauer, ad loc., is on broadly the right lines.   φάτις εἰσιν ... | ἀνδρῶν μνηστήρων: (objective gen. dependent on φάτις) 'the news of the suitors (killed by me) will spread'. Odysseus had expressed himself similarly to Telemachus (cf. κλέος φόνου; 138ᵃ = 363ᵃ), and indeed his fears turn to reality: cf. xxiv 412–13 (with ὅσσα for φάτις/κλέος). 362ᵇ = xii 429ᵇ; Il. xviii 136ᵇ; 363ᵃ =138ᵃ etc.; 363ᵇ ~ iv 537ᵇ (ἔκταθεν).

364-5. 364 = iv 751, xv 49, xix 602. The authenticity of these lines (disputed by Autenrieth, Nauck, van Leeuwen; cf. Ameis–Hentze, Anhang iv, 96–7) cannot be seriously doubted: without them the prospective τάδ᾽ of 361 is left hanging in the air. The command expressed by the infinitive ἧσθαι ('stay sitting quietly') is linked with the warnings given in the (negative) imperative, μηδέ ... ἐρέεινε. Line 365 is closely associated with vii 31 (μηδέ τιν᾽ ἀνθρώπων προτιόσσεο μηδ᾽ ἐρέεινε). The two verbs suit the context better in vii, but are perfectly appropriate here too: Penelope is to avoid contact, preferably to keep out of sight altogether, and certainly not to speak to anyone (so that no questions are asked).

366-72. Odysseus and his three companions arm themselves and leave the city. Odysseus thus puts into action the plan announced at 137–40 and 359–63, to retreat to the country holding where Laertes lives, and to await the outcome there. The lines prepare for the continuation of the action as described in xxiv 205 ff.

366. ~ Il. iii 328; 366ᵃ = viii 416ᵃ.

367. ὦρσεν: here 'roused'.

368. ἔντε᾽ ... ἀρήϊα: as at Il. x 407; cf. τεύχε᾽ ἀρήϊα, xix 4 (ἀρήϊα τεύχεα, xvi 284 etc.).   χερσὶν ἐλέσθαι: as at viii 68 etc.

369. οὐκ ἀπίθησαν: as at xv 98 etc. 369ᵇ resumes and varies the thought from 366ᵇ.   χαλκῷ: 'with the bronze weapons'; cf. δύσετο χαλκόν, xxii 113.

COMMENTARY

370. (= xxiv 501; 370ᵃ = xxii 399ᵃ). **θύρας:** here the courtyard gate which Philoetius had shut at Odysseus' behest at xxi 240–1 (κλήϊσεν . . . θύρας εὐερκέος αὐλῆς, xxi 389), not the door to the μέγαρον (xxi 236). On the details cf. S. Hiller, *WS* NF iv (1970), 14–27, esp. 21.

371. φάος: 'the (first) light of day' (cf. 347–8).   **ἐπὶ χθόνα:** 'over the earth'.

372. Athena herself intervenes to protect them by 'enveloping them in νύξ', i.e. making them invisible to other eyes. The poet uses here a motif common in the *Iliad*, that of divine intervention in human affairs in the form of spreading (or lifting) a protecting mist or darkness, variously described as ἀήρ, ἀχλύς, νέφος ἀχλύος, ὀμίχλη, but also as νύξ (cf. *Il.* v 506–6; xvi 567); cf. J. T. Kakridis, 'The Motif of the Godsent Mist in the Iliad', in *Homer Revisited* (Lund, 1971), 89–107.

BOOK XXIV: INTRODUCTION

There can hardly be any part of the *Odyssey* as it now stands which has been subjected to closer scrutiny by the analytical critics than the last book. We should not be surprised by the very different conclusions reached by such attempts to account for its genesis; this is not the place to discuss these theories in detail. Here it must suffice to note that, besides the theory that the last book is a secondary addition to an already complete *Odyssey* (e.g. R. v. Scheliha, L. A. Stella, M. Müller, H. Eisenberger), there has been considerable support for the view that the epic as we know it represents the reworking of an older, shorter poem (or a conflation of several older poems) by a redactor usually termed 'the *B*-poet', on whose poetic gifts widely differing verdicts have been passed, so that he has been variously styled 'a bungling compiler' and 'a poet with an architectural sense of construction'. Critics who hold this latter theory (and they include Wilamowitz, Schwartz, Focke, von der Mühll, Merkelbach, and Schadewaldt) attribute both the ending of the existing text and other passages (especially the so-called Telemachy, and some of the Phaeacis) to the hand of this redactor. As most of these scholars judge the appended conclusion to begin not at xxiv 1 but at xxiii 297 (or 344), most of the argument is closely linked with problems which have already been discussed in connection with the Alexandrians' verdict on xxiii 296 ff. (cf. n. ad loc.).

Our own opinion is that the 'conclusion' of the *Odyssey* was always an integral part of the compositional plan of the author who created the *Odyssey* as we know it. This judgement is based on a number of observations which can only be briefly summarized here. Most important is the fact that the narrative of the last book is so carefully prepared for throughout the rest of the poem, and in such various ways, that a failure to fulfil the expectations aroused by both direct announcements and indirect indications would have been profoundly disappointing and irritating to the poet's audience. Moreover the peculiarities of language, style, composition, and content identified in xxiv do not by any means warrant the conclusion that the passage must be attributed to a poet other than the author of the text up to xxiii 296/344; on the contrary these features of xxiv point to the same hand as in the preceding 23 books. Finally it must not be forgotten that without its conclusion the epic would lack the balance and the sense of direction, both inward and outward, towards the goal set out at the beginning, that we find in the overall structure of the composition. An abrupt breaking off, before this goal was reached, would seriously undermine the well-grounded hypothesis that the author of the *Odyssey* consciously modelled his poem on the example of the *Iliad*, particularly with regard to its external construction. So, just as after the death of Hector the events narrated in xxiii–xxiv form an essential part of the *Iliad*, so here too, in the *Odyssey*, after the death of the suitors and the reunion of the hero with his wife, a place must be given to reconciliation, the restoration of the rightful ruler to his old rights, and the re-establishment of divinely instituted order. It is an encouraging sign that in the last few decades the number of scholars defending the 'authenticity' of the conclusion to the *Odyssey* has been steadily rising. We can give here only a selection of names:

Woodhouse, *Composition*, 232–3 *et passim*.
Heubeck, *Dichter*, 36–40.
H. Hommel, 'Aigisthos und die Freier', *Studium Generale* viii (1955), 237–55.
K. Fiedler, *Der Schluss der Odyssee* (diss. Marburg, 1957).
W. B. Stanford, 'The Ending of the Odyssey', *Hermathena* xciv (1965), 5–20.
Besslich, *Schweigen*, 123–5, 98–101.
S. Bertman, 'Structural Symmetry at the End of the Odyssey', *GRBS* ix (1965), 115–22.
Bona, *Studi*, 115–22.
F. Müller, *Darstellung und poetische Funktion der Gegenstände in der Odyssee* (diss. Marburg, 1968), 116–22.
J. Dingel, 'Der 24. Gesang der Odyssee und die Elektra des Euripides', *RMus.* cxii (1969), 103–9.
Thornton, *People*, 115–19 *et passim*.
Erbse, *Beiträge*, 97–109, 166–244.
C. Moulton, 'The End of the Odyssey', *GRBS* xv (1974), 153–69.
H.-A. Stössel, *Der letzte Gesang der Odyssee* (diss. Erlangen/Nuremberg, 1975).
W. Krehmer, 'Volk ohne "Schuld"', *ZA* xxvi (1976), 11–22; D. Wender, *The Last Scenes of the Odyssey* (Leiden, 1978).
A. Heubeck, 'Zwei homerische Peirai', *ZA* xxxi (1981), 73–83.
On the older literature cf. Ameis–Hentze, *Anhang*, iv 94 ff.
A. Heubeck, *Die homerische Frage* (Darmstadt, 1974), 128–30.

The various arguments put forward by analytical and unitarian critics cannot be discussed here in detail; but an attempt will be made to respond to the different lines of argument in the notes on particular words, lines, and passages, and to present there a clear standpoint on these issues. Works listed above that do not appear also in the List of Bibliographical Abbreviations are cited in the commentary by author's name and 'op. cit. (Introd.)'.

Book xxiv is clearly divided into three sections, each of which is self-contained:

1. the so-called deutero-nekuia (1–204);
2. the recognition scene between Odysseus and Laertes (205–412);
3. the fight with the suitors' relatives, and the peace brought about by divinely imposed oaths (413–548).

BOOK XXIV: COMMENTARY

1-204. The deuteronekuia abruptly transfers the scene of the action, which had run continuously since xvi. Suddenly we are transported to a scene far away, in the underworld. The poet describes the arrival in Hades of the souls of the slaughtered suitors, and their meeting with the spirits of heroes who fought at Troy. The suitors witness an exchange between Achilles and Agamemnon; and one of them, Amphimedon, converses with Agamemnon. Changes of scene are common enough in the first two of the three main parts of the *Odyssey*; there is however no parallel in the poem for this abrupt switch from the main line of the story to a brief glimpse of events in the underworld, before resuming the action on earth at 205. Perhaps this peculiarity was one of the reasons which induced Aristarchus to reject 1–204 as spurious, especially as the lines could apparently be omitted without disturbing the continuity of the text. The scholia give us a wealth of other possible reasons for Aristarchus' negative view (ad xxiv 1); these often contrast the critics' ζητήσεις with the λύσεις of those scholars who did not feel able to support Aristarchus' judgement. The ζητήσεις concern above all the subject-matter and conceptions (including religious beliefs) presented in the athetized passage. Insofar as they continue to play a role in modern thinking on the subject they are given ad loc.; they are also discussed in detail by G. Petzl, *Antike Diskussionen über die beiden Nekyiai* (Meisenheim, 1969), 44–66; cf. further Stanford, ad loc.; Stössel, op. cit. (Introd.), 15–20; K. A. Garbrah, *Würzburger JB* NF iii (1977), 7–16. In this connection it should also be remembered that Aristarchus' well-attested athetesis of the deuteronekuia ill accords with the widely accepted interpretation of the scholion to xxiii 296, which would have us believe that he thought the authentic text of the *Odyssey* finished at that point, and so viewed the rest of the transmitted text as post-Homeric interpolation (cf. n. on xxiii 297–xxiv 548). We should not dismiss lightly the objections regarding the deuteronekuia as an integral part of the epic (Bona, *Studi*, 107–9, reviews briefly the various attempts to condemn 1–204 on analytical grounds). However, since there is no scope in the present context to discuss all these arguments in detail (cf. the bibliography given above), the following points should be noted. (1) With an account of events in the world of the dead, the nature of the subject matter precludes the kind of preparation which we find for episodes belonging to the main narrative (e.g. the revenge on the suitors, the reunion of the hero with his wife, or even the action of xxiv 205 ff.). Nevertheless we may see an indication of the scene to follow (at 1–204) at xx 345–72, especially 351–7, where the seer Theoclymenus announces to the suitors his fearful vision of the future (cf. particularly εἰδώλων δὲ πλέον πρόθυρον, πλείη δὲ καὶ αὐλή | ἱεμένων Ἔρεβόσδε ὑπὸ ζόφον 354–5); cf. Thornton, *People*, 5. (2) Admittedly, the outward form, with its interruption of the flow of action to present a scene quite remote from the main narrative, is, as has already been observed, unparalleled in the *Odyssey*; the device of switching the scene of action, used so extensively elsewhere, particularly in the first two thirds of the poem, is of a quite different order, as shown most recently by R. Friedrich, *Stilwandel*, 12–47 *et passim*. The nekuia is, however, comparable, so far as concerns the technique governing its insertion in the narrative, with Iliadic episodes which likewise are peripheral to the main action. There are many instances in the *Iliad*, as here, of an episode inserted between the departure of heroes from one place and their arrival at their destination; so that the uneventful period of their journey takes on a certain borrowed colour (for a complete catalogue of these episodes see W. Theiler, in *Festschrift f. E. Tièche* (Bern, 1947), 163 n. 52); the best-known example is probably the interval between Hector leaving the battlefield and arriving in the city, filled in with an account of the meeting between Diomedes and Glaucus (vi 119–236). The peculiar demands of the situation here, and the effect required, have prompted the author of the *Odyssey* in this one case to return to the formal episode-technique of the *Iliad*. (3) In terms of the poetic function assigned to the deuteronekuia there are two aspects we should consider, one of which lies at a much deeper level than the other. On the one hand we can observe the poet's virtuosity in building up from a series of incomplete accounts and references a full and very vivid picture of the events from the burial of Hector to the Achaeans returning home in triumph. These episodes are not related in the *Iliad*, but must surely have been treated already in poetic form in the oral tradition. The picture painted by the author is a very full one, but would nevertheless have remained incomplete without the account which Agamemnon gives Achilles of the latter's own death and burial (36–94), especially since precisely this element in the saga, as neo-analytic research has shown, in all probability already played a significant part in pre-Homeric heroic poetry. A more important consideration, however, is that the poet was concerned from the very beginning to set the fate of Odysseus and his family against the background of the vicissitudes of Agamemnon's house. This contrast in the fates of the two heroes pervades the entire work. It is particularly emphasized in the opening books (i, iii, iv) and at the centre of the poem (xi). Now, after Odysseus' return home, reunion with his wife, and revenge on the suitors, the poet obviously wishes to remind us of this contrast. It is deepened by the introduction of another hero, the greatest of all who fought at Troy, Achilles (cf. the earlier reference at xi 467–540). The ἀρετή of Penelope, who was both clever and courageous, can be highlighted once more, for the last time, by Agamemnon. Odysseus, who suffered most and longest, can at the end of his labours enjoy an ὄλβος (192), which is not only the diametric opposite of the ὀλοὴ μοῖρα of Agamemnon (28), but which even outshines the ὄλβος of Achilles (36). In the epic treatment of the *Odyssey*'s essentially novelistic subject-matter this comparison of the heroes' fates to round off the poem is as necessary as the Telemachy (or, as we shall see, the account of the meeting with Laertes, and the σπονδαί with the Ithacans). Cf. U. Hölscher, 'Die Atridensage in der Odyssee', in *Festschrift f. R. Alewyn* (Cologne/Graz, 1967), 1–16, esp. 9–12; Thornton, *People*, 4–10; R. Friedrich, *Stilwandel*, 160–1; Stössel, op. cit. (Introd.), 32–4; W. Krehmer, *Gnomon* xlviii (1967), 538–9; Wender, op. cit. (Introd.), 19–44.

1–4. Ἑρμῆς: the contracted form of the god's name is given here (as at v 54 etc.), although uncontracted Ἑρμείας (as at 10) is used more frequently. This should not be regarded as an 'abnormality' (Shipp, *Studies*, 360); cf. Meister, *Kunstsprache*, 154–6. On the pre-history of the name-form cf. (besides Meister, loc. cit.) after the decipherment of the linear B tablets, among others, Hoekstra, *Modifications*, 40 n. 1; C. J. Ruijgh, *RÉG* lxxx (1967), 12; Ventris–Chadwick, *Documents*, 543 (root form *e-ma-a₂* /*Hermāhās/*). The god's epithet κυλλήνιος is derived from his birthplace, on the Arcadian Κυλλήνης ὄρος (cf. *h.Merc.* 1–10), which was also a centre of his cult. The fact that this is the only occurrence of the epithet in Homeric epic does not support an analytical position, especially since his other titles δῶτορ ἑάων (viii 335) and σῶκος (*Il.* xx 72) are also *hapax legomena*. More striking is the fact that the god is here assigned the role of ψυχοπόμπος, leading the souls of the departed down to Hades. Nowhere else in Homer is this office associated with Hermes; this is in keeping with the idea that on leaving the body ψυχαί normally passed directly to the underworld without the services of a guide (vi 11, x 560, etc.; and numerous examples in the *Iliad*) or occasionally led by κῆρες θανάτοιο (xiv 207 cf. *Il.* ii 302, xiii 416). Moreover xxiv 1 ff. does not take account of the idea that the souls of the dead could not pass into Hades until the body has been buried, although this particular idea is confined in the epics to the fates of Patroclus (cf. esp. *Il.* xxiii 69–74) and Elpenor (*Od.* xi 53–5, xi 51–80, xii 9–15). We should hardly be surprised that xxiv embodies yet another variant of the many ideas on the fate of the soul after death, as there were clearly many conflicting views, and no generally accepted orthodoxy on the subject in ancient Greece (cf. the excellent remarks of O. Regenbogen, in *Kleine Schriften* (Munich, 1961), 17). Here the poet clearly saw good reason (primarily, poetic reason) to introduce Hermes as the conductor of souls. For the situation here is quite unusual: instead of a single ψυχή, here is a whole crowd of ψυχαί, all travelling a common path to Hades. It is quite reasonable to give this group a guide. Hermes was pictured in ancient religious thought, which is partly echoed in the epics, as the guide par excellence, and this makes him particularly suited to the role assigned to him here. Whether this was an invention of the poet's, or whether, as seems more likely (cf. Erbse, *Beiträge*, 234), Hermes' πομπὴ ψυχῶν was a part of common religious belief in the archaic period, is almost impossible to determine, and in the last analysis not of any great importance. In addition the poet may have been influenced by the wish to offer a counterpart in xxiv to the co-operation between Athena and Hermes portrayed at the beginning of the poem (i, v): as Athena brings Odysseus and his men safely to Laertes, so Hermes conducts the souls of the suitors to Hades; cf. Thornton, *People*, 4–5. A poetic model for the scene can, however, be seen in the last book of the *Iliad*, which indeed influenced the concluding scenes of the *Odyssey* in several respects. In the *Iliad* Hermes accompanies old Priam on his visit to Achilles, ensures his safety, and helps him on the return journey to the city (with the body of Hector). The parallel between the escort's role in both passages is underlined by the poet's use here (incidentally as in v) of quotation from the *Il.*: 3ᵇ–4 (= v 47ᵇ–48) = *Il.* xxiv 343ᵇ–4. But whereas the lines are firmly rooted in context in the *Iliad* (Hermes uses his wand in the manner described, to send men to sleep at 445–7, and to wake the sleeping Priam at 677–89) here xxiv 2ᵇ–4 are merely ornamental (in fact an *epitheton ornans*, cf. Stössel, op. cit. (Introd.), 40–1). The magic wand of the Iliadic Hermes has become almost a shepherd's staff as the god keeps his 'flock' of souls together. **ἐξεκαλεῖτο:** sc. δόμων or μεγάρου Ὀδυσσῆος. 3ᵃ = v 233ᵃ etc. **θέλγει:** 'enchants', here almost 'closes'. Constr.: ἀνδρῶν ... ὧν (sc. ὄμματα θέλγει) ἐθέλει. τοὺς δ' (demonstr. 'the others') ... ἐγείρει: still belongs to the rel. τῇ-clause. **ὑπνώοντας:** (only found in this line = v 48, both from *Il.* xxiv 344): the form has not been satisfactorily explained; cf. Meister, *Kunstsprache*, 90–2; Chantraine, *Grammaire*, i 366; Shipp, *Studies*, 99. It can hardly be formed from (factitive) ὑπνόω (which is not found in Homer); more likely an artificial creation from ὕπνος.

5. τῇ (sc. ῥάβδῳ) ῥ̓ ἄγε (sc. ψυχάς) resumes ἐξεκαλεῖτο ... ἔχε δὲ ῥάβδον. **τρίζουσαι:** refers, as at *Il.* xxiii 100–1 (ψυχή ... ᾤχετο τετριγυῖα) to the murmurous fluttering of the souls in flight, as is apparent from the comparison at 7–9.

6-8. The tightly controlled form of the comparison (cited in Plato, *R.* iii 387) rests on the key word τρίζειν which prepares for 6–8 (τρίζουσαι, 5), stands at the centre of the simile itself (τρίζουσαι, 7), and rounds it off in the ὥς-clause (τετριγυῖαι, 9). The noisy flight of the souls is likened to the sound of bats (νυκταρίδες) unsettled and fluttering around (ποτέονται) in the corner (loc. μυχοῖ lies behind μυχῷ; cf. Ruijgh, *Élément*, 164) of a large cave (6ᵇ = xiii 363ᵇ) when one (τις) of the colony (ὁρμαθός: *hapax*, from ὅρμος, 'chain') falls from the rock face, and the others secure their hold on each other above (ἀνά). The passage recalls xi 605–6: κλαγγὴ νεκύων ἦν οἰωνῶν ὥς, | πάντοσ' ἀτυζομένων. The similarity is particularly striking because the Greeks classified bats as birds (cf. Stössel, op. cit. (Introd.), 41–2). The resemblance to the similes of xxii 384–8 and 468–71 was pointed out by von der Mühll, *Odyssee*, col. 765. **ἀποπέσησιν:** with striking metrical lengthening of ἀ- as in ἀπονέεσθαι (ii 195 etc.) and a number of other forms; Wyatt's explanation, *Lengthening*, 84–7, is probably to be preferred to that of A. Hoekstra, *Mnemosyne* xxxi (1978), 1–26, esp. 18–20.

9-10. τετριγυῖαι ἄμ' ἦισαν: picks up τρίζουσαι ἔποντο (5) as ἄρχε ... σφιν does ἄγε κινήσας. **ἀκάκητα:** (elsewhere only *Il.* xvi 185, also with reference to Hermes) is one of those formulaic divine/heroic epithets in

COMMENTARY

-τᾰ (where we would normally expect -της) which are probably petrified vocative forms; for further details see Risch, *Wortbildung*, 37–8. The etymology and meaning are obscure; a detailed bibliography is given by W. Spoerri, *LfgrE* s.v. εὐρώεις (as at xxiii 322): cf. x 512n.

11–14. The mythological–geographical details of the route to Hades given here are certainly striking. They have frequently given rise to analytical speculation (cf. for example Kirk, *Songs*, 249). Leaving aside the phrase πὰρ δ' ἴσαν Ὠκεανοῦ τε ῥοὰς, 11 (for which cf. παρὰ ῥόον Ὠκεανοῖο ᾖομεν, xi 21–2; cf. also x 508–11) and the mention of the meadow of asphodel as the place where the souls will stay (13–14; xi 539, 573), we find here topographical particulars such as Λευκὰς πέτρη, Ἡελίοιο πύλαι, and δῆμος ὀνείρων, which do not appear elsewhere in Homeric epic. On the other hand xxiv omits such details as the ἄλσεα Περσεφόνης (x 509–10), the Cimmerian country and people (xi 14–15) and the river which souls have to cross to reach Hades (*Il.* xxiii, 72–3; *Od.* x 513–15). All this however does not argue against attributing both nekuiai to one and the same author, who must have had available to him a wealth of legendary and religious material from epic and oral tradition, from which he could make his selection. There would be a difficulty here only if the details given in xxiv contradicted the general concept of the underworld prevalent in the archaic period; but there is in fact no contradiction between the account here and popular geographical mythology. The 'Leucadian Rock' is certainly not Cape Leukatas on the island of Leukas, or indeed any other spot in the real world (cf. R. Hennig, *Klio* xxxv (1942), 331–40). Like the underworld itself, and its surroundings, it lies in the mythical west, by the stream of Oceanus (cf. W. Karl, *Chaos und Tartaros in Hesiods Theogonie* (diss. Erlangen/Nuremberg, 1967), 95–106). It may in early times have become proverbial, 'threshold of death' (cf. Sappho's leaf from the Leucadian Rock; Euripides, *Cyc.*, 163–7); cf. Wilamowitz, *Untersuchungen*, 73; Ameis–Hentze, *Anhang*, iv 99; Ameis–Hentze–Cauer, and Stanford, ad loc.; E. Janssens, 'Leucade et le pays des morts', *AC* xxx (1961), 381 ff.; Erbse, *Beiträge*, 235. The sun god steers his team of horses through the πύλαι Ἡελίοιο after the sun has set. These gates are also thought of as being in the west, exactly opposite the point where the sun rises in the morning (iii 1, xii 3–4); cf. Ameis–Hentze–Cauer, and Stanford, ad loc.; W. Karl, op. cit., 103; and the different (and hardly credible) views of A. Lesky, 'Aia', *WS* lxiii (1948), 31 (= *Ges. Schriften* (Bern/Munich, 1966), 33). We should not be surprised by the fact that the δῆμος ὀνείρων is also placed in the mythical west. The φῦλον ὀνείρων is descended from Nyx (Hes. *Th.*, 212), who lives in the west; a full and convincing account is in W. Karl, op. cit., 69–94.   πὰρ ... ῥοὰς: if the interpretation adopted here is correct (cf. xi 14–19n.), then only the second of the alternatives offered by Chantraine, *Grammaire*, i 123, can be correct, the first being 'au delà du cours de l'Océan...', and the second, 'le long de...'.   εἴδωλα καμόντων is (like xi 476b) obviously taken from *Il.* xxiii 72b. The exact meaning, and genesis, of this formulaic expression are difficult to

360

determine. In any case καμόντων here almost has the meaning of θανόντων ('images of those who have their labours behind them', O. Regenbogen, op. cit. (1–4n.), 17); for a detailed discussion see W. Bergold, *Der Zweikampf des Paris und Menelaos* (Bonn, 1977), 96–7, who refers to *Il.* iii 274–9, where the reading καμόντας is preferred.

15-22. On arriving in Hades the souls of the suitors 'discover' (εὗρον: 'they found before them', 'they met') the spirits of Achilles and those heroes who were particularly close to him; they see this group joined by the souls of Agamemnon to the comrades slain with him and then witness a conversation between Achilles and Agamemnon (23–98). Only then does Hermes bring the suitors in closer (ἀγχίμολον . . . ἦλθε, 99), and one of them, Amphimedon, is brought into the conversation (99–204). There is no contradiction between 15ff. and 99ff., as suggested by, among others, Page, *Odyssey*, 119. The poet is rather using here (as in other passages) an epic pattern drawn from tradition, and clearly discernible in the *Iliad*; cf. *Il.* xviii 1ff., where Antilochus finds Achilles by the ships (εὗρε, 3) just when the latter is pondering the fate of Patroclus (6–15), and then approaches (ἐγγύθεν ἦλθεν, 16) to give Achilles the tragic news. Similarly in xviii 368ff. Thetis comes upon (εὗρ', 372) Hephaestus as he is finishing a work of art (373–80), and then places herself at his side (ἐγγύθεν ἦλθε, 381), where he notices her. And finally an example from the *Odyssey* itself: Odysseus looks for his father, and finds him in the garden (εὗρεν, xxiv 226); he watches the old man at work, and considers what he should do (227–42), until finally he approaches (παριστάμενος, 243) and addresses him. The whole problem is correctly analysed by, among others, Thornton, *People*, 5ff.; Erbse, *Beiträge*, 236; Eisenberger, *Studien*, 324 n. 17; Fenik, *Studies*, 78–80, 96 (with additional examples). Other critical objections have concerned the chronological difficulties: apparently the souls of Achilles and Agamemnon meet for the first time only now, after so many years (although this encounter ought to have taken place before Odysseus' own descent to Hades); and Achilles seems to know nothing of his burial; cf. Kirk, *Songs*, 249. But the poet was prepared to risk this difficulty for the sake of the poetic advantages of the passage, which lie in the content of this exchange of news in the underworld: once more (before the poem comes to its conclusion) the good fortune of Odysseus and the fame of Penelope are highlighted by contrast with the fates of the other heroes; cf. Hölscher, op. cit. (1–204n.), 1–16, esp. 9–12; Thornton, *People*, 7ff.; Stössel, op. cit. (Introd.), 43–77; Wender, op. cit. (Introd.), 34–44.

15. 15ᵇ = xi 465ᵇ, *Il.* i 1ᵇ, etc.

16-18. = xi 468–70; cf. also iii 109–12. Here and in these other passages Antilochus, son of Nestor, is placed on the same level as Patroclus and Ajax (cf. also 73–9), whereas in the *Iliad* he is given a subsidiary role (both in general and in relation to Achilles, his principal function being to bring the news of Patroclus' death); furthermore, the poet of the *Odyssey* knows the story of his death at the hands of Memnon, son of Eos (iv 187–8; cf. also xi 522). All this indicates that the poet knew an extended version of the saga later recorded in the post-Homeric *Aethiopis*, in which Achilles killed Memnon in revenge for Antilochus' death, and thereby consciously brought forward his own death; cf. the collection of testimonia and fragments in Bethe, *Odyssee*, 167–9. However, since the author of the *Odyssey* cannot have known the actual *Aethiopis*, a written composition of later date, his knowledge of events not directly mentioned in the *Iliad*, but presupposed by that epic (as has been clearly shown by neo-analytical research), must have come from familiarity with a poetic treatment of the saga in pre-Homeric oral tradition. Here he combines, and seeks to reconcile, this material with the account of events given in the *Iliad*. Material from this pre-Iliadic epic, which we must postulate, and which also appears to have included a description of Achilles' funeral, has also been used in the account which Agamemnon gives to Achilles, 36–94 (a passage which reads like a summary of a fuller epic narrative). On the methodology and results of neo-analytical research cf. the instructive and comprehensive account given by W. Kullmann, 'Zur Methode der Neoanalyse in der Homerforschung', *WS* xv (1981), 5–42 (with a very full bibliography); on the particular problems of xxiv 36–97 see the cogent discussion by H.-A. Stössel, op. cit. (Introd.), 44–8.

19. ὥς: here approx. 'so, as indicated'. The heroes already named, Patroclus, Antilochus, and Ajax (οἱ μὲν) form a circle round Achilles (κεῖνον); cf. Eisenberger, *Studien*, 324 n. 17.

20–2. = xi 387–9. The spirits of Agamemnon and his companions approach this first group (ἀγχίμολον), just as they approached Odysseus in the first nekuia. On 22 cf. Agamemnon's description at xi 409–26, and Proteus' account to Menelaus, iv 512–37.

23. ~ 105.

24–202. The contributions of the two pairs of speakers are balanced in terms of length, as well as in content and attitude: Achilles, 24–34, Agamemnon, 36–97; Agamemnon again, 106–19, and Amphimedon, 121–90. Together the speeches form the preparation for, and justification of, Agamemnon's summing up of the fate of Odysseus (192–202), which is the point of the whole scene; elucidated by Thornton, *People*, 7 ff.; Fenik, *Studies*, 148–9.

24–35. Achilles laments the bitter fate of his great adversary, the most powerful commander at Troy, Agamemnon. He would rather have wished him a glorious death in the field. We should not be troubled by the illogicality presupposed by this scene, an illogicality which has indeed only rarely excited comment until recently. On the one hand Achilles' speech implies that strangely the souls of Agamemnon and Achilles are now meeting for the first time in Hades, nearly ten years after the death of the former; on the other hand Achilles is clearly aware of the fate which befell Agamemnon on his arrival home. The poet's intention here is to provide a particularly vivid contrast between the ὄλβος of Achilles, described at length by Agamemnon (36), and the tragic end of the career of Agamemnon, which would have been well known to his audience, and which therefore needs only to be briefly indicated by Achilles. The difference between the two

heroes here is that Achilles found a glorious death in battle, and was buried with the highest honours.
24. 24ᵇ = vii 164ᵇ etc. On the construction of περὶ + gen. (ἀνδρῶν ἡρώων) cf. xxiii 166–7 n. The antithesis to the μὲν clause (24–7) begins at ἤ τ' ἄρα, 28.
26. ~ xix 110.
27. = iii 220.
28–9. ἤ τ(ε): introduces here (as often elsewhere) the antithesis to the preceding statement: 'now, however'; cf. Ruijgh, τε épique, 798.   ἄρα: 'as it turned out'.   καί σοι ... ὀλοή: 'it was your fate too that μοῖρα ὀλοή (death) would claim you before your time, prematurely (πρωί)'. ἀλεύεται: must be aorist subj.; cf. Chantraine, Grammaire, i 369; Shipp, Studies, 360.
30. ὡς ὄφελες: (... ἐπισπεῖν) 'how you should have ...', i.e. 'how much I wish that you had ...'.   τιμῆς ἀπονήμενος: aor. middle; Chantraine, Grammaire, i 382.   ἧς περ ἄνασσες: 'in enjoyment of the royal honours, the royal state which you held'. On ἀνάσσειν τιμῆς cf. LfgrE col. 796. 30; the same combination is found elsewhere only in the problematical Il. xx 180, on which see E. Heitsch, Aphroditehymnus, Aeneas und Homer (Göttingen, 1966), 80; H. Erbse, RMus. cx (1967), 11 ff.
31. 31ᵃ = 27ᵃ etc.; 31ᵇ (~ 22ᵇ) = Il. ii 359ᵇ etc.
32–3. = i 239–40, xiv 369–70.
34. ~ v 312 (after Il. xxi 281).
35. = 191.
36–97. Agamemnon praises the ὄλβος of Achilles, which consists in what Agamemnon is to report, his glorious death and the high honours accorded at his funeral. Agamemnon's account is one of those many passages, most of them in direct speech, which together give a comprehensive picture of the Postiliaca (including the return of the heroes). It can hardly be doubted that the poet is here basing his account on an oral epic treatment of the material (a pre-Homeric 'Aithiopis' or 'Achilleis'). It is no less probable that the author of the Iliad had drawn important elements of xvi-xxiii from the same source in making the man who took Achilles' place, Patroclus, bear Achilles' fate, as correctly perceived in principle by D. Mülder, Die Ilias und ihre Quellen (Berlin, 1910), 159 ff. Our poet was therefore familiar with both the pre-Homeric presentation of the material, and its transformation in the Iliad; we shall have cause to refer to both 'sources'. It is however practically certain that he does not directly 'quote' from either, but simply uses them as a model for various motifs. Since he rarely lifts material word for word from the Iliad (although cf. 39–40n.), then it is probably reasonable to assume that the same applies to the use made in xxiv 36–97 of any pre-Homeric Aethiopis, as A. Dihle, Homer-Probleme (Opladen, 1970), 17 ff., has emphasized; for a different view cf. H. Pestalozzi, Die Achilleis als Quelle der Ilias (Erlenbach and Zurich, 1945), passim; W. Kullmann, Die Quellen der Ilias (Wiesbaden, 1960), 29–50 passim.
36. The line is phrased in anticipation of 192, which opens Agamemnon's

speech of 192–202, where he contrasts the ὄλβος of Achilles with the immensely greater ὄλβος of Odysseus; cf. van der Valk, *Textual Criticism*, 239. 36ᵇ (= *Il.* ix 485ᵇ etc.) used in the *Odyssey* only here.

37. The ὅς-clause (from here to σεῖο, 39) is used with causal sense. Agamemnon chooses his words with reference to his own οἴκτιστος θάνατος (34). **ἐν Τροίῃ:** 'in the area round the city of Troy'. Ἄργος here probably refers to the whole of Greece, so that ἑκὸς Ἄργεος means 'far from the (Greek) homeland'; cf. G. Steiner, *LfgrE* s.v. (with extensive bibliography). **ἀμφὶ ... σ':** used in a purely local sense, in contrast to περὶ σεῖο (39), where the body is the prize for which they fight.

39–40. 39ᵃ ~ *Il.* xvi 775ᵃ; 39ᵇ–40 = *Il.* xvi 775ᵇ–6; cf. also *Il.* xvii 26–7: αὐτὸς δ' ἐν κονίῃσι μέγας μεγαλωστὶ τανυσθεὶς | κεῖτο. The three similar passages (of *Il.* xvi, xviii, *Od.* xxiv) have sometimes been thought to echo a passage from a pre-Homeric oral composition, referring to Achilles; cf. Pestalozzi, op. cit., 18; Schadewaldt, *Welt*, 168 n. 65; Kullmann, op. cit., 38. This is surely not an instance of the repeated use of a traditional phrase from the rich store of formulaic expression. Rather we have here the adoption of a phrase formulated with regard to a specific situation. This non-formulaic poetic phrase seems to have been coined originally with reference to Cebriones, Hector's charioteer from *Il.* viii onwards. The expression λελασμένος ἱπποσυνάων fits Cebriones exactly; it is not so meaningful, though it is not inappropriate, when used of Achilles; cf. earlier opinions expressed by W. Diehl, *Die wörtlichen Beziehungen zwischen Ilias und Odyssee* (Greifswald, 1938), 124; U. Hölscher, *Gnomon* xxvii (1955), 395; A. Dihle, op. cit. (36–7 n.), 22–5; Erbse, *Beiträge*, 193–4 (and n. 72). **στροφάλιγγι (κονίης):** only here and *Il.* xvi 775, xxi 503; στροφάλιγξ, 'whirl', is derived from verb στρέφω; cf. Risch, *Wortbildung*, 175. **μέγας μεγαλωστί:** (only here and *Il.* xvi 776, xviii 26): 'great in your greatness'; adv. μεγαλωστί is an *ad hoc* artificial creation from μεγάλως; cf. Risch, *MH* xxix (1972), 69 n. 10 (= *Kleine Schriften* (Berlin, 1981), 171 n. 10); *Wortbildung*, 366. **ἱπποσυνάων:** ἱπποσύνη, hapax in the *Odyssey*: 'art of steering a chariot'.

41. **πρόπαν ἦμαρ:** 'the whole day'. The genesis of this much discussed phrase, in which προ- obviously strengthens the meaning of πᾶν, has been convincingly explained by Leumann, *Wörter*, 98–9: it begins with pre-Homeric formulations such as *πρὸ πανῆμαρ (normal coalescence of πᾶν ἦμαρ) ἐμαρνάμεθα (or δαίνυντο), in which πρὸ was loosely associated with the verb ('we fought on'); in the development of the epic language the phrasing was completely restructured to πρό-παν ἦμαρ producing this most unusual function of προ- in πρόπαν.

42. 42ᵃ = *Il.* vii 376ᵃ, xv 58ᵃ. **παῦσεν:** here used in an absolute sense, 'he made an end of it'.

44. ~ *Il.* xviii 233.

45. **λιαρῷ:** (cf. v 268 etc.) here 'lukewarm'; on the cleansing of a corpse with ἄλειφαρ (attested in Myc.: *a-re-pa* /aleiphar/), here 'oil for anointing', cf. M. Andronikos, *Archaeologia* W, 3, 25. For the detail of the scene

which is only indicated in 44–5 cf. the extended description *Il.* xviii
343–53.

46. 46ᵃ = iv 523ᵃ; on 46ᵇ cf. iv 198 and above all the detailed account at *Il.* xxiii
135–53 (which refers to the burial of Patroclus). On the offering of hair in
ancient ritual cf. Andronikos, op. cit., 18–20.

47–9. Thetis rises from the sea with the Nereids (ἀλίῃσιν) to raise the lament
(βοή). This is surely a motif from the old 'Aethiopis', which must have
exerted a similar influence on the *Iliad*'s description of how Thetis, with the
Nereids, raises the lament (xviii 51), and emerges from the sea to comfort
her son weeping for Patroclus (xviii 65 ff.). ἐπὶ πόντον ὀρώρει:
'echoed across the sea'. On 49 cf. xviii 88, *Il.* iii 34, xiv 506; and the similar
reaction of the Myrmidons when Thetis brought Achilles his weapons (*Il.*
xix 14–15). Cf. G. Kurtz, *Darstellungsformen menschlicher Bewegung in der Ilias*
(Heidelberg, 1966), 143 n. 71.

50–7. These lines demonstrate clearly that the poet was not simply following
a pre-Homeric epic. The role given to Nestor here exactly corresponds to
the way he is presented in the *Iliad*. There are also parallels with some of
the scenes in the *Iliad* which can hardly be fortuitous. The readiness to flee
on board the ships as fast as possible recalls the situation in *Il.* ii where the
Achaeans are strongly inclined to return home (142–54), and it is only with
the greatest difficulty that Odysseus dissuades them (182 ff.). Nestor's intervention here is introduced in the same terms as at *Il.* vii 325–6 and ix 94–5,
where he also gives good counsel to the Achaeans. Finally 54 is modelled
on *Il.* iii 82; cf. Diehl, op. cit. (39–40n.), 125.

50. As early as Aristarchus (schol. on 1) there has been felt to be some inconsistency between 43 and 50ᵇ (= *Il.* vii 432ᵇ): ἄλογον δὲ καὶ ἐπὶ τῶν νεῶν
ὄντων αὐτῶν λέγειν, ὅτι δείσαντες τὰς Νηρηίδας ἔφυγον ἐπὶ τὰς ναῦς; cf.
also Garbrah, op. cit. (1–204n.), 12, 14. There is in fact no such inconsistency: the Achaeans first bring the body back to the camp by the ships,
where, at a given time, they carry out the rites for the dead; when Thetis
appeared, however, they were on the point of running to the ships to
escape. (ἐπὶ νῆας can mean both.) For a correct interpretation see Stössel,
op. cit. (Introd.), 49–50.

51. 51ᵇ = ii 188ᵇ (which refers to the prophet Halitherses).

52. ἀγορήσατο: ('he spoke in the assembly') fits better in the context of the
passages 'cited', *Il.* vii 326 and ix 95; cf. Diehl, op. cit. (39–40n.), 125.

54. μὴ φεύγετε: the present form (similarly ἴσχεσθ', 'Halt!') is certainly
strange in this context since the Achaeans had not yet started to flee, cf.
Shipp, *Studies*, 361. But here too the language is influenced by the Iliadic
model cited here: ἴσχεσθε and μὴ βάλλετε ('Cease firing!'), the parallel
words at *Il.* iii 82, make perfect sense in their context.

55. = 47.

56. ἀντιόωσα: (metrical lengthening from -ώσας -άουσα) + gen. 'caring
about, concerned for'.

57. This line describes the reaction to 54 (ἴσχεσθ'–ἔσχοντο) just as *Il.* iii 84
follows on from 82 (57ᵃ = *Il.* iii 84ᵃ). There the Achaeans gave up the μάχη

(throwing missiles and shooting at Hector), and so here, in response to Nestor's appeal, μὴ φεύγετε, they abandon their φόβος (*hapax* in the *Odyssey*), i.e. the hasty withdrawal to the ships to escape. The idea that here, exceptionally, φόβος means 'panic, fear' rather than 'flight in panic' cannot be accepted; cf. J. Gruber, *Über einige abstrakte Begriffe des frühen Griechischen* (Meisenheim, 1963), 19; Stössel, op. cit. (Introd.), 50–1.

58. ἁλίοιο γέροντος: Nereus.

59. 59ᵃ = iv 719ᵃ etc.; 59ᵇ = *Il.* xvi 670ᵇ, 680ᵇ (in a similar context). Here σε must be supplied: 'they dressed you in immortal robes (presumably chiton and pharos; cf. *Il.* xxiv 580–1).'

60. This passage has given rise to a number of questions. Aristarchus objected that the reference to nine Muses is un-Homeric. In fact elsewhere in the *Odyssey* there is reference to only one Muse (i 1, vii 63, 73, 481, 483). The situation is a little different in the *Iliad*, which in some places recognizes the single Muse ([i 1], ii 761), but elsewhere refers to several (but not a fixed number; i 604, ii 484, 491, 594, 598, xi 218, xiv 508, xvi 112). The question of whether Hesiod, who refers always to nine Muses (*Th.* 60, 77–9, 916–17), was influenced by *Od.* xxiv 60, or whether in fact both poets were drawing on material from an older source (an 'Aethiopis'?), has been much discussed by Erbse, *Beiträge*, 194–7. He offers important arguments in favour of the former possibility: ἐννέα πᾶσαι, as had already been observed by Ameis–Hentze–Cauer, ad loc., can at 60 only mean 'nine in all' (a substantial number, made clearer by the typical number nine); on the other hand Hesiod may have seen an opportunity to change the meaning of πᾶσαι, here used as a predicate, into a descriptive adjective ('all nine Muses'), and so fix the number of Muses at nine in conformity with his triadic and enneadic scheme. 60ᵇ (= *Il.* i 604ᵇ) is probably an inherited formulaic expression (< ἀμειβόμεναι ϝοπὶ καλῇ), as has been convincingly argued by Chantraine, *Grammaire*, i 124, and Hoekstra, *Modifications*, 56 n. 3. It is not, however, possible to determine exactly the meaning of ἀμείβεσθαι in this expression. In the context of the passage of the *Iliad*, on which this is based, it is possible to envisage Apollo as a sort of cantor (ἀοιδὸς ἐξάρχων) singing verses to which the Muses respond in chorus. In the different context of 60 the poet appears to have given the phrase a different meaning: the situation pictured may perhaps be most closely compared with the lament for Hector, *Il.* xxiv 720–2. Despite the difficulties in this passage (721ᵇ may be corrupt) it is quite clear that the poet pictures ἀοιδοί, who may be professional musicians, performing as θρήνων ἔξαρχοι, while the women ἐπιστενάχοντο, i.e. respond, as a kind of chorus, with cries of mourning between the verses (θρῆνοι) of the ἀοιδοί. In the light of this scene it seems reasonable to suppose that at xxiv 58–62 the Muses act as ἀοιδοί (θρήνεον, 61), while the role taken in the earlier passage by the Trojan women is here assigned to the Nereids (οἴκτρ' ὀλοφυρόμεναι, 59); as interpreted by Ameis–Hentze–Cauer, ad loc. The half-line taken from *Il.* i 604 is thus seen not to be used 'proprio sensu' in its new context. For an extensive discussion of ritual lament see Andronikos,

Archaeologia W, 12; M. Wegner, *Archaeologia* U, 29 and 34; G. Petersmann, 'Die monologische Totenklage der Ilias', *RMus* cxvi (1973), 3–16. The mourning Nereids were probably a feature of pre-Iliadic descriptions of the burial of Achilles (which may have prompted the poet of the *Iliad* to introduce a Nereid scene in xviii). This does not, however, necessarily follow for the Muses, and these may have been introduced by the author of the *Odyssey*.

62. The exact meaning of the γὰρ-clause cannot be exactly determined, largely because of the uncertainty of the meaning of the verb. (ὑπ)-ὤροϱε is a reduplicated, thematic aorist from ὄρνυμι. As with the analogous forms ἤγαγεν and ἤϱαϱεν, we would expect here a transitive meaning ('set in vigorous motion'); and indeed in most instances ὤϱοϱε certainly is transitive, *Il.* ii 146, *Od.* iv 712, xxiii 222, and even *Od.* xix 201, where the object 'north wind' can easily be supplied. It is true that at *Il.* xiii 78, *Od.* viii 539 and xxiv 62 one is more inclined to give the verb an intransitive sense ('rose up'), which could have developed under the influence, for example, of the intr. perf. ὄϱωϱε; cf. Ameis–Hentze–Cauer, ad loc.; Schwyzer, *Grammatik*, i 749; Chantraine, *Grammaire*, i 397–8; H. Rix, *IF* lxx (1965), 29–49, esp. 29–30 n. 14; Shipp, *Studies*, 366. However, in all three cases, with different arguments, it is possible to show that the verb has a transitive character. Thus, with ὑπώϱοϱε at 62 we should supply an object which, though not explicitly stated, is to be understood from the context: 'The clear-singing Muse so roused [the mourning of the Argives]'. This interpretation avoids the very dubious assumption that μοῦσα here means exceptionally 'the song (of the Muses)'; and λίγεια applied to a person is entirely plausible (cf. λιγὺς ἀγορητής, *Il.* i 248 etc.). One detail does disturb: the use of the singular. Should it be understood as a collective? Or does the poet mention only the one Muse, the leader, as representing the whole group (ἐξάϱχουσα)? Cf. A. Heubeck, 'Homerisch ὤϱοϱε', *Zeitschr. f. vergl. Sprachforschung* xcvii (1984), 88–95, esp. 94 ff.

63. 63ᵃ = v 278ᵃ, vii 267ᵃ; 63ᵇ = *Il.* xxiv 73ᵇ. **ὁμῶς:** here 'uninterrupted'. **νύκτας τε καὶ ἦμαρ:** (sing.!) on the genesis of this unusual phrase cf. Meister, *Kunstsprache*, 33 n. 3. The long delay before the funeral is not easy to explain. Possibly we should see the influence of some pre-Iliadic Achilles epic. Or perhaps we should simply conclude that such superhuman heroes deserve an unusually long period of mourning between death and burial.

65. ἔδομεν πυρί: Andronikos, *Archaeologia* W, 121–31, correctly points out that Homer speaks only of cremation, and thus describes a practice which became increasingly popular in Greece from the protogeometric period onwards and in many areas prevailed completely. The poet nowhere allows us to discern even a vague memory of the custom prevalent in Mycenaean times of interment. We can therefore reasonably assume that (as in other areas of daily life) even the poetic description of the funeral rites largely reflects the customs of Homer's day.

65ᵇ-6. ~ *Il.* xxiii 166. An extensive description of the procedure is given in *Il.* xxiii 166–83. **ἕλικας:** cf. i 92 n.

67-8ᵃ. Achilles' body is burned ἐν ἐσθῆτι θεῶν, i.e. wearing the ἄμβροτα εἵματα given by the Nereids (59). The poet deliberately omits here any reference to the usual ritual burning of a dead warrior's weapons (cf. for example *Il.* vi 416–18; *Od.* xi 74, xii 13). In the version of the legend known to the author of the *Odyssey* (cf. xi 543–64) the armour of Achilles, which had been made for him by Hephaestus, is indeed not consigned to the flames, but ignites the fateful ὅπλων κρίσις between Odysseus and Ajax. For the detail that Achilles is burned (ἐν) ἀλείφατι πολλῷ | καὶ μέλιτι γλυκερῷ cf. *Il.* xxiii 170, where Achilles had placed amphoras of honey and unguent (ἄλειφαρ: cf. 45) on the pyre of Patroclus. In both passages the reference is to the ritual offering of honey and oil for the dead; cf. Andronikos, op. cit. (65 n.), 25–6.

68ᵇ-70. τεύχεσιν ἐρρώσαντο: 'they moved fast, rushed forward with their arms', i.e. 'they performed an armed dance round the burning pyre'; cf. Leumann, *Wörter*, 287 (who refers to *Il.* xxiv 616). A similar honour, a threefold procession round the body, had been accorded to the dead Patroclus after his corpse had been recovered from the battlefield (*Il.* xxiii 4–16). On the custom cf. Andronikos, op. cit. (65 n.), 14–15. **καιομένοιο:** sc. σέο. 70 = *Il.* ii 810, viii 59. **πέζοι θ' ἱππῆές τε:** 'infantry and those who fight from chariots'.

71. 'When the flames of Hephaestus had finished their work on your body, had consumed the corpse . . .'. φλὸξ Ἡφαίστοιο as at *Il.* ix 468 etc.

72-5. The following morning (ἠῶθεν) the bones of Achilles were collected, and laid in an amphora filled with unmixed wine and oil. The golden amphora was a gift from Thetis for her son, and said to have been presented by Dionysus. The poet refers here to the ἀμφιφορεύς mentioned in the *Iliad*, albeit in a passage which has been regarded as suspect since ancient times, xxiii 92; cf. W. Diehl, op. cit. (39–40 n.), 125–6, who argues for the authenticity of the line.

72. τοι: ethic dat.

74. The line was wrongly athetized by Aristarchus (on account of the reference to Dionysus); cf. van der Valk, *Textual Criticism*, 116; G. A. Privitera, *Dioniso in Omero e nella poesia greca arcaica* (Rome, 1970), 49–95.

76-9. 77 ~ *Il.* xxi 28; 76 ~ 18 above. This golden amphora now holds the mingled (μίγδα) bones of Achilles and those of Patroclus, which until then had been preserved in a golden bowl (φιάλη; cf. *Il.* xxiii 243–4, 252–4); and so Patroclus' wish (*Il.* xxiii 91–2) is fulfilled. While the poet's main intention in 76–7 is to forge the link with the *Iliad* (xxiii), he is also influenced by the content of his pre-Iliadic source, in which Antilochus probably played the role that the *Iliad* attributes to Patroclus. So the bones of Antilochus are kept alongside those of Achilles and Patroclus, although slightly separated (χωρὶς, i.e. in a separate vessel); cf. W. Kullmann, op. cit. (36–97 n.), 40–2; K. Reinhardt, *Die Ilias und ihr Dichter* (Göttingen 1961), 362. For the phrasing of 79 cf. 18; for the content cf. *Il.* xxiv 574–5, which do not necessarily contradict 79. Lines 77–9, condemned by Pestalozzi, op. cit. (36–97 n.), 24, as inauthentic (78–9 appear to have been regarded as

suspect in ancient times, possibly on account of the apparent contradiction
with *Il.* xxiv 574–5), are undoubtedly authentic precisely because of the
reference to the *Iliad*. Moreover 80 would make little sense if 77–9 are
omitted; cf. Reinhardt, op. cit., 351 n. 1.

80–1. ἀμφ' αὐτοῖσι: i.e. round the bones of the heroes laid in amphoras, the
Achaeans build a burial mound (cf. the somewhat more detailed description at *Il.* xxiii 255–6), and so fulfilled the wish expressed by Achilles at *Il.*
xxiii 243–8 (μέγαν καὶ ἀμύμονα τύμβον ~ *Il.* xxiii 247, εὐρύν θ' ὑψηλόν τε).

ἱερὸς στρατός: in connection with στρατός the word ἱερός has lost some
of its original, religious meaning, but not all the religious connotations:
'filled with unusual inner strength'; cf. R. Wülfing–von Martitz, *Glotta*
xxxviii (1960), 272–307, esp. 300ff.; J. P. Locher, *Untersuchungen zu ἱερὸς
hauptsächlich bei Homer* (Bern 1963), 56ff.

82. ἀκτῇ ἔπι προὐχούσῃ: cf. ἀκροτάτη πρόεχ' ἀκτή, xii 11. 82ᵇ = *Il.* vii 86ᵇ.

83. τηλεφανής: (*hapax*) 'visible from far off'.   **ἐκ ποντόφιν:** (~ ἐκ
πόντου) 'from the sea'; on -φι- formations cf. Meister, *Kunstsprache*, 135–
46; Chantraine, *Grammaire*, i 234–41.

84. γεγάασι: (perf.) 'they live'. Lines 82–4 probably indicate that the poet
knew of a τύμβος which lay on the Trojan coast, and which was reputed to
be the tomb of Achilles. And indeed there was such an Ἀχιλλήϊον, first
referred to in literature by Alcaeus, fr. 14 Diehl (354 L–P, Voigt). It is of
course possible that it was not until later, after Homeric times, that the
Aeolians identified the striking tumulus on Sigeion with the monument to
Achilles described in the *Odyssey*. The problem is a complex one, and
cannot be discussed at length in the present context. It is intimately related
to the question of the original concept of Achilles, and the pre-Iliadic
tradition of the hero's fate after death. The version of the legend presupposed by Homer, which has the soul of Achilles descend to Hades, is
not in accordance with the (post-Homeric) *Aethiopis* attributed to Arctinus,
according to which Thetis snatches her son from the pyre, and transports
him to the Λευκὴ νῆσος (Procl. § 66; cf. Kullmann, op. cit. (36–97 n.), 54,
additionally 40–2), i.e. elevates him to hero status, or deifies him. There is
some merit in the argument that the cyclic *Aethiopis* follows the tradition of
pre-Homeric epic, whereas Homeric poetry itself had rationalized the old
legend; cf. for example K. Rüter, *Odysseeinterpretationen*, 67 n. 25. The view
adopted here, which makes a clear distinction between a pre-Homeric oral
epic about Achilles, and the (written) *Aethiopis* composed with a knowledge
of the Homeric poem, meets the objections expressed by A. Dihle, op. cit.
(36–97 n.), 17 ff., about the neo-analytical approach. In any event it is worth
remembering that from an early date Achilles was worshipped as a god
among Greek settlers on the Black Sea as Ποντάρχης; there was a cult,
among other places, on an island called Λεύκη at the mouth of the
Danube. On all these questions cf. the comprehensive study by
H. Hommel, 'Der Gott Achilleus', *Sitzungsberichte der Heidelberger Akad.
Wiss.* (1980) i, who thinks that Achilles was originally a god of the dead.

85–92. It seems probable that Thetis had instituted funeral games in honour of her son in the pre-Homeric Achilles epic. If this supposition is correct, there is also an indirect reference to this older description at *Il.* xxiii, where Achilles holds games in honour of his 'substitute', Patroclus. For the post-Homeric *Aethiopis* an ἀγών in honour of Achilles is guaranteed by the testimony of Proclus (§ 67 Kullmann).

85–6. Achilles had provided prizes out of his own store (*Il.* xxiii 256–61). Here Thetis begs valuable ἄεθλα from the gods, and places them at the centre of the competitors' arena (μέσῳ ἐν ἀγῶνι as at *Il.* xxiii 507; cf. *LfgrE* s.v. ἀγών) for the best of the Achaeans. 86ᵇ = *Il.* xi 227ᵇ etc.

87. The line is the same as xi 416 (except that τάφῳ, 'solemn obsequies', replaces φόνῳ); similarly 90 ~ xi 418, with θηήσαο replacing ὀλοφύραο. However, while at xi 416 we should follow Aristarchus and some of the MSS in reading ἀντεβόλησας, here the majority reading ἀντεβόλησα gives a better sense (van der Valk, *Textual Criticism*, 149, and J. Bechert, op. cit. (xxiii 5n.), 264–5). This does mean that the (original) structural correspondence of xi . . . μὲν . . . ἀντεβόλησας, 416, and ἀλλά . . . ὀλοφύραο, 418, is here abandoned in favour of a switch between first and second person—hence the variant ἐπεθήπεα for θηήσαο, which is surely an ancient conjecture.

89. ζώννυνταί: must be taken as subjunctive. The form is certainly strange in comparison with δαινύῃ (viii 243, xix 328): one would expect ζωννύωνται (with metrical ῡ). Schulze, *Quaestiones*, 331, Schwyzer, *Grammatik*, i 792, and Chantraine, *Grammaire*, i 458, may be correct in assuming here an old athematic subjunctive characterized by lengthening of indicative -νυ- to -νῡ-; cf. the extensive discussion by Erbse, *Beiträge*, 197–8. ἐπεντύνονται: better ἐπεντύνωνται (Thiersch). Certainly we cannot agree here with Shipp, *Studies*, 360, who sees both verbs as regular indicatives, and assumes 'a quite abnormal syntax'. ζώννυσθαι refers to putting on the ζῶμα ('loincloth') worn by competitive boxers and wrestlers (*Il.* xxiii 683; cf. also 710), but also by soldiers (*Il.* iv 187 = 216); cf. Marinatos, *Archaeologia* A, 12). Line 89ᵇ is perhaps to be understood as 'when the young men . . . prepare for competition' (ἐπ' ἐντύνονται ἄεθλα), with ἄεθλον used here in its secondary meaning 'competition' (originally 'prize'; cf. 85 and 91). It is possible that the shift in meaning to 'competitive games' began with this complex of meanings (originally 'when they prepared for competition'); cf. in addition S. Laser, *LfgrE* s.v. ἄεθλον.

90. ~ xi 418; cf. 87n. θηέομαι: 'regard with wonder'; cf. H. J. Mette, *Glotta* xxxix (1961), 49–71, esp. 50.

91. ἐπὶ σοί: 'in your honour'. 91ᵇ = 85ᵇ.

92. ἀργυρόπεζα Θέτις: only once in the *Odyssey*, but frequent in the *Iliad*. 92ᵇ = *Il.* xxiv 749ᵇ (of the dead Hector).

93–7. Here Agamemnon takes up the thought expressed by Achilles at 28–34, and confirms Achilles' view from his own experience. He contrasts the glorious fate of Achilles with his own miserable end on returning home, and so prepares indirectly for the comparison, inspired by the next speech, that of Amphimedon (121–90), between his own fate and that of Odysseus, which surpasses even the glorious destiny of the son of Peleus.

93–4. ὥς: introduces Agamemnon's summing up. In dying not only did Achilles not lose his ὄνομα, but he also won 'noble κλέος' (undying fame) which will last for all time (αἰεί) among all men (94ᵃ = i 299ᵃ, xix 334ᵃ). We should not overlook the fact that the poet here forecasts immortality for the *Iliad*.

95. 'But what pleasure can *I* have in the fact that I survived the war?' At 95ᵃ Agamemnon 'cites' Achilles' words of *Il.* xviii 80; 95ᵇ = i 328ᵇ etc.

96. 96ᵇ = iii 194ᵇ. For Zeus' responsibility cf. μοῖρ' ὀλοή, 29; to a certain extent Aegisthus and Clytaemestra were only instruments in the hand of the supreme god.

97. 97ᵇ = iv 92ᵇ (which also refers to Clytaemestra). The extent of Clytaemestra's responsibility for her husband's death is variously indicated in those passages of the poem which describe the fate which awaited Agamemnon on his return. His words here, at 97, are closest to the account at xi 405–34, but go further in accusing Clytaemestra of having taken part in the murder herself, as Aegisthus' accomplice. In the earlier saga known to the poet Clytaemestra had joined in planning the murder, but had not herself been involved in the execution of the plan. The extreme formulation of 97 prepares indirectly for the praise of Penelope. On the details cf. P. Bergman, *Der Atridenmythos in Epos, Lyrik und Drama* (diss. Erlangen/ Nuremberg, 1970), 4–41.

98. = iv 620 etc. The line concludes the encounter between Achilles and Agamemnon (19ᵇ–97), and serves as a transition to the exchange between Agamemnon and the suitor Amphimedon. On the formal structure of the series of scenes from 15 cf. 15–22 n.

99–100. Together with the souls of the suitors, who up to now had stood apart, Hermes now approaches the group around Agamemnon and Achilles.   **διάκτορος ἀργεϊφόντης:** (99ᵇ = i 84ᵇ etc.) the god is designated here by means of his most common titles, neither of which has yet been satisfactorily explained (cf. i 38 and 84 nn.). On διάκτορος see the attractive theory of H. Koller, *Glotta* liv (1976), 214, and R. Janko, *Glotta* lvi (1978), 192–5 (with extensive bibliography), who suggest a development from *δι-άκ-τωρ, 'escort' (ἡγεμών; cf. verb forms ἄγε, 6, ἦρχε, 9, κατάγων, 100, which suggest the office of ψυχοπόμπος). On ἀργεϊφόντης cf. Chantraine, *Dictionnaire* s.v., and latterly Koller, op. cit., 211–16 (*ἀργεϊ φάων > *ἀργεϊφῶν > ἀργεϊφόντης). **Ὀδυσῆϊ:** dat. of the agent.

101. τὼ δ': Achilles and Agamemnon.   **ἐσιδέσθην:** on middle cf. J. Bechert, op. cit. (xxiii 5n.), 222.

102–4. 102 ~ 20; 104ᵃ = *Il.* xiii 641ᵃ; 104ᵇ = iv 555ᵇ. Amphimedon, son of Melaneus, and one of the boldest of the suitors (xxii 242–4), had fallen by the hand of Telemachus (xxii 277–84). The ties of hospitality linking the house of Agamemnon and Amphimedon's family, expounded in detail at 114–19, are an invention of the author's, introduced to establish a prior relationship between Agamemnon and Amphimedon, which provides a basis for the present conversation; there is no question of this detail having been present in the older epic tradition; cf. Stössel, op. cit. (Introd.), 64–5.

105. ~ 23.

106–19. Agamemnon asks Amphimedon what fate met him and his companions.

106. τί παθόντες ... ἔδυτε: 'What fate have you suffered that you have made your way below?' ἐρεμνὴν γαῖαν: appears as a periphrasis for the underworld only here in Homeric epic; more frequent is ἔρεβος, 'darkness, place of darkness', from which ἐρεμνός (< *ἐρεβ-νός; similarly ἐρεβεννός < *ἐρεβεσ-νός) is derived; cf. Chantraine, *Dictionnaire* s.v. ἔρεβος. The acc. is used in its 'lative' function expressing the goal towards which the action expressed by the verb proceeds.

107–8. Agamemnon is struck by the fact that Amphimedon and all his companions form a 'select' group 'of the same age' (i.e. they are all equally youthful): 'One [the omission of τις is strange; cf. Shipp, *Studies*, 360] could hardly have made a better job (οὐδέ κεν ἄλλως) of picking out, and bringing together, the best men in a city.' Agamemnon therefore supposes that the group must have met their end in some common venture. The various forms which such a venture might have taken are reviewed in the lines which follow.

109–13. The threefold question (ἦ—ἦ—ἦέ) which Agamemnon puts to Amphimedon is an almost exact verbal parallel to the question put to Agamemnon himself by Odysseus at xi 399–403; on the problems of content and language (esp. μαχεούμενον, xi 403: -οι, xxiv 113) cf. xi 399–403 n. With this (certainly intentional) reusing of the lines in a different context there is, besides the necessary slight alteration of language, also an alteration of formal syntax (which does not greatly affect the meaning), in 113: in xi 403 Odysseus had considered whether enemy forces (ἀνάρσιοι ἄνδρες) had killed Agamemnon (σε) while he fought for, i.e. to conquer, their city and womenfolk (μαχεούμενον); at xxiv 113, however, Agamemnon's supposition is that enemy forces fighting (μαχεούμενοι) to save their city and women had killed the attacking suitors. In a sense he is not far from the truth, for Odysseus had been fighting (with the aid of his three companions) to rescue his city and his wife from the 'enemy' and had been victorious.

114–19. Agamemnon seeks to justify his request for information by reminding Amphimedon that he is a ξεῖνος (cf. 104 n.). The poet assumes here, as at xi 447–8, that in collecting allies for the campaign against Troy Agamemnon had come to Ithaca, stayed in the house of his old friend Melaneus, and had from there established his relationship with Odysseus; cf. Finley, *World*, 119. It is not certain to what extent the story here is influenced by a pre-Iliadic version of the legend. The old saga (or pre-Iliadic epic) would have included an embassy to Ithaca (as to the other Achaean chiefs), but it is far less certain whether Agamemnon would have been named as leader, or member, of this and similar missions. The relationship of hospitality between Agamemnon and Melaneus is certainly an invention of the author of the *Odyssey* (cf. 102–4 n.), and the post-Homeric *Cypria* appears to know only of an embassy consisting of

Menelaus, Nestor, and Palamedes; cf. Procl. *Chr.*, 103, 25–7 Allen = § 22 Kullmann.

114. On 114ᵇ cf. i 187: ξεῖνοι... εὐχόμεθ᾽ εἶναι. **εὔχομαι**: (in the non-religious context) 'I (proudly, solemnly, firmly) maintain'; cf. L. C. Muellner, *The Meaning of Homeric* εὔχομαι *through its Formulas* (Innsbruck, 1978), 83–8.

115. **ἣ οὐ μέμνῃ ὅτε...:** as at *Il.* xv 18ᵃ etc. ἢ οὐ (synizesis!). μέμνῃ (contracted) for expected μέμνηαι (*Il.* xxi 442). δῶ: cf. i 176n. and bibl. The discovery of Myc. *do-de* /dō-de/ 'into the house' on Theban linear B tablets (TH Of 26 for example) has thrown new light on the genesis of the Homeric form; cf. M. Lejeune, *Studi micenei ed egeo-anatolici* xvii (1976), 79–84.

116–17. 116ᵇ = viii 518ᵇ. 117ᵃ = xi 372ᵃ; 117ᵇ = viii 500ᵇ. It is not clear what σὺν ἀντιθέῳ Μενελάῳ belongs with: connecting it with κατήλυθον (and ὀτρυνέων) presupposes Menelaus' participation in the embassy (first recorded in the *Cypria*; cf. 114–17n.); but taking it with ἕπεσθαι produces a rather imprecise effect. Perhaps we should assume with Stössel, op. cit. (Introd.), 67–8, a construction ἀπὸ κοινοῦ.

118–19. Line 118 presents considerable difficulties; cf. latterly Stössel, op. cit. (Introd.), 229. The reading δ᾽ ἄρ᾽ given in all manuscripts (even P.) must be preferred to Aristarchus' reading (cf. schol. on *Il.* x 48), favoured by von der Mühll, δ᾽ ἐν, which is surely a conjecture designed to avoid the awkward dative μηνὶ οὔλῳ. This dative is best explained by Chantraine, *Grammaire*, ii 76, as a 'comitative' dative (of time), 'en un mois entier'; somewhat differently by Palmer, *Companion*, 135, as 'instrumental', originally 'by means of'. πάντα is difficult to understand, and possibly corrupt (Schwartz, *Odyssee*, 332; von der Mühll, ad loc.); on the older attempts at emendation cf. Ameis–Hentze, *Anhang*, iv 102. Line 118 probably means that Agamemnon and his companions had taken a month altogether (πάντα?) over their mission, the journey to Ithaca, the stay there (with the difficult task of persuading Odysseus to take part in the campaign), and the return journey; a similar interpretation is given in Ameis–Hentze–Cauer, and Stanford, ad loc. It is improbable, as some have suggested, that the period μηνὶ οὔλῳ refers only to παρπεπιθόντες. **οὖλος**: Attic ὅλος, both from *ὅλϝος. **εὐρέα πόντον**: (for εὐρὺν) as at *Il.* vi 291, ix 72, an artificial formation modelled on εὐρέϊ πόντῳ (i 197); cf. K. Witte, *RE* viii, 2225, 2236–7; Hoekstra, *Modifications*, 112. 119ᵃ = *Il.* xxiii 37ᵃ. **σπουδῇ:** '(only) with difficulty'. **παρπεπιθόντες:** redupl. aor. of παραπείθω, 'win over, prevail upon' (cf. xxii 213). 119ᵇ = xviii 356ᵇ.

120. ~ 35, 191.

121–90. Amphimedon's reply.

121. = xi 397; *Il.* ii 434, etc. This formulaic line of solemn address, omitted from some MSS, has been regarded by some as a late interpolation; cf. Ameis–Hentze, *Anhang*, iv 102, and latterly von der Mühll. The repeated address of 122, διοτρεφές, is indeed striking, but not in fact without parallel; cf. xi 92–3, 473–4, 617–18. Furthermore 121 is very close to

109–13, just as the similar-sounding xi 397 is close to 399–403 (= xxiv 109–13); the poet's intention is clearly to recall the similar conversational situation in the first nekuia; cf. Stössel, op. cit. (Introd.), 68.

122–4. 122ᵇ = xv 155ᵇ; 123ᵇ ~ i 169ᵇ etc. Amphimedon responds first to Agamemnon's second question of 115–19 (μέμνημαι answers ἦ οὐ μέμνῃ, 115). Only then does he turn to the first, and more important, question of 106–13, and at 123–4 undertakes to fulfil Agamemnon's request εἰπέ μοι εἰρομένῳ. **καταλέξω**: on καταλέγειν cf. T. Krischer, op. cit. (xxiii 225 n.), 146–58; Amphimedon promises an objective account which will include all the important events, but exclude the inessential. **θανάτοιο τέλος**: (as at v 326 etc.): the gen. narrows down the meaning of the word with which it is constructed, i.e. 'the end consisting of death'; cf. A. Heubeck, *Glotta* l (1972), 139–40.

125. ~ xx 290. **μνώμεθ'**: imperf.

126. ~ i 249 (= xvi 126). **ἐτελεύτα**: like τελευτὴν ποιῆσαι, i 249–50, xvi 126–7: 'make an end (by marrying one of the suitors)'.

127. The suitor remains unaware of the real reason for Penelope's indecision, and gives his own interpretation of her behaviour (which from his point of view is entirely plausible), which accords with the explanation he gives of subsequent events in 167 ff. **θάνατον ... μέλαιναν**: as at ii 289 etc.

128–46. This is the third account of Penelope's ruse. The earlier accounts were given by Antinous (ii 93–110) and later by Penelope herself (xix 139–56). The wording in all three accounts is broadly similar (on the parallel xxiv 143 = ii 107ᵃ = xix 153 see below). The very minor differences reflect the differences in perspective and attitude of the speaker (the standpoint of a suitor or Penelope). For the most part these variations are superficial, for example ἡμῖν μετέειπε, ii 95 and xxiv 130, compared with αὐτοῖς μετέειπον, xix 140. A few more significant differences appear where the speaker concerned relates events from an individual viewpoint to justify his/her own actions: ii 93 = xxiv 128 against xix 138; ii 108–9 = xxiv 144–5 against xix 154–5; and significantly δόλῳ, ii 106 = xxiv 141, as opposed to ἐγώ, xix 151. This threefold presentation of the same material has seemed objectionable to many critics and has given rise to analytical inferences. It has been much debated which of the three passages is original and which are borrowings (by later poets). Many different conclusions have been reached, of which only the most important can be mentioned here. Priority has been given to the passage in ii by E. Bethe, 'Odyssee-Probleme', *Hermes* lxiii (1928), 81–92; to the account in xix by Wilamowitz, *Heimkehr*, 39, Focke, *Odyssee*, 319, B. Stockem, *Die Gestalt der Penelope in der Odyssee* (diss. Cologne, 1955), 48, and Page, *Odyssey*, 121; and to the version in xxiv by Schwartz, *Odyssee*, 118 and 302. That all three accounts are derived from a common source, which has not survived, is argued by Büchner, 'Penelopeszenen', 129–67; von der Mühll, *Odyssee*, 705 and 765 (who suggests a Thesprotis as a source; somewhat differently in col. 735); Merkelbach, *Untersuchungen*, 63; F. Wehrli, 'Penelope und Telemachos',

MH xvi (1959), 228–37, esp. 229 n. 2; and Rüter, *Odysseeinterpretationen*, 190–2. A useful critical review of these discussions is given in Bona, *Studi*, 107–29; cf. also Eisenberger, *Studien*, 54 n. 27; Stössel, op. cit. (Introd.), 231. Against analytical interpretations it must be remembered that: first, the account of the ruse is indispensable in all three passages, fulfilling a different poetic function in each context; second, the episode is recounted at each of three compositionally important places in the epic, at the beginning of the open confrontation with the suitors, at the turn of events in favour of Odysseus, and after the confrontation with the suitors is over, cf. W. Krehmer, *Zur Begegnung zwischen Odysseus und Athene (Od. xiii, 187–440)* (diss. Erlangen/Nuremberg, 1973), 39–43; third, the device of repeating an episode with largely the same wording is wholly in accord with the technique of archaic epic, and should indeed recall in each instance the context in which the account was previously heard, cf. Krehmer, op. cit., 39–48; fourth, there are no contradictions either between the three accounts, or with their respective contexts, cf. F. M. Combellack, 'Three Odyssean Problems', *California Studies in Antiquity* vii (1973), 17–46, esp. 34–5, Wender, op. cit. (Introd.), 34–7; and fifth, there is no proof, nor is it likely, that the poet 'quoted' more or less word for word an independent source at three points in his epic. On the other hand he must surely have known a version of the story, probably in oral epic form, in which Penelope's web was central to the action, as opposed to its marginal position in the *Odyssey*; it is a reasonable supposition that in this older treatment the discovery of the deception coincided with the return of Odysseus; cf. Woodhouse, *Composition*, 66–71, esp. 70–1; Lesky, *Homeros*, 116; W. Kullmann, 'Die neue Anthropologie der Odyssee und ihre Voraussetzungen', in *Didactica Classica Gandensia* xvii–xviii (1977/8), 37–49, esp. 39–40; idem, *WS* NF xv (1981), 5–42, esp. 35–8. For an explanation of individual points of language see ii 93–110n.

128–9. ἀλλὰ δόλον τόνδε ἄλλον ἐνὶ φρεσὶ μερμήριξε | στησαμένη μέγαν ἱστὸν ... ὕφαινε: the introduction to the account of the weaving is almost identical with the opening of the parallel passage in ii 93–4 (ἡ δὲ δόλον ...). In xix 138–9 the formulation is markedly different: φᾶρος μέν μοι πρῶτον ἐνέπνευσε φρεσὶ δαίμων | στησαμένη μέγαν ἱστὸν ... ὑφαίνειν. The account of xix omits the striking introduction ἀλλὰ δόλον τόνδε ἄλλον (ἐγὼ δὲ δόλους τολυπεύω, xix 137, seems to lead better to 138–9), and moreover φᾶρος, which seems to suit the context better, is dependent on ὑφαίνειν. However the passages in ii and xxiv are no less clearly formulated: ii 97 (= xxiv 128) is preceded by ii 89–92 (the same ideas are expressed in xxiv 126–7), which refer to the δόλοι of Penelope; in both cases, however, δόλος ὅδε ἄλλος means that Penelope resorted to the trick of weaving alongside other deceptions, rather than that the weaving and the scheming against the suitors were two separate actions each occupying a period of three years, such as Antinous indicates in ii. Both passages (ii 88–9 and xxiv 106–7) refer then to the same period of three years; correctly interpreted by Thornton, *People*, 150 n. 13, against the misconceptions of

Woodhouse, *Composition*, 70–1; Page, *Odyssey*, 120–1; Wehrli, op. cit. (128–46 n.), 228–37; and Kirk, *Songs*, 244–5. There is only one (unimportant) difference in the information given in the accounts of ii and xxiv: according to Antinous some weeks elapsed between the discovery of the deception (which clearly took place shortly before the point at which the poem opens) and the completion of the handiwork; whereas Amphimedon places the display of the completed work at the very time of Odysseus' return (147). Incidentally the form of words used to describe the weaving of the shroud, both at xix 139 and ii 94 (= xxiv 129), is quite 'correct', and in keeping with Homeric usage. In some instances ἱστός clearly retains its original meaning of 'loom' (i 357 = xxi 351 = *Il.* vi 491); however usually it refers to the finished article made at the loom; this is particularly clear at ἱστὸν τεχνῆσαι (vii 110 v.l.), 'to produce a web with craftsmanship, skilfully'; cf. *Il.* iii 125–6 and xxii 440–1, where the phrase ἱστὸν ὑφαίνειν is amplified by elaboration of ἱστὸν as δίπλακα πορφυρέην; and Hes. *Op.* 64, πολυδαίδαλον ἱστὸν ὑφαίνειν. An intermediate range of meaning is apparent in v 62 and x 221–3. ἱστὸν ἵστασθαι probably meant originally then 'to set up a web', i.e. to set, stretch the warp; cf. G. Wickert-Micknat, *Archaeologia* R, 41–6. It is significant that ὑφαίνειν (129) can also be used with the object δόλος (δόλους καὶ μῆτιν ὕφαινον, ix 422, the subject being Odysseus!): with the action ἱστὸν ὑφαίνειν Penelope can also be said to δόλον ὑφαίνειν, and similarly in connection with her web she can say ἐγὼ δὲ δόλους τολυπεύω (xix 137), using a phrase drawn from the technical language of spinning and weaving; cf. Wickert-Micknat, op. cit., 46 n. 209. ἱστός is also indirectly attested in Myc. Greek: cf. gen. pl. *i-te-ja-o* /histej-jāhōn/ PY Ad 684, 'weaving women'.

142–3. Line 142 (= ii 107 = xix 152) sounds formulaic, as does 143, though the latter is uncertainly attested, both here and in the two parallel passages; cf. von der Mühll, ad loc. ii 107a ('add. pauci codd.'), xix 153 ('om. nonnulli'), xxiv 143 ('om. complures'). The wording of this same line is also used as the second half of a similar formulaic expression in x 469–70 (with the variation μακρὰ τελέσθη; but again x 470 is only poorly attested), and in Hes. *Th.* 58–9 (59 is certainly genuine; cf. M. L. West, ad loc.). Since a similarly expanded expression is found at xi 294–5 (= xiv 293–4 = *h.Ap.* 349–50) it is reasonable to suppose that xxiv 143 (and ii 107ᵃ and xix 158) may well be genuine. Cf. also x 469–70 n.

147–90. Following on from the account of Penelope's web Amphimedon relates the events from the arrival of Odysseus in Ithaca to the killing of the suitors. He summarizes the action of xiii–xxiii, and so continues the summary given by Odysseus to his wife in xxiii 310–41 (cf. Heubeck, *Dichter*, 38) in a similarly subjective vein. This subjective colouring of the account (cf. 127 and 128–46 nn.) is apparent from the outset (147–50), with the juxtaposition of the completion of the φᾶρος and the hero's return. καὶ τότε δή, 149, does not mean 'on the same day', but that the events took place at approximately the same time (cf. Bona, *Studi*, 111); nevertheless Amphimedon's account does shorten the period—of some weeks, according to the indications given elsewhere in the poem—between the discovery of Penelope's deception and the appearance of the hero. This is quite understandable in view of the poet's intention to allow Amphimedon to relate the events from his own standpoint. The suitor omits the lapse of time between the two events, and so omits any mention of the phase in which he and his companions established themselves in Odysseus' house and squandered his possessions, and thus clearly put themselves in the wrong (cf. Erbse, *Beiträge*, 236–7). Amphimedon thus shifts attention away from the outrage committed by the suitors, and implies that the fault lay mainly with Penelope, who had for so long kept the suitors at arm's length by her ruses. It is undoubtedly true that the older saga did closely associate in time the completion of the shroud and the return of Odysseus, but the idea that the poet here deliberately echoes the earlier version of the story, or even quotes from the older work (as suggested for example by Woodhouse, *Composition*, 70–1, and Lesky, *Homeros*, 116), is hardly convincing. The suitor gives his own version of events as he remembers them, and in order to present himself in the best light. This is also true with regard to another detail of his story, where he speaks of a conspiracy between the couple over the trial of the bow, in other words bringing forward the reunion of Odysseus and Penelope to a time before the trial of the bow (167–9). Here too there can be no question of the poet drawing on an earlier form of the story (as Merkelbach suggests, *Untersuchungen*, 7). As Finsler, *Homer* ii 438, correctly emphasizes, the whole episode must have seemed to the suitor on reflection to have been pre-arranged by the couple. Cf. further Bona, *Studi*, 123; H. Vester, *Gymnasium* lxxv (1968), 429; Thornton, *People*, 106–8; Eisenberger, *Studien*, 272 n. 19.

147. εὖθ': 'just as'.   ἱστός: here 'web' (cf. 139, 145).
149. καὶ τότε δή: introduces the main clause.   κακός ... δαίμων: cf. O. Tsagarakis, *Nature and Background of Major Concepts of Divine Power in Homer* (Amsterdam, 1977), 111–12. The δαίμων is κακός because it has brought the suitors to an evil end.
150-3. 150 ~ iv 517; 152ᵃ = iv 633ᵇ; 152ᵇ = viii 445ᵇ, xiii 425ᵇ; 153 ~ xvi 169. Aristarchus considered the passage suspect: πῶς δὲ καὶ ὁ Ἀμφιμέδων ἐπίσταται τὴν ἐν τοῖς ἀγροῖς ἐπιβουλήν; It is futile to ask where Amphimedon acquired his knowledge: the poet simply attributes this (accurate) piece of information to him. The similarity of wording (150 ~ iv 517 etc.) is perhaps intended once more to draw attention to the contrasting fates of Odysseus and Agamemnon.   τὼ δὲ: Odysseus and Telemachus.   ἀρτύναντε: 'having prepared/planned'.
154-5. ἤ τοι ... αὐτὰρ ...: cf. xxiii 113n.
155. ~ xxii 400.
156. 156ᵇ = xxiii 95ᵇ.
157. = xvi 273, xvii 202, 337.
158. = xvii 203, 338. Since with τὰ δὲ λυγρὰ περὶ χροΐ εἵματα ἕστο the line repeats the formulation of 156 κακὰ χροΐ εἵματ' ἔχοντα in an almost intolerable way, it is difficult to avoid the conclusion of F. A. Wolf that 158 should

COMMENTARY

be excised; the identical xvii 203 and 338 are, however, unobjectionable. The origin of the interpolation has been plausibly accounted for by Stössel, op. cit. (Introd.), 73. For the older literature see Ameis–Hentze, *Anhang*, iv 103. The authenticity of the line has also been questioned by von der Mühll and Schadewaldt.

159. ἡμείων: (as also at 170 and elsewhere; cf. ὑμείων, xxi 318 etc.) is a purely poetic form with metrical lengthening (< ἡμέων); cf. Chantraine, *Grammaire*, i 271. **τὸν ἐόντα:** 'that it was this man (τὸν: demonstr.); cf. xxiii 116.

160. 160ᵇ = ii 29ᵇ.

161. ἐνίσσομεν: from ἐνιπή, 'rebuke, threat'; -ίσσω < *-iqʷi̯ō; a later form is ἐνίπτω; cf. Frisk, *GEW*, and Chantraine, *Dictionnaire* s.v. ἐνιπή; 'scold, abuse, threaten'. **βολῆσιν:** refers to the three missiles thrown at Odysseus, xvii 462 ff., xviii 394 ff., xx 299 ff.

162–3. τῆος: (synizesis): 'for a period of time'. τῆος is Nauck's conjecture; it would be better to retain the unanimously transmitted τέως (with synizesis) μὲν: it is unlikely that an original τῆος was replaced in the course of transmission by τέως μὲν; cf. Chantraine, *Grammaire*, i 11. However it is possible that the formulaic usage reflects a pre-Homeric prototype *αὐτὰρ ὁ τῆος . . .; cf. Hoekstra, *Modifications*, 34–5. **ἐτόλμα:** (τολμάω here 'endure') to be taken with τετληότι θυμῷ (= iv 459ᵇ etc.), and βαλλόμενος καὶ ἐνισσόμενος with ἐνὶ μεγάροισιν ἑοῖσι (= xix 573ᵇ).

164–6. Amphimedon describes the concealment of weapons in the store-room, planned by Odysseus and Telemachus at xvi 281–98, but somewhat differently carried out at xix 1–46 (cf. the convincing arguments of Erbse, *Beiträge*, 3–41). He had not witnessed this himself, but, like Melanthius (xxii 139–41), he had, as one of the suitors caught in the hall, drawn the right conclusion. He is also correct in his general assumption of divine support (164 ~ *Il.* xv 242), although it was in fact Athena, not Zeus, who stood by Odysseus' side with counsel and aid (xvi 282, xix 6, 34–5). On 165–6 cf. xvi 284–5; ἀρήϊα τεύχεα . . . | ἐς μυχὸν ὑψηλοῦ θαλάμου καταθεῖναι ἀείρας, and further xix 4, 17. The closing of the door (ἐκλήϊσεν ὀχῆας: 'he bolted the door') is not mentioned in xix. More precise technical details of the mechanism of bolts are given in xxi 46–50. Cf. R. F. Willetts, 'Homeric Doors', Ἐπετηρὶς τοῦ Κέντρου Ἐπιστημονικῶν Ἐρευνῶν (Λευκωσία) v (1971/2), 35–41.

167–77. Amphimedon's account of the trial of the bow (recounted in full in xxi) is brief, but contains all the essential points. The speaker is mistaken only in his perception of how the contest came about: he assumes that Odysseus was responsible, whereas the competition was planned and launched by Penelope (xix 573–81; xxi 1 ff.); and he supposes a collaboration between Penelope and her husband (cf. πολυκερδείῃσιν, 167), thus implying a reunion before the trial. The suitor was indeed bound to have gained the impression that the action had been deliberately plotted by the pair with the express intention of bringing about the suitors' death; cf. 149–90n. The analytical approach of Wilamowitz, *Untersuchungen*, 59,

378

Merkelbach, *Untersuchungen*, 6–7, and Kirk, *Songs*, 245, has rightly been criticized by Bona, *Studi*, 125, Thornton, *People*, 106–18, Eisenberger, *Studien*, 323–4, and Moulton, op. cit. (Introd.), 162.

167. πολυκερδείῃσιν: cf. xxiii 77.

168. = xxi 3.

169. 169ª = ix 53ª; 169ᵇ = xxi 4ᵇ.   αἰνομόροισιν: (elsewhere only ix 53, and *Il.* xxii 481) 'having a terrible fate'.

170. ἡμείων: cf. 159n.

171. ~ xxi 185.

172. 172ᵇ = xxi 314ᵇ. The action is described in detail at xxi 378–9.

173-5. In these lines Amphimedon refers back to the events preceding the handing of the bow to Odysseus, at xxi 273–8. On ὁμοκλέομεν cf. xxi 360, 367. Line 174 refers to Odysseus' speech of xxi 275–84, and 175 recalls Telemachus' order to Eumaeus (who is surely the one meant by μιν) at xxi 369–75. οἷος is remarkable because Penelope also agreed to Telemachus' idea at xxi 331–40; however, it was the son who conveyed the order.

176. After the parenthetic 173–5 Amphimedon resumes from 172.

177. = xxi 328.

178-85. The report of the suitors' murder echoes many of the phrases used in xxii 1–389, which in their turn repeatedly recall the model of battle scenes in the *Iliad*.

178. 178ª = xx 128ª (cf. xxii 2); 178ᵇ = xxii 3ᵇ.

179. 179ª = xi 68ª. The description of the suitors as βασιλῆες occurs also at i 394, xviii 64; cf. also xxii 52.

180. 180ª = iii 58ª.   βέλεα στονόεντα: as at *Il.* xvii 374 etc.

181. 181ª = xxii 266ª; 181ᵇ = xxii 118ᵇ.

182. = *Il.* xi 366 = xx 453. Again Amphimedon assumes correctly a divine hand in the action (cf. 164).   ὅ: = ὅτι.   σφι: Odysseus and his three companions are meant.   ἐπιτάρροθος: (used only this once in the *Odyssey*, but frequently in the *Iliad*, 'helping, helper', used only of gods (esp. Athena), is obviously an 'extended' form from original ἐπίρροθος, 'hastening (to bring aid), helping'; cf. B. Forssman, in *Lautgeschichte und Etymologie* (Wiesbaden, 1980), 180–98, esp. 181–4; Frisk, *GEW* s.v. ἐπίρροθος; Chantraine, *Dictionnaire* s.v. ῥόθος.

183. 183ᵇ = xiv 262ᵇ, xvii 431ᵇ.   αὐτίκα: is surprising, because the fighting described in 183–5 is obviously the second phase of the battle (xxii 257–309), which took place after Amphimedon had fallen (xxii 284).

184-5. These lines are almost identical to xxii 308–9; cf. also *Il.* x 483–4, xxi 20–1.

186-90. Amphimedon's final words are indispensable, above all for the sake of the contrast with 43–94 (cf. Eisenberger, *Studien*, 324; Erbse, *Beiträge*, 234). They also point forward to Odysseus' confrontation with the suitors' kinsmen at the end of xxiv.

187. ἀκηδέα: here in a passive sense (as for example also at vi 26, xix 18, xx 130) 'uncared for (κῆδος)'; in its specialized meaning 'unburied' only here and *Il.* xxiv 554. On the content of the line cf. xxii 435–56.

188. ἴσασι: (on the form cf. xi 122n.; on the striking length of the first syllable cf. Hoekstra, *Modifications*, 91 n. 2) here used in an absolute sense, 'they do not know at all'.

189. βρότον: on the origin of the secondary, specialized meaning 'blood from a wound' (*hapax* in the *Odyssey*, often in the *Iliad*, e.g. vii 425) cf. Leumann, *Wörter*, 124–6. **ὠτειλέων:** in the *Odyssey* only here and xix 456 (here with synizesis -έων) 'wounds', not normally used of a wound from a missile; cf. H. Trümpy, *Kriegerische Fachausdrücke im griechischen Epos* (diss. Basle, 1950), 93; however, cf. *Il.* xviii 351, xix 25; cf. Bergold, op. cit. (11–14n.), 159 n. 2. The etymology is obscure, cf. Chantraine, *Dictionnaire* s.v.

190. 190ᵇ = *Il.* xxiii 9ᵇ etc. **κατθέμενοι:** sc. ἐν λεχέεσσι, cf. 44. **γοάοιεν:** uncontracted (cf. *Il.* xxiv 664 γοάοιμεν) cf. Chantraine, *Grammaire*, i 78; Shipp, *Studies*, 37.

191–204. The scene in the underworld closes with a speech from Agamemnon, 192–202. It is of great significance, on various counts. From the compositional point of view the speech completes the outward structure of the conversation between the spirits in Hades; it is also the goal to which the conversation has been heading. It follows on from two pairs of speeches balanced against each other in terms of subject and number of lines accorded to each: 11:62 (Achilles:Agamemnon); 14:70 (Agamemnon:Amphimedon). The first exchange contrasted the inglorious death of Agamemnon with the glorious end of Achilles; the second exchange culminates in the indirect celebration of the homecoming of Odysseus. The final speech from Agamemnon functions as a kind of summary: the ὄλβος of Odysseus not only far excels the fearful fate of the victorious commander Agamemnon; it even surpasses the heroic destiny of the man who won undying fame at the cost of an early death. The parallelism between Agamemnon's greeting to Achilles (ὄλβιε Πηλέος υἱέ, 36) and the same hero's address to Odysseus (ὄλβιε Λαέρταο πάϊ, 192) makes the contrast particularly clear. Agamemnon's celebration of Odysseus' fate, recalling as it does Achilles' words of 24–34, and Agamemnon's reply (95–7), significantly takes the indirect form of eulogy of the wife whose unexampled ἀρετή has until this point hardly been praised directly and in so many words. The fact that the poet chooses to put this commendation into the mouth of Agamemnon is particularly important: in the first nekuia the same hero had been moved by his experience of Clytaemestra to recommend suspicion towards all women. Even Penelope had not been entirely excepted (xi 427–34, 441–3, 454–6). Finally we cannot fail to notice how Agamemnon's speech acts as the climax of the contrasting treatment of the fates of the two families, which has been a leitmotiv throughout the work from the very opening of i. Cf. Woodhouse, *Composition*, 205–7, 232–3; Hölscher, op. cit. (1–204n.), 1–16; Thornton, *People*, 7–10; Erbse, *Beiträge*, 232–3; Fenik, *Studies*, 148–9.

191. = 35. The formulaic line is unusual here because it names Amphimedon (τόν) as the listener to whom the speech is addressed, whereas in fact it introduces a speech directed to the absent son of Laertes.

192. The line recalls 36, not only by its identical opening, ὄλβιε, but also by the emphatic formality of the address occupying the whole hexameter. πάϊ: with two syllables is *hapax*.

193. σὺν μεγάλῃ ἀρετῇ: the sense demands that it be taken with ἄκοιτιν, not ἐκτήσω. This is an unusual construction; cf. Shipp, *Studies*, 360.

194-6. ὥς ... ὥς ...: with a double exclamation Agamemnon gives the reasons for his statement at 192. ἀγαθαὶ φρένες: recalls iii 266, where Nestor says of Clytaemestra that she τὸ πρὶν ... φρεσὶ ... κέρχητ᾽ ἀγαθῇσι; cf. iii 266 n. κουριδίου: cf. xi 430 n.

196. 196ᵇ = *Il.* ii 325ᵇ, vii 91ᵇ.

197-8. ἀρετῆς: picks up the theme of ἀγαθαὶ φρένες. τεύξουσι δ᾽ ... Πηνελοπείῃ: the clause amplifies and justifies the earlier τῶ-clause: the κλέος of Penelope will be immortalized in song. It is significant for the poet's conception that here the gods are named as the authors of the song to Penelope: they inspire the earthly poets. On the other hand the poet is well aware of the worth of his own achievement: his own κλέος will be immortal alongside the κλέος of Penelope. ἐπιχθονίοισιν: (substantive here as at xvii 115) loc. dat., 'among mankind'. The meaning of ἀοιδὴν χαρίεσσαν is emphasized by the contrasted statement (199-201) that a στυγερὴ ἀοιδή will be the portion of Clytaemestra throughout mankind (ἐπ᾽ ἀνθρώπους, 201 ~ ἐπιχθονίοισιν, 197). The ἀοιδή will be στυγερή because it will speak of evil deeds (κακὰ ἔργα); correspondingly, the attribute χαρίεσσα surely also refers to the content, the ἀοιδή 'bringing joy' because it describes joyful things; cf. Latacz, op. cit. (xxiii 13 n.), 101.

199. οὐχ ὥς: introduces an elliptical expression. The meaning is that 'she did not behave like the daughter of Tyndareus, who ...'. Similar constructions are found in xx 426, *Il.* xix 403, and frequently later in Attic prose; cf. Shipp, *Studies*, 301 and 360. Τυνδαρέου κούρη: Clytaemestra; cf. xi 298-304 n. On the form Τυνδαρέου for Τυνδαρέω cf. Chantraine, *Grammaire*, i 197; for a theory on the morphology and etymology of the name see A. Heubeck, 'Amphiaraos', *Die Sprache* xiv (1971), 8-22, esp. 21-2. On 199ᵇ cf. κακὰ μήσατο θυμῷ, *Il.* vi 157ᵇ, xiv 253ᵇ.

200-2. 202 = xi 434. δέ τ᾽ ... | δέ τε ...: cf. Ruijgh, τε *épique*, 696; the conjecture by Schwartz, *Odyssee*, 333, δ᾽ ἔτι, 201, is superfluous. χαλεπὴν φῆμιν: 'evil reputation'. ὀπάσσει: here 'will attach'.

203-5. 203 = xxiii 288 etc. 204ᵇ = *Il.* xxii 482ᵇ. Ὣς οἱ μὲν ... οἱ δ᾽: with this formulation, so characteristic of development of the story line in Homer, the change of scene is clearly marked; 203-4 draw to a conclusion the scene in the underworld (1-202), while 205ff. bring the story back to events on earth, which the poet had abandoned at xxiii 372. On the technique of occupying a period lacking incident, e.g. the marking of time spent on a journey, with description of events elsewhere, cf. xxiii 366-72 and xxiv 1-204 nn. ἑστάοτ᾽: the dual refers to Agamemnon and Amphimedon; on the form cf. xxiii 46 n.

205-412. This episode, which reaches a climax in the reunion of Odysseus and Laertes, forms the central section of xxiv. This scene has been carefully

COMMENTARY

prepared long in advance: thus critics who, doubting the authenticity of the whole of the conclusion (xxiii 297–xxiv 548), regard the episode as a post-Homeric interpolation, must also remove as spurious the majority of those passages which clearly have the function of preparing for this encounter. This is of course hardly practical, and indeed it would be most surprising if after all the ἀναγνωρισμοί described by the poet in such detail in the second half of the epic he did not include a reunion of Odysseus with his father, an episode which is most effective in the form of a recognition scene. The fact that the scene is presented in such detail, and with a poetic quality no less than that evident in the recognition scenes with son and wife, is also evidence of authenticity. We cannot discuss here in any great detail the various interpretations which have been placed on this scene, nor the reasons for questioning its authenticity: we must refer the reader to the bibliography given in the Introduction, and to the discussion of individual passages.

Laertes is frequently mentioned in the poem, although, of the twenty-one passages in which he is named, the only significant ones are those in which the poet clearly intends to give us, by means of a series of interlocking snippets of information, a provisional general picture of the man: his outward circumstances, appearance, and state of mind—a picture which the description of xxiv confirms and completes; cf., among others, W. B. Stanford, *Hermathena* vi (1965), 10; Thornton, *People*, 115–16; Wender, op. cit. (Introd.), 57–60. In this connection we should mention the following passages: i 188–94; ii 96–102 (= xix 141–7 = xxiv 131–7); iv 110–12, 735–41; xi 187–96; xv 353–7; xvi 117–20, 137–45. Finally, the journey to the farm is carefully prepared by xvi 138 and especially xxiii 137–40.

205. The line is taken with only minor alterations from *Il.* xxiv 329; κατέβαν is retained, although strictly speaking it is suited only to the context of the *Iliad* because here there is no question of anyone 'going down'; κατα-βαίνειν must mean here (like κατέρχεσθαι, xi 188) merely 'go to'. On the other hand πεδίονδ' ἀφίκοντο has been deliberately altered to ἀγρὸν ἵκοντο; there have already been many references to Laertes' ἀγρός (i 190, xi 188, xxiii 139, 359). οἱ δ': Odysseus and his companions. τάχα δ': δὲ introduces the main clause (as at xix 330, xx 57, xxii 217).

206. τετυγμένον: this participle used usually of buildings or parts of buildings ('well constructed'), is used here of the ἀγρόν; here, then, '(well) cultivated'.

207. κτεάτισσεν: (used elsewhere of Laertes: πολλὰ κτεατίσσας, ii 102 = xix 147 = xxiv 137): 'gained, acquired ownership of'; cf. *Il.* xvi 57: δουρὶ κτεάτισσα sc. κούρην. The exact sense is disputed (cf. Stanford, ad loc.); but it clearly means that with his own hands and with great effort Laertes has brought a piece of land into cultivation, and so made it his own property (in addition to his τέμενος) (cf. W. Richter, *Archaeologia* H, 12 with n. 49); this must have been at the beginning of his reign since he was able to show his young son the trees planted there, and to give him some of them (cf. 336–44). On the description of the farm which follows, and which

382

recalls in many respects the description of Eumaeus' homestead (xiv 4–28), cf. Müller, op. cit. (Introd.); Richter, op. cit., 24–5.

208. οἶκος: probably means here the whole farmyard. κλισίον: (*hapax*) was obscure even to Aristarchus (cf. van der Valk, *Textual Criticism*, 114); Dorotheus of Askalon is said to have devoted a whole book to this one word in his λέξεων συναγωγή: and modern scholars too have come to no definite answer; cf. Ameis–Hentze, *Anhang*, iv 104; Richter, op. cit. (207n.), 24; Erbse, *Beiträge*, 199–200; Frisk, *GEW*; and Chantraine, *Dictionnaire* s.v. κλίνω. κλισίον may refer to an outhouse for the farmhands, built 'round' (scil. round the αὐλή?). πάντῃ: probably replaces an older (but still Homeric?) form *πάντη; cf. Chantraine, *Grammaire*, i 249; Risch, *Wortbildung*, 358.

209. σιτέσκοντο: (*hapax*) 'they were accustomed to eat'; on the form cf. P. Wathelet, loc. cit. (xxiii 94–5n.). ἴζανον: see Chantraine, *Grammaire*, i 316.

210. δμῶες ἀναγκαῖοι: the exact meaning of the expression, found only here, is disputed; cf. the list of explanations to date in Stössel, op. cit. (Introd.), 87–8; specifically on δμώς cf. G. Ramming, *Die Dienerschaft in der Odyssee* (diss. Erlangen/Nuremberg, 1973), 3–18; G. Wickert-Micknat, *Unfreiheit im homerischen Zeitalter* (Wiesbaden, 1983), 155–9. We have here probably not men who have experienced the ἦμαρ ἀναγκαῖον (*Il.* xvi 836), i.e. who have lost their freedom by being captured in war, but free citizens in reduced circumstances due to debt or loss of their κλῆρος, and therefore obliged to earn their living in the service of another; cf. Wickert-Micknat, op. cit, 171. A similar expression is to be found at 499: ἀναγκαῖοι πολεμισταί. τοί οἱ φίλα ἐργάζοντο: 'who carried out his wishes; who worked for him'.

211. Σικελὴ γρηῦς: we discover now that the old servant named at i 191 (ἀμφίπολος, probably a purchased slave) comes from Sicily; only later (386–90) do we also learn that she is the wife of the servant mentioned soon afterwards (222), Dolius (first introduced at iv 735). The poetic technique of παραλείπειν καὶ ὕστερον φράζειν is particularly clear here. The fact that Sicily and the western Mediterranean beyond lay well within the poet's horizons is shown by the frequency with which the island is named (Σικανίη, xxiv 307; also Σικελός, xx 383, xxiv 366, 389). As we know from reliable historical reports (e.g. the founding of Syracuse in 733 BC) and archaeological finds, the Greeks formed close links with the West by the beginning of the 8th century at the latest, and soon founded colonies; cf. T. J. Dunbabin, *The Western Greeks* (Oxford, 1948); A. Schenk Graf v. Stauffenberg, *Trinakria und Grossgriechenland* (Munich, 1963), 351–4 *et passim*; A. Heubeck, *Archaeologia* X, 82 (with bibl.). Here, as in other places (as, for instance, in his references to the Phoenicians) the poet projects back into the heroic world the ideas and conditions of his own time; cf. Stössel, op. cit. (Introd.), 88–91. πέλεν: 'she was in charge'. γέροντα: Laertes.

212. 212ᵃ ~ vii 256ᵃ etc.; 212ᵇ = i 185ᵇ. The iterative form κομέεσκεν is found elsewhere only at 390.

COMMENTARY

213-18. With a short speech Odysseus dispatches his son and the herdsmen Eumaeus and Philoetius (δμώεσσι, 213) into the δόμος of the farm. So the poet sets the scene for Odysseus and his father to meet alone, with an obvious similarity to the scene at xiv 5–28. There too Odysseus is at first to be alone with Eumaeus; to that end the poet has all four servants of the herdsman occupied outside the house at the time of Odysseus' arrival.

215. δεῖπνον: (acc.) is used as a predicative ('as a meal') of the object συῶν ὅς τις ἄριστος.

216-18. Odysseus announces his intention to 'put his father to the test' (πειράομαι + gen.), and at 217–18 explains his reason and the (ostensible) purpose of this 'trial': he wishes to know whether, after this long separation, his father will recognize him. This test has been frequently criticized as cruel and unnecessary, e.g. by Wilamowitz, *Heimkehr*, 82; von der Mühll, *Odyssee*, 766; R. v. Scheliha, *Patroklos* (Basle, 1943), 19–20; Kirk, *Songs*, 250. The occasional attempts to justify Odysseus' action, on the grounds that it is in his nature to test everything (cf. for example Focke, *Odyssee*, 378; J. T. Kakridis, *Homer Revisited* (Lund, 1971), 160–1; Stanford, ad 116–18) are hardly convincing. The subsequent narrative, however, shows that although Odysseus carries out the πεῖρα as announced, the purpose is actually quite different from that given: the ostensible reason stated turns out to have been only a (necessary) pretext, as Odysseus cannot, and does not wish to, reveal the true purpose of his πειρᾶσθαι to his companions. This will be a most unusual πειρᾶσθαι, the meaning of which only becomes clear from the interpretation of the recognition scene; it is most certainly not a 'test'.

217. αἴ κε ... ἦέ κεν: used in a double question only here; elsewhere ἤ κε is always used. The aorist subjunctives ἐπιγνώῃ and φράσσεται (short vowels; cf. Chantraine, *Grammaire*, i 454) have a future meaning when used with κε. **φράζομαι ὀφθαλμοῖσιν:** 'recognize with one's eyes'.

218. 218^b = xix 231^b. **ἀγνοιῇσι:** on the unusual metrical lengthening (-οι- < -ο-) cf. Wyatt, *Lengthening*, 168. Schwyzer, *Grammatik*, i 661, correctly conjectured that -ῃσι has replaced Homeric -ῃσι in transmission (following Wackernagel); cf. A. Heubeck, *Archaeologia* X, 110 n. 595. **ἀμφὶς:** here 'apart, away'; cf. *LfgrE* 688. 78.

219. 219^a = vi 71^a. This is not a distribution of weapons, as Merkelbach, *Untersuchungen*, 154, supposes; Odysseus hands the weapons which he had donned at xxiii 366 to the servants to take into the house. He does not wish to meet his father armed; cf. Erbse, *Beiträge*, 98; Eisenberger, *Studien*, 319.

221. ἆσσον: here with gen. (ἀλωῆς), 'nearer to'. **πολυκάρπου ἀλωῆς:** recalls the γουνὸς ἀλωῆς οἰνοπέδοιο mentioned in i 193 and xi 193 as the place where Laertes is accustomed to spend his time; on ἀλωή cf. i 193n. **πειρητίζων:** obscure; used elsewhere with gen., acc., or inf., here it is used absolutely, and cannot have its usual meaning ('test, try, prove'); the meaning is probably that Odysseus goes into the garden to see if he can find his father there.

222. The simple epic form of expression used in similar situations elsewhere (cf. for example *Il.* i 327–9: τὼ δ'. . . βάτην . . . | . . . | τὸν δ' εὗρον) is here both negated and expanded: ἆσσον ἴεν . . . οὐδ' (!) εὗρεν Δολίον; it is not until 226 that we come to τὸν δ' οἷον πατέρ' εὗρεν; this heightens our awareness of the importance of the scene to come between son and father alone (cf. 213–18 n.).

Dolius has already been mentioned several times in the poem (iv 735–9, xvii 212, xviii 322, xxii 159); of these references the first is particularly important. There we learn that he is an old δμώς given to Penelope by her father on the occasion of her marriage, and that he now keeps a κῆπος πολυδένδρεος. This Dolius is now (iv 737–8) to go to Laertes and seek his advice in connection with Telemachus' journey. Dolius' close relationship with Laertes has already, then, been established. This is reinforced by the reference to his 'tree-filled garden' (iv 736), which Odysseus also mentions, xxiii 139 and 359–60 (πολυδένδρεον ἀγρὸν), as the place where his father is to be found. Other passages name Dolius as the father of the faithless servant Melanthius and the equally wicked maid Melantho. Later (389) we discover that he is married to the Sicilian maid mentioned at 211 (cf. n.); again it only becomes clear at 387 that the υἷες of 223 are also sons of Dolius (in all they number six, as indicated at 497). Earlier critical opinion was that there are two or three characters by the name of Dolius in the poem: Penelope's servant; the father of the two miscreant servants; and the father of six fine sons; cf. Ameis–Hentze, *Anhang*, iv 104–5, and the similar arguments put forward by Erbse, *Beiträge*, 238–40 (with a summary of previous research). We must emphasize, however, that there is no compelling reason to postulate more than one servant Dolius; cf. Stanford (ad xxiv 222), Fenik, *Studies*, 191–2; Ramming, op. cit. (210 n.), 17–18, 77–8; Eisenberger, *Studien*, 315–16 with n. 3; Stössel, op. cit. (Introd.), 91–3; Wender, op. cit. (Introd.), 54–6. On phonetic grounds there can also be no question of his name being connected with δοῦλος, as M. Lambertz, *Glotta* vi (1915), 1–17, Erbse, *Beiträge*, 239, and Frisk, *GEW* iii, 77, assume. δοῦλος comes from Myc. do-e-ro/dohelos/. The name Dolius is derived from the appellative δόλος, a 'vox media', which can have a pejorative sense in some contexts, but which can also have a positive meaning: certainly the epithet δολόμητις is in no sense negative when applied to Odysseus; cf. A. Heubeck, *Bibliotheca Orientalis* xxx (1973), 481.   ὄρχατον: formed from ὄρχος, which as an agricultural term means 'row (of trees, vines etc.)' (vii 127, xxiv 341), and so comes to refer to the orchard or vineyard laid out in rows (vii 112; *Il.* xiv 123). Homeric usage distinguishes the ὄρχατος from arable and pasture, a distinction which is also expressed physically in the enclosure of the ὄρχατος (on 224–5 see below). The poet must mean this ὄρχατος when referring to the γουνὸς ἀλωῆς οἰνοπέδοιο (i 193; xi 193; cf. also xxiv 221, 224, 336) and κῆπος πολυδένδρεος (iv 737, and further xxiv 338 of Laertes). As has long since been observed, there is a correspondence between Laertes' orchard and the—albeit idealized—garden of Alcinous (vii 112–31), which is also described as ὄρχατος (112), πολύκαρπος ἀλωή (122; cf. xxiv 221) and κῆπος (129), and which, like all gardens, is

COMMENTARY

surrounded by a ἕρκος (113); for the details see W. Richter, *Archaeologia* H, 96–8 *et passim*. **ἐσκαταβαίνων:** is to be understood in a similar sense to that in κατέβαν, 205 (cf. n.).

223. δμώων: the servant Dolius appears here as master of other servants, as does Eumaeus (cf. xiv 24–8, 449–52), who has a similar position and role (cf. also 213–18n.). **υἱῶν:** sc. of Dolius; cf. 387 etc.

224–5. The reason is given for the absence of Dolius and his men: they had gone away (ᾤχοντ' in plpf. sense), with Dolius in charge (he is the γέρων of 225; ὁδὸν ἡγεμόνευε as at vi 261, x 501) 'to gather αἱμασιαί to be used (inf. expressing purpose) for the garden wall (ἕρκος)'. The garden is, then, like that of Alcinous (vii 113), surrounded by a ἕρκος, consisting of αἱμασιαί. The exact meaning of this word, which appears elsewhere in Homer only at xviii 359 (αἱμασιὰς λέγων), is as unclear as its etymology; cf. Pisani, *LfgrE* s.v., and Chantraine, *Dictionnaire* s.v.; Richter, *Archaeologia* H, 107 n. 786. It might mean stones and/or (thorny) brushwood, particularly in view of xiv 10, where a detailed description is given of the αὐλή (there, as at ix 184 and *Il.* xxiv 452, 'courtyard wall') built by Eumaeus: (δείμαθ'...) ῥυτοῖσι λάεσσι καὶ ἐθρίγκωσεν ἀχέρδῳ (xiv 8–10); on the thorny twigs of the ἄχερδος (*hapax*) cf. *LfgrE* s.v.

226–31. Having been told that Odysseus has at last found his father (εὗρεν, 226) we do not hear of further developments until 252 ff. The intervening lines are used by the poet to describe Laertes at work, amplifying the brief indication given at i 193, ἑρπύζοντ' ἀνὰ γουνὸν ἀλωῆς οἰνοπέδοιο, and xi 191, κακὰ δὲ χροῒ εἵματα εἵται. The passage is comparable to the 'insert' between xiv 5 (where Odysseus meets Eumaeus) and 37 ff. (the conversation between Odysseus and Eumaeus), which is entirely devoted to a description of the home and present activity of Eumaeus. There is a similar sequence of scenes at the beginning of xxiv: the suitors find the souls of the heroes (εὗρον, 15), while Agamemnon and Achilles are engaged in conversation (19–98); the suitors approach, and then are drawn into the conversation (99 ff.); cf. xxiv 15–22 n., and Fenik, *Studies*, 96.

226. 226ᵇ = 336ᵇ; *Il.* xx 496ᵇ, xxi 77ᵇ. **ἐϋκτιμένη:** used in a similar way to τετυγμένον, 206 (cf. n.).

227. λιστρεύοντα: (*hapax*), from λίστρον, 'tool for levelling or digging' (xxii 455, *hapax*; cf. Risch, *Wortbildung*, 42). φυτὸν λιστρεύειν probably means the same as φυτὸν ἀμφελάχαινε (242, *hapax*), picking up the half line 227ᵇ, i.e. 'digging round, breaking up the soil round the plant (shrub, tree)'; cf. Stanford, ad loc.; Richter, *Archaeologia* H, 126. **ῥυπόω:** 'be dirty'; ῥυπόωντα with unusual metrical lengthening; cf. Meister, *Kunstsprache*, 87.

228. ῥαπτόν: here 'patched'. **ἀεικέλιον:** 'disreputable, unseemly'; cf. *LfgrE* s.v.

229. κνημῖδας: Laertes' κνημῖδες (here 'leggings to protect the shins') are made of leather. It is impossible to determine what the poet had in mind by way of the appearance, construction, and material of the κνημῖδες ('greaves') worn by soldiers, especially since there have been no archaeological discoveries from the so-called dark ages up to 700 BC to help. The single occurrence of χαλκοκνημίδες as an epithet of the Achaeans (*Il.* vii 41), and two references to greaves made of tin (*Il.* xviii 613, xxi 592), do not prove that the poet did not have in mind leather shin-protectors, with (perhaps only in some cases) strips of metal sewn on. For an extensive discussion of this difficult question see H. W. Catling, *Archaeologia* E, 143–61. **ῥαπτάς:** here 'sewn'. **γραπτῦς:** (*hapax*) 'scratch'; from γράψω, 'scratch'; cf. Risch, *Wortbildung*, 40–1.

230. **χειρῖδάς:** (*hapax*) 'gloves', derived from χείρ, like κνημίς from κνήμη; cf. M. Meier, -ιδ-: *Zur Geschichte eines griechischen Nominalsuffixes* (Göttingen, 1975), 65. **βάτων:** (*hapax*) 'brambles, thorns'.

231. **κυνέην:** original meaning 'dogskin cap', there being no doubt as to the derivation from κύων; cf. Chantraine, *Dictionnaire* s.v. κύων; there is no basis for the doubts expressed by Hoekstra, *Modifications*, 99 n. 4, who refers to this as 'popular etymology'. κυνέη later became a more general term meaning 'cap, helmet', which could be made of bronze (κυνέη πάγχαλκος, xxii 102), leather (κ. ταυρείη, *Il.* x 257), weasel skin (κ. κτιδέη, *Il.* x 335, 458), or, as here, goatskin; cf. J. Borchhardt, *Homerische Helme* (Mainz, 1972); *Archaeologia* E, 57–74. **πένθος ἀέξων:** this expression, transmitted without variant and evidently not queried by ancient scholars, has been doubted by modern scholars (older literature in Ameis–Hentze, *Anhang*, iv 105; the more recent literature in J. Dingel, *RM* cxii (1969), 105–6), and there have been a number of conjectures: πνῖγος ἀλέξων, W. Schulze; ψῦχος ἀλέξων, V. Bérard; αἶθος ἀλέξων, W. Schadewaldt (translation); Eisenberger, *Studien*, 318 n. 5. These conjectures, however, can only be justified if one regards 231ᵇ as a causal or modal phrase relating only to 231ᵃ. In fact 231ᵇ belongs with the whole description, 226–31: Laertes' self-inflicted suffering also increases his grief for the son whom he believes to be dead; cf. Stanford, ad loc.; Erbse, *Beiträge*, 200. In addition πένθος ἀέξων is to a certain extent a 'quotation' from xi 187–96, a passage which prepares for xxiv 226–31 (κακὰ δὲ χροῒ εἵματα εἶται, 191), and which delineates the psychological state of Laertes with the unambiguous and undisputed 196–7, μέγα δὲ φρεσὶ πένθος ἀέξει (!) | σὸν νόστον ποθέων. It is also significant that 231ᵇ recalls μέγα δὲ φρεσὶ πένθος ἔχοντα, 223.

232. 232ᵃ = xv 59ᵃ; *Il.* v 95ᵃ etc.

233. ~ vii 218; 233ᵇ ~ xi 195ᵇ; cf. 231 n.

234. 234ᵇ = xi 391ᵇ etc. **βλωθρὴν:** (only here and *Il.* xiii 390 = xvi 483): etymology and exact meaning unknown; perhaps 'tail'; cf. Bechtel, *Lexilogus*, 82; Chantraine, *Dictionnaire*, and *LfgrE* s.v. **ὄγχνην:** (vii 115 etc.) 'pear tree'.

235-40. The formulaic 235 (= iv 117, x 151; and variations) introduces one of the 'decision' scenes typical of Homeric epic to which C. Voigt has devoted a monograph, *Überlegung und Entscheidung, Studien zur Selbstauffassung des Menschen bei Homer* (diss. Marburg, 1934; repr. Meisenheim, 1972). There are several main distinguishable types: in one form the formulaic line is followed by the naming of the alternatives considered (ἢ . . . ἠε + opt.; cf. *Il.* i 188–93; *Od.* xxiii 85–7); in another the subject considers how best to

COMMENTARY

reach a specific goal (ὡς . . . + opt.; cf. *Il.* ii 3–4); a third possibility is also raised by the use of μερμηρίζειν with infinitive, where there is hardly any question of deliberation since μερμήριξα simply means then 'I came to the decision'; cf x 151, 438. Lines 235–40, transmitted almost without variant, present a striking, and most unusual, contamination of different constructions, with μερμήριξα governing three closely related infinitives, but attached to it an ἤ + opt. clause. While many interpreters regard this unusual combination as a justifiable exception (van der Valk, *Textual Criticism*, 217; Chantraine, *Grammaire*, ii 296) or as intentional on the part of the author (Erbse, *Beiträge*, 200–2), we should in this case consider very carefully whether we have here an interpolation, albeit a very early one, which owes its origin to the model provided by iv 117–19 (iv 117 = xxiv 235; iv 119 = xxiv 238; but cf. also xxiii 85–7) where a 'normal' construction with ἠὲ . . . ἤ is involved; as suggested by A. Nauck, A. Kirchhoff, van Leeuwen, V. Bérard, Wilamowitz (*Heimkehr*, 81 n. 3), Voigt (op. cit., 36–7), von der Mühll (*Odyssee*, 766); Stössel (op. cit. (Introd.), 96–7). If we assume that we have here an interpolation, the difficulties both of construction and of the sequence of thought disappear. It is entirely reasonable that Menelaus should consider whether to leave the initiative to Telemachus, to mention his father, or 'whether he should question him, and himself test him in detail' (iv. 119), the equivalent second alternative in xxiv 238 does not make a great deal of sense. What does ἕκαστά . . . πειρήσαιτο mean here? Above all it is not up to the new arrival (in xxiv, Odysseus), but to the 'host' to do the questioning; thus Penelope is right to consider this course when faced with Odysseus at xxiii 86 (ἤ . . . φίλον πόσιν ἐξερεείνοι); and in xxiv it is Laertes who directs the decisive questions to the unknown stranger, τίς πόθεν εἰς ἀνδρῶν; πόθι τοι πόλις ἠδὲ τοκῆες; (298). Finally the effect is truly poignant when Odysseus, overcome by the pitiful sight of his father (226–31), thinks (μερμήριξε aorist!) to give way to his first impulse, and directly introduce himself without any prior πεῖρα (216). We therefore assume that in this passage the third of the three types mentioned above is present.

236. περιφῦναι: 'embrace'.

237. The optative in indirect statement (ὡς ἔλθοι) is, as has been earlier observed (cf. Ameis–Hentze, *Anhang*, iv 105; Page, *Odyssey*, 104; Shipp, *Studies*, 361) quite unparalleled in Homeric epic. It is questionable whether the difficulty can be avoided by taking the ὡς-clause as an indirect question ('how he . . .'; cf. Palmer, *Companion*, 158; Chantraine, *Grammaire*, ii 224; Erbse, *Beiträge*, 200–1; Wender, op. cit. (Introd.), 46). It is probably more reasonable to assume that the poet thoughtlessly transferred to the quite different context of xxiv 236 the construction of xvii 539 = xviii 384, in which the optative (after εἰ) is quite correct (. . . ἔλθοι καὶ ἵκοιτ' ἐς πατρίδα γαῖαν); cf. E. Tagliaferro, *Helikon* xi/xii (1971/2), 474–82.

239–40. The formulaic 239 (= x 153 etc.; on similar expressions cf. Voigt, op. cit. (235–40n.), 38–9) introduces the conclusion to which the decision scene has come (here 240); ὧδε also (unlike, for example, ταῦτα, *Il.* xvi 715) points forward: '(to act) in the following manner'. If our rejection of

238 is correct, then the closest parallel is in x 151–5, where Odysseus decides (μερμήριξα aorist!) to go to the house of Circe, and reconnoitre, but on further reflection (φρονέοντι, 153) modifies his decision: he will first (πρῶτ', 154) return to the ship, bring food for his men, and send them out on duty (before he returns to Circe). Here Odysseus comes to the decision to reveal his identity to his father immediately, but then, on further consideration (φρονέοντι) decides instead first (πρῶτον) to carry out his planned πεῖρα (and only then to reveal his identity). The inner logic of this delay of the moment of recognition by the πεῖρα will emerge from the dialogue to come (244 ff.), as will that which is meant by the scarcely translatable phrase, κερτομίοις ἐπέεσσι πειρηθῆναι. These difficult, and, we think, so often misinterpreted, words become clear only after the first part of the plan (πρῶτον) has been carried out: see 315–17 n. On δοάσσατο cf. Ruijgh, Élément, 130; Chantraine, Dictionnaire s.v. δέατο. In 240 ἐπέεσσι πειρηθῆναι the reading given by all our medieval MSS has been convincingly defended by Erbse, Beiträge, 202–4, citing T. Stifler, Philologus lxxix (1924), 323–54. The reading transmitted in P.²⁸, ἔπεσιν διαπειρηθῆναι, regarded by Wilamowitz, Heimkehr, 81 n. 3, as Homeric, and adopted by von der Mühll in his edition (cf. also Stanford, ad loc.), cannot, for various reasons, be accepted. The vulgate reading, despite the doubts expressed by Page, Odyssey, 104, and von der Mühll ('rhythmo reluctante') and others, is metrically unobjectionable.

241. After the long retardation, which, however, arises from the situation, and the development planned by the author, the poet can at last resume from 226. Odysseus, having found his father, approaches (ἰθὺς belongs with αὐτοῦ). τὰ φρονέων: picks up φρονέοντι, 239, but with the sense altered to 'with this intention (to carry out the πεῖρα)'.

242. κατέχων κεφαλὴν: this expression uses the verb in its original meaning ('hold downwards, down to the ground'); there is no cause to object to such a use (Schwartz, Odyssee, 135 n. 2; Page, Odyssey, 104); cf. van der Valk, Textual Criticism, 52–3; Erbse, Beiträge, 204; Wender, op. cit. (Introd.), 46. On ἀμφιλαχαίνω cf. 227 n.

243. 243ᵃ = 516ᵃ; 243ᵇ = xvi 308ᵇ. The sequence ὁ μὲν . . ., 242 (Laertes): τὸν δὲ . . ., 243 (also Laertes) is unusual, but not unreasonable.

244–79. Odysseus' speech follows in three parts: first 244–55, second 256–64, and third 265–79. The first part refers to the person addressed, and contains a double contrast, of the splendid κομιδή of the garden compared with, as Odysseus says, the poor κομιδή which Laertes allows himself; and then again the contrast between the poor care for outward appearance and the overall impression given by the old man, which suggests a king rather than a slave. Odysseus' question as to the man whom the other serves, the garden's owner, rounds off this section of the speech, and leads at the same time to the second part, in which Odysseus asks for confirmation of what he has just learnt from a passer-by, that he is in Ithaca. This thought is then developed, as Odysseus adds that he was unable to discover from this man whether one was still alive who had once been a guest of his. The key word

389

COMMENTARY

ξεῖνος leads on to the third part, in which Odysseus elaborates that he had taken the son of Laertes into his home, and showered him with gifts. This third part of the speech incorporates many elements from earlier 'cover-stories', particularly that of xix. Overall, however, it is in every element directed to the particular situation. It is calculated by Odysseus, with a sure psychological understanding, so that he presents himself as a man to be taken seriously, understanding, and credible, and, step by step, so as to arouse the attention, interest, and finally the curiosity of the old man to whom it is addressed. By posing questions, awaking memories, and stirring long-suppressed feelings, Odysseus forces his father not only to answer the questions put, but to ask questions in return, and so, step by step, to emerge from his self-inflicted isolation and apathy.

244. **ἀδαημονίη:** (*hapax*) is an abstract in -ίη regularly formed from ἀδαήμων; Risch, *Wortbildung*, 116. It is however to be noted that most abstracts from -μων adjectives are formed -μοσύνη (examples in Risch, 53). We should therefore consider, with Erbse, *Beiträge*, 205 (cf. *LfgrE* s.v.), whether the ancient variant ἀδαημοσύνη is not to be preferred. **οὐκ ἀδαημονίη σ' ἔχει:** an unusual construction (Kirk, *Songs*, 250, 'anti-traditional'), but not without parallel: κλέος and σέβας also occur as subjects of transitive ἔχειν. It should therefore be read as 'you are not ruled by ignorance'. **ἀμφιπολεύειν ὄρχατον:** depends on ἀδαημονίη, '(inability) to tend the garden (as ἀμφίπολος)'.

245. **ἔχει:** intrans. ἔχειν in connection with an adverb, meaning 'to be in a certain state, condition', is unusual in Homer, but quite possible; examples in Erbse, *Beiträge*, 205–6 (cf., for example, xii 435): 'The care of the garden is in excellent condition.'

246–7. Recounting all that Laertes tends amplifies what was indicated by πολύκαρπος ἀλωή in 221. The φυτόν named at the outset (227) is probably meant as a general term covering all the plants, which also appear in the description of Alcinous' garden (vii 114–28). Parallels to the unusual synaloepha in ὄγχνη, οὐ are to be found in Erbse, *Beiträge*, 206–7. **πρασιή:** a collective in -ιή derived from a substantive (from πράσον, 'leek'), 'bed of leeks, vegetable garden'; Risch, *Wortbildung*, 117.

248. The line is modelled on the very common formulaic line ἄλλο δέ τοι ἐρέω, σὺ δ' ἐνὶ φρεσὶ βάλλεο σῇσι (xi 454 etc.); the variation in the second half is modelled on *Il.* vi 326 (οὐ μὲν καλὰ χόλον τόνδ' ἔνθεο θυμῷ). The model, with its (indicative!) ἔνθεο, accounts for the unusual imperative construction μὴ ἔνθεο (μὴ + aor. imper. elsewhere only *Il.* iv 410, xviii 134); cf. E. Tagliaferro, *Helikon* xiii/xiv (1973/4), 420–9.

249–50. The contrast in thought between 249–50 and 244–8 is underlined by the formal correspondence: the unusual construction of 249 recalls that of 244; and οὐκ ἀγαθὴ κομιδή recalls εὖ ... κομιδή, 245. **αὐχμεῖς:** (*hapax*), 'are dry', is here used in an extended meaning, 'are uncared for'. This extension of meaning makes excellent sense, for the state of αὐχμεῖν will soon come to an end with a bath and anointing (366); cf. *LfgrE* s.v. **ἀεικέα ἔσσαι:** (cf. εἶμαι, xxiii 115) recalls 227–31.

251. The particular point of this sentence here gives rise to a most unusual construction, with regard to the double use of οὐ: the first οὐ negates only the expression ἀεργίης ἕνεκ', while the second οὐ negates the whole clause. The meaning is that 'it cannot be for any laziness on your part that your master does not allow you proper care (cf. κομιδή, 245, 249)'; cf. Chantraine, *Grammaire*, ii 337. **ἀεργίης:** (*hapax*), regularly derived with the abstract suffix -ίη from ἀεργός (xix 27), like κακοεργίη (xxii 374) from κακοεργός (xviii 54); cf. Erbse, *Beiträge*, 208. -ι- has metrical lengthening; there is no cause to postulate an older form *ἀεργείης; cf. Wyatt, *Lengthening*, 160–1; Risch, *Wortbildung*, 116 n. 130.

252-3. **τοι ... ἐπιπρέπει:** (*hapax*) '(Nothing of a slave) appears in you'. **δούλειος:** (*hapax*) the usual adjective is -ιος (δούλιος, xiv, 340 etc.); -ιος can sometimes be replaced for metrical reasons by -ειος, which was originally restricted to adjectives derived from metrical objects; cf. besides δούλειος also γυναίκειος, ἵππειος and others; Risch, *Wortbildung*, 132. It is not possible here to explain it as a Doric form (Shipp, *Studies*, 362). **εἰσοράασθαι:** a loosely attached infinitive ('when one looks at you'). **εἶδος καὶ μέγεθος:** (cf. v 217 etc.) an acc. of respect; cf. Bechert, op. cit. (xxiii 5 n.), 404. 253ᵇ (= *Il.* iii 170ᵇ) is the positive complement to 252–3ᵃ.

254-5. **ἔοικας:** (the unanimous reading) is syntactically not impossible: 'you look like someone ⟨to whom it would be more appropriate⟩ ... to sleep in a soft bed'; cf. Chantraine, *Grammaire*, ii 302. Bentley's conjecture ἔοικεν seems, however, to fit better, and it has won almost universal acceptance (even by Chantraine, ad loc.). The meaning then would be: 'it would be more appropriate for such a man ⟨as you⟩ ... to sleep'. The point of the passage, which (with the possible exception of ἔοικας) is certainly not corrupt (despite Stanford, ad loc.), becomes clear when we recall xi 188–95, which describes the actual conditions in which Laertes sleeps. The unusual optative in the ἐπεί-clause evidently has here less of a potential meaning (Palmer, *Companion*, 171) than an iterative sense; but a proper parallel for this use, later so common, is not to be found among the examples cited by Chantraine, *Grammaire*, ii 224–5. 255ᵇ is altered for metrical reasons from τὸ γὰρ γέρας ἐστὶ γερόντων (*Il.* iv 323, ix 422; cf. also *Od.* xxiv 190, 296, etc.).

256. = i 169 etc.

257. The first part of the speech ends with the question, who is Laertes' master? **τεῦ:** (= τίνος) is to be taken with ἀνδρῶν; cf. the formulaic half line τίς πόθεν εἰς ἀνδρῶν, vii 238ᵃ etc.

258. = i 174 etc. The formulaic line introduces the second part of the speech, which begins with Odysseus' second question (καὶ τοῦτ').

259. The meaning is: 'whether this country (τήνδε), where I have arrived, is really (ἐτεόν: adv.) Ithaca'; cf. xiii 328.

260. **οὗτος ἀνήρ:** 'the man there'. **νῦν δή:** 'just now'.

261-4. 262ᵃ ~ xix 98ᵇ, 264 = iv 834. **ἀρτίφρων:** (*hapax*) is probably a compound of the type βωτιάνειρα, formed like ἀρτιεπής and ἄρτιπος; cf. Bechtel, *Lexilogus*, 261; Risch, *Wortbildung*, 192; Erbse, *Beiträge*, 207–8; *LfgrE* s.v. For the meaning cf. οὔτε φρεσὶν ᾖσιν ἀρηρώς, x 553; i.e. approx.

COMMENTARY

'sensible (~ πεπνυμένος)'. It is possible that ἀρτίφρων is supposed to suggest the expression φρεσὶν ἄρτια εἰδέναι τινι, approx. 'have the right attitude, display loyalty towards another' (e.g. xix 248; cf. C. Calame, LfgrE s.v. ἄρτιος), where ἄρτια appears close to ἤπια. The reason given in the following ἐπεί-clause for the description of the man as οὔ τι μάλ' ἀρτίφρων could support this idea: the man questioned did not show himself very obliging; he 'did not trouble himself' (τόλμησεν) to give more exact news of the ξεῖνος in question. Odysseus suggests that the failure to give an answer was not due to ignorance, but to unwillingness. The identity of the ξεῖνος is not yet revealed. It becomes clear only from the third part of the speech, although even then Odysseus is not mentioned by name.

265–79. With the formulaic 265 (= xv 318) Odysseus introduces the third part of his speech, the subject of which has already been indicated by the key word of 263, ξεῖνος. The guest is said to have been the son of Laertes of Ithaca, and he had been well received, and honoured with many gifts. The closest parallel, both in terms of content and structure, is xix 185–202, part of the tale told by Odysseus to Penelope.

267. ~ xix 350; 267ᵃ = viii 39ᵃ.

268. = xix 351. In both instances φιλίων (for the later φίλτερος) is a comparative from φίλος; cf. Risch, Wortbildung, 90. It is used as a predicate ('as more welcome, honoured') to the subject τις βροτὸς ἄλλος; cf. Erbse, Beiträge, 209; Wender, op. cit. (Introd.), 47–8 (arguing against Page, Odyssey, 105).

269. εὔχετο: cf. 114 n.   γένος: acc. of respect.

270. Ἀρκεισιάδην: 'son of Arceisius'; cf. iv 755.

271–2. = xix 194–5.

273. ξεινήϊα: (on the unusual derivative from ξεῖνος cf. Risch, Wortbildung, 127–8), used elsewhere invariably as a substantive, could also be so used here, as object of the verb, with δῶρα in apposition ('as a gift'); Erbse, Beiträge, 209. Since, however, ξεινήϊος was originally an adjective formed from ξεῖνος, only later used in the neuter form ξεινήϊον (sc. δῶρον) as a substantive, it is also possible that we have here the older formulation ξεινήϊον δῶρον, 'guest-gift'. A parallel can be found in the development of ξείνιος, the (regular) -ιος derivative from ξεῖνος: ξείνιον δῶρον > ξείνιον, 'guest-gift'.

274. = ix 202; cf. also Il. xix 247 ~ xxiv 232.   χρυσοῦ εὐεργέος: the gold is 'well fashioned', i.e. worked into jewellery.   τάλαντα: the weight of the Homeric 'talent', mentioned only in relation to gold, is not known; it may be significantly less than the Mycenaean talent (29 kg.), and even less than the Attic talent (± 25.8 kg.).

275. 275ᵃ = ix 203ᵃ.   πανάργυρον: 'made completely out of silver'. ἀνθεμόεντα: 'with many flowers, decorated with floral patterns'.

276–7. = Il. xxiv 230–1. Exact identification of the various woven articles is not possible. χλαῖνα means the smaller kind of (woollen) wrapper used as a cloak as well as a blanket; it is ἁπλοΐς because it is simple, i.e. not folded (as opposed to μεγάλη, xiv 521, διπλῆ, xix 226, or ἐκταδίη, Il. x 134); τάπης means a thick woollen blanket used (like the κῶας) as an underblanket; φᾶρος is the larger linen cloak, and χιτών a tunic made of wool and sewn together; cf. xxiii 155 and 179–80nn.; S. Marinatos, *Archaeologia* A, 6–11; S. Laser, *Archaeologia* P, 1–15. ἐπὶ τοῖσι: 'in addition to the items mentioned'.

278. 278ᵇ = *Il.* ix 128ᵇ etc. χωρὶς δ': 'but further, in addition'.

279. 279ᵃ = ix 334ᵃ. εἰδαλίμας: (*hapax*) an artificial form, created by analogy with the common κυδάλιμος: the εἶδος of women corresponds to the κῦδος of men; the meaning is, therefore, 'beautiful'; cf. Leumann, *Wörter*, 248; Bechtel's alternative explanation, *Lexilogus*, 110, is less convincing.

280–301. Laertes' reply shows that Odysseus' words have achieved their intended effect. The speech had been designed to present the speaker as sensible, understanding, and trustworthy, and, particularly in the last section, to recall to the old man a vivid picture of the brilliant and highly honoured son. The speech brings tears to Laertes' eyes (280), and prompts his curiosity to learn more. This indicates that Odysseus has succeeded in penetrating the wall of apathy with which his father has surrounded himself (cf. 244–79 n.). Laertes' reply is also divided into three sections: first he responds to the direct and indirect questions of the second part of Odysseus' speech, and refers to the third part (281–6); then in the second part (287–96) he asks questions in return, responding to the third part of Odysseus' address to him; and finally (297–301) he asks the vital questions about the identity of the man addressing him. Laertes' reply does not take account of the first part of Odysseus' speech (but cf. 289 and 293nn.); cf. Stössel, op. cit. (Introd.), 100–1.

280. 280ᵇ = 234ᵇ etc.

281–2. ἦ τοι μὲν ...: (cf. xxiii 113n.), contrasted with ὑβρισταὶ δ' ... ἐρεείνεις: in 259. At 282 Laertes gives an explanation for the strange behaviour of the man approached by Odysseus (260–4).

283. δῶρα ... ταῦτα: 'the gifts mentioned before' (273–9). ἐτώσια is used as a predicate of δῶρα ('as useless, in vain'). χαρίζεο: here 'give in friendship'; cf. Latacz, op. cit. (xxiii 13n.), 114. Laertes' mode of thinking is entirely in keeping with the archaic expectation of return gifts (cf. θέμις, 286); cf. Finley, *World*, 73–4.

284. In 284–6 Laertes explains 283. εἰ γὰρ ... κίχεις: (2nd sing. imperf. of κιχάνω; cf. Chantraine, *Grammaire*, i 299–300): 'for if you met'. On εἰ γὰρ cf. D. Tabachovitz, *Homerische εἰ-Sätze* (Lund, 1951), 48–9. Ἰθάκης ἐνὶ δήμῳ: as at i 103.

285. σ' εὖ δώροισιν ἀμειψάμενος: (σ' = σοι) 'matching (your gifts) with ample gifts in return'; cf. Erbse, *Beiträge*, 211 (somewhat differently, *LfgrE*, i 622. 46–8 s.v. ἀμείβω).

286. ξενίῃ ἀγαθῇ: 'with splendid hospitality'. ξενίη (only here and 314) is a regular -ίη abstract formed from ξένος (which does not appear in Homer) /ξεῖνος (both from *ξένϝος, Myc. ke-se-nu-wo /ksenwo-/ etc.); cf. ξένιος, xiv 158 etc. On the coexistence of ξεν-/ξειν- see Meister's convincing

COMMENTARY

discussion, *Kunstsprache*, 202–9. **ἡ γὰρ θέμις:** (as at iii 45 etc.) cf. 283n. **ὅς τις ὑπάρξῃ:** 'when one has begun the process'. ὑπάρχω (*hapax*) is used here in the sense of the simple verb (e.g. xxii 437), further examples do not appear again until the fifth century; cf. Erbse, *Beiträge*, 211.

287. This line (= 256) introduces the second part of Laertes' response.

288. **πόστον:** (*hapax*) 'which (in the ordinal series)'; probably derived by haplology from *ποσ(σ)οστός by analogy with ordinal numbers such as ἐεικοστός (322) etc., with the accent from πόσος; cf. Chantraine, *Dictionnaire*, 921. The next example is in Aristophanes, *Pax* 163. Analytical objections are rejected by Stössel, op. cit. (Introd.), 162 (with bibl.). **ὅτε:** 'since'.

289. **ἐμὸν παῖδα:** with these words (cf. also 293) Laertes inadvertently reveals his identity, and thus indirectly answers the question put to him at 257. **εἴ ποτ᾽ ἔην γε:** this obscure formulaic expression (cf. xix 315, *Il.* iii 180, etc.) is discussed at length by W. Bergold, op. cit. (11–14n.), 71 n. 1: 'if he was that once', meaning 'if it must now be that he was that (and is no longer)'; cf. also Thornton, *People*, 155 n. 19.

290. ~ xix 301. On the deliberate repetition of δύστηνον with δύσμορον cf. Erbse, *Beiträge*, 212.

291. 291ᵃ ~ xiv 135ᵃ. At ἥ the subject of the relative clause changes.

293. **περιστείλασα:** περιστέλλω (*hapax*). The basic meaning is uncertain, perhaps 'to clothe/cover in a shroud', then 'solemnly bury' (as in Attic). **τεκόμεσθα:** again betrays Laertes' identity (cf. 289).

294. **πολύδωρος:** 'bringing in many gifts (δῶρα-ἔεδνα)', applied to a wife given away (normally by her father) for many gifts; cf. πορὼν ἀπερείσια ἔδνα, xix 529 (which refers to the groom); G. Wickert-Micknat, *Archaeologia* R, 82, 90–1.

295. **κώκυσ᾽:** 'mourned'; with acc. only here; criticized by Schwartz, *Odyssee*, 136 n. 2, as 'decadent'. ἐν λεχέεσσιν (as at 44) belongs with πόσιν.

296. 296ᵇ = 190ᵇ. καθελεῖν ὀφθαλμούς: 'close the eyes' as at xi 426.

297–8. Laertes introduces the last part of his speech with the same line used by Odysseus to begin the second section of his address (258). He poses the crucial question, as to the stranger's identity, using the same formulaic words (298) employed by Circe (x 325), Eumaeus (xiv 187), and Penelope (xix 103) when questioning Odysseus (cf. also i 170, xv 264). On the construction and meaning of the question cf. S. West, ad i 170.

299. **δαί:** a typical Atticism; cf. i 225 and *Il.* x 408. The reading δέ has been defended by van der Valk, *Textual Criticism*, 172–3, and Erbse, *Beiträge*, 212–13. The different views presented by Schwartz, *Odyssee*, 33 (δ᾽ ἥ), von der Mühll, ad loc., Shipp, *Studies*, 362, and S. West, ad i 225 (δαί), are less convincing.

300–1. Laertes considers two possibilities, that Odysseus had come in his own ship (cf. xiv 247) or as a paying passenger (ἔμπορος; cf. M. Schmidt, *LfgrE* s.v.) on a ship that was not his own (νηὸς ἐπ᾽ ἀλλοτρίης; cf. ii 318–20, where the speaker is Telemachus). **οἱ δ᾽ ...:** 'have the others (the crew), after setting you down (trans. aor. ἔβησα), sailed away (intrans. aor. ἔβην)?' On this clearly intentional and quite legitimate play on words cf. Erbse, *Beiträge*, 212 (who argues against Page, *Odyssey*, 109). In fact with the second alternative Laertes has hit on the right answer.

302. = v 214 (τὴν) etc.

303-14. Odysseus replies with a formulaic introduction (303 ~ i 179 etc.). He answer Laertes' questions in reverse order: 304-8 respond to 298-301 (the third section), 309-13ᵃ to 288 (from the second section), and 313ᵇ-14 to the thought behind 282-6 (the first section).

304-6. The names given in this fictitious biography are improvised on the spur of the moment, and are obviously meant to be seen through and decoded, not so much by Laertes, who does not react to them, but by the audience. Ἀλύβαντος: the stranger comes from Ἀλύβας, a fictitious place, thought by ancient scholars to be in South Italy (= Metapontum), probably because the island of Σικανίη is named in 307, and because of other place-names in Magna Graecia formed with -αντ- such as Τάρας, Ἀκράγας (?). Behind the form, and the metrical scheme (i.e. the place-name Ἀλύβη (τηλόθεν ἐξ Ἀλύβης, ὅθεν ..., *Il.* ii 857) and the personal name Ἀρύβας (κούρη δ' εἴμ' Ἀρύβαντος ..., xv 426). The choice of name may have been suggested by ἀλάομαι: Odysseus is the ἀλαόμενος *par excellence*; cf. Stanford, ad loc.; Erbse, *Beiträge*, 101. Thornton, *People*, 117, on the other hand, thinks of ἀλύω. Ἐπήριτος: the fictitious name of the stranger, should certainly not be connected with ἔρις etc. (as suggested by, among others, Finsler, *Homer*, ii 440; Erbse, *Beiträge*, 101); it is ultimately identical with arch. ἐπάριτος, 'picked, chosen' (X. *HG* vii 4); cf. also Lacon. Πεδάριτος (Th. viii 28)—Ion. Μετήριτος, νήριτος (sc. ὕλη: Hes. *Op.* 511), all from the root ἀρι-, 'count'; cf. Leumann, *Wörter*, 246-7; Ruijgh, *Élément*, 161-2. Ἀφείδαντος: the name of the father, Ἀφείδας, is formed by analogy with, on the one hand, Φείδας (*Il.* xiii 691; cf. also Φείδων, xiv 361; on which cf. Risch, *Wortbildung*, 230) and, on the other, Ἀ-δάμας (*Il.* xii 140), Ἀ-κάμας (*Il.* ii 823 etc.). It is not clear whether the poet was thinking here of the man who 'did not spare' the suitors, or of one 'who does not spare his property', i.e. 'generous'; cf., among others, Wilamowitz, *Heimkehr*, 70 n. 1; B. Mader, *LfgrE* s.v. Πολυπημο-νίδαο: the meaning of the name given to the grandfather is equally problematic. The unanimously attested form makes us think of the one 'who has suffered much' (so interpreted by Thornton, *People*, 117); but Cobet's conjecture that the transmitted form conceals Πολυπάμων (cf. πολυπάμων, 'owning much property', *Il.* iv 433; abbreviated form Πάμμων, *Il.* xxiv 250) ~ πολυκτήμων, is very attractive; on the details cf. Wilamowitz, *Untersuchungen*, 70 n. 1; Ameis-Hentze, *Anhang*, iv 107; Bechtel, *Lexilogus*, 281-2; H. v. Kamptz, *Homerische Personennamen* (diss. Jena, 1956; repr. Göttingen, 1982), § 26a; Erbse, *Beiträge*, 101; Risch, *Wortbildung*, 52 and 148; Chantraine, *Dictionnaire* s.v. πέπαμαι. On the formulaic word-order of 305 (similarly, for example, *Il.* ii 625, *Od.* xviii 299, etc.) cf. P. Wathelet, *ŻA* xxix (1979), 31. **δαίμων:** cf. O. Tsagarakis, op. cit. (149n.), 105–12.

307. 307ᵇ = v 99ᵇ. **Σικανίης:** according to Hdt. vii 170, and Th. vi 5 *Σικανίη* is the old form of *Σικελία*; cf. 211n. **ἐλθέμεν:** inf. expressing result.

308. = i 185. Odysseus responds to 299–301. On the ancient variant reading *μοι ἠδ' ἔστηκεν* see van der Valk, *Textual Criticism*, 146.

309–10. 310 = xix 223, *Il.* xxiv 766. These lines are in response to 288–9. *δή = ἤδη*.

311–14. **δύσμορος:** rounds off (with enjambment) 309–10, just as *δύσμορον* (290) concludes the question at 288–9. Odysseus goes on to enhance the credibility of his (fictitious!) tale to Laertes with a *τέρας* (also an ad hoc invention) which promised good fortune. **ἤ τέ:** to a certain extent expresses an antithesis to what has gone before, approx. 'though'; cf. xxiv 28n. **ἐσθλοὶ:** (*ὄρνιθες*) is explained by *δέξιοι*: the birds flew to the right, as the observer looked north, and so foretold a happy outcome. **οἷς ... ἰών:** the parallel elements of the relative clause offer a carefully constructed syntactical chiasmus: *χαίρων μὲν ἐγὼν ἀπέπεμπον... χαῖρε δ' ἐκεῖνος ἰών.* **ἐώλπει:** from *ἔλπω*; cf. xx 328. **ἔτι:** (approx. 'again later') belongs with *μείξεσθαι*. **ξενίῃ:** (on the form cf. 286n.) 'in hospitality'. **διδώσειν:** (but cf. also *διδώσομεν*, xiii 358) is an unusual form (a 'monstrum rhapsodicum' according to Page, *Odyssey*, 109; similarly Kirk, *Songs*, 250). This reduplicated future can hardly have any specialized meaning; a point emphasized by Shipp, *Studies*, 139, arguing against Chantraine, *Grammaire*, i 442. The form is rather an artificial creation in response to the demands of the metre, modelled on e.g. *ἀγλαὰ δῶρα διδοῖτε*, xi 357ᵇ, *ἀ. δ. διδοῦσιν*, xviii 279ᵇ. See further Schwyzer, *Grammatik*, i 783; Chantraine, *Grammaire*, i 448. Line 314 again refers back to 373–8 and 284–7.

315–17. Odysseus' words have the same effect on Laertes as the news of Patroclus' death on Achilles (315–17ᵃ = *Il.* xviii 22–4ᵃ). There can be no doubt either that the use of these lines from the *Iliad* is intentional or that they have a quite different function in this context. Lines 315–17 are after all preceded not by a report of Odysseus' death, but by news of a favourable omen. With well-considered words Odysseus has succeeded in breaking down his father's self-control, but also, at the same time, releasing him from the paralysis of emotion, lethargy, and apathy: he has recalled his father to life and self-awareness. In helping his father to give expression to his grief Odysseus has prepared the way forward to the moment of recognition. Indeed the anagnorisis would not be possible, or credible, were it not prepared by this spontaneous self-revelation (235–7) as the emotions, stirred up by Odysseus, rise to a sudden peak. In this sense we see more clearly the meaning of the comment that it seemed better to Odysseus in relation to his father *πρῶτον κερτομίοισ' ἐπέεσσιν πειρηθῆναι* (240). His intention is not to put his father to the test, and certainly not to do so with 'teasing', 'mocking', 'humiliating', or 'heartlessly cruel' words; and indeed no such language is used at any point. On the contrary: Odysseus' words are calculated, by their tendency simultaneously to conceal and reveal truth, from beginning to end to bring about an inner change in his father, and to make him capable of recognition. The intention described at 240 corresponds, then, to that expressed elsewhere as ἐρεθιζέμεν | κερτομίοισ' ἐπέεσσι (*Il.* iv 5–6); cf. Thornton, *People*, 115–18. In certain situations the speaker attempts to prompt a quite specific and essential emotional response in the other by means of the suggestive power of cleverly chosen words to draw the other man out (Thornton: 'provoking': on the broad range of meanings of κερτόμια ἔπεα cf. W. Bergold, op. cit. (11–14 n.), 136 n. 1). Here the aim of the πειρᾶσθαι, which is only a first step (πρῶτον!), is to create in the father the right mood, itself a precondition for Odysseus' successful revelation of his identity (for it to be accepted and believed by Laertes); cf. A. Heubeck, 'Zwei homerische πεῖραι', *ζΑ* xxxi (1981), 73–83, esp. 74–9. See also Thornton, *People*, 115–18; Stössel, op. cit. (Introd.), 98–109; W. Krehmer, *Gnomon* xlviii (1976), 537–8. Of those interpretations which more or less differ from this we should mention von der Mühll, *Odyssee*, 766; W. Theiler, in *Festschrift für É. Tièche* (Bern, 1947), 146–7; Erbse, *Beiträge*, 97–109; Moulton, op. cit. (Introd.), 163–4; Fenik, *Studies*, 47–50; Wender, op. cit. (Introd.), 57–60.

315. ἐκάλυψε: 'covered, darkened'.

316. αἰθαλόεσσαν: (αἰθαλόεις from αἴθαλος, -η, 'soot') 'sooty, black'.

317. 317ᵇ = *Il.* xxiii 225ᵇ (cf. also *Il.* xxiv 123; *Od.* vii 274).   ἀδινά: used here almost as an adverb, 'close together, following close on each other; violently'. Intensity of emotion is still expressed in Homer by quantitative expressions (cf. compounds in πολυ- such as πολυπενθής etc.); cf. B. Snell, *Die Entdeckung des Geistes* (Hamburg, 1948²), 32–3.

318-19. ἀνὰ ῥῖνας δέ οἱ ἤδη | δριμὺ μένος προῦτυψε: the intensity of Odysseus' reaction (ὠρίνετο θυμός) on seeing his father weeping with despair is described in words which are almost untranslatable and which recall, as von der Mühll, *Odyssee*, 766, rightly notes, the equally unusual description of xix 211–12. The strange phraseology cannot, however, be criticized; correctly defended by Erbse, *Beiträge*, 99 n. 3, and 214, against Kirk, *Songs*, 206–7, 250, and *MH* xvii (1960), 204 ('strained, bizarre, and indeed almost meaningless'). At the sight of his father Odysseus' heart is deeply stirred; and a sharp, stabbing pressure (pang) rose up to his nose (προτύπτειν, normally a term used in descriptions of fighting, e.g. *Il.* xiii 136 etc., is used here in an unfamiliar context), a pressure 'presaging tears' (Ameis–Hentze–Cauer, ad loc.).

320. Now at last Odysseus does what he briefly considered at 236–7, and then immediately rejected (239–40).   ἐπιάλμενος: precedes περιφὺς; once again the poet uses atypically a term usually used in battle description (e.g. xiv 220, xxii 305; cf. προῦτυψε, 319) to emphasize the violence of Odysseus' reaction.

321-60. On the skilful construction of the recognition scene see Besslich, *Schweigen*, 123–5.

321-6. Odysseus speaks.

321. Two thoughts are combined (as in xxi 207) in the short sentence with which Odysseus identifies himself: 'That man, after whom you ask (cf. 298), is me, your son, and he is standing before you (ὅδε).'

322. = xvi 206, 484, xxi 208.

323-6. After revealing his identity (μέν, 321) Odysseus abruptly turns to a new thought (ἀλλ', 323): he tells Laertes to stop mourning; time is pressing, he says (324), though his point is not immediately clear, he adds briefly the news of his revenge on the suitors. This prepares for the continuation of the story-line, for Laertes cannot be satisfied with the stranger's bald assertion that he is his son (329-30), and furthermore 326-7 give food for thought. Laertes' words at 351-5 show that he had rightly understood Odysseus' parenthetic remark of 323ᵇ.

323. ~ iv 801, xv 8, xxi 228.

324. 324ᵃ = 265ᵃ, xv 318ᵃ.   **ἔμπης:** 'in spite of all that' (i.e. 'although there would be much more to say').

325. Cf. xviii 236, 247.

326. 326ᵇ = xxiii 64ᵇ.

327-9. 329 ~ xxiii 273; 329ᵇ = xiii 344ᵇ. Laertes responds, apparently quite unmoved by Odysseus' words, and still in the grip of profound despair. In a matter of fact way he asks for evidence of the truth of this assertion ('if you really are Odysseus, my son, returned'), ignoring 323-6. All this should not surprise us, for it would not be in character for Laertes to give free reign to his joy until reliable confirmation of the stranger's claim has been produced; his attitude is the same as that of his son towards Athena in xiii (esp. 324-54), and of Penelope towards her husband in xxiii. Lines 352-5 show that Laertes has not in fact overlooked 323-6.

331-44. Odysseus' reply simply concerns his father's request at 328-9. He furnishes not one, but two σήματα, showing his scar (331-5), and pointing out the trees his father had given him as a boy (336-44). This double presentation of proof is not, as might appear, gratuitous. The scar has become an essential feature of the recognition topos in the poem, having almost led to a premature identification of Odysseus by Penelope in xix, having served as entirely adequate proof to the herdsmen (σῆμα ἀρι-φραδές, xxi 217), and having been reported to Penelope by Eurycleia (xxiii 73-7). But just as Penelope in response to the nurse rejected the scar in favour of a more sure σῆμα known only to herself and her husband, namely the secret of the bed, so here Odysseus offers his father a further 'sign' known only to the two of them: no one could tell simply by looking at them that the trees belonged to the son. The intentional parallel with xxiii is unmistakable. Cf. Müller, op. cit. (xxiii 181–2 n.), 36 n. 4; Erbse, *Beiträge*, 108–9; Stössel, op. cit. (Introd.), 107–8.

331. οὐλὴν... τήνδε: 'the wound here'; Odysseus points to it.   **φράσαι ὀφθαλμοῖσι:** cf. 217 n.

332-5. 332-3 ~ xix 393-4, 465-6; on 334-5 cf. xix 412, 460; 335ᵇ = iv 6ᵇ etc. Odysseus briefly summarizes the story of xix 393-466.   **οἰχόμενον:**

'when I had gone there'. **ὄφρ᾽ ἂν ἑλοίμην:** 'so that I could receive'.
δεῦρο μολών: on the content cf. xix 399-412.
336-44. The second *σῆμα*. Now we see that the many references to Laertes'
garden (*γουνὸν ἀλωῆς οἰνοπέδοιο,* i 193 = xi 193; *ἀγρὸν πολυδένδρεον,*
xxiii 139, 358; *πολυκάρπου ἀλωῆς,* xxiv 221) were in fact preparing for the
recognition scene.
336. 336ᵇ ~ 226ᵇ (cf. n.). **εἰ δ᾽ ἄγε ... εἴπω:** construction as at ix 37; cf.
Chantraine, *Grammaire,* ii 207.
337. ἕκαστα: sc. *δένδρεα.*
338. παιδνὸς ἐών: as at xxi 21.
339. ὠνόμασας: aor. only here; 'named, identified by species'.
340-1. Cf. vii 114-16. **ὄρχους:** (cf. 222n.) refers to the 'rows' of vines;
cf. 212-14. **ὧδ᾽:** either 'at every opportunity' (Ameis–Hentze–Cauer,
ad loc.) or (better?) 'as follows'. **ὀνόμηνας:** used with fut. inf., i.e.
almost like *ὑπισχνέομαι,* lacks close parallels in epic; cf. Page, *Odyssey* 107;
Shipp, *Studies,* 362. Nevertheless the related *ὀνομάζω* is so used with the
sense of 'specify' in two passages of the *Il.* (xviii 449 and esp. ix 515), so that
we are led to expect, or supply, a future infinitive to follow (cf. *εἰ μὲν γὰρ μὴ*
δῶρα φέροι, τὰ δ᾽ ὄπισθ᾽ ὀνομάζοι (sc. *οἴσειν, δώσειν*) | *Ἀτρείδης,* ix 515-
16), and to understand the meaning 'promise'.
342-4. διατρύγιος: (*hapax*) probably not 'interspersed with fruit trees and
vines' (Schwyzer, *Grammatik,* ii 449; Shipp, *Studies,* 362), but rather 'ripen-
ing at different times': Risch, *Wortbildung,* 114, 'diversis temporibus fructus
ferens' (Ebeling, *Lexicon* s.v.; similarly 'each row bore grapes in succession', LSJ s.v.; cf. also Erbse, *Beiträge,* 214-15; *LfgrE* s.v.). This interpretation is confirmed if we follow Ameis–Hentze, *Anhang,* iv 107, and
Erbse, *Beiträge,* 214-15, in taking *ἔνθα δ᾽ ἀνὰ σταφυλαὶ παντοῖαι ἔασιν,* 343,
as a parenthetic amplification of *ὄρχοι διατρύγιοι,* and furthermore if in
the description of Alcinous' wonderful garden (vii 112-32, esp. 122-6) we
take *πάροιθε δέ τ᾽ ὄμφακές εἰσιν* | *ἄνθος ἀφιεῖσαι, ἕτεραι δ᾽ ὑποπερκάζουσιν*
(vii 125-6) as an elaboration of the expression *σταφυλαὶ παντοῖαι.* Cf.
Richter, *Archaeologia* H, 133 and 145-6 **ἤην:** (also given at xix 283,
xxiii 316, *Il.* xi 808) is not objectionable; cf. Meister, *Kunstsprache,* 109;
Chantraine, *Grammaire,* i 289. **ἀνὰ:** as an adverb is rare; but cf. in a
similar context *μέλανες δ᾽ ἀνὰ βότρυες ἦσαν, Il.* xviii 562; cf. Wender, op.
cit. (Introd.), 49. **ἔασιν:** is not likely to be corrupt, as Schwartz,
Odyssee, 333, supposes; his conjecture *ἔησαν* seems unnecessary. If we
assume that *ἤην· ἔνθα ... ἔασιν* (343; see above) is parenthetic, then the
construction *ὁππότε* with iterative optative in 344 is no longer problematic
(cf. Erbse, *Beiträge,* 215; Chantraine, *Grammaire,* ii 259, gives a different
explanation); thus 'whenever the seasons of Zeus (with their different
weather conditions) press down on them with their power'.
345-50. Laertes, wrenched out of apathy by the *κερτόμια ἔπεα* of his son, and
set free to mourn just a moment before, is now so overcome by his son's
convincing *σήματα* that he briefly loses consciousness (*ἀποψύχοντα,* 348; cf.
347-8n.), and must be supported in Odysseus' arms. The poet uses a

formulaic phrase (345 = iv 703, v 297, 406, xxii 68, *Il.* xxi 144), which always denotes complete mental and physical effects induced by a deeply disturbing situation or piece of news, but which does not in other cases result in fainting. The addition of 346, however, recalls in particular Penelope's reaction to Odysseus naming the secret of the bed, xxiii 205–6 (= xxiv 345–6). Odysseus' father reacts in the same way as she had done, but more dramatically, since he actually loses consciousness (cf. 348–9).

345–6. Cf. xxiii 205–6 n.

347–8. 347ª = xv 38ª. The passage τὸν δὲ ποτὶ οἱ (sc. approx. κλινόμενον) | εἷλεν ('took, seized') is taken from *Il.* xxi 507 with the addition of ἀποψύχοντα as required by the context. Active ἀποψύχειν is unique in Homer. Whereas middle ἀποψύχεσθαι (*Il.* xi 621, xxi 561, xxii 2; on the details cf. LSJ s.v.), with ἱδρῶ as its object, is connected with ψῦχος, and means 'to cool off the sweat', active ἀποψύχειν means roughly 'to lose consciousness (ψυχή)', like ψυχὴν ἀποκαπύειν, *Il.* xxii 467; cf. Erbse, *Beiträge*, 216.

349. The very similar v 458 (~ *Il.* xxii 475) describes strength returning to Odysseus after he had collapsed in total exhaustion (ἄπνευστος, ἄναυδος, ὀλιγηπελέων; κάματος) on the shore. The repetition of the line here shows that Laertes' collapse is only temporary (cf. 245–50 n.). Laertes soon recovers his breath (ἄμπνυτο as at *Il.* v 697; xxii 475; cf. Ruijgh, *Élément*, 134), and his strength (θυμός) returns (ἀγέρθη). On the terminology and its meaning, cf., among others, B. Snell, op. cit. (315 n.), 17–42, and the literature given in Heubeck, *Frage*, 188–9.

350. = iv 234 ~ xix 214.

351–5. Laertes responds now to his son's news given at 324–6. His words are prefaced by an invocation of Zeus and the other Olympians, which expresses the new spirit of the *Odyssey*. Laertes sees the retribution on the suitors as an act of divine justice, an expression of a far-reaching theodicy; cf. W. Burkert, *RMus* ciii (1960), 130–44, esp. 141; Friedrich, *Stilwandel*, 135. At the same time his words at 353–5 also show that he has seen the point of his son's counsel in 324–6 to make haste (χρὴ σπευδέμεν, 324).

351. For Ζεῦ followed by pl. θεοὶ cf. xx 98.

352. This line responds to 325–6. **ἐτεόν:** here adverbial.

353. 353ª = *Il.* i 555ª etc. Laertes fears the vengeance of the suitors' kinsmen, just as Odysseus had done, xx 41–3, xxiii 117–22 (cf. n.), 137–40, 362–5, xxiv 324.

354. Ἰθακήσιοι: here denotes specifically the families of the suitors.

355. πάντῃ: cf. 208 n. ἐποτρύνωσι: here 'dispatch (in haste)'. The use of the verb with ἀγγελίας means that we probably have here not ἡ ἀγγελίη, 'a message', but ὁ ἀγγελίης, 'a messenger'. On the morphologically strange formation of ὁ ἀγγελίης from the older (and regular) ἡ ἀγγελίη in the course of the epic tradition cf. Leumann, *Wörter*, 168–73; B. Forssman, *Münchner Studien zur Sprachwissenschaft* xxxii (1974), 41–64; H. Erbse, in *Le Monde grec: Hommage à Claire Préaux* (Brussels, 1972; 1978²), 68–74. Κεφαλλήνων: the form has raised objections (cf. Wilamowitz, *Untersuchungen*, 73), but should not have done. It is modelled on *Il.* ii 631–6 and iv 350, where Odysseus' men are referred to collectively as Κεφαλλῆνες; cf. also *Od.* xx 210, xxiv 378, 429. D. Mülder, *RMus* lxxx (1931), 1–35, esp. 11–15, has argued convincingly that the alternating use of the quasi-identical terms Ἰθακήσιοι and Κεφαλλῆνες is governed by the demands of metre. Cf. Stössel, op. cit. (Introd.), 109–10.

357–60. Odysseus does not deny the danger he himself had pointed out, but urges his father to take heart. At the same time he tries to steer the conversation indoors, where his companions are waiting.

357. = xiii 362, xix 436, *Il.* xviii 463.

358. 358ᵃ ~ *Il.* xviii 266ᵃ.

359. ~ xxiii 367. **ἔνθα:** 'thither'. Lines 359–60 recall 214–15.

360. 360ᵇ ~ *Il.* xxiv 263ᵇ. **προῦπεμψ':** the only Homeric form in which -ου- formed by crasis is in the stressed half (*longum*) of the foot; in every other case -ου- could theoretically be read, because it is in the unstressed, second half of the foot, as uncontracted -οε- (‿ ‿). There is, however, no reason to find this objectionable; cf. Erbse, *Beiträge*, 217.

361–83. Odysseus and Laertes arrive at the house; Laertes bathes, and his appearance is enhanced. The bath scene (partly through the choice of words) deliberately recalls the parallel scenes of vi 224–5 (cf. also xviii 69–70) and xxiii 153–63. It is fruitless to speculate about any one scene being derived from the others: each suits its own context. This bath scene serves to present the 'rejuvenated' Laertes as a worthy fellow combatant alongside the younger men, and to fit him for his ἀριστεία, for he will in fact be the first to kill one of the enemy (525–30). In this sense the scene 365–71 indicates how the story will end.

361. 361ᵃ = *Il.* vi 232ᵃ; 361ᵇ ~ xv 454ᵇ.

362. = xv 28, 85.

363. ~ 359, xxiii 367.

364. 364ᵇ = xv 500ᵇ.

365. 365ᵇ = xxiii 153ᵇ. **Τόφρα:** 'meanwhile'. **ᾧ ἐνὶ οἴκῳ:** has less force here than at xxiii 153.

366. 366ᵇ = xxiii 154ᵇ. **ἀμφίπολος Σικελή:** cf. 211 n.

367. 367ᵃ ~ xxiii 155ᵃ. In place of φᾶρος and χιτών only the χλαῖνα is named here.

368. = xviii 70 (which refers to Odysseus). **ἤλδανε:** 'filled out'.

369. 369ᵃ ~ vi 230ᵃ, [xxiii 157ᵃ]; 369ᵇ = viii 20ᵇ, xviii 195ᵇ. **ἰδέσθαι:** on the middle see Bechert, op. cit. (xxiii 5 n.), 152–3.

370–1. ~ xxiii 163; 370 = iii 468, 370ᵃ = xxiii 163ᵃ, 370ᵇ ~ xvi 178ᵇ; 371ᵇ = ii 5ᵇ, iv 310ᵇ.

372. = i 122 etc.

373. 373ᵇ = xxiii 81ᵇ.

374. 374ᵃ ~ 253ᵃ. **εἶδός τε μεγεθός τε:** acc. of respect as at 253.

375. This formulaic line is very common in the *Odyssey*, but with Telemachus as subject (i 368 etc.).

376–82. This speech of Laertes' clearly recalls the Iliadic Nestor; indeed Laertes here assumes an almost Nestorian role, for often in such critical situations Nestor had expressed the wish that his youthful strength could be restored, and retold the story of one of his earlier exploits as an example to inspire his listeners (*Il.* vii 132–57; xi 670–762; xxiii 629–43). The close connection with the Iliadic model is amply illustrated by the borrowing of 376 word for word from *Il.* vii 132. The difference between the situation here and the three comparable scenes with Nestor is that Laertes speaks of his past exploit, the capture of Nericus, only after the new event (the slaughter of the suitors), and so his speech is not exhortatory, looking forward to new deeds, but retrospective (379–82). In view of the difference in context the formal framework of the paradigmatic tale is significantly altered from the *Iliad* (e.g. in xi: εἴθ' ὡς ἡβώοιμι..., 670: ὡς ἐών..., 762) to: αἰ γάρ... οἷος..., τοῖος ἐών... (on the construction cf. 379–80 n.).

377–8. 377ᵇ = iii 4ᵇ. Laertes tells how, as Lord of the Cephallenians (cf. 355 n.) he conquered the town of Νήρικος (as read by von der Mühll and others, not Νήριτος). Νήρικος is thus in somewhat awkward apposition to ἀκτὴν ἠπείροιο; the sense probably is 'the city on the coast of the mainland'. The geographical details remain unclear, and have given rise to much speculation. The town may have stood where, in Homeric times, Leucas (later to become an island) was still connected by an isthmus to mainland Acarnania (before the cutting made by the Corinthians; Strabo x 451 ff.). The town Nericus is later mentioned in Th. iii 7 in connection with an Athenian campaign against Leucas and Acarnania. Νήρικος has no connection with the mountain Νήριτος on Ithaca (ix 22 etc.). On the details cf. Ameis–Hentze–Cauer, ad loc.; Bechtel, *Lexilogus*, 160 (unreliable on individual points); Stubbings, in *Companion*, 400; Simpson–Lazenby, *Catalogue*, 103.

379–80. 370ᵇ = 325ᵇ etc.; 380ᵃ = *Il.* vii 137ᵃ. **τοῖος ἐών**: here Laertes elaborates on the wish introduced with αἰ γάρ (376), with the infinitives ἐφεστάμεναι καὶ ἀμύνειν: 'oh if only I, as the man who conquered then, could have helped you yesterday'; on the unusual construction (cf. further vii 313 in the disputed, but certainly genuine passage vii 311–16; cf. Hainsworth, ad loc.; Shipp, *Studies*, 330, differs) cf. Palmer, *Companion*, 155; Chantraine, *Grammaire*, ii 318. **χθιζὸς**: like ἡματίη, xix 203. **ἐφεστάμεναι**: cf. ἐφέστασαν, xxii 203.

381–2. κε: belongs with ἔλυσα (past unreal) and with ἐγήθεις. On 382 cf. xxiii 47; cf. Hoekstra, *Modifications*, 122.

383. = iv 620 etc.

384–5. 384 = xvi 478; 385 = i 145 etc. While 383 (οἱ μὲν) refers to Odysseus and Laertes, οἱ δ' ἐπεὶ οὖν resumes from 364, and refers to those who were already in the house, viz. Telemachus, Eumaeus, and Philoetius (H. Reynen, *Glotta* xxxvi (1958), 40–1). 385–6 refer to all five men (οἱ μὲν, 386).

386. δεῖπνῳ ἐπεχείρεον: this unusual expression (the verb is used in Homer only here and in the related 395), instead of the expected formula of i 149 etc., is necessitated by the context: those in the house were about to eat (ἐπεχείρεον imperf.!) when Dolius and his sons appeared on the scene.

The meal is delayed until after the intermediate episode (which lasts until 411); 412 resumes from 386. Against the objections of Page, *Odyssey*, 108, see Erbse, *Beiträge*, 271; Eisenberger, *Studien*, 317–18 n. 5.

387. Dolius and his team return from the work described at 222–5. On the figure of Dolius cf. 222 n. σὺν: here adv. 'together with him'. υἱεῖς: only here and 497, xv 248; elsewhere υἷεες or υἷες.

388–90. ἐξ ἔργων (cf. 224) μογέοντες is an unusual expression; cf. Schwartz, *Odyssee*, 136 n. 2; Page, *Odyssey*, 108. Normally μογέω is transitive, 'suffer' (e.g. in the formulaic πολλὰ μογήσας, ii 343 etc.); there are in addition only two passages in which the participles μογέων and μογέοντες respectively are used absolutely to mean 'only with difficulty, with great effort': *Il.* xi 636 and xii 29. There may be a development from such usage to the expression in xxiv 388, which can hardly mean anything other than 'worn out from working in the fields'; cf. Erbse, *Beiträge*, 218. προμολοῦσα: the mother had in the meantime gone out to the fields, and fetched Dolius and his sons (with, of course, the news that Odysseus had returned). Only now do we learn that the 'Sicilian maid', who has appeared before (cf. 211 n.), is Dolius' wife. σφεας: her husband and sons. ῥα γέροντα | ἐνδυκέως κομέεσκεν: as at 211–12. κατὰ ... ἔμαρψεν: (sc. αὐτον) tmesis.

391. φράσσαντό: cf. 216–18.

392. ἔσταν: 'they remained standing'. τεθηπότες: cf. xxiii 93–5 n. (τάφος), 105–7 n. (τέθηπεν). On the content cf. 388–90 n.

393. ἐπέεσσι καθαπτόμενος: 'addressing (him) courteously'.

394. ἀπεκλελάθεσθε: (*hapax*) has unusual, but unobjectionable, strengthening of normal ἐκλελάθεσθε with the additional prefix ἀπό ('wholly and completely'); explained by Erbse, *Beiträge*, 219. θάμβευς: refers to the behaviour of those who have just arrived, described as τεθηπότες; on the etymological relationship of θάμβος, τέθηπα (and τάφος) cf. Chantraine, *Dictionnaire* s.v. θάμβος. The scansion ‒ ‒ of the genitive of a neuter in -ος, as in θάμβευς, is otherwise unattested in Homer (Page, *Odyssey*, 108), but can be accepted in view of scansions such as ἐρέβευς (∪ ∪ ‒), xi 37, and θέρευς (∪ ‒), vii 118; cf. Chantraine, *Grammaire*, i 58; Erbse, *Beiträge*, 219–20. The poet could have written -εος (εο); cf. in the Naxian Nicandre inscription (IG xii 5, 1425b; *CEG* 404. 3) Δεινομένεος (‒ ∪ ∪ ‒).

395. ἐπιχειρήσειν: cf. 386 n.

396. 396ᵇ ~ ix 545ᵇ.

397–407. The exchange with Dolius follows the pattern of the last part of the scene with Laertes: 397–8 ~ 345–8; 399–405 (403–5: concern about Penelope) ~ 349–55 (353–55: fear of the suitors' kinsmen); 406–7 ~ 356–7; cf. Fenik, *Studies*, 191–2. The doubts expressed by Schwartz, *Odyssee*, 333, about the authenticity of 403–8 are not justified.

397–8. χεῖρε (dual) πετάσσας | ἀμφοτέρας (pl.) as at *Il.* xxi 115–16; on the construction cf. Schwyzer, *Grammatik*, ii 47 n. 8. Ὀδυσεῦς: this form of the gen. (alongside the common Ὀδυσσῆος and Ὀδυσῆος, as well as the unique Ὀδυσσέος of *Il.* iv 491) is quite unparalleled: normally -ε(ϝ)ο-

COMMENTARY

is not contracted; Chantraine, *Grammaire*, i 34. Did the poet intend
*Ὀδῦσεος (with εο pronounced as a diphthong, corresponding to
Ὀδυσσέος taken as scanning ∪ –⁴ –)? Other scholars assume that the text
is corrupt, and offer conjectures: ἄμφω Ὀδυσσῆος, Nauck; Ὀδυσέως,
Bérard. There is an extensive discussion in Erbse, *Beiträge*, 220–1. **ἐπὶ
καρπῷ:** ('wrist') with λαβών, χεῖρ'(α) with κύσε.
399. = xx 198 etc.
400–1. **ἐελδομένοισι:** (ἐέλδομαι: 'wish for, long for') predicative with ἡμῖν
(cf. xx 209), as is ὀϊομένοισι. Only the reading οὐδ' ἔτ' can be correct;
Ruijgh, τε *épique*, 707.
402. 402ᵇ = viii 413ᵇ. **οὐλέ:** (*hapax*), originally voc. of οὖλος, Attic ὅλος,
is used here as an imperative ('*salve*') in conjunction with χαῖρε (cf.
Chantraine, *Dictionnaire* s.v. ὅλος); literally 'be happy and well'; cf. Latacz,
op. cit. (xxiii 13 n.), 50. **μάλα:** an ancient conjecture (cf. van der Valk,
Textual Criticism, 36); μέγα (vulgate) is supported by *h.Ap.* 466.
403–5. In view of the close personal bond between Dolius and Penelope (iv
735–41) his question should not be criticized as 'impertinent and inappropriate' (Schwartz, *Odyssee*, 333), for it shows his loyalty and devotion; cf.
Stössel, op. cit. (Introd.), 113.
403. = 258, 297, etc.
405. **ὀτρύνωμεν:** deliberative subjunctive.
407. The line is modelled on *Il.* xiii 275; the reply sounds more abrupt than
intended.
408. = xvii 602. **αὖτις:** in xvii Eumaeus does sit down *again*, but this is
not true of Dolius and αὖτις is difficult to explain here; it may be an
instance of careless repetition of a line from another context; cf. R. Führer,
LfgrE i, col. 610, 23–7 s.v. αὖτις. The ancient variant αὖθι κάθιζεν seeks to
avoid this difficulty. **ἐπὶ δίφρου:** the δίφρος, probably a stool without a back or arms, is for the servants' use: Odysseus and his companions
sit on κλισμοί and θρόνοι (385); cf. S. Laser, *Archaeologia* P, 37 *et passim*.
409–10. The meaning behind this abbreviated account is that the sons of
Dolius crowd round Odysseus, and greet him (δεικανόωντ' only at xviii
111ᵃ = xxiv 410ᵃ, and *Il.* xv 86; on the etymology and form of δεικανάομαι
cf. the investigations of B. Forssman, *Die Sprache* xxiv (1978), 3–24). On
410–11 cf. x 397ᵇ ἔφυν τ' ἐν χερσὶν ἕκαστος. **ἐν ... φύοντο:** belong
together, and χείρεσσι is an instrumental dat.: 'they grew on him with their
hands, they clasped him by the hand'.
411–12. **ἐξείης δ' ἕζοντο:** 411 resumes with a verbal echo from 385. After
the arrival of Dolius and his sons all present can now begin the meal which
Odysseus and his men had wanted to start earlier (385). While iv 624
(= xxiv 412) refers to the preparation of the meal, 412 refers to the meal
starting (almost in the sense of οἱ δ' ἐπ' ὀνείαθ' ἑτοῖμα προκείμενα χεῖρας
ἴαλλον, i 149 etc.). But just as at 386 the typical development of the action is
interrupted: there is here no conventional line to close the meal (αὐτὰρ ἐπεὶ
πόσιος κτλ., i 150 etc.). Instead, in keeping with the Homeric pattern of
marking time (cf. xxiv 1–204 n.), the lull in the action caused by the meal is

occupied by a glance at the action taking place elsewhere (the gathering of the suitors' kinsmen in the city, 413–71; and the gods' conversation, 472–88); and the meal does not end until 489(~ i 150). The uncharacteristic sequence of events is indicated by the phrases Ὣς οἱ μὲν . . ., which prepares for the change of scene (Ὅσσα δ' . . .); cf. Arend, *Szenen*, 72; Freidrich, *Stilwandel*, 204 n. 121. It is worth noting that the change of scene announced with 412 also occurs after the identical iv 624, in that instance from Sparta to Ithaca: μνηστῆρες δὲ . . . (625).

413–548. The final part of the last book is devoted to the confrontation and reconciliation with the suitors' kinsmen. This is the goal to which the whole of the poem has been directed, for from the first the action has been leading not just to the hero's return, his revenge on the suitors, and reunion with those nearest to him, but also to the restoration of the old order in Odysseus' kingdom. In keeping with the importance of this concluding scene (σπονδαί) for the inner and outward structure of the poem it is carefully prepared—like the recognition scene with Laertes, but also, of course, the reunion with Penelope, the battle with the suitors etc. This preparation begins in the very first books, but increases in intensity towards the close of the epic. So there can be no doubt that the assembly of the Ithacans in xxiv 413–71 is intended as a structural counterpart to the popular assembly in ii 1–259, just as the interchange between Zeus and Athena at xxiv 472–88 is conceived in parallel to the similar divine scene at i 22–95. The structural parallels are underlined by the similar constellations of characters: in both i and xxiv the Olympian conversation is conducted by Athena and Zeus; and the roles played in the popular assembly in xxiv by Antinous' father Eupeithes, on the one hand, and on the other by the herald Medon and the prophet Halitherses, correspond to those played in ii by Antinous himself, Halitherses, and Mentor. Furthermore Odysseus' fear that revenge on the suitors would provoke vengeance from their families is first expressed in his exchange with Athena (xx 40–2), and reappears in his conversations with Telemachus (xxiii 117–40), Penelope (xxiii 361–5), and Laertes (xxiv 324–6); all these passages would be pointless if Odysseus' fear were not realized. The poet has, however, also carefully indicated well in advance the futile result of the kinsmen's enterprise. Twice at the beginning of the epic Telemachus speaks words of crucial significance in defiance of the suitors (i 376–80 = ii 141–5). The key word is νήποινος: the complaint that the βίοτος of Odysseus is being wasted, νήποινος, without the suitors paying for it, is followed by an imprecation that Zeus may exact vengeance, and see that they perish, νήποινοι; this means here, in ironic adaptation of the meaning in i 377 = ii 142, that they should not count on revenge after their bloody end. Zeus' acknowledgement of Telemachus' prayer by sending an omen in the form of two eagles (ii 146ff.) is intended to foreshadow the action to come in xxii and xxiv: the suitors will not only meet their just deserts; their deaths will be unavenged. Telemachus' words therefore point to the essential goal of the whole epic narrative: Zeus and his daughter will replace the old patriarchal system of justice, which has until now prevailed with remorseless consistency, as in accordance with the law of the vendetta bloodshed repeatedly calls for further bloodshed; in its place they will establish a new moral order, one based on a justice guarded and supported by the gods. We should also note that the σπονδαί restore the relationship between Odysseus and the demos of Ithaca, who had played such a cowardly and inglorious role in the assembly of ii. The old harmony between people and ruler, which had been sadly interrupted (cf. ii 230–41; 230–4 = v 8–12), is restored. Doubts as to the authenticity of the σπονδαί are regularly expressed, latterly by Müller, loc. cit. (xxiii 153–63 n.) and Eisenberger, *Studien*, 314–26. For the counterarguments cf. esp. Heubeck, *Dichter*, 36–40; H. Hommel, 'Aigisthos und die Freier', *Studium Generale* viii (1955), 237–45; 'Aischylos Orestie', *Antike und Abendland* xx (1974), 14–24, esp. 17–19; Erbse, *Beiträge*, 139–42; Stössel, op. cit. (Introd.), 115–37; W. Krehmer, 'Volk ohne Schuld', *ZA* xxvi (1976), 11–22; *Gnomon* xlviii (1976), 339; B. Andreas and H. Flashar, *Poetica* ix (1977), 249–50; Wender, op. cit. (Introd.), 63–71.

413. 413ᵇ = ii 383ᵇ ~ *Il.* v 495ᵇ. **Ὅσσα δ':** signals the scene-change from the farm to the πτόλις (cf. 411–12 n.), where the news (ὅσσα) of the slaughter of the suitors is spreading. ὅσσα appears here as a superhuman being, who goes through the town as an ἄγγελος; the model of *Il.* ii 93–4 (Ὅσσα . . . | ὀτρύνουσ' ἰέναι, Διὸς ἄγγελος) appears to be an influence; but even at i 282, where ὅσσα appears at first to be used purely as an abstract, the following line, ἐκ Διός, ἥ τε μάλιστα φέρει κλέος ἀνθρώποισι, shows that here too personal conception is involved. On the complex meanings of so-called abstracts in early Greece cf. J. Grüber, op. cit. (57 n.), 87–9 (on ὅσσα in particular, 31). **πάντη:** cf. 208 n.

414. **θάνατον καὶ κῆρ':** cf. 127.

415. ~ ix 401, xi 42. **οἱ δ':** the meaning is deliberately kept vague: in 416 ff. it probably refers first of all only to the families of the suitors; however, in the ensuing ἀγορή (420 ff.) we are probably meant to think (as in ii) of the whole Ithacan people gathered together (cf. 443, 454). There is no universally accepted explanation of what ὁμῶς refers to and means; cf. Stanford, ad loc.; perhaps it goes both with ἀΐοντες (in the temporal sense) and with ἐφοίτων (local: 'together').

416. **μυχμῷ:** (*hapax*) 'moaning, groaning', is formed with the suffix -σμος from the root found in Attic μύζειν, μύξαι, 'groan'; cf. Risch, *Wortbildung*, 46. **δόμων προπάροιθ':** cf. πάροιθεν μεγάροιο, iv 625; probably in the αὐλή.

417. **ἐκ ... οἴκων:** the physical layout is indicated in xxii 448–51 (the women carry the dead suitors from the μέγαρον, and lay them down ὑπ' αἰθούσῃ . . . εὐερκέος αὐλῆς) and xxiii 49 (the bodies lie ἐπ' αὐλείῃσιν); so the families find the corpses in the αὐλή, near the πρόθυρον ('courtyard gate'), where apparently the courtyard wall (ἕρκος) was made into an open portico (αἴθουσα), presumably by pillars within the courtyard; cf. S. Hiller, 'Die Aithusa bei Homer', *WS* NF i (1970), 14–27. In the circumstances οἴκων (pl.!) can only mean (uniquely in Homer) 'the whole palace

complex, the palace'. **ἔκαστοι:** (in explanatory apposition to the subject οἱ) means here the individual families of the dead suitors. It is questionable whether, as Schwartz, *Odyssee*, 333, and others claim, the text is really corrupt here; for an extensive discussion of the textual questions see Stössel, op. cit. (Introd.), 257 n. 3. It is in any case noticeable that the narrator is in haste here: his intention is evidently to see the corpses buried before the σπονδαί.

418-19. The meaning of these lines is clear: while the Ithacan families bury their sons, the bodies of those from more remote parts of Odysseus' kingdom (cf. xvi 122-4; *Il.* ii 631-5) are placed on fast ships to be transported home. But the construction is unusual. The use of πέμπειν with infinitive is common enough, but the passages which evidently served as models, *Il.* xvi 454-5, 671-3 ~ 681-3, are constructed differently. Perhaps the poet inferred from them (and used in his own distinctive fashion) a construction πέμπειν τινί meaning 'to hand over to someone'; normally, of course, we find πέμπειν τινί τι, 'to send someone something' (v 167).

420. 420ᵃ = xvi 361ᵃ. **εἰς ἀγορὴν:** the meaning here initially is a meeting of the suitors' families; as the scene develops the poet wishes to give the impression (by the appearance of Halitherses and Medon) of a regular assembly of the people as in ii (cf., for example, 438). **ἀχνύμενοι κῆρ:** as at xii 250.

421. = ii 9 etc.

422. Cf. *Il.* vii 94, 123. **δ':** on δέ, which connects the main clause to the preceding subordinate clause, cf. Chantraine, *Grammaire*, ii 356-7.

Εὐπείθης: father of Antinous (i 383 etc.), appears here in person for the first time; on his significant name see H. Mühlestein, *ŽA* xxi (1971), 46-7.

423. **ἄλαστον:** 'violent'. The etymology is obscure, possibly formed from alpha privative and the root λαθ- (λανθάνω), and originally meaning 'unforgettable'; Chantraine, *Dictionnaire* s.v. ἀλάστωρ. **πένθος:** with objective gen., 'pain on account of another'.

424. −21.

425. = ii 24. **τοῦ:** objective gen. with δάκρυ.

426-62. On the inner links within the triad of speeches (Eupeithes, Medon, Halitherses) cf. Besslich, *Schweigen*, 98-101.

426-37. Eupeithes urges the people to revenge. It should be noted that the projected vengeance is quite within the moral and legal bounds of convention; cf. Finley, *World*, 89.

426. 426ᵃ = iv 663ᵃ, xvi 346ᵇ; 427ᵇ = *Il.* iv 298ᵇ etc. **μέγα ἔργον:** 'an evil deed' (similarly iii 261, xi 272, xix 92). Besides ἔργον, μήσατ'(ο) also governs the personal accusative Ἀχαιούς (by analogy with e.g. βλάπτω τινά); a parallel construction is also to be found at xviii 27, ὃν ἂν κακὰ μητισαίμην (differently, for example, at xxiii 96).

427-9. **τοὺς μὲν ... τοὺς δ' ...:** the reasons for the accusation are given in a double form, with, however, the emphasis on the second element. The syntax of 427-8 is unusual: after the participial construction of 427, in which τοὺς μέν (those who took part in the expedition to Troy) is the object

407

of ἄγων, we have in 428 a subdivision of the μέν-part into two complementary μέν and δέ clauses, in which first νῆας, and then λαούς ('crew') are the object of ὤλεσε. τούς δ', 429, refers, of course, to the suitors.   ἐλθών: 'on his return'.   Κεφαλλήνων: cf. 355 n.

430. ἱκέσθαι: sc. to avoid our revenge.

431. = xiii 275 (~ xv 298). On Elis and the Epeians cf. Il. ii 615–24.

432. ἴομεν: a short vowel subjunctive (hortatory); where exactly they are going to go is not mentioned yet.   καί ἔπειτα: 'in time to come'; similarly ii 60.   κατηφέες: (hapax) 'covered with shame'; from this κατηφείη (Il. iii 51 etc.); on the morphology cf. Risch, Wortbildung, 82, and on the (uncertain) etymology cf. Chantraine, Dictionnaire s.v. (with bibl.).

433. = Il. ii 119; 433ᵇ = xxi 255ᵇ; τάδε prepares for 434–5.

435. ἐμοί γε: 'at least for me, as far as I am concerned'.

436. ζώέμεν: here 'live longer'.   μετείην: here a genuine optative (unlike ἄν... γένοιτο, 435).

437. ἀλλ' ἴομεν: after the explanation given in 433–5, ἴομεν of 432 is emphatically repeated.   φθέωσι: (with synizesis -εω-) short vowel subjunctive of ἔφθην resulting from quantitative metathesis (cf. φθέωμεν, xvi 383); cf. Meister, Kunstsprache, 159; Chantraine, Grammaire, i 64, 71, 459. περαιωθέντες: περαιόομαι (hapax), from περαῖος (ἀντιπέραια, Il. ii 635): 'travel across (from one coast to another)', as indicated, for example, at 430–1; differently περάω with acc., 'travel (the seas)'; cf. Erbse, Beiträge, 221–2.   ἐκεῖνοι: Odysseus and his men.

438. 438ᵃ = Il. i 357ᵃ (δάκρυ χεών as at 425); 438ᵇ ~ ii 81ᵇ.

439–40. 439ᵃ = xx 173ᵃ. The lines recall the escape of the herald Medon and the singer Phemius (xxii 330–80).   ἐπεί... ἀνῆκεν: 'after sleep had left them, when they had woken up'. The poet rather artificially contrives to have the pair hear nothing of the preceding activity (415–20).

441. ἐν μέσσοισι: 'among them'. 441ᵇ (~ xxi 122ᵇ): all are astonished that these men are still alive.

442. 442ᵇ = iv 696ᵇ, 711ᵇ, xxiii 361ᵇ.

443–9. Medon speaks as though he had heard Eupeithes' speech. His account of Odysseus killing the suitors with the aid of a god in the form of Mentor must be retained, as it fulfils a vital function (despite Wilamowitz, Untersuchungen, 71–2, who sees the speech as a later insertion intended to establish a connection with xxii). At 443–4 Medon to a certain extent corrects Eupeithes' words at 426; and the reference to divine aid alters the mood, emphasized by the phraseology, from οἶκτος to χλωρόν δέος (438: 450); Medon prepares the ground for the effect of the following speech from Halitherses. The differences between Medon's account (445–6) and the poet's description of the help given by Athena (xxii 205–40, 297–309) are small and superficial; they arise from the speaker's wish to show that divine intervention decisively influenced the outcome of the fight.

443–4. 443ᵃ = 454ᵃ, 444ᵃ = i 79ᵃ.   γάρ: presupposes an (unspoken) warning in κέκλυτε... Ἰθακήσιοι: listen to me, not Eupeithes! The violent deeds of which Eupeithes has spoken were contrived by Odysseus 'not

without the will of the gods' (similarly vi 240).   τάδε μήσατο ἔργα:
deliberately picks up the wording of 426, μέγα ἔργον μήσατ'.

445. θεὸν ἄμβροτον: as at *Il.* xx 358 etc.

446. Cf. xxii 205–6.

447–9. 449ᵇ = xxii 118ᵇ.   **δὲ:** adversative; the meaning is 'it was, however,
not Mentor but an immortal god, who . . .'.   τοτὲ μὲν . . . τοτὲ δὲ: 'at
one moment . . . at the next', refers to the double role played by Athena in
xxii: at one moment appearing before Odysseus (φαίνετο) to encourage
him (cf. xxii 205–40, esp. 226–35), and then driving the suitors wild with
fear (ὀρίνων) by a charge (θῦνε) through the μέγαρον (cf. xxii 297–309).
The action in xxii was a little different: there it is by raising the aegis that
Athena produces panic among the suitors (cf. ἐφέβοντο κατὰ μέγαρον, xxii
299), and the charge is made by Odysseus and his men (ἐπεσσύμενοι κατὰ
δῶμα, xxii 307).

451–62. The third speaker in the assembly, the prophet Halitherses, tries to
build on the groundwork of Medon's contribution, and counter the arguments of Eupeithes, and so frustrate the latter's plans: the Ithacans themselves are really responsible for what has happened, because they had
failed to curb the behaviour of the suitors, but of course the greatest guilt
was borne by the suitors themselves, for which they have now got their just
deserts. The verbal echoes of Eupeithes' speech are particularly striking,
but there are also equally significant, and deliberate, echoes of Halitherses'
speech in the assembly of ii, where his arguments had not prevailed against
the suitors. The skill of the poet's technique in establishing verbal connections between widely separated passages is particularly apparent here; cf.
Erbse, *Beiträge*, 240–1. There is no justification for W. Theiler's theory,
MH vii (1950), 108l, that 450–60 are an interpolation.

451–4. 451–2ᵃ = ii 157–8ᵃ; 452ᵇ = *Il.* i 343ᵇ, iii 109ᵇ, xviii 250ᵇ (referring to the
prophet Poulydamas); 453–4 = ii 160–1. The various verbal parallels are
very significant: Halitherses is introduced in almost the same terms as at ii
157–60. At 452 the prophet's gifts are characterized in true Homeric
fashion: he is not credited with supernatural mantic powers but with
wisdom and clear understanding which enable him to draw conclusions
about the future from the past.   πρόσσω καὶ ὀπίσσω: 'back into the
past and forward into the future' cf. LSJ s.v. ὀπίσω. At 454ᵃ Medon's opening words (443ᵃ) are deliberately repeated.

455. τάδε ἔργα: Halitherses refers back to 426 (μέγα ἔργον) and 444 (τάδε
ἔργα): the ἔργον of Odysseus, carried out with the help of the gods, can
only have been caused by your κακότης, i.e. that of the entire Ithacan
people.

456–60. These lines explain the above: you did not follow my counsel (ii 161–
78) and that of Mentor (ii 229–41; 161 = 229!), to curb the actions of the
suitors; 457 refers back to ii 167–8 (καταπαυέμεν: καταπαύσομεν) and 239–
41 (Mentor); 458–60 are intimately connected with ii 235–8 (Mentor); for
458 cf. ii 236, for 460 cf. ii 238 (460ᵇ = ii 238ᵇ). μέγα ἔργον (458) refers once
more back to 426: it is not Odysseus who has done evil, but the suitors.

458. 458ᵇ = xii 300ᵇ.

459. = xviii 144.

460. 460ᵃ = xxi 333ᵃ; 460ᵇ = ii 238ᵇ.

461–2. ὧδε: looks forward to the warning μὴ ἴομεν of 462, which is in stark contrast to Eupeithes' re-iterated ἴομεν (432, 436). The fear expressed in Eupeithes' concluding words (μὴ . . . ἐκεῖνοι) (436) is countered by the prophet with a much more serious danger, 'that no one meet trouble which he has brought on himself'. The prophet here expresses a thought which is particularly dear to the author of the *Odyssey*: some misfortune is the result of fate, but some is self-incurred; cf. i 7, 32–43; xxii 416; xxiii 67.

463–6. In ii Halitherses had spoken entirely in vain; here he does find support from at least a section of the crowd. It is probably not possible to come to a wholly convincing decision as to the reference of οἱ δ', 463, τοὶ δ', 464, and σφιν, 465; it seems, however, most likely that οἱ δ' and σφιν refer to the supporters of Eupeithes, τοὶ δ' to those of Halitherses, and 463ᵇ is parenthetic. This is the view taken by Wilamowitz, *Untersuchungen*, 72; Erbse, *Beiträge*, 241; Stössel, op. cit. (Introd.), 127 (with detailed argument); the editions of Stanford and von der Mühll; and Schadewaldt's translation. The other interpretation (that a majority support Halitherses) is to be found in Ameis–Hentze–Cauer, ad loc.; Schwartz, *Odyssee*, 129 n. 1; Wilamowitz, *Heimkehr*, 83; Focke, *Odyssee*, 381; Besslich, *Schweigen*, 99 n. 24. Evidence for the interpretation adopted here is to be found in the phrases ἀνήϊξαν (cf. ἐσσεύοντο, 466) and μεγάλῳ ἀλαλητῷ ('war cry': *Il.* xii 138, xiv 393), which better suit people preparing to fight than those who respond to the words of the prophet. In spite of the prophet's warning the supporters of Eupeithes, who are in the majority (464ᵃ), leap from their seats, fired with enthusiasm for battle, and hasten to arms, while the others, shaken by the seer's arguments, remain seated in their places (αὐτόθι).

πλείους: (hapax) the fact that the contracted form is Homeric is shown by ἀρείους, i 48, and *Il.* xvi 557, in both instances used in the metrical position ∪ – –⁶; on the other hand at xxiv 464 the form πλέονες could equally well have been used; cf. Chantraine, *Grammaire*, i 55. ἅδε: aorist of ἀνδάνω. μῦθος: here 'plan, counsel' sc. of Halitherses. Εὐπείθει (– – –⁶): the contracted ending -ει (< -εΐ < -ehi) can be used, although rarely, in the stressed half of the foot (*longum*); but its position here at the end of a line is unique in Homer. The poet may have been prompted to bend the rules of metrical convention by the wish to make the play on words Εὐπείθει | πείθοντ' as effective as possible; cf. Meister, *Kunstsprache*, 128–9; Page, *Odyssey*, 109; Erbse, *Beiträge*, 222–3. ἐπὶ τεύχεα ἐσσεύοντο: ἐπὶ with acc. in the sense of 'to fetch' is unusual (Hoekstra, *Modifications*, 104, cites only iii 421); here we have borrowing from *Il.* ii 808ᵇ.

467. = 500, *Il.* xiv 383. νώροπα: in the *Odyssey* only here (and 500), but common in the *Iliad* in the formula νώροπι(-α) χαλκῷ(-όν); meaning and etymology unknown; a bibliography is given in Chantraine, *Dictionnaire* s.v. χαλκόν: here 'armour'; cf. xxii 113, where it means helmet and shield.

468. 468ᵃ = ii 392ᵃ.   εὐρυχόροριο: cf. vi 4 n.

469. ἡγήσατο: 'took command'.   νηπιέῃσι: abstract noun from νήπιος 'folly'. On the morphological problems cf. Chantraine, *Grammaire*, i 83; Risch, *Wortbildung*, 133; S. West, i 297 n.; on pl. νηπιέῃσι (as at *Il.* xv 363, xx 411) cf. Chantraine, *Grammaire*, ii 31: the plural use of abstract nouns (cf. ἀτασθαλίῃσιν, i 7, ἀφροσυνάων, xxiv 457 etc.) expresses the multiplicity of aspects of abstract meaning.

470-1. 471ᵃ = xiii 6ᵃ, *Il.* i 60ᵃ.   φῆ δ' ὅ γε: 'he at least believed'.   οὐδ' ἄρ' ἔμελλεν: with following fut. inf., as at x 26 and frequently in the *Il.* (e.g. xii 3): 'but it was not given to him (by fate)...'. Such authorial *vaticinia ex eventu* are not common in Homer; the best known example is κακοῦ δ' ἄρα οἱ (i.e. Πατρόκλῳ) πέλεν ἀρχή, *Il.* xi 604.   αὐτοῦ: 'there', i.e. in the coming battle.

472-88. A scene set among the gods on Olympus. The sudden change of scene from earth to Olympus has many parallels in the *Iliad*, e.g. iii 461 : iv 1; xvi 430:431-2; xviii 355:356; xxii 166ᵃ:166ᵇ; in the *Odyssey* cf. xiii 125ᵃ:125ᵇ. The technical skill of the structure is unmistakable: just as the poet has filled the time taken by the meal at the farm with the account of events in the city (cf. 411-12 n.), so now the time which Eupeithes and his men need to travel from the city to the farm is filled with a conversation on Olympus. From 489 the three strands of the narrative will be skilfully bound together, as the meal draws to an end (489), the suitors' kinsmen approach the farm (493), and—just at the right moment—Athena also appears on the scene (502), having come from Olympus in haste (488). It is quite clear that the assemblies of the gods in i (26-95) and xxiv are closely connected (cf. Stössel, op. cit. (Introd.), 130): just as Zeus and Athena agreed to set events on earth in motion, and so arranged for Odysseus' return, so now they look to bring events to a final, and happy, end. It is equally unmistakable that this divine scene in xxiv is based on Iliadic models, above all iv 1-74 (cf. Heubeck, *Dichter*, 44; Moulton, op. cit. (Introd.), 165; H. Schwabl, *WS* NF xii (1978), 6 n. 3) and xxii 166-87 (W. Theiler, *MH* vii (1950), 109; M. Müller, *Athene*, 155-6; Moulton, op. cit. (Introd.), 165-6), which show certain similarities to the scene in xxiv (but also to that in i) in situation and theme. In all these cases questions are decided by reference to the decrees of fate, or to decisions taken long before the thematic parallels have also influenced the wording of the scene in xxiv, which will be discussed ad loc.

472. αὐτὰρ: emphatic, marks the change of scene.   Ζῆνα Κρονίωνα: found only here; cf. also Δία Κρονίωνα, xiv 406, and in the *Il.* Ζῆν'... Κρονίδην, v 756.

473. = i 45, 81; *Il.* viii 31.

474. 474ᵃ = 114ᵃ.   τί νύ: can introduce either a dependent or an independent question; cf. Chantraine, *Grammaire*, ii 292.

475-6. ~ *Il.* iv 15-16 ~ 82-3. The (deliberate) parallel between the double questions in the *Iliad* and *Odyssey* is in contrast to the different answer: in the *Iliad* Zeus seeks the continuation of the struggle; here he seeks to end it.

προτέρω: 'furthermore'. **φύλοπιν αἰνὴν: φύλοπις,** 'battle', in the *Odyssey* only here and xi 314, xvi 268, common in the *Iliad*, particularly in the formula found here (e.g. v 496). **ἀμφοτέροισι:** 'both parties'. **τίθησθα:** (as at ix 404) only this form of the 2nd sing. present (with the secondary ending -σθα) is found in Homer. The choice of the trisyllabic form (instead of a possible *τίθεις or *τιθεῖς) was apparently dictated by the trisyllabic τίθησι (3rd sing.) in the model verse *Il.* iv 83. On the difficult problems of inflection cf. Chantraine, *Grammaire*, i 298–9, 469–70.

477. = i 63 etc.

478. Cf. iv 492, xi 463; *Il.* i 550.

479–80. = v 23–4. Which pair of lines was composed first (or, as the analytical critics would ask, which poet composed the lines, and which borrowed them) is almost impossible to decide; cf. Wilamowitz, *Untersuchungen*, 70; *Heimkehr*, 82; Ameis–Hentze–Cauer, ad loc.; Focke, *Odyssee*, 76 n. 1; Heubeck, *Dichter*, 53; M. Müller, op. cit. (xxiii 153–63n.), 157 n. 41; Stössel, op. cit. (Introd.), 131. It is, however, noticeable that νόον, 479, on the one hand clearly refers to νόος, 474, but that on the other hand Zeus can at best only guess that Athena had already thought of the plan which he presents at 480–6 (ἐβούλευσας . . . αὐτή; there is no mention of this previously) and has therefore already indirectly answered her question; in this respect v 23 seems to suit its context better. Line 487 (πάρος μεμαυῖαν) shows that Zeus was right to assume that his plan agreed with what Athena had in mind. Neither passage makes very clear what κείνους refers to; but in the context it must refer to the suitors (punished or to be punished). The antithesis expected after ἤ τοι is quite clearly formulated in v (Τηλέμαχον δὲ . . ., 25), but it is also present in xxiv: the context shows that Zeus is contrasting the suitors (ἤ τοι κείνους) with the Ithacan people as a whole (cf. 483–6); cf. also C. J. Ruijgh, *Mnemosyne* xxxiv (1981), 283–4.

481. 481ᵃ = xiii 145ᵃ; xvi 67ᵃ, *Il.* iv 37ᵃ. Now Zeus turns to actually answering the questions asked in 474–6. He gives the impression of leaving the decision to Athena, but adds his own opinion on what the right course of action is (ἐπέοικεν sc. ῥέζειν).

482–5. Zeus' plan is that following the just punishment of the suitors a treaty should be sworn, by which Odysseus will enjoy the privilege of kingship for life, and the kinsmen of the suitors will forgo revenge, so that unity, prosperity, and peace will reign as formerly. This plan is of the greatest importance in the history of ideas: it means nothing less than the abolition of the law of the blood-feud, which had hitherto prevailed without qualification; in its place is established a new political order based on justice and law, and validated by the gods, in which a just and benevolent king ensures wealth and freedom (cf. ii 234, v 8–12, xi 136–7, xix 109–14). The poet is here the advocate and herald of a new age. Cf. Hommel, op. cit. (Introd.), 242; U. Hölscher, in *Festschrift für R. Alewyn* (Cologne/Graz, 1967), 12; Erbse, *Beiträge*, 140; Friedrich, *Stilwandel*, 162. The construction ὅρκια . . . ταμόντες ὁ μὲν (Odysseus) βασιλευέτω . . . ἡμεῖς δ' (θεοί) . . . θέωμεν (where we would expect οἱ δέ, i.e. the citizens, but particularly also the families of the suitors, ἐπιλαθέσθων) contains a slight inconcinnity, which is surely deliberately introduced to emphasize the decisive role of the gods in the establishment of the new order; cf. Ameis–Hentze–Cauer, ad 483; Stanford, ad 485; Erbse, *Beiträge*, 223 n. 147.

482. ἐπεὶ δὴ: (as at iv 13, viii 452, xxi 25, *Il.* xxii 379, xxiii 2) contains the unusual prosodic sequence ∪ –¹ –², thus introducing a στίχος ἀκέφαλος. Explanations differ; cf. for example Meister, *Kunstsprache*, 42–4; Wyatt, *Lengthening*, 219–21; E. Tichy, *Glotta* lix (1981), 56; S. West, iv 13 n.; Hainsworth, viii 452 n.

483. 483ᵃ = *Il.* ii 124ᵃ, iii 73ᵇ.   **ὅρκια:** on ὅρκος, ὅρκιον, etc. cf. Leumann, *Wörter*, 79–97; on the genesis of the expression in 483 see W. Bergold's convincing account, op. cit. (11–14 n.), 43–4 n. 2: ὅρκια τάμνειν, 'kill animals for sacrifice to solemnize an oath' > 'conclude a treaty'; ὅρκια πιστὰ τάμνειν 'conclude a reliable treaty'.

484. παίδων τε κασιγνήτων: both objective genitives, dependent on φόνοιο.

485. ἔκλησιν (sc. φόνοιο) θεῖναι (cf. σκέδασιν θείη, i 116, xx 225; similarly in Erbse, *Beiträge*, 223): 'cause to forget'. ἔκλησις (*hapax*) is regularly formed from ἐκλανθάνεσθαι (cf. esp. ἐκλέλαθον, *Il.* ii 600, 'they made to forget'); cf. J. Jones, *Glotta* li (1973), 12–13; Risch, *Wortbildung*, 39. Subj. θέωμεν, due to quantitative metathesis, is to be read with synizesis; cf. Chantraine, *Grammaire*, i 71.   τοὶ δ᾽: after ὁ μὲν and ἡμεῖς δ᾽, means all the inhabitants of Ithaca.   ἀλλήλους φιλεόντων: here approx. 'they are to live in harmony with each other'; on the complex meaning of φιλεῖν cf. M. Landfester, *Das griechische Nomen 'philos' und seine Ableitungen* (Hildesheim, 1966), 108–9.

486. πλοῦτος: in the *Odyssey* only here and xiv 206.   εἰρήνη: *hapax* in the *Odyssey*.

487–8. =*Il.* iv 73–4, xxii 186–7 (cf. 473–88 n.); further 487 = *Il.* xix 349; 488 = i 102, *Il.* i 44, ii 167, vii 19, xxiv 121.   πάρος μεμαυῖαν: before approaching Zeus Athena had already intended to do what in fact turns out to be the νόος of Zeus. Both deities are equally interested in reconciling the Ithacans.

489. οἱ δ᾽ (Odysseus and his men) ἐπεὶ οὖν: refers back to 412. The replacement of the conventional pair of lines marking the beginning and end of a meal (i 149–50 etc.) by 412ᵇ and 489 is necessitated by the insertion of 413–88, which describe action occurring elsewhere while the meal is taking place at the farm. The distance between 412 and 489 requires changing αὐτὰρ ἐπεὶ... to οἱ δ᾽ ἐπεὶ οὖν..., where οὖν provides a link with 412; cf. H. Reynen, *Glotta* xxxvi (1958), 41–2.   σίτοιο μελίφρονος: replaces πόσιος καὶ ἐδητύος where the adjective fulfils the function of including the wine (cf. πόσιος) in the meal; cf. μελίφρονα οἶνον, vii 182, xiii 53.   ἐξ ἔρον ἕντο: as at i 150 etc.

490. = xxii 261.

491. ἴδοι μὴ ...: as at xiii 215–16 an expression of fear finds its way into the phrase; meaning 'someone should keep a look out, for I fear that they (sc.

COMMENTARY

the suitors' kinsmen) may already be at hand. ὦσι: contracted only here and *Il.* xiv 274. For an explanation of this and similar (Attic) forms see Erbse, *Beiträge*, 224 (with further bibl.), who, probably correctly, suspects corruption here; the poet probably wrote ἕωσι (with synizesis ϝῳ); cf. also Schwartz, *Odyssee*, 136 n. 1.

493. 493ᵃ = xx 128ᵃ. τοὺς δέ: the suitors' kinsmen.

494. ~ xix 3 (= xxii 150, xxiii 112).

495. οἴδε: the demonstrative, along with ἐγγύς, emphasizes that they are close at hand. ὁπλιζώμεθα: ὁπλίζομαι meaning 'put on armour' only here and in the *Iliad* (viii 55; cf. also ἀφωπλίζοντο, *Il.* xxiii 26). θᾶσσον: the comparative form is used in exhortation (cf. vii 151-2, x 72) to mean 'as quickly as possible'; cf. Chantraine, *Grammaire*, ii 150.

496. ~ *Il.* xxiii 131. On 496ᵇ cf. xxii 113ᵇ, xxiii 366ᵇ, 369ᵇ, xxiv 467ᵇ.

497. (οἱ δ' ...) τέσσαρες ἀμφ' Ὀδυσῆ': refers to Odysseus and his three comrades in arms (Telemachus and the two herdsmen). The unusual expression (cf. Schwyzer, *Grammatik*, ii 416; Chantraine, *Grammaire*, ii 88) can be explained as an expansion of such regular phrases as τοὶ δ' ἀμφ' Ὀδυσῆα (xxii 281), 'Odysseus and his companions', by explanatory τέσσαρες: 'namely four (in total)'. υἱεῖς οἱ Δολίοιο: similarly, for example, τιμῆς τῆς Πριάμου, *Il.* xx 181; in these and similar expressions we see the gradual development of the demonstrative pronoun into an article; cf. Chantraine, *Grammaire*, ii 163; Erbse, *Beiträge*, 224-5.

498. ἐν δ' ἄρα: (sc. τοῖσι) 'in their midst'; on 498ᵇ cf. xxii 201ᵃ.

499. πολιοί: only here 'grey-haired' (in this sense commonly in Attic drama); elsewhere πολιός is used by Homer only as an epithet of γένειον and κάρη. Page's objections (*Odyssey*, 111) are dealt with by Erbse, *Beiträge*, 225. ἀναγκαῖοι (cf. 210) πολεμισταί: 'fighters against their will' (amplified by πολιοί); the opposite is ἐθέλοντες, e.g. *Il.* iv 224; cf. also *Il.* iv 300, viii 56-7.

500. = 467. The repetition of the line is intentional: the preparations for battle by Eupeithes' men and those of Odysseus are described in exactly the same terms.

501. = xxiii 370. ἄρχε δ' Ὀδυσσεύς: (ἦρχε codd.) parallel to τοῖσιν δ' Εὐπείθης ἡγήσατο, 469.

502. During the preparations for battle Athena has completed her journey to Ithaca; now the different strands of the threefold narrative are drawn together; cf. 472-88 n.

502-3. = xxii 205-6 (additionally 504 ~ xxii 207). Once again the repetition of a line is deliberate (cf. 500 n.): Athena intervenes in the battles of xxii and xxiv in the same guise, that of Mentor. It is, however, no less important that Athena in the shape of Mentor had already supported Telemachus in his first confrontation with the other Ithacans (ii 267 ff.); now (xxiv 502 ff.) she undertakes the task of bringing the conflict to an end.

504. = v 486 ~ xxii 207.

505. ~ xviii 214, xxii 163.

506. τόδε γ' εἴσεαι: 'you will know how to …'; τόδε prepares for 508. **ἐπελθών | … ἵνα:** 'when you have come there, where …'.

507. ἀνδρῶν μαρναμένων: (= *Il.* xv 715) depends on ἄριστοι. **κρίνονται:** here 'measure themselves in battle'; cf. *Il.* ii 385, xviii 209.

508. Odysseus quotes here the advice given by Hippolochus to his son Glaucus: μηδὲ γένος πατέρων αἰσχυνέμεν, *Il.* vi 209; πατέρες in both passages mean 'maiores', 'forefathers'.

509. ἠνορέῃ: (*hapax* in the *Odyssey*, frequent in the *Iliad*), 'manhood': abstract in -έη (< Aeol. -έᾱ < ίᾱ; cf. Νεστόρεος with Aeol. -ρε- for -ρι-); Aeol. *ἀνορέᾱ is probably a retrograde formation from the compound *εὐάνορέᾱ (-ίᾱ); cf. Leumann, *Wörter*, 109–10; Risch, *Wortbildung*, 133. **πᾶσαν ἐπ' αἶαν:** (as at *Il.* viii 1ᵇ etc.) 'throughout the whole world'.

510. = i 388 etc.

511–12. 511ᵃ = xx 233ᵃ, *Il.* iv 353ᵃ etc.; 512ᵇ = iv 157ᵇ etc. F. A. Wolf's conjecture, τῷ δ' ἐπὶ θυμῷ (cf. xvi 99, *Il.* xiii 485), is convincing; cf. Erbse, *Beiträge*, 225. Construction: 'You will see how in this (my) spirit I will in no way shame you …'.

514. ἡμέρη ἥδε: 'this day, today'. **θεοὶ φίλοι:** (as an exclamation used only this once) should be accepted as an explanation of extreme joy.

515. υἱός θ' υἱωνός τ': as at *Il.* v. 531. **δῆριν:** (only here and *Il.* xvii 158) 'battle, conflict; here (honourable) competition'; on δῆριν ἔχουσιν cf. μάχην ἔχουσιν, *Il.* xiv 57.

516–27. Athena's command to Laertes to begin the fighting (516–20) should be understood as part of the poet's plan to echo the divine action at the opening of *Il.* iv. There too Athena had, with the agreement of Zeus, prompted an individual to open the hostilities, Pandarus (iv 92–114); the difference, however, is that in that instance she had led a fool astray, and caused a fresh outbreak of hostilities. Here though her action may appear to contradict the common intention of Zeus and his daughter described by the poet at 472–88, it is in fact designed to prepare the way for achieving the ultimate aim, which is of course the swift reconciliation of the warring parties; for peace cannot come about until the suitors' kinsmen, bloodthirsty as they are, have learned by experience the sheer hopelessness of their cause, and are forced to recognize that the suitors fell νήποινοι by the will of the gods, and are therefore not entitled to be revenged (cf. i 380). In the action which follows the goddess will assume the task of ending as quickly as possible the hostilities which she has unleashed (cf. 528 ff., 541 ff.). The poet has the brief battle begin with its most important action, the death of Eupeithes at the hands of Laertes, in order to give Laertes too a moment of ἀριστεία (prepared in 365–82). By describing this fighting, like that of xxii, in Iliadic language (because of the similarity in material) the poet lends an aura of heroic grandeur and dignity to the proceedings.

517. Ἀρκεισιάδη: Laertes; cf. 270. **φίλταθ' ἑταίρων:** as at *Il.* xiii 249, xix 315; similarly *Il.* xxiv 748. Athena can speak in this way when in the guise of Mentor.

518. κούρῃ γλαυκώπιδι: only here and *Il.* xxiv 26.

415

519. = 522. **ἀμπεπαλὼν ... ἔγχος:** found otherwise only in the *Iliad* (iii 355 etc.), *ἀμπεπαλών* is redupl. aor. of *ἀναπάλλω*, 'swing, lift up; draw (ready to throw)'. **προΐει:** here (unlike 522 and its use in the *Iliad*) imperative. **δολιχόσκιον:** cf. xix 438.

520. = *Il.* 482; cf. also *Il.* xv 252, xix 110.

521–2. Laertes follows Athena's instructions exactly: 521 ~ 518 (he prays to the goddess who is in fact standing next to him!); 522 = 519 (*προΐει* in 522 is now imperf. indic.).

523. **χαλκοπαρῄου:** (*hapax* in the *Odyssey*; in the *Iliad* used only in the formula *κυνέης διὰ χαλκοπαρῄου*, xii 183 etc.): 'having bronze cheek(-piece)s with bronze cheek-guards'. It is almost impossible to decide between -η- and -η(ηι)-; either *παρειαί* (< *παράϝαί*), 'cheeks', or *παρήϊον*, 'cheek-piece' (Myc. *pa-ra-wa-jo/parāwaiō/* dual) could have served as the final element of the compound; cf. Chantraine, *Dictionnaire*, s.v. *παρειαί* and *χαλκός*. On the archaeological questions see J. Borchardt, *Archaeologia* E, 57–74.

524. = *Il.* v 538, xvii 518, iv 138. **ἥ** sc. *κόρυς*. **εἴσατο:** (cf. xxii 89) 'went'. **χαλκός:** here the bronze tip of the spear.

525. = *Il.* iv 504 etc.; 525ᵃ = xxii 94ᵃ. **ἀράβησε:** (*ἀραβέω*) 'rattle, clang'.

526. 526ᵇ = xxii 141ᵇ. **ἔπεσον:** (*ἐμπίπτω* with dat.) 'fall upon' (cf. *Il.* xvi 270).

527. 527ᵇ = xvi 474ᵇ; *Il.* xiii 147ᵇ etc. Apart from the alteration of *νύσσοντες* to *τύπτον δὲ* = *Il.* xiii 147 etc. (cf. Shipp, *Studies*, 364); *τύπτω* here 'hit, wound (wish a slash or jab)', in conjunction with *ἔγχεσιν* also xxii 308. **ἀμφίγυος**, used only in the dat. pl. with *ἔγχεσιν*, is a possessive compound meaning literally 'having a *γύη (curve, bend) either side' (cf. Risch, *Wortbildung*, 177, 188). The sense has never been entirely satisfactorily explained: 'beidseitig gebogen' (with reference to the bronze point; cf. *LfgrE* s.v.) or ('a deux pointes flexibles' (Chantraine, *Dictionnaire* s.v. *γύη)? Cf. Trümpy, *Fachausdrücke*, 59.

528–30. These lines are modelled on passages in the *Iliad* in which an unreal conditional construction (*καί νύ κε δή ..., εἰ μή ...*) is used to describe the intervention of a god to prevent an outcome which is not decreed by fate, or which does not lie in the gods' plans; e.g. iii 373–4, v 311–12; cf. Reinhardt, op. cit. (xxiii 168–72 n.), 107 ff. In making Athena achieve her object here with a loud cry the poet may have been thinking of *Il.* xviii 217–18; cf. W. Theiler, *MH* vii (1950), 109. **ἀνόστους:** a regular formation ('having no return home'; cf. Risch, *Wortbildung*, 183) is a *hapax*, like *ἀ-νόστιμος*, iv 182. **Ἀθηναίη ... αἰγιόχοιο:** as at xiii 252, *Il.* v 733 etc. **φωνῇ** is used to emphasize *ἤϋσεν* as at *Il.* iii 161 with *ἐκαλέσσατο*. **κατὰ δ' ἔσχεθε:** (*κατασχέθω*) 'hold back'. **λαὸν ἅπαντα** refers to Eupeithes' men (cf. *Ἰθακήσιοι*, 531; *τοὺς δὲ*, 533), who in spite of the successes of Odysseus and Telemachus are still the attackers.

531. **ἴσχεσθε:** with gen. 'refrain from'.

532. **ἀναιμωτ(ε)ί:** 'without (further) bloodshed'; on the formation cf. Risch, *Kleine Schriften* (Berlin, 1981), 167–75: *ἀναιμωτεί* is the linguistically

correct form. The second half of the line is modelled on διακρινθεῖτε
τάχιστα, Il. iii 102ᵇ. The Iliadic passage 95–110 with διακρινθήμεναι (97)
also allows us to be more precise about the meaning of the verb: 'separate
(peacefully, on the basis of a treaty)'.

533. 533ᵃ = ii 296ᵃ; 533ᵇ = xii 243ᵇ (~ xxiv 450ᵇ), Il. vii 479ᵇ.

534. ~ xii 203 with τεύχεα (with -ες) for ἐρετμά; τεύχεα in this case refers
above all to the shield; cf. Il. xvii 760, xxi 301; cf. Erbse, Beiträge, 227–8.

535. 535ᵇ = Il. ii 182ᵇ, x 512ᵇ ~ xx 380ᵇ; but whereas in the Iliad ὄπα depends
on ξυνέηκε/ἄκουσε, here with different syntax it is the object of φωνησάσης
and so we have a new combination here, ὄπα φωνεῖν: a procedure which,
as Leumann, Wörter, passim, has shown, is not unusual; cf. Erbse's
convincing discussion, Beiträge, 228–9.

536. 536ᵇ = xii 328ᵇ (cf. n.).

537. 537ᵃ = viii 305ᵃ, Il. viii 92ᵃ.

538. = Il. xxii 308; the poet uses here only the first line of a simile referring
to Hector (308–10). οἴμησεν: 'he charged after (the enemy)'.
ἀλεὶς: 'crouched (ready to spring)'; part. from aor. ἐάλην, present εἴλω,
εἰλέω (common in the Iliad; in the Odyssey only here and in the form
ἔλσας, v 132, vii 205), 'draw oneself together'. ὑψιπετήεις: 'flying
high' (only here and Il. xxii 308) is an artificial expansion of synonymous
ὑψιπέτης (xx 243; Il. xii 201, 219, xiii 822); cf. Risch, Wortbildung, 154.

539–44. By her double intervention, setting on Laertes to begin the battle,
and warning the Ithacans to halt the fight, Athena has achieved her first
objective, of creating the preconditions for the surrender of Odysseus'
enemies and a peaceful end to the conflict. At the same time her efforts
have brought about a situation which she and Zeus had not considered:
Odysseus is on the point of ruthlessly massacring his opponents. Zeus now
takes the initiative, and warns his daughter to carry out the plan as agreed;
Athena obeys, and in turn commands Odysseus to lay down his arms
(542–4 are in parallel to 531–2). It is significant that the father of gods
orders events indirectly: his warning thunderbolt is not directed towards
Odysseus drunk with success, but (unlike the model passage Il. viii 130–6,
where it warns Diomedes) towards Athena, to remind her of her duty.

539. ψολόεντα κεραυνόν: cf. xxiii 330–2 n.

540. 540ᵇ = iii 135ᵇ. ὀβριμοπάτρης: (elsewhere only i 101, Il. v 747, viii
391), epithet of Athena, 'having a mighty father'; cf. Risch, Wortbildung,
186.

542. = v 203 etc.; cf. Hainsworth, v 203 n.

543. 543ᵇ = Il. ix 440ᵇ etc. νεῖκος ὁμοιίου πτολέμοιο: also xviii 264.
On ὁμοιίος cf. S. West, iii 236 n.; further Chantraine, Dictionnaire s.v., and
above all Wyatt, Lengthening, 174–8. ἴσχεο is parallel to ἴσχεσθε, 531.

544. This line is undoubtedly modelled on Il. xx 301, where the poet found
the unusual construction μὴ + κεχολώσεται (fut. indic.); he is probably
also influenced here by such phrases as μή πώς μοι μετέπειτα χολώσεαι
(aor. subj.), Il. xiv 310; cf. Chantraine, Grammaire, ii 331, Shipp, Studies,
144.

545. = *Il.* xxii 224. χαῖρε δὲ θυμῷ is hardly surprising, despite the view expressed by Ameis–Hentze–Cauer, ad loc. The sight of Mentor fills Odysseus with confidence, and hope for ending the battle against a much greater force; these are legitimate grounds for joy; cf. Latacz, op. cit. (xxiii 13 n.), 71, 144.

546. 546ᵇ = iii 136ᵇ, *Il.* iii 321ᵇ ~ *Od.* xxiv 476ᵇ, *Il.* iv 83ᵇ.   ὅρκια ... ἔθηκε: (*hapax*). Athena carries out her father's wish of 483–6 by having the feuding parties swear unity (μετ' ἀμφοτέροισιν), a secure basis for future peace (κατόπισθε; cf. xxii 40).

547. = xiii 252, 371.

548. = 503: the beginning and end of Athena's decisive intervention in the fighting are significantly marked by the same words. The naming of the goddess in the last lines is also an appropriate end to the whole work, for she had set events in motion, ensured that they followed the intended course with numerous interventions, and now brought about the conclusion towards which the entire poem has been directed: the return of the hero, reunion with his wife, and the restoration and renewal of the old order on Ithaca. As the result of her efforts the situation desired by Zeus (485–6), marked by φιλία, πλοῦτος, and εἰρήνη, can now be made reality.

INDEX OF GREEK WORDS
(CUMULATIVE)

419

INDEX OF GREEK WORDS (CUMULATIVE)

GENERAL INDEX (CUMULATIVE)

metonymy II 167, III 29, 30, 49–50, 65, 206

metre: absence of spondees II 272; acephalous verses I 194, 199, 275–6, 329, II 57, 141, III 151, 413; and apostrophe III 33; caesura, bucolic III 54, 166, mid-line III 87–8, 123, penthemimeral III 44, third-foot III 33, trochaic III 18; consonantalized ι I 197–8, I 272; effect of spondees II 254; elision of diphthong I 216, II 44, 138, 201, III 20; Hermann's Bridge I 105, 123, 237; hiatus I 88, 94, 103, 146, 243, II 156, 158–9, 177, 195, 200, 204, 210, 212, 219, 220, 241, 262, 265, 268, 271, 274, III 160, 169, 171, 174, 177, 178, 229, 237, 254, 269–70, 294, double III 250, 'illicit' III 86, initial III 290, see also digamma; iambic III 242; irregularity III 288, 410; other unusual practices I 123, 132, 146, 230, 361, II 45, 99, 104, 187, 240, 248, 255, III 60, 111; related to passion of speaker II 270; short vowel before ζ I 106, II 270; spondaic III 37, 40; synecphonesis I 104; synizesis II 16, 29, 58, 183, 210, 211, 212, 263, III 38, 40, 65, 76, 85, 93, 99, 101, 153, 159, 167, 169, 173, 176–7, 203, 242, 245, 259, 298, 378, 408; trochaic III 113; and vocabulary III 37, see also metathesis, quantitative

metrical alternatives II 26, 95, 96, 127, see also formulae

metrical lengthening I 69, 88, 102, 111, 144, 156, 206, 257, 262–3, 308, 325, 353, 372, 380, II 16, 17, 22, 37, 47, 50, 53, 70, 92, 112, 141, II 194, 141, 142, 156, 162, 173, 174, 176, 177, 191, 193, 203, 205, 207, 218, 229, 237, 241, 245, 248, 252, 261, 265, 266, 274, III 21, 24, 79, 80, 82, 85, 170, 171, 174, 176, 186, 187, 192, 193, 199, 202, 223, 226, 229, 236, 252, 254, 272, 338, 350–1, 359, 365, 378, 384, 386, 391

metrical shortening III 60, 222, 286

middle voice (verb) II 137, 161, 163–7, 215, 220, 228, 232, 248, 250, 269, 270, 272, 285, III 48, 171, 181, 185, 205, 296, 306, 309, 315, 323, 348

middle-passive voice (verb) III 48

Minos II 111, III 85

'Minyans', 'Minyan' and Aeolian mythology II 92, 94, 180, 246–7

Moly II 51, 60–1

mulecart (ἀπήνη) I 297–8

Murnaghan, S. III 8 n. 5, 9

Muses I 68, 69, 350, II 128, III 366–7

music III 205, see also lyre

Mycenae II 244

Mycenaean forms I 70, 75, 208, 267, 299, 304, 312, 323, 340, 352, 365, 374, 376, II 16, 17, 21, 22, 23, 25, 26, 28, 31, 34, 36, 43, 56, 61, 63, 65, 85, 86, 93, 94, 95, 97, 119, 123, 141, 157, 165, 167, 173, 178, 179, 180, 182, 186, 188, 189, 193, 194, 200, 205, 207, 208, 212, 240, 241, 247, 248, 249, 256, 257, 271, 282, III 21, 51, 117, 159, 165, 235, 269, 277, 293, 299, 305, 307, 322, 328, 334–5, 364, 373, 376, 416; Linear B texts I 99, 159, 160, 190, 348, 373, II 150, 154, 162–3, 168, 171, 175, 181, 196, 236, 253, 286

myth, solar III 82

names II 195; derived from place II 14; eponymous III 27, 97; exchange of II 12–13, 33; indicating conception of character I 73, 97, 121–2, 154, 177, 257, 293–4, 324, 348; intrusive I 152; invented I 353, II 25, 33, 39, 186; non-Greek II 124, 133, 170, 207, 270–1, 286; odd compounds I 99, 123; papponymic I 83, II 105; patronymic I 77, 80, 91–2, 126, 162, 194, 195, 214, II 13, 43, 166, 196, 207, 215, 217–18, 237, 258, III 31, 258, 260, 269, 278, 280, 338; power associated with II 39, 40; significant III 27, 34–5, 38, 40, 47, 52, 77–8, 81, 86, 111, 246, 385, 407

narrative technique I 12–18, 290, 295, 317, 331, 345, 353, II 3–4, 8–11, 147–9, III 7–8, 12, 14, 55; adumbration of later events I 85, 89, 106, 109, 112, 151, 152, 195, 200, 209, 212, 256, 292, 299, II 9, 10, 23, 25, 30, 31, 32, 35, 40, 45, 49, 52, 53, 55, 56, 66, 68, 80, 81, 88, 90, 91, 97, 98, 100, 104, 109, 118, 121, 124, 125, 126, 134, 135, 278; anecdote I 320–1; closing cadence III 73, 106, 127; contrasts II 10, 46, 79, 101, 102;